Understanding Family Problems

RPH

Understanding Family Problems

A Psychological Approach

Neil Frude
University of Wales College of Cardiff

JOHN WILEY & SONS
Chichester · New York · Brisbane · Toronto · Singapore

Other Wiley Editorial Offices

John Wiley & Sons, Inc., 605 Third Avenue,
New York, NY 10158-0012, USA

Jacaranda Wiley Ltd, G.P.O. Box 859, Brisbane,
Queensland 4001, Australia

John Wiley & Sons (Canada) Ltd, 22 Worcester Road,
Rexdale, Ontario M9W 1L1, Canada

John Wiley & Sons (SEA) Pte Ltd, 37 Jalan Pemimpin #05-04,
Block B, Union Industrial Building, Singapore 2057

Library of Congress Cataloging-in-Publication Data:
Frude, Neil.
    Understanding family problems :   a psychological approach / Neil
  Frude.
        p.   cm.
    Includes bibliographical references.
    Includes index.
    ISBN 0 471 91741 9
      1. Family—Mental health.   2. Problem families—Mental health.
  3. Stress (Psychology)   4. Life change events—Psychological
  aspects.   I. Title.
      [DNLM: 1. Family—psychology.   2. Interpersonal Relations.
  3. Life Change Events.   4. Psychology, Social.   5. Stress,
  Psychological.   WA/308/F944u]
  RC455.4.F3F78   1990
  155.9'24—dc20
  DNLM/DLC
  for Library of Congress   90-12399
                                                                    CIP

British Library Cataloguing in Publication Data:
Frude, Neil
    Understanding family problems   :   a psychological approach.
    1. Families. Personal problems
    I. Title
    362.82

    ISBN 0 471 91741 9
    ISBN 0 471 92276 5 (pbk.)

Typesetting by Thomson Press (India) Ltd., New Delhi
Printed in Great Britain by Biddles Ltd, Guildford, Surrey.

For Kathleen, Annette, and Benedict

For Kathleen, Annette, and Benedict

Contents

Contents

Preface

This book provides a review of a number of major problems that families commonly face. It considers how and why these problems arise, how families attempt to cope with them, and how professionals can best help families to deal with them. The approach taken is psychological, rather than sociological, and there is some discussion, in various parts of the book, of the relationship between these two levels of analysis.

In the first two chapters a number of basic conceptual issues are raised and a distinction is drawn between 'the individual's family' and 'the family unit'. The first chapter reviews evidence relating to the 'provisions of relationships' and explores a major theory that has been used to explain how individuals make decisions regarding their close relationships. The second chapter focuses on 'the family unit' and explores the systems theory approach to the analysis of interactions within families. The characteristics of 'healthy' and 'dysfunctional' families are considered using this perspective, and there is a general analysis of how families respond to stress.

Subsequent chapters provide detailed reviews of a limited number of major 'family concerns'—problems that commonly give rise to profound hardship and disruption. Four major areas are covered: illness and handicap, conflict and violence, separation and divorce, and dying and bereavement.

The aim of the book is to review the findings from a wide range of empirical studies in order to provide an analysis of how such problems affect families; and although there is no attempt to provide details on intervention techniques or to provide guidelines for therapy, much that emerges from the reviews has a direct relevance for self-help, lay intervention, and professional practice. Each chapter includes material that has considerable implications for those who deal with families facing the type of difficulty discussed. Busy health professionals, psychologists, social workers, and teachers usually come face to face with a wide range of family problems and have little time to become acquainted with the vast literature relating to each of these. Those in any of these professions should find the book informative and will be able to draw conclusions that will directly affect their practice.

Any book that focuses on problems within families, or stressful events that affect families, necessarily 'accentuates the negative' about family life. However, it would be unfortunate indeed if the reader were to develop a pessimistic view of family life. Although there is much hardship, stress, and violence within families, there is also so much that is positive. One conclusion that might be drawn from the body of literature reviewed in this volume is that many families and individuals are incredibly resilient in the face of severe difficulties—they often survive the most formidable conditions and recover from the most appalling situations. As we shall see in Chapter 1, the majority of people place a very high positive value on their family relationships.

Recent demographic changes mean that fewer people now live in the traditional family arrangement than was the case in past decades. More people cohabit than ever before, and a proportion of such relationships are homosexual. There are more divorces and, partly related to this, more single-parent families. Also related to the increasing divorce rate is the greater incidence of 'blended families' formed when a divorced person with custody of one or more children remarries. Dual-career marriages are also much more common than they were in previous times. Family size has declined markedly, while longevity has greatly increased. Behind each of these 'aggregate changes' are millions of stories of how particular families have been formed and have developed. Any conclusion drawn regarding 'how families are affected by X' or 'how families cope with Y' is necessarily limited in its range of application. Each family is unique, and yet there are discernible patterns that permit certain generalizations to be made. Thus information derived from studies of families in one context may provide pointers for how families in a somewhat different context may be helped to cope. My aim in writing this book has been to gather and integrate information from a wide variety of sources. Practitioners will be best placed to judge how this information can be applied.

This book was completed during a period of study leave. I am grateful to the University of Wales, College of Cardiff for granting me the time to finish the manuscript, and to the Faculty of Psychology, University of Amsterdam, for accommodating me during a six-month stay. In particular I would like to thank my family for granting me the freedom to consider family problems 'at a distance', and Jan Hoogeboom, Harri Vorst and Pieter Kempe for making my stay in Amsterdam particularly rewarding.

N. F.

1

The Individual and the Family

The first part of this chapter makes a conceptual distinction between 'an individual's family' and 'a family unit' and then addresses the rather difficult issue of how each of these terms may be defined. Some studies of the family focus on individuals, and treat family relationships primarily as an important part of the person's social context, whereas others focus on the family unit as a whole, and regard individuals as sub-elements within that unit. There is no great incongruity between these approaches, and in many ways they are complementary, but they are somewhat different. The remainder of the chapter is concerned with an examination of two issues that relate to 'the individual's family'. The first theme is the impact of close relationships on the individual's well-being and health, and various sources of evidence are used to draw a conclusion about whether, in general, adults benefit from their involvement in intimate relationships. The second theme is how individuals make decisions regarding their social relationships. Chapter 2 focuses on issues concerning 'the family unit'. In later chapters particular problems such as family violence, divorce, and bereavement, are discussed in detail, and evidence from studies that have adopted either of the two major approaches is used to provide an account of how such problems arise and how they affect individuals and the family system.

Thus the first two chapters illustrate two different ways of approaching the analysis of family life. Both are valuable and provide useful routes to understanding. But despite the fact that they overlap somewhat, and that they frequently provide complementary analyses, the difference between them is fundamental. Not only do they represent different ways of analysing interactions within the family, but they even employ the concept of 'family' in two significantly different ways. This conceptual issue needs to be addressed before we explore questions about 'the individual's family'.

THE INDIVIDUAL'S FAMILY AND THE FAMILY UNIT

How might we identify a particular family unit? One possible strategy would be to ask a person to list members of his or her family, and then to consider that collection of people as 'the family unit'. Unfortunately there is a major problem with this proposal. If we were to ask two married people each to draw up a list of 'my family' we might well find that the two lists differ somewhat. The wife might include, for example, an uncle to whom she feels especially close, whereas the husband might not consider that his wife's uncle is part of his family. Certainly the uncle in question would be likely to include in the list of *his* family members certain people who would not feature in either of the original lists. Thus if we think of each person being surrounded by a circle of people whom they identify as members of their own family, it is likely that very few circles would be completely co-extensive. Even for marital partners the overlap would in many cases be only partial

Another example will clarify this further. Suppose that a man has been married twice and that his first wife has custody of children from their marriage. He may well consider that those children are members of his family. His former wife will also consider that the children are members of her family. Both ex-partners may agree, however, that they are no longer members of the same family, and the man's second wife will probably not regard the children of her husband's first marriage as members of her family. It can be seen that an individual's list of his or her family members does not provide a satisfactory basis for identifying a particular family *unit*. An individual may simultaneously be in two or more families, and his or her 'family' may therefore include some people who never interact together. In the example given above the remarried man may consider his current wife and his two children from his previous marriage as 'his family', but the four of them may never have met together and would not be regarded as a 'family unit'. A 'family unit' is more than a 'collection' of people—it is an interacting and interdependent *group*. 'An individual's family' may be simply an 'assembly' or 'collection' of those people who each have a very special relationship with the individual (but not necessarily with each other), whereas 'a family unit' is 'an organization' or 'a group' in which each member has a very special relationship with *each* of the other members.

An examination of 'the individual's family' is likely to differ from an examination of 'the family unit' in terms of the concepts and the level of analysis employed. In addition, however, the membership of the groups that are examined might well be different. Having distinguished between these two concepts it would be appropriate to offer a definition of each, but unfortunately this is by no means an easy task. Few people experience confusion when using the term 'family', and most feel that they have a clear idea of what the word means. But like some other common words it proves very difficult to define precisely. This is partly because the term is used in several different ways and the meanings only partially overlap. It would be tempting to avoid the matter of definition if it were not for the fact that it bears on a number of important substantive issues. A little further exploration is therefore needed.

First we will consider how 'the individual's family' might be defined in such a way that, at least in principle, we could identify the people who would count as members of a particular person's family. The task is to identify the individual's family members, with the eventual aim of gaining insight into the experience and behaviour of that individual. Other people identified as members of the individual's family, however, would be of interest only in so far as they help us to understand the individual. They are therefore treated simply as a (rather special) part of the individual's social background, or social environment.

If the ultimate goal is to increase the understanding of how an individual responds to family members and is influenced by them, then the criteria used to define the membership of 'the individual's family' must be appropriate to this aim. They must be closely related to the individual's experience. In other words, they must be of direct psychological relevance. If we were primarily concerned not with psychological issues but with legal issues, for example, or with genetic issues, then we would employ quite different criteria in our bid to define family membership. For example, suppose that a man has a brief sexual encounter with a woman, unknowingly leaves her pregnant, and later has a son or daughter that he knows nothing of. He may die never having met the child and never even suspecting the child's existence. This scenario is not in the least implausible, and in fact happens rather frequently. Now the question arises, is this 'unknown' child part of the man's family? According to biological criteria the answer must be 'yes'. According to legal criteria the answer is also 'yes' (witness the men who react with bewilderment when presented with a 'paternity suit'). But, if the child remains 'unknown', is he or she a part of the man's family in any *psychologically* meaningful way? In this case the answer must surely be 'no'.

On the other hand, suppose two people cohabit but do not get married and do not have children. They may cohabit for nearly a lifetime, other people may treat them in every respect as though they were married, and their relationship may be psychologically as 'close' and 'meaningful' as it is for any married couple. Would we wish to claim that, simply because they have never signed legal papers, one partner is not a member of the other's 'family'? In a legal context, of course, relevant documentation may be of crucial importance in settling matters such as rightful inheritance, but in terms of the psychological functioning of an individual who is involved in such a partnership, or the nature of the relationship between the two people, the legal status of the union may be immaterial.

These two examples illustrate that using legal and biological criteria to identify who is and who is not a member of an individual's family would lead us to include some people who play little (or even *no*) part in the individual's social life, and to exclude some who play the most critical role. Similar problems are encountered with another criterion that is sometimes incorporated as an element in definitions of the family—'common residence'. An individual may have lived in very close proximity with another person (a prison cell-mate, for example) for many years and yet would not consider that person to be a member of his or her family. On the other hand, some of those who are considered by individuals to be members of their family may not reside with them.

For the purposes of psychological analysis we need to establish criteria of family membership that reflect how the individual regards certain other people, relates to them emotionally, and interacts with them. Such criteria will allow specific people to be identified as members of the individual's family whether or not there is a legal tie or a blood tie, and whether or not they share a home together. The individual's emotional response to such people will clearly be relevant, but although high emotional dependence might be a *necessary* criterion, it cannot be a *sufficient* criterion. If it were, then an adolescent's passion for a new date would be adequate reason to regard the beloved as a member of the young person's family, but this is clearly not how the term 'family' is used. Some of those who have a profound psychological effect on the individual (and might therefore count as 'significant others') would not number among the person's family members (such people might include close friends, an employer, a teacher, a fiancé, and a mistress or lover). The distinction between those who are and those who are not members of the individual's family must depend on more specific components of the person's feeling about them. It is difficult to avoid the apparently circular conclusion that a person is a member of an individual's family if that individual regards them as a member of his or her family. However, this is no more circular that defining the membership of a club as the set of people who have been admitted as members. But even if we adopt this tactic, we are still left with the question of which factors are salient to an individual's recognition of someone as a member of their family. Individuals are likely to differ in this respect, but in many cases such recognition will be associated with feelings of affinity, obligation, intimacy and emotional attachment.

Thus we are left with the conclusion that an individual's disposition towards a person is the most appropriate criterion for deciding whether or not that person should be identified as a member of the individual's family. One consequence of this proposal is that the 'selection' depends only on the subjective response of the individual and not at all on the disposition of others. In many cases, of course, selection is symmetrical, so that Jack includes Jill as a member of his family and Jill includes Jack as a member of her family. But such reciprocation will not always occur. A person may even be a member of another individual's family without realizing it, and some of those whom an individual regards as a member of their family might take exception to the individual's 'claim'. Situations such as this can arise when one person is unable to relinquish strong positive feelings for their ex-partner following separation or divorce, for example, or, more generally, when one person 'disowns' another but the other person still feels a strong attachment. Even many years after the legal event of divorce one or both of the ex-partners may still regard their former spouse as a member of their family. If such an appraisal is common to both then, psychologically, the two people have not managed a separation. In many cases, however, one person still regards their ex-partner as a family member, but the other does not.

It would be gratifying if having established, at least in principle, criteria for deciding who should be regarded as a member of an *individual's* family, we had thereby provided a solution to the problem of the membership of a family *group*. However, it has already been shown that the necessary congruence between different individuals' judgements of who is and who is not a member of their family cannot be guaranteed. Thus another strategy must be used to identify the membership of a family group. Standard definitions of the family unit can provide only limited assistance in this task. The family (unit) has been described as 'an arena of interacting personalities' (Nye and Berardo, 1966) and as 'a set of mutually contingent careers' (Farber, 1964). It is interesting that neither of these definitions makes reference to any biological, legal, or residential criteria, and that they both imply that the family is 'an entity' or 'a thing in itself'. However, neither sufficiently differentiates between a family unit and other types of group (such as a sports team or a stable group of co-workers).

A more specific definition might be devised by employing a strategy similar to that used to define 'an individual's family', but this time requiring that each individual who is to be included in the group recognizes every other member of that group as a member of their own family. Thus if two partners each regard the other as a member of their family, and there is no-one else whom they *both* recognize as a member of their family, 'the family unit' consists of just the two. If, however, there is also a third person whom they both recognize as family members, and that person recognizes each of the other two individuals as members of their own family, then the family unit will consist of the three people. Using this strategy it would be possible, at least in principle, to identify particular 'family units' by starting with a particular individual's list of family members and then examining the lists of each of those members in order to establish the most extensive group for which each member claims every other member as one of their own family.

Thus membership of both 'the individual's family' and 'the family unit' are seen to depend ultimately on how individuals are disposed towards those to whom they are affiliated. In the first case, however, membership depends only on one individual's judgements, whereas in the second it depends on a *correspondence* between a number of individuals' perceptions. One problem that would be encountered in operationalizing such a scheme would be the fact that young children (whom we would of course wish to be included in family groupings) do not have the feelings or make the kinds of sophisticated judgements about relationships implied in the procedures that would be involved. This problem might be overcome in a number of ways, but the simplest would be to make their membership of a family unit dependent on 'claims' made by adults.

The analysis provided may seem very far removed from any practical concern, but in fact it is highly relevant to a number of important real-world issues. For example, how should we judge whether an adopted child has become a family member? If we use a legal criterion, of course, there is little problem. The child is recognized as a full family member as soon as the relevant papers are signed. But the psychological reality is more complex. In some cases an adopted child becomes part of 'the family' very soon after moving into the home, whereas in other cases this process takes a considerable time (and in some cases it may never happen). It is clear that some children who experience long-term fostering become members of the foster family, but that many do not. In some cases a distant relative who moves into a family, or a lodger, or a divorced person's long-term companion, becomes a 'family member' even though there are no formal or legal ties with any other individual in the family. If such a person regards all of the others as members of their own family, however, and if each of the other people includes the individual as a member of their own family, it would seem irrational to exclude that person when conducting any psychological investigation or making any psychological analysis of the family unit.

A major advantage of the type of definition offered is that it excludes all cases where there is a blood tie, a legal connection, or common residence, but where there is no mutual recognition of family membership. On the other hand, if the definition relies on psychological criteria, particular cases of non-traditional groupings such as those involving gay couples, heterosexual cohabiting couples, and even some communes, would be identifiable as 'family units'. This is appropriate because, in terms of interactional style and level of psychological interdependence, the relationships within such units resemble those within traditional families more than they resemble relationships between friends, for example, or between employers and employees. The issue is not simply that of when it is appropriate to use the term 'the family'. The important question concerns when it is appropriate to regard a group of people as a family and to analyse their interactions and their relationships using a 'family' approach.

The question of whether it is appropriate to apply 'family analysis' to non-traditional intimate groupings has become more significant as relationship patterns have become more diverse. Half a century ago the majority of families consisted of two parents who were married to each other, most families included a number of children, and close relationships were maintained with many other people who were related by blood or in law. Today, however, many children live in single-parent households or with one natural parent and a stepparent. Families are smaller, so that many children have no siblings, and close relatives often have little contact with each other. Furthermore, an increasing number of couples choose not to have children, more people now live alone, and more are entering into a long-term homosexual partnership. The proportion of people now involved in 'non-traditional family forms' has increased dramatically, so that these days the 'modal' family pattern (two married parents residing together with two or more natural children) can hardly be said to represent the majority of 'families'.

THE IMPACT OF THE FAMILY ON THE INDIVIDUAL

We now turn to an examination of two issues that relate to 'the individual's family'. The first of these concerns the impact of family life on the individual. The second concerns how individuals make decisions about their family relationships.

THE SIGNIFICANCE OF CLOSE RELATIONSHIPS

Close relationships are significant both for the individuals involved and for society as a whole. For society, particular benefits derive from the organization of individuals into family groups, and these can be listed in terms of categories that are sometimes referred to by sociologists as the 'functions' of the family. They include the regulation of sexual behaviour and reproduction, the provision of basic needs such as food and shelter, the protection and socialization of children, and the provision of emotional support for individuals. The family unit is also recognized as a basic economic and 'consumer' unit.

The task of assessing the significance of family life for the individual has been approached in a number of ways. For example, people have been interviewed and asked to identify the advantages or disadvantages they experience as a result of their involvement in close relationships. Another strategy involves examining the events that make a special impact on people, and then assessing how far these derive from their family life. Following a different approach, comparisons are made of the happiness, health, or longevity of groups of people whose personal circumstances differ significantly (those who are married, single, or divorced, for example).

INDIVIDUALS' EVALUATIONS OF CLOSE RELATIONSHIPS

Weiss (1974) interviewed people who had been involved in a close relationship but were now without a partner. The interview focused on individuals' feelings about what had been missing from their lives since the relationship had ended. In his analysis of the responses, Weiss identified six basic 'provisions of relationships'—attachment, social integration, reassurance of worth, a sense of reliable alliance, the opportunity for nurturance, and guidance. Each of these provides certain benefits for the individual. 'Reassurance of worth', for example, refers to the fact that in their interactions with an intimate, people may feel 'valued' and 'respected'. Those who lack self-confidence may benefit particularly from such appreciation, but most people's self-regard is enhanced when a significant person shows recognition of their efforts and acknowledgement of their worth.

Thus people recognize that they derive certain benefits from close relationships. Indeed, when they are asked what makes them most happy, what provides them with satisfaction, and what gives meaning to their lives, they emphasize their close relationships much more than other aspects of their life such as their job, leisure interests, health or wealth (Freedman, 1978). People recognize that their own happiness is largely dependent on the behaviour and well-being of 'significant others', and on the quality of key relationships. But they also acknowledge that these same relationships often provoke anger, anxiety and sadness. Irritations and conflicts within the family frequently rouse people to intense anger, and many aspects of their family relationships lead them to become profoundly distressed. Even those whose family members are healthy and happy, and who enjoy warm and close relationships, may worry about the longer-term future. They may appreciate that many 'good' relationships eventually become conflictual and end in sadness and bitterness. They may worry that the partner will become violent or abandon the relationship, or that a family member will become seriously ill. Anxiety may also be generated by a concern about how they would manage following the partner's or the parents' death.

Thus individuals recognize that their close relationships are sources of happiness, comfort, and joy, on the one hand, and frustration, tension and distress on the other. However, most people seem to judge that on balance they derive important benefits from their close relationships. During times of bitter conflict or special adversity they may of course regret their involvement, but the majority of people evaluate their close alliances positively. Those who are not involved in a close relationship often feel that something is missing from their lives, and they may actively seek out someone with whom they can form a special association. Similarly, couples are often highly motivated to enhance the quality of their lives by having children. Thus most people seem to have a positive evaluation of close relationships. However, it is important to check such subjective evaluations against more tangible criteria.

LIFE-EVENT STUDIES

Considerable attention has been paid in recent decades to the impact of 'life events'. In a seminal study, Holmes and Rahe (1967) interviewed a large number of people about events that they felt had recently had a special influence on their lives. The researchers then constructed an inventory of incidents that many people had experienced, and asked 'judges' to assess the impact that each of these would be likely to have. 'Getting married' was given the base score of '50 units' and other events were then judged against this standard. The event considered likely to have the most impact was the death of the spouse (100 units), and strong effects were also predicted for divorce, the birth of a child, loss of employment, etc. The study was not designed specifically to examine the impact of changes relating to family relationships, but it is clear from even a cursory examination of the list drawn up by Holmes and Rahe (and from similar inventories that have subsequently been compiled—for example by Paykel, McGuinness, and Gomez, 1976) that many events that have the most significant implications for individuals are related to aspects of their family life.

Although many life-event inventories include both positive events (such as marriage) and negative events (such as the death of a spouse) greater emphasis is usually placed on unfavourable occurrences. However, a compilation of positive life events (Argyle and Henderson, 1985) also reveals that many items are associated with family relationships. Another recent innovation in this field involves the charting of relatively minor positive and negative events and changes of circumstance. These are sometimes referred to as 'uplifts' (positive) and 'hassles' (negative), and it has been shown that they often make a significant impact on the individual (Kanner et al., 1981). Inventories that list these less conspicuous events are once again found to include many items relating to family life.

Those who have a partner and children generally experience more events than those who live alone. People who are surrounded by a number of family members tend to lead lives that are filled with incident. Some of the events and changes they experience would generally be regarded as favourable while others would be judged as unfavourable. People who have many close relationships will experience more 'entrances' (such as the birth of a child) and more 'exits' (the death of a family member, marital separation, or a young adult leaving home) than those who are relatively isolated. They will frequently experience more 'uplifts' (such as birthdays, anniversaries, and school successes) and more 'hassles' (such as minor illnesses of family members, or occasions of family discord). Such events will have both a direct effect on the individual, and indirect effects resulting from the impact of the change on other members of the family. Thus a father will be personally affected by an adolescent leaving home, but will also be influenced by the impact that this has on his wife and other children.

Those who live alone and have few personal ties will avoid many unfavourable and potentially detrimental events, but they will also miss out on positive changes. A life that is relatively free of incident or disturbance may also be without much interest or excitement. While early studies of the impact of life events stressed the potentially damaging effects of too much change, recent thinking has placed more emphasis on the benefits that people gain through experiencing at least a modest degree of incident and transition in their lives.

CLOSE RELATIONSHIPS, HEALTH, AND WELL-BEING

So far it has been established that people recognize both costs and benefits of their intimate relationships and that, in general, they judge such relationships as rewarding. Life-event studies indicate that those involved in close relationships lead 'fuller' lives, experiencing more positive and more negative events. A reasonable hypothesis based on such findings would be that people who are integrated into an intimate social network actually might have a greater sense of well-being, and better physical and psychological health, than those who do not have such relationships.

Comparisons of the self-reports of married people, single people, the widowed, and the divorced, concerning their happiness, loneliness, and stress do indicate that those who are currently married have fewer problems and have a greater sense of positive well-being. For example, in a study by Glenn (1975), 36% of married women described themselves as 'very happy' compared to under 20% of women who were widowed, divorced or never-married. Surveys also indicate that relatively few married people are lonely. Those who are single (i.e. have never married) report moderate levels of loneliness, and those who are separated, divorced, or widowed appear to experience the most loneliness (Peplau and Perlman, 1982). Married people also report less stress than those in any of the other groups (Cargan and Melko, 1982). In one relevant area, however, the pattern is somewhat different, although perhaps not surprising. Hughes and Gove (1981) found that married people had relatively high scores, compared with other groups, on a measure of 'manifest irritation'.

All of these comparisons are based on self-evaluations by people in the different groups, and together they suggest that those who are currently married are better off. The same pattern emerges from studies that have used more objective indices. An extensive body of research has confirmed that, in general, those who are involved in intimate relationships are healthier, both physically and mentally, than those who are not. Overall, married people have better physical health than those who have never married or are divorced or widowed. They are less likely to suffer from a wide range of ailments, including asthma, diabetes, ulcers, tuberculosis, cancer of the mouth and throat, hypertension, strokes and coronaries (Lynch, 1977; Reed et al., 1983; Cohen and Syme, 1985). Married people also tend to make a better recovery from illnesses and operations than those who are not married (DiMatteo and Hays, 1981). The advantage associated with being married is even apparent in statistics relating to death rates. Married people have a lower rate of early mortality than those who are single, widowed or divorced (Verbrugge, 1979; Berkman and Syme, 1979; Morgan, 1980; Perlman and Rook, 1987).

Studies of mental health reveal a broadly similar pattern (Bloom, Asher and White, 1975; Gove, 1972). Examinations of both psychiatric admission rates and self-reports of people in the general community show that married people experience the fewest psychological symptoms. The frequency of such symptoms is intermediate among widowed and never-married adults, and highest among the divorced and separated. Those who are not currently married are also more likely to use drugs and to contemplate suicide (Cargan and Melko, 1982). In general it seems that intimate relationships are particularly important in maintaining health (Reis, 1984), although other social contacts (for example, with neighbours and work colleagues) may also be significant (Berkman and Breslow, 1983). There is some evidence that for women, more than for men, contacts with friends and distant relatives may provide an adequate substitute for immediate family contacts (Madge and Marmot, 1987). There remains some controversy about whether a high number of casual contacts can offer the same 'health protection' as the presence of one or more intimates, but there is general agreement that those with very little social contact are at high risk and that the availability of a key intimate is of particular significance.

The overall advantage established for the married with regard to health and well-being is clearly an 'average' effect, and hides the fact that many people suffer substantially as a result of an unsatisfactory or violent marriage. As a group, those who have been divorced for a number of years fare substantially better than those who still endure a highly conflictual marital relationship (this will be discussed in Chapter 8). Violent family relationships place people in immediate danger of injury as well as imposing severe distress (marital violence will be considered in Chapter 7). Thus it is clear that the general advantage derived from being involved in an intimate relationship will not hold in every case. The health and well-being of many people is placed in jeopardy by those who are close to them, and they might be substantially better off without these relationships.

Thus while marriage often seems to lower the risk of loneliness, emotional distress, and physical illness, the quality of the marital relationship is all important (Gove, Hughes, and Style, 1983). If the marriage is especially good, then the benefits may be considerable. For example, one large prospective study found that husbands who had an especially loving relationship with their wives were at a much lower risk of developing angina (Medalie and Goldbourt, 1976). On the other hand, marriages that are conflictual or under threat may increase stress and have serious adverse effects on both psychological well-being and physical health. Certain styles of family interaction have also been identified as increasing the risk of particular 'psychosomatic' disorders. For example, Martin (1977) concluded from a review of studies of asthma, that 'when asthma develops without strong allergic predisposition, many features of antagonistic, mutually frustrating family interactions are present' (p. 331).

Many studies suggest that being in an environment in which events are unpredictable and largely uncontrollable may produce chronic anxiety that can lead to the development of peptic ulcers. An individual may feel that other members of his or her family behave capriciously and that their own behaviour has little impact, and such a state of affairs may lead to the onset of an ulcer in a person who is constitutionally at risk. In other families an individual may be frequently placed in circumstances in which high levels of anger and hostility are generated, but in which open expression of such feelings is strongly discouraged. In such a situation the chronic inhibition of aggression may exacerbate hypertension (McClelland, 1979). Thus both positive and negative aspects of the quality of a relationship appear to have substantial effects on an individual's psychological and physical condition.

For those who are no longer with a partner, the quality of the former relationship may also have a profound effect on their state following the separation or loss. Widows whose marriages were conflictual generally make a poorer recovery following the death of their spouse than those whose marriage was more harmonious (this issue will be discussed further in Chapter 10), and many qualities of their former marriage are relevant to how well a divorced person is able to cope. The length of time since a bereavement or divorce is of course a major factor determining the individual's physical and emotional state. In both cases an acute reaction, that is often very intense, is normally followed, after some time, by a substantial recovery.

In trying to account for variation in well-being and health within groups of married, single, widowed or divorced people, it is also necessary to consider whether there might be systematic variations with such global variables as social class, sex, and race. The issue of whether there is an overall gender difference in how people are affected by the presence or absence of close relationships has proved particularly controversial. At one stage the claim was made that 'while marriage is good for men, it is not good for women' (Bernard, 1973), and this provoked a lively debate. There is still an absence of total consensus on this matter, but the conclusion reached by many of those who have examined the evidence in detail is that although the advantages of being married, as gauged by health indices, may be somewhat greater for men than for women, the married of both sexes do appear to be happier and more healthy.

EXPLANATIONS

In spite of the many exceptions there appears to be a clear positive association between various indicators of health or well-being and the individual's involvement in close relationships. How can this be explained? One possibility is that the associations, or correlations, do not in fact reflect a causal connection between the two variables being studied. Thus the association might arise from the fact that those who are favourably placed with respect to some other variable (higher social status, for example) are both more likely to be healthy and more likely to be involved in close relationships. Various studies that have attempted to ascertain whether some such factor might be responsible for the association between health and marital status, however, have failed to discover any variable that can satisfactorily explain the connection in this way.

If the association between health and relationship status is indeed causal then we still need to establish which is the cause and which is the effect. It is possible that the state of an individual's health determines whether they become involved in or are able to maintain a relationship. Thus rather than relationship status being a causal determinant of health, an individual's state of physical or mental health may partly determine whether they are able to sustain a relationship. Those who are very depressed or highly anxious, for example, and those who have a chronic physical illness, may find it more difficult to find a partner, or their condition might threaten an ongoing relationship. There is some evidence that this type of explanation accounts for *some* of the association, but it cannot explain all of it. Other evidence supports the assumption that an individual's involvement in close relationships does play an important role in determining whether or not they will become mentally or physically ill.

The question of how good-quality intimate relationships serve to protect people from mental and physical afflictions has a number of possible answers, and it is likely that several provide at least part of the explanation. One account explains the association not in terms of the advantages conveyed by intimate relationships, but in terms of the legacy of severe stress associated with the ending of a relationship. Thus the relatively poor physical and psychological health of the divorced and the widowed might be a residual effect following the particularly intense distress that accompanied the marital breakdown or the death of the partner. Some support for this hypothesis comes from the fact that individuals are often in an especially poor state immediately after separation or bereavement and that, in most cases, their health and disposition gradually improve with time. However, problems do often remain, and it is likely that these are not merely the long-term effects of the primary stress but reflect current factors such as loneliness and financial hardship.

Another explanation of the relationship between social integration and health focuses on the fact that the presence of other people helps to regulate and to impose certain demands on the individual. Those who are involved in important relationships have more rules to follow and their behaviour is monitored by people who care about their health and welfare. Rook (1985) identified regulation as one of the basic functions of intimacy. Social integration encourages compliance with certain 'rules' or 'norms', making the individual's life more orderly and more predictable, and reducing the chances that they will engage in dangerous practices (Hughes and Gove, 1981). Those who are socially isolated are more likely to expose themselves to danger and to act in ways that increase risks to their health. Following divorce (and, to a lesser extent, bereavement), some people's lives become quite disordered. They may eat and sleep irregularly, and they tend to smoke more and to drink more alcohol. It is clear that many disorders that have a relatively high incidence among those who are not married (including throat cancer, strokes, and cirrhosis of the liver) are related to smoking and the use of alcohol. Those who are involved in a satisfactory relationship may feel less stressed (and thus have less 'need' of the comfort or escape that may be derived from smoking or drinking), and they are also likely to be influenced by their 'significant others' to avoid behaviours that could jeopardize their health.

Another approach suggests that those who have good personal relationships are better able to cope with stress. For example, married people are probably subjected to at least as many stressful events as those who are not married (indeed, they may be subjected to considerably more), but they may be protected from adverse effects by certain benefits that they derive from their relationship with their partner. This proposal has two principal variations. According to the first (the 'increased well-being hypothesis'), relationships enhance an individual's personal strength, making them more resilient in the face of stress and better able to cope. According to the second ('the social support hypothesis') individuals may be helped to contend with stress through the provision of emotional and practical support by other people at times of particular stress. These two accounts, of course, do not conflict (they may both explain some of the effect) and there is now a considerable body of evidence supporting each (Cohen and Wills, 1985).

According to the 'increased well-being hypothesis', those involved in intimate relationships are less vulnerable to stress because they have an increased sense of well-being. Wills (1984) suggested that social support strengthens the individual's feeling of being in control and assures them that they are valued. As a result self-esteem is increased, and this increases psychological tolerance and resistance to stress. People who have an intimate relationship are unlikely to experience chronic loneliness, they have the opportunity to exert some degree of influence over other people, and they are likely to feel 'needed' by others. It is suggested that such feelings of control, satisfaction, and well-being provide the individual with a general strength and resilience that will be useful in resisting the impact of stressful events.

The 'social support hypothesis' suggests those who have close relationships are better able to cope with stress (and thus exhibit fewer symptoms) because comfort and assistance are available to them during difficult times. Sharing a problem with others may help to attenuate adverse effects, and other people provide emotional support and assist in practical ways (MacFarlane *et al.*, 1983). Those who have to face challenging situations without social support are more likely to show detrimental effects. In a summary of the available evidence,

Cobb and Jones (1984) concluded that social support does indeed play a significant role in alleviating the negative impact of stressors. Both the well-being hypothesis and the social support hypothesis can explain why negative life events tend to have less impact on those who are married than on those who are not (Thoits, 1982).

In line with the social support hypothesis is the evidence that intimates often act informally as 'resident therapists' and so guide or 'treat' the person who faces a threatening situation. People seem to 'consult' with their partners, relatives, and close friends during times of personal difficulty. They often report that they gained considerable emotional support from such contact and that it helped them to survive a highly distressing period of their lives. Thus Griffith (1985) asked individuals to list the people they 'really depended on' when personal problems arose, and found that the spouse was the most frequently cited source of support. Nye and McLaughlin (1982) also found that informal psychotherapy takes place in the majority of marriages, and such support is evidently very important in protecting individuals against many adverse effects of stress (Kessler and Essex, 1982). In a study of the social origins of depression among women, Brown and Harris (1978) found that the presence of an intimate and confidant was associated with low vulnerability to stressful events.

The various explanations that have been considered are all psychological in nature, but some recent accounts have focused on the effects of social support on physiological vulnerability. A number of research findings indicate that warm interpersonal relationships may bring about certain physiological changes which make the individual more resistant to illness. Thus Ganster and Victor (1988) suggested that interpersonal warmth might lead to a release of certain neurochemicals which counteract the harmful biochemical changes resulting from stress, and Kennedy, Kiecolt-Glaser and Glaser (1988) provided evidence supporting the view that intimate relationships may attenuate stress-related decreases in immune function, thus reducing the risk that the stress will actually provoke a disease.

In the light of all of the evidence it seems reasonable to conclude not only that most people positively evaluate their close relationships, but that such relationships often confer substantial advantages. The presence of an intimate appears to be far more significant in 'protecting' the individual than the presence of more distant friends and acquaintances. On the other hand, there are certain dangers inherent in close relationships. They sometimes become difficult and disagreeable and can lead to much distress. The fact that many people choose to persist with an unhappy alliance rather than bringing it to an end is perhaps further testimony to the high value that is generally placed on intimacy, or it may reflect a general apprehension about being alone.

Assessments of how family relationships affect personal well-being tend to represent the individual as merely 'reacting' to changes of circumstance. Thus life events are said to have an 'impact' on the individual, and people are portrayed as simply responding to transitions in relationships. But people are proactive as well as reactive, and make many important choices about how they will live. They make decisions about how they will relate to other people, and some actively choose to abandon their most significant relationship. In addition to the initiatives people take regarding such critical questions, they are constantly evaluating situations, making judgements about their best course of action, and assessing how others respond to their actions. How the individual makes decisions regarding his or her relationships is the second of the two substantive themes explored in this chapter, and this provides an opportunity to introduce a theory that has been increasingly influential in recent years— 'social exchange theory'.

SOCIAL EXCHANGE THEORY

The evidence reviewed above suggests that individuals gain a great deal, overall, from their family relationships. But this does not directly explain why individuals decide to enter or to remain in relationships, or why they sometimes decide to leave them. People don't get married because they have read research reports suggesting that marriage would be good for their health. How then can we explain why people make the choices they do about relationships? How does an individual decide whether to enter into a relationship, to get married, to have children, or to leave a marriage? Why do some married people choose to have an affair, and why do some adolescents choose to run away from home?

For each of these questions many alternative explanations are available. There are hundreds of 'mini-theories' that offer to explain particular aspects of family life, and some of these will be encountered in later chapters. However, there is one 'macro-theory' that offers an explanation for all of these issues, and many more besides, and it therefore deserves special consideration. Although the approach does not find favour with all of those concerned with the analysis of family life, it does offer a very useful framework for explaining the decisions that individuals make about their close relationships. The theory is familiar to social psychologists as 'social exchange theory'. Although we will consider the theory as a way of explaining individuals' family-related choices or decisions, it can also be elaborated to explain the behaviour of whole family units and even much larger systems, including cultures.

INDIVIDUALS' DECISIONS

'Social exchange theory' is based on the view that people act rationally and make choices that they think will provide the best 'pay-off'. Thus they seek rewarding interactions, relationships, and statuses. A reward is basically anything that the individual finds pleasurable or agreeable, and a cost is anything that the person dislikes or finds disagreeable. By evaluating the likely rewards and costs of alternative courses of action, the person seeks to maximize 'profit'. People judge the value of their best course of action against a general standard based on their previous experience ('the comparison level') and against the value of the 'next-best' action, situation, or relationship (the 'comparison level for alternatives'; Thibaut and Kelley, 1959). If no profitable course of action is open then the individual will follow the direction that seems likely to involve the least cost.

The choice between alternative actions depends on estimates of the probabilities of various possible outcomes. People differ profoundly in their estimates of the likely consequences of an action, so that while some are optimistic and assign a very low probability to negative outcomes, others are unduly pessimistic. The evaluation of any particular reward also differs between individuals, so that some place a higher value that others on social approval, for example, or security, or independence. People's evaluations change with their changing circumstances and moods, and may be grossly distorted when they are highly emotionally aroused. Thus when an individual has been intensely angered by another person's action, the infliction of pain on that person may be judged as having paramount reward value. Thus even the violent action of an enraged person may be seen as 'rational' given the value that the aggressor assigns to hurting the victim. The evaluation process is often very complex, involving not only many probability assessments but also the analysis of a large number of cost and reward elements. This process of appraisal, however, is usually automatic and unconscious. People sum up complex social situations 'implicitly' rather than by systematically working through a series of calculations, just as, when catching a ball, a person does not explicitly work out the complex mathematics of the trajectory. Individuals are often quite unaware of various elements involved in their assessment, and it has to be acknowledged that some people are very scornful of the idea that their preferences and actions represent the outcome of a strategic evaluation process.

DECISIONS IN THE SOCIAL CONTEXT

The theory can be used to explain decisions such as a person's choice of where to go for a holiday, but from its inception social exchange theory was particularly concerned with complex social decisions and social behaviour. Thus very early on it was suggested that such intricate concepts as 'respect', 'trust' and 'liking' could be understood as forms of interpersonal reward (Newcomb, 1961). Other important social rewards include approval (social disapproval is a cost), autonomy, the agreement of other people, and freedom from ambiguity. Material gains, especially money, are also important sources of reward, and people take these into consideration when they are making a decision.

In order to gain a reward a person often has to incur some costs, and the action will be profitable only if the rewards outweigh the total cost. The benefit gained by entering into a relationship, for example, may be somewhat reduced by a consequent reduction in the individual's autonomy. Any valued relationship imposes limitations on the person's choices, if only because it means that the person must avoid actions that will challenge or end the relationship. Sometimes there is a conflict between the short-term and long-term pay-offs likely to follow from an action. Thus a person might be uncertain about whether or not to be unfaithful to their spouse because there is a conflict between the reward of immediate pleasure and the danger that an affair might jeopardize their highly valued marriage.

Just as chess players 'look ahead', and predict their opponent's likely response to their move, so those making choices in social situations gauge the likely response of others. Certain general norms help the individual to make relevant predictions. Thus there is a general 'norm of reciprocity'; people who reward others expect to be rewarded in return. This norm is learned early on in socialization (it is related to the principle of 'fairness'), and is later 'enforced' by the fact that non-reciprocity may bring high costs in the form of social disapproval, retribution, or non-cooperation in future interactions. People also have specific expectations about how the person with whom they are interacting is likely to respond. If we 'know' somebody we have some idea of how they will evaluate a situation and how they will react to our action. Thus we are likely to be influenced in our behaviour by what we think the other person's reaction will be. In choosing a present for somebody, for example, we draw upon our knowledge of what gives them particular pleasure.

Almost all interactions between people have some 'reward' (or gain) and 'cost' (or loss) implications for both participants. Sometimes one person's loss is another's gain, so that the total gains (expressed as positive units) and losses (expressed as negative units) add up to zero. If a group of friends are playing cards for money, for example, then at any stage in the game the summed losses of all participants must equal the summed gains. If one member of the group leaves, the others can work out what s/he has won or lost by working out their own losses and gains. If they find that between them they have a net gain, they know that the other person must have lost that amount of money. The losses equal the gains, so the sum of the losses and the gains is 'zero'. Many interpersonal interactions have this property, and they are generally referred to as 'zero-sum games'. But some interactions do not have a net zero outcome. If two people decide to take a walk together they may both gain enjoyment, so that there is a net profit, or if two people invest jointly in an enterprise that fails, they both suffer a cost. Either of these two types of interaction are referred to as 'non-zero-sum games'.

DECISIONS IN THE CONTEXT OF CLOSE RELATIONSHIPS

So far social exchange theory has been considered in its application to simple social situations. How can the theory be applied to the analysis of close relationships? Although many people prefer not to think of close relationships in this way, it is clear that even such complex concepts as 'commitment', 'duty' and 'love' can be viewed in terms of rewards and costs and the kinds of 'games' that have been described. In close relationships, rewards are derived from such sources as the enjoyment of mutual activities, supportive communication, and the display of physical affection (Levinger, 1982). Costs may result, for example, from conflicts or duties.

Thus if we ask why a person decides to get married, social exchange theory would provide an answer in terms of the benefits the person feels will be gained by entering into the marriage. They may look forward to such immediate rewards as companionship, sexual pleasure, the 'high status' of being married, and so forth, and to an immediate curtailment of certain costs incurred by being single (such as living with parents, or experiencing loneliness). They may also look forward to longer-term benefits (children, a high standard of living, etc.). The particular partner is chosen as having high 'value' (the judgement of value may include a consideration of the person's intelligence, wealth, humour, sensitivity, status and physical attractiveness), and as being the 'best choice' in terms of the available alternatives.

The consideration of rewards and costs in the context of long-term relationships benefits from an extension of the simple 'economic' metaphor. For example, in the context of a long-term relationship an act that is charitable (and thus 'costly') in the short term can be explained by reference to longer-term outcomes. Generous actions strengthen the relationship, and a stronger relationship is likely to produce more rewards in the long term. Acts that are rewarding to partners, friends or family members, serve to validate and maintain the relationship. Where sharing is extensive, as in marriage, a generous action may contribute to the general fund of goodwill, and no immediate reciprocation may be expected. People also value close relationships *in themselves*, and they are rewarded by the happiness and well-being of those who are important to them. They also derive great satisfaction ('reward') from the fact such people treat them with respect and express love and admiration. Family members may feel a personal sense of pride when a partner or child is successful in some enterprise. A father, for example, may be pleased that his child has beaten him in a game of skill. Although at the simplest level such a defeat would be considered a personal cost, it is clear that when pride and identity aspects are taken into consideration the situation can be seen as rewarding for the father.

Those who are critical of attempts to explain interactions within intimate relationships in cost and reward terms often make the error of thinking that such analyses are exclusively concerned with the individual's short-term and 'selfish' gratification. But social exchange theory is not limited in this way, and has no difficulty in accounting for actions that are charitable, dutiful or self-sacrificing. It will be recognized that the social exchange account of behaviour in close relationships is compatible with the 'provisions of relationships' identified by Weiss (1974), and discussed earlier in the chapter, and can help to explain why supportive and gratifying actions occur regularly in successful relationships.

When a relationship has been on-going for some time, it may have built up a healthy 'credit balance' in the eyes of both partners. Such a relationship will be relatively stable and will not be threatened if one partner's action suddenly imposes high costs on the other. Similarly, if it is expected that the relationship will have a long future, people are prepared to invest (i.e. accept costs) in order to achieve gains at a later time. In some ways, therefore, close relationships would seem to be less reactive to immediate pay-offs from interactions than more transient relationships. But although good long-term relationships have this quality of resilience, intimate relationships also involve many highly rewarding and highly costly interactions, and are subject to many special expectations about profits and losses.

Thus within the marital relationship one partner might expect the other to make frequent gestures of affection, to take responsibility for a range of household tasks, to engage in sexual activity regularly, to remember birthdays and anniversaries, and so on. The rules that apply to a marriage are more numerous than those apply to friendship, for example (Argyle and Henderson, 1985), and many of these prescribe that rewards should be given by one partner to the other. Many rules also impose high costs on the partner, so that the marital relationship is a context in which high-cost and high-reward interactions occur very frequently. It is therefore just as well that the effects of specific interactions are attenuated in such relationships. This attenuation reflects both the long-term 'credit' and 'investment' nature of such alliances, and the fact that people involved in close relationships would generally incur very high costs if they were to opt out of the relationship.

Close relationships that are recognized in the wider society (such as marriage and the parent–child relationship) are also subject to social expectations and regulations, and the breaking of rules may attract substantial social disapproval. Thus many sources of reward and cost act together to impose a certain 'inertia' on family relationships, so that members are less likely to abandon the family in order to gain short-term rewards.

The distinction between zero-sum and non-zero-sum games is particularly important for the analysis of interactions within close relationships. Some types of marital interaction (such as those involving the personal allocation of limited joint resources) take the form of zero-sum games, whereas others do not. Thus if two people agree to get married they both assume that each will benefit as a result. Some activities can be either zero-sum or non-zero-sum. If both partners positively enjoy sex, for example, their sexual activity together will be non-zero-sum. But if only one of them enjoys sex, their sexual encounters will be rewarding for one but costly for the other. Clearly this is likely to have profound effects on the nature, frequency and quality of their sexual contact. To take another example, if a wife wishes to work outside the home and the husband feels that this will enable him to enjoy a better standard of living, the situation is not competitive. But if the husband feels that he will lose as a result of his wife's employment, and he therefore wants her to remain at home, they will have competing interests. When the decision is finally made one partner is likely to feel that they have won and the other is likely to feel that they have lost.

Any close relationship involves many zero-sum and non-zero-sum games, but the proportion of each will vary. Ideally, family relationships should feature a high proportion of non-zero-sum games. Thus it is preferable for a married couple to engage in many mutually rewarding activities than for them to be constantly competing with each other for rewards. With limited financial resources and certain chores to be accomplished, some zero-sum situations will always arise. But any negative effects of these (particularly for 'the loser') may be offset by the couple's involvement in projects which are beneficial to both. The more zero-sum games a couple play the more frequently they are likely to engage in conflict.

APPLYING THE THEORY

The Marital Situation

Social exchange theory has been used to explain such variables as marital quality, marital satisfaction, marital stability, and marital power, and to account for associations between these variables. One of the major advantages of this theory, compared with many others, is that it generates a wide range of testable hypotheses about marital and other types of family relationship. Some applications of social exchange theory to understanding marital relationships will be briefly described before we consider how the theory can be used to explain decisions regarding family composition, and how it can be applied to the analysis of parent–child relationships.

It has already been suggested that the theory can be used to explain the individual's choice of a marital partner. The chosen partner will have high 'value' on salient characteristics. Individuals differ as to which attributes they regard as important in a partner, but physical attractiveness, intelligence, and status are often relevant to the choice that is made. Certain special talents or achievements, such as musical skill or sporting attainments, may be crucial to the choice made by some individuals, but central to any evaluation of a potential partner will be judgements about how responsive, caring, and affectionate they will be. Obviously a choice can only be made from those who are 'available' to be chosen, i.e. those who are prepared to respond positively. The person chosen will be 'best choice' in terms of their value compared with the values of possible alternatives.

Social approval or disapproval by friends and relatives regarding the choice of partner can help to explain the general tendency for people to marry someone who is similar to themselves. Thus disapproval of family members regarding a 'mixed marriage' in terms of race or religion will tend to influence a person to choose someone from the same type of background. Another factor that may lead someone to choose a partner with similar interests and values has been suggested by Nye (1982). He proposed that people who have similar values will engage in more non-zero-sum games than those who have markedly different values. Thus by choosing to marry someone with the same interests, an individual maximizes the proportion of non-zero-sum games likely to arise within the relationship (needless to say, the person who proposes or accepts a proposal of marriage will not be thinking in these terms!).

Lewis and Spanier (1982) presented an exchange theory of marital quality. The rewards and costs of the marital relationship for both partners determine the quality of the marriage, and the stability of the relationship reflects both this quality and the rewards and costs that are judged as likely to come from external sources (including other possible relationships, and the social disapproval that may follow marital dissolution). Levinger (1965) suggested that marital stability is directly related to the degree of attraction between the partners and to the strength of the barriers to dissolution, and is inversely related to the attractiveness of alternative relationships.

Nye and McLaughlin (1982) proposed that if an individual's partner plays various marital roles effectively the marital relationship will be highly rewarding and the individual will have a high degree of marital satisfaction. If a husband likes to eat well, for example (and if he believes that it is part of his wife's role to prepare his meals), the fact that his wife is a good cook will contribute to his overall marital satisfaction. In order to test their general hypothesis these authors examined the association between individuals' marital satisfaction and their perceptions of their partner's competence in various family roles. They assessed people's feelings about whether their partner was effective in the recreational role, in the child-care role, etc., and found that perceived competence in such roles was significantly related to marital satisfaction. The highest correlation with marital satisfaction was obtained, for both men and women, with their perception of the partner's effectiveness in the 'therapeutic' role. Those who felt that they could rely on their partner for support during times of personal difficulty were also likely to be generally satisfied with their marriage.

Nye suggested that social exchange theory could be used to explain why families develop and maintain a certain degree of structure with regard to roles and routines. If there were no established roles, no task would be allocated to any particular family member and each chore and responsibility would be open to negotiation. This would be highly inefficient and would probably generate frequent conflict. But when roles have been established, each family member recognizes and accepts their own and other members' responsibilities. The family will then function successfully, and without members feeling unduly burdened, as long as each person is willing and able to play their role effectively. The initial process of allocating roles may be delicate and conflictual. A newly married couple, for example, may find it difficult to establish an arrangement that is agreeable to both partners. When a major change occurs, for example if a child is born or if the husband becomes unemployed, the previously established role structure may need to be revised, and some families find it much easier than others to adapt to such new conditions.

In zero-sum situations, the 'player' most likely to win is the one with the most power. There are 'domains of power', so that a mother may be more powerful in the area of child-care, for example, and her husband may be more powerful with respect to major family expenditure. Bahr (1982) used social exchange theory to provide an analysis of power relationships within marriage. A partner who has a high level of control within the relationship is able to make the other comply with requests that they find disagreeable. Those who have more 'resources' (more status, for example, or more money) can exert more control because they have greater potential for rewarding their partner. Similarly, those who are more effective in their performance of family roles are able to deliver more rewards to their spouse, and this gives them more power. The more dependent a person is on their partner for rewards the less power they have in the relationship. Those who derive many rewards from outside the marriage (from a job, for example, or from an extramarital relationship) are less dependent on the rewards they receive from their partner, and will be more powerful as a consequence.

The degree of power exerted within marriages ranges along a continuum from very low levels to very high levels, but for analytic purposes we can distinguish between 'high control' and 'low control' marriages. In some cases power is distributed asymmetrically between the spouses, so that one has substantially more power than the other, and in others the power of both partners is about equal. This gives rise to a fourfold classification first used by Blood and Wolfe (1960). In 'syncratic' marriages there is a high degree of control, but each partner is able to exert control over the other. In 'autonomic' marriages there is low control, so that neither partner controls the other and they therefore act more or less independently. Both of these arrangements are symmetrical. Where the relationship is asymmetrical with regard to power, the marriage may be 'husband-dominated' or 'wife-dominated'.

The analysis of marital relationships provided by social exchange theory offers explanations for many situations observed in particular marriages, and also suggests many general hypotheses concerning the relationship between such concepts as marital satisfaction, role competence, and marital power. For example, a man who is judged by his wife as incompetent in his role as 'provider' (for example, if he is seen as not motivated to work) will tend to lose power. Since he provides fewer rewards, his wife is likely to be less satisfied with the marriage.

A more extensive example will illustrate how the theory can be used to predict more elaborate interactional sequences. If a husband judges that his wife has lost interest in sex then his devaluation of her as a sexual partner would be likely to reduce his overall satisfaction with the marriage. This dissatisfaction might lead him to provide fewer rewards for his wife (perhaps by showing her less affection), and at the same time he might seek a more 'profitable' relationship. Thus marital stability might be reduced, and the husband's power in the relationship would be likely to increase. With more power, however, he would be able to win in more zero-sum confrontations. As a result, the marriage might once again become profitable for him, and stability might therefore be regained. The end-result of the wife's loss of interest in sex, in this hypothetical case, will be a change in the balance of power, although the story also includes a temporary destabilization of the relationship. Many alternative scenarios could be described, but the example illustrates how social exchange theory can be used to trace developments in a marital relationship, and demonstrates that the theory is certainly not limited to a consideration of immediate personal pay-offs. The example also shows how the theory predicts certain compensatory and stabilizing adjustments following changes in the reward value of the relationship for one or both partners. In this respect social exchange theory shows some similarity to the major approach to be considered in Chapter 2–systems theory.

Fertility and Child-rearing

So far the discussion has focused mainly on the marital relationship, but social exchange theory can also be used to explain many other aspects of family life, including decisions regarding fertility, and parent–child relations. A number of studies have examined adults' judgements of the rewards and costs involved in having children, and thus their perception of 'the value of children'. Children are commonly seen as rewarding because they relieve loneliness, provide love and companionship, bring happiness, supply stimulation, and increase self-esteem (Hoffman and Manis, 1982). Children are also recognized as generating substantial costs, including those of high financial outlay, a greatly increased workload, and substantial loss of freedom. The rewards increase with the number of children, but so do the costs, and the rise in costs may be steeper, so that at a certain point having further children will cease to bring a net reward. At this point, therefore, according to this analysis, the couple will choose not to have further children. Thus the theory can explain decisions regarding family size as well as a couple's initial decision about whether or not to have children. When partners agree about the desirability (or the 'profitability') of having a child, they will not be in conflict, but if they make different evaluations then their aspirations will be different and they will be engaged in a zero-sum game in which one will win and one will lose.

Decisions about fertility are based on estimates of the likely rewards that a child (or a further child) will provide, and the likely costs involved in their care. It must be remembered, of course, that many conceptions are unplanned and unwanted. Social exchange theory is only relevant in such cases to the extent that it can help to explain decisions made about the initial sexual activity (particularly regarding contraceptive non-use) and about voluntary abortion, and the analysis it might offer of the anticipated rewards and costs that will follow the birth of the child. When a child is born, whether planned or not, the parents may find that the estimates made of the costs and rewards have to be drastically revised. In some cases such a revision is a happy one, and parents who had underestimated the appeal of the infant, or overestimated the costs involved, will be pleasantly surprised. Sometimes, however, the reality comes as an unpleasant shock. If the baby is handicapped, for example, the parents may downgrade certain anticipated long-term rewards, and may need to increase their estimate of the costs likely to be involved in the child's care. Most parents faced with this situation, as we shall see in Chapter 4, revise their expectations very effectively and in such a way that a high evaluation of the child is maintained. A few are unable to achieve this without professional intervention, however, and in some cases the parents decide that they will not be able to care for the child.

Very high levels of cost are incurred by the continued care of any child. If the child provides many benefits, however, by showing affection, achieving developmental and educational goals, and complying with parental requests, the rewards will outweigh the costs and the child will continue to be loved and cherished. If a parent fails to develop or maintain such a positive evaluation then the child may be at risk of maltreatment. The powerful rewards that most people experience as a result of seeing their children growing up healthy, happy, and intelligent can explain why parents are apparently so self-sacrificing. But strong social sanctions also operate to encourage parental benevolence and to reinforce inhibitions against mistreating children.

Decisions made in the context of a close relationship rely only partly on expectations of how intimates will respond. They also reflect the rewards and costs that might come from friends and neighbours, distant relatives, or societal agencies such as the police, the tax authorities or the social service department. The relevant sanctions may be positive or negative in character, and whereas some operate informally (for example, when grandparents express pleasure following the birth of a grandchild, or when relatives show their disapproval of a divorce), some are managed in a formal way (as when the State gives financial support for those with children, or intervenes in a case of child abuse). Thus government policies, social management practices, and the 'social climate', all play a part in determining individuals' decisions. Nye (1982) has suggested that political changes and social developments can also be explained in terms of social exchange theory, because organizations and groups, including the wider society, also act to minimize costs and maximize profits.

Children's Decisions

Children, of course, do not opt into the family relationship, but their total vulnerability in the early years, and their dependence throughout the years before adolescence, means that they derive extensive rewards from their interactions with other family members. In a few cases a decision is made on their behalf that they would be better off in an alternative situation, and if a child is to be adopted, for example, the professionals involved in choosing a family for the child will often engage in an exercise that is straightforwardly one of 'profit maximization'. They will choose to place the child in the situation where he or she is likely to derive the most benefit and to be at least risk of rejection or maltreatment.

It is very easy to understand many child behaviours in terms of profit maximization. Children seek excitement and novelty, and are highly motivated to attain tangible rewards. Parents are concerned to bring up their children so that they are considerate and thoughtful, and the different values and interests of the parents and the child may lead to frequent conflicts. Children comply if they judge that compliance will be profitable, and for most children parental approval and disapproval act as very powerful rewards and costs. Disciplinary encounters can be seen as zero-sum games. The child wants to continue banging the drum, for example, and the parent wants the noise to stop. One will win and the other will lose. Because parents have many powerful sanctions at their command they have the potential to control situations so that the child experiences more rewards or fewer costs by discontinuing an undesirable activity. However, the effective use of this power demands considerable skill, and some parents are more skilled than others at administering cost and reward contingencies.

During adolescence a number of important changes take place. The adolescent is more competent than the younger child and has less need for the security offered by the parents. At the same time influences beyond the home may become more powerful sources of reward, so that the balance between security and autonomy changes in favour of greater independence. If the adolescent is able to derive substantial rewards from outside the home the parents will lose some of their power over the young person. At the same time the adolescent's reduced family orientation is likely to mean that he or she will provide fewer rewards for other family members and may be seen as deficient in the performance of family roles. Thus for a number of reasons the quality of the parent–adolescent relationship may decline, and in some cases it will break down, with the adolescent either running away or being ejected by the parents. Adolescents who have experienced high costs in the home context (as a result of frequent marital conflict, for example, or abuse), and those who have a very high estimation of the rewards obtainable elsewhere, will be more likely to seek independence at a younger age. Some continue to place a high value on the security and other benefits offered by the family and may thus have very little motivation to leave home.

THEORY AND INTERVENTION

Social exchange theory has been discussed at some length because there is a high level of current interest in the theory, it provides many testable hypotheses, and it is one of the few viable 'macro-theories' that can be used to explain many aspects of family life. It is not difficult to see how the kind of analysis provided by the theory can be used to shed light on many family problem issues and to suggest useful methods of intervention. An unhappy marriage, for example, may be characterized as one in which one or both partners derive few rewards. If a partner who holds most of the power in the relationship manages resources selfishly, the other is likely to be dissatisfied. Those who judge that their partner is incompetent in an important role are likely to be disenchanted with the relationship. Couples who engage in many zero-sum games are likely to experience frequent conflict and to incur high costs. If a marriage is low in terms of its 'residual balance' of rewards (if it is 'bankrupt') then it will be especially vulnerable to any interaction that proves costly to a partner, and such a person may judge that an alternative lifestyle (living alone or with another partner) is likely to be more profitable for them. People seek to enhance their self-esteem, to receive social approval, to maintain relationships that are profitable, and to maximize the profits they derive from these relationships. Together, these motivations can explain many of the decisions that people make, and many of the actions they engage in, within the context of close relationships.

Intervention in cases where a relationship is in difficulties might involve attempts to enhance its profitability for both partners. Some people have little insight into their partner's evaluation of rewards and costs. In such cases, improving the communication about relevant attitudes and preferences might prove very constructive. Encouraging both partners to give more rewards to their spouse (for example, by showing more affection or spending more time with them) might enhance the quality of the marriage, or a couple might be shown how to resolve conflicts by means of negotiation rather than fighting. Some methods aim at changing the power balance within the relationship or at changing partners' perception of their spouse's effectiveness in particular marital roles. All of these interventions can be seen in terms of their effect in increasing the overall level of rewards (or reducing the costs) exchanged in the course of the couple's interaction.

When explanations of the family unit, rather than of an individual's family decisions, are discussed in the next chapter, another major theory—systems theory—will be introduced. However, it should be noted that social exchange theory could be used to provide accounts of whole-family interaction and that systems theory could be applied to an analysis of individuals' decision-making. Thus both theories can in principle be used to explain both an individual's decisions and the behaviour of the family unit, and a comprehensive and truly satisfactory account of the family may eventually emerge as a result of a closer alignment between the two theories.

REFERENCES

Argyle, M. and Henderson, M. (1985) *The Anatomy of Relationships*. Harmondsworth: Penguin.

Bahr, S. J. (1982) Exchange and control in married life. In: F. I. Nye (ed.), *Family Relationships: Rewards and Costs*. Beverly Hills, CA: Sage.

Berkman, L. F. and Breslow, L. (1983) *Health and Ways of Living: The Alameda Country Study*. New York and Oxford: Oxford University Press.

Berkman, L. F. and Syme, S. L. (1979) Social networks, host resistance and mortality: a nine-year follow-up study of Almeda residents. *American Journal of Epidemiology*, **109**, 186–204.

Bernard, J. (1973) *The Future of Marriage*. New York: Bantam.

Blood, R. O., Jr and Wolfe, D. M. (1960) *Husbands and Wives*. New York: Free Press.

Bloom, B. L., Asher, S. R. and White, S. W. (1979) Marital disruption as a stressor. *Psychological Bulletin*, **85**, 867–894.

Brown, G. W. and Harris, T. (1978) *The Social Origins of Depression*. London: Tavistock.

Cargan, L. and Melko, M (1982) *Singles: Myths and Realities*. Beverly Hills, CA: Sage.

Cobb, S. and Jones, J. M. (1984) Social support, support groups and marital relationships. In: S. W. Duck (ed.), *Personal Relationships—5: Repairing Personal Relationships*. London: Academic Press.

Cohen, S. and Syme, S. L. (eds) (1985) *Social Support and Health*. New York: Academic Press.

Cohen, S. and Wills, T. A. (1985) Stress, support and the buffering hypothesis. *Psychological Bulletin*, **98**, 310–357.

DiMatteo, M. R. and Hays, R. (1981) Social support and serious illness. In: B. H. Gottlieb (ed.), *Social Networks and Social Support*. Beverly Hills, CA: Sage.

Farber, B. (1964) *Family: Organization and Interaction*. San Francisco, CA: Chandler.

Freedman, J. L. (1978) *Happy People*. New York: Harcourt Brace Jovanovich.

Ganster, D. C. and Victor, B. (1988) The impact of social support on mental and physical health. *British Journal of Medical Psychology*, **61**, 17–36.

Glenn, N. D. (1975) The contribution of marriage to the psychological well-being of males and females. *Journal of Marriage and the Family*, **37**, 594–600.

Gove, W. R. (1979) The relationship between sex roles, marital status and mental illness. *Social Forces*, **51**, 34–44.

Gove, W. R., Hughes M. and Style, C. B. (1983) Does marriage have positive effects on the psychological well-being of the individual? *Journal of Health and Social Behaviour*, **24**, 122–131.

Griffith, J. (1985) Social support providers: who are they? Where are they met? And the relationship of network characteristics to psychological distress. *Basic and Applied Social Psychology*, **6**, 41–60.

Hoffman, L. W. and Manis, J. D. (1982) The value of children in the United States. In: F. I. Nye (ed.), *Family Relationships: Rewards and Costs*. Beverly Hills, CA: Sage.

Holmes, T. H. and Rahe, R. H. (1967) The Social Readjustment Rating Scale. *Journal of Psychosomatic Research*, **11**, 213–218.

Hughes, M. and Gove, W. R. (1981) Living alone, social integration and mental health. *American Journal of Community Psychology*, **87**, 48–74.

Kanner, A. D., Coyne, J. C., Schaefer, C. and Lazarus, R. S. (1981) Comparison of two modes of stress measurement: minor daily hassles and uplifts vs. major life events. *Journal of Behavioural Medicine*, **4**, 1–39.

Kennedy, S., Kiecolt-Glaser, J. K. and Glaser, R. (1988) Immunological consequences of stressors. *British Journal of Medical Psychology*, **61**, 77–85.

Kessler, R. C. and Essex, M. (1982) Marital status and depression: the importance of coping resources. *Social Forces*, **61**, 484–507.

Levinger, G. (1965) Marital cohesiveness and dissolution: an integrative view. *Journal of Marriage and the Family*, **27**, 19–28.

Levinger, G. (1982) A social exchange view of the dissolution of pair relationships. In: F. I. Nye (ed.), *Family Relationships: Rewards and Costs*. Beverly Hills, CA: Sage.

Lewis, R. A. and Spanier, G. B. (1982) Marital quality, marital stability and social exchange. In: F. I. Nye (ed.), *Family Relationships: Rewards and Costs*. Beverly Hills, CA: Sage

Lynch, J. J. (1977) *The Broken Heart*. New York: Basic Books.

MacFarlane, A. H., Norman, G. R., Streiner, D. L. and Roy, R. G. (1983) The process of social stress: stable, reciprocal and mediating relationships. *Journal of Health and Social Behaviour*, **24**, 160–173.

Madge, N. and Marmot, M. (1987) Psychosocial factors and health. *Quarterly Journal of Social Affairs*, **3**, 81–134.

Martin, B. (1977) *Abnormal Psychology: Clinical and Scientific Perspectives*. New York: Holt, Rinehart and Winston.

McClelland, D. (1979) Inhibited power motivation and high blood pressure in men. *Journal of Abnormal Psychology*, **88**, 182–190.

Medalie, J. H. and Goldbourt, U. (1976) Angina pectoris among 10,000 men. *American Journal of Medicine*, **60**, 910–921.

Morgan, M. (1980) Marital status, health, illness and service use. *Social Science and Medicine*, 14, 633–643.

Newcomb, T. M. (1961) *The Acquaintance Process*. New York: Holt, Rinehart and Winston.

Nye, F. I. (1976) *Role Structure and the Analysis of the Family*. Beverly Hills, CA: Sage.

Nye, F. I. (ed.) (1982) *Family Relationships: Rewards and Costs*. Beverly Hills, CA: Sage.

Nye, F. I. and Berardo, F. (1966) *Emerging Conceptual Frameworks in Family Analysis*. New York: Macmillan.

Nye, F. I. and McLaughlin, S. (1982) Role competence and marital satisfaction. In: F. I. Nye (ed.), *Family Relationships: Rewards and Costs*. Beverly Hills, CA: Sage.

Paykel, E. S., McGuinness, B. and Gomez, J. (1976) An Anglo-American comparison of the scaling of life-events. *British Journal of Medical Psychology*, 49, 237–247.

Peplau, A. and Perlman, D. (1982) *Loneliness*. New York: Wiley.

Perlman, D. and Rook, K. S. (1987) Social support, social deficits, and the family: Toward the enhancement of well-being. In: S. Oskamp (ed.), *Family Processes and Problems: Social Psychological Aspects*. Beverly Hills, CA: Sage.

Reed, D., McGee, D., Yano, K. and Feinleib, M. (1983) Social networks and coronary heart disease among Japanese men in Hawaii. *American Journal of Epidemiology*, 115, 384–396.

Reis, H. T. (1984) Social interaction and well-being. In: S. W. Duck (ed.), *Personal Relationships—5: Repairing Personal Relationships*. London: Academic Press.

Rook, K. S. (1985) The functions of social bonds: Perspective from research on social support, loneliness and social isolation. In: I. G. Sarason and B. R. Sarason (eds.), *Social Support: Theory, Research and Application*. The Hague: Martinus Nijhoff.

Thibaut, J. W. and Kelley, H. H. (1959) *The Social Psychology of Groups*. New York: John Wiley.

Thoits, P. A. (1982) Conceptual, methodological and theoretical problems in studying social support as a buffer against life stress. *Journal of Health and Social Behaviour*, 23, 145–159.

Verbrugge, L. M. (1979) Marital status and health. *Journal of Marriage and the Family*, 41, 267–285.

Weiss, R. S. (1974) The provisions of social relationships. In Z. Rubin (ed.), *Doing Unto Others: Joining, Molding, Conforming, Helping, Loving*. Englewood Cliffs, NJ: Prentice-Hall.

Wills, T. A. (1984) Supportive functions of interpersonal relationships. In: S. Cohen and L. Syme (eds.), *Social Support and Health*. New York: Academic.

2
The Family Unit

Even if we knew everything about each of the individual members of a particular family, we would still not know everything about the family unit. Relationships cannot be understood by examining people as individuals, no matter how extensive the analysis might be. Relationships are the links and contiguities that connect people; they are 'between' people rather than 'within' one or more individuals. Each family member has a relationship with each other member, with particular sub-groups of people ('the children', for example), and with the family as a whole. But even an examination of all of these relationships would not amount to an analysis of the family unit. The family unit has 'emergent properties'; it is more than the sum of its parts.

In this chapter a number of issues concerning 'the family unit' will be explored. First we consider a useful metaphor for the family unit—that of 'the organism'—before introducing 'systems theory'. This allows us to examine many important aspects of the structure and interactions of whole families and to differentiate between families that function well and those that are dysfunctional. Family responses to stressful events are then investigated.

THE FAMILY AS 'AN ORGANISM'

If the family is not simply a collection of individuals, but is 'a thing in itself', what kind of thing is it? In Chapter 1 it was shown that although everyone 'knows' what a family is, the matter of definition is rather complex. Similarly, everyone is very well acquainted with family interaction but the task of providing a more formal analysis is by no means easy. Part of the complexity stems from the fact that the family can be considered in a number of different ways. It can be seen, for example, as a sub-unit within society, or as an interacting group of individuals. Although these characterizations are rather different, both are valid, and many others could be suggested. The particular goal of a psychological analysis is to understand the interactions that occur within the family group, although this often requires consideration of the social context and the social identity of the family.

When attempting to analyse something that appears particularly complex, it if often instructive to explore certain basic issues by employing a convenient metaphor. In some ways families are *like* tribes, committees, hanging mobiles, kaleidoscopes, etc. We will take just one metaphor, and consider the family *as if* it were a living organism. Like organisms, families have a structure and organization, they carry out certain functions, and they interact with the wider environment. More metaphorically, families can be said to have an 'anatomy', a 'physiology', and a 'mentality', and to follow a developmental 'life-course'. Like organisms, families may develop 'disorders' and often suffer 'stress' and 'injury' as a result of adverse environmental events.

STRUCTURE

Family units have a structure or '*anatomy*'. As was shown in Chapter I, it is not always easy to establish the membership of a family unit (and thus, in terms of the metaphor, to recognize the boundary of the organism). Families are not watertight units. A member of one family may also be a member of one or more other families, and in some cases (if a person has been 'disowned' or is 'missing in action', for example), boundary issues may be very difficult to resolve.

Various structural patterns can be mapped onto family groups. For example, family form or structure can be construed in terms of gender and generation, yielding 'positional roles' such as those of 'father', 'eldest daughter', 'grandmother', etc. Or the family can be analysed in terms of particular 'process roles' that members play in the 'family drama'—roles such as 'the breadwinner' or 'the peacemaker'. Structure can also be examined in terms of communication pathways or power relationships. Using any one of these perspectives it is often possible to identify particular sub-groups. Thus sub-groups might be distinguished on the basis of positional roles (the parental sub-group, for example), or patterns of alliances between members (thus there may be 'rival factions', 'strong coalitions', or 'an isolated member'). Thus any particular family unit might be analysed structurally in many different ways, and any accurate description may be useful and revealing.

FUNCTION

Physiology is that part of biology which is concerned with the functioning of the organism. Just as, for the living organism, anatomy and physiology are closely linked, so structural aspects of the family relate to the functioning of the group and the processes that it engages in. As applied to living organisms the term 'function' has two related meanings. First there are certain things that the organism is required to do in order to survive or to fulfil certain 'necessary' tasks (such 'functions' include respiration and reproduction). Secondly, the term relates to how organisms work or perform (i.e. '*how* they function'). This distinction is relevant in family analysis, too, for families can be said both 'to have certain functions' and 'to function in certain ways'.

As part of society, families have a reproductive function and facilitate the transmission of the culture from one generation to the next. These are important societal functions of traditional families, but they are not performed by, for example, couples who opt to remain childless, or gay families. But families of all types regulate members' behaviour and promote their individual interests. They offer protection and support, and generally enhance individuals' well-being. Thus these functions would appear to be universally applicable to family units (although this does not mean that they are adequately fulfilled in all particular cases). The question of *how* families function could be seen, in terms of the organic metaphor, as a 'physiological' issue or as a 'psychological' issue (i.e. how do families *behave*). We will consider family behaviour and family experience under the 'psychology' heading.

PSYCHOLOGY

Many living organisms are capable of learning, and those that are highly advanced can also be said to experience the world and to have a 'mentality'. It is clear that individual members of a family learn, think and feel, but can the family *as a unit* be said to learn or to have a 'mentality'? In one sense the term 'family behaviour' simply refers to the behaviour of individuals within the family context, and this presents no special problem. The key question is whether it is ever legitimate to refer to the behaviour *of* the family. It is certainly possible to recognize that some families have a particular 'style' of interaction and to identify regular behavioural sequences (sometimes referred to as 'scripts' or 'schemata'). Behavioural strategies that are in some way 'successful' (for example, those that are effective in relieving tension) tend to be repeated and to become incorporated into the family repertoire. Thus families do evolve interaction patterns that it would seem appropriate to regard as features of the family unit rather than of individuals.

The appropriateness of ascribing behaviour and learning to families can also be supported by a further argument. In their descriptions of the rites and rituals that occur in tribal societies, anthropologists refer to *tribal* rites and *tribal* rituals, and clearly regard these as features of the society rather than of individuals. Families also engage in 'rites' and 'rituals' (for example, they may develop their own special ways of celebrating birthdays or of remembering a family member who has died). Such behavioural patterns might well be labelled '*family* rites' and '*family* rituals'.

The next question is whether a 'family unit' can be said to have a 'mentality'. Within most families certain beliefs, attitudes, and values will be generally held, and where there is a high degree of consensus between family members, the terms 'family belief' or 'family myth' might be employed. But if such terms simply reflect an overlap or agreement between individuals then they hardly represent a 'family mentality'. Yet if we consider how consensus develops in a family we find support for the proposition that in some ways a family unit may be said to have 'a mind of its own'. Within a group, certain 'synergies' may be produced. For example, the fact that a couple *share* the same belief may have a far more powerful effect than the fact that each of the two individuals holds the belief. Similarly, a sequence or pattern of actions may have a significance beyond that of the actions considered separately, just as a melody is more than a series of individual musical notes. Studies of interactional processes in groups other than the family have provided evidence that group decisions, group behaviours, and group experiences are not merely 'averages' of individual members' judgements, action tendencies, or experiences. What emerges as a result of the group process is often something that would not have been predicted from a knowledge of the individuals' initial positions.

The phenomenon of 'groupthink' has been painstakingly analysed by Janis (1972), and there have now been many experimental demonstrations of decision shifts and the emergence of novel behaviours or experiences as a function of group interaction. Such phenomena have been demonstrated in laboratory settings with groups of strangers convened especially to take part in the experiment. These groups have no interactive history, the tasks they face are usually artificial, and the group members have little commitment to the group or to any individual within it. The fact that substantial 'emergent' effects can be demonstrated even in these circumstances strongly suggests that similar (and perhaps far more powerful) effects emerge in family units.

Sociologists concerned with 'the sociology of knowledge' have provided detailed analyses of how families 'construct reality' (e.g. Berger and Luckmann, 1966; Reiss, 1981). A consensus view of neighbours, agencies, world events, and the family itself, emerges as a result of interactive processes. Many such processes operate in a subtle fashion and are difficult for an outside observer to recognize. Non-verbal communication, and what is *not* said, may be as important in the reality construction process as messages that are more explicit. Those working within the field of family therapy have also provided many illustrations of how families construct reality, and they too regard these constructions as attributes of the family unit rather than of individual members. Therapists have been especially concerned to report cases in which a family belief, of 'myth', helps to generate or maintain a symptom. But all families engage in mythologizing to some extent, and many myths are benign or helpful in their effect. Past events may be selectively recalled and re-worked to meet the needs and aspirations of the family, and present threats may be characterized or 'appraised' so that an optimistic and encouraging outlook is maintained.

DEVELOPMENT

Living things grow, develop, and eventually die. Families, too, pass through a developmental sequence, They are 'formed', they undergo changes, and in the end they 'die'. A phrase that is sometimes used to describe this sequence of transitions is 'the family career'. Different types of family unit follow different career pathways, and many of these have not yet been examined in any detail. Considerable attention has been paid, however, to the developmental patterns of 'traditional' families. Various analysts have distinguished a number of 'modal' developmental stages. Some have chosen to divide the 'family life cycle' into four such stages, while others have differentiated between seven, eight, 12, or even more. Duvall (1977) formulated eight stages, starting with the married couple who have no children and ending with the ageing family— a stage that lasts from retirement until death. Any characterization of the family career in terms of a fixed number of stages will necessarily be rather simplistic. Such schemes tend to over-emphasize the uniformity of development and often demarcate between phases at rather arbitrary points (for example, Duvall's stage II ends when the eldest child is $2\frac{1}{2}$ years old).

Nevertheless, such models have been useful in mapping broad patterns of change, and the delineation of stages has facilitated the recognition of certain systematic shifts that tend to occur in the course of development. Families that are at the same stage of development are likely to be somewhat alike in their interactional style and to face similar 'tasks' or problems. Thus many 'young families' experience pressures that are somewhat different from those faced by families with adolescent children. In order to provide a developmental analysis of data from their major study of intact families, Olson and McCubbin (1983) distinguished seven stages: young couple; childbearing; school age; adolescent; 'launching'; 'empty nest'; and retirement. This study indicated, for example, that marital happiness tended to decrease at the childbearing stage and then increased again during the 'empty nest' stage.

The numerous shifts and transitions that occur during development require the family to adapt. Thus when the first child is born the married couple must assume parental roles. The nature of their interaction will change and the family boundary is expanded to include the infant. The birth of another child will affect the relationship that the parents have established with their firstborn. During the family career there are likely to be several 'entrances' and 'exits' (as new members enter or leave the group), and there will be other changes as family members get older. As children grow up their dependency decreases and they are able to communicate more effectively and to assume more responsible roles. Thus family structure changes radically and repeatedly over the course of normal development. But in addition to the adjustments made in response to 'maturational' changes, the structure may need to adapt in response to 'non-normative' family events, and to pressures that originate outside the family.

INTERCHANGES WITH THE ENVIRONMENT

Living organisms are constantly engaged in exchanges with their environment. Certain ecological conditions make it easy for them to survive, whereas others continually present a threat. Families, too, are heavily influenced both by their immediate physical and social environment, and by the wider social context. For example, family interaction patterns are partly dependent on the structure and resources available in the home. Architectural features will determine the degree of privacy that can be achieved, and the availability of labour-saving devices may reduce conflicts about chores. But families also partly design their physical environment to meet their particular needs. Thus the allocation of rooms to particular individuals or to particular functions will reflect aspects of family interaction. The fact that the marital partners have separate bedrooms, for example, is likely to indicate something significant about the nature of their relationship. Families are also affected by the material resources and facilities available in the neighbourhood. Thus efficient transport between the home and the workplace will mean that workers are able to spend more time at home and are less likely to arrive from the workplace tired and frustrated. The social environment also has a major influence on the family. Contact with neighbours, with relatives, with special-interest groups, and with agencies such as the police, social services and schools all make a substantial impact on families.

The processes that occur within any family reflect the sociohistorical context. Anthropological studies show how family patterns differ from culture to culture, and historical studies (e.g. Shorter, 1975) reveal how family structures, values, and practices have changed over time. A number of significant themes can be identified in the evolution of 'the family' in Western culture. One substantial change has been that family units (as defined in terms of the criteria of high intimacy, frequent interaction, and close alliance) have contracted, so that they now include fewer members. In previous centuries most family units included many people who were related by blood or legal ties. Kinship apparently had greater psychological relevance, and family units included many individuals who would now be regarded only as members of 'the extended family'. Most contemporary family units, at least in the majority of Western cultures, include only two generations and do not include the parent's siblings, nephews or nieces.

Another important change has been the increased diversity of family forms, with far fewer people now living in what is termed 'the traditional family'. There has also been a substantial increase in the direct involvement of social agencies in many aspects of family life. Provision of educational, medical, counselling and legal services has meant that many duties and rights that families previously exercised independently now come under public scrutiny and receive support or bring sanctions from outside agencies. These days, groups of professionals offer help and advice on almost every aspect of family life, the events of birth and death have become increasingly medicalized, and many aspects of child socialization have been taken over by schools. There have also been momentous changes in the climate of opinion on many issues that are of key importance to family life, and quite disparate attitudes and provisions exist in different societies regarding, for example, contraception, abortion, divorce, the care of the elderly, and sexual behaviour. Social ideologies, mores and provisions all have profound effects on interaction and experiences within individual families.

PATHOLOGY AND TRAUMA

Just as organisms often develop disorders or ailments due to some internal malfunction, so families sometimes become distressed as a result of an intrinsic and dysfunctional interactional pattern. Certain styles of interaction are likely to create a tense atmosphere within the family, or to impair communication, so that there is an overall reduction in the family's ability to function effectively. This may lead to the development of a medical or psychological symptom in one or more members. Alternatively, it may create a high level of family conflict, or might lead one or more members to withdraw from the family unit. In some cases there is a gradual reduction of family well-being and an erosion of competence until a crisis or symptom is eventually precipitated. In other cases the poor functioning of the family becomes apparent only when circumstances require change (for example, when a child is born, or when an adolescent in about to leave home). Coping with such normative changes demands a certain flexibility, and families that are resistant to change will find it particularly difficult to adapt.

Many families are also exposed to stressful events that are non-normative and may originate outside the family. Extreme examples are the sudden unemployment or imprisonment of a family member, or an environmental disaster that deprives the family of its home. Even families that have functioned well in normal circumstances may be severely disrupted by such misfortune. It is not simply that individual family members are stressed; the event produces changes in family structure. Roles may be realigned, and established behavioural patterns may change radically. In the face of extreme adversity some families are able to unite and to act in an adaptive and coordinated fashion, whereas others are thrown into crisis. Pursuing the organic metaphor, families may be said to differ in terms of their 'constitutional strength', their 'resistance', and their 'immunity'.

The metaphor of the family as an 'organism' has allowed us to explore a number of important aspects of the family unit. Although thinking about the family *as if* it were a living organism has been instructive, this method of inquiry is limited, and it is necessary to take the further step of examining the structure and processes of family units more directly. One approach that offers many insights into family life, is 'systems theory'. To consider the family 'as a system' is not simply to employ another metaphor, for whereas families are not living organisms they certainly *are* interactive systems.

THE FAMILY AS A SYSTEM

In Chapter 1, social exchange theory was used to examine how individuals make decisions regarding their family relationships. In this chapter we introduce a theory that provides an account of the family as a unit. 'General systems theory' was initially formulated by the biologist von Bertanlanffy in the 1920s and was then developed by mathematicians, engineers, and others before being applied to social organizations, including small groups, the family, and whole societies (Bertanlanffy, 1968; Buckley, 1967). Systems theory is better at providing descriptions than at making specific predictions about families, and it might therefore be more appropriate to view it as a conceptual tool rather than as a testable theory. 'Systems thinking' has had a special impact on the development of therapeutic strategies, but has also provided useful insights into many of the complex processes that occur within families.

In the following sections some basic concepts of systems theory are introduced; we then explore the nature of the family as a system; and we consider the relationship between system dysfunction and family problems.

SYSTEMS THEORY

A system is a set of elements, the relationships between them, and the relationships between the attributes or characteristics of the elements. A system is more than simply a collection because there are comparatively stable relationships between the elements (i.e. there is structure) and because the different parts of the system are causally linked. Systems theory employs the concept of 'circular causality'. According to this, a cause produces an effect which then has many repercussions, some of which have an impact on whatever was originally the cause. Any observation of a system takes place at a particular point in time, and at that moment any identifiable effect will already have produced changes in whatever is recognized as the cause of that effect. The process of observation imposes some degree of 'stasis' on a system that is in reality highly dynamic and interactive. Thus although causes precede their effects, the connections between *observed* causes and effects are viewed as circular, rather than linear.

Information is transmitted within the system and is used to maintain stability, to bring about structural changes, and to facilitate interaction with other systems. By employing information feedback loops systems may behave in ways that can be described as 'goal-seeking' or 'purposive'. Negative feedback allows a system to maintain stability, as in the case of the most commonly quoted example, a thermostat. A thermostat is controlled by negative feedback, so that when the temperature increases above a certain level the heating is switched off, but when the temperature decreases sufficiently the heating is switched on. The process of maintaining stability is labelled 'homeostasis'. The capacity for such control is engineered into certain mechanical systems and occurs naturally in all biological and social systems. In the case of the heating control a positive feedback loop would promote further heating when the temperature was high and this would clearly be maladaptive. Although the effect of positive feedback is often destructive, it can also be useful in introducing variety into the actions performed by the system and allowing it to change or develop from one stable state to another. This is often useful in producing adaptation to a sustained change in environmental conditions, but such adaptation demands a certain degree of flexibility. The process of adaptive structural development is referred to as 'morphogenesis'.

A system is a structure of elements, each of which is likely to play different roles within the system. The role or roles played by any element will depend upon its intrinsic characteristics and its position in the system structure. Within the system as a whole, several sub-systems may be discernible (indeed, each element can be regarded as a sub-system), and the whole system may also be identified as a sub-system within a wider system. The identification of a system is dependent on there being a recognizable external boundary. Boundaries that offer only a partial or transitory separation are described as 'permeable', and systems with a permeable boundary are described as 'open'. Open systems have more influence on the environment, and are more responsive to the environment, than 'closed' systems (i.e. those that have a relatively impermeable boundary).

If the boundaries around sub-systems are excessively permeable, the limited partition between them will limit their capacity to function autonomously. In many cases the resulting lack of 'specialism' will hinder the effective functioning of the system as a whole (reducing its capacity to adapt to change, for example). At the other extreme, if the boundaries between sub-systems are highly impermeable, feedback and communication between the sub-systems will be reduced. Each will work relatively independently and this, too, will limit the effectiveness of the system.

Because systems have some degree of continuity of structure over time, they behave in a somewhat orderly manner. Thus an observer may identify certain patterns in the system's behaviour, and make certain predictions about how it will act. Identified behavioural patterns may be regarded as the 'rules' that the system follows, and recurring goal-directed behaviours may be recognized as 'strategies'. Some highly complex systems (and especially social systems) have such elaborate feedback and internal communication characteristics that they may be said to be 'self-aware'. Individual elements may be able to recognize their own position in the system, and the positions of other elements, and may have a realistic appreciation of the identity and characteristics of the system as a whole. Systems that are self-aware have a greatly increased capacity to maintain or change their structure and can respond more flexibly to new situations.

FAMILY SYSTEMS

Families are systems, and the members of the family unit are the elements. The system also encompasses the relationships between the members and between their various attributes as individuals. Stability is maintained by homeostatic processes that preserve the integrity and structure of the system. Thus families need to sustain an appropriate balance between the autonomy of individual members and the cohesiveness of the unit as a whole. If the family environment has become too restrictive, actions that foster independence may reduce cohesion to a more acceptable level. On the other hand, if family members have become too distant from one another then an increase in joint activities or a display of warmth may strengthen the bonds between them. In either case negative feedback is operating to maintain the status quo. A positive feedback loop, however, may destabilize the family system, as when conflict produces more conflict. Such a vicious circle can lead to an escalation that may become violent and out of control. Negative feedback operating in a conflict situation may attenuate the hostility, thereby reducing the tension and restoring equilibrium.

The operation of a positive feedback loop is sometimes productive, for example when it enables the family to adapt its structure in changing circumstances (this is the process of 'morphogenesis'). Adjustments will be necessary as individuals mature, and as members enter or leave the group, and most family systems need to undergo several radical structural changes during their lifespan. Whereas the presence of infants or young children, for example, demands a relatively cohesive system, a family with adolescent members will need to allow more autonomy. In addition to the radical structural changes that take place at times of major developmental transition, more subtle adaptations are continually taking place.

Family structure can be analysed in terms of roles or relationships. The systems approach tends to define the individual in terms of his or her role within the group, although each individual can also be viewed as a distinct sub-system. It is possible to map several different role structures onto a family group and a number of sub-systems (such as the parental sub-system) may be identified. The degree of permeability of the boundaries between such sub-systems has important consequences for how well the system is able to function as a unit. Thus if the boundary between the parent and child sub-systems is highly permeable there will be a lack of generational structure and this may reduce the effectiveness of the system (for example, in its role of socializing children). The boundary around the system gives the family unit an identity, but this external boundary must have some degree of permeability. Families are therefore open systems (some families are more open than others), that continually influence and respond to the wider physical and social environment. The impact of such external systems as the school, the factory, and the health service, may have a critical effect on how a family functions.

No family operates in a totally chaotic fashion, and interaction within any family is therefore systematic and repetitive to some degree. Families tend to develop particular styles of interaction, some of which appear goal-directed or 'strategic', and some recurring behavioural patterns may be identified as 'routines', 'habits', 'customs', or 'rituals'. Any regular pattern of behaviour may be described as 'rule-following' and will generate expectations about future actions, but many rules also operate as directives. Prescriptive rules help the system to regulate the behaviour of individual members and the relationships between sub-systems, and an infringement of such a rule often brings sanctions and may lead to conflict. If a rule has never been made explicit it may be especially difficult to resolve the issue of a possible transgression by means of negotiation. Some systems are flexible and some are rigid in their application of rules and in their capacity to modify rules as circumstances change.

Families are communication systems, and family communication is continual because even silence (what people do not say, or what they avoid saying) often has significance. Thus it is impossible for members not to communicate. The verbal content of a communication is accompanied by non-verbal behaviour that often has a special implication for the relationship between the informant and the recipient of the message. Effective communications are clearly transmitted, with a close similarity between the verbal and non-verbal elements. Because there is constant communication between elements, the sub-systems, and the system as a whole, a family can be said to be 'self-aware'. Each family evolves its own 'construction of reality' and a principal component within this is the representation of the family itself.

FAMILY SYSTEMS AND FAMILY PROBLEMS

If a family is well structured, with boundaries that are somewhat permeable, and if it communicates effectively, it is likely to function well. On the other hand, families that are structurally deficient, or in which messages are poorly transmitted, are likely to be dysfunctional. But although a dysfunctional family is likely to have appreciable problems, observing that a family has a problem does not imply that it must be dysfunctional in terms of its properties as a system. It is therefore necessary to make the distinction between 'a dysfunctional family' and 'a family with a problem'. Some family problems are 'intrinsic' and arise as a direct result of system dysfunction, but others are caused by the impact of particular stressors and hardships on families that, according to systems criteria, would be judged as having good structural properties.

Conflict, violence, or the symptomatic behaviour of one or more family members may be the result of structural or process dysfunctions that are intrinsic to the particular family system. But some families encounter serious difficulties only when a major change of circumstances demands a substantial developmental transition. Thus a family that has been happy, well-functioning and symptom-free for many years may encounter difficulties when an adolescent child is about to leave home. In other cases a family that has been successful, and has coped well with developmental transitions, will collapse when faced with a major catastrophe. Thus the destruction of the family home by fire, the sudden imprisonment of a member, or some other disaster may create intense pressures that seriously threaten the stability of even the most resourceful family system.

Just as individuals differ in the strength of their 'constitution', so families may be seen as constitutionally strong or weak. Systemic dysfunction saps constitutional strength, but so do a number of other factors, including recent experience of major stress. Although a particular family's capacity to withstand pressure will be somewhat consistent, vulnerability will also fluctuate somewhat. In some cases a stressful event will occur when the family is especially susceptible, perhaps because it is in the process of undergoing a developmental change or is still recovering from the impact of an earlier stressor. Some adverse incidents thus occur at more opportune times than others, and events sometimes conspire to deal a 'combination punch' that few families would be able to withstand. Thus even strong families may be critically damaged by extreme adversity.

A family may be left vulnerable as a result of previous misfortune, but the system's experience of overcoming stressful situations may have enabled it to develop a number of strategies that will prove useful when later setbacks occur. Some such strategies amount to methods for solving practical problems, while others relate to structural adaptations. Thus a family may learn that one member is especially good at coordinating family activities during times of crisis, or the family may learn that by making the external boundary more permeable, and accepting help, pressures on the family are somewhat reduced. Thus a family may be strengthened or 'immunized' against some of the worst effects of later adversities. It may also learn to anticipate certain difficulties and to take successful avoiding action.

DIFFERENCES BETWEEN FAMILIES

Before considering in more detail the characteristics of well-functioning families and the various ways in which family systems may be dysfunctional, we will address a more general question—What important contrasts can be made between families as systems? Families clearly differ in their basic structure (one-parent families, childless couples, etc.), in their stage of development, and their cultural setting. But are there fundamental systems characteristics that can usefully differentiate between families whatever their shape, stage of development and sociohistorical context?

A number of therapists and research teams have identified dimensions that appear to be helpful in making such differentiations, and two dimensions in particular regularly emerge from such analyses. These will be discussed in the context of a brief examination of the 'circumplex model' devised by Olson and his colleagues (Olson, Russell and Sprenkle, 1979). The circumplex model actually discriminates between families in terms of three dimensions—'communication', 'cohesion' and 'adaptability'. The communication dimension ranges from supportive, empathic and clear communication, at one end, to critical and unclear communication at the other. Good communication within the family system enables members to express their needs and preferences as they relate to the other, more prominent, dimensions of the model. 'Adaptability' refers to the ability of the system to change its structure, roles, and rules in response to both situational and developmental pressures. A family that has a very low degree of adaptability is described as 'rigid' and a family that has a very high level is described as 'chaotic'. As the labels imply, a family's location at either of these extremes is regarded as maladaptive. Thus both rigid and chaotic families are likely to experience special problems, particularly when faced with a need to change. Families located between the extremes are less likely to have difficulties in making adaptations. Such families are labelled 'structured' if they show a tendency to maintain the status quo, and 'flexible' if they are more adaptable.

In rigid families, roles are strictly defined, the power structure is inflexible, leadership is authoritarian, and discipline is managed in an autocratic way. Rules are treated as if they were immovable laws and are not subjected to negotiation or compromise. In chaotic families, on the other hand, there are few clear rules, so that there is continual wrangling and few decisions are ever reached. There is little or no consistency of power structure, and positive and negative sanctions are delivered in an irregular and rather arbitrary way. Children receive little guidance, and discipline is inconsistent. As a result, they are often confused about what behaviour is appropriate and the parents find it difficult to control them. In families that fall between these two extremes, rules are subjected to negotiation and issues are discussed in a democratic manner. Power is exercised fairly and carefully. Children are disciplined effectively, and their needs and wishes, as well as those of the parents, are taken into consideration. The role structure is generally stable but there is also some degree of flexibility, so that the family is able to adapt when necessary.

The other dimension, 'cohesion', relates both to the emotional bonding between family members and to their autonomy as individuals. Families that are very low on the cohesion dimension are said to be 'disengaged'. The bonds between members are extremely weak and each individual functions as an autonomous unit. There is little family unity or sense of family identity. At the other extreme the 'enmeshed' family has an extremely high level of cohesion. Members identify with the family so closely, and the bonds are so tight, that there is little sense of individual identity. Many enmeshed families are relatively 'closed' to the outside world and show little interest in matters that do not have an immediate significance for the family. Between the two extremes are families that strike a balance between closeness and individual autonomy. Some of these families (those labelled 'separated') tend towards low cohesion while others (labelled 'connected') show a tendency towards high cohesion. Members of families in the mid-range of the cohesion dimension are intimately involved with each other, share many common concerns, and identify with the family unit, but they also have their own interests and are able to maintain a degree of independent functioning.

Olson's model combines the two major dimensions to create a 'space' in which any particular family can be located. Although, conceptually, each dimension is a continuum, families are classified into one of four 'types' on each dimension. Thus, employing both dimensions, a particular family would be located in one of 16 cells in a 'four by four' grid. An enmeshed family, for example, would be further classified as 'enmeshed–rigid', 'enmeshed–structured', 'enmeshed–flexible' or 'enmeshed–chaotic'. Families that are extreme on both dimensions are labelled 'extreme'; those that are extreme on only one dimension are 'mid-range'; and those that occupy a middle position on both dimensions are 'balanced'. The hypothesis is that balanced families are likely to function better than extreme or mid-range families. They will be more effective in fulfilling their objectives and dealing with internal differences, and few complications will be generated in the course of their day-to-day interaction. They will also be relatively effective in adapting to developmental demands and in meeting pressures imposed by special hardships or misfortune.

Although the circumplex model provides a particularly lucid and well-formulated analysis of family differences, the two major dimensions have long been recognized by clinicians and researchers as being of of special significance (e.g. Angell, 1936; Minuchin, 1974). Empirical exploration of the model has confirmed the existence of the two dimensions and shown them to be independent (a review is provided by Russell and Olson, 1982). Thus a family's rating on one dimension does not predict its position on the other. There is also empirical support for the hypothesis that extreme families function less well than those that are balanced (Sprenkle and Olson, 1978; Olson and McCubbin, 1983).

Olson and his colleagues have developed 'family adaptability and cohesion evaluation scales' ('FACES III' is the current version) to measure members' perceptions of family functioning. This enables a particular family to be located in terms of the two key dimensions. The results of studies indicate, however, that members of the same family often hold quite different views of their family on these dimensions. Olson and McCubbin (1983) found that, in general, wives rated the family as higher on cohesion than did their husbands, and that adolescents of both sexes viewed the family as much less cohesive than did their parents.

To categorize a family in terms of the circumplex model, the FACES scores obtained from members are compared with pre-established norms. However, these norms derive from large-scale studies of intact families in the United States and it has become apparent that they may not be directly applicable to non-traditional families or to those from other cultures. This does not mean that the dimensions are any less relevant in these cases, but only that the distribution of scores for such families may be somewhat different from those in the original sample. Cultural and sub-cultural differences in the average levels of cohesion and adaptability may reflect differences in values. Thus in the Puerto-Rican and Italian cultures a particularly high value is placed on emotional and physical togetherness, and the same is true of some religious groups such as the Mormons and the Amish (Olson and McCubbin, 1983). Within the relevant cultural context, families that conform to these ideals might function very well, although in terms of the general norms associated with the circumplex model they would be classified as enmeshed. Thus there may well be significant differences in the levels of cohesiveness and adaptability that characterize optimal functioning in different contexts.

A comparable argument can be made with respect to non-traditional family forms. Thus in a study of well-established lesbian relationships it was found that a large majority of these family units would be classified, according to the standard criteria, as enmeshed and chaotic (Zacks, Green and Marrow, 1988). However, the authors of this study argue that because many women place a high value on emotional closeness, the extreme cohesion scores may simply reflect the fact that two women are involved in the relationship. Similarly, lesbian women are likely to have become adaptable in the face of social prejudice, and this might be reflected in the high scores for adaptability. Most of the women reported a high level of satisfaction with their relationship and there was no evidence to suggest that the relationships were dysfunctional. Thus special care must be taken in applying the terms 'enmeshment' and 'chaos' too readily to families that differ in form or culture from those studied in the original research. But although the levels of cohesion and adaptability differ significantly between populations, these dimensions do seem to be applicable to the full range of family groups.

OPTIMAL FAMILIES

Judging by a number of criteria, many families appear to function very well. Individual members are satisfied with their family relationships and are psychologically healthy. There is relatively little conflict, and the family is able to adapt easily and successfully to developmental changes and to cope well with most stressful events. Such families are variously labelled 'healthy', 'well-functioning', 'energized' or 'optimal'. It would be wrong to imagine that such families never become distressed, however, for in the face of disaster they may experience very grave crises and may need help in order to remain a viable unit. But these family systems generate few problems, and in all normal circumstances they function well.

Many theorists, clinicians and researchers have suggested qualities that characterize such families, and many of the descriptions they have provided reflect the conceptual framework of systems theory. The following 'portrait of the optimal family' includes attributes that are frequently cited in the literature (sources include Beavers, 1977; Epstein, Bishop and Levin, 1978; Fisher and Sprenkle, 1978; Lewis *et al.*, 1976; Minuchin, 1974; Olson and McCubbin, 1983; Olson, Sprenkle and Russell, 1979; Pratt, 1976; Satir, 1972; Stinnett *et al.*, 1980; Straus, 1968; Textor, 1989).

In healthy families, members have warm and close relationships with one another. Each identifies with the family as a whole and has a sense of 'family pride'. Despite the cohesiveness of the unit, however, individuals are granted autonomy and members retain their own identity. Such families have an external boundary that is semi-permeable, permitting help and supportive information into the system but avoiding intrusion by deviant or disruptive environmental influences. As 'open' systems they are able to take advantage of input (including information and practical help), and by interacting with neighbours and the community they are able to maintain a positive relationship with the wider system.

The internal structure is clear, and boundaries (for example, between the parental sub-system and the child sub-system) are adequately maintained. Power is distributed relatively equally within generations, but not between generations. Thus although the parents share power, they remain in control of their children. Minuchin (1974) and others regard a clear hierarchical structure as a prerequisite for effective family functioning. However, healthy families are not inflexible in their power structure and are able to make suitable adjustments when developmental pressures or changes of circumstance require. Roles are clearly differentiated and are complementary. Individuals are assigned to particular tasks and acknowledged to have specific rights and duties, and they do not experience internal conflict regarding the various roles they play within the family. Although roles are clearly defined, substantial flexibility is maintained. Thus when one person is temporarily unable to play a particular role, another person takes over. Such replacement is smooth, and is understood and accepted by family members. Furthermore, there are no problems of readjustment if a person becomes available to resume a former role.

There are clear rules that are understood and supported by all members. Infringement brings appropriate sanctions, but there is some flexibility in applying rules, and they change with circumstances and with the stage of family development. Thus rules concerning how the children should behave are revised continually as the children get older. Rule changes are explicit and often follow a process of negotiation. Healthy families engage in open and effective communication. The meaning of messages is clear and it is always apparent to whom the message is addressed. Questions are clearly asked and plainly answered, and all transactions have a clear ending (Satir, 1972). The way in which a message is expressed is almost always congruent with the verbal content.

Members are able to communicate their opinions, hopes and fears freely and without anxiety. Individuals are not 'forbidden' to express their sentiments openly or to experience many different types of feeling. Nevertheless, not all aspects of family life are seen as suitable for open discussion, and the need for privacy is respected. Healthy families recognize issues of conflict and tackle them constructively. They discuss matters openly, engage in negotiation, and often arrive at resolutions by compromise. Thus conflict is not merely regulated, but differences are also satisfactorily resolved; healthy families are not torn apart by disagreements or fights. When disputes occur between individuals, other family members do not ignore the fact, or align with one party against the other, but attempt to arbitrate or bring about a reconciliation, and after a conflict has subsided measures are taken to strengthen relationships. Healthy families are effective in dealing with conflict, just as they are effective in solving a wide range of problems and achieving many goals. They have a wide range of strategies within their repertoire, respond flexibly, generate new tactics, and learn by experience. Thus strategies that have proved beneficial in the past are likely to be used again.

All families 'construct reality' (Reiss, 1981) and develop a collective impression that encompasses many aspects of the world, including the family, neighbours, relatives, and the physical environment. This construction is sometimes labelled 'paradigm' (Reiss, 1981), 'world view' (Minuchin and

Fishman, 1981), or 'family cosmology' (Solomon, 1976). This representation of the world is continually being negotiated and elaborated. Sometimes the re-editing process is explicit. One person may offer an opinion that meets with general acceptance and is incorporated into the family view. Or such an opinion may meet with criticism or challenge, and the family may negotiate until 'the truth' of the matter is settled. More often, the process is implicit. Most actions and messages draw upon many shared assumptions, and if an interaction proceeds smoothly, and does not give rise to misunderstanding or challenge, then these assumptions will be reinforced. Healthy families show a congruence between their beliefs, attitudes, and values, and maintain a coherent vision that is unique and yet remains 'in touch' with the general social consensus. In their perception of personalities, issues and events, such families are never totally unrealistic. They have a tenable view of the extent of their responsibility and of their ability to control events, and their prognoses about the likely outcome of troublesome situations are neither over-optimistic nor unreasonably pessimistic.

These families do not insist the each member subscribe totally to the general consensus. It is recognized that individuals have their own perspective and have many experiences beyond the family. Members are encouraged to share such experiences, and the family's collective outlook on the world is often revised on the basis of individuals' accounts. Members are realistic in judging themselves, other family members, and the unit as a whole, and they have a fair impression of how they are perceived by other members. But although appraisals within healthy families are marked by a 'realism', members do collaborate to create certain collective 'myths'. However, the myths held by healthy families are harmless in their effect, being used mainly to foster solidarity and to enhance the family image.

DYSFUNCTIONAL FAMILIES

There are many different ways in which a family may be dysfunctional, and so the term 'the dysfunctional family' does not refer to any one family type. Just as any one of a whole range of faults may bring about the failure of a machine, many different departures from optimal functioning may render a family dysfunctional. And just as no machine will show every conceivable mal-function, so no family will be dysfunctional in every possible way. Optimal families manage to achieve a balance between extremes, and whereas some dysfunctional families will be extreme in one direction, others will be extreme in the other. The diverse nature of dysfunctional families is recognized in the oft-quoted aphorism, the first sentence from Tolstoy's *Anna Karenina*, which states: 'All happy families are alike, but each unhappy family is unhappy in its own way.' However, all dysfunctional families are limited in some important respect. They may be unable to deal successfully with routine practical matters, the general climate within the home may be conflictual or chaotic, or some aspect of family interaction may generate physical or psychological symptoms in one or more members.

Family dysfunction may result from excessive cohesiveness ('enmeshment') or from a lack of closeness between family members ('disengagement'). In enmeshed systems individual members may be so engulfed by their family roles and relationships that they lack autonomy and lose their own identity. An enmeshed system is unable to benefit from the varied input of experience, opinion, and information that occurs when each individual makes a distinct contribution. There may be little respect for or encouragement of individual autonomy, and there may be particular difficulties when older children wish to become independent. In disengaged families, on the other hand, individuals may be so detached from family matters that there is little sense of family identity and it is difficult for the group to function together as an effective system. Members have only a weak attachment to the family unit and provide each other with little support or guidance. The system thus exerts meagre influence or control over the individuals within it. The family therefore fails to function effectively in rewarding members and regulating their behaviour, and individuals who operate without the guidance and constraint of the family system may feel isolated and alienated, or they may be influenced more by peers or by other systems than by their own family unit.

Dysfunctional families may have extremely permeable, or extremely impermeable, outer or inner boundaries. Families that have an impermeable external boundary derive few benefits from their environment. These closed families may refuse offers of support or aid and may treat those who offer help as intruders. On the other hand some families are too open. They are so much influenced by external factors that they show little self-determination and have a poor sense of identity. Such families may come to rely too heavily on outside help and approval, and retain little privacy. When the boundaries within the system are too permeable, as in enmeshed families, distinctions between sub-systems are unclear and there is a lack of separation between the sub-groups. Problems are especially likely to occur if the boundaries between the generational sub-systems become blurred, one effect of this being to weaken the hierarchical power structure. On the other hand, if the boundaries are impermeable, some members will have little access to some of the sub-systems, and communication will be impaired. An individual or a sub-system may become almost totally dissociated from the others.

Sometimes an unorthodox sub-system structure develops. Thus in the case of 'triangulation', one of the marital partners withdraws from the other and forms a tight and enmeshed relationship with one of the children. The father may develop an alliance with one of his daughters, for example, that is so close and exclusive that the mother and other children are disregarded. This is likely to generate a number of problems. In maintaining discipline, for example, it is important for the parental sub-system to be well integrated and distinct, and for both of the parents to share power. However, like other dysfunctional structural patterns, triangulation may represent an attempt to solve a serious problem that exists within the system. Thus father–daughter triangulation may prevent the father from becoming disengaged from the system as a whole. If the marital sub-system is weak or conflictual then the special cross-generational relationship may be vital in holding the system together and preventing the breakup of the family.

A family may also be dysfunctional because roles are poorly defined. If few rights or duties are assigned to particular individuals then many issues will need to be repeatedly negotiated. In other families there will be a lack of coordination between roles, or individuals may experience severe internal conflict about the various roles that they are expected to play. If there is little flexibility in the system a vital role may be left unfilled when the customary occupant is absent or indisposed, and without a suitable replacement the system may be seriously impaired in its ability to function effectively. Rigid systems are the most likely to experience difficulties in making such substitutions, and if they do manage to re-allocate a role they may later experience difficulties in restoring the original arrangement.

Communication in dysfunctional families may be inadequate in a variety of ways. Many ambiguous messages may be delivered, or those who receive messages may systematically distort their meaning. There may be a frequent incongruity between the verbal content of a message and the way in which it is expressed. Thus verbal remarks that are benign in their literal meaning may be spoken in a tone that conveys suspicion or disapproval, and this may create an atmosphere of innuendo and insinuation. Communication may be poorly coordinated, so that individuals or sub-systems frequently fail to act as messengers, or distort the messages that they are expected to convey. Sometimes a particular sub-system appears intransigent, disregarding any suggestions or appeals expressed by other sub-systems. If there is very little sharing of information, some members will remain ignorant of certain facts that would be of benefit to them. A failure to disseminate knowledge may also obstruct the process of finding a solution to problems that might be resolved by the pooling and integration of information. Within the family system certain issues may be strenuously avoided in all interaction, and the effects of secrets may be to undermine the trust between members and to inhibit communication.

Many features that are over-represented in dysfunctional families are likely to promote conflict between individuals or between sub-systems. Thus in enmeshed families, an individual who attempts to behave independently may attract disapproval and reprimand. Other members may complain about an action that is interpreted as 'disloyal'. Conflict is likely when a rigid family system struggles to cope with a situation that demands a flexible response.

Individuals in disengaged families may be annoyed by the family's failure to provide them with adequate rewards; and ambiguous communication will generate many misunderstandings. Conflict often arises over issues concerning the rules that operate in the family. Such clashes may concern what these rules are, whether they are valid, whether a rule has been broken, and what the consequences of infringement should be. Explicit rules allow the relevant issues to be addressed directly, but in dysfunctional families many rules are implicit.

Families respond to conflict in different ways, and many dysfunctional families engage in responses that are ineffective or destructive. Some regard differences of interest or of opinion as contests between rival factions rather than as obstacles to be overcome by communal strategies and collaborative efforts. Differences may be quashed by the exercise of unilateral power rather than resolved by discussion and negotiation. Many dysfunctional families are unfamiliar with strategies that would be useful in de-escalating a conflictual situation. Tactics involving the use of humour, compromise or apology may be quite alien to a family in which hostility has frequently escalated to become uncontrolled, and even violent. Quarrelsome incidents may leave a residue of hostility and permanently damage relationships.

While it is clear that many dysfunctional families engage in destructive conflicts, a family's resolute avoidance of all confrontation is also regarded as problematic. Denial of differences between members or sub-systems in terms of interests, values or attitudes may reflect a fear that a conflict incident might prove 'lethal' to the fragile system. Chronic inhibition of conflict, however, means that many problematic issues remain unresolved. This can produce resentment and unhappiness, reduce the stability of the system, and generate symptoms in family members. Some individuals may come to recognize that disagreements usually lead to bitter fights and damage relationships without ever satisfactorily resolving any issue, and they may become inhibited about ever voicing dissension. In order to keep the peace they may inhibit expression of many of their feelings and, eventually, suppress the feelings themselves.

Conflict is one type of problem that all families must frequently deal with, but many other problem issues also call for a solution. Families that are inflexible, and those that are chaotic, develop only a limited repertoire of strategies. Rigid families will tend to apply the same strategy over and over again, failing to explore alternatives. They may persist in using a strategy that is patently unsuccessful. Chaotic families are rather inept at generating, using and evaluating the effect of different strategies. They tend to follow an arbitrary route from one unsuccessful strategy to the next, learning little from their repeated failures. A frenzied search for a solution sometimes leads to a rapid oscillation between two extremes of interactional style. Thus a child's extreme defiance may be met with alternating periods of highly indulgent or very strict discipline as the family struggles to establish whether the behaviour is more tolerable under an authoritarian or a liberal regime. When a member threatens to leave the family there may be a rapid alternation between actions likely to either increase or decrease family cohesion.

Some attempts to find an effective strategy for dealing with a major problem will result in the family arriving at a solution that has unfortunate side-effects for one member. Thus in the case of 'scapegoating', one individual, usually a child, is blamed for the family's problems. The individual becomes the focus of concern (this may take the form of anxiety, anger, or blame) and attention is deflected from the initial problem. For example, if severe discord between the parents threatens the family's survival, a problem with the child's health or behaviour may distract concern away from the marital sub-system. In some such cases the child's condition will also be held accountable for the problems within the marital relationship. Thus the presence of the symptom (or the supposed symptom) has survival value for the system as a whole, and in such a case it will be in the family's interest to maintain the complaint.

Jackson (1957) observed that when an individual's psychiatric condition improved there was often a negative reaction from the other family members. He suggested that the patient's recovery often disturbs an equilibrium that has been established, and that the system reacts ('homeostatically') in a bid to regain its stability. Systems theory has helped therapists and others to identify a number of such processes and strategies that may create or maintain particular symptoms. If a therapeutic team concludes that a problem, or supposed problem, with a member's behaviour or health is the result of a scapegoating strategy they will attempt to change the system dynamics so that the fundamental problem is eliminated and the symptom therefore rendered 'unnecessary'.

Some dysfunctional families construct reality in a highly idiosyncratic or even bizarre way. The general 'world view' that they evolve may be highly incoherent or inconsistent with established facts. In extreme cases there may be a *'folie a familie'*—a shared view that is so at odds with the general consensus that it amounts to a kind of madness. Eccentricity in the collective appraisal style is more likely in a closed system, when family views are not validated against external sources of information and opinion. Thus a family may arrive at an unreasonable judgement about the physical health of a member, and neglect to check their assessment against professional opinion.

Families may arrive at a faulty appraisal or judgement because their grasp of the relevant facts is unsound, for because they make illogical deductions. Sometimes a family member who has somewhat eccentric views exerts a disproportionate influence over the reality construction process and introduces strange ideas that are adopted by other members. But unusual and inaccurate family judgements often serve a particular emotional function. There may be a strategic reason why a family wishes or 'needs' a particular explanation and strives to maintain a view despite the availability of information that discredits their position. Thus dysfunctional families may form the view that they are 'fated' and have little control over events. This impression of their own helplessness may be used to justify inactivity, failure to solve a problem, or excessive dependency on external agents. In other cases certain matters (particularly other people's motives) are systematically misconstrued in order to sustain feelings of anger, bitterness or resentment. Some families maintain an unrealistic confidence in their ability to face hardship, or they take an over-optimistic view of the likely outcome of problematic situations. Their assessment of how a scenario is likely to develop will be based more on hope than on judgement.

Many dysfunctional families create myths that conceal the truth about important family matters. Thus some families with a history of frequent physical violence deny to themselves and to others that 'real violence' has ever occurred. Families may try to convince others (particularly relatives and therapists) of the validity of their delusions. Myths commonly held by dysfunctional families have been described by a number of clinicians. Thus 'myths of harmony' paint a glowing picture of family life. Members subscribe to the fiction that their relationships are harmonious and that the family is self-sufficient and free of conflict. 'Rescue myths' offer the promise that 'help is on the way'—that a child, or a distant relative, or a therapist, for example, will offer a complete solution to the family's current problems (Stierlin, 1973).

Thus many of the problems that are observed within families can be attributed to the effects of some structural or process dysfunction. Some such problems arise because the family system is unable to fulfil important tasks, failing to provide adequate rewards for family members, for example, or failing to regulate the individual's behaviour. Some problems do not arise because of some basic inadequacy of the system but reflect an ill-fated attempt to solve a problem. Thus a child's symptom may represent an attempt by the system to prevent family breakup at a time of severe marital disharmony. Dysfunctional systems are not only likely to develop problems because of some intrinsic malfunctioning, but they also find it difficult to cope with developmental changes, and they are easily thrown into crisis by stressful events. However, it must be remembered that even those families that are able to cope very well in normal circumstances may become seriously disturbed when they meet with a critical misfortune.

FAMILIES AND STRESS

In the 1930s, Angell (1936) studied the reactions of families to a sudden loss of income during the Depression. He identified two major factors that were clearly associated with the degree of impact of financial hardship—'family integration' and 'family adaptability'. These are very similar to the cohesion and adaptability dimensions of the circumplex model. Hill (1958) incorporated Angell's two factors (as 'family resources') into 'the ABC-X family crisis model'. This has remained highly influential, and recent research following in this tradition has been enhanced by major developments in the understanding of how individuals respond to stressful events. Concepts and research findings from both these fields of study have been integrated to provide detailed accounts of the responses of family members and family systems. Recent research has focused particularly on the processes that individuals and families use to reduce and manage stress, and to limit its adverse effects.

Chapter 1 included a discussion of how an individual's physical and psychological health may be affected by 'stressors'—life events that require changes in the person's lifestyle. 'Stress' is the physiological and psychological response to one or more stressors, and the effect of several stressors is often cumulative. It was established in the earlier discussion that many stressful events arise within the family, that individuals differ in their resilience to stress, and that adverse consequences are moderated by a number of factors, one of the most significant being social support.

Stressors that originate within the family have direct effects on all members, and on the relationships between them. Considerable alterations of the structure and processes of the family unit may be needed. But even when a stressor originates outside the family and makes a direct impact on only one member, this has consequences for other family members and for the family unit. Much of the social support individuals receive comes from the family, and some families offer better support than others. Cohesive families, for example, are likely to provide more comfort and reassurance than disengaged families. Flexible families are able to take pressure off a member by reallocating roles and tasks during periods of acute stress, whereas rigid families are less able to do this.

Thus stressor events often disrupt the family's functioning and generate a state of tension, or 'family stress'. 'Distress' is the unpleasant experience associated with this tension, and certain costs related to stressor events are referred to as 'family hardships' (for example, illness may bring financial hardship). Residual tension resulting from the impact of previous stressors, and strains associated with roles or relationships, are labelled 'prior strains' (Pearlin and Schooler, 1978; Olson and McCubbin, 1983). Stressors and strains often have a cumulative effect, and the accumulation is referred to as 'pile-up'.

High levels of stress produce negative consequences. Family conflict may become intense, for example, or one or more members may experience physical or psychological symptoms. Such conflicts or symptoms are then likely to act as additional stressors, so that a vicious circle may develop. The impact of stressors may be so great that the family unit is unable to perform its normal functions and is said to be in a state of 'crisis'. Essential tasks may be neglected, rules may fail to operate, and the family's behaviour may become unpredictable. But such extreme reactions are not inevitable, and many families that are 'under stress' would not be said to be 'in crisis'. Many families prevent crisis by engaging in cognitive and behavioural activities that limit the adverse effects of stressors, and maintain stress at a tolerable level. Such activities are collectively labelled 'coping'.

According to the 'ABC-X family crisis model' (Hill, 1958), a stressor event ('A') interacts with the family's strengths and resources for meeting that event ('B'), and the family's perception of the event ('C') to produce an impact ('X'— stress, or crisis). Although Hill employed the term 'crisis', this was broadly defined, and his model is equally applicable to less critical responses to stress. The model emphasizes that the impact of a stressor depends not only on the nature of the event but also on the family's resources and perceptions. Since this model was first introduced many modifications and elaborations have been suggested. The most radical revision was proposed by McCubbin and Patterson (1982) who developed 'the double ABC-X model'. This focuses on stressors and strains, family resources, and family coping, and emphasizes the dynamic nature of the family's response to stress. Thus the 'A' element includes not only the original stressor event but also stressors that result from the family's efforts to cope. Situational and developmental stressors combine with residual tension from prior strains and hardships to create a 'pile-up'. The 'B' element includes not only pre-existing family resources but also those that the family develops in response to the stress (especially coping strategies). The 'C' element is extended beyond the perception of the stressor event to include the family's perception of the effects of the stress and its own attempts to cope with the tension. Finally, the 'X' element includes family adaptation as well as stress or crisis.

Families differ profoundly in their response to stressor events. Some survive and continue to function well even after the impact of a series of major stressors, while others seem unable to manage even the slightest misfortune. The variation in the family's resilience reflects many different factors, including their perception of the stressor, the strengths of the family system as a whole and the sub-systems within it, the range of strategies that the family has for solving problems, and the degree and quality of contact with external sources of help. Families differ in the extent to which they generate serious stressful situations, in their resilience to the immediate impact of a stressor, and in their capacity for longer-term readjustment or regeneration.

Certain family stressors, including conflict, violence, marital breakdown, and several psychological symptoms, are more likely to occur in 'dysfunctional' families than in those that ordinarily function well. How an event is perceived is an important determinant of the impact it makes, and whereas some families are fairly realistic in their appraisal, others are unduly pessimistic. Some families have more strengths and more resources than others. Those that are resilient to the effects of stressors find it relatively easy to move from one stable state to another, and can therefore readjust rather readily. Some families seem little affected by certain stressors, but the absence of crisis does not mean that the system has remained passive and untouched by the event. Apparent composure following misfortune may reflect the effectiveness of the system in dissipating tension. Some families are very efficient in meeting a potential crisis and protecting themselves from the chaos and disruption that a stressor sometimes provokes.

FAMILY STRESSORS

In her review of family stress, Boss (1987) suggested a number of dimensions that could be used to differentiate between stressors. Thus although many stressors are unpleasant and unfavourable events, some are favourable. Even positive events such as the family moving to better accommodation or winning a major lottery may demand considerable adaptation. 'Developmental' stressors are events that normally occur at some stage in the 'family career', whereas 'non-normative' stressors include episodes such as serious illness or disability, sudden loss of employment, a family member receiving a long prison sentence, or a young child being taken into care. Adaptation in such cases may be especially difficult because the event is unlikely to have been anticipated and there are fewer social 'blueprints' to guide the family in its response.

Some stressors are unforeseen, whereas others follow a period of anticipation, and some forewarning may allow a family to prepare emotionally for the approaching change, and to engage in the process of 'anticipatory coping'. For example, the birth of a child demands major changes of the system, but many useful environmental and psychological preparations are normally made during the months of pregnancy. Other events, however, strike with no forewarning and catch the family when it is totally unprepared. The term 'disaster' refers to serious, adverse and unanticipated changes such as the sudden death of a young person or the birth of a handicapped child.

Stressors differ in strength, i.e. in their intrinsic power and disruptiveness. Thus the untimely death of a family member is an especially powerful stressor whereas a minor illness is far less severe. However, the effects of even very slight stressors ('hassles') may be considerable. Sometimes a rather minor event triggers a chain of responses in a family that creates severe stress within the system, or many hassles may accumulate to make life increasingly tedious and difficult to manage. Some stressors originate inside the family, whereas others are instigated externally, and whereas some are chronic, others are acute. Chronic stressors (sometimes labelled 'strains') are stressful situations rather than events, and the effect of these may be especially severe when they persist at a time when the family also has to cope with other stressors or with normative developmental changes. Some stressors are willingly taken on by the family (a move to a better house, for example) whereas others are non-volitional. Stressors also differ in the extent to which they are controllable or adjustable.

A number of studies have attempted to assess the nature and frequency of family stressors. In their study, Olson and McCubbin (1983) found that major stressors and strains were experienced at all stages of the family life cycle, although there was a distinct tendency for a major 'pile-up' to occur during the adolescent and 'launching' stages. Families in their large sample reported a wide variety of stressors and strains, including financial difficulties, intrafamily conflicts, tension between the demands of work and family, losses of relatives and friends, and illnesses.

FAMILY APPRAISAL

The level of stress provoked by an event depends critically on the understanding that the family has of it, including how they explain its origin and how they judge its likely implications. Any powerful change will decrease familiarity and increase uncertainty, thus generating additional stress, and a family will therefore benefit if it is able to reduce ambiguity and strangeness by forming some clear understanding of what is happening. But while it is important that they develop *some* interpretation, different images of the stressor will differ in their capacity to minimize stress. For example, a view of the event as externally caused, controllable to some degree, and variable in its effects, may lessen the emotional impact and encourage attempts at control. If, on the other hand, family members regard the event as intractable, they will judge that any effort made to influence the situation would prove futile.

It has already been noted that if a stressful event is foreseen the family is better able to cope, and one reason for this may be that in anticipating the event a family is often able to change its outlook to accommodate the possibility of such a change. It may then be able to evaluate the potential effects and to determine ways in which these might be allayed. The value of anticipation has been established separately for bereavement, marital separation, and major changes in health, and in each of these cases it is known that important cognitive processes take place in the period between the initial alert and the onset of the event. The family's attribution of the cause of a critical event may be especially significant. There is likely to be speculation about how the change arose, why it occurred when it did, and why it happened to the family. Responsibility or 'blame' for an adverse event may be attributed internally or externally. The more the family is able to attribute the event to external factors, rather than to a person or relationship within the family, and the more the cause is seen as momentary, accidental, and unlikely to occur again, the less disruption will result. If the family attributes blame internally this may diminish family pride and increase feelings of guilt or inferiority. In other cases the blame will be attributed to a particular family member, and this may amount to an instance of scapegoating.

Judgements about stressful events partly reflect the family's general 'appraisal style' and their overall 'paradigm' or construction of reality. Thus their outlook may be generally optimistic or pessimistic, and whereas some families subscribe to the view that most events are controllable, other families are fatalistic. Families differ in their readiness to attribute events to coincidence, accident, or the influence of some supernatural agent. Views about the nature and origin of a problem will also depend on more specific knowledge and theories about, for example, disease or handicap. Thus explanations of why a family member has developed a particular disease will reflect general knowledge concerning pathology and medicine, and information derived from the media, friends and professionals. Family myths will sometimes be created specially to provide an explanation for some aberrant event. Thus information from many sources is consolidated in a bid to clarify what is happening. Families often negotiate over their explanation of events. Propositions and counter-propositions are aired and discussed before a consensus view emerges, although in some cases total consensus is not achieved, and different members, or different sub-systems, maintain disparate views.

It can be seen that the family's perception of a stressor event is not simply a passive process, but is highly active and 'constructive'. Neither is the process 'objective', for the view the family forms will often be influenced by the need to minimize stress. Thus one way that families attempt to reduce the impact of a stressor (i.e. how they cope) is by forming a 'convenient' view of the event. Modifying perception is often a highly effective coping technique, and although constructive modification takes a number of different forms, in many cases it amounts to 'taking a more positive view'. For example, the family may minimize the likely effects of the stressor, or may draw comparisons that make the event seem more favourable (i.e. it could have been a lot worse). Another powerful phenomenon is that of 'reframing'. To 'reframe' an event is to place it within another 'frame' which fits the 'facts' equally well but changes its meaning entirely. Thus something that is initially regarded as 'a disaster' may be reframed so that it is seen as 'a challenge'. Watzlawick, Weakland, and Fisch (1974) provided many examples of how families reframe events, and showed that this practice often helps them to cope (indeed, reframing is now used by therapists as a powerful intervention technique). Some families adopt the strategy of 'passive appraisal' and decide that things will take care of themselves in time. In certain circumstances (where the consequences of the event really are unmanageable) such an attitude of resignation may at least have the virtue of conserving energy and maintaining the system at its current level of functioning.

Although it is generally assumed that an adaptive impression of a stressor event is one which fosters an optimistic view, emphasizes controllability, focuses attention on the stressor, increases awareness, and encourages the active monitoring of changes, this is not always the case. Sometimes it is in the best interests of the family to 'deny' the reality of the stressor, to ignore unfavourable aspects, or to maintain an unrealistic optimism with regard to the likely outcome (Pearlin and Schooler, 1978). In some cases a false hope will help to maintain the system through an initial danger period. Thus even misperception may be functional. Fantasy, superstition and myth may help to maintain a relatively cheerful and emotionally supportive atmosphere when a more accurate view would lead to dejection and apathy.

The occurrence of a major stressor can have profound effects on the way the family perceives events and may challenge many fundamental assumptions. It may undermine beliefs that the world is 'just' and that events are predictable, and increase the suspicion that the universe is either malevolent or chaotic. Families that develop such views are likely to feel that planning for the future would be pointless. Following the sudden death of a family member, for example, people sometimes report that they no longer feel sure of anything, and that the future seems totally precarious.

The family anticipates the likely consequences of the stressor, monitors its impact, and evaluates how well individuals and the system are managing. Some families see themselves as powerful, and assume that they will be competent in controlling events and maintaining stability, whereas others consider themselves to be vulnerable and ineffectual. The family's perception of its own mastery may reflect the religious and cultural environment, but to a large extent it will derive from recent experiences in dealing with misfortune. If many previous attempts at mastery have been unsuccessful, the family may conclude that it is inept or that events are essentially uncontrollable. Such beliefs will encourage a passive response, although such families may derive some comfort from casting themselves in the role of 'helpless victim'. In certain cases this view will be adaptive. On the other hand, success in previous efforts will encourage some families to feel confident about their mastery of difficult situations. Families that judge themselves as having triumphed over the current adversity may derive great satisfaction from their accomplishment. They may regard the family as stronger, more united, and more effective than ever before, and they may feel that they will be able to contend with the future, no matter what that future may bring.

COPING RESPONSES

It is clear that families are not passive. They do not simply surrender to the impact of a stressor, but actively engage in a variety of coping processes in a bid to combat the stressor and to minimize stress. If these efforts are successful then crisis will be avoided. Initial efforts are directed towards minimizing or reducing the impact of the stressor ('resistance coping'), but at a later stage the strategies are directed more towards reorganizing and stabilizing the system ('adaptive coping'). Appraisal modification (reframing, passive appraisal, etc.) is one form of cognitive coping strategy, but coping also includes a variety of behavioural, interactional, and structural moves. The capacity of a family to manage stress depends on the resources it has and how well it uses them (Olson and McCubbin, 1983). Resources include both enduring qualities that provide resilience (these are referred to as 'strengths'), and responses that can be brought into play to deal with stress ('coping strategies'). Families with many existing strengths and coping strategies will be resilient to adverse effects of stressor events, although new strengths and strategies may also be developed in response to threat.

Family strengths include moderate cohesiveness and adaptability, explicit rules, the flexible operation of these rules, an effective power structure, good communication, high accord, and family pride. The family's overall strength is increased if the sub-systems function well, for example if there is good communication within the marital sub-system and it is effective in resolving conflict. Assets of individual members, including such qualities as personal resourcefulness, good humour, emotional stability, and satisfaction with their relationships also reinforce family strength. Olson and McCubbin (1983) found that families that were able to maintain stress at a low level had many strengths. Members were in agreement on many issues, their communication was effective, they shared many leisure activities, and they had a high level of satisfaction with their family, friends, and the general of quality of life. This study found that certain strengths were more apparent and more significant at some stages of family development than at others.

The other major resource that enables families to moderate stress is the repertoire of coping strategies available to the family unit, sub-systems, and individual family members. This includes behaviours that seek to evade, escape or directly modify the stressor; judgements made about the stressful event and its aftermath; and any response that attempts to control the emotional reaction to the stressor (Lazarus, 1966). Coping by the family unit involves interactions with the family, and between the family and the community, and has the aim of maintaining a favourable family structure, enabling the system to continue to perform its functions and to overcome obstacles. A key function during periods of tension is that of providing emotional support for members. Thus individuals' efforts are directed at personal emotional survival, the support of other members, and the maintenance of family functioning, while coping at the family level is directed at maintaining the structure and functioning of the system, and supporting individual members. Sometimes, however, there is an incongruity between the coping efforts of individual members and of the family system. Thus individuals who seek escape through the use of alcohol will probably reduce their contribution to effective family functioning. Such incompatibility is more likely to occur in disengaged families than in those that are cohesive.

Some coping strategies are internal to the family, whereas others involve external systems as sources of information or aid. Some families are highly self-reliant whereas others readily seek help. The most resourceful families operate with some degree of autonomy, and do not become over-dependent, but they are also able to request and accept help from outside. Some internal coping strategies involve modifying appraisals (of the stressor, of its effects, and of the responses of individuals and the family unit) while others involve changing aspects of the family structure to enable the system to function more effectively under difficult conditions. One structural change that may be particularly useful is that of increasing the permeability of the external boundary so that more contact is made with the extended family or with social agencies. Other structural changes involve re-allocating roles or redistributing tasks. For example, a family that is normally democratic in its decision-making may give a member 'executive power' during an emergency. Family rules may also be modified to allow for the changed circumstances, or there may be a shift in the degree to which members are expected to conform to certain rules. Some families attempt to cope by becoming more tolerant, and some by becoming more authoritarian.

Family cohesion may be increased as members join together to resist a challenge to their collective welfare or prosperity. They may feel united and bound together in their shared misfortune. As a result of sharing their fears and hopes, discussing their problems openly, and employing such diversionary tactics as humour and small talk, they may feel closer together than ever before. Threats imposed by a stressor often provoke intense family discussion, and the urgency of the situation may encourage straight talking and frank disclosure. Thus communication may become more explicit and more revealing, and in some cases the breakthrough in rapport will continue to have positive effects in the long term. It is especially constructive if, in a climate of adversity, a family is able to overlook perennial differences and conflicts, and to disregard less serious issues so that attention can be focused on the major problem. Many families, when under acute pressure, do manage to establish a temporary cessation of hostilities, and many achieve a rare spirit of compromise. Thus in general the family may function more effectively in a climate of near-crisis than it does under normal circumstances.

In addition to the general forms of adjustment considered so far, many coping strategies are tailored specifically to particular problems. Thus if the principal wage-earner suddenly becomes unemployed, the family may respond by increasing its financial resourcefulness. Patterns of family spending are likely to change abruptly and the family might use the extra time together to pursue new activities or interests and thus enhance family cohesion. Families employ a whole range of tactics, and change their interactions, in order to cope with specific problems. In some cases problem-solving techniques are used to combat the stressor directly, so that a family faced with a sudden loss of a salary, for example, may explore various ways of increasing the overall income.

Many coping strategies draw on resources from outside the family, but although some families attempt to cope with stress by becoming more open, others become more closed. They may remain committed to keeping their difficulties secret, and hiding the problem from the outside world, particularly if the problem generates feelings of shame, embarrassment or guilt. In general, however, it would seem to be more adaptive for a family that is under stress to become more open, and many do seek out friends and relatives during times of difficulty (Olson and McCubbin, 1983). Other potential sources of help include church organizations, and self-help groups, including those that are specifically committed to helping with the type of problem that is confronting the family (alcoholism, bereavement, family violence, for example, or many categories of chronic illness and handicap). Such groups help the family by informing them about the problem and about available resources, by encouraging them to communicate their experiences, and by describing strategies that have been 'tried and tested'. As well as informal community services, many social agencies and professional services offer help in terms of advice, counselling, and practical aid. Some families are more ready than others to seek help from a professional therapist.

Although external help may be of special benefit during a period of acute stress, it may also make a significant contribution during the weeks and months that follow. Hill (1949) suggested that the immediate impact of a severe stressor event provokes family disorganization, but that this is normally followed by recovery. Finally, he suggested, the family achieves a new stable structure. Thus there is a sequence of disruption, recovery and reorganization, and the family structure that emerges in the final stage may be more or less favourable than that which formerly prevailed. Regeneration is likely to be easier for families in which members continue to communicate effectively with one another and consult widely with outside agencies. Thus a family's experience of high stress, or even of a period in which it has failed to function ('a crisis') may emerge stronger in its structure and 'wiser' in terms of its range of strategies and its recognition that adversity can be successfully overcome.

The more numerous a family's strengths and coping strategies, the more protected it will be from the adverse effects of a stressor event. Families that are dysfunctional as a result of deficiencies or defects in their normal structure and functioning will generally have relatively few strengths and few strategies, and are likely to be especially exposed and vulnerable. However, it is not enough that the family simply *has* many resources; it must also be active in using them. In some cases a family that will be so disabled by the impact of a stressor that it will be unable to mobilize its available resources and will thus be prevented from coping effectively.

SUMMARY AND CONCLUSION

In Chapter 1 some definitional issues were first examined, and the distinction was made between the individual in the family context and 'the family unit'. The effect of the family context on individuals' health and well-being was reviewed, and social exchange theory was used to provide an explanation of how individuals make decisions regarding their personal relationships. In Chapter 2 the focus changed to the family unit. Several issues were explored using the metaphor of 'the family as an organism' and systems theory was then introduced. This was employed to provide an account of the relationship between family functioning and family structure, and to explore some important ways in which family systems differ. Particular attention was paid to cohesion and adaptability, two factors that empirical research and clinical studies have suggested are critical in determining how a family functions, how it accomplishes developmental changes, and how it copes with the impact of stressor events. Systems thinking was also used to examine the characteristics of optimal, or 'healthy', families and those that are 'dysfunctional'. The point was emphasized, however, that all families experience stress and that the integrity of even the most well-functioning family may be challenged by powerful adverse circumstances. An account was then given of various features of family stressors, and this was followed by an analysis of appraisal processes and the role of family resources (strengths and coping strategies) in minimizing stress.

The family problems to be considered in subsequent chapters vary widely in their nature and effects. Some, like family conflict and violence, are generated by interactions within the family. These reflect individuals' psychology, the nature of particular relationships, and broader structural features of the family group. In many cases the relationship between the family and the wider system is of particular relevance. Some families seem especially vulnerable because they are socially isolated, while in other cases it is clear that the community imposes special pressures that create or exacerbate tensions within the family. Many problems derive from the impact of a powerful non-normative event such as the birth of a handicapped child or the serious illness of a family member, while in other cases a stressor situation or event is 'normative' but no less disruptive, as when an elderly family member is dying or has recently died.

Each of the chapters that follows will provide an examination of how individuals and families respond to severe stress, whether this stress origin- ates within or outside the family. An account will be given of why some relationships become highly conflictual, why some adults launch aggressive attacks on their children or their partner, and how such incidents affect all members of the family. The interactional processes leading to marital separation and divorce will also be considered, and an account will be given of how adults and children fare after a marriage has been dissolved. Reviews of the impact of illness, handicap, and bereavement will illustrate and draw upon many of the descriptions of individual and family processes presented in the two introductory chapters. It will be seen how individuals make decisions regarding difficulties in their family relationships and how they respond to adverse family circumstances. Following the examination of family processes given in the present chapter, attention will be given to the issues of how family systems minimize stress and how they make structural adaptations following the impact of particular types of stressor.

Although families can be devastated by serious troubles, in many cases both individuals and family units manage to endure the most formidable upsets and tragedies. The extent to which individuals and families are able to accommodate to severe misfortune is often remarkable. Thus despite the high number of people whose family circumstances cause them to experience serious psychological symptoms, and despite the very high (and increasing) number of family relationships that end in breakdown, the overall picture that emerges from an examination of the research on family problems is in many ways one of persistence, resourcefulness and resilience.

For some individuals, and some families, however, the outcome is much less favourable, and it is sometimes possible to identify selective 'risk factors' that play a part in determining the intensity of adverse effects. Some of these factors are specific to particular kinds of problem, but a number have a more general relevance. Thus successful coping and adaptation is more likely if the family has a history of functioning well, and if it has overcome previous adversity. The adjustment process also tends to operate more smoothly if there has been some forewarning of the event, or if a difficult episode has developed gradually. In such circumstances there will have been some anticipation of the stressor, and the responses needed to contend with it, so that if the worst fears are realized there will be less of a shock and previously rehearsed coping strategies may be used to attenuate the stress.

Some time after a stressor event has made its immediate impact, individuals and family systems usually recover from their initial confusion and disorder. Thus following divorce or bereavement there is typically a gradual attenuation of the negative effects that may have been apparent soon after the loss. The adage 'Time will heal' suggests that time alone is necessary for the process of recovery, but in reality the alleviation of distress and the restoration of stable functioning is largely the result of active processes. What might once have been described simply as a consequence of 'natural healing' or 'natural recovery' is now better understood as the result of dynamic responses and adaptations by the individual and the family system. Individuals take time to make complex cognitive adjustments and to incorporate powerful new facts into their scheme of things. They engage in a continuous process of constructing and reconstructing a coherent (though not necessarily objective) account of what happened and why. In many cases their evaluations will reflect a concern with self-protection and the maintenance of self-esteem.

Individuals may also have to change certain of their former cognitive and behavioural routines. For example, a newly divorced person may have to relearn how to think in terms of 'I' rather than 'we', and may have to adapt their behaviour in order to perform actions that were formerly shared. Family systems, too, must modify their 'paradigm' to accommodate new facts and must engage in the process of restructuring. They may have to modify rules, to re-assign roles, and to develop novel behavioural routines. Such adaptation takes time, and a successful new structure may emerge only after a long period of trial and error. In addition, the recovery of both the individual and the family is somewhat dependent on how other people and other systems regard them, and the expectations they have of them. The change of circumstances following a major event may entail a change of identity for the individual or the family, and recovery may be aided or inhibited by powerful social responses, including blame, pity, kindness, humiliation, envy and confusion.

Although it has been emphasized that individuals and families often display an extraordinary capacity for self-preservation, and manage to cope very well with various potentially devastating occurrences, many families benefit greatly from help provided by people and agencies outside the family. Such help may come from relatives; friends; neighbours; voluntary organizations; professionals such as the clergy, lawyers and doctors; or psychologists and psychiatrists. One of the ways in which professionals can develop more effective ways of supporting troubled families is by strengthening their understanding of how problems arise within family units, how individuals make decisions about their relationships, and how family systems struggle to solve problems and to cope with stress. There are clearly important lessons to be learned from well-functioning families and from those that are adept at contending with serious misfortune. Family members are often able to provide first-hand accounts of the processes that helped them and their family to persevere and survive through major difficulties, but in many cases only detailed research employing less familiar concepts and more elaborate hypotheses can provide satisfactory explanations. By understanding what happens in families that are successful in their struggles against adversity, professionals are likely to be better placed to aid recovery in families with fewer resources or less experience of overcoming hardship and distress.

REFERENCES

Angell, R. C. (1936) *The Family Encounters the Depression*. New York: Charles Scribner's Sons.

Beavers, W. (1977) *Psychotherapy and Growth: A Family Systems Perspective*. New York: Brunner/Mazel.

Berger, P. L. and Luckmann, T. T. (1966) *The Social Construction of Reality*. New York: Doubleday.

Bertanlanffy, L. von (1968) *General Systems Theory*. New York: Braziller.

Boss, P. (1987) Family stress. In: M. B. Sussman and S. K. Steinmetz (eds.), *Handbook of Marriage and the Family*. New York: Plenum Press.

Buckley, W. (1967) *Sociology and Modern Systems Theory*. Englewood Cliffs, NJ: Prentice-Hall.

Duvall, E. (1977) *Marriage and Family Development*. Philadelphia: J. B. Lippincott.

Epstein, N. B., Bishop, D. S. and Levin, S. (1978) The McMaster model of family functioning. *Journal of Marriage and Family Counselling*, **40**, 19–31.

Fisher, B. L. and Sprenkle, D. H. (1978) Therapists' perceptions of healthy family functioning. *International Journal of Family Counseling*, **6**, 1–10.

Hill, R. (1949) *Families Under Stress*. New York: Harper.

Hill, R. (1958) Generic features of families under stress. *Social Casework*, **49**, 139–150.

Jackson, D. (1957) The question of family homeostasis. *Psychiatric Quarterly*, **31**, 79–90.

Janis, I. L. (1972) *Victims of Groupthink*. Boston, MA: Houghton Mifflin.

Lazarus, R. (1966) *Psychological Stress and the Coping Process*. New York: McGraw-Hill.

Lewis, J. M., Beavers, W., Gossert, J. T. and Philips, V. A. (1976) *No Single Thread: Psychological Health in Family Systems*. New York: Brunner/Mazel.

McCubbin, H. I. and Patterson, J. M. (1982) Family adaptation to crises. In: H. McCubbin, A. Cauble and J. M. Patterson (eds.), *Family Stress, Coping and Social Support*. Springfield, IL: Charles C. Thomas.

Minuchin, S. (1974) *Families and Family Therapy*. Cambridge, MA: Harvard University Press.

Minuchin, S. and Fishman, H. C. (1981) *Family Therapy Techniques*. Cambridge, MA: Harvard University Press.

Olson, D. H., McCubbin, H. I. and associates (1983) *Families: What Makes Them Work?* Beverly Hills, CA: Sage.

Olson, D. H., Russell, C. S. and Sprenkle, D. H. (1979) Circumplex model of marital and family systems. II: Empirical studies and clinical intervention. In: J. Vincent (ed.), *Advances in Family Intervention, Assessment and Theory*. Greenwich, CT: JAI.

Olson, D. H., Sprenkle, D. H. and Russell, C. S. (1979) Circumplex model of marital and family systems. I: Cohesion and adaptability dimensions, family types and clinical application. *Family Process*, **18**, 3–28.

Pearlin, L. and Schooler, C. (1978) The structure of coping. *Journal of Health and Social Behavior*, **19**, 2–21.

Pratt, L. (1976) *Family Structure and Effective Health Behaviour: The Energized Family*. Boston, MA: Houghton Mifflin.

Reiss, D. (1981) *The Family's Construction of Reality*. Cambridge, MA: Harvard University Press.

Russell, C. S. and Olson, D. H. (1982) Circumplex model of marital and family systems: Review of empirical support and elaboration of therapeutic process. In: D. A. Bagorozzi, A. Jurich and R. Jackson (eds.), *New Perspectives in Marriage and Family Therapy*. New York: Human Sciences.

Satir, V. (1972) *Peoplemaking*. Palo Alto, CA: Science and Behaviour Books.

Shorter, E. (1975) *The Making of the Modern Family*. New York: Basic Books.

Solomon, N. (1976) Homeostasis and family myth: An overview of the literature. *Family Therapy*, **3**, 75–85.

Sprenkle, D. H. and Olson, D. H. (1978) Circumplex model of marital systems. IV: Empirical studies of clinic and non-clinic couples. *Journal of Marriage and Family Therapy*, **4**, 59–74.

Stierlin, H. (1973) Group fantasies and family myths: Some theoretical and practical aspects. *Family Process*, **12**, 111–125.

Stinnett, N., Chesser, B., DeFrain, J. and Knaub, P. (1980) *Family Strengths: Positive Models for Family Life*. Lincoln. NA: University of Nebraska Press.

Straus, M. (1968) Communication, creativity and problem-solving ability of middle- and working-class families in three societies. Reprinted in M. Sussman (ed.), *Sourcebook in Marriage and the Family* (3rd edn). Boston, MA: Houghton Mifflin.

Textor, M. R. (1989) The 'healthy' family. *Journal of Family Therapy*, **11**, 59–76.

Watzlawick, P., Weakland, J. and Fisch, R. (1974) *Change: Principles of Problem Formation and Problem Resolution*. New York: W. W. Norton.

Zacks, E., Green, R-J. and Marrow, J. (1988) Comparing lesbian and heterosexual couples on the circumplex model: An initial investigation. *Family Process*, **27**(4), 471–484.

3

Family Responses to Physical Illness

In Chapter 1 it was reported that involvement in intimate relationships appears to reduce a person's vulnerability to a variety of physical ailments. The quantity and quality of social contact seem to affect susceptibility to infections, malignancies and various psychosomatic disorders. On average, married people are healthier than the single, widowed or divorced, and they also tend to live longer.

One explanation of why good relationships help to safeguard health suggests that frequent contact with intimates enhances an individual's well-being. Those who are part of a social network are likely to feel valued and have more opportunities to exert control. Their general outlook may be more positive, and they may develop a high level of self-confidence. It is suggested that the personal strengths derived from frequent and harmonious social contact increase the person's capacity to cope with adversity. Another hypothesis focuses on the role of social support at times of stress. Partners and confidants can help individuals through a difficult period by listening to them, giving advice, expressing emotional support and providing practical aid. Intimates may also help to regulate the individual's behaviour, and make it less likely that he or she will engage in dangerous actions. Although most explanations of the association between social intimacy and positive health refer solely to psychological processes, there also appear to be links between the quality of social support and various biological indices. For example, those who are involved in close relationships show less of a decrement in their immunological function following the impact of a stressful event than those who are socially isolated.

This chapter focuses on how individuals and family systems respond to the physical illness of a family member. Serious illness often makes a profound psychological impact not only on the patient but also on other individuals in the family, and on the family system. The effect of family variables on patient recovery will also be examined. In the second part of the chapter, special attention is paid to the impact of children's physical disorders. Other issues that relate to physical illness (including handicap, dying, and bereavement) are considered in later chapters.

As part of their 'world view', families have beliefs and attitudes covering a wide range of issues relating to health and disease. Thus they may have a common attitude towards the medical profession and the value of particular forms of treatment. They may share a general view of whether sick people are usually helpless victims of affliction or whether illness is more often the result of personal failure or neglect. The ideas that families hold regarding the nature and effects of infections, malignancy and toxins are often quite unrelated to conventional medical thinking, and in some cases they might be regarded as rather eccentric, yet the medical myths they construct often have a powerful influence on how families interpret symptoms, how they treat a sick member, and how they respond to medical advice (Hardwick, 1989).

Most families have particular beliefs relating to the promotion of health and the prevention of illness. Some families are highly concerned about the need to maintain a balanced diet, to take regular exercise, to avoid smoking and smoky atmospheres, and to limit the intake of alcohol. Other families seem unconcerned about some or all of these issues. Several studies have reported family patterns in attitudes towards diet, exercise, smoking and the use of alcohol. Parental attitudes are associated with a number of potentially hazardous aspects of children's behaviour. Obese children tend to come from families in which sweets are frequently offered as rewards and in which children are encouraged to eat more (Baranowski and Nader, 1985), and the risk that a child will smoke is greater if its parents smoke (Nolte, Smith and O'Rourke, 1983).

RESPONSES TO SYMPTOMS

When some people feel unwell they prefer to keep the fact to themselves. This may reflect an attempt to 'deny' that they have the symptom, or they may wish to protect other family members from 'unnecessary anxiety'. Other people immediately disclose any discomfort and are quick to seek reassurance and support. Before a reliable diagnosis has been established the family may attempt to make its own diagnosis and to assess the likely seriousness of the problem. The judgements made by the family will be based on collective experience and expertise, and may draw on information from formal education, the media, myths, 'old wives' tales', and experiences of earlier illnesses. Some family members will have more influence than others as the family considers the nature of the complaint, and it seems that within many families the mother is credited with the most dependable understanding and intuition regarding health issues (Litman, 1974). Family discussions concerning the health of the person who feels unwell will tend to be optimistic, and if a serious disorder is suspected then the worst fears are likely to remain unspoken.

Communal denial may provide some relief from anxiety, but in certain cases it can prove dangerous. Refusal to acknowledge that a condition may be serious, for example, may delay the decision to summon medical aid. In a study of coronary patients, Hackett and Cassem (1969) found that the median delay between the onset of pain and the summoning of professional help was two hours for patients who were alone at the time, or who had acted independently, and 12 hours for those who had discussed with their family whether or not help should be called. In many cases the pain caused by an acute myocardial infarction ('heart attack') is misattributed by other family members to 'indigestion' or 'heartburn', and when the correct diagnosis is established other family members may feel guilty about having under-estimated the seriousness of the patient's condition. The patient, in turn, may be annoyed that others failed to appreciate the degree of his or her suffering and failed to respond to the condition with due alarm.

Thankfully, few disorders present a family with such an acute threat as when a member suddenly develops severe chest pains. The most common symptoms, such as those of influenza, lower back pain, headaches and diarrhoea, are usually attributed quite accurately to relatively non-threatening and non-emergency conditions, and such minor ailments usually disappear without medication, or are relieved following the administration of a home remedy. It is estimated that about three-quarters of illness episodes are managed within the home without specialist assistance being called for (Turk and Kerns, 1985). Families often develop a consensus about the effectiveness of self-medication and other home treatments, and may establish a repertoire of remedies for the various afflictions that commonly affect members. Thus in the case of headaches, some families put their faith in aspirin, others rely on paracetamol, and some take the view that it is best to avoid all medication. Some family medicine chests are filled with a bewildering array of pills and potions whereas other families have a disdain of all such remedies, regarding the use of palliatives and painkillers as either unwise or immoral.

There are substantial differences between families in the frequency with which they consult physicians. Just as some individuals are 'frequent consulters' so some families seem to seek professional advice and assurance with great regularity. There are a number of reasons why members of some families consult regularly. One obvious possibility is that such families encounter considerably more illnesses than others. This may be a consequence of frequent cross-infection, or the fact that the family lives in an environment which is dangerous or unhygienic. In some cases a congenital susceptibility will affect several members. A severe family stress may also simultaneously produce symptoms in several members. For example, the serious illness of one person may create such stress within the family that other members soon begin to complain of physical symptoms.

The frequency of consultation also reflects 'thresholds' for becoming alarmed about a symptom, and for soliciting professional help. Some families are ever vigilant for possible signs of ill-health. The slightest skin blemish, muscle twitch or ache is enough to trigger a worry about whether this might signal some serious malady. As soon as any minor symptom becomes apparent, such families may seek immediate reassurance from a physician. Thus they may have a rather low threshold for judging that it is necessary or advisable to summon expert help. At the other extreme, some families are very hesitant about calling for medical assistance (Gorton *et al.*, 1979). Reluctance to consult a physician may result from a number of different attitudes or dispositions. A family may lack confidence about its own judgement, for example, and may be anxious about whether the symptom will be regarded by the physician as too trivial to have merited professional attention. Some families are profoundly sceptical about the expertise of medical personnel, and some families are so 'closed' that they are reluctant to involve any 'outsider' in what they regard as 'a family matter'. And in some cases a family member, or the family as a whole, will be afraid to consult a physician because they have grave fears about the possible outcome of the diagnostic process.

RESPONSES TO DIAGNOSIS

Even when a physician is consulted, the diagnostic issue may remain ambiguous for some time. The family may have to wait for test results or may be told to seek further advice. Prolonged ambiguity about the nature or seriousness of the disorder places a particular stress on family members. They may feel that they have no 'right' to react with strong emotions because their worst fears have not yet been confirmed by professional opinion. Family members will not wish to upset the patient by appearing to anticipate the worst possible outcome, and they may therefore hide their anxiety. The patient will also endeavour to remain optimistic. But while they wait to discover whether grave news is in store, all family members are likely to engage in a number of anticipatory coping strategies. The tension generated by continuing uncertainty can place immense pressure on family relationships.

When a reliable diagnosis is established, the patient and other family members will actively assess the meaning and implications of the information they have been given. If the news is unequivocally good there is likely to be profound relief, but if it is confirmed that the condition is serious, chronic, disabling or life-threatening, this is likely to generate substantial stress. Such news might provoke a personal crisis for the patient, and the family will need to make significant cognitive and structural adjustments. Some of these adjustments will be directed towards minimizing the impact of the diagnosis. Such 'resistance coping' is likely to include some reappraisal of the situation, perhaps using 'denial', 'reframing' or 'passive appraisal.' Rapid changes may also take place in the style of family interaction. Thus it seems that the diagnosis of a serious illness often produces a sharp increase in family solidarity (Kaplan *et al.*, 1977). Later there will be 'adaptive coping', which is likely to involve a number of structural changes. It appears that in many cases such adaptations are successful in allowing the family to continue to function effectively (Zahn, 1973).

Just as families attempt to understand the significance of a member's symptom, and engage in a diagnostic exercise, so they make attributions about the causes of a disease. If a physician diagnoses influenza, for example, there may be speculation about how and when the person contracted the disease. The patient might be berated for not having taken due precautions, or there may be recriminations against certain family members for not having provided the patient with adequate protection. The picture that families construct of how an illness might have arisen is often totally at odds with orthodox medical opinion. Judgements may be largely based on myths and old wives' tales, but however bizarre the family's assessment of the nature and origins of the disease, their understanding will form the basis for the emotional response to the patient. In some cases the view may be taken that the illness is deserved, or has even been 'deliberately' brought on by the patient. In most cases, however, the patient will be seen as a victim, and this view will cause the family to treat him or her with sympathy, forbearance and indulgence, rather than with reproach or criticism.

When a serious illness has been diagnosed, the patient is likely to ask 'Why me?', and family members will wonder why the disease struck the patient when it did, whether they were responsible in any way, and whether the patient's illness has implications for their own future health. The majority of seriously ill patients do speculate about the possible causes of their illness and about factors that may have precipitated the affliction or would have been effective in preventing it. Thus cancer patients may hold themselves or other people responsible for the disease, or may attribute it to stress. Some of these patients adopt a more fatalistic view or feel that they have simply been 'unlucky'. Those who have suffered a heart attack often attribute their condition to stress, and tend to underrate or deny the contribution of diet and smoking (Turnquist, Harvey and Andersen, 1988).

People tend to attribute their own problems to external factors, but often ascribe other people's difficulties to internal or personality factors. This general bias has been demonstrated in numerous social psychology experiments and is also evident when patients and members of their families consider the causes of an illness. Thus wives of heart-attack victims are more likely than their husbands to identify personality aspects (such as 'being a workaholic') as responsible for the attack (Rudy, 1980). Similarly, the husbands of women suffering from cancer of the breast or cervix are more likely than their wives to attribute the malignancy either to chance or to personality factors (Gotay, 1985). By making internal attributions about the patient's condition, family members may seek to avoid any suggestion that they themselves bear some responsibility for the condition. The wife of a heart-attack victim would wish to avoid the conclusion that family stress, or the food she provided, had contributed to the husband's condition, and the husband of a cervical cancer patient would wish to dispute any suggestion that his sexual activity or lack of cleanliness might have endangered his wife's health.

In general, patients who arrive at a firm conclusion about what caused their illness are likely to adjust better than those who fail to make a clear causal attribution (DuCette and Keane, 1984). Explaining the illness may be one important step towards coming to terms with it. However, the nature of the explanation is also significant. A number of studies indicate that patients who hold themselves in some way responsible for what has happened to them may have a more favourable psychological response than those who attribute it to chance or blame other people. Attributing an illness to a controllable aspect of one's own behaviour may carry the implication that if high-risk activities (such as smoking or drinking excessively) are avoided the physical condition will improve and no recurrence will follow. It is tempting to suggest that if patients are encouraged to 'take responsibility' for the illness this might facilitate good adjustment, but there is no direct evidence to support the use of such a strategy, and even the link between self-blame and favourable psychological outcome must be regarded as rather tentative (Turnquist, Harvey and Andersen, 1988).

Thus different families hold distinct health belief paradigms and theories of illness. Patients and their families actively endeavour to assign a meaning to symptoms. They interpret physical signs and often make a tentative diagnosis, and they use their own criteria when assessing whether the condition is improving or deteriorating. They propose possible remedies, monitor the effects of treatments, and decide when the situation demands expert help. Some families tend to play a waiting game, 'allowing nature to take its course', whereas others more readily call for the assistance of health professionals. Families also develop theories about the likely cause of an illness and 'blame' may be apportioned to various external sources and to members of the family (including the patient). In addition they may hold quite different beliefs or ideas about which medicines or other forms of treatment are most effective. All of these variations in family response may be highly significant in determining how families interact with health professionals, the steps that are taken to ensure adequate care, and the attitudes that individuals have towards their own symptoms. Ultimately, therefore, the family's response to the initial signs of physical disorder, and their response to the diagnosis, may have a substantial effect on how well the patient is able to cope with the affliction.

THE IMPACT OF ILLNESS

After the shock or relief aroused by the 'official' diagnosis, the family will continue in their efforts to cope with the patient and his or her affliction. The impact of the illness will depend on a large number of factors, some of which relate to the nature (or perceived nature) of the illness itself, and some of which relate to situational factors or to aspects of the family structure and functioning. There are likely to be adaptations of the family system, and individual members will respond in different ways, reflecting their personality, their roles and responsibilities within the family, and the quality of their relationships with the patient and other family members. Illness factors include effects on the patient's physical and mental functioning, the assumed cause of the problem, and the likely outcome of the affliction. The immediate effect of an illness may be very different from its long-term impact and there are likely to be marked changes with improvements or deteriorations in the patient's condition.

ILLNESS DIMENSIONS

Time-course

One of the factors that is of special relevance in considering the impact of an illness on the patient and the family is the suddenness of onset. Conditions such as Alzheimer's disease, Parkinson's disease and arthritis, for example, usually progress slowly. An initial slight memory loss, tremor or stiffness may develop very gradually into a severely disabling condition, and during this time the patient and family will have time to adjust and adapt to the illness. Although such illnesses may impose major changes in family structure, these may evolve very gradually as the result of many marginal adjustments. A heart attack or a serious stroke, however, may bring sudden critical shifts. There will be immediate changes in how the family view the patient and the unexpected nature of the event may catch the family totally unprepared. There will have been little or no rehearsal for handling the situation, no 'anticipatory coping' and the shock may bring severe disruption to the family structure. Members who formerly provided strength and resolution in the family may now appear weak. Those who were formerly content to leave control to others may take on new responsibilities. Certain relationships may strengthen in response to the emergency, while others may weaken. The system may be thrown into a state of crisis, with sudden shifts and role reversals. Such reorganization is by no means always chaotic or arbitrary; sometimes the changes in family alliances, roles and responsibilities that mark the immediate response to a major stressor set the pattern for the future and prove successful in maintaining the functioning of the family unit.

Degree of Disability

Another dimension on which illnesses differ is in the degree of physical impairment or infirmity involved. Some disorders are crippling, perhaps restricting the patient to a wheelchair, some confine the patient to bed, and some produce serious sensory disabilities. Some afflictions demand constant nursing of the patient, and in some cases major problems of incontinence will arise. On the other hand there are many disorders, including many that are serious, in which—at least at some stages—there is no infirmity. A person who cannot move about freely, or who needs special attention in order to perform everyday functions, will clearly place more hardship and responsibility on other members of the family. In extreme cases the extent of this problem will necessitate constant specialist nursing care and the patient may be hospitalized. Some patients, and some caregivers, adapt much more readily than others to the loss of independence resulting from an illness. Issues of pride, dignity and personal freedom may come to the fore, and constant caring often has profound effects of the level of intimacy between members. Caregivers who formerly interacted with the patient for less than half of the day, and who had many regular social contacts outside the family, may now find that they are constantly needed by the patient, and their opportunities to meet with others may be drastically curtailed. The practical aspects of caring may be psychologically daunting and physically demanding and result in frustration and exhaustion that lead to a deterioration of the relationship. Such problems may be further exacerbated if the patient responds badly to the state of increased dependency.

In addition to the burden of caring, the loss of the fully functioning family member will place an extra share of routine chores on the shoulders of other family members. A sick mother may become unable to play her usual part in childcare activities, so that the father, in addition to caring for his wife, has to take on many extra childcare tasks. Disablement of someone who was previously employed may entail a loss of job and income, and other wage-earners may have to stop working, or refuse promotion or offers of extra work, in order to play their part in looking after the patient. Infirmity may decrease opportunities for taking holidays and engaging in shared activities outside the home, and it may totally disrupt the sexual behaviour of the married couple. Clearly, different types of illness will be placed in different positions on the two dimensions of illness so far discussed—time-course and disability. If a major disablement occurs suddenly (for example, as the result of a serious stroke or an accident) then the impact on the family will be different from that imposed by the same degree of disablement resulting, after many years, from a progressive disorder such as arthritis or multiple sclerosis.

Psychological Impairment

A further illness dimension of major relevance is that of the degree of psychological change brought about as a direct result of the illness. In addition to the serious emotional reactions that some patients experience as the result of their serious illness (to be considered below), some disorders disturb normal brain functions and lead directly to profound emotional changes or to a pronounced intellectual deterioration. Among the illnesses that bring about such changes are Alzheimer's disease, Korsakoff's syndrome and Huntington's chorea. Strokes and brain tumours may also produce direct psychological effects. The symptoms most commonly found are amnesia, confusion, and dementia, although some of these disorders may also bring about direct changes in emotional response, or produce hallucinations and delusions.

Alzheimer's disease is the most common physical disorder in which emotional functioning is directly affected. It is the most prevalent cause of 'senile dementia' and affects between 5% and 10% of all people over 65. It involves the progressive degeneration of brain tissue and this produces a gradual deterioration in intellectual ability, emotional integration, and skilled performance. Most patients survive for around eight years following the initial deterioration, and over this period the progressive dementia may lead to complete incontinence and loss of self-care skills. The need for constant nursing in the latter stages of the disorder means that relatives who look after these patients are subjected to severe long-term stress. They face many practical difficulties and become increasingly restricted in their activities. Many of these families find it difficult to maintain social contacts outside the home, and as a result of their arduous and disturbed lifestyle a majority of families with an Alzheimer's patient experience serious emotional problems.

Other conditions that may directly lead to profound psychological transitions include traumatic brain injury and stroke, although many of the emotional changes that follow such traumas are the result of psychological responses to other effects, rather than the direct result of anatomical changes. The symptoms that clinicians regard as primary (notably memory loss) are often not those which cause most disturbance to relatives. Family members are more likely to be distressed by secondary symptoms such as increases in irritability, stubbornness, and 'childish' behaviour (Brooks and McKinlay, 1983). Such adjustments in personality may lead family members to withdraw from the patient so that, in the longer term, brain-injured patients themselves may feel more troubled by the adverse changes in their social life than by their primary symptoms. As time goes on family members come to attribute the difficult behaviour not to a dysfunction of the brain but to alterations in the patient's personality (Kerns and Curley, 1985). This fundamental shift, by which the patient ceases to be seen as a victim and is progressively held to blame for undesirable behaviours, is likely to lead to frequent conflict and can place relationships in jeopardy. A reduction in the patient's social perceptiveness may also add to the emotional estrangement between the brain-damaged person and other family members. Such a decrement may increase self-centredness and reduce empathy for other people's feelings (Lezak, 1978).

Other Dimensions

Many other dimensions on which it is possible to range particular illnesses have a special relevance to the impact on family life. One is the degree of pain or discomfort involved. Some illnesses cause extreme agony and distress whereas others are relatively benign in their day-to-day impact on the patient's comfort. Another dimension is 'stability'. Some longer-term illnesses are relatively stable in their effect, whereas others follow a path of frequent remissions and relapses. It may not be known from one day to the next whether there is likely to be a sudden improvement or a setback, and the unpredictability may make many aspects of practical management very difficult and undermine morale. Illnesses also differ in their long-term prognosis. For many illnesses complete recovery is to be expected, whereas for others there can be no realistic hope of substantial improvement. Some are life-threatening whereas others have no particular implication for life expectancy. Although there are certain links and correlations between different dimensions, it is possible to find a disorder to fit almost any imaginable profile, and the dimensions are thus relatively independent. For example, some severely disabling conditions (such as a serious stroke) have a sudden onset whereas others (such as multiple sclerosis) develop gradually over a long time-span. Similarly, some painful illnesses (such as cancer) are life-threatening whereas others (such as arthritis) are not.

A few disorders, notably Huntington's chorea, provide a direct threat to the long-term health of other family members because of their hereditary nature. Huntington's disease usually begins in middle age and involves the progressive deterioration of brain tissue. The symptoms eventually include dementia, irritability, depression and hallucinations, as well as the spasmodic 'choreic' movements which give the disorder its name. Each child of an affected parent has a 50% chance of inheriting the disorder, and until recently it was not possible to determine which children would be affected until the symptoms made their appearance. The potential impact of this disorder on family life is especially profound, for there will not only be grave concern for the identified patient but also a longer-term fear concerning younger members of the family. Those who have a parent with the disease clearly have very good reason to worry about their own future health, and they need to consider the implications for planning a family of their own. Consultation with a genetic counselling service would seem to be essential for anybody who is in such an unfortunate position.

Some illnesses stigmatize the patient whereas others do not. Some cancer patients feel stigmatized, for example, and many friends and families of AIDS patients feel reluctant to disclose the nature of the diagnosis to others. With this disease the attribution of causality takes on a special importance. However much physicians may stress the fact that all those who suffer from AIDS are equally 'victims', there is considerably more public sympathy for the patient who is assumed to have contracted the virus from a blood transfusion than for one who is assumed to have been infected during a casual homosexual encounter. Within families of AIDS patients, members are often embarrassed about the revelation of homosexuality and feel that the illness brings notoriety to the family (Frierson, Lippman and Johnson, 1987).

Some diseases are stigmatizing in another way, because the disease itself, or treatment, has produced some disability or disfigurement. Some patients loathe the thought of being seen in wheelchair, or using a walking frame. The patient recovering from a mastectomy must learn to live without her breast and may feel unattractive and 'less of a woman'. The colostomy patient may develop a profound self-consciousness, with chronic fears about hygiene and odours. Diabetic and other patients may feel stigmatized by their dietary restrictions, especially when eating with strangers, and the chemotherapy patient may feel highly embarrassed by the loss of hair resulting from treatment.

THE PATIENT'S PSYCHOLOGICAL RESPONSE

Another key factor influencing how the family as a whole, and particular members of the family, respond to the illness is how the patient responds psychologically. Clearly this will largely reflect the nature of the disease— including the degree to which it is life-threatening, painful, stigmatizing, and disabling. Yet people also differ profoundly in their psychological resilience to illness. Some patients are defiant and withstand misfortune with great courage and endurance. Others are easily overcome. They quickly lose confidence and become highly anxious, angry or depressed. Some of these patients will attempt to hide their emotions, but some will be unable or unwilling to endure their suffering alone. Although the type of response reflects the individual's personality, it is also greatly influenced by the reactions and expectations of those around. Family members may inhibit the patient's expression of negative emotions, they may 'permit' such expression, or they may encourage it.

Those who are sick often attempt to cope by appraising their situation in the most optimistic way. They may count on an early and complete recovery, although this is more realistic for some conditions than for others. Others engage in the process of denial and constantly distract themselves from the fact of their illness. Many struggle to maintain a normal lifestyle even though disabled or in pain, and show a dogged determination not to 'give in' to the illness, and others cope by using alcohol or other drugs to deaden the psychological, as well as the physical, pain. In some cases patients endeavour to counter their anxiety by acting aggressively or with an exaggerated assertiveness. Typically, however, the psychological response to a serious physical illness is some degree of anxiety or depression. Patients may feel a sense of hopelessness, disappointment about the restrictions placed on their normal activities, a fear for the future, and a sense of injustice.

The patient's own psychological reaction is likely to play a major part in determining how other members of the family respond. If the patient chooses to 'play down' the impact of the illness, for example, other family members are likely to join in the conspiracy of maintaining a cheerful façade and pretending that the illness is of little consequence. In such circumstances, discussion of the topic may become taboo. Other patients tend to dwell on the illness, persistently alluding to it and constantly demanding recognition of their special condition. They may be demanding and aggressive, or miserable and weepy. Some patients feel that family members are too demanding and do not make sufficient allowance for the illness, whereas others feel that they are being treated, quite inappropriately, as severely disabled or seriously afflicted. The actual level of support is likely to be less important than the patient's perception of the support (Taylor, Wood and Lichtman, 1983). For their part, family members may feel that the patient is behaving inappropriately, either by making too few adjustments to compensate for the affliction, or by exaggerating the importance of symptoms. A suspicion may arise that the patient is attempting to capitalize on the illness and using it to manipulate the feelings and action of others.

In the process of coming to terms with the illness, the patient and other family members adopt new roles. The 'sick role' includes certain rights and obligations; the patient is exempted from many normal duties and the family acknowledges that the individual is not responsible for his or her present 'sick' state. On the other hand the patient is obliged to have the desire to get well, to minimize the extra burden on other members of the family, and to comply with any treatment requirements. One or more members of the family may take on the role of 'nurse' or 'caregiver'.

THE RELATIONSHIP BETWEEN PATIENT AND CAREGIVER

The problem of dealing with the illness is likely to become especially critical if the patient's disability requires intensive care by a family member. In such a circumstance the patient's attitude will be particularly important in determining how the family adapts. The task of caring for a person who is distraught and defeated is quite different from that of caring for someone who is aggressive and argumentative. Some patients will appear to resent the care being given to them, or will argue that not enough is being done. Others will be constantly thankful and appreciative, and attempt to lighten the psychological burden of those who nurse them and provide for their needs. The patient's response to care will depend largely on their appraisal of the spirit in which such care is provided. A patient who judges that the caregiver is performing tasks resentfully may feel depressed or angry as a consequence. On the other hand, if the caregiver is seen as positive, agreeable and relaxed then the patient is likely to remain calmer and to feel less of a burden.

When constant care is necessary, structural changes to the family system are required and, in particular, one member of the family is likely to adopt the role of 'principal caregiver'. In some cases it will be 'obvious' which person should take on such a role, but in other cases there may be difficult negotiations about which member or members will fulfil this role. The interaction between the patient and this key caregiver is likely to be prolonged, intense, and intimate, and a nurse–patient sub-system is likely to be a forceful component of the adapted system. In some cases the boundary around this sub-system will be relatively impermeable, with other family members playing little part in the patient's care. Within this sub-system cohesion may become very high, so that each individual becomes highly dependent on the other, and the interactions between them become very intense.

Within this context there will be many opportunities for the development of escalatory patterns. These may take the form either of 'vicious circles' or 'virtuous circles'. The patient who is difficult, who issues demands in an assertive and critical way, and who shows little appreciation of the help being given, will impose a heavy burden on the caregiver, who may then attempt to minimize contact with the patient. This may generate further resentment on the part of the patient, who is likely to accuse the caregiver of 'lacking concern'. In such a situation the caregiver will be unlikely to derive much satisfaction from the role of nurse and may come to resent the sacrifices that have had to be made in looking after the sick person. In such circumstances the patient is unlikely to be able to maintain a positive self-image as someone who is responding to adversity with fortitude and forbearance. Critical comments by the caregiver might make them feel unloved and unlovable. This may lower self-esteem and lead to depression or anger, and this in turn will make them more difficult to care for. Open strife may develop between caregiver and patient, with each feeling victimized by the other, and the quality of the interaction may deteriorate until few of the favourable aspects of the pre-illness relationship remain intact.

At the other extreme, the experience of caring and being cared for may greatly enhance the relationship between caregiver and patient. The patient may be appreciative of the added burden on the caregiver and be at pains to minimize demands. The caregiver may take great satisfaction in being able to ease the patient's discomfort and admire the way in which the pain and infirmity are being confronted. Aware of being recognized by the caregiver as 'a model patient', or as 'courageous' and 'heroic', the patient will attempt to live up to this image, perhaps hiding the full extent of the suffering, making allowances when care is less than optimal, and requesting rather than demanding further help. In such a scenario each performer will feel their dignity to be maintained and each will be able to take pride in their achievement. They will develop an increasing respect for the other person and will be able to communicate the conviction that a difficult situation is being faced sensibly, sympathetically and bravely. The extreme dependence of the patient on the caregiver may be reciprocated as the caregiver develops the 'need to be needed'.

The above sketches are extreme and idealized. In most patient–caregiver relationships there will be points of tension *and* points of relative ease. The quality of the interaction may change from day to day, perhaps reflecting the patient's physical state, the fatigue or ill-health of the caregiver, and other events happening within the family. The sketches are also essentially dyadic, and ignore other members of the family, whereas in most families the caregiver–patient sub-system will not be disengaged from the rest of the system. Input from other family members may increase or decrease the level of tension within this pivotal relationship. Indeed, in some families the role of 'principal caregiver' will be shared by several people. Such an arrangement will spread the burden of care, but it might also prove unstable and lead to frequent conflicts about whether individuals are taking a reasonable share of the responsibility. If one individual is allocated to the role of caregiver, then their satisfaction with the role is likely to depend critically on how other members react. If they openly acknowledge the special contribution that the caregiver is making to the patient's happiness and to the overall functioning of the family then the role may be fulfilling. But if family members seem to take for granted the extra effort being expended by the caregiver, or if they appear to resent reduced attention to their own needs, the caregiver is likely to become dissatisfied and frustrated.

FAMILY STRESS: INDIVIDUALS

Both for those who take on the special caregiver role, and for other members of the patient's family, a serious illness may prove highly stressful. Sometimes this stress will result in psychological disturbances—frequently depression or anxiety states—and sometimes it will precipitate a physical illness. The results of several research studies suggest that the partners of chronically ill patients experience at least as much stress as the patients themselves (Kerns and Turk, 1984). In some cases the symptoms developed by another member of the family may resemble those of the patient. Thus in one study it was reported that a quarter of the wives with husbands who had suffered a myocardial infarction developed cardiac-like symptoms, including chest pains and shortness of breath (Stern and Pascale, 1979). Some illnesses will be seen by family members as having direct implications for their own physical health, whereas others will not. Thus partners of AIDS patients may fear that they have or will contract the disease, and those who have a parent with cancer or Alzheimer's disease may fear that they will be similarly affected at some time in the future. If, as a result of the stress induced by one family member's illness, other family members do develop symptoms, they may also adopt a sick role, and this may radically change the overall role structure within the family. The relative severity of the two (or more) sets of symptoms, and the comparative importance of individuals' needs, may become significant issues that generate substantial conflict.

The risk of a physical or psychological disorder developing in a caregiver or other member of the family is related to many of the factors discussed previously in this chapter. Clearly the severity, time-course and nature of the disorder are highly important. The degree of support given by medical personnel is also highly influential, as is the support given by relatives and others. The patient's response to the illness, and to care, is also extremely critical. Factors affecting the well-being of family members, especially of caregivers, have been most extensively studied for cases of dementia, and in reviewing the relevant literature, Morris, Morris and Britton (1988) draw a number of conclusions that might well apply to other chronic illnesses. The burden on the caregiver often centres on the 'daily hassles' they experience, frequently as a result of the patient's irritating and frustrating demands. The particular problems that create stress for those who care for the demented patient include sleep disturbance, nocturnal wandering, incontinence and dangerous behaviour. Relatives often experience difficulty in sleeping and may become preoccupied with fears about the possibility of a further deterioration of the patient's mental state (Rabins, Mace and Lucas, 1982), and those who act as the principal caregiver run a high risk of becoming depressed or of suffering from other psychiatric disorders (Coppel et al., 1985; Gilleard, 1984).

Several studies suggest that caregivers are more likely to be adversely affected if they are closely related to the patient. Close family members often experience considerable distress as a result of prolonged caregiving, and this effect appears to be more pronounced for husbands and adult sons than for wives and adult daughters. When the caregiver is a member of the extended family, or is unrelated to the patient, they suffer fewer problems of psychological adjustment. Such people are likely to be less 'emotionally involved', but patients might also be more gracious and less demanding of those who are not closely related to them. Another possibility is that those who are not close family members are less intensely involved in the caregiver role, spend less time with the patient, and may retain the option of removing themselves from the situation.

The quality of the pre-illness relationship between the patient and the caregiver also seems to be an important determinant of the distress experienced by the caregiver. If the relationship was close and mutually rewarding, the caregiver is likely to fare relatively well (Gilleard et al., 1984). If the pre-illness relationship had been very positive the caregiver and patient are likely to continue to treat each other well when constant care becomes necessary, although in chronic conditions such as dementia even the relationships with the most auspicious history may eventually become distressed. Morris, Morris and Britton (1988) found that there was a significant reduction in intimacy between demented patients and those who were caring for them within the family, and the research also indicated that the relationships that had declined most in intimacy were those in which the caretaker had become depressed.

Depression among relatives who provide care for Alzheimer's patients is more common among those who feel that they have little control over the patient's behaviour. Pagel, Becker and Coppel (1985) found that spouse caregivers tended to be more depressed if they attributed the cause of the patient's disturbed behaviour to themselves, and Morris (1986) found significant associations between caregivers' levels of depression and the degree to which they regarded the difficulties they were experiencing as stable and global (i.e. affecting many aspects of their lives). In Morris's study, and others, depression has also been shown to reflect the caregiver's estimation of how well they are able to cope with the patient's difficult behaviour. It therefore seems that the caregiver's emotional response does not simply reflect the 'objective difficulties' they face, but depends critically on their individual appraisal of the situation, and on the attributions they make about the nature, causes and likely outcome of the problems they have encountered in caring for the patient.

Although the focus of this section has been on the effects of an adult's illness on other adults within the family, and particularly on the principal caregiver, children are often adversely affected by the illness of a parent (or a sibling). Parental illness is often experienced by children as a major stressor (Gersten et al., 1974) and may produce psychological or physical disorders (Garmezy and Rutter, 1983). For children, as for adults, social support seems to be a protective factor (Wolchik, Sandler and Braver, 1987).

FAMILY STRESS: RELATIONSHIPS

A serious illness of one person will not only affect the health and well-being of other family members as individuals, but will also have an impact on all of the relationships between members. The disability of a husband or wife, for example, will change not only the marital sub-system but also the relationships each of the parents has with the children. Thus the structure of the whole family unit will change as a result of the serious affliction of any member.

When one of the marital partners is ill, the marital relationship is likely to be most affected, and it will change in many ways. The time that the couple spend together may increase dramatically, there may be a comprehensive re-allocation of roles and tasks. The wife of a man who is seriously ill may find herself making many more decisions than she was prior to her husband's illness, and the husband of a sick or disabled wife may have to learn new skills to perform domestic tasks, such as cooking and ironing, that were previously undertaken by his wife. The degree and nature of the couple's intimacy may change significantly. The patient is likely to become more dependent on their partner than they were previously, and the caregiver may gain considerable power. The opportunities for the caregiver to reward the patient will be increased while the opportunities for the patient to reward the caregiver will decrease. Despite the additional time spent together, the couple may have fewer opportunities to engage in joint recreational activities.

There are a number of ways in which one partner's illness may lead to an attenuation or cessation of the couple's sexual contact. Sometimes the pain or disability caused by the illness will make a normal sexual relationship impossible. Sometimes the psychological sequelae of the illness (particularly depression or acute anxiety), or treatment side-effects, will make the patient unable or unwilling to engage in intercourse. In some cases a disease will have increased the patient's self-consciousness or body image to such a degree that they feel themselves to be unattractive or 'neutered'. Men and women who have undergone surgery for rectal or intestinal cancer often have severe and long-term difficulties in sexual adjustment (Devlin, Plant and Griffin, 1971). Colostomy patients often remain highly self-conscious of the stoma. They may live in continual fear of spillage and odours, and wish to avoid the embarrassment that they would experience during sexual contact (Druss, O'Connor and Stern, 1969). Many women who have had a mastectomy remain highly self-conscious about their appearance and feel themselves to be no longer sexually attractive. The disfigurement caused by the removal of a breast may make them very reluctant to resume an active sex life. For different reasons, cervical cancer patients may also experience considerable difficulties in sexual adjustment (Andersen, 1987).

Despite the high level of stress that an illness may bring to a marriage, however, there is little evidence to suggest that marital satisfaction is diminished as a result. Many studies have failed to find a significant association between marital satisfaction and the disability of one of the partners (Brown, Rawlinson and Hardin, 1982). It seems that the impact of an illness affects couples in very different ways. Although the impact may be disastrous for some, marital satisfaction for some couples actually seems to improve as a result of the impact of an illness. In such cases it may encourage emotional expression, and foster psychological intimacy and 'solidarity'. The lack of any clear association between illness and marital happiness is consistent with the view that good reactions and negative reactions balance out across couples. In the majority of cases a serious illness will have a very significant effect on how the marriage is perceived and valued by partners, and on how they interact, but it seems that many couples manage to accommodate to the situation in a constructive way.

FAMILY STRESS: THE FAMILY SYSTEM

A similar picture emerges when we examine the impact of a member's illness on the functioning of the family as a whole. Some family systems are thrown into crisis, but others respond to the challenge by implementing changes that have favourable long-term effects. Thus family cohesion may increase, there may be more open expression of affection and commitment, and problem-solving may improve. Some families are 'energized' as a result of their exposure to a major illness (Pratt, 1976), and it appears that as many families are brought together by the impact of a serious illness as are pushed apart (Litman, 1974). A family's high resilience should not be taken as evidence that it is 'untouched' by the illness, however, for the maintenance of effective functioning often reflects the fact that many adaptations have been made and that the system has coped well. If the effects on the family take the form of adaptive changes then stress may be maintained at a tolerable level and crisis thereby prevented.

How well a particular family copes with an illness will depend on aspects of the illness itself, the quality of functioning of the family before the illness, and the precise nature of the changes that are made to defend against stress. 'Illness factors' relate to the nature of the particular illness, and include the suddenness of onset, the degree of life-threat, the level of disability, the likelihood of recurrence, the intensity of pain experienced, and the level of care needed by the patient. A family will generally be better able to adapt the more slowly an illness develops. Severe disability will often reduce the patient's capacity to maintain family duties and responsibilities in a way that a less disabling condition will not. The nature of the illness has a profound influence on how the patient responds psychologically, and this is critical in determining how the illness affects the family system. On the other hand, the reactions of other family members, and of the family system, also play a major part in determining how the patient responds, so that there is a dynamic interaction between the responses of the patient and the family.

Effectiveness of coping will also reflect the family's general structure and functioning, and particularly its resources—strengths and coping strategies. In terms of the dimensions of the circumplex model, outlined in Chapter 2, families at the extremes of the two major dimensions would be expected to fare less well than those in a mid-position. Within enmeshed families, for example, emotional over-involvement between members might lead each individual to treat an illness as a personal affliction. At the other extreme, disengaged families have little cohesion, and some members might regard another's illness primarily as a personal inconvenience. When illness strikes, such individuals would be expected to withdraw emotionally from the patient and the family, although social pressures and personal needs might prevent them from abandoning the situation entirely. Less extreme families would seem better equipped to cope effectively. Members retain a sense of autonomy, and will maintain a personal perspective on the patient's illness, while also having empathy, providing support for the patient, and playing a constructive role in the various adjustments made by the system. Similarly, on the adaptability dimension, rigid families will find it difficult to make the necessary adapations while, at the opposite extreme, chaotic families will lack the coordination necessary to respond in a sustained and satisfactory way. Between these two extremes, families will be able to make adjustment but will not be overwhelmed by the changes.

Illness often leads to major adjustments in a family's role structure. If constant care of the patient is necessary, one or more family members may need to take on the caregiver role. The degree to which this role is shared, and the style and quality of the relationship that develops between patient and caregiver(s), are often critical, and if one person is called upon to devote much of their time and energy in this way, other roles and duties that they would normally perform may have to be taken over by others. The patient, too, may be unable to play a normal part in family life. Thus an illness is likely to increase the burden of chores and responsibilities while reducing the number of people available to shoulder this burden. In many cases the problem is solved by other family members taking on new responsibilities. Thus older children may step into roles vacated by a sick adult and may perform tasks and undertake commitments that would normally be assigned to those of a more mature age. An older child may act as a 'mother' to younger children, for example, or might be allocated other duties that would normally be performed by an adult family member.

The composition of the family (and the position of the patient in the family structure) will clearly be important in determining how the family adjusts to an illness, and adjustment will also depend on the family's stage of development. The diagnosis of a life-threatening disorder will have a quite different impact if the patient is the young mother of three young children or is a 70-year-old man living with younger family members. The impact of a mother's illness will depend critically on the age of the children, and disability in an older man is likely to have more effect if he is still of working age than if he has been retired for a number of years. An illness will also be more disruptive if it occurs during a transition between two 'stages', when the family already has an agenda for change. A chronic illness may continue to impose a strain on the family system across several stages of family development, and the impact is likely to be different at each of these stages.

An illness is likely to be coped with more adequately if the family is 'open' and maintains a high level of contact with the wider community. Friends, relatives, neighbours, self-help groups, and various social agencies, may all be important sources of aid. Practical help and emotional support from outside the family often improve the well-being of those who live with someone who is seriously ill. For example, Morris (1986) reported that informal social support was associated with relatively low rates of depression and stress among those caring for a partner suffering from dementia. Physicians clearly have a special role to play in keeping the family informed about the patient's condition and notifying the family about local resources, and many families also gain advice and comfort from meeting with other families that are striving to cope with the same illness (Kahan et al., 1985). Sharing experiences with those who face similar problems may encourage the expression of feelings, reduce isolation, and help the family to realize that the problems it faces are by no means unique.

TREATMENT, RECOVERY, AND REHABILITATION

Just as social support appears to have the protective effect of reducing an individual's vulnerability to illness, so it may aid the return to health following a period of sickness. A number of studies indicate that the presence of supportive family members helps the patient to recover from illness and surgery (DiMatteo and Hays, 1981). Among women suffering from breast cancer, for example, the quality of family support is positively related to adjustment (Bloom, 1982), and prognosis following myocardial infarction is less favourable for those who are socially isolated than for those who are surrounded by friends and family (Ruberman et al., 1984). Litman (1966) studied the relationship between social support and recovery from a variety of illnesses, and found that whereas three-quarters of patients whose families provided strength and reassurance recovered well, three-quarters of those whose families were not supportive had a poor rehabilitation record.

Family interaction may also be critical in determining the extent to which a patient complies with treatment and participates in rehabilitation programmes (O'Brien, 1980; Turk, Meichenbaum and Genest, 1983). The interest, concern and encouragement of family members may increase patients' compliance with demanding treatment regimes. They may be persuaded to take medication regularly, to exercise, and to avoid dangerous behaviours such as smoking. In some cases, however, the family has a negative effect on patient expectation or compliance. Some families have a poor understanding of what is to be expected following symptomatic recovery and continue to regard the former patient as highly susceptible. In some cases anticipatory grief remains even when all immediate threat to the patient's life has been removed, and in other cases the family's fear of recurrence (particularly of cancer or a heart attack) may increase the patient's level of anxiety. In a bid to alleviate their own fears, however ill-founded these may be, families of heart-attack survivors sometimes believe that there will be no recurrence as long as the patient remains inactive and does not attempt to revert to a normal lifestyle. Families and patients need to be provided with accurate information so that they may adopt a realistic view of the dangers and the possibilities of a complete rehabilitation. In some cases family members differ in their views of whether the patient is fit and able to resume normal activities and responsibilities, and such a diversity of opinion can generate considerable conflict.

During the recovery phase the family may find it difficult to reverse adaptations that were implemented to cope with the illness. A rigid family system, in particular, may perpetuate the 'sick role', and a return to the pre-illness structure may be prevented by the tendency for 'successful' adaptations to be maintained. In some cases the attention paid to the patient's health will have been useful in distracting the family from other concerns such as the threat of a marital breakup, and the system may therefore have a vested interest in maintaining its concern with the patient's physical condition. In some cases this will include a strategic denial by the family that recovery has occurred. Sometimes the patient, too, will have little incentive to vacate the sick role. An indulgent family may have accommodated so extravagantly that the role has been accompanied by major privileges, and in such a circumstance there may be relatively few benefits to be gained by rehabilitation and the resumption of pre-illness tasks and responsibilities.

RESPONSES TO CHILDHOOD ILLNESS

The association between family stress and childhood illness is complex. On the one hand, a child's affliction is usually a source of stress for all members of the family; on the other hand, stress may play an important part in precipitating or maintaining an illness (Lask and Fosson, 1989). A high level of family stress appears to increase the risk of childhood accidents (including accidental poisoning, burns, and fractures) and is associated with the onset of a number of childhood diseases, especially those involving the gastrointestinal and respiratory systems (Beautrais, Fergusson, and Shannon, 1982; Greene *et al.*, 1985). Family events have also been associated with the development and course of many chronic childhood illnesses including diabetes and asthma (Leaverton *et al.*, 1980; Lask and Matthew, 1979), and there is evidence to suggest that even the inception of some childhood cancers may be linked to family stress.

EMOTIONAL RESPONSE AND ILLNESS MANAGEMENT

Family members have important roles to play in helping to comfort the sick child and in managing practical aspects of the special care that is required when illness strikes. But family members also respond emotionally to the sick child, and a strong emotional reaction may interfere with the efficiency of their management. Some parents become so emotionally burdened as a result of the child's disorder that they are unable to reassure or comfort the child or to undertake tasks that would improve the child's condition. Although anxiety is usually the predominant emotion generated in such circumstances, elements of guilt, depression and anger may also be present.

In a study of 50 mother–child pairs attending a paediatric out-patient clinic, Bush *et al.* (1986) showed that the mother's behaviour had a major influence on the child's response to a medical examination. The children of mothers who used distraction were more at ease than those of mothers who showed agitation or who anxiously tried to reassure the child. Parents are intuitively aware that their own anxiety may adversely affect the child, and they usually try to control their emotional response in order not to alarm the child. They may attempt to maintain psychological control by employing various coping strategies. Some parents make use of 'denial', an irrational and emotional refusal to accept that a threat is real. Others distract themselves from the immediate problem by devoting their energies to diverting and time-consuming activities. Other coping strategies involve seeking comfort from other people, searching for information about the illness and, if the child is hospitalized, avoiding visiting the child too often. This latter strategy may be misunderstood by relatives and medical professionals as signifying that the parent lacks strong feelings towards their son or daughter. But sometimes such 'distancing' signifies that a highly involved mother or father considers that being with the seriously ill child would prove too distressing and might adversely affect the child's self-control.

The child who is sick is often treated by the parents as extremely delicate and vulnerable. They may extend special privileges and arrange treats and there may be a reluctance to apply the normal standards of discipline. The child may be shielded from additional stresses and overprotected. If such handling extends over a long time, however, the protectiveness may prevent the development of skills and inhibit the growth towards maturity. In extreme cases the parents' 'babying' of the child will lead to a regression of behaviour, so that soiling, wetting, thumbsucking and other behaviours return after an absence of several years.

The degree to which a child's illness disturbs the family equilibrium depends on many variables, including the age of the child, the presence or absence of siblings, the personalities of the parents, and the nature of the illness itself. More serious illnesses and accidents may require that the child be hospitalized, but in the majority of cases a parent will nurse the child in the home. Some common disorders are well understood by parents as frequently occurring in childhood (for example, measles, whooping cough and chicken-pox). They have a limited time-course and present little threat. Other disorders, like diabetes, asthma and epilepsy, are less well understood by parents and have implications for long-term health. And some diseases, like leukaemia, are immediately life-threatening and often require painful medical or surgical intervention.

An implicit danger in examining clinical research findings such as those reviewed in this chapter is that negative aspects tend to be over-represented. While it is true that the onset and maintenance of a child's illness may reflect dysfunctional family patterns, and that a child's illness may generate family stress, it needs to be emphasized that families also play important positive roles in protecting children from illness, in managing effective treatment regimes, and in helping children to cope with their affliction. Parents play the major role in the prevention of disease by employing high standards of hygiene, regulating diet, presenting the child for immunization, and maintaining the home as a safe environment. They constantly monitor their children's health and consult physicians when they are anxious about a symptom that might indicate the onset of an ailment. They therefore act to safeguard the child and remain highly vigilant for any sign that all is not well. Indeed, Mechanic (1965) found that most mothers were more concerned with their children's health than with their own.

The family environment can also act as a buffer against disease. A happy atmosphere, with high affection and low tension, may well protect children from certain kinds of illness. For example, Rutter and Cox (1985) demonstrated that good relationships between parents and children can safeguard children against adverse reactions to stress. Apley (1982) coined the term 'emotional vitamins' to describe the positive aspects of parenting that make children more resilient and less predisposed to illness. And family factors play an important role when disease does strike. Emotional support and practical help by members of the child's family will often serve to minimize the child's suffering, to aid a speedy recovery, and to attenuate the longer-term repercussions of the illness. The child suffering from a chronic disorder will benefit in the long term, and will be helped to maintain a good psychological adjustment, by continuing to be accepted as a normal family member. In response to a child's suffering the family may in fact become more united and more determined to work together to help and protect the afflicted child. One study revealed that many families with an epileptic child were particularly good at making decisions together, and this was presumed to reflect the family's experience in coping with the stress imposed by the child's disorder (Ritchie, 1981).

In the remainder of this chapter, five major topics within the area of the family and childhood illness are reviewed. After a brief discussion of children's understanding of illness the effects of hospitalization are examined. Next, family responses to chronic childhood illness are discussed, and then the special case of childhood cancer is explored in some detail. Finally, the subject of childhood psychosomatic disorders is considered. A number of related topics are dealt with in later chapters. Childhood handicap is examined in Chapter 4, and children's conceptions of death and dying, and their response to a terminal illness, are discussed in Chapter 9. The child's response to bereavement is considered in Chapter 10.

CHILDREN'S UNDERSTANDING AND RESPONSES TO ILLNESS

Young children have a very limited comprehension of the nature and causes of illness (Eiser, 1985). At a very early stage they are likely to regard illness as a kind of moral infringement and when are sick they may consider that this represents a punishment for some previous misdemeanour. When they hear of someone being ill they may judge that the person should be blamed for the affliction. As cognitive development proceeds, however, they construct a more realistic account. They begin to understand that people are 'stricken' by illness and that symptoms are merely the signs of some underlying illness process. They become less confused about issues such as infection and contagion and they learn to make important distinctions between different types of illness.

The fact that young children's ideas about illness may be quite different from those of adults has certain implications for paediatric care. For example, Burbach and Peterson (1986) suggest that young children who take a moral view of illness may be reluctant to report symptoms, thereby endangering their health. It would seem very important for health professionals to understand children's conceptions of illness in order to be able to communicate well with their young patients, but research has shown that medical personnel often have a very poor understanding of children's concepts of illness (Perrin and Perrin, 1983). It is probable that in some cases this will substantially reduce the effectiveness of interventions. Those who may need to talk with children about their condition or help them to make 'an informed decision' about their treatment clearly need to have a keen appreciation of the level of understanding of their paediatric patients. Insight into a child's comprehension will also allow health professionals to increase their effectiveness in reducing patients' anxieties and increasing their compliance with a treatment regimen. There are clear implications, too, for health education. In the absence of an adequate understanding of the meanings of health and illness concepts for young children, lessons by teachers, and media advertising campaigns, may be totally inappropriate for the target age group.

Although children's general concepts of health and illness are limited by the extent of their general cognitive maturity, within such limits their specific understanding of their own malady will principally reflect what their parents tell them and how their parents behave. Young children who are sick may not be able to form a sophisticated understanding of the nature of their medical condition, but within the limits of their cognitive ability they will certainly acquire some notion of whether their illness is serious or not and of how long their discomfort is likely to last.

The parents of young children may have to convince them that there is no need to feel responsible for the affliction, and that being ill is not 'naughty'. Children also gain an impression of what their illness means from subtle cues manifest in their parents' behaviour. Evident anxiety about the condition will alarm the child, changing both the way they *think* about the illness and the way they *feel* about it. Thus children use their parents both as sources of information and as emotional models. Just as they may acquire fears by observing a parent's alarm in the presence of certain insects, or when hearing thunder, so evident parental distress about the illness, the treatment, or hospitalization, is likely to upset them. The child's distress may then increase the parents' concern and begin to unnerve other relatives, so that a kind of 'emotional contagion' spreads through the family.

HOSPITALIZATION

About one in three children are admitted to hospital some time during their childhood, and for a quarter of all children the first hospital admission occurs during the first five years of life. In nearly a half of these cases the child undergoes surgery, the most common operations being tonsillectomy and adenoidectomy, appendectomy, circumcision, hernia repair and squint correction (Butler and Golding, 1986). Whether or not surgery is involved, the experience of hospitalization often proves very upsetting for the child, and adverse reactions appear to reflect a number of different factors. Among the most important of these are the separation from parents; the effect of the strange physical and social environment; and the fear, pain and discomfort that may result from particular diagnostic and therapeutic procedures. However, children of different ages respond to hospitalization in quite different ways, and the emotional reaction also depends on the child's previous experiences of separation and the nature of any psychological preparation for admission and treatment. The disturbance is likely to be especially severe if the child is admitted under emergency conditions, and if painful medical procedures such as lumbar punctures or bone marrow aspirations are involved.

THE AGE FACTOR

Young babies, up to the age of about six months, show little or no anxiety in response to hospitalization, and as long as they are stimulated with interesting toys, and receive social stimulation from nurses and other children, they fare relatively well (Rutter, 1981). Older babies tend to cry more than they would normally, and may show various other signs of missing their parent/s and their familiar surroundings. When a parent visits, infants of this age tend to cling and cry, and when children return home they often show a great reluctance to be separated from a parent even for short periods of time. Between the ages of 18 months and four years the child's response to hospitalization is most intense, with many showing extreme panic and anger. Behaviour tends to regress, and screaming, withdrawal, rocking, bed-wetting and sleep disturbances are relatively common. In many cases the child continues to be disturbed for several weeks or months following the return home. However, such adverse effects are not found for all children and are often absent if the parent is able to remain with the child throughout the period of hospitalization.

PREVIOUS SEPARATION EXPERIENCES

A child's previous experience of separation from the parents seems to have marked effects on the response to hospital admission. If the child has not had the opportunity to feel secure when left in a situation away from a parent (for example, when attending a nursery school or when staying overnight with grandparents) then hospitalization brings two simultaneous novel and potentially shocking elements—being separated, and being in a strange situation where distressing medical procedures are performed. Thus children who have no experience of previous separations may be terrified by the unfamiliar hospital setting. The child who has been used to separations and to novel environments therefore has a distinct advantage, but a history of previous separations does not, of itself, guarantee immunity from adverse reactions. The quality of antecedent separation experiences is also important; if they have been negative then the child may have become sensitized to separation and may respond with a particularly high degree of distress to hospital admission. Children often need a considerable period of time to recover psychologically from one hospital experience, and if a second admission follows closely on the first they are likely to display considerable emotional and behavioural disturbance.

MINIMIZING DISTRESS

Most parents attempt to prepare the child emotionally for a hospital stay. The older child can be reassured that there is a good reason for admission, that the stay will be temporary, that visiting will be regular, and that certain 'fringe benefits' will be gained (lots of toys to play with, other children to meet, a regular supply of ice cream, etc.). During the stay it is likely that certain painful procedures will need to be performed (injections, surgery and a variety of examinations), and it is helpful if professionals keep parents informed about what is likely to be involved so that the parents can help to prepare the child for particular interventions.

Providing such information and offering emotional support for the parents often reduces their anxiety and this in turn appears to lessen the child's distress (Wolfer and Visintainer, 1979). This reflects the general finding that children's anxiety about hospitalization is closely related to the tension shown by the parents. Mahaffey (1965) provided mothers of young children about to undergo surgery for the removal of tonsils and/or adenoids with support and information about the surgical procedures involved. Mothers in a control group did not receive this special attention. Compared to the children of the control mothers, the children of mothers in the experimental group cried less, made fewer calls for help, and displayed fewer behaviour problems after the operation. This demonstrates the value of health professionals working closely with the parents, and is an interesting variation on the many studies indicating that provision of emotional support and information to an adult patient prior to a surgical procedure generally aids postoperative recovery.

Preoperative psychological preparation of the children themselves aims to provide information, to encourage the expression of emotions, and to foster a trusting relationship with medical personnel. Various methods have been introduced to accomplish these goals. For example, several films and videotapes have been produced to help allay fears of hospitalization and surgery. With titles such as 'Scott goes to hospital' and 'Christine has an operation', these often present a somewhat nervous but brave child (the 'model') who is shown experiencing the kinds of procedures that the patient is about to undergo. Several controlled studies have shown that such films are often effective in reducing a young patient's fear (Melamed, 1977). Other techniques shown to be effective include puppet therapy, role playing, and play with 'hospital-relevant' toys (Eckhardt and Prugh, 1978).

For the younger child, especially, the major problem associated with hospitalization may be the separation anxiety, and there are a number of ways in which this can be reduced. Encouraging the child to play with familiar toys, and with dolls that have 'accompanied' them to hospital, is one useful strategy. 'Aunting' is another; one or two particular nurses are assigned to care for the child so that relationships begin to be formed and the child can recognize 'special' people among the many strangers encountered in the hospital. And it is of course particularly useful if parents and relatives make frequent visits. Many hospitals now permit sick children to be visited at any time, and some allow parents to stay during the period of treatment ('rooming in'). There is good evidence that rooming in does help the child to adjust emotionally, both during the hospital stay and in the period after discharge (e.g. Brain and Maclay, 1968).

In some cases, however, parents may find that close proximity to the sick child for extended periods raises their own anxiety level to an unbearable degree. Thus parents are likely to be the best judge of what arrangements will be best for them and for the child. For illnesses that are particularly sensitive to emotional effects a constant round of reunions and partings may make the child's condition worse. In the 1930s Peshkin observed that some asthmatic children improved considerably when they were removed from the home environment, and noted that some of these children had asthma attacks when their parents visited. He developed the extreme view that in some cases children would benefit from a long period of separation from their parents (up to two years!), a process he labelled 'parentectomy'. At the other extreme some paediatricians have suggested that because hospital treatment can have highly disruptive effects on the child and the family, the removal of the child from the home should be regarded as an option of last resort. It has also been argued that for non-urgent treatments it may be preferable to delay hospitalization until the child is older and more able to cope with the psychological stresses imposed by separation and treatment.

When the child returns home from hospital there may be further problems of readjustment, and the reunion with the parents is sometimes attended by considerable emotional disturbance. This psychological aftermath is usually short-lived, but if there have been a number of hospital admissions, and particularly if the family is disturbed or if the quality of the parent–child relationship is not good, persistent behavioural problems can occur (Butler and Golding, 1986; Quinton and Rutter, 1976).

CHRONIC CHILDHOOD ILLNESS

Almost all children suffer periodically from minor illnesses which are relatively short-lived, but some develop serious long-term conditions such as epilepsy, arthritis and diabetes that may impose a chronic stress on the child and other members of the family. The child's illness may make considerable demands on the parents' resources of time, energy and finance, and family roles are likely to change, with the chronically sick child taking on a 'patient' role and a parent (usually the mother) taking on the 'nurse' role. Attention may be focused almost exclusively on the patient, with other members' needs and concerns taking a much less prominent place. Sometimes shared anxiety over the child's condition serves to unite an otherwise discordant family. The child's illness may distract the family from other areas of conflict or concern, or it may provide a useful scapegoat for disappointments and difficulties. Overall, however, the emotional impact of the child's illness is negative. Families with a chronically ill child show relatively high rates of marital conflict, and individuals within such families become vulnerable to a variety of emotional problems. Anger and guilt are often experienced, but anxiety and depression appear to be the most common adverse responses (Sabbeth and Leventhal, 1984). The stress of caring for a chronically ill child may also produce a marked reduction in the parents' self-confidence, this effect being more pronounced for mothers than for fathers (Johnson, 1985).

MANAGEMENT BY PARENTS

Parents often become very knowledgeable about the disease afflicting their child, and this knowledge is often useful in helping them to control the child's symptoms (Johnson, 1985). The parents of many chronically ill children are expected to carry out regular, complicated and sometimes painful procedures to aid the management of the illness. Thus in the case of a child with a serious renal condition the parents may be involved in home dialysis procedures, and in the case of childhood diabetes the parents need to make regular tests to monitor blood sugar levels and to administer insulin by injection. Parents of children who suffer from a range of disorders, including diabetes, cystic fibrosis, coeliac disease and phenylketonuria, must enforce firm dietary restrictions.

The example of dietary constraint provides a useful illustration of how the management of chronic illness may have considerable ramifications for family life. First the parents must learn details of the nature of dietary regime to be followed, and they must discipline themselves to ensure that all of the food provided for the child is 'safe'. They must inform any relatives, friends, teachers and group leaders who may ever offer food to the child about the special diet. They also have to deal with the child's feelings of deprivation or embarrassment at not eating the same food as siblings, peers and parents. At the earliest possible age the child needs to be given some understanding of the reason for the dietary regime and encouraged to develop self-discipline. The parents will also need to decide how to respond when the restrictions are breached.

Thus the single issue of dietary control involves the parent in a number of tasks—the task of developing a special dietary expertise, the task of constantly monitoring the young child's food intake, the task of educating the child and others about the diet, the task of disciplining infringements, and finally the task of handing control over to the child at a suitable stage. But dietary control is only one aspect of the child's special needs, and for any serious chronic illness there are likely to be a number of such issues, each of which may be vital for the child's safety. Thus the management of diabetes involves, as well as dietary restriction, sugar level monitoring and insulin injection. As the child grows older the parents must decide, in consultation with their medical advisers, when the child can be left alone to manage the various health-maintaining procedures. The process of handing over such control to the child is usually gradual and associated with considerable parental ambivalence. On the one hand the parents may wish to encourage the child to become independent, while on the other they may fear that he or she will not be sufficiently conscientious or competent. A fear for the child's continued safety may make them wary of relinquishing direct supervision. In diabetes, control of management tasks is generally passed to the child in a number of stages. Most children are judged to be capable of self-injection by the age of 10 years, whereas the accurate self-testing of sugar levels is not usually possible until the age of 12 or 13 years.

PSYCHOLOGICAL EFFECTS ON THE CHILD

Although chronic illness does increase the risk that a child will develop emotional and behavioural problems, many such children seem to cope relatively well, and only a small minority are clearly psychologically disturbed as a result of their illness (Kellerman *et al.*, 1980). Naturally, the magnitude of the psychological effect will depend on the effects and time-course of the illness and on the nature of treatment. Frequent or long-term hospitalization is associated with relatively high risk of distress, and some illnesses produce physical effects which directly change the child's emotional state. Thus the fact that some children with epilepsy become withdrawn and socially isolated could be the result of either a psychological reaction to the illness or a direct effect of interference with normal brain activity (Hoare, 1987).

A number of family variables have also been shown to be associated with children's psychological responses to chronic illness. In one major study Pless, Roghmann and Haggerty (1972) found that although children with chronic ailments were generally at risk of poor mental health, many of those whose family situation was favourable and supportive were relatively well adjusted. Similarly, it has been shown that epileptic children who come from well-functioning families are likely to make a good adjustment (Bagley, 1971). A poor parent–child relationship is also associated with a high frequency of persistent behavioural problems in children who have had a number of successive hospital admissions (Quinton and Rutter, 1976). Furthermore, aspects of the family environment are likely to make an impact on the course of the illness itself. Studies that have followed patterns of illness and family discord over a number of years suggest that a rise in the level of conflict is often followed by a deterioration in health (e.g. Koski and Kumento, 1975). Negative life changes, many of which are associated with aspects of family life, have been shown to affect the urine ketone levels of child diabetics (Brand, Johnson and Johnson, 1986) and the pulmonary functioning of children with cystic fibrosis (Patterson and McCubbin, 1983).

Thus the general atmosphere within the family, and particular stressful family events, appear to have important effects on the course of a chronic illness and on the child's psychological response. Specific family responses to the disease and the sick child are also important. If parents and siblings attempt to 'normalize' the situation the child is liable to retain a 'normal' self-image, but if their responses constantly focus on the medical condition then the child is likely to treat the illness as an intrinsic and central personal attribute. A parental tendency towards treating the chronically ill child as special, vulnerable, and 'damaged' may have a negative effect, bringing about a secondary, psychological, disablement. Johnson (1980) found that overcontrol, overanxiety, overindulgence, and rejection were all detrimental to the health of diabetic children. Overindulgence during periods of illness may bring 'secondary gain', with the child deriving certain benefits (for example, added attention, or opportunities to miss school) from being ill.

A family that 'rewards' a chronically ill child excessively during acute phases of the illness will do little to increase motivation towards recovery. The responses of such families may therefore have the effect of discouraging the child's compliance with certain demands of the medical treatment programme. Many chronically sick children do consider that their parents and siblings treat them more favourably when they are ill (Peterson, 1972) and there is evidence that they sometimes attempt to capitalize on such sympathetic responses. Thus in the case of asthmatic children, Matus (1981) found that increased attention by the family, and special indulgences and treats given during an acute phase, sometimes prompt a child to neglect medication or to engage in actions likely to cause an asthmatic attack. Fortunately, many parents are aware that the child may use an illness to manipulate family members, and they often take steps to ensure that this does not happen (Johnson, 1985).

EFFECTS ON SIBLINGS

Although other children in the family usually feel considerable sympathy for a brother or sister who is suffering from a chronic illness, they also tend to view the parents' behaviour towards the sick child as excessively lenient and overprotective (Cairns *et al.*, 1979). Siblings may feel that all of the parents' attention and concern is focused on the ailing child and that their own needs are undervalued or disregarded. If the parents make a point of openly emphasizing the courage, suffering, and vulnerability of their sick offspring, then the healthy siblings are likely to feel jealous, excluded, and isolated. Their self-esteem may suffer and they may exhibit behaviour difficulties or withdrawal. While the results of a number of studies suggest that the siblings of chronically ill children are especially vulnerable to psychosomatic disorders, and frequently engage in attention-seeking behaviours (Ferrari, 1984), a few studies have failed to discover adverse consequences (Johnson, 1985). If problems are identified they may reflect the sibling's anxiety over the child's illness, or the parent's changed behaviour towards them, or a general stressful atmosphere within the family.

CHILDHOOD CANCER

'Childhood cancer' is the generic name for a number of diseases of varied aetiology. About 1500 cases of cancer are diagnosed annually in children from the UK (approximately 7500 in the US), and just a few decades ago childhood cancer was considered to be a short-term and invariably fatal disease. Due to medical advances over half of these children now survive, although this still leaves the disease as a major cause of death in childhood. Families therefore face the situation of caring for a child who has a serious chronic illness, where many of the treatment procedures are painful and have aversive side-effects, and in which the chances of long-term survival remain uncertain.

Some studies have suggested that psychological factors may play a part in the onset of childhood cancer. For example, Jacobs and Charles (1980) found that whereas 50% of a group of children with cancer had experienced parental loss during the preceding years, only 16% of a matched control group had experienced such a loss. There were also significant differences between the groups (with more of the cancer group being adversely affected) in terms of the number of changes of residence and the frequency of family disputes they had experienced. However, the hypothesis that psychological factors play a significant part in the aetiology of childhood cancers remains highly controversial, and the major factors known to be involved in causation (genetic, immunological, etc.) are all biological.

THE PARENTAL RESPONSE

When parents are told that their child has cancer they generally respond with a shock and numbness that can last for several days or weeks. Following this immediate reaction some parents develop a severe anxiety state, or depression, and many others have trouble sleeping and eating and remain preoccupied with the diagnosis and its significance. Some may infer from the diagnosis of cancer that their child will soon die, and it is very important that health personnel present a realistic picture of the likely prognosis. Thankfully, following recent advances, this information is likely to provide some hope and encouragement. If parents have too pessimistic a view of the outcome they may communicate this to the child, providing added distress, and they may begin to engage in psychological strategies that assume that the child will die. They may withdraw their emotional investment in the child or indulge in a mental rehearsal for the loss of the child—a process known as 'anticipatory mourning'. Such attempts to prepare for a future loss may prove useful if the child does eventually die, but if the child survives then the parent–child relationship may suffer severely as a result of the parents' premature bereavement response (Kemler, 1981).

Some months after the diagnosis the majority of parents are found to be coping remarkably well (Marky, 1982), although a substantial minority continue to have persistent problems. About a quarter remain clinically anxious or depressed (Maguire, 1983), and levels of alcohol abuse, work difficulties and sexual problems tend to increase. Although there is frequently a sharp increase in marital discord, the incidence of separation and divorce does not appear to increase during the crisis involved in caring for the child with cancer (Van Dongen-Melman and Sanders-Woudstra, 1986). If the parents judge that a course of treatment is proving effective, their estimate of the child's chances of survival will rise. They may still describe themselves as 'living from day to day', but for many the 'black cloud' of the child's possible death becomes a less and less prominent feature.

In a study of how families cope with childhood leukaemia during the six months following diagnosis, Kupst et al. (1983) found that most families managed reasonably well and that there were relatively few 'pathological' reactions. The risk of psychological distress was found to be related to the child's age (mothers with younger children fared less well than those with older children), lack of social support, and the presence of other stressors (including marital problems, financial hardship, and employment difficulties). The strategies employed by those who were apparently coping well were also studied. No single effective psychological tactic was identified, but a variety of coping strategies seemed to work for different people and for different families. Some remained optimistic and pinned their hopes on a happy outcome, while others adopted a more fatalistic stance. Some maintained a dogged self-reliance while others made use of all the social support they could muster. Several individuals accepted the reality of the crisis at one moment but would later engage in emotional 'denial'. As in many other studies of childhood and adult illness, the findings from this research suggest that rather than constituting a hazardous evasion of the situation, denial can be a useful way of avoiding a particularly adverse and disabling response. It therefore seems that some degree of self-distraction and emotional escape may have a positive outcome.

Distraction from prolonged and distraught rumination on the child's fate may also be imposed by the various practical demands likely to be made on the parents. Thus some degree of home-nursing will be required, and while in some cases this may involve little more than making sure that medication is taken regularly, in others more difficult procedures have to be carried out, as when parents are asked to maintain catheters. Parents are also likely to be preoccupied with keeping a brave face for the sake of the child and they may spend a good deal of effort in providing their own brand of informal psychotherapy. This is likely to involve helping the child to prepare for and cope with an aggressive treatment regime and its side-effects. Treatments that are carried out in the home, the special attention demanded as the result of the child's anxieties, and frequent hospital appointments, are all likely to prove highly disruptive of normal family life.

In addition to the emotional pressures inflicted on a family by the care of a child with cancer, the financial burden has also been identified as a frequent source of considerable hardship. Because specialist paediatric cancer centres are few and far between, the child often has to be taken some distance to attend for regular clinic sessions. The direct cost of travel may be high, but in addition there are likely to be many incidental costs (including expenditure on food and accommodation, as well as loss of pay) and together these often represent a significant proportion of the family's total budget. Thus the economic cost, together with the time and energy required to organize and realize frequent visits, may add considerably to the impact of the child's illness on the family (Lansky *et al.*, 1979; Bodkin, Pigott and Mann, 1982). Financial hardship may thus cause added distress at a time when the child and other family members are particularly emotionally vulnerable.

Most parents, it must be emphasized, cope well with all these difficulties. Those who develop serious psychiatric problems need specialist attention, but the question arises of whether anything can be done to help prevent such severe adverse reactions and to improve the well-being of those who, although they would not be diagnosed as suffering from a psychological disorder, are certainly functioning under a very heavy emotional burden. Medical personnel have a key role to play in providing support and information. Parents appreciate being kept closely informed about developments in the child's condition, especially if they are positive. But parents are also likely to benefit from discussing issues that worry them with other people. Close relatives may provide invaluable support, but it is generally agreed that additional professional psychological help should be offered to the parents of a child with cancer.

EFFECTS ON SIBLINGS

The limited available evidence suggests that because of the life-threatening nature of the disease, siblings of children who are suffering from cancer may be even more distressed than the siblings of children with other kinds of chronic illness. They may feel confused, isolated, guilty, and somewhat envious of the attention being given to the child with cancer, and there is good evidence that their needs are often neglected as a result of the parents' preoccupation with the sick child (Spinetta, 1981). Among the symptoms reported as common in these siblings are jealousy, irritability, social withdrawal, anxiety, and loss of self-esteem (Lansdown and Goldman, 1988). In some cases siblings are called upon to act as bone marrow donors, but there is no evidence to show that this opportunity to help with the treatment significantly reduces their feelings of being disregarded.

The distress and the behaviour problems so often evident in these siblings might be prevented by the parents' recognizing that all of their children are especially vulnerable at this time of family stress. Social workers and medical personnel may need to remind parents that the siblings need special attention. As well as being properly cared for and being encouraged to accept that they are still important and cherished members of the family they should be kept informed of what is happening to the sick child and what is likely to happen in the future. They may need to be reassured that they are not to blame in any way for their brother's or sister's condition, and they should be prompted to express their anxieties and other feelings. Medical professionals can assist the family by supplying information that parents will pass on to the siblings, and by conducting family sessions in which problems are discussed with the parents and all of the children together.

FAMILY RELATIONSHIPS

In view of the substantial and multiple difficulties confronted by the families of children who have cancer, it is remarkable that so many seem to cope well. Attempts to maintain some degree of stability involve a number of processes, some of which may involve fundamental changes in family expectations, rules and roles. Kupst *et al.* (1983) found that the adequacy of coping of mothers, fathers and the child with cancer were all related, so that some family units seemed to be coping better than others. Families that coped well were found to be more open in terms of communications between members, and communications with staff.

A strategy that seems to be effective in maintaining family stability is that of normalizing the situation as far as possible (Chesler and Barbarin, 1987). The less that the family sees itself as 'stricken' the more it will be able to function adaptively. An open sharing of information and feelings seems to aid the coping process dramatically, and the family may benefit by sharing feelings with others and by learning about how other families in similar situations are managing. Many parents feel that it would be beneficial for their family to meet with others facing a similar trauma and some join self-help groups that are set up with the aims of encouraging families to share information and to provide mutual help and comfort. A number of hospitals have taken the initiative in forming such groups. Some arrange for families to meet on the ward, while others consider it more appropriate for families to meet well away from the hospital setting (Gilder *et al.*, 1978).

In a minority of cases families fare very poorly after a child has been diagnosed as having cancer. It has already been noted that many marriages suffer. There may be a substantial increase in the level of marital discord and problems may be encountered in the sexual relationship. The fact that the child's siblings are often distressed has also been discussed. They frequently feel confused and isolated and may feel with some justification that they take second place as the parents devote most of their time and energy to the care of the sick child. The reason for these negative changes appears to be that the attention of the parents (and particularly of the mother) focuses primarily on the patient and that little effort is expended in the maintenance of other relationships. The strong, and even obsessional, alliance between a parent and the sick child may totally dominate the family structure so that all other relationships are threatened and may weaken.

Although changes of this kind occur to some degree in many families with a childhood cancer victim, in a few cases the mother–sick child relationship comes to totally dominate the family system. The so-called 'symbiotic syndrome' (Lansky and Gendel, 1978) is an extreme form of 'triangulation' in which mother and child engage in a very close, exclusive and maladaptive relationship. The onset of such an alliance often seems to be triggered by a stressful event such as a loss, the birth of a sibling or hospitalization. The child regresses to a much earlier level of development, maintaining a foetal position, bottle feeding, using infantile speech or insisting on being carried everywhere. The highly anxious mother is likely to accede to the child's evident wish to be treated like a baby, particularly if she feels that the illness is placing the child's life under threat. Thus the clinging together of mother and child can be interpreted as resulting from an acute anxiety caused by the anticipation of permanent separation.

The relationship becomes exclusive, with the child withdrawing from other children, and with both the mother and child retreating from the father and siblings. Mother and child may become a housebound pair, constantly together and even sleeping alone in the same bed. Sometimes they may prefer to remain in the hospital together rather than returning home to be part of the family. Although such closeness provides immediate comfort for the mother and child, the consequences are likely to be seriously detrimental in a number of respects. Not surprisingly, such over-intimate alliances can have traumatic effects on the marriage and seriously damage the relationships between the mother and the child's siblings. The mother may thus draw herself well away from those who will be able to provide the most support and the most comfort if the child dies. Mothers who have been involved in such symbiotic relationships with the sick child respond to the child's death very badly indeed. Some refuse to accept that the child has died, and others have suicidal thoughts or hallucinate the continued presence of their special child. Although Lansky and Gendel report a number of cases of the symbiotic syndrome in the context of childhood cancer, they suggest that this maladaptive coping strategy is not limited to such cases but can also occur when a child has another chronic life-threatening disease.

THE CHILD'S RESPONSE

Although many once held that it was kinder to protect the child from the knowledge of the diagnosis (and, particularly, of the potentially fatal outcome of the disease) there is now a consensus that attempting to maintain silence may prove harmful. Although a child's knowledge that imminent death is a possibility may greatly increase the anxiety (Spinetta, 1974), it seems that open communication is to be preferred to a guarded approach involving long-term suppression of information. The child will certainly perceive cues from the parents and other relatives that the disorder is serious, and it is often held that children have a right to know about the gravity of their condition. Some authors (notably Spinetta, 1980) have provided guidelines for parents who face the task of disclosing to a child that s/he is suffering from a serious and possibly lethal illness. A child who has been informed about the disease is more likely to ask questions, and the answers will often offer reassurance to counter the appalling fantasies constructed by children who have been 'shielded' from the true diagnosis. The informed child is also better able to understand why aggressive and painful treatments are necessary. Thus the parents have a very important role to play in communicating information to the child, and they generally seem to do this very effectively. Susman *et al.* (1982) found that the conceptions of cancer held by the patient and parent were similar; they often had a similar perception of the illness, they shared many of the same feelings, and they tended to hold comparable views about the likely outcome.

As in other types of childhood illness, there is a clear association between the anxiety of the parent and the child's distress. A parent who is evidently anxious about the illness may cause the child to panic; or if the child is highly distressed, perhaps as a result of painful treatment or frequent hospitalization, this is likely to increase the parents' anxiety. Initially, distress is caused by the diagnosis and fears about the eventual outcome. Later, it is likely to be elicited by the effects of medical procedures used to examine and treat the child. All of the major therapeutic interventions used to combat childhood cancer (radiotherapy, chemotherapy and surgery) are 'aggressive treatments' that have unpleasant side-effects. Bone marrow aspirations, lumbar punctures, and injections with chemotherapeutic agents are painful, and some interventions also produce nausea and vomiting. Hair loss is another frequent treatment side-effect, voice characteristics may change as a result of hormone administration, and in some cases disfiguring surgery, including limb amputation, may be necessary. Bone marrow transplants are likely to involve hospitalization lasting between two and three months, and some of the drugs used in treatment suppress the immune system so that the child must remain isolated from other people, including the family, in order to prevent infection. All of this is likely to be highly disturbing to the child and the family.

It is hardly surprising that children with cancer often develop psychological problems. Fear of death, the pain and problems of the illness itself, hospitalization, and the nature of the treatment and its side-effects, often produce profound disturbances of emotion and behaviour. Anxiety and depression are common, and the child's conduct is often regressive. The child may withdraw and become emotionally detached from those around, or extreme clinging behaviour may be displayed towards the parents. Sometimes the 'symbiotic syndrome' develops as mother and child form a tightknit and exclusive relationship. The fact that there are adverse reactions is hardly surprising given the extreme stresses faced by the child, and it is much more remarkable that a proportion of children who suffer from cancer do *not* show appreciable psychological disturbance. To some extent this may reflect a high level of resilience that characterizes many children, but there is also evidence that many families help by providing a high level of emotional support, keeping the child well informed, answering questions and allaying unnecessary fears. Clinics can also assist in the prevention and treatment of psychological distress by engaging in open communication with the child, by teaching anxiety reduction techniques such as relaxation, and by making use of art therapy and play therapy techniques.

THE CHILD AT SCHOOL

The young cancer patient's continued attendance at school is an important aid to maintaining 'normality', but for a number of reasons absences are likely to be frequent. Lansky *et al.* (1975) reported a relatively high incidence of school refusal (or 'school phobia') among children with cancer, and suggested that this often reflected a fear of separation from the mother. The parent who feels highly protective is less likely to force the child to attend, particularly if there is some danger that class-mates may respond in a heartless way. Hair loss, for example, will identify the child as 'different' and may bring ridicule, and peers may stigmatize a child they know to be a cancer victim. Eiser (1980) examined the experiences of teachers with a pupil suffering from leukaemia. Half of the teachers reported some difficulties in teaching the child, but the major problem identified was frequent interruptions in schooling. The average attendance rate for these children was just 67%, with many of the absences being due to clinic appointments, acute symptoms, or the need to avoid infection.

When treatment drastically reduces the efficiency of the immune system common childhood diseases such as chicken-pox and measles may prove fatal, so children have to be shielded from the possibility of infection by peers. Eiser found that attendance rates improved substantially when chemotherapy was discontinued. As a result of the recurring absences most of the children had fallen behind their peers academically and some were receiving remedial teaching even though they were described as being of average or above-average ability. Being placed in a remedial class is likely to threaten a child's self-esteem, and sensitive action by the teacher will be required to avoid children concluding that they lack basic competence.

The teachers in Eiser's study felt that most parents had done a good job of briefing them about the child's condition. A majority of parents visited the school regularly and had kept the teacher informed about the progress and side-effects of the treatment. Most teachers recognized that their own behaviour towards the child with leukaemia was particularly lenient and attentive, but Eiser points out that school may be the only situation in which these children are not perceived primarily in terms of their illness, and that teachers have a vital role to play in encouraging a 'normal' self-concept. It is essential that teachers, as well as parents, be as fully informed about the child's condition as possible, and it is especially useful if the teacher is able to make contact with the health professionals responsible for the child's medical supervision. On a more general level, a number of training packages for teachers have been developed. These aim to enhance teachers' understanding of cancer and to provide them with practical suggestions about how a child suffering from this illness may best be helped to adjust in the school situation (Ross and Scarvalone, 1982).

LONG-TERM OUTCOME

About 40% of children with cancer will die of the disease, perhaps after a long course of promising remissions and responses to treatment followed by disappointing relapses. Eventually these children and their families will be faced with the painful process of coping with the child's dying weeks and days, and the parents will later confront the harrowing task of contending with their bereavement (relevant issues are discussed in Chapters 9 and 10). But happily an increasing number of children diagnosed as having cancer do survive in the long term and a number of studies reveal that the majority of these go on to lead happy and well-adjusted lives.

Li and Stone (1976) conducted a follow-up study of 142 adult survivors of childhood cancer and found that most were doing well at college or in work. For the majority there was no clear evidence of long-term psychological disturbance following their illness and they had not experienced difficulties in establishing close personal relationships. This positive outcome is highly encouraging, especially in view of the fact that a small proportion of the patients had developed a further primary tumour and that several others had persistent medical conditions arising from their cancer or from the therapeutic regime. Holmes and Holmes (1975) also found that most survivors of childhood cancer were well adjusted. Of more than 100 '10-year survivors' interviewed, one-quarter considered themselves to be 'markedly' or 'moderately' disabled as a result of the cancer, but despite this some 90% of the group reported that their history of serious illness had had no particular effect on their present life.

A small proportion of those interviewed in this study did say that the after-effects of their cancer were still serious, but some also claimed that it had had a positive influence on their lives. A few who had suffered brain damage were clearly psychologically impaired, but others had become 'overachievers' who were highly successful in a number of fields, and the overwhelming majority were enjoying a normal or near-normal lifestyle. Positive effects were also evident in a study by O'Malley *et al.* (1979). They found that many survivors claimed that their successful treatment made them feel specially privileged at having been spared from death, or had made life more meaningful, or had left them with a debt to society. One-third also felt that the experience of cancer had some effect on their career choice, and it was found that many had opted to work in health-related fields.

On the other hand this study revealed that not all of the former patients were doing well. Twelve per cent of the group appeared to have a marked psychological difficulty—usually anxiety, depression, or major mood swings —and many more had at least one mild psychiatric symptom. Some said that they lived cautious lives, avoiding risks and paying close attention to their health, and nearly a quarter felt that having cancer had made it more difficult for them to make or maintain friendships. Some social contacts seemed to have a fear that the cancer might be contagious, and others appeared to be repulsed by the patient's loss of hair or amputation. But although many patients reported that they lost friends or were ostracized because of their cancer when they were a child or adolescent, few experienced such difficulties as adults, and most had told their close friends about the illness.

When asked for their advice to those who have to care for children with cancer, a clear majority of survivors felt that children should be told that they have the disease, although they acknowledged that this could lead to distress. They also recommended that psychological support should be made available to the child and other members of the family. Looking back, most people felt that they had received good support from their family throughout their illness, and they recalled a number of coping strategies that had proved useful following the diagnosis. A very common, and apparently effective, method was emotional detachment or 'denial'. Other research on childhood cancer survivors has indicated that a good long-term psychological outcome is more likely if the patient is part of a supportive family where problems are openly discussed and the expression of feelings is encouraged. This evidence provides further support for the view that families facing the daunting task of caring for a child with cancer can do a great deal to help the patient during the illness phase and in the period of recovery.

CHILDHOOD PSYCHOSOMATIC ILLNESS

The discussion so far in this chapter indicates that childhood illnesses have psychological effects on the young patient and on other members of the family, and that psychological factors may have profound effects on the management and course of both acute and chronic disorders. Even where the cause and nature of the illness are undeniably biological, it seems that emotional, cognitive and behavioural elements are often important in exacerbating or attenuating the disorder and in influencing the course of recovery. But there are also many conditions in which emotional stress appears to be responsible for the initial development of a physical illness, and these tend to be labelled 'psychosomatic'. Among the childhood disorders categorized in this way are non-organic recurrent abdominal pain, certain bladder and bowel disorders, some cases of asthma, and some skin disorders such as eczema and urticaria.

Although psychological elements play a part in the aetiology of at least some cases of these disorders, however, they develop only in children who have a particular biological vulnerability, and environmental conditions may also play a crucial role. In most cases a complex interaction between these biological, environmental and psychological conditions is responsible for instigating an acute attack of the illness. But this is also true of many illnesses that are not usually identified as 'psychosomatic'. Thus we should recognize that psychological factors can play an important part in almost all physical illnesses, influencing the individual's vulnerability, and the onset and course of the disease, while acknowledging that such influences play a more central role in some kinds of disorder—those we recognize as psychosomatic—than in others (Lask and Fosson, 1989).

A number of studies have demonstrated the fact that family factors can affect a child's vulnerability to infectious disease. For example, Meyer and Haggerty (1962) monitored the life events within families over a one-year period, while periodically taking swabs from the children's throats in order to measure the level of streptococcal infection. It was found that stressful family events were followed by an increase in the bacterial level, and this therefore suggested that family stress can increase children's vulnerability to infection.

The part played by family stress in modifying the course of an illness has been demonstrated for a number of conditions, principally—though not exclusively—those recognized as psychosomatic (Lask and Matthew, 1979; Leaverton *et al.*, 1980; Patterson and McCubbin, 1983). One such disorder is recurrent abdominal pain. This affects about 10% of children at some time during their childhood (Apley and Hale, 1973) and tends to occur most frequently in the morning. It appears that children with certain temperaments (for example, those who are timid, 'highly strung', or 'perfectionist') are more vulnerable to the condition than others, but the pattern of the development of symptoms also reflects parental attitudes and responses. Parents tend to take very different views of the child's complaint; some identify the pain as psychogenic and tend to play it down, whereas others worry that there might be a serious organic problem and seek constant medical reassurance (Faull and Nicol, 1986). As demonstrated in the case of many other conditions, a high level of parental anxiety about a child's illness will be communicated to the child, and the child is likely to respond with increased distress. In the case of a psychogenic complaint such distress is likely to exacerbate the symptom. As well as this general effect, particular episodes of psychosomatic abdominal pain can often be seen as a reaction to specific stressful events occurring within the family or at school.

The most significant research linking family factors to psychosomatic illness in children is probably that concerning asthma. Between 5% and 10% of school-aged children show some signs of asthma (Ellis, 1983), and roughly twice as many boys as girls are affected. Biological vulnerability factors always play an important role in this illness, and there is a well-established hereditary factor. The relatives of asthmatic children are more likely than others to suffer not only from asthma but also from eczema, a skin disorder that is also stress-related (Butler and Golding, 1986). It is true that in many cases of asthma psychological factors seem to be of little importance, with the intermittent asthma attacks triggered either by environmental conditions (e.g. a high pollen count or a smoky atmosphere) or by infection. But in other cases the illness is clearly exacerbated by psychological factors. Some of the research in this area has focused on the question of whether certain personality characteristics may predispose a child to develop asthma. Although it has been shown that asthmatic children tend to exhibit a number of neurotic characteristics such as high dependency, high anxiety and obsessiveness, it now seems probable that these represent the psychological response to the condition rather than predisposing personality traits (Rees, 1980).

Studies on the parent–child relationship suggest that a number of parental characteristics including overprotectiveness and perfectionism play a causal role in asthmatic attacks (Cheren and Knapp, 1980). Clinical evidence and systematic studies have indicated that the symptoms of some asthmatic children are relieved as a result of separation from the parents. Thus Purcell et al. (1969) measured the amount of wheezing and the number of asthma attacks in a group of children identified as 'primary psychological cause' asthmatics. Measurements were first taken during a period of normal family life, then during a two-week period when the parents lived away from home (the children were cared for by a substitute mother), and again after the family had been reunited. It was found that the children experienced significantly less wheezing, and suffered fewer asthma attacks, during the separation phase than during either of the other phases. They also required less medication when their parents were absent.

In a study of asthma, diabetes, and other complaints, Minuchin and his colleagues (Minuchin, 1974; Minuchin et al., 1975) found additional support for the hypothesis that family interactions play an important role in determining the course of chronic conditions. They suggested that certain characteristics of families are related both to the aetiology and to symptom exacerbation of chronic psychosomatic illnesses in children. The maladaptive family characteristics identified by the group include enmeshment, overprotectiveness and rigidity. Minuchin also suggested that many families of children with psychosomatic symptoms strive to avoid open conflict. They fear change and, because conflict might challenge the established order within the family, many contentious issues are never addressed or brought out into the open. The parents may inhibit expression of conflict because they are concerned that this will adversely affect the child. Another dysfunctional pattern reported by Minuchin involves conflict between the husband and wife, with the child entering into a coalition with one or other parent. Minuchin does not claim that dysfunctional family patterns are sufficient by themselves to cause the psychosomatic symptomatology, and is careful to acknowledge that the child's physical vulnerability is another important factor.

The fact that family relationships seem to play such an important role in the onset and course of childhood illnesses such as diabetes, asthma, eczema and recurrent abdominal pain suggests that it might be appropriate to adopt a treatment approach that does not focus solely on the 'identified patient', but which also involves the parents or the whole family. Such a treatment could perhaps change unhealthy parental attitudes or modify dysfunctional family patterns in such a way that the child's symptoms would be relieved. In some cases a vicious circle may have developed, with the parent's anxiety causing stress to the child, thus exacerbating the disorder and giving the parents even greater cause for concern. If parents involved in such a cycle were helped to take a calmer view of the child's condition this might prevent the escalation, and would hopefully generate a 'virtuous circle' (i.e. lower parental anxiety should lead to a reduction in the child's symptoms, and the parents would then have less cause for concern).

In other cases therapy might be directed at changing parental anger or guilt about the child's disorder. As these attitudes are bought out into the open, and as change is facilitated, pressures that are maintaining the child's symptoms may be reduced. Another approach focuses on changing inappropriate family relationships or communication patterns. After a diagnostic family procedure has identified particular dysfunctional features of family interaction an attempt is made to modify these so that future interactions are less likely to promote or maintain symptoms. The expression of latent conflicts may be encouraged, for example, or overprotectiveness may be challenged and changed. There is good evidence that family therapy is often effective in modifying family patterns (Gurman, Kniskern and Pinsoff, 1986), and this approach to intervention has been used successfully to relieve psychosomatic symptoms in children (Lask and Kirk, 1979; Lask and Fosson, 1989). Such therapy is offered in addition to any conventional medical treatment recommended for the condition.

REFERENCES

Andersen, B. L. (ed.) (1987) *Women with Cancer: Psychological Perspectives*. New York: Springer-Verlag.

Apley, J. (1982) One child. In: J. Apley and C. Ounsted (eds), *One Child*. London: Spastics International Medical Publications.

Apley, J. and Hale, B. (1973) Children with recurrent abdominal pain: how do they grow up? *British Medical Journal*, No. 3, 7–9.

Bagley, C. (1971) *The Social Psychology of the Child with Epilepsy*. London: Routledge and Kegan Paul.

Baranowski, T. and Nader, P. R. (1985) Family health behaviour. In: D. C. Turk and R. D. Kerns (eds.), *Health, Illness and Families: A Life-Span Perspective*, New York: Wiley.

Beautrais, A. L., Fergusson, D. M. and Shannon, F. T. (1982) Life events and childhood morbidity: A prospective study. *Pediatrics*, 70, 935–940.

Berkman, L. F. and Breslow, L. (1983) *Health and Ways of Living: The Alameda County Study*. New York and Oxford: Oxford University Press.

Bloom, J. R. (1982) Social support, accommodation to stress and adjustment to breast cancer. *Social Science and Medicine*, 16, 1329–1338.

Bodkin, C. M., Pigott, T. J. and Mann, J. R. (1982) Financial burden of childhood cancer. *British Medical Journal*, 1347–1349.

Brain, D. J. and Maclay, I. (1968) Controlled study of mothers and children in hospital. *British Medical Journal*, No. 1, 278–280.

Brand, A. H., Johnson, J. H. and Johnson, S. B. (1986) The relationship between life-stress and diabetic control in insulin-dependent diabetic children and adolescents. Unpublished manuscript, University of Florida. Reported in Johnson (1985).

Brooks, D. N. and McKinlay, W. (1983) Personality and behavioural change after severe blunt head injury. *Journal of Neurology, Neurosurgery and Psychiatry*, 46, 336–344.

Brown, J. S., Rawlinson, M. E. and Hardin, D. M. (1982) Family functioning and health status. *Journal of Family Issues*, 3, 91–110.

Burbach, D. J. and Peterson, L. (1986) Children's concepts of physical illness: a review and critique of the cognitive-development literature. *Health Psychology*, 5, 307–325.

Bush, J. P., Melamed, B. G., Sheras, P. L. and Greenbaum, P. E. (1986) Mother–child patterns of coping with anticipatory medical stress. *Health Psychology*, 5, 137–157.

Butler, N. R. and Golding, J. (eds.) (1986) *From Birth to Five: A Study of the Health and Behaviour of Britain's Five Year Olds*. Oxford: Pergamon.

Cairns, N., Clark, G., Smith, S. and Lanksy, S. (1979) Adaptation of siblings to childhood malignancy. *Journal of Pediatrics*, 95, 484–487.

Cargan, L. and Melko, M. (1982) *Singles: Myths and Realities*. Beverly Hills, CA: Sage.

Cheren, S. and Knapp, P. (1980) Gastrointestinal disorders. In: H. Kaplan, A. Freedman and B. Sadock (eds.), *Comprehensive Textbook of Psychiatry: III*. Baltimore, MD: Williams and Wilkins.

Chesler, M. A. and Barbarin, O. (1987) *Childhood Cancer and the Family: Meeting the Challenge of Stress and Support*. New York: Brunner/Mazel.

Cohen, S. and Syme, S. L. (eds.) (1985) *Social Support and Health*. New York: Academic Press.

Cohen, S. and Wills, T. A. (1985) Stress, support and the buffering hypothesis. *Psychological Bulletin*, 98, 310–357.

Coppel, D. B., Burton, C., Becker, J. and Fiore, J. (1985) Relationships of cognitions associated with coping reactions to depression in spousal caregivers of Alzheimer's patients. *Cognitive Therapy and Research*, **9**, 253–266.

Devlin, B. H., Plant, J. A. and Griffin, M. (1971) Aftermath of surgery for anorectal cancer. *British Medical Journal*, **3**, 413–418.

DiMatteo, M. R. and Hays, R. (1981) Social support and serious illness. In: B. H. Gottlieb (ed.), *Social Networks and Social Support*. Beverly Hills, CA: Sage.

Druss, R. G., O'Connor, J. R. and Stern, L. (1969) Psychologic response to colectomy: II. Response to a permanent colostomy. *Archives of General Psychiatry*, **20**, 419–427.

DuCette, J. and Keane, A. (1984) 'Why me?': An attributional analysis of a major illness. *Research in Nursing and Health*, **7**, 257–264.

Eckhardt, L. O. and Prugh, D. (1978) Preparing children psychologically for painful medical and surgical procedures. In: E. Gillert (ed.), *Psychological Aspects of Pediatric Care*. New York: Grune and Stratton.

Eiser, C. (1980) How leukaemia affects a child's schooling. *British Journal of Social and Clinical Psychology*, **19**, 365–368.

Eiser, C. (1985) *The Psychology of Childhood Illness*. Chichester: Wiley.

Ellis, E. F. (1983) Asthma. In: R. E. Behrman and V. C. Vaughan (eds.), *Nelson Textbook of Pediatrics*. Philadelphia: Saunders.

Faull, C. and Nicol, R. (1986) Abdominal pain in six-year olds: an epidemiological study in a new town. *Journal of Child Psychology and Psychiatry*, **28**, 251–260.

Ferrari, M. (1984) Chronic illnesses: psychological effects on siblings—I. Chronically ill boys. *Journal of Child Psychology and Psychiatry*, **25**, 459–476.

Frierson, R. L., Lippman, S. B. and Johnson, J. (1987) AIDS: Psychological stresses on the family. *Psychosomatics*, **28**, 65–68.

Ganster, D. C. and Victor, B. (1988) The impact of social support on mental and physical health. *British Journal of Medical Psychology*, **61**, 17–36.

Garmezy and Rutter, (eds.) (1983) *Stress, Coping and Development in Children*. New York: McGraw Hill.

Gersten, J. C., Langner, T. S., Eisenberg, J. G. and Orzek, L. (1974) Child behaviour and life events: undesirable change or change per se? In: B. S. Dohrenwend and B. P. Dohrenwend (eds.), *Stressful Life Events: Their Nature and Effects*. New York: Wiley.

Gilder, R., Buschman, P. R., Sitarz, A. L. and Wolff, J. A. (1978) Group therapy with parents of children with leukemia. *American Journal of Psychotherapy*, **32**, 276–287.

Gilleard, C. J. (1984) *Living with Dementia: Community Care of the Elderly Mentally Infirm*. London: Croom Helm.

Gilleard, C. J., Belford, H., Gilleard, E., Whittick, J. E. and Gledhill, K. (1984) Emotional distress among the supporters of the elderly mentally infirm. *British Journal of Psychiatry*, **145**, 172–177.

Gorton, T. A., Doerfler, D. L., Hulka, B. S. and Taylor, H. A. (1979) Intrafamilial patterns of illness reports and physician visits in a community sample. *Journal of Health and Social Behaviour*, **20**, 37–44.

Gotay, C. C. (1985) Why me? Attributions and adjustment by cancer patients and their mates at two stages in the disease process. *Social Science and Medicine*, **20**, 825–831.

Gove, W. R., Hughes M. and Style, C. B. (1983) Does marriage have positive effects on the psychological well-being of the individual? *Journal of Health and Social Behaviour*, **24**, 122–131.

Greene, J. W., Walker, L. S., Hickson, G. and Thompson, J. (1985) Stressful life events and somatic complaints in adolescents. *Pediatrics*, **75**, 19–22.

Gurman, A., Kniskern, D. and Pinsoff, W. (1986) Research on the process and outcome of marital and family therapy. In: S. Garfield and A. Bergin (eds.), *Handbook of Psychotherapy and Behavior Change, 3rd edn*. New York: Wiley.

Hackett, T. P. and Cassem, N. H. (1969) Factors contributing to delay in responding to the signs and symptoms of acute myocardial infarction. *American Journal of Cardiology*, **24**, 651–658.

Hardwick, P. J. (1989) Families' medical myths. *Journal of Family Therapy*, **11**, 3–27.

Hoare, P. (1987) Children with epilepsy and their families. *Journal of Child Psychology and Psychiatry*, **28**, 651–655.

Holmes, H. A. and Holmes, F. F. (1975) After ten years, what are the handicaps and life styles of children treated for cancer? *Clinical Pediatrics*, **9**, 819–823.

Jacobs, T. J. and Charles, E. (1980) Life events and the occurrence of cancer in childhood. *Psychosomatic Medicine*, **42**, 11–24.

Johnson, S. B. (1980) Psychosocial factors in juvenile diabetes: a review. *Journal of Behavioural Medicine*, **3**, 95–116.

Johnson, S. B. (1985) The family and the child with chronic illness. In: D. C. Turk and R. D. Kerns (eds.), *Health, Illness and Families*. New York: Wiley.

Kahan, J., Kemp, B., Staples F. R. and Brummel-Smith, K. (1985) Decreasing the burden in families caring for a relative with a dementing illness. *Journal of the American Geriatrics Association*, **33**, 664–670.

Kanner, A. D., Coyne, J. C., Schaefer, C. and Lazarus, R. S. (1981) Comparison of two modes of stress measurement: Minor daily hassles and uplifts vs. major life events. *Journal of Behavioural Medicine*, **4**, 1–39.

Kaplan, D. M., Smith, A., Grobstein, R. and Tischman, S. E. (1977) Family mediation of stress. In: R. H. Moos (ed.), *Coping with Physical Illness*. New York: Plenum Press.

Kellerman, J., Zeltzer, L., Ellenberg, L., Dash, J. and Rigler, D. (1980) Psychological effects of illness on adolescents: I—Anxiety, self esteem and perception of control. *Journal of Pediatrics*, **97**, 126–131.

Kemler, B. (1981) Anticipatory grief and survival. In: G. P. Koocher and J. E. O'Malley (eds.), *The Damocles Syndrome*. New York; McGraw-Hill.

Kennedy, S., Kiecolt-Glaser, J. K. and Glaser, R. (1988) Immunological consequences of stressors. *British Journal of Medical Psychology*, **61**, 77–85.

Kerns, R. D. and Curley, A. D. (1985) A biopsychosocial approach to illness and the family: neurological disease across the lifespan. In: D. C. Turk and R. D. Kerns (eds.), *Health, Illness and Families: A Life-Span Perspective*. New York: Wiley.

Kerns, R. D. and Turk, D. C. (1984) Depression and chronic pain: the mediating role of the spouse. *Journal of Marriage and the Family*, **46**, 845–852.

Koski, M. and Kumento, A. (1975) Adolescent development and behaviour: a psychosomatic follow-up study of childhood diabetics. *Modern Problems in Pediatrics*, **12**, 348–353.

Kupst, M. J., Schulman, J. L., Maurer, H., Morgan, E., Honig, G. and Fochtman, D. (1983) Psychosocial aspects of pediatric leukemia: from diagnosis through the first six months of treatment. *Medical and Pediatric Oncology*, 11, 269–278.

Lansdown, R. and Goldman, A. (1988) The psychological care of children with malignant disease. *Journal of Child Psychology and Psychiatry*, 29, 555–567.

Lansky, S. B., Cairns, N. U., Clark, G. M., Lowman, J., Miller, L. and Trueworthy, R. (1979) Childhood cancer: nonmedical costs of the illness. *Cancer*, 43, 403–408.

Lansky, S. B. and Gendel, M. (1978) Symbiotic regressive behaviour patterns in childhood malignancy. *Clinical Pediatrics*, 17, 133–138.

Lansky, S. B., Lowman, J. T., Vats, T. and Gyulay, J-E. (1975) School phobias in children with malignant neoplasms. *American Journal of Disorders of Childhood*, 129, 42–46.

Lask, B. and Fosson, A. (1989) *Childhood Illness—The Psychosomatic Approach: Children Talking with their Bodies*. Chichester: Wiley.

Lask, B. and Kirk, M. (1979) Childhood asthma: family therapy as an adjunct to routine management. *Journal of Family Therapy*, 1, 33–50.

Lask, B. and Matthew, D. (1979) Childhood asthma: a controlled study of family psychotherapy. *Archives of Disorders of Childhood*, 54, 116–119.

Leaverton, D. R., White, C. A., McCormick, C. R., Smith, P. and Sheikholislam, B. (1980) Parental loss antecendent to childhood diabetes mellitus. *Journal of the American Academy of Child Psychiatry*, 19, 678–689.

Lezak, M. D. (1978) Living with the characterologically altered brain injured patient. *Journal of Clinical Psychiatry*, 39, 592–598.

Li, F. P. and Stone, R. (1976) Survivors of cancer in childhood. *Annals of Internal Medicine*, 84, 551–553.

Litman, T. J. (1966) The family and physical rehabilitation. *Journal of Chronic Diseases*, 19, 211–217.

Litman, T.J. (1974) The family as a basic unit in health and medical care: a social behavioural overview. *Social Science and Medicine*, 8, 495–519.

Madge, N. and Marmot, M. (1987) Psychosocial factors and health. *Quarterly Journal of Social Affairs*, 3, 81–134.

Maguire, G. P. (1983) The psychosocial sequelae of childhood leukaemia. In: W. Duncan (ed.), *Paediatric Oncology*. Berlin: Springer-Verlag.

Mahaffey, P. R. (1965) The effects of hospitalization on children admitted for tonsillectomy and adenoidectomy. *Nursing Research*, 14, 12–19.

Marky, I. (1982) Children with malignant disorders and their families. *Acta Paediatrica Scandinavica*, Supplement 303.

Martin, B. (1977) *Abnormal Psychology: Clinical and Scientific Perspective*. New York: Holt, Rinehart and Winston.

Matus, I. (1981) Assessing the nature and clinical significance of psychological contributions to childhood asthma. *American Journal of Orthopsychiatry*, 51, 327–341.

McClelland, D. (1979) Inhibited power motivation and high blood pressure in men. *Journal of Abnormal Psychology*, 88, 182–190.

Mechanic, D. (1965) Perception of parental response to illness. *Journal of Health and Human Behavior*, 253, 6–19.

Medalie, J. H. and Goldbourt, U. (1976) Angina pectoris among 10,000 men. *American Journal of Medicine*, 60, 910–921.

Melamed, B. G. (1977) Psychological preparation for hospitalization. In: S. Rachman (ed.), *Contributions to Medical Psychology:* Volume I. Oxford: Pergamon.

Meyer, R. J. and Haggerty, R. J. (1962) Streptococcal infections in families. *Pediatrics*, **29**, 534–549.

Minuchin, S. (1974) *Families and Family Therapy*. Cambridge, MA: Harvard University Press.

Minuchin, S., Baker, L., Rosman, B., Liebman, R., Milman L. and Todd, T. (1975) A conceptual model of psychosomatic illness in children. *Archives of General Psychiatry*, **32**, 1031–1038.

Morris, L. W. (1986) The psychological factors affecting emotional wellbeing of the spouse caregivers of dementia sufferers. M.Sc. thesis, University of Newcastle upon Tyne.

Morris, R.G., Morris, L. W. and Britton, P. G. (1988) Factors affecting the emotional wellbeing of the caregivers of dementia sufferers. *British Journal of Psychiatry*. **153**, 147–156.

Nolte, A. E., Smith, B. J. and O'Rourke, T. (1983) The relative importance of parental attitudes and behaviour upon youth smoking behaviour. *Journal of School Health*, **53**, 264–271.

O'Brien, M. E. (1980) Hemodialysis regimen compliance and social environment: a panel analysis. *Nursing Research*, **29**, 250–255.

O'Malley, J. E., Koocher, G., Foster, D. and Slavin, L. (1979) Psychiatric sequelae of surviving childhood cancer. *American Journal of Orthopsychiatry*, **49**, 608–616.

Pagel, M. D., Becker, J. and Coppel, D. B. (1985) Loss of control, self-blame and depression: An investigation of spouse caregivers of Alzheimer's disease patients. *Journal of Abnormal Psychology*, **94**, 169–182.

Patterson, J. M. and McCubbin, H. I. (1983) The impact of family life events and changes on the health of a chronically ill child. *Family Relations: Journal of Applied Family and Child Studies*, **32**, 255–264.

Perlman, D. and Rook, K. S. (1987) Social support, social deficits and the family: Towards the enhancement of well-being. In. S. Oskamp (ed.), *Family Processes and Problems: Social Psychological Aspects*. Beverly Hills, CA: Sage.

Perrin, E. C. and Perrin, J. M. (1983) Clinician's assessments of children's understanding of illness. *American Journal of Diseases of Children*, **137**, 874–878.

Peterson, E. (1972) The impact of adolescent illness on parental relationships. *Journal of Health and Social Behaviour*, **13**, 429–437.

Pless, I., Roghmann, K. and Haggerty, R. (1972) Chronic illness, family functioning and psychological adjustment: A model for the allocation of prevention mental health services. *International Journal of Epidemiology*, **1**, 271–277.

Pratt, L. (1976) *Family Structure and Effective Health Behaviour: The Energized Family*. Boston, MA: Houghton-Mifflin.

Purcell, K., Brady, K., Chai, H., Muser, J., Molk, L., Gordon, N. and Means, J. (1969) The effect of asthma in children of experimental separation from the family. *Psychosomatic Medicine*, **31**, 144–164.

Quinton, D. and Rutter, N. (1976) Early hospital admissions and later disturbances in children: An attempted replication of Douglas's findings. *Developmental Medicine and Child Neurology*, **18**, 447–459.

Rabins, P.V., Mace, N. L. and Lucas, M. J. (1982) The impact of dementia on the family. *Journal of the American Medical Association*, **248**, 333–335.

Reed, D., McGee, D., Yano, K. and Feinleib, M. (1983) Social networks and coronary heart disease among Japanese men in Hawaii. *American Journal of Epidemiology*, 115, 384–396.

Reges, L. (1980) Etiological factors in asthma. *Psychiatric Journal of the University of Ottawa*, 5, 250–261.

Reis, H. T. (1984) Social interaction and well-being. In: S. W. Duck (ed.), *Social Relationships, 5: Repairing Social Relationships.* London: Academic Press.

Ritchie, K. (1981) Research note: interactions in the families of epileptic children. *Journal of Child Psychology and Psychiatry*, 22, 65–71.

Ross, J. W. and Scarvalone, S. A. (1982) Facilitating the pediatric cancer patient's return to school. *Social Work*, 27, 256–261.

Ruberman, W., Weinblatt, E., Goldberg, J. D. and Chaudhary, B. S. (1984) Psychosocial influences on mortality after myocardial infarction. *New England Journal of Medicine*, 311, 552–559.

Rudy, E. B. (1980) Patients' and spouses' causal explanations of a myocardial infarction. *Nursing Research*, 29, 352–356.

Rutter, M. (1981) *Maternal Deprivation Reassessed.* Harmondsworth: Penguin.

Rutter, M. and Cox, A. (1985) Other family influences. In: M. Rutter and L. Hersov (eds.), *Child and Adolescent Psychiatry: Modern Approaches.* Oxford: Blackwell.

Sabbeth, B. F. and Leventhal, J. M. (1984) Marital adjustment to chronic childhood illness: a critique of the literature. *Pediatrics*, 73, 762–768.

Spinetta, J. J. (1974) The dying child's awareness of death: a review. *Psychological Bulletin*, 81, 256–260.

Spinetta, J. J. (1980) Disease-related communication: how to tell. In: J. Kellerman (ed.), *Psychological Aspects of Childhood Cancer.* Springfield, IL: Charles C. Thomas.

Spinetta, J. J. (1981) The sibling of the child with cancer. In J. J. Spinetta and P. Deasy-Spinetta (eds.), *Living with Childhood Cancer.* St. Louis, MO: C. V. Mosby.

Stern, M. J. and Pascale, L. (1979) Psychosocial adaptation post-myocardial infarction. *Journal of Psychosomatic Research*, 23, 83–87.

Susman, E., Hersch, S., Nannis, E., Strope, B., Woodruff, P., Pizzo, P. and Levine, A. (1982) Conceptions of cancer: Perspectives of child and adolescent patients and their families. *Journal of Pediatric Psychology*, 7, 253–261.

Taylor, S. E., Wood, J. V. and Lichtman, R. R. (1983) It could be worse: selective evaluation as a response to victimization. *Journal of Social Issues*, 39, 19–40.

Turk, D. C. and Kerns, R. D. (1985) The family in health and illness. In: D. C. Turk and R. D. Kerns (eds.), *Health, Illness and Families: A Life-Span Perspective.* New York: Wiley.

Turk, D. C., Meichenbaum, D. and Genest, M. (1983) *Pain and Behavioural Medicine: A Cognitive-behavioural Perspective.* New York: Guilford Press.

Turnquist, D. C., Harvey, J. H. and Andersen, B. L. (1988) Attributions and adjustment to life-threatening illness. *British Journal of Clinical Psychology*, 27, 55–65.

Van Dongen-Melman, J. E. W. M. and Sanders-Woudstra, J. A. R. (1986) Psychosocial aspects of childhood cancer: A review of the literature. *Journal of Child Psychology and Psychiatry*, 27, 145–180.

Wills, T. A. (1985) Supportive functions of interpersonal relations. In: S. Cohen and L. Syme (eds.), *Social Support and Health*. New York: Academic Press.

Wolchik, S. A., Sandler, I. N. and Braver, S. L. (1987) Social support: its assessment and relation to children's adjustment. In: N. Eisenberg (ed.), *Contemporary Topics in Developmental Psychology*. New York: Wiley.

Wolfer, J. A. and Visintainer, M. A. (1979) Pre-hospital psychological preparation for tonsillectomy patients: effects of children's and parents' adjustment. *Pediatrics*, **64**, 646–655.

Zahn, M. A. (1973) Incapacity, impotence and invisible impairment: their effects upon interpersonal relations. *Journal of Health and Social Behavior*, **14**, 115–123.

4

The Handicapped Child and the Family

INTRODUCTION

In Western industrial societies between 2% and 3% of the population are substantially and permanently handicapped. This figure includes both the physically disabled and the intellectually handicapped, and it means that approximately one in 15 families is directly affected. This chapter considers how the presence of a disabled person affects family well-being and family functioning. It considers the impact of the birth of a handicapped baby, the relationship between the child and the parents, and the special problems which face the handicapped themselves, their parents, and their siblings. It also considers the difficult decision that sometimes has to be made about whether a child should be placed in an institution, and issues affecting the family's quest for the best educational and occupational opportunities for their handicapped member.

Much of the content of the previous chapter, concerning the effects on the family of a child's illness, is also relevant to this chapter. Yet the overlap is only partial. Illnesses may or may not be handicapping, the handicaps may or may not result from an identifiable medical condition. Although membership of one of a number of minority groups within society (being gay, for example, or being black) is sometimes described as a handicap, this chapter will be concerned with physical handicap and mental handicap. 'Mental handicap' refers here to intellectual deficiency rather than to 'mental illness', and whereas some mental handicap results from identifiable abnormalities (such as the chromosomal abnormality present in Down's syndrome), in other cases there is no specific reason for the person's limited intellectual capacity—just as some people are naturally highly intellectually gifted, others are 'naturally' intellectually retarded.

It would clearly be a mistake to generalize too readily about 'the handicapped person' because there are very important differences between various types of handicap and there are different levels of severity. There is, however, some justification for considering these very different conditions together, because all handicapped people are restricted in various ways in what they can achieve. All handicaps confer limitations and increase reliance on other people, at least in the early years. Typically, family members take up the commitment to provide the necessary additional care for the disabled person. In some instances this may amount to just a moderate adaptation of the normal family lifestyle, but in many cases it demands a radical adjustment to normal care patterns and a long-term responsibility which places an onerous burden on parents and, to a lesser extent, on siblings. For the child who is partially deaf the family may need only to make sure that a hearing aid is available from the earliest possible age, and that they take special care when communicating with the child. Profoundly disabled people, however, may need continuous protection, aid, and nursing throughout their lives.

Another characteristic shared by handicapped people is that they are stigmatized. People have somewhat similar attitudes towards, for example, mentally retarded individuals and thalidomide victims. Handicapped people are often viewed by others as 'imperfect', 'damaged' or 'abnormal', and those with a particular disability are often treated as if their handicap were global. Strangers may behave towards those with a speech impairment as if they were also intellectually retarded, and treat those who lack motor coordination as if they were also deaf. When someone is identified and labelled as 'handicapped' other people tend to respond in characteristic ways, treating the individual as 'less of a person'. The terms 'Mongol', 'imbecile' and 'cripple' may be rarely used today to describe the handicapped, but many of the attitudes that coincided with the use of these terms live on. Such prejudices have a restrictive and damaging effect on the handicapped themselves and on their friends and families. It is not surprising that people who suffer from a slight disability will often go to considerable lengths to hide their 'imperfection' and to escape the damaging 'handicapped' label.

Some handicaps have become more readily identified as the medical, educational and psychological sciences have developed. For example, children are now tested regularly for academic achievement so that a mild mental retardation may shown when in a previous age it would have remained undiagnosed. On the one hand, such identification is beneficial because it may identify a need for special educational provision, but it can also have a damaging effect by labelling people who are only marginally handicapped as 'different'. Disabilities have no intrinsic psychological value but are given a meaning within a particular society. The attitudes towards the disabled which feature in that society determine the extent to which the handicapped person suffers a secondary social handicap. Despite considerable changes of attitude over the past decades, disability still has a widespread negative evaluation that often restricts educational, recreational and vocational opportunities. In many cases such constraints do more to inhibit the development and lifestyle of the disabled person than the limits imposed by the handicapping condition itself. In addition, the negative evaluation produces rejection and humiliation that insult and upset disabled people and those who care for them.

THE BIRTH OF A HANDICAPPED CHILD

THE PARENTS' RESPONSE

All expectant parents have at least fleeting anxieties during the period of pregnancy about whether the child will be healthy and free of handicap. In some tragic cases the baby is born dead, and the parents confront the harrowing situation of coping with the loss of an 'unknown' infant (the issue of bereavement in the case of the stillborn baby is discussed in Chapter 10). Usually, however, the newborn baby will be declared fit and sound and the parents can feel reassured, but some babies are very weak or ill at the time of birth and need to be taken to special care units. Although the period of separation from the baby may be disturbing and disheartening for the parents, most will be encouraged by the knowledge that the child will 'pull through' and will have a good chance of living a perfectly normal life. In a small proportion of cases the situation is much less promising, however, for it will be immediately apparent that the child is handicapped, and the information that the newborn child is deformed or disabled will come as a grave shock to the parents.

Parents of handicapped children are frequently critical of how they were told about the child's condition. They complain that they were not given enough information, that they were not told together, or that the news was given to them when many other people were present (Cunningham, 1979). Even before they are told of the handicap, parents are often aware that something is amiss from the responses of midwives and others present at the infant's delivery. Some report that they could tell immediately that there was something seriously wrong with the baby from the hushed silence, from the way that professionals looked at one another, or from clear signs of embarrassment and evasion. The time between their initial suspicion and the confirmation of a serious problem is often remembered by parents as one of unbearable intimidation and alarm.

There is a clear relationship between the way in which parents are informed of the child's handicapping condition and their acceptance of the problem. Those who receive information which is straightforward, detailed and unambiguous have less difficulty in coming to terms with the situation than those for whom the communication is vague, hurried, and brief (Svarstad and Lipton, 1977). Although the initial communication is of great importance this needs to be followed up by many more opportunities for the parents to discuss matters with physicians, nurses, counsellors and social workers. The parents may be so shocked by the news that they fail to take in much of what is being said. Further questions will occur to them as they consider the implications of the diagnosis, and their emotional state may change rapidly. It is therefore very important that nurses and others should be at hand to review information, to give advice, and to help the parents to deal with their anguish and apprehension.

MacKeith (1973) described the feelings experienced by parents when a handicapped child is born. He identified two competing biological responses. On the one hand there is a tendency to pity and protect the helpless child, but on the other hand there is a natural revulsion at the abnormal appearance of the baby. This feeling of revulsion is likely to predominate during the initial stage, and MacKeith suggested that it was this that led handicapped and malformed children in some primitive communities to be removed and either killed or left to die of exposure. Today a malformed baby may be taken away to a special care unit, to protect the mother from her own feelings.

MacKeith also noted that the birth of a handicapped baby is likely to invoke feelings of 'reproductive inadequacy'. Babies are normally shown off with pride, and parents typically seek to identify with the infant, and to 'claim' it, by pointing to particular parental features in the baby's appearance. Parents are congratulated at having produced 'a fine baby', and to have delivered a healthy infant is seen as an achievement. By implication, therefore, to give birth to an abnormal baby is to fail, and many parents faced with such a misfortune do experience a sense of failure or humiliation. They may also suffer an intense feeling of loss. By the time the child is born many mothers have already 'made friends' with the baby as they think it will be. In giving birth to a handicapped child they sometimes feel as though they have lost the child they expected, and their grief for the lost healthy infant may bring about an acute bereavement reaction.

Parents of the newborn handicapped child experience an assortment of emotions including shock, revulsion, embarrassment, guilt and anger. They are likely to feel embarrassed at having to announce to friends and relatives, who will have anticipated a joyful outcome of the pregnancy, that the baby has been born handicapped. Sometimes the couple have to accept congratulations on the birth before they are able to convey the news that all is not well, and people who learn of the baby's condition may find themselves embarrassed and unsure about what they can say or do to ease the parents' pain.

As when they face other types of trauma, people search for possible explanations of what caused the handicap. In their sorrow, despair and anger, the parents of a newborn handicapped child may be unrealistic in their hypotheses about why the child is not normal. The common lack of understanding about the medical nature of handicapping conditions, and the preponderance of myths and old wives' tales concerning congenital handicap, may contribute to fantasies about what led to the abnormality. Mental retardation, especially, is poorly understood and greatly feared, and can attract extravagant 'theories'. The parents of a newborn handicapped infant may attribute blame to themselves, perhaps recalling a past 'sin', or citing some shock experienced during pregnancy. Such parents therefore take upon themselves a specific responsibility for triggering the handicap, while others experience a less tangible guilt by holding themselves responsible for bringing a handicapped child into the world to face, as they see it, a lifetime of adversity, indignity and meagre opportunity.

Anger is another common feature of the initial psychological response. The parents may feel frustrated and violated, and seek a target for their outrage. They are likely to regard the birth of the disabled child as a nightmare which they have done nothing to deserve. Their anger may also involve a feeling that 'a bargain has been broken'. They had bargained to care for and protect a normal child for 16 years or so, but not to spend a lifetime coping with a handicapped child. Their anger may be displaced to a more visible target. It may be turned inward, or directed towards the partner. Sometimes the hostility is expressed towards the child itself, and not infrequently it is directed towards professionals involved in the pregnancy or birth, or to those who offer help following the recognition of the baby's condition.

At this time of crisis the parents are likely to become very sensitive to other people's actions and they may respond intensely and aggressively to those who show little sign of appreciating their torment. The responses of nurses, paediatricians, and other professionals (as well as friends and relatives) are of crucial significance at this time, and a delicate balance has to be struck between joining with the parents in their grief and providing them with hope and encouragement. Some deformities, such as a cleft lip, look particularly serious in the newborn, and honest reassurance may be tactfully provided if the parents appear to over-estimate the severity of the handicapping condition. Hope may also be instilled by commenting in a sensitive way about the achievements of older children with the same condition. On the other hand, professionals need to be wary of presenting too slight a picture of the handicap, or too optimistic a prognosis. Many parents at this stage will reject attempts to reconcile them with the child's condition and they will not take kindly to anybody who fails to acknowledge the extent of their personal tragedy.

Where the handicap is less obvious, but is suspected by medical personnel, it may be some time before the parents are told of the uncertainty about the child's condition. Sometimes the physicians need to await test results before confirming their diagnosis, and they may be wary of alarming parents before they are sure that something is amiss. However, there is good evidence that parents appreciate being kept fully informed of what is going on, and many of those who have faced this situation report considerable resentment over what they remember as the evasive tactics of the health professionals and the 'deliberate' delay before they were told that their baby was handicapped (Gath, 1978).

Couples differ in their ability to stand up to the stress and their capacity to engage in various coping strategies. They differ in how they judge their problem, and in their ability and willingness to think constructively about how they will contend with practical demands. Some concern themselves mainly with immediate matters, whereas others focus on the longer-term future for the child and the family. Some couples persist in denying the extent of the problem they face. They insist, unrealistically, that there has been a mistaken diagnosis or that the child will 'grow out of it' and develop normally. Others take a completely different stance. Not only do they accept the diagnosis, but they seem to adopt the worst possible picture of the likely outcome. They actively resist adjustment to the situation and vigorously maintain their anguish, refusing to acknowledge that life may yet prove bearable. They are reluctant to 'make the best' of the situation and appear to feel that accepting the handicap, and preparing to deal with the difficulties, would be to submit too easily to a monstrous outrage. They are loathe to resign themselves to what they may view as a life sentence of hardship, distress and disappointment.

A number of studies have sought to identify factors that would allow us to predict the degree of stress likely to be experienced by parents who discover that their newborn infant is handicapped. On the whole there has been little consensus between such studies, and the various factors that have been examined appear to contribute rather little to an accurate prediction of the emotional impact on the parents. This disappointing result, following considerable research effort, may stem from the fact that there has been a tendency for researchers to examine demographic variables such as the sex of the child, the number of children in the family, the age of the parents and social class, rather than psychological variables such as the parents' knowledge about handicap, their general attitudes towards handicapped people, their previous level of psychological adjustment, and their overall feelings about children and child-rearing.

The severity of the apparent handicap is certainly associated with the degree of trauma experienced by the parents. Obviously, the birth of a baby with a very minor handicap will, on average, cause less stress to the parents than the birth of a baby with multiple and severe defects. But as well as the severity of the condition, the precise nature of the condition is also important. In particular, it seems that parents respond less traumatically when they learn that their child has a sensory or motor handicap (such as blindness or a limb deformity) than when they are told that the child has a condition that will severely limit intellectual development. Even this generalization, however, is open to qualification. Several researchers have suggested that whereas the announcement of a child's intellectual handicap may be more traumatic for parents who place a high value on academic achievement, disclosure of a serious physical handicap may prove more disturbing for parents who place a high premium on physical fitness or athletic prowess.

Much of the evidence linking demographic variables to the degree of trauma experienced by parents of handicapped babies emanated from a series of studies conducted by Bernard Farber and his associates in the 1950s and 1960s. Although some of these early findings have received support from later research, other studies have failed to confirm some of the relationships originally identified. Thus Farber (1960) reported that the initial level of stress was related to the sex of the baby and that, overall, more disappointment and distress followed the birth of a handicapped boy. Later studies, however, have indicated that this may be true only if the parents have markedly different expectations and ambitions for boys and girls. The Farber team also found that fathers tend to experience a markedly greater impact when the handicapped child is a boy and that mothers may experience more trauma when the child is a girl. This finding has been confirmed by some recent studies (Lamb, 1983). Kramm (1963) also confirmed the fact that the adverse impact is often especially high when the infant is the couple's first child.

Several studies (e.g. Farber, 1960; Giannini and Goodman, 1963) reported that middle-class parents show more distress in response to the birth of a disabled baby than do working-class parents. For middle-class parents a diagnosis of severe mental retardation, in particular, may precipitate an extremely unfavourable reaction, with the situation likely to be viewed as a 'tragic crisis'. One reason advanced for such a social class effect is that middle-class parents tend to anticipate that their offspring will do well academically and eventually take up a professional career. On learning of the child's severe intellectual impairment these expectations are suddenly shattered. By contrast, it is suggested, working-class parents are more concerned with the 'here and now' and with the immediate strain that the child will place on their limited family resources.

Relatively little attention has been paid by researchers to the relevance of the parents' personalities, although Farber (1959) did indicate that the personal adjustment of the parents before the birth of the child was significantly associated with the degree of stress experienced. On the other hand, many studies have examined the nature of mothers' and fathers' reactions and these reveal an association between the type of reaction and the parent's sex. Mothers tend to respond with a more overt expression of their feelings and are likely to be preoccupied with how they will cope in the forthcoming months, whereas fathers tend to focus on longer-term issues, including the financial implications and the likely impact of the handicap on the child's eventual social and occupational status (Lamb, 1983). Fathers often have greater difficulty in adjusting and often conceal their attitudes towards the child (Zelle, 1973).

THE DECISION TO PLACE A CHILD IN AN INSTITUTION

Despite the intense shock of having given birth to a child who is handicapped, outright rejection of the infant is very rare. In some especially severe cases there is no option but for the child to be cared for in an institution. Although the knowledge that this course of action is unavoidable may serve to reduce the immediate stress on the family, it is unlikely to entirely relieve feelings of guilt. Friends and professionals can do much to allay the emotional conflict and suffering by assuring the parents that the baby will receive high-quality nursing care that would be impossible in the home setting. Most parents who are forced by the severity of the handicapping condition to give the child over to a residential home or hospital eventually manage to come to terms with this, and the conviction that they have 'done the right thing' tends to grow over the weeks and months. There are marked differences between families, however, in the degree to which they wish to maintain contact and acknowledge the child as a full, but absent, member of the family. In systems terms, some of these families will experience considerable ambiguity regarding the boundary of the family unit.

For other parents of the severely handicapped, a difficult decision may need to be made about whether or not to 'put the child away'. They are faced with the stressful task of deciding whether they will try to manage a child who will need constant and intensive care, or whether they will surrender the child to full-time professional care. Where the option to keep the child is barely viable the parents know that the choice of rearing the child at home will place a very heavy burden on the family. They are in a much more difficult position than either parents with a profoundly handicapped child who simply would not be able to rear the child at home, or those with a less severely handicapped child, who face a somewhat less daunting burden of caring. Thus parents in the intermediate position suffer particularly high levels of stress when a decision must be made. On the one hand they may realize that the residential care will offer the child immediate medical supervision and special training facilities. But they may also feel that the child will suffer from a lack of family support. If the parents can reassure themselves that the residential home will provide a compassionate and stimulating environment, and that the decision to give the child into care is being made for the sake of the child, rather than in a 'selfish' way, they are likely to elect for the residential option without feeling too much guilt about having 'abandoned' or 'discarded' their offspring.

The decision to place the child in residential care reflects not only the degree and nature of the child's handicap but also certain factors in the family. Few children are 'put away' because of physical handicap; it is usually a severe intellectual disability (often accompanied by multiple physical problems) that leads to this course of action. In a study of family factors relating to the decision to institutionalize, Graliker, Koch, and Henderson (1962) failed to find a relationship with social class, religion, or the age or level of education of the parents. But they did find a tendency for first-born severely handicapped children, rather than later-borns, to be institutionalized.

ADAPTATION

The immediate reaction of the parents to the news of their baby's handicap is typically one of shock and panic. Combined with depression, anger and guilt, this initial period has been labelled the stage of 'disintegration' (Miller, 1968). In the following days and weeks, however, the couple usually struggle to come to terms with the reality of their plight and they enter the 'adjustment' stage. They re-think their plans, begin to accommodate emotionally, and seek any information that is likely to prove useful or reassuring. They may gain further knowledge about the condition from professionals and from books, and they will also begin to learn about available resources and possible intervention procedures. In some cases they will be informed about corrective surgery or medical treatment that will improve the child's condition.

At this time the parents also begin to develop a close attachment to the infant. Any physical deformity that caused them acute distress in the first hours and days after the birth will now have less impact. As the revulsion fades the protective urge comes to dominate, and the parents are likely to derive great comfort from seeing the baby behave in ways that other babies behave. The fact that the handicapped infant feeds well, or cries 'normally', or looks untroubled when asleep, will encourage the parents and promote the attitude that their offspring, although different from others, is a delicate human being who needs and deserves their love and care. The time when the handicapped baby first makes eye contact is recalled by many mothers as the point at which they started to make a positive adjustment and to relate to the infant as a developing and engaging individual.

The adjustment process is likely to be slow and painful. Parents have to come to terms with a lifestyle that may be radically different from the one they had envisaged. In addition to the efforts and anxieties involved in normal child-rearing many extra demands are likely to be made on them and they may feel that their efforts will ultimately bring less return in terms of the child's achievements and independence. Olshansky (1966) spoke of adjustment as the process of coming to terms with 'chronic sorrow'—a continual extension of an acute grief reaction. In view of the tragic fact, he maintains, this response is perfectly understandable and justifiable, and professionals should avoid labelling distressed parents as 'neurotic'. They should not attempt to eliminate the sorrow or coerce the parents into accepting the child. Instead, they should help the family to work slowly towards developing their relationship with the infant, and should provide advice and assistance with the practical problems of caregiving.

During this phase the parents will also meet a variety of social reactions to their child's condition. Friends and relatives will typically rally round and promise help and support, although some will find it difficult to hide their confusion and embarrassment. Some strangers will be unable, or unwilling, to conceal their feelings about the child, and the parents may find that some people avoid them, some appear embarrassed, and others treat them in a brash or condescending way. They may soon learn that the fact that a child is handicapped can stigmatize the parents as well as the child. Occasionally people will behave in a boorish way, but stigmatization is more often evident through more subtle behaviours such as excessive and inappropriate courtesy (Goffman, 1963). Parents may also come to resent the way that some professionals treat them as though they themselves were patients, and will react strongly against the kind of stereotyping that identifies them as 'handicapped parents'. In their efforts to resist such identification they may also reject any suggestion that they should make contact with the parents of other handicapped children. In some cases their refusal to accept the status of parents with 'special needs' may lead them to avoid professionals who could offer useful guidance and help, and to forgo contact with groups, societies and centres that might contribute a good deal of practical advice and psychological support.

During the adjustment phase the couple will typically have to survive many difficult incidents. They will have to explain to many people, some of whom will have appalling preconceptions, the nature of the child's condition. They may have to suppress feelings of envy when they see parents with normal babies. And they may still have to resist the temptation to blame someone, or some thing, for their predicament. Usually, however, they do manage to cope successfully with such challenges, and their concerns turn more to the day-to-day problems of caring for a child for whom they are now feeling more and more warmth and commitment (Menolascino and Egger, 1978).

There follows a third stage which can be labelled 'reintegration' (Miller, 1968). During this stage the couple strive to put things into perspective and to integrate the child into the family. They attempt to make the best of the difficult situation and learn to cope with the special problems of childcare. Most parents by this stage have come to accept that their child is different and that they must contend with the burden imposed by the child's special needs. There are, however, a minority of parents who still hold out some hope that the child has been misdiagnosed, and that the judgements made by the paediatricians will turn out to be erroneous. Much has been written about the phenomenon of 'shopping around', of taking the child from one medical specialist to another in the hope that some expert will pronounce the child normal or at least less seriously handicapped than has been claimed. It seems, however, that only a very small proportion of parents engage in such an exercise. Two family therapists (Pollner and McDonald-Wikler, 1985) have described a case in which a whole family judged and treated their retarded child as normal, overlooking all signs of handicap and ignoring reports from doctors and teachers. The family's attribution of competence to the child, and their failure to make due allowances for the handicapping condition, had profound adverse consequences for the child. The authors quote this as an example of how a family can construct its own reality and defend its representation of events against all external influences.

Almost all parents of a young baby find that the tasks of constant caring are demanding, fatiguing and emotionally draining, and some handicapped babies, though not all, make more demands on their parents than non-handicapped infants. For some there will be the special hardship of having to make regular and frequent clinic visits, some will need to cope with particular feeding or sleeping difficulties, and others may have to learn specific nursing routines to help with the baby's medical needs. Even if the infant proves particularly delightful and responsive, however, the parents may be aware that the child will never be able to become fully independent. Even more than other parents, they are likely to see their handling of the child as a duty and a sacrifice. Although some parents develop a particular devotion towards the handicapped child who is highly dependent and vulnerable, others find it difficult to commit themselves wholeheartedly. They may continue to regard the child as damaged or imperfect, and if the infant lacks social responsiveness there is a high risk that the parents will persist in maintaining some degree of emotional detachment.

LATER IDENTIFICATION

In many cases a handicap is not evident immediately at the time of birth, or in the weeks that follow, but becomes apparent as the child fails to thrive or develop in the normal way. Deafness, for example, is not usually diagnosed until the child is several months old, and milder forms of mental handicap may not become evident until considerably later. Of the children who will eventually be diagnosed as mentally handicapped only one-third are diagnosed before the age of 12 months and only two-thirds are diagnosed before they start school.

For a number of reasons the psychological response of the parents of children diagnosed as handicapped at a later stage is quite different from that of parents who learn of the disability immediately after the birth. Generally, the emotional impact on the parents is less severe. One reason for this is that the disability is likely to be less serious. Another important factor is that before the diagnosis is made the parents will probably have developed a strong attachment to the infant. No initial feelings of distress or revulsion will have pre-empted the growth of a close bond between parents and child.

The indication that all is not well may come gradually, and in many cases it will be the parents themselves who first suspect that there is something amiss. At first their fears may remain unspoken, and they may strongly dismiss any suggestions from others that the child has some handicapping condition. Later they may be forced to acknowledge that something could indeed be wrong, although at first their anxieties may be hesitatingly expressed. A series of medical opinions may successively challenge the parents' attempts to maintain that the child is healthy and normal. Their reluctance to accept an unfavourable diagnosis may lead the parents to 'shop around' among medical experts for the most favourable diagnosis, or prognosis, or for a 'cure'. Thus, as with some of those for whom the child's handicapping condition is evident at birth, the parents may adopt the strategy of denial.

Because the process of diagnosis is likely to be progressive, the parents are unlikely to be faced with a sudden shock. Having been alert for some time to the possibility of a handicapping condition they will have had the opportunity to prepare themselves emotionally for a positive diagnosis. Although they are likely to receive the outcome of the analysis of the child's condition with alarm, therefore, they are unlikely to respond with total panic. Similarly, their view of the child will not change radically as a result of the diagnosis, since in the course of anticipating the news they are likely to have adjusted their impressions and expectations of the child.

The gradual process of diagnosis often involves an incidental educational element. As the various alternative assessments of the child's level of functioning become apparent, the parents may become aware of the possibilities for providing help. During their frequent contacts with various professionals they may receive advice about possible schooling arrangements, remedial prospects, and aid available through social service departments. As a result of their information-seeking, conversations with friends and an increased sensitivity to media coverage they may also have become aware of various local facilities available for the handicapped. Those who are relatively late in learning of their child's handicap are also less likely to suffer from the effects of stigmatization. Like the parents themselves, friends, neighbours and relatives will have developed relationships with the child and are likely to treat the child as a normal boy or girl rather than as handicapped.

Thus there are many reasons why a later diagnosis generally involves less distress for the parents, but the gravity of the disappointment and anxiety provoked by such a diagnosis at any stage should not be underestimated. Confirmation that their child is suffering from a lifetime disabling condition is always profoundly disheartening for parents. They need to adjust their view of the child's future and their own. Critical to the impact made by such a diagnosis is the way in which the process of informing the parents is handled.

This is a task calling for the utmost sensitivity, and many parents are able to recall, long afterwards, precise details of how the news was communicated to them. While many report that the professional's attitude was compassionate and responsive, some recall that they were treated in a callous and uncaring way. It is clear that, following disclosure of a child's disability, all parents should be offered advice and counselling, but unfortunately such resources are not always made available.

THE PSYCHOLOGICAL DEVELOPMENT OF THE HANDICAPPED CHILD

THE NEEDS OF HANDICAPPED CHILDREN

In her book *The Needs of Children*, Mia Kellmer Pringle (1975) stresses that handicapped children have the same basic needs as other children. All children need love and security; they need new experiences; they need their achievements to be recognized; and they need to be given responsibility. Providing for these needs in the case of handicapped children often makes special demands on those who care for them. If the parents feel vulnerable and insecure, this will tend to undermine the child's confidence and morale. Parents may have to work harder to convey their love and appreciation to the child. Intellectual, sensory and motor handicaps all, in their various ways, reduce the child's ability to gain new experiences, so that family members and teachers need to be particularly active and ingenious in order to provide a wide range of stimulation. Parents may also have to overcome practical difficulties, for example in transportation, and to cope with people's reactions to the child's odd appearance or embarrassing behaviour, if they are to enrich the child's knowledge of the world by organizing regular visits to the park, the swimming pool and the shops.

Difficulties will also be encountered in meeting the handicapped child's need to accomplish tasks which merit praise. Such children will often achieve less than other children, and Pringle emphasizes that parents and teachers should make due allowance for the child's condition. The criteria used to judge the accomplishments of the disabled child should be adapted to reflect their capabilities, and praise should reflect effort rather than results. Finally, in order to foster self-respect and self-acceptance, the child should be encouraged to shoulder responsibilities. The development of self-care skills, such as those involved in feeding, cleaning and toileting, reduces the burden on parents while enhancing the child's independence and self-esteem. Parents need to judge when the child is realistically capable of taking on particular duties, and they may have some difficulty in steering a course between extending too much protection or too little.

DIFFERENCES BETWEEN TYPES OF HANDICAP

Clearly, the psychological development of a handicapped child will depend to some degree on the nature and degree of the handicap. It will also partly depend on the individual's personality, but to a large extent it will reflect how the child is treated by other people, and especially by family members. Children who are totally blind, but have no other disabilities, are generally able to achieve the same levels of intellectual and emotional development as non-handicapped children. Because it limits communication, however, profound deafness often restricts intellectual development and frequently results in poor educational progress. The situation is vastly improved if help with communication is given at the earliest possible age, and developmental delays in cognitive functioning are significantly reduced if the deaf child receives early training in both sign language and lip reading. It is interesting to note that the deaf children of deaf parents receive manual language training at an earlier age and perform better on language tasks than those with hearing parents (Brill, 1969). Most studies of the development of thalidomide victims found that they made excellent progress both intellectually and emotionally, although the victims who also had a hearing loss were adversely affected in terms of their language and emotional adjustment (Pringle, 1975).

Children with cerebral palsy are often retarded intellectually and educationally, although it is difficult to determine the extent to which this is due to the biological effects of the condition itself and the extent to which it reflects psychosocial consequences. Children with spina bifida also range very widely in terms of their cognitive development. In the case of mental handicap, developmental delays and relatively poor levels of attainment are found across a wide range of psychological functions. The degree of impairment in particular areas of performance will tend to reflect the general level of intellectual functioning, but there are likely to be areas in which a particular mentally handicapped child will under- or over-achieve compared to others of the same overall level of intelligence. Although they may not reach a high degree of emotional and social maturity, many mentally handicapped children are perfectly well adjusted and become socially accomplished. As in the case of other handicapped children, their progress depends largely on how well they are able to communicate. A significant delay in language acquisition often constrains other important areas of psychological growth, and early training in communication skills often brings widespread benefits (Cheseldine and McConkey, 1979).

MULTIPLE HANDICAPS

In a high proportion of cases, handicapped children are multiply handicapped, or have additional medical conditions that adversely affect their development.

About a third of Down's syndrome children have a convergent squint, for example, and a third have a congenital heart defect. A relatively high proportion of other mentally retarded children have a hearing loss or visual disturbance. Between a third and a half of children with cerebral palsy are also mentally handicapped, and this group also shows a relatively high frequency of epilepsy and hearing impairments, as well as visual problems and difficulties with speech (Dinnage, 1970). Thus many families with a handicapped child will simultaneously face a number of problems that combine to make the tasks of caring for and educating the child especially difficult.

SECONDARY HANDICAPS

For many disabled children the 'primary handicap' creates further difficulties that can be recognized as 'secondary handicaps'. Thus disabled children often have limited opportunities to explore the world, and restriction in their play can adversely affect their cognitive development. Cashdan (1968) showed that both mentally and physically handicapped children with a mental age of four years have less familiarity with objects and everyday situations than normal four-year-olds. The child's handicap sometimes makes it difficult for parents to arrange for the child to play with other children, and the resulting lack of exposure to peers may seriously hinder the development of social motivation and social skills. If, as a consequence, the child fails to develop a natural responsiveness and empathy, he or she may not be found attractive by other children. Thus a mutual antipathy may develop between the handicapped child and other children, and this may lead the child to remain in a rather withdrawn state even when there are opportunities to interact with others. Such an impairment of social drive can clearly be regarded as a form of secondary handicap.

The limited communication skills of deaf children may place heavy restrictions on what they are able to learn. Providing instructions to these children is more difficult, and there are limits to how far the child is able to benefit in the normal way from story-telling, listening to broadcasts, and joining in the games and fantasies of hearing children. Lacking stimulation, they are unlikely to fully develop their intellectual potential. Their inability to communicate easily with other children, and with adults, may curtail the extent to which they are able to form social relationships, and this in turn may adversely affect their emotional adjustment. Such a gloomy sequence of inferences could easily be provided to demonstrate the potential secondary handicapping effects of many different forms of disability. It is important to realize, however, that there are many effective ways of intervening to prevent such complications arising from the initial handicapping condition. If deaf children are speedily introduced to communicating with signs, for example, this will prevent many of the problems that would have resulted if they had remained silent and relatively isolated from others.

In many cases the early years provide a special 'window of opportunity' for intervention. Children who suffer from a sensory, motor or intellectual disability may realize their full potential if effective interventions and training systems are used to promote cognitive, social and emotional development. Following the growing recognition of the importance of early intervention, various programmes have recently been designed to help parents to teach and stimulate the child. Methodical use of these programmes is often effective in fostering optimal growth, for example, in cognitive and language skills. Special toy libraries and playgroups have also been established so that handicapped children, including those from poor homes, may have an opportunity to explore an extensive range of games and playthings and to interact with children of a similar age. Older handicapped children, and handicapped adults, often make strenuous efforts themselves to overcome restrictions that their disability threatens to place on their lives. The philosophy of 'normalization' that has gained increasing influence in recent decades has encouraged many people to assist the handicapped in making full use of their capacities.

IDENTITY: SOCIAL AND EMOTIONAL DEVELOPMENT

The social and emotional development of handicapped children may be deficient for a number of reasons. For some, including those with a severe mental handicap, limitations will arise directly from the primary handicap. The child's low intellectual capacity will impede the development of social skills and emotional maturity. Other handicapped children will have been prevented from developing a sophisticated social awareness by having had very limited exposure to social situations. There are a number of reasons why such exposure may have been restricted. Some parents have very few social contacts themselves, and having a disabled child tends to reduce the frequency of visits to friends, neighbours and relatives. Other parents may keep their child away from social gatherings because they are embarrassed, or because they feel that other people will be made uncomfortable by the child's presence, or because they fear that the child will become anxious. There is a particular difficulty if the child has a serious disfigurement. Physical appearance is crucially important in determining how strangers (adults and other children) respond, and the child who has an odd facial cast or is misshapen may encounter such cruel responses from people outside the family that the parents decide they can best protect the child from embarrassment and misery by keeping them away from the public gaze. Determined attempts to protect children from emotional upset by limiting their interactions, however, may seriously inhibit their emotional development. Children who learn that other people are to be avoided are likely to develop a severe social anxiety. And children who become highly self-conscious about their handicap are likely to lack self-confidence and to develop emotional problems as a result of feeling different and 'inferior'.

Handicapped children do tend to be restricted in their peer relationships. In a study comparing handicapped children with non-handicapped controls, Clarke, Riach and Cheyne (1977) found that disabled children were more likely to be isolated, to play alone, and to act as passive observers of other people's activities. They also communicate less with other children and are less likely to engage in imaginative play. In a study of Down's syndrome children, Byrne, Cunningham and Sloper (1988) found that those who were least restricted in their friends and play activities tended to be more socially mature and generally had few behaviour problems.

At some stage the child will come to realize that he or she is handicapped and therefore different from most other children. The disability may feature as highly salient, or of little importance, in the child's overall concept of self. Those with an intellectual handicap may have a special difficulty, even when they are adolescents and adults, in realizing how they are different from others. The importance given to the disability feature, how it is understood, and the emotional response to it, reflect above all the significance attributed to the condition by the parents. Children's understanding of their disability derives mostly from how the parents act, and what they say or imply. In a frequently quoted statement, two early researchers highlighted the importance of parental attitudes: 'The child seems to adopt the same attitude to the disability that his parents do. If they worry about it, so does he. If they are ashamed of it, he will be sensitive too. If they regard it in an objective manner, he will accept it as a fact and not allow it to interfere with his adjustment' (Allen and Pearson, 1928). Many later studies provide clear support for the view that the psychological adjustment of the young handicapped child depends principally on the attitudes of the parents, and a study by Pless and Pinkerton (1975) suggested that the attitude of the mother was especially important in determining how the child adjusts. For the older disabled person the attitudes of teachers, peers and strangers may also become very important, but those who have had the benefit of a highly positive parental influence will by this time have gained a strong sense of their own identity and will be relatively immune to any outside challenge to their self-confidence.

Children who regard the handicap as a dominant feature of their identity may have very few opportunities for identification with other people or with fictional characters. Heroes in stories and television programmes are rarely depicted as disabled. The child may even face difficulties in identifying with the non-handicapped parents, and many developmental theories claim that such identification is essential for the growth of a well-adjusted personality. Children who have a handicapped parent are clearly liable to have less difficulty in this respect. In one important study (Brill, 1969) it was found that deaf children whose parents were also deaf had a better psychological adjustment than deaf children who had hearing parents. There are a number of plausible explanations for this finding, but it is probable that the child's closer identification with the disabled parents is partly responsible for their relative advantage.

The person who has a profound or 'obvious' handicap has no option but to concede that they are disabled and to acknowledge that other people will identify them as such. Many are able to accept their circumstances, and maintain a good psychological adjustment. If they are able to present themselves as 'handicapped but normal' then other people are likely to treat them accordingly. Overall, most handicapped people are fairly well adjusted although a minority never manage to come to terms with their predicament and retain a high level of anxiety and self-consciousness about their condition. There are, however, many people who are less profoundly, or conspicuously, handicapped and several studies have indicated that such 'marginally handicapped' people tend to have more serious adjustment problems than those who are severely disabled.

Thus whereas blind children (without other handicaps) are generally as emotionally stable as non-handicapped children, partially sighted children are, on the whole, less well adjusted (Pringle, 1967). A study of Cowen and Bobgrove (1966) showed that, both for blindness and deafness, a moderate sensory impairment is more often associated with adjustment problems than is a profound impairment. The most likely explanation would seem to be that the moderately handicapped person is faced with an identity problem, able to claim partial membership in two worlds but not completely acceptable in either. Such people face a difficult dilemma. They may be constantly unsure about whether they will be treated as handicapped or as normal. In this precarious position, feelings of tension will swiftly alternate with feelings of relief. When such individuals attempt to hide their disability, and to pass as 'normal', they will be judged by normal criteria and no allowances will be made for their special difficulties. But when they reveal their handicap they are likely to expose themselves to prejudice and stigmatization. Because stereotyping tends to blunt differences of degree, they may suffer by being identified with those who are much more disabled and much more limited in their capabilities.

There is a danger that a handicapped child may become so preoccupied with the disability that this will produce a chronic lack of motivation and distort the whole personality. On the other hand, some disabled children develop an over-optimistic view of their capabilities and may face bitter disappointment at a later stage. Thus some mentally handicapped children maintain expectations about their future life and their likely attainments that are totally unrealistic. While they remain within a sheltered setting they are somewhat protected from 'harsh realities', but when they are later forced to accept their limitations they may experience considerable frustration and disillusionment. One potential benefit claimed for the integration of the handicapped into normal schools and normal social environments is that this encourages a realistic self-evaluation, and allows disabled children to arrive at a more valid appraisal of how their own skills, attitudes and interests compare with those of their non-handicapped peers. As we shall see, however, the assumed benefits of normalization have been widely questioned.

EMOTIONAL AND BEHAVIOURAL ADJUSTMENT

Although many handicapped people cope well psychologically with their disability, others are never able to come to terms with it. Some remain in a chronic state of frustration and anger, while others feel anxious or even guilty about their condition. Some of those who are frequently dejected seem continually envious of those who are not handicapped. Studies of children with a variety of handicapping conditions have shown a relatively high frequency of behaviour problems and poor emotional adjustment. Thus Breslau (1983) found that children with cerebral palsy were more likely to be anxious and aggressive than controls, and Gath and Gumley (1987) reported a high rate of behaviour problems among retarded children, including those with Down's syndrome. This study compared Down's syndrome children with other retarded children, and with the siblings of both groups. Parents reported more problem behaviours, especially 'hyperactivity', for both of the handicapped groups than for the siblings. In another study of Down's children, Byrne, Cunningham and Sloper (1988) found that, compared to non-handicapped children, a significantly higher number of the disabled children had sleeping problems and problems of incontinence. In addition, more of the handicapped children had fears and more were described as 'attention-seeking'. Factors predictive of behaviour problems included the child's developmental status (more advanced children were less likely to exhibit problem behaviours), and the father's employment status (if the father was unemployed the child tended to have more behaviour problems). Problems were also more common where the mother had a poor emotional adjustment and a poor relationship with the child. Clearly there is a problem of interpretation here, for it is likely that those children who had special difficulties thereby contributed to the mother's distress.

Findings suggesting a relatively high rate of behaviour problems among handicapped children must be placed in proper perspective. It is certainly not the case that all handicapped children, or all children with a particular type of disability, have behavioural or emotional problems, and some psychological difficulties arise directly from the biological nature of the handicap. In some cases problems stem from the child's individual response to the disability, whereas in other cases they arise from the parents' handling of the child. Faced with challenging, highly demanding, or disagreeable behaviour by the child, parents may respond in such a way that the behaviour is exacerbated rather than controlled. Reports of the incidence of problems also tend to be one-sided and fail to capture positive aspects of the situation. The parents of many handicapped children report several aspects of the 'special' child's behaviour that give them particular pleasure. Several mothers in the Byrne, Cunningham and Sloper (1988) study, for example, reported that their Down's syndrome children had an especially happy and loving nature, while others expressed considerable enjoyment of the child's very distinctive sense of humour.

THE HANDICAPPED CHILD AT SCHOOL

Although many handicapped children attend special schools, there has been increasing pressure in recent years (by parents and some educationalists) to incorporate children with a variety of handicaps into normal schools. This strategy of integrated education is intended to bring about 'normalization' and is generally referred to as 'mainstreaming'. Various 'half-way' schemes have also been devised. Some children, for example, spend only part of the school week in the normal class and receive supplementary training from a special education teacher. A number of assumptions lie behind the thinking that mainstreaming will be beneficial to handicapped children. It is assumed that integration will serve to reduce the isolation of the handicapped child and will provide greater experience in social interaction with non-handicapped peers. Another assumption is that attendance at a normal school will result in less stigmatization than attendance at a special school. It is claimed that the handicapped will benefit from being exposed at a relatively early age to those who are more proficient than they are, and that this will enable them to make realistic assessments of their own talents and limitations. A further argument is that in many ways the normal classroom bears more resemblance to the real world than does the special classroom, and a final point made by those who advocate mainstreaming is that integrating the disabled will serve to reduce the prejudices of non-handicapped children and make them more accepting of people with limited intellectual ability or physical competence.

These seem very reasonable hypotheses, but many people have voiced their disquiet with the mainstreaming strategy. They argue that the disabled are less protected in the integrated school, that their self-confidence is likely to be damaged as their limited performance becomes apparent, and that they will fail to develop skills fully because the education they receive will not be tailored to their special needs and abilities. It is also argued that normal schools do not have the favourable staff:pupil ratio of special schools, that the teachers have often not been trained to deal with the handicapped, and that they do not have enough time to devote to children who seriously lag behind the majority of the class. The arguments for both sides are often expressed with some force, and the issue of mainstreaming remains highly controversial. Ideally, the validity of various beliefs about mainstreaming would be tested by means of studies comparing handicapped children who have been exposed to integrated and segregated education. If the children were comparable in other ways, then assessments of their achievements, self-confidence, aspirations and peer relationships should allow us to appraise any real advantages of one arrangement over the other.

Unfortunately, despite several studies conducted to establish the effects of integration, the results have been mixed, and no clear picture has yet emerged. While a number of studies do show some advantage for integrated education, other studies point to certain disadvantages. Harvey and Greenway (1984) examined the self-concepts of physically handicapped children who attended integrated or special schools and found that those who attended normal schools had lower self-esteem. These authors suggested that continuous comparison with normal peers leads handicapped children to evaluate themselves negatively. In a similar vein, Cope and Anderson (1977) found that physically disabled children who attended special schools had lower anxiety than those who attended special units attached to normal schools.

The claim that the integration of the handicapped into normal schools will have the effect of reducing other children's prejudices against the disabled has also been challenged. Several studies indicate that children's attitudes to the handicapped can be positively influenced as a result of their meeting disabled children (for example, Newberry and Parish, 1987) but although there may be a sharp gain in positive evaluation after a limited number of meetings some residual antipathy often remains and the initial gain may not be maintained if the children continue to interact over a longer timespan. In a study of the social adaptation of mainstreamed retarded children, Taylor, Asher and Williams (1987) found that such children were often rejected by their non-handicapped classmates and that they were often highly anxious about their classroom interactions. Teachers judged their handicapped pupils as more socially anxious and less cooperative than most other children. Although this study did not compare mainstreamed retarded children with those who attended special schools, the results clearly indicate that the integrated classroom does not necessarily embody the spirit of high tolerance, cordiality and cooperation between handicapped and non-handicapped children that was hoped for and expected by those who first advocated the mainstreaming approach.

It may still be too early to draw any firm conclusion about the relative effects of the two educational strategies, and it is likely that the variations between different schools in terms of atmosphere, special provisions for the handicapped, and levels of teachers' special training, are so pronounced that any clear advantage for either segregated or integrated education cannot yet be identified. It has been claimed that although mainstreaming is beneficial 'in principle', the attitudes and practices of particular teachers do not always reflect the spirit of the approach, and that this may be why integration programmes often fail to achieve the aims inherent in the mainstreaming philosophy (Macmillan, Jones, and Meyers, 1976).

THE EFFECTS OF A HANDICAPPED CHILD ON THE PARENTS

THE PARENTS' EXPERIENCE OF THE CHILD

Those with handicapped children are likely to have a number of special parenting problems. Parents may find it difficult to understand or interact with a child who has limited communication skills or behaves in unpredictable ways. If the child appears to show little social responsivity there is a danger that the parents will 'reciprocate' and show few positive emotional responses. Cashdan (1968) found that, on average, both mentally and physically handicapped children were shown less affection by their mothers than were normal children. Although some mothers of the handicapped lavished much affection on their handicapped child, others gave very little affection (and this was particularly the case where the child was physically handicapped). Blind children cannot provide reinforcement for their parents by making eye contact, and deaf children do not make the same engaging vocalizations as other children. Such deficits may have serious adverse effects on the formation and maintenance of a good parent–child relationship. Parents may fail to appreciate the significance of many of the child's actions and disregard cues that should convey the child's affection and appreciation. The few parents who share a disability with the child are in a much better position to understand and communicate with their offspring, and it is easy to see why deaf parents report greater ease in rearing their deaf children than do hearing parents (Schlesinger and Meadow, 1972).

Jones (1979) compared mother–child interaction patterns in families of non-handicapped children and Down's syndrome children, and showed that Down's children were less likely to take the initiative. Consequently their mothers tended to be more directive, and this then further reduced the extent to which the handicapped child took an active part in maintaining the interaction. The recommendation from this study was that mothers of such children should reduce their own activity level in order to provoke the child into instigating social exchanges. Special features of the interaction between cerebral palsied children and their parents have also been reported. One study (Kogan, Tyler, and Turner, 1974) found a progressive reduction of warm positive interactions between mothers and children during play sessions. Kogan (1980) explained this by suggesting that the mothers derived relatively little reward from the child's behaviour, and he recommended ways of preventing the decline in congenial interaction. The intervention methods he advised were aimed at modifying the parents' attitudes and expectations, and teaching them to behave in ways that would stimulate the child to provide more positive feedback.

The quality of the relationship between parent and child may be considerably improved if the parents are helped to 'read' the meaning of the child's actions. A notable example of such intervention is to be found in Fraiberg's work with the mothers of blind children (Fraiberg, 1977). Blind children begin to smile at the same time as sighted babies, but they smile less often. The fact that they are unable to make eye contact can detract markedly from the parents' feelings of intimacy with the child, and the apparent avoidance of mutual gaze means that parents sometimes feel 'rejected'. Fraiberg found that as a result of such feelings many of the mothers gradually withdrew their emotional investment in their blind child. They tended to play with the child relatively infrequently, and many claimed that they felt little love towards their blind son or daughter. In a bid to remedy this unfortunate state of affairs, Fraiberg engaged mothers in a programme in which they were trained to accurately interpret the child's various cues and signals. She found that such training increased the mothers' attachment to their child and also changed the children's behaviour. Mothers spent more time playing with the child, and children reduced the extent to which they engaged in various stereotyped behaviours (such as rocking, head-banging, and continual sucking) that are often exhibited by handicapped children.

Mentally retarded children soon begin to fall behind other children in their achievements so that, for example, at a time when most parents are celebrating the fact that their child is successfully toilet-trained, parents of the handicapped may have to contemplate many more years of dealing with incontinence. Retarded children may also be 'clinging'. Hewett (1970) found that approximately a third of the cerebral palsied children in her research sample were described by their mothers as 'demanding', and that many wished to be with the mother all of the time. But parents generally learn to cope with such difficulties, and many emphasize that life with the child actually presents relatively few problems of control. Thus most of the mothers in Hewett's study described their handicapped child as easy to manage, and Gath (1978) found that most parents of Down's children reported that they were not particularly difficult to care for. Indeed many of Gath's parents claimed that the child was relatively undemanding and caused less night-time disruption than non-handicapped siblings.

Apart from the problems parents may face in dealing with the child at home, two other issues often give rise to concern. Even when the child is still young, the parents may experience frequent despair about the adversity that the child is likely to meet in the longer term. They may be haunted by the spectre of the child as a vulnerable adult faced with hardship, injustice and social isolation. More immediately, they may be embarrassed and humiliated by the child's responses in social situations, and by other people's reactions to such behaviour. The child's ungainly movements or unintelligible speech may attract stares and puzzled or pitying looks. Temper tantrums may be frenzied and frequent, and deficiencies in social awareness and an ignorance about social norms may lead the child to make indelicate statements in public, or to engage in activities that other people find embarrassing or offensive.

Many parents of the handicapped seem to adapt naturally to their child's limitations and behavioural style. They become adept at understanding poorly expressed needs, they learn to take pride in accomplishments that would be of hardly any significance in the case of other children, and they develop a 'thick skin' in social situations. Parents scale down their expectations of the child, and this realism prevents life from becoming one long series of disappointments. Whereas parents of non-handicapped children are often pleased when their child's development appears to be 'advanced', the parents of handicapped children need to be satisfied with slower progress. Later, they often derive great pleasure from the fact that their initial expectations were placed at too low a level and that the child is now seen to be achieving much more than they had anticipated.

OVER-PROTECTION AND DISCIPLINE

One way in which some parents fail to bring out the best in their handicapped offspring is by over-protecting them. Certain parental actions may bring about the 'secondary handicap' of over-dependency. Because the child lacks certain independent skills the parents may engage in 'helpful' behaviours that actually prevent the child from developing worthwhile skills. Thus the parent may continue to assist in dressing or toileting tasks rather than allowing the child to persist alone until, after many failures, the skill is acquired and the activity is added to the child's repertoire. Another form of over-protection occurs when the child is kept away from potentially embarrassing or difficult social situations outside the home. This may have the effect of inhibiting the development of social awareness and social skills. Parents should be helped to realize that for all children, including the handicapped, attempting actions beyond their capacity and meeting new and difficult situations are essential predeterminants of successful learning. Children benefit from making errors and from being exposed to a certain degree of risk. Thus the parents' struggles to protect the handicapped child from all hazards, all setbacks and all rebuffs are likely to reduce the opportunities for learning and for the enrichment of experience.

Over-protection may reflect the parents' anxieties, and their desire to make life as easy as possibly for the handicapped child, but in some cases what appears to be over-protection can be seen as parental accommodation to the extreme over-dependency of the child. It is often difficult to determine how far the child's over-dependency stems from the parents' over-protection and how far the reverse is the case. Children certainly differ widely in their timidity and in their eagerness to explore the environment, and it would be a mistake to ascribe all of the variation in children's dependency to differences in parental style. By nature, some children seem to be extremely adventurous and fearless, and they may be said to be 'over-independent'. Such children often fail to appreciate physical dangers and may engage in extremely hazardous exploits,

so that their parents have to struggle continually to protect them by cur-
tailing their exploratory behaviour.

Another form of over-protection involves a failure to demand reasonably
high standards of behaviour from the child. Some parents find it impossible to
apply any form of discipline to their handicapped offspring, and this can lead to
the child becoming 'wild'. By allowing the child to behave selfishly and
defiantly, however, the parents neglect an extremely important aspect of the
child's socialization, and any delinquency that results may make the child's life
very difficult at school and in other social settings. The question of discipline
creates problems for many parents of handicapped children, particularly when
the child is young. Parents often adjust their criteria of acceptable behaviour so
that actions that would be judged as 'naughty' and punished if engaged in by
other children of a similar age are disregarded or dealt with more leniently.
Partly, this reflects the fact that parents of the handicapped make allowances
for the child's lack of understanding or coordination, but it may also reflect a
general reluctance to chastise a child who is seen as psychologically vulnerable.

In one study (Byrne, Cunningham and Sloper, 1988) half of the mothers of
Down's syndrome children reported that they were less strict with the handicapped child than with their other children, whereas only 8% felt that they
were more strict with the handicapped child. But handicapped children are by
no means exempted from all punishment. Many parents report that they try to
treat all of their children in the same way, and the special allowances made for
the handicapped child tend to diminish as the child gets older. Gath and
Gumley (1987) found that parents of adolescents with Down's syndrome
demanded similar standards of politeness and obedience from the handicapped
as they did from non-handicapped siblings. It was found, however, that
parents had higher expectations of the siblings and exerted much more control
over their retarded children. Some of the greatest differences concerned safety
restrictions.

In a few extreme cases parents make no allowances for the handicapped
child and use excessive punishment. The parents' own frustration, and their
resentment of the child, may lead to harshness, rejection and cruelty. There is
evidence that handicapped children are more at risk of being physically abused
than other children, although it must be stressed that only a small minority of
handicapped children suffer physical maltreatment.

THE FATHER'S ROLE

Lamb (1983) provided a review of studies that have specifically examined the
role of fathers in the care of handicapped children. In general it appears that
fathers of the handicapped tend to play a relatively minor role in the child's
upbringing, and there is little evidence to suggest that many of them increase
their participation in household tasks in order to reduce the additional burden

on the mother. Indeed, it seems that there is a tendency for fathers of handicapped children to decrease, rather than increase, their involvement with the family. In systems terms, therefore, fathers in many of these families become disengaged from the rest of the family. There is also evidence that they are more concerned than mothers are about the child's behaviour outside the home. It needs to be said that the rather dismal picture of fathers of the handicapped presented by the results of studies is a modal picture, and that there are many exceptions to the general rule. Thus some fathers do maintain a high profile within the family, relieve their wives of chores, and take a full part in caring for the handicapped child. It is unfortunate that this is an uncustomary development, particularly because lack of commitment by the father has obvious adverse consequences for other members of the family.

THE EMOTIONAL EFFECTS OF CARING

It is commonly acknowledged that the presence of a handicapped child creates stress for the parents by imposing physical strain, financial hardship, and emotional stress, and a number of studies suggest that these difficulties sometimes contribute to a deterioration in the parents' health. Baldwin (1976) found that the large majority of mothers in his study group, and about half of the fathers, reported that either their physical or mental health had been adversely affected by the child, and Quine and Pahl (1985) found that over half of the mothers of mentally handicapped children were depressed. In a review of studies of the parents of physically disabled children, Philp and Duckworth (1982) concluded that 'there is reasonably firm evidence that the parents of children with disablement are more likely than parents of children without disablement to suffer from stress, anxiety and depression'.

Gath (1978) noted that despite the high rate of depression she found in a group of mothers of Down's children, few had consulted a physician or psychiatrist for help. They generally attributed their mental state to the child's condition, but they usually considered their emotional state to be a natural and understandable response to a difficult situation rather than 'an illness'. Despite their problems, most of the mothers in this study said that they derived a great deal of enjoyment from their interaction with their children. Fathers may be less forthcoming about the brighter side of life with a handicapped child, however. Zelle (1973) found that fathers often have more trouble adjusting and often conceal their feelings about the child, and Gath (1978) described many of the fathers she studied as 'tired' and 'irritable'.

Byrne, Cunningham, and Sloper (1988) discovered high levels of maternal stress in families with a Down's syndrome child, but noted that for a number of mothers there were no appreciable signs of tension. Stress problems tended to be more acute in those whose handicapped children were exhibiting behaviour problems and in those whose children were hostile to one another. 'Non-stressed' mothers were more satisfied with their lives. They tended to have time to themselves and had more opportunities for holidays and excursions outside the home. In addition, these women were usually helped with chores and decisions by other members of the family. A similar picture emerged from a study by McKinney and Peterson (1987). They found that both the characteristics of the handicapped child and the amount of support given by the husband were highly predictive of the degree of distress experienced by the mothers of disabled children.

Most of the mothers who participated in the study by Byrne, Cunningham, and Sloper (1988) felt that they had changed considerably following the birth of the child. Many indicated that they were less concerned with trivia and had become less materialistic. They cited many positive changes in their lives and reported fundamental shifts in their values and priorities. Positive findings have also emerged from other research. In her study of mothers of Down's children, Carr (1988) found that although a minority reported that the lifestyle imposed by the presence of the handicapped child often made them feel lonely, many others said that the child provided them with company or reported that they had made many friends through the child. One mother spoke of 'terrific compensations'. So although many studies indicate that emotional well-being is often adversely affected by the child's handicap, long-term detrimental effects are by no means inevitable. Many parents of the handicapped manage to cope well and maintain their emotional strength, and many come to recognize that there are many positive aspects to life with a disabled child.

Most of the studies of parents of the handicapped have dealt with families in which there is a severe disability. The issue of the health of those parents whose children are marginally handicapped has rarely been addressed, and it is possible that where there is uncertainty about whether the child is most appropriately regarded as disabled or not disabled some parents might experience particularly high levels of stress. They might be unsure about whether they should inform friends and relatives of the child's condition and about how hard they should strive to gain access to normal schooling. They may also be unsure about what aspirations they should have for the child's long-term future. Faced with such doubts and uncertainties such parents might well feel insecure, and their internal conflict might well give rise to anxiety.

EFFECTS ON MARITAL ADJUSTMENT

It would seem reasonable to assume that the stresses and hardships placed on families as a result of the birth of a handicapped child will often have adverse consequences for the parents' marriage. Despite numerous studies on this issue, however, no clear consensus of findings has emerged. It appears that some marriages do suffer, but that many do not, and in a number of cases the presence of the disabled child appears to strengthen, rather than weaken, the emotional tie between the parents. Thus the 'reasonable assumption' fails to reflect the wide range of marital effects and, in particular, fails to take account of the fact that in some ways life with the disabled child may increase people's commitment to their family and their marriage.

Early studies of the impact of a handicapped child on the parents' marriage generally failed to find either detrimental or beneficial effects, although one study did indicate that working-class marriages were somewhat threatened by the presence of an older mentally handicapped boy (Farber and Jenné, 1963). Several more recent studies have reported parents' assertions that the handicapped child helped to strengthen the marital relationship. Thus in a study of families with a Down's child, Byrne, Cunningham, and Sloper (1988) found that one-third of the mothers claimed that the child's presence had improved the marriage while only one-sixth reported that it had had an adverse effect. Recent reviews (e.g. Longo and Bond, 1984) conclude that a child's learning difficulties are not associated with an increased rate of divorce.

A somewhat less favourable picture, however, has emerged from other studies. Gath (1978) reported that the marital relationship tended to be less healthy in families of a child with Down's syndrome than in the families of non-handicapped children, and a similar deleterious effect was reported by Pahl and Quine (1984) and Lonsdale (1978). Tew, Payne, and Lawrence (1974) found that while the birth of a child handicapped by spina bifida seemed initially to foster solidarity between the couple, the quality of many of the marriages deteriorated over time. Eventually the divorce rate in their sample was twice the national average.

Unfortunately, it is not possible to instil order into this mixed array of findings by showing reliable evidence that some forms of handicap have more effects on a marriage than others. Gath (1988), for example, found that in families with a Down's child half of the marriages were described as warm and harmonious, whereas in the families of children with other forms of intellectual retardation only a quarter of the marriages were described in this way. On the other hand, Quine and Pahl (1985) failed to find such a difference. In Carr's (1988) study, a quarter of the mothers of Down's children claimed that the birth of the handicapped baby had adversely affected their marriage. Some of these women also claimed that the child's condition had instilled a fear of future pregnancies and that this had caused serious disruption to the sexual relationship.

THE PRACTICAL COSTS TO PARENTS

We have seen that many parents cope well with the undeniable stresses of continually caring for a handicapped child. Although there is a fairly high risk that the mother, in particular, will be depressed, and although the child's presence *may* place some strain on the marriage, relatively few parents or marriages 'fall apart' under the burden of caring. However, this should not be taken as evidence that there is little stress involved in the situation. The parents often face considerable stress, and the fact that so many seem to survive and to remain cheerful and optimistic is testimony to their ability to meet the challenge of bringing up a handicapped child and to cope with all of the practical and emotional problems that this entails.

In many parents' accounts of their difficulties the emphasis is placed on the practical hardships rather than on the emotional burden. Parents highlight particularly the financial difficulties and the physical burden of everyday care. It generally costs much more to keep a handicapped child than a non-handicapped child. Special aids are often needed; the practical difficulties involved in using public transport may mean that taxis often have to be taken; and if the child is incontinent this will bring further expense (as well as substantially increasing the workload). The child's frequent demands for attention and need for constant care may deny the mother the opportunity to take a job outside the home. Carr (1988) found that even when the handicapped person was 21 years old the mother was less likely to be working outside the home. Only one-third of such mothers were working, compared to two-thirds of a matched control group.

One of the major sources of practical difficulty in caring for a physically handicapped child is the child's lack of mobility, both inside and outside the home. Butler, Gill, and Pomeroy (1978) showed that ambulatory problems were responsible for the main housing difficulties of families with such a child. Nearly half of the children in this study were unable to manage the stairs by themselves and had to be carried from floor to floor. It is also often impossible, or extremely difficult, for the parents and child to use public transport, and it may be difficult for them to gain access to public buildings. Although wheelchair access to public amenities has improved considerably in recent years, many still remain inaccessible to the disabled, bringing frustration and disappointment and restricting the handicapped person's opportunities to enjoy and benefit from the full range of normal activities.

THE EFFECTS ON SIBLINGS

ADVERSE EFFECTS

There are number of reasons why we might expect the presence of a handicapped child in the family to have adverse effects on siblings.

It might be expected that with all the extra care needed by the disabled child, non-handicapped siblings will receive less attention, and will therefore feel that they are less important to the parents. Or parents might exert increased pressure on siblings to achieve excellence at school, or on the sports field, in order to somehow 'compensate' for the limitations of the disabled child. From a very early age, children become very concerned about fairness and tend to protest if they see other children being treated more favourably than they are. Siblings of the handicapped may find it difficult to appreciate why certain expectations and demands are applied to them but not to their disabled brother or sister. They may not understand that the parents' apparent inconsistency represents a higher order of justice.

Adverse effects may also stem from a sibling feeling stigmatized because their brother or sister is disabled. Playground gibes may cause them to lose confidence or to respond aggressively. Byrne, Cunningham and Sloper (1988) reported that a quarter of the mothers of Down's children knew that another child in the family had at some stage been teased about the fact that they had a handicapped sibling. Another possible source of difficulty for siblings is the distress of parents. If there are adverse effects on the mother's emotional well-being, for example, or if the burden of caring for the handicapped child produces marital conflict, then the siblings as well as the handicapped child are likely to suffer as a result. Thus if siblings of the handicapped are shown to be at a high risk of experiencing emotional or behavioural problems this might reflect the fact that their parents are disturbed, or treat them unfavourably, rather than being a direct effect of the presence of the handicapped child.

When a child's disability becomes known, at birth or some time later, parents often anticipate difficulties for the siblings and, indeed, they may be reluctant to inform their other children about the infant's condition. Gath (1978) found that, in the case of babies born with Down's syndrome, parents often waited for some time (in some cases several months) before relating the news to the siblings. Although a few children did show distress following the disclosure, most displayed little reaction, and several parents recalled their relief at watching the sibling play with the baby 'just like before'. Some parents feel that they need time to come to terms with the reality of the handicapping condition in order to present a brave front when explaining to the other children that their new brother or sister is 'different'. In such cases a delay may be helpful, for there is evidence that siblings' responses to the handicapped child largely reflect the feelings of the parents. All young children depend on their parents to paint a picture of the world and they usually accept and respond to whatever picture they are given. The parent who presents the newborn handicapped as lovable, pleasing, and welcome can therefore expect that their children will regard the baby in the same way.

Having outlined a number of reasons why we might expect certain adverse effects on siblings, and having discussed the fact that parents often anticipate problems, the key question is whether these children do often have difficulties. A number of studies have indicated that siblings are adversely affected by having a disabled brother or sister. Gath (1974), for example, found a relatively high rate of disturbance at school among the older sisters of the handicapped, and she suggested that this often resulted from a heavy burden of care placed upon them. A further study by Gath and Gumley (1987), however, failed to replicate this finding. Breslau, Weitzman and Messenger (1981) studied the siblings of children with a variety of handicaps and found evidence of greater isolation and delinquency compared to the control group, and Breslau (1983) found that siblings of children with cerebral palsy had relatively high levels of anxiety and aggression.

RISK FACTORS

Other studies have reported few adverse effects, and in general the evidence suggests that siblings are not devastated by the presence of the retarded or physically handicapped child, and that living with a handicapped child does not always have detrimental effects on siblings' behaviour or mental health (Carr, 1985). But some *are* affected, and it would clearly be valuable to identify factors that increase or decrease the risk of a sibling responding adversely. Fortunately, some information on this question is available. For example, studies of the relationship between effects on the siblings and the nature and severity of the handicapping condition suggest, in line with the rather pronounced effects found for those who are 'marginally handicapped', that the siblings of mildly handicapped children may be *more* affected than siblings of the severely handicapped. Thus Grossman (1972) found that the siblings of mentally handicapped children had a better psychological adjustment when that child also had a severe physical disability, and the author suggested that this was because when the child had a visible defect siblings could identify their brother or sister more clearly as 'handicapped'. On the other hand, Grossman suggested, the presence of a child whose handicap was 'hidden' generated more discomfort in the siblings.

Findings from later studies could be construed as further evidence that siblings are more accepting of a handicapped child, and less disturbed, if they are able to regard the child as dramatically different from themselves. In a study of the self-esteem of the siblings of physically handicapped children, Harvey and Greenway (1984) showed that the siblings of those who attended normal schools had lower self-esteem than the siblings of those who attended special schools. Certain mentally retarded children, notably those with Down's syndrome, have a distinctive appearance and are easily recognized as handicapped. Many of those who are retarded for some other reason, however, have a normal appearance. Thus it might be predicted that siblings of Down's children would be less disturbed than siblings of other retarded children, and this was indeed reported by Gath and Gumley (1987). They found that whereas the siblings of Down's children were doing as well as controls at school in terms of behaviour, reading attainment, and general attainment, the siblings of other retarded children tended to have difficulties, especially with reading, and exhibited various behaviour problems. A number of other explanations for this finding could be put forward, however, and not every study has produced results in line with the current hypothesis. A fairly high level of disturbance has been reported among siblings of children with spina bifida (Tew, Payne, and Lawrence, 1974), for example, whereas many of these children are severely physically disabled.

Another important predictor of the degree of disturbance among the siblings of handicapped children appears to be the extent to which the handicapped child is behaviourally disturbed, or 'deviant'. Gath and Gumley (1987) compared parents' reports of the behaviour of retarded children and their nearest age siblings, and found that where the handicapped child had been rated as 'deviant' the siblings were also more likely to be disturbed. The results of this study also suggested that siblings (most commonly sisters) who took a major parenting role and had a heavy load of domestic chores were especially likely to have behavioural problems. In the Gath and Gumley study, in common with most other studies in this area, the sex and age of the sibling did not seem to be of overall significance in determining the risk of disturbance. On the other hand, the relative ages of the handicapped child and the sibling have frequently been cited as relevant. Thus Byrne, Cunningham and Sloper (1988) found that there were fewer problems where the Down's syndrome child was the oldest than when he or she was the youngest or a middle child. Relatively poor relationships between the siblings were also found to be more common when the Down's syndrome child had several behaviour difficulties.

Thus the body of research on sibling effects indicates that some, but by no means all, of the siblings of handicapped children seem to be adversely affected by the presence of the disabled child. Various reasons for such detrimental consequences may be suggested, but so far there has been little examination of the processes that may lead to these effects. We cannot even be sure of the extent to which they are 'direct' effects of the disabled child's presence and how far they may reflect parental distress. Siblings of children who are marginally handicapped, or whose disability is inconspicuous, appear to be at higher risk of disturbance than the siblings of those who are seriously and manifestly disabled. If the handicapped child has a behavioural disorder then the siblings are also likely to be behaviourally disturbed, but siblings who are older than the handicapped child are less likely to show distress or to be disruptive. Another 'protective factor' appears to be a high level of positive family functioning. Gath and Gumley (1987) showed that siblings of mentally retarded children were less likely to be deviant if the family was judged to be cohesive.

SIBLINGS' ACCOUNTS

There is a limit to the understanding that can be achieved by simply measuring the attainment or psychological health of siblings, or by interviewing parents to determine their impressions. Few studies have gathered accounts directly from siblings to ascertain the nature of their feelings and attitudes about life with their disabled brother or sister, but interesting results have been obtained from the one or two that have. Some researchers have interviewed older children, and others have asked adults to recall relevant aspects of their childhood. In an interview study with children, Hart and Waters (1979) found that siblings expressed a need for more information so that they could best help the handicapped child. They wanted to know more about the disability, more about how they should respond to the disabled child, and more about available resources. They also felt that it would be useful to have contact with the siblings of other handicapped children. In addition, many of these older siblings expressed some anxiety about whether they were at increased risk of having a handicapped child of their own, and this makes clear the need for adolescent and adult siblings of the handicapped to have access to a genetic counselling service.

In a survey of adults, Cleveland and Miller (1977) recorded recollections of a childhood spent with a disabled brother or sister. The non-handicapped siblings generally recalled that their relationships with the parents and the handicapped child had been good. It was found, however, that the male respondents in particular were often rather ill-informed about the nature of the disability, and a high proportion of the female respondents recalled that many demands were made upon them by parents struggling to care for the handicapped child. In some cases sisters felt that they had been over-burdened by such chores and responsibilities, but the researchers noted that many more of them than would be expected had gone on to choose a career in one of the caring professions.

EFFECTS ON FAMILY FUNCTIONING

STRESS AND ADAPTATION

So far this chapter has described the effects of the birth of a handicapped child, and has considered studies of how the disabled child, the parents and the siblings are affected by the handicap. We are now in a position to integrate the findings of these studies with further evidence, to present a description of how overall family functioning may be affected by the presence of the handicapped child.

It is clear that the birth of a handicapped child places a considerable stress on the family, and that the system needs to make special adaptations in order to accommodate. Farber (1959) outlined a number of stages in the family's response. He suggested that at first families often attempt to deal with the new situation by maintaining their prevailing structure, functions, and outlook.

They hold on to their existing roles and values, perhaps seeking to deny the reality of the handicap and to maintain a 'fiction of normality'. At a later stage, however, adherence to the old organization and the old routine is found to be impractical and they are forced to acknowledge that the child's condition will have a major impact on the family. Relationships between family members are then revised, and activities beyond the home are likely to become more and more restricted. The siblings take on special responsibilities, and this may involve a rearrangement of age roles and sex roles. Generally, Farber suggested, such adaptation is sufficient to maintain adequate family functioning, but if the care of the child remains too disruptive and too emotionally taxing the family will be forced to reject or 'freeze out' their disabled member. This is a very rare phenomenon, he suggests, because families are extremely adaptable and tolerant.

Farber's account is useful, but it fails to allow for the considerable differences between families. Flexible families, for example, are more likely to be able to change their expectations and to accept the fact of the child's disability, whereas rigid families may hold on for a long time to hopes that the child has been misdiagnosed or that there will be a sudden improvement in the condition. Such families may resist all attempts to help them, because they regard this as accepting a reality that they wish to deny. The presence of a handicapped child places many physical demands on the family, and in the longer term these are likely to lead to structural changes. Research by Dupont (1980), and others, has indicated that in most cases the major part of the extra burden is taken up by the mother. Fathers typically play a relatively minor role in rearing the handicapped child, and only a few become significantly more involved in providing practical support for their wives. Many fathers, indeed, seem to react by detaching themselves emotionally from the child and disengaging from the family.

The precise nature of the father's response, however, may be critical in determining how the rest of the family copes. In one early study (Peck and Stephens, 1960) a high degree of association was found between how the father viewed the handicapped child and the perceptions of other family members. The researchers suggested that the father's reaction might set the general pattern for the family's response to the child. More recent studies indicate that when several members of the family help with practical tasks, and when decision-making is shared, the mother tends to suffer less emotional distress and the children tend to be less disturbed (e.g. Byrne, Cunningham and Sloper, 1988). Thus by his active participation in family affairs the father can play a major part in helping to reduce the distress of other family members and in maintaining good family functioning. The fact that many fathers seem so reluctant to engage in such a role is therefore particularly unfortunate. But it would be inappropriate to ascribe fathers' withdrawal simply to selfishness or apathy. To some degree their retreat probably reflects their emotional difficulty in coming to terms with the child's condition, and their conviction that they would prove inept in dealing with the child's special care demands.

The increased burden of chores often leads to siblings taking on more responsibilities than other children of their age. Older girls, in particular, may become highly involved in caring for the handicapped child. Thus the structure within the sibling sub-system may be profoundly affected, and the boundary between this sub-system and the parental sub-system may be blurred as a result of one or more of the children taking on 'adult' roles and responsibilities. In addition, a child who is severely mentally handicapped may always be treated as 'the youngest' or as 'the baby of the family'.

THE DIRECTION OF EFFECTS

There has been much discussion in this chapter of associations found between the levels of psychological adjustment of different family members. A handicapped child who shows behaviour problems is likely to have a mother who is distressed. A handicapped child who is 'deviant' is likely to have siblings who are described in the same way. How well an individual copes is also related to how well particular relationships within the family are maintained, and to how well the family is faring as a unit. Maternal stress is associated with poor support by the husband. Siblings are less likely to have behaviour problems if the family is cohesive. But although such associations are often taken to imply a particular causal connection, other interpretations are possible.

For example, from the evidence of an association between low support from the husband and a high risk of depression in the mothers of handicapped children it is tempting to conclude that poor spouse support somehow *causes* mothers to be depressed. But several plausible alternative explanations are possible. For example, a wife's depression may lead the husband to withdraw and thus give less support; or, since the measure of support is usually the wife's account, depressed mothers may underestimate the support they receive from their spouse; or low support by the husband may simply be a sign of the fact that he, too, is depressed, so that the association reflects the fact that some *couples*—perhaps those facing serious financial hardship, or those whose handicapped child has acute behaviour problems—are more depressed than others.

Thus although the fundamental question implicit in much of what has been discussed in this chapter is 'How does the presence of a handicapped child affect the family?' the findings of many of the studies quoted permit alternative interpretations. The basic problem is that of attempting to understand 'the direction of effects'. An association between a parent's emotional adjustment and a child's behaviour problems could as easily be explained in one direction (the child causes the parent effects) as in the other (the parent causes the child effects). Such studies therefore often raise a question that is complementary to the one originally posed: 'How far does the family influence the handicapped child?'

A recent study attempted to shed light on the question of the direction of effects (Mink and Nihara, 1987). Evaluations of the psychosocial adjustment and self-esteem of handicapped children were made and these were then correlated with a number of indicators of family functioning (including parental warmth, family conflict and family cohesion). Further complex analyses allowed the researchers to examine the direction of effects. It was found that in harmonious and cohesive families the family tends to influence the child, whereas in other families the child tends to influence the family. This conclusion, although considerably more refined than those from most studies in the field, is probably still far too simplistic. As with almost all family issues, the relationship between the behaviour and experience of the handicapped child and other members of the family is very complex, with many intricacies and many convolutions. Few studies systematically refer to differences between families. While it remains impossible to do justice to this complexity by presenting the results of group studies, however, such research does have the fundamental value of showing us 'what is the case'. It may not be able to tell us why.

FAMILY COMPOSITION

The presence of a handicapped child can critically affect attitudes to family planning and family composition, and thus influence the eventual family structure. In some cases the parents increase their desire to have another child, perhaps hoping that the birth of a normal child will somehow 'dilute' the effects of the disability. Overall, however, it seems that the birth of a handicapped child more often reduces the parents' desire to have more children. Although in some cases this may be because the parents fear that a further child might also be born with a handicap, it is more often because the increased burden of caring for the handicapped child persuades them that they would be unable to cope with further offspring. Clearly, the severity and nature of the handicap are important factors here, and a genetic counsellor might well be able to provide important information about the risk that any further child will be handicapped.

THE RESILIENCE OF FAMILIES

Many critical adjustments are made by family members to meet the needs of the handicapped child while maintaining their own emotional well-being and the integrity and functioning of the family system. It is usually the mother who makes most adjustments and does the most to make sure that the family continues to function well. Largely through her efforts the marital relationship, parent–child relationships, and child–sibling relationships usually remain relatively stable and positive in tone. Although there have been a number of reports of adverse effects of a handicapped child on general family functioning, including increased role tension and increased conflict (Lyon and Preis, 1983), there is considerably more evidence that, despite their hardships, most families cope well.

This conclusion contrasts with the assumption made by many professionals. Blackard and Barsch (1982) surveyed both parents and professionals to compare their judgement of the impact of the severely handicapped child upon the family, and found that, compared to parents' responses, professionals over-estimated the degree of negative impact. These authors also found that the problems reported by the families concerned practical hardships rather than adverse psychological reactions. Similarly, Jacobson and Humphrey (1979) reviewed the literature and concluded that the disruptive effects of a handicapped child have often been overstated while the positive effects have generally been ignored. The buoyancy evident in many of these families should not be misconstrued as an indication that the presence of a handicapped child produces little hardship or stress—there is overwhelming evidence to the contrary—but it provides testimony to the fact that families use a variety of effective strategies in minimizing such stress. They show considerable stamina and resilience in the face of misfortune, and often adapt with vigour and determination. Adaptation is not accomplished in a single phase, but is a continuing process requiring considerable flexibility. The strain may so reduce families' reserves of energy and their capacity to make further adjustments that they are more vulnerable to other normative or non-normative family life events. On the other hand, the experience in dealing with one major setback may provide families with confidence, coping skills, and courage to face other major problems with additional fortitude. Some families manage to cope well for years before the strain of caring for the child eventually takes its toll in terms of extreme family disruption (Farber, 1959), but it is clear that most families manage to persevere successfully with their lifelong task.

HELPING THE FAMILY WITH THE HANDICAPPED CHILD

INFORMATION AND AID

A number of research studies provide guidelines for professionals who are involved in helping families with handicapped children. It is clear that when a handicapped child is born parents need and appreciate information about the child's condition and about the eventual prognosis. They want to be given as much information as early as possible, and to be provided with a realistic, rather than an over-optimistic, view. A sympathetic approach is welcomed, but many parents object strongly to any attempt to reconcile them too easily to the child's condition. Many parents need time to come to terms with their suffering and will respond aggressively to professionals who seem intent on humouring them. At a later stage they will respect those who are able to point to hopeful signs in the child's condition or to offer support by providing access to resources. Help is appreciated more when it is given in a spirit of collaboration, with professionals involving the parents as team members and providing copies of any reports written about the child. Parents welcome information about local community resources and warnings about deficiencies in service provision.

Families with handicapped children benefit from practical help, and may also need emotional support. The need to attend regular clinic appointments can present problems, particularly for those who do not have their own means of transport. The professional may be able to arrange appointment times so that they present less hardship for parents, and may be able to make arrangements for transporting the family to the clinic. The care of older physically handicapped children may be made considerably easier if special aids are provided, and professionals from a number of disciplines may help families to discover what aids are available, how they can be obtained, and how simple versions can be improvised. Parents may need to be shown how best to lift a child, and how best to manage sleeping, feeding, toileting, and bathing.

Professionals may also put parents in touch with local self-help groups, but should be sensitive to the fact that some parents prefer to avoid contact with the families of other handicapped children. Others are pleased to meet regularly with parents facing similar problems, and some become highly involved in the organization of self-help groups. They may also join with other parents in lobbying for improved local resources to meet their children's needs. Professionals can also help by arranging alternative care for the child at times of special difficulty or family emergency. The mothers of handicapped children often say that they 'cannot afford to be ill', and illness often instigates an acute stress in these families. If the mother has to spend some time in hospital, and no substitute care can be arranged with friends or relatives, a social worker may need to make alternative arrangements. The child may be taken into temporary care, or a live-in nurse provided, or extra support may be given to the family so that the remaining members are themselves able to cope with the child.

Because the handicapped child often has special needs, and requires special handling skills, the parents may be highly reticent about asking other people to baby-sit for short periods or to look after the child while they take a holiday. In some cases their reluctance is a realistic reflection of the childcare difficulties, but in other cases it indicates the parents' over-protection of the child. A social worker may be able to arrange suitable 'respite care' and encourage the parents to accept that both they and the child might benefit from a short time apart.

PARENT TRAINING

Professionals may also be able to advise the parents about whether an early intensive training programme would prove beneficial to their child, and how they might go about arranging such a programme. The parents may have seen or heard media coverage of 'wonder methods' for improving the mobility or the intellectual attainments of handicapped children and wish to discuss these with someone whom they know and trust. A number of intervention programmes involve the parents as the child's teachers. Typically, psychologists or specially trained teachers train the parents to teach the child in a structured way. One such method is the Portage Approach, a home-teaching service for mentally handicapped young children originally developed in Portage, Wisconsin (Shearer and Shearer, 1972). Parents are instructed by a visiting teacher to become more effective teachers of their children. The parents learn how to select tasks, how to train the child, and how to monitor achievements in a highly organized way. This system has been shown to be very successful in developing the skills of pre-school mentally handicapped children (Pugh, 1981).

Several other 'enrichment' programmes have been developed. Hanson (1981) described a method for providing Down's children with enhanced stimulation from the age of a few months, and claimed that this helps to overcome the developmental decline usually shown by these children. Controversial programmes initiated by Glenn Doman in the United States, and at the Peto Institute in Hungary, attempt to affect the neurological structures controlling movement and coordination by intense and repeated 'forced' limb exercises. These are directed primarily at brain-damaged children, especially those with cerebral palsy. All of these methods rely heavily, although not exclusively, on the parents and are very demanding of time and effort. They are certainly not suitable for all handicapped children, and some of the claims made for some of the methods are almost certainly excessive. The professional adviser needs to be able to curb unbridled optimism in a sensitive way while fostering parents' enthusiasm to provide intensive stimulation for their child.

As Byrne, Cunningham, and Sloper (1988) point out, there is some risk that intervention methods employing parents as skills-teachers will place strains upon the parent–child relationship and undermine the parents' confidence. These authors express more enthusiasm for interventions aimed at improving the parent–child relationship. A number of such methods have already been described, including Fraiberg's method of training parents to understand the behavioural cues of their blind children. Crawley and Spiker (1983) lay stress on teaching parents to closely observe their children's behavioural cues, and Affleck *et al.* (1982) have developed a wide-ranging method for enhancing relationships between parents and their handicapped children. Their programme includes exercises designed to improve 'turn taking' in parent–child interactions, and methods for developing parents' recognition of the child's preferred level of stimulation.

Professionals may also help the family to make choices about educational placement. They may encourage parents to seek a nursery school placement and later assist in arranging suitable schooling. A teacher with special responsibility for the education of handicapped children, or an educational psychologist, will have a good knowledge of special schools and training facilities in the locality and will be aware of the policy of local normal schools regarding the integration of the handicapped. The parents might need to discuss the potential advantages and disadvantages of mainstreaming.

COUNSELLING

In addition to providing help with practical problems, professionals can provide emotional support. Parents may benefit during the period after the baby's birth by talking with a counsellor about their feelings of anxiety, depression, guilt, and anger. Like other parents, those who have handicapped children may lack confidence in their ability to manage the child. They may need to be reassured that their endeavours are proving effective, and may derive considerable comfort from the fact that someone outside the family acknowledges their efforts and understands their exhaustion. Fears about possible adverse effects on siblings may be relieved as a result of informed discussion, and in some cases the siblings themselves will need psychological intervention to help with problems. If the marriage is in difficulties, marital counselling is likely to be useful. With the counsellor acting as a neutral third party, and current family issues as agenda items, marital therapy may help the husband and wife to understand how their partner feels about the handicapped child.

In some cases the issue of the advisability and desirability of a further pregnancy will have placed a special strain on the couples' sexual relationship. An interview with a genetic counsellor may help to allay unnecessary fears and may help the couple to explore together their hopes and ideals for the future shape of their family. Genetic counselling with the parents may also help to reduce any residual feelings of guilt about being 'responsible' for the handicap. When such counselling is available for older siblings it may reduce their fear that they are at high risk of parenting a disabled child. Sometimes the family issues that need resolution concern the wider family dynamics, and these may be explored and treated by inviting all members of the family, including the handicapped child, to participate in a series of family therapy sessions (Berger and Foster, 1986).

THE HANDICAPPED IN ADOLESCENCE
AND ADULTHOOD

THE HANDICAPPED ADOLESCENT

At different stages in their lives handicapped people face different challenges, meet different obstacles, and encounter different types of prejudice. Going to school, changing schools, and seeking work are examples of transitions which may place a special stress on the handicapped person and the family. Adolescence is often a time of particular tension. At this time disabled people may feel increasingly stigmatized because they attend a special school, and as they see others of their age becoming more independent and developing a social and leisure life of their own, their feelings that they are 'different' and 'inferior' may become more intense. When others begin to seek and form romantic attachments the handicapped may feel considerable apprehension about whether they will be able to attract others or whether they will suffer long-term rejection, loneliness, and sexual tension. This is also the time of transition from school to work, and the handicapped have special reason to fear that they will not be able to obtain satisfactory and rewarding employment.

There may also be fresh anxieties for the parents at this time. They may have fears about the child becoming delinquent, or sexually uncontrolled, and the fact that the child is becoming an adult may focus their attention on the longer-term prospects for work and care. There is likely to be some tension, as there is between most other adolescents and their parents, about what degrees of independence and freedom are appropriate at a particular age, and enmeshed families will experience more difficulty in 'letting go' of the adolescent. A young person who wants to be treated as an adult may cause alarm, especially if the family has been somewhat over-protective. Parents may realize that the child has little awareness of the potential dangers of being exploited socially, financially, and sexually beyond the safe haven of the home. On the other hand, they may wish to encourage independence and exploration, and may be depressed by the fact that their disabled youngster seems unable or unwilling to cope autonomously.

The adolescent may go through a rebellious or aggressive stage that taxes the parents profoundly. Many parents, however, seem to contend well, and by this time have evolved a number of tactics for managing difficult behaviour. Carr (1988) found that older children with Down's syndrome were usually fairly easy to manage and often responded well to encouragement and persuasion. Most parents recognized this and had developed special skills that they found useful for gaining compliance. This study showed that by the age of 21 most people with Down's syndrome were left alone at home for short periods, while some were able to use public transport, to visit friends, and to go shopping alone.

Adolescence is traditionally regarded as a time when many identity issues are resolved and many aspects of the individual's social personality develop. For the handicapped, this may be a period when drastic revisions are made in their attitudes to their disability. Some gain a new determination to achieve the highest possible standard of excellence in a particular field or to take part in the widest possible range of activities. Those who are wheelchair-bound may take part in competitive sports, including specially adapted versions of team games. For handicapped people, as for their peers, adolescence is often a period when independence and self-determination become very highly prized.

Handicapped people may realize at this stage that it is largely up to them how they regard their disability. They may remain highly self-conscious about their handicap or may regard it as of secondary importance. Many come to appreciate that their own lack of self-consciousness about their disability may help others to ignore it. Some welcome open discussion about the handicap and some even develop a repertoire of humorous references to the disability. Others, however, remain embarrassed and prefer to avoid any allusion to the condition. Many discover that confidence breeds confidence, whereas self-consciousness leads to withdrawal and a consequent reduction in morale. Studies comparing well-adjusted and poorly adjusted handicapped people show that the well-adjusted are more confident, less aggressive and less anxious, and have higher self-esteem. Other people are likely to find such personality features highly attractive and will therefore be eager to get to know the handicapped person. Interaction will build further confidence, whereas social anxiety and withdrawal are likely to become self-perpetuating.

The issue of how 'up-front' to be about the handicap poses a special problem for those who are marginally handicapped. As long as their disabling condition remains concealed they will avoid the effects of stigmatization. But the person who attempts to hide a handicapping condition is in a precarious situation because he or she may suffer sudden censure and rejection if the disability becomes apparent. It is particularly unfortunate that situations offering the most gain for hiding the marginal disability, such as meeting potential dating partners or attending job interviews, may also bring the greatest penalties when the handicap is discovered. Thus the person is liable to face a critical choice about how open to be about the disability, and the anxieties this dilemma generates may considerably increase the threat of situations that are already highly stressful.

For the handicapped person, the chance to work offers may benefits. It provides some degree of financial independence; it also establishes a regular pattern to the day and week, thus reducing monotony; and it extends the opportunities for making social contacts. Some handicapped people are able to manage in normal employment, some are assigned to positions reserved for those with particular disabilities ('niche jobs') and some work in sheltered workshops. For those who cannot be employed, even in sheltered workshops, there are special care units where training is given in basic life skills (toileting, cleaning, simple cooking, use of the telephone, road safety, etc.). These also provide an orderly schedule and a regular change of environment for the handicapped person, and they give the family a period of relief from the management of their disabled member.

MOVING AWAY FROM HOME

As handicapped people become more mature they generally become less dependent on their parents and adapt more easily to new situations. Some, of course, have handicaps which place relatively few limitations on the vocational and social aspects of their lives. They may move away from home, attend college, make close friendships, find good jobs, and eventually settle down to a family life of their own. Thus those who are blind and deaf may differ very little in their adolescence and adulthood from those who are not handicapped. The same is true of some people with cerebral palsy, spina bifida, and mild forms of intellectual retardation. But for many others the handicap places severe limitations on their independence, and they face many more barriers. Yet, even for the most restricted, attendance at school, holidays away from the family, and experience in a work situation or special care unit, are likely to have increased their adaptiveness and self-reliance.

For many of these handicapped people and their parents there will come a time when consideration needs to be given to the possibilities for a more independent lifestyle. The parents may have become increasingly aware that their disabled son or daughter will outlive them, and that some form of institutional, sheltered or independent home will eventually become necessary. They are likely to see an advantage in the move being planned, and implemented gradually, rather than being instigated hastily in an emergency. For some parents the handicapped person's move away from the home will come as a relief, and the parents may look forward to enjoying time to relax together without constant restraint and worry. Others, however, regard the departure as a necessary evil and feel that their lives will be empty when their handicapped child leaves. Whatever their feelings, the parents are likely to appreciate that a successful move towards independent living is a major achievement for the disabled person, an affirmation of maturity and a highly positive pointer towards a favourable future.

The provision of various forms of sheltered accommodation has been increased in recent years. The idea is that those with relatively minor handicaps will be able to lead somewhat independent lives if the social and physical environment is adapted to their needs and abilities. An increasing number of mentally handicapped adults live in hostels, and there has also been a major growth in community care. In one version of such care, the 'group home', a small number of handicapped adults live together in a house in the local community, with help and supervision by a team of professional and volunteer caregivers. Each of the residents is encouraged to undertake chores and to develop skills that will aid their independent living. They are also encouraged, as far as possible, to make shopping trips alone and to take part in community activities.

RIGHTS AND 'NORMALIZATION'

One of the great advantages of several handicapped adults living together in this way is that they can form a relatively permanent social group. The development of close relationships between residents is inevitable in such a situation, and is generally encouraged. Different communities, however, have different philosophies when it comes to the issue of sexual liaisons. Typically, sexual attraction and sexual liaisons between adults who are physically disabled present few problems. Relationships may be encouraged and counselling provided to help the couple overcome any physical problems that affect their sexual behaviour. There is often more of a problem in dealing with the sexuality of the mentally handicapped. Such disabilities rarely prevent sexual thoughts, feelings or expression. The mentally handicapped may have to be taught that masturbatory arousal is only to be indulged in privately and, when two mentally handicapped adults are physically attracted to one another, those who help to care for them must make decisions, or follow guidelines, about whether sexual behaviour is to be encouraged, merely 'permitted', or actively discouraged. They may need to make an assessment of whether any exploitation is involved, of whether contraceptive advice and provision are to be offered, and about how the relationship is likely to be regarded by the other residents.

Further problematic issues concern whether the partners should be allowed to share a room, whether their parents should be informed of the liaison, and whether the couple should be encouraged or permitted to place their arrangement on a more permanent and formal footing. Clearly the answers to many of these questions will depend on the severity of the handicap of each partner but, whatever the level of handicap, these issues are likely to prove delicate and difficult. Some people staunchly defend the mentally handicapped person's 'right to sexuality', whereas others feel that the retarded person cannot be made fully aware of all of the relevant concerns and dangers. Different agencies and communities have developed different practices in response to these issues, but the subject is still hotly debated.

The concern over the sexuality of the mentally handicapped is one important aspect of a wider issue. There is some controversy about the degree to which the goal for such people should be that of 'normalization'. On the one hand it is argued that all possible attempts should be made to develop the person's repertoire of skills so that they are able to become involved in normal activities and relationships. This philosophy contends that the mentally handicapped have precisely the same rights as other individuals, and that to treat them as 'impaired' or 'unsound' amounts to denying them their dignity. Professionals who follow this way of thinking are likely to assert that handicapped individuals themselves are the best judges of their own interests, that they should be allowed to make mistakes, and that they should be held responsible for their misdemeanours.

The contrasting point of view states that it is unrealistic to aim towards a normal lifestyle for those who have a serious degree of intellectual impairment, and that to strive too energetically towards such a goal may place too heavy a demand on the handicapped individual. Those who support this view would claim that they recognize the rights of the mentally handicapped but that such people also have additional rights, including the right to be protected and the right to remain partially dependent. They would further argue that the 'normal' culture has evolved standards, rules and roles for the convenience and regulation of mature, knowledgeable and discriminating adults, and that just as we extend certain privileges to young children, and make fewer demands on them, so we should make special allowances for those who have limited intellect. Those who advocate this position would agree that the handicapped should be helped to develop their skills to the greatest possible extent, but would argue that they should not be expected to conform to the routines and expectations of a conventional lifestyle.

CONCLUSION

In this chapter we have examined how the birth of a handicapped baby affects the parents, and how the family adapts to accommodate to the needs of the disabled child while continuing to meet its other commitments. The birth of any baby, and the rearing of any child, generates a good deal of stress within families, but when the child's abilities are more limited than normal, and the level of dependency is consequently greater, the pressures on the family can be intense. We have seen that most families cope remarkably well with the situation. Soon after the initial shock has passed, the parents begin to revise their expectations and begin to adjust to the situation. Despite their initial forebodings many mothers soon become highly emotionally attached to the child, and often recognize special positive aspects of the child's personality. Many fathers, however, seem to find it extremely difficult to play their full part in family affairs, and many of these become disengaged from the family. Older siblings usually relate very well to their handicapped brothers and sisters and are often recruited to help with childcare and other day-to-day chores. Practical hardships and constraints may limit outings and holidays, however, and the parents often face severe financial pressures. Mothers often report sheer physical exhaustion as a result of tending constantly to the child's special needs. Despite all this, most family members, and most family systems, manage to come through the difficulties and to survive the substantial pressures. Adjustments are made in expectations, in personal values, and in roles, but individuals generally get by, and as a result of considerable adaptations the family system usually remains intact.

Some families of the handicapped manage well simply by exercising their own intrinsic resources. It may be a matter of pride to them that they do not need to rely upon outside aid. But most families are happy to accept the help that may be offered by relatives, self-help groups, and professionals. In particular, they are thankful for assistance with practical matters, and for any advice or training that will help their handicapped child to achieve the highest possible level of attainment and to gain maximum independence, happiness, and satisfaction. Parents usually take full responsibility for care and development during the child's early years, but they may continually worry about the long-term future. Later, the family may be satisfied that by virtue of the disabled person's increased maturity and independence, or through accommodation offered by a group home, a sheltered hostel, or an institution, the handicapped person will continue to be protected and valued when the parents are no longer available to give their support.

REFERENCES

Affleck, G., McGrade, B. J., McQueeney, M. and Allen, D. (1982) Relationship-focused early intervention in developmental disabilities. *Exceptional Children*, **49**, 259–261.

Allen, F. H. and Pearson, G. H. J. (1928) The emotional problems of the physically handicapped child. *British Journal of Medical Psychology*, **8**, 212–235.

Baldwin, S. (1976) *Some Practical Consequences of Caring for Handicapped Children at Home*. University of York: Social Policy Unit.

Berger, M. and Foster, M. (1986) Applications of family therapy theory to research and interventions with families with mentally retarded children. In: J. J. Gallagher and P. M. Vietze (eds.), *Families of Handicapped Person: Research, Programs and Policy Issues*. Baltimore, MD: Paul H. Brookes.

Blackard, M. K. and Barsch, E. T. (1982) Parents' and professionals' perceptions of the handicapped child's impact on the family. *Journal of the Association for the Severely Handicapped*, **7**, 62–69.

Breslau, N. (1983) The psychological study of chronically ill and disabled children: Are healthy siblings appropriate controls? *Journal of Abnormal Child Psychology*, **11**, 379–391.

Breslau, N., Weitzman, M. and Messenger, K. (1981) Psychologic functioning of siblings of disabled children. *Pediatrics*, **67**, 344–353.

Brill, R. G. (1969) The superior IQs of deaf children of deaf parents. *The California Palms*, **15**, 1–4.

Butler, N., Gill, R., and Pomeroy, D. (1978) *Handicapped Children—their homes and life styles.* University of Bristol: Department of Child Health.

Byrne, E. A., Cunningham, C. C. and Sloper, P. (1988) *Families and their Children with Down's Syndrome: One Feature in Common.* London: Routledge.

Carr, J. (1985) The effect on the family. In: A. M. Clarke, A. D. B. Clarke, and J. M. Berg (eds.), *Mental Deficiency—The Changing Outlook.* London: Methuen.

Carr, J. (1988) Six weeks to twenty-one years old: a longitudinal study of children with Down's syndrome and their families. *Journal of Child Psychology and Psychiatry*, **29**, 407–431.

Cashdan, A. (1968) Mothers bringing up physically handicapped children. In: J. Loring and A. Mason (eds.), *The Subnormal Child.* London: Spastics Society.

Cheseldine. S. and McConkey, R. (1979) Parental speech to young Down's syndrome children: an intervention study. *American Journal of Mental Deficiency*, 83, 612–620.

Clarke, M. M., Riach, J. and Cheyne, W. M. (1977) Handicapped children and pre-school education. University of Strathyclyde: Report to Warnock Committee on Special Education.

Cleveland, D. W. and Miller, N. (1977) Attitudes and life commitments of older siblings of mentally retarded children. *Mental Retardation*, **15**, 38–41.

Cope, C. and Anderson, E. (1977) *Special Units in Ordinary Schools.* London: University of London, Institute of Education.

Cowen, E. L. and Bobgrove, P. H. (1966) Marginality of disability and adjustment. *Perceptual and Motor Skills*, **23**, 869–870.

Crawley, S. B. and Spiker, D. (1983) Mother–child interactions involving 2 year olds with Down's syndrome: a look at individual differences. *Child Development*, **54**, 1312–1323.

Cunningham, C. (1979) Parent counselling. In: M. Craft (ed.), *Tredgold's Mental Retardation.* London: Baillière-Tindall.

Dinnage, R. (1970) *The Handicapped Child: Research Review*, Vol. 1. London: Longman (in association with the National Bureau for Co-operation in Child Care).

Dupont, A. (1980) A study concerning time-related and other burdens when severely handicapped children are reared at home. *Acta Psychiatrica Scandanavica*, **62** (Suppl. 285), 249–257.

Farber, B. (1959) Effects of a severely mentally retarded child on family integration. *Monographs of the Society for Research in Child Development*, **24**, No. 2.

Farber, B. (1960) Perceptions of crisis and related variables in the impact of a retarded child on the mother. *Journal of Health and Human Behaviour*, **1**, 108–118.

Farber, B. and Jenné, W. C. (1963) Family organization and parent–child communication: Parents and siblings of a retarded child. *Monographs of the Society for Research in Child Development*, **28**, No. 7.

Fraiberg, S. (1977) *Insights from the Blind.* New York: New American Library.

Gath, A. (1973) The school age siblings of mongol children. *British Journal of Psychiatry*, **123**, 161–167.

Gath, A. (1974) Siblings' reactions to mental handicap: a comparison of the brothers and sisters of mongol children. *Journal of Child Psychology and Psychiatry*, **15**, 187–198.

Gath, A. (1978) *Down's Syndrome and the Family: The Early Years.* London: Academic Press.

Gath, A. (1979) Parents as therapists of mentally handicapped children. *Journal of Child Psychology and Psychiatry*, **20**, 161–165.

Gath, A. and Gumley, D. (1986) Behaviour problems in retarded children with special reference to Down's syndrome. *British Journal of Psychiatry*, **149**, 156–161.

Gath, A. and Gumley, D. (1987) Retarded children and their siblings. *Journal of Child Psychology and Psychiatry*, **28**, 715–730.

Giannini, M. J. and Goodman, L. (1963) Counselling families during the crisis reaction to Mongolism. *American Journal of Mental Deficiency*, **67**, 740–747.

Goffman, E. (1963) *Stigma: Notes on the Management of Spoiled Identity*. New York: Jasson Aaranson.

Graliker, B., Koch, K. and Henderson, R. (1962) Teenage reactions to a mentally retarded sibling. *American Journal of Mental Deficiency*, **66**, 838–843.

Grossman, F. K. (1972) *Brothers and Sisters of Retarded Children: An Exploratory Study*. Syracuse, NY: Syracuse University Press.

Hanson, M. J. (1981) Down's syndrome children: characteristics and intervention research. In: M. Lewis and L. A. Rosenblum (eds.), *The Uncommon Child*. New York: Plenum.

Hart, D. and Walters, J. (1979) *Brothers and Sisters of Mentally Handicapped Children: Family Involvement with Services in Haringey*. London: Thomas Coram Research Unit, University of London, Institute of Education.

Harvey, D. H. P. and Greenway, A. P. (1984) The self-concept of physically handicapped children and their non-handicapped siblings: an empirical investigation. *Journal of Child Psychology and Psychiatry*, **25**, 273–284.

Hewett, S. (with Newson, J. and Newson, E.) (1970) *The Family and the Handicapped Child*. London: George Allen and Unwin.

Jacobson, R. B. and Humphrey, R. A. (1979) Families in crisis: research and theory in child mental retardation. *Social Casework: The Journal of Contemporary Social Work*. December, pp. 597–601.

Jones, O. H. M. (1979) A comparative study of mother–child communication with Down's Syndrome and normal infants. In: R. Schaffer and J. Dunn (eds.), *The First Year of Life*. Chichester: Wiley.

Kogan, K. L. (1980) Interaction systems between preschool handicapped or developmentally delayed children and their parents. In: T. M. Field, S. Goldberg and A. M. Sostek (eds.), *High Risk Infants and Children: Adult and Peer Interaction*. New York: Academic Press.

Kogan, K. L., Tyler, H B. and Turner, P. (1974) The process of interpersonal adaptation between mothers and their cerebral palsied children. *Developmental Medicine and Child Neurology*, **16**, 518–527.

Kramm, E. R. (1963) *Families of Mongoloid Children*. Washington, DC: US Government Printing Office.

Lamb, M. E. (1983) Fathers of exceptional children. In: M. Seligman (ed.), *The Family with a Handicapped Child: Understanding and Treatment*. New York: Grune and Stratton.

Longo, D. C. and Bond L. (1984) Families of the handicapped child: research and practice. *Family Relations*, **33**, 57–65.

Lonsdale, G. (1978) Family life with a handicapped child: the parents speak. *Child: Care, Health and Development*, **4**, 99–120.

Lyon, S. and Preis, A. (1983) Families of severely handicapped persons. In: M. Seligman (ed.), *The Family with a Handicapped Child: Understanding and Treatment.* New York: Grune and Stratton.

MacKeith, R. (1973) The feelings and behaviour of parents of handicapped children. In: D. Boswell and J. Wingrove (eds.), *The Handicapped Person in the Community.* London: Tavistock Publications and the Open University.

Macmillan, D., Jones, R. and Meyers, C. (1976) Mainstreaming the mentally retarded: some questions, cautions and guidelines. *Mental Retardation,* **14**, 3–13.

McKinney, B. and Peterson, R. A. (1987) Predictors of stress in parents of developmentally disabled children. *Journal of Pediatric Psychology,* **12**, 133–150.

Menolascino, F. J. and Egger, M. (1978) *Medical Dimensions of Mental Retardation.* Lincoln, NA: University of Nebraska Press.

Miller, L. G. (1968) Toward a greater understanding of the parents of the mentally retarded child. *Journal of Pediatrics,* **73**, 699–705.

Mink, I. T. and Nihara, K. (1987) Direction of effects: family lifestyles and the behaviour of TMR children. *American Journal of Mental Deficiency,* **92**, 57–64.

Newberry, M. K. and Parish, T. S. (1987) Enhancement of attitudes towards handicapped children through social interactions. *Journal of Social Psychology,* **127**, 59–62.

Olshansky, S. (1962) Chronic sorrow: a response to having a mentally retarded child. *Social Casework,* **43**, 190–193.

Olshansky, S. (1966) Parent responses to a mentally defective child. *Mental Retardation,* **4**, 20–25.

Pahl, J. and Quine, L. (1984) *Families with Mentally Handicapped Children: A Survey of Stress and of Services Response.* Canterbury: Health Services Research Unit, University of Kent.

Peck, J. R. and Stephens, W. B. (1960) A study of the relationship between the attitudes and behaviour of parents and their mentally retarded children. *American Journal of Mental Deficiency,* **64**, 839–844.

Philp, M. and Duckworth, D. (1982) *Children with Disabilities and their Families: A Review of Research.* Windsor: National Foundation for Educational Research.

Pless, I. B. and Pinkerton, P. (1975) *Chronic Child Disorder: Promoting Patterns of Adjustment.* London: Henry Kimpton.

Pollner, M. and McDonald-Wikler, L. (1985) The social construction of unreality: a case study of a family's attribution of competence to a severely retarded child. *Family Process,* **24**, 241–254.

Pringle, M. L. Kellmer (1967) *The Emotional and Social Adjustment of Physically Handicapped Children.* Occasional papers No. 11. London: National Foundation for Educational Research.

Pringle, M. L. Kellmer (1975) *The Needs of Children.* London: Hutchinson.

Pugh, G. (1981) *Parents as Partners.* London: National Children's Bureau.

Quine, L. and Pahl, J. (1985) Examining the causes of stress in families with severe mentally handicapped children. *British Journal of Social Work,* **15**, 501–517.

Schlesinger, H. S. and Meadow, K. P. (1972) *Sound and Sign: Childhood Deafness and Mental Health.* Berkeley, CA: University of California Press.

Shearer, M. S. and Shearer, D. E. (1972) The Portage project: A model for early childhood education. *Exceptional Children*, **39**, 210–217.

Svarstad, B. L. and Lipton, H. L. (1977) Informing parents about mental retardation. *Social Science and Medicine*, **11**, 645–651.

Taylor, A. R., Asher, S. R. and Williams, G. A. (1987) The social adaptation of mainstreamed mildly retarded children. *Child Development*, **58**, 1321–1334.

Tew, B., Payne, E. H. and Lawrence, K., M. (1974) Must a family with a handicapped child be a handicapped family? *Developmental Medicine and Child Neurology*, **16** (Suppl. 32), 95–98.

Zelle, R. S. (1973) The family with a mentally retarded child. In: D, P. Hymovich and M. Underwood Barnard (eds.), *Family Health Care*. New York: McGraw-Hill.

5

Conflict and Violence

INTRODUCTION

It is a rare family indeed that has no conflict. Marital conflict and conflict between children and parents is very common, and most families are able to live with the fact that from time to time they will engage in rather hostile exchanges. Families that manage to avoid open conflict are often considered dysfunctional, stemming from the belief that any intimate living arrangement will inevitably involve at least occasional clashes of opinion and differences of interest, and that mutual engagement over such difficulties is more likely to lead to a solution than denial of the problem and the strenuous avoidance of confrontation. A certain degree of conflict, then, is acknowledged to be healthy and desirable, although it is clear that some confrontations will be damaging. It is important to understand family conflict because of the serious adverse effects it can have on relationships and because it is sometimes a precursor of serious physical violence. There has therefore been a considerable exploration of the field, despite the fact that, being a very intimate and private concern, family conflict is not an easy subject to study. Much is now known about how family conflict begins and how it escalates, and particular attention has been paid to cases in which physical aggression is used by one family member on another.

In this and the next two chapters a number of aspects of family conflict and violence will be discussed. This chapter deals with marital and adolescent–parent conflict before considering the question of why there is so much violence in the family. The general issues raised in the chapter are then illustrated by focusing on one particular class of family violence—'elder abuse'. Chapters 6 and 7 consider in detail the two forms of family violence that have given rise to most concern and have generated the most research—the physical abuse of children and marital abuse.

CONFLICT

Conflict often arises when one person voices their disapproval of something another person has done. In response to this complaint the other person may defend their behaviour, and the two parties will then begin an argument about the issue, and about whether the complaint is justified or not. Some arguments begin when a 'conflict of interests' becomes apparent. For example, a confrontation may arise over how some limited resource (such as money, or free time) should be shared. The conflict becomes hostile when one or both of those involved becomes angry. Anger is generated when a person experiences a situation as irritating (for example, when an adolescent continually plays loud music, or a baby constantly cries), or when they judge a situation to be either 'costly' (for example, if an evening out has been spoiled, or if additional chores have to be carried out), or 'transgressive' (for example, if a person has broken a promise or has failed to remember a birthday). Almost all of the situations that generate anger can be analysed in terms of some combination of perceived irritants, costs, and transgressions (Frude, 1980, 1989).

For example, suppose a young person is forbidden to go to a late-night concert. This will certainly involve a 'cost' to the teenager (the threatened loss of attendance at the concert) but he or she may also feel that a parent has no right to exercise such control now that they have achieved 'young adult' status, and that by behaving in an 'authoritarian' way the parent has acted 'out of line' (a transgression). From the parent's point of view, the teenager's attendance at the late-night concert might produce anxiety (a cost). If the child challenges their authority this is likely to be seen as a transgression; and if the issue is constantly raised with a groan this might also prove irritating. Family members often find each other irritating, and costs ('look what I've given up for you'; 'you never let me do what I want') and transgressions ('you've no right'; 'you're being unfair') frequently trigger both inter-generational and marital conflicts.

Once a conflictual interaction has begun it will often escalate, with words and actions becoming progressively harsher, and other issues being brought into the dispute. An original complaint about a partner being late may produce a retaliatory comment about laziness ('I was late because I had to feed the cat— you wouldn't feed the cat'), and the argument may then progress to generalizations (often employing the words 'always' or 'never'). It may also become more wide-ranging, as the combatants use stored-up resentments as further ammunition for their attack. Eventually the conflict may become a general verbal assault by one person on the behaviour and personality of the other. Ultimately there will be an end to the conflict, sometimes as the result of a compromise and sometimes as the result of one person 'backing down'. Occasionally both partners in the conflict become aware that prolonging the fight will cause long-term damage and agree to end the confrontation 'for the sake of the relationship' while maintaining their different opinions. When the conflict episode has ended, the partners typically engage in actions such as apologizing, forgiving, and resolving not to fight again, and thus attempt to heal any damage that has occurred and to prevent further outbreaks of hostility.

MARITAL CONFLICT

Almost all married couples argue at least occasionally, and a number of studies have established lists of the topics that are often the focus of such arguments. Typical issues of conflict include money, children, sex, chores and tasks, friends and in-laws. Sometimes a fierce argument is triggered by what appears to be a very trivial concern—one partner forgetting to replace the cap on a toothpaste tube, for example, or a partner failing to comment on what the other is wearing. Such trivial matters have been labelled 'tremendous trifles', but those who have analysed marital conflicts in detail report that the surface issues often hide some important 'hidden agenda'. Thus the toothpaste cap incident might really concern the issue of emotional closeness. The complaining partner might reason in the following way: 'He knows that I get irritated when I find the toothpaste cap left off. I have mentioned it repeatedly, and even pleaded with him to replace the cap. He ignores my pleas, showing that my happiness means little to him, and if my happiness means little to him then he doesn't really love me'. Thus what appears at first to be a trivial matter is now seen as far more important. Toothpaste cap replacement has become a crucial test of whether love is reciprocated.

Several authors have attempted to provide a list of the fundamental issues that underlie most marital conflicts. Gottman *et al.* (1976) suggest that most arguments really concern status ('My partner is not treating me as an equal'), positiveness ('My partner doesn't care about me') or responsiveness ('My partner is not interested in me'). In an alternative formulation, Patterson, Hops and Weiss (1975) hypothesize that conflict develops when one partner's behaviour fails to match the expectations or hopes of the other. Thus an action, or a failure to act in a certain way, may produce a disappointment that threatens one person's satisfaction with the relationship. In some cases a partner may really behave very badly, so that an objective observer would agree that a reasonable expectation has been flouted. In other cases, however, such an observer might feel that the expectation itself was unreasonable.

People enter into marriage with certain expectations, beliefs and fantasies about their partner and the relationship, and some of these are likely to be over-idealistic. For example, a newly-married person might believe that 'As long as we love each other ... my partner will do everything for me ... we will never quarrel ... my partner will accept everything I do (never ignore me, or criticize me, or be angry with me), ... and our sex life will be perfect.' When the reality falls short of one of these ideals the person may conclude that 'our love is not real' and respond in a dejected or angry way. Clearly, the more unrealistic the prior expectations, the more likely it is that there will be disappointment and hostility. Epstein and Eidelson (1981) found that the holding of unrealistic beliefs about the relationship was highly predictive of the degree of distress within the marriage. Unrealistic expectations held by partners in distressed marriages were found to include the belief that sexual interaction should always be perfect, and the belief that any serious disagreement would be profoundly damaging to the relationship.

A number of researchers have examined the differences in conflict interactions between couples whose marriage is troubled and those whose marriage is generally agreeable. Even when couples are asked to participate together in artificial conflicts that have been contrived in a psychology laboratory, many aspects of their communication can be shown to be related to measures of their marital satisfaction. Faced with experimental conflict resolution tasks, distressed couples find less agreement and engage in more negative behaviours than do non-distressed couples. Jacobson (1981) suggested that individuals in distressed marriages frequently attempt to control their partner's behaviour by using aversive control tactics such as withdrawing rewards or administering punishments and Jacobson *et al.* (1985) found differences in how partners in distressed and non-distressed marriages explained their spouse's annoying behaviour. Those in troubled marriages tend to attribute their partner's uncooperative or negative behaviour to internal and stable factors such as the partner's personality rather than to external and temporary factors such as their having had a particularly difficult day. An extensive series of studies focusing on the attributions made by marital partners has been conducted by Fincham and his colleagues (e.g. Fincham, Beach and Baucom, 1987). This team found that distressed individuals tended to make hostile attributions about their partner's negative behaviours but to see their own actions as positively motivated. Thus distressed spouses tend to discredit positive behaviour by the partner and to focus instead on negative aspects, and they often judge that these are caused by internal, stable and global factors. Fincham and Bradbury (1987) reported that for women, but not for men, subsequent levels of marital satisfaction can be predicted on the basis of the attributions made about the partner's behaviour at an earlier time.

Bornstein and Bornstein (1985) concluded from their review that partners in distressed marriages often have difficulty in accurately perceiving the meaning of their spouse's communications. Those with marital difficulties also have a tendency to repeat their own position rather than addressing the issues raised by their partner. They make more complaints and criticisms, they tend to resort readily to sarcasm, and their communications are more likely to be uncontrolled and 'uncensored'. As well as these general findings of differences between high-conflict and low-conflict couples, it has become clear that many couples develop a particular style of conflict engagement and escalation that can be identified across different situations. Thus one couple might escalate conflicts rapidly, fight 'below the belt', and always introduce issues relating to the in-laws, whereas another couple will maintain a high degree of civility throughout and never make reference to other relatives. Some couples make a swift transition from the verbal to the physical, so that their arguments usually end in a general brawl. As we shall see, the issue of a couple's 'conflict style' may be crucial to an understanding of at least some cases of marital violence.

Information of the kind reviewed here has been used to devise intervention strategies for couples seeking help with conflict. For example, Bornstein and Bornstein (1985) have described in detailed a behavioural programme aimed at reducing the frequency of negative interactions and increasing the frequency of positive exchanges. The programme also teaches couples how to problem-solve together to reach consensus and compromise. Effective communication skills, particularly listening skills, are also taught. In their work with distressed couples, these authors have found that even a small reduction in the number of negative interchanges often produces a significant increase in marital satisfaction.

So far we have considered conflict that arises as a consequence of one partner annoying the other for some reason (failing to meet expectations, for example, or engaging in some action or inaction that the other person finds irritating). But conflict sometimes begins when one partner deliberately sets out to start an argument, or feels angry for some reason and displaces this anger onto the spouse. The first of these situations, involving 'strategic conflict', will occur when a person is so dissatisfied with the relationship that they are willing to risk damaging it, or even wish to do so. They use marital fighting as a vehicle to communicate their dissatisfaction to the partner, to hurt them, and to strike at the integrity of the relationship. Thus if an individual has become involved in a serious extra-marital affair they may set out to destroy the existing relationship by initiating frequent arguments. When engaging in 'conflict therapy' with a couple, the therapist must be sure that both partners are genuinely motivated to maintain and improve the relationship.

Sometimes the anger expressed in marital conflict does not have its origin in the couple's interaction, but results from annoyance generated in another context. Thus a mother who has had a particularly difficult day with a child, and is feeling very aggravated, may displace her anger onto her husband; or a man who has been annoyed by someone at work may bring his anger home. When people are angry they are more easily annoyed, and in such circumstances an action by the partner that would normally pass unnoticed might attract a highly critical response. Sometimes a long-term difficulty at work, or with the extended family, or with a child, can lead to regular and bitter arguments between the couple. They may fail to recognize why the fights are occurring, and a therapist will sometimes be able to help them recognize and deal with the problem. Understanding that the quarrels are caused by external stress and do not reflect a problem intrinsic to their relationship may bring relief to a discordant couple and enable the irate partner to find less destructive ways of dissipating the tension.

INTER-GENERATIONAL CONFLICT

Children, including young babies, often irritate their parents. Crying, waking at inconvenient times, and eating in a fussy or messy way are frequent sources of irritation. The child's behaviour often imposes severe costs (of time, effort and money), and is often judged to be transgressive ('naughty' or 'defiant'). As a consequence, parents often become angry with their children, but only some of these cases can appropriately be said to involve 'conflict'. Young babies do not engage in contests with their parents, although the parents may sometimes feel that they are at cross-purposes with the infant. As the child gets older, however, there may be frequent disciplinary struggles that can properly be labelled 'conflicts'. Often the child wishes to do something that the parent disapproves of and tries to prevent or stop. Threats may be issued, followed by minor disciplinary sanctions, and the parent and child may engage in a 'battle of wills'. Most parents develop the skills necessary for controlling the child effectively and are able to prevent situations from becoming critical, but disciplinary confrontations can prove dangerous if the parent experiences a rapid rise in anger and has few inhibitions about using severe and inappropriate forms of physical punishment.

In many cases the most intense and stressful inter-generational conflicts occurs when the child reaches adolescence. 'Launching' is one of the critical developmental stages of the family life cycle, and some family systems experience great difficulty in allowing the older children to achieve independence. Teenagers spend more time with their peers and increasingly take their values from the peer group (Cooper and Ayers-Lopez, 1985), and many of these values will be incompatible with those of the parents. In their bid for increased independence adolescents often question their parents' decisions and challenge their right to impose rules. Parents may fear that the adolescent will be unable to avoid the dangers associated with drugs, crime and sexual experiences without their guidance. They may be particularly alarmed when they see how rapidly their influence is waning and how quickly the teenager's involvement with the family is declining. In an attempt to alleviate their own anxieties, and to protect the young person, they may explore various ways of re-establishing their control, and this often leads to a power struggle that is the focus of most serious parent–adolescent conflict. Young people wish to become more independent, to control their own lives and to make their own rules, while parents wish to retain a substantial degree of power and influence. In many cases both adolescents and parents over-estimate the degree of power that they hold (Jessop, 1981), and such incongruous presumptions do nothing to improve the quality of family communication.

The achievement of autonomy is a gradual process, rather than a single event, and the struggle for independence may therefore continue over many years. The constant confrontation can prove very debilitating for all those involved, and it is therefore not surprising that the presence of an adolescent in the family has been found to be associated with high levels of stress (Olson and McCubbin, 1983). Eventually, when the family system adapts and the young person is able to achieve a satisfactory level of autonomy, the tension often wanes and a new stable equilibrium is established. Adolescents who move away from the family home at a relatively early age often experience a strengthening of attachment to the family as a result. Clearly, living away is likely to pre-empt many fights over issues relating to independence.

FAMILY VIOLENCE

Some marital and inter-generational conflict escalates from verbal attacks to physical violence. Such episodes may involve a two-sided brawl and the aggression is usually somewhat restrained, perhaps taking the form of shoves and pulls. Sometimes, however, one person attacks the other in a brutal and dangerous way. In some cases, therefore, conflict leads to serious injury, and in numerous cases every year it actually leads to the death of a family member. But although there is a definite link between family conflict and family violence it would be wrong to regard them merely as different aspects of the same phenomenon. Many incidents of violence, particularly those involving the physical abuse of young children and some cases of marital and elder abuse, do not originate in *mutual* antagonism or follow a prolonged quarrel, but reflect the unilateral response of the perpetrator towards the victim. Although such attacks commonly follow 'provocation' by the victim, many incidents of violence do not arise from arguments, and some violent episodes do not therefore result from conflict. It is also clear that not every occurrence of conflict ends in violence. In most cases disputes and arguments end without any resort to physical aggression.

Family violence is not a unitary phenomenon. There are differences between classes of family violence (marital abuse, child abuse, abuse between siblings, etc.) as well as major distinctions within each of these. Yet there are fairly strong associations between the different types, so that child abuse and marital abuse, for example, tend to occur in the same families. Estimates of the incidence of family violence differ widely, depending mostly on the criteria used to define 'violence', but extreme aggression leading to injury or even death is by no means uncommon. The person most likely to murder an adult is their spouse, and a vicious attack by a parent is one of the most frequent causes of death among young children. Clearly, fatalities represent just the tip of a very large iceberg of suffering and injury.

EXPLANATIONS OF FAMILY VIOLENCE

Different explanations of family violence reflect, to a large degree, different ideologies. Before presenting accounts of child abuse, marital abuse and 'elder abuse' in this and the following two chapters, it is necessary to give brief consideration to a number of theoretical questions. This will set the scene and provide a justification for the approach to be taken. For many other family problem issues, such as illness and bereavement, there are few ideologically contentious aspects, and such discussion is hardly necessary, but in attempting to analyse family violence different authors and researchers start from quite different theoretical perspectives and make highly contrasting assumptions about the nature of the problem.

There are two main approaches to answering questions concerning the nature of family violence and why it occurs. The first approach focuses on cultural norms and attitudes. It maintains that family violence is very common, and that this reflects the fact that society condones and even encourages brutality within the home as a way of maintaining the cultural status quo. In particular, child abuse is said to reflect and maintain the view that parents 'own' their children, and marital violence (which is treated as synonymous with 'wife-beating', i.e. violence inflicted by a man on a woman) is seen as reflecting and supporting socially approved and encouraged male dominance or patriarchy. Thus according to the feminist/social stratification explanation of marital abuse (e.g. Dobash and Dobash, 1979), the aggression that husbands direct at their wives mirrors the wider conflict in society regarding the gender-linked allocation of resources and power.

The second approach to explanation focuses on family interaction and psychological processes. It does not deny the relevance of the cultural climate but does not accord it the prominence assigned by the first approach. It treats violent incidents as exaggerated (and 'deviant') forms of behaviour that have their origin in conflict and disciplinary situations and reflect both the anger and the lack of inhibition of the assailant. Explanations within this approach may be 'psychiatric' (explaining violence in terms of the personality and/or the psychopathology of the perpetrator) or 'interactional' (explaining the violence in terms of the relationship and interactions between the assailant and the victim, or in terms of aspects of the family system). The account of family violence to be presented in this and the next two chapters will follow the second approach and will place particular emphasis on interactional issues. Societal factors such as poverty and the high rate of unemployment are acknowledged to play an important causal role, but their effect is examined through the psychological effects that such conditions have on the individuals who engage in acts of violence.

The two approaches assign a quite different importance to the various half-hearted threats, and pushes and pulls, that feature as a part of life in many families. Those who follow the first approach, and take a highly cultural or political view, are apt to regard any corporal punishment administered to a child, including a slap, as abusive and as reflecting a general misuse of children. Similarly, they are likely to regard one marital partner grabbing or pushing the other as an 'attack'. Such actions, however, are not deliberate attempts to inflict hurt or injury on the other person (they are usually intended to restrain or prevent some action) and are not usually considered to be 'violent' by either of the people involved. There is clearly a difficulty about where it is most appropriate to draw the line between behaviour that is 'tolerable' or 'legitimate' and that which should be considered abusive. Because different researchers use quite different criteria in their working definitions of 'violence', there is often some difficulty in assessing the frequency of the use of unacceptable force from research reports. In the case of interactions between young siblings, for example, much of what some researchers would define as 'violence' might be seen by the 'assailant' and 'victim' merely as 'sparring' or 'play-fighting'.

THE CULTURAL CLIMATE

It is often claimed that there is a widespread cultural approval of family violence. It is true that we generally accord little significance to the limited use of corporal punishment on children, marital pushes and pulls, and occasional fights between young siblings. It is also true that people refrain from becoming involved in the affairs of other families (that is true of all aspects of family life, and reflects a cultural value regarding the 'privacy' of the family). But people certainly do not approve of children being injured or of wives being beaten up. The reason that the question 'Have you stopped beating your wife?' is regarded as unfair is precisely because it gives the person a choice between two socially *unacceptable* replies. Abusers are rarely proud of their actions, and are much more likely to be ashamed of any violence they have shown towards their children or their spouse. The presence of other people does not facilitate attacks (as it would if this were a socially encouraged form of behaviour) but acts as a powerful inhibitor of violence. Following an attack, most abusers strive to minimize what they have done (often blaming the action on the effects of alcohol, for example, or stress) rather than boasting about their achievement. The majority of people do not attack their spouse or their children and most consider that hurting a wife or a child is 'vicious' and 'cowardly'. Sympathy is extended, quite properly, to the victim, and there are frequent popular calls for the perpetrators of family violence to be severely punished. In view of all this, it is difficult to maintain that society condones and encourages family violence, except, of course, if we are referring to actions which most people would not consider to be violent.

  This does not mean that we can confine our analysis to cases in which serious injury occurs, however, or where the victim feels abused or the attacker acknowledges that their behaviour constitutes abuse. Some people fail to recognize that the attacks they make, or the attacks made on them, are abusive when most others would have no doubt that serious violence had occurred. Gelles (1987), for example, found that some wives who had been beaten by their husbands accepted the violence without complaint and that a few felt they had 'deserved it'. The toleration shown by such women does not make the aggressive behaviour tolerable. A line between 'acceptable' and 'unacceptable' behaviour has to be drawn somewhere, and any such line will reflect a value judgement. But a value judgement that labels the 90% or so of parents who occasionally use a slap as a means of disciplining the child as 'violent parents' is unhelpful, and detracts attention from the plight of those children who are under threat of serious injury. Slapping is not 'good' and is probably best avoided, but the parent who uses a slap to prevent a child touching a hot iron does not become, through that action, a 'child abuser', and we should avoid analyses that imply otherwise.

One common objection to the interactional account concerns the role assigned to the victim. According to the interactional view, the victim's behaviour (a child's constant crying, for example, or a wife's complaint about her husband's drinking) often triggers the anger that results in violence. The criticism often levelled at such accounts is that in some way they *blame* the victim for what has occurred, or at least they they detract from the blame attributed to the aggressor. A more outrageous misinterpretation suggests that such analyses imply that the victim deliberately provokes attacks—that the victim 'wants' to be hit. Neither of these characterizations of the interactional account is warranted. The victim's behaviour might well be said to *provoke* the assault, but it is not claimed to be a sufficient *cause* of the attack and it is certainly not regarded as a *justification* for the brutality. The assailant's response is seen to depend upon the interpretation of the situational 'trigger', the emotional response that follows from this, and an intention to hurt the victim. The responsibility for the attack clearly rests with the assailant, and in almost all cases it rests *solely* with the assailant. There *are* instances of deliberate provocation to violence, where a court of law might consider that the victim should take some share of the blame, but these are rare. The constant, harrowing and annoying crying of a baby who is teething painfully cannot justify a vicious attack, but it may well help to explain it. And in this case, at least, surely no one could accuse those who construct an interactional account of implying that the baby must share some of the blame or is in some way 'asking to be attacked'?

The above discussion is not merely relevant to academic concerns. Definitional criteria, assumptions that are made about cultural attitudes, and ideological beliefs that affect our examination of the relevant evidence, all play a major part in determining our view of the nature of family violence, how it arises, and how it may best be prevented and treated. Explanations of family violence have become something of an ideological battleground, and it is necessary to address certain contentious points before presenting an analysis of child abuse, marital abuse and elder abuse in terms of interactions between perpetrators and their victims.

WHY IS THERE SO MUCH VIOLENCE IN THE FAMILY?

Nothing in the foregoing discussion does anything to undermine the judgement that family violence is all too common, or to deny that violence is especially likely to occur in family situations. However, rather than attempting to explain this in terms of societal pressures on families *to be* violent, as some analysts would, the approach to be adopted here will focus on the psychological strains and frustrations that arise for individuals, and between individuals, in the course of family life. We will consider why such tensions are likely to generate violent attacks by one family member on another. One obvious reason why family violence may be considerably more common than street violence, or violence towards neighbours, friends and work colleagues, relates to the intensity and frequency of contact between family members. People who live together, eat together, sleep together and play together will be in close proximity for so much of the time that strong emotions, including anger, are likely to be generated on at least some of the occasions when they interact. There are likely to be many times when one person's behaviour annoys another, and in some cases such annoyance will initiate a chain of events that eventually results in a physical assault. The first step towards answering the question of why there is so much violence in the family therefore involves considering family situations that are likely to generate anger.

An analysis of situations in terms of irritants, costs and transgressions can help in this task. The high level of contact between members means that a person's irritating habits (an adult who frequently sighs or who snores loudly, for example, or a baby who cries with a pitiful yelp or 'grizzles' continually) are likely to prove very annoying. Strangers and acquaintances are only exposed to some of a person's irritating habits. In public, or when visitors are in the home, people are somewhat inhibited in their behaviour. Thus the display of some particularly irritating and unsociable habits (such as teeth-scraping or nose-picking) may be reserved for the family audience. Irritants can be very annoying and may be 'the last straw' leading to an attack, but they are rarely sufficient alone to arouse profound anger. If another member complains to the person about the behaviour, of course, the criticism may initiate a conflict sequence. A request for the person to stop the irritation may be disregarded, or lead to increased and 'deliberate' repetition, in which case the irritation experienced by the complainant will usually increase and the behaviour will come to be judged as *deliberately* offensive.

More important than irritants are the perceived costs of another person's behaviour. In the discussion of social exchange theory, in Chapter 1, it was noted that family members are in a very powerful position to confer benefits on each other and to exact costs. Children, and babies in particular, demand a great deal of attention and many costs of time, effort and money are necessarily involved in their care. If parents feel aggrieved about such costs, and especially if they feel that the benefits provided by the child are few (if they judge that the child is unresponsive to them, for example, or does not provide the interest and company that they expected) then they may react angrily to a situation that involves further expense of time or effort (for example if an infant soils a nappy immediately following a change, or if a child refuses to eat food that has taken a long time to prepare). Between older children and their parents, and between the husband and wife, there may be disputes over the allocation of the space, money or physical resources that they share. Thus if there is one television set, and two people want to watch different channels at the same time, there is an immediate conflict of interests. The matter might be settled amicably, by compromise or a generous gesture, or the person whose interests are thwarted may simply accept the situation, but such issues have also been known to generate violent clashes. Negative outcomes are much more likely where the differing interests concern more important shared resources such as money, or the allocation of shared duties such as household chores. People who feel that they are doing too much of the work or receiving too few of the joint resources are likely to object, and their complaint will often lead to conflict.

Not all of the costs and benefits incurred in family life emerge from interactions that can be recognized as 'zero-sum games' (i.e. where one member's loss is another's gain). Many benefits reflect what one person gives to another without any loss on their part—affection, for example, or comfort. The application of social exchange theory to the study of intimate relationships has shown how people depend on their 'significant others' to provide them with many such benefits. Thus a married person expects the partner to show concern and interest, to administer 'therapy' in times of personal difficulty (Nye and McLaughlin, 1982), to provide emotional comfort and security, and to share sexual pleasure. If such rewards are not forthcoming then a 'cost' is experienced. Children, too, expect their parents to provide comfort, interest and praise, and parents expect their children to be affectionate, to appreciate their efforts and to 'reward' them with interest and achievement. When an expectation is thwarted the deprived individual is likely to be disappointed or angry and may lodge a complaint. People have many more reward expectations of family members than they have of more distant relatives, acquaintances or strangers, and they soon feel deprived and resentful if they judge that these are not being fulfilled. Thus the family situation is marked by a particularly high potential for non-fulfilment of expectations, and this can lead to disappointment, anxiety and sometimes anger.

Other costs and benefits arise from the behaviour of family members beyond the home. One person's achievement may be a source of pride to other family members; or their failure or misdemeanour may bring disappointment or disgrace. A wife will be embarrassed by the fact that her husband has been arrested for drunkenness, and may experience a personal loss of pride. On the other hand, the career success of one family member will usually be a source of pride (and thus a benefit) to other members of the family. Parents take pride in the achievements of their children, so that a child's academic success is experienced as a reward, whereas academic failure is perceived as a cost. If the child gets into trouble outside the home the parents are also likely to experience this as a major cost. It is clear that a very high level of interdependence differentiates family relationships from other types of relationships, and the intense reward–cost environment of the home can help to explain why there is so much domestic violence.

Families (and individuals) subscribe to many implicit and explicit rules about behaviour, and on many occasions it will be judged that someone has broken a rule. Such transgressions often provoke an angry response. The rules that operate within families are more numerous and are often less well defined than the rules that operate within other types of social relationship. They also vary from family to family, although there are general rules that operate within most (Argyle and Henderson, 1985). The terms 'should' and 'should not' often feature prominently in both marital and inter-generational conflicts, and some parents of very young babies even apply rules to the infant's behaviour and regard particular behaviours as transgressive. Family conflict very often begins when one member complains to another about a failure to adhere to a rule. Sometimes the dispute that follows focuses on whether a rule has actually been broken (as when there is a contest about whether or not one partner acted in a flirtatious way towards another person) and sometimes it focuses on the legitimacy of a rule (thus a partner may defend the right to be flirtatious as long as it is 'harmless fun' and does not lead to infidelity).

Some rules embody attitudes to structural features of the family (especially the power structure) and some disputes about rules, and accusations of rule infringement, therefore amount to confrontations concerning the family structure. Struggles for power ('a limited resource') may become apparent when rights are called into question (as when teenagers challenge their parents' right to determine the time at which they should arrive home after an evening out). Clearly, such disputes are much less likely to occur beyond the family situation, and this therefore provides another illustration of why family conflict (sometimes leading to family violence) should be so common.

So far we have simply outlined a number of ways in which family situations have a high potential to provoke anger. Many of the situations that commonly arise in the course of family life are likely to be judged as irritating, as 'costly', or as involving a transgression. The discussion so far has indicated why the family context has the potential to prove more annoying than most other social situations. The fact that people spend so much of their time engaged in family interaction means that a high frequency of annoyance is to be expected. Indeed, in view of the numerous potential sources of annoyance within the family context, it might be wondered why anger is not the predominant emotion generated within the family. However, if family members are positively inclined towards one another they are likely to avoid behaving in ways that may upset and annoy others, and they are also likely to adopt a charitable view of other members' potentially annoying behaviour. Efforts to act 'acceptably' and to judge 'charitably' are more likely to be found when the general family atmosphere is positive and when relationships are warm and friendly. In such families responsiveness, accommodation, and an inclination to judge other people's actions favourably will add to the harmonious interactive style and annoyance will be relatively rare. And if intense aggravation is rarely generated there will be less chance of resentment and complaint, with the result that the likelihood of conflict, escalation and violence will be considerably reduced. Sometimes, however, relationships within the family are not sufficiently favourable to promote accommodation, or the nature of an individual's action is such that intense annoyance will occur despite a general congeniality.

The relatively high frequency of family violence does not simply reflect the common occurrence of annoying situations, however. In most other social contexts people are very reluctant to make open complaints and may endure annoying behaviours without comment. With members of their own family, people are less inhibited. Thus in addition to a high frequency of annoyance in family situations, there is also a relatively high probability of transition from annoyance to complaint. And whereas in other contexts a complaint is likely to lead to the immediate cessation of the annoying behaviour, perhaps with an apology, family members will often be far less reticent about defending themselves and engaging in angry verbal exchanges. The more frequent such verbal battles have been in the past the less reluctant will the contestants be to enter the fray. Familiarity is one reason why marital partners or adolescents and their parents may be more likely to enter into a quarrel than two strangers. Conflict with a stranger is unpredictable and may suddenly prove dangerous. Engaging in conflict with a family member, however, usually means sailing in well-charted waters and is rarely perceived as dangerous (although of course it may prove to be so). A further point is that a person may often judge that it is *worth* entering into a fight with a family member because if the issue is resolved in their favour then important long-term benefits will follow. This again reflects the especially high level of interdependence between those in the same family. Because the outcome of a dispute with a stranger is less predictable, may prove perilous, and is unlikely to have important long-term implications, such conflict is much more likely to be avoided.

The next step along the pathway that we are tracing, from annoyance to violence, is the escalation of conflict, and there are a number of reasons why conflicts between family members who regularly engage in verbal battles might escalate quickly. They are likely to have developed habitual patterns in their confrontations, and each person will be aware of the kinds of comments that will cause the most distress to the other. There may be little verbal sparring before a rapid onslaught of insults and disparagements focuses on the opponent's personality, family of origin or other sensitive areas. The fact that family members know each other's past history, and have a keen appreciation of any special areas of vulnerability, means that they have the 'advantage' of being able to inflict maximum hurt. In addition, long-standing issues of dispute may soon be brought to the surface whenever family members engage in any substantial clash.

The general verbal free-for-all involved in this type of conflict is likely to instigate extremely high levels of anger in both parties. The other person's attack is likely to be judged as mean and unjustified, and the manner of their attack (be it with grimaces and cruel mimicry, or with an apparent cold detachment) is likely to cause extreme irritation. The insults and accusations may be hurtful and reduce self-esteem, thus proving highly 'costly' to the individual, and many of the actions that the other person engages in are likely to be seen as breaking rules ('transgressions'). Such transgressions may include unfairly attacking people who are not present to defend themselves, or raising matters that the person considers to have long been settled. Some individuals will feel that the other person's transgressions during the conflict episode both merit and justify a physical attack.

The transition from the verbal to the physical is more likely to occur between family members than between strangers or acquaintances. Parents may feel that they have a right to discipline a child using physical methods, and may feel that such action is the only means they have of controlling the child. Undoubtedly, some men feel that they have a similar right to chastise their wife. Thus it is often perceived by one family member to be legitimate to push, pull, or slap another, and if such behaviour becomes habitual there are likely to be occasions on which the aggression escalates beyond mere swats and tugs to become much more forceful. If physical coercion is commonly used then part of the pathway leading to physical abuse will be established, and the fact that previous assaults have passed without serious repercussions will do nothing to curb the attack. The issue of 'family privacy' is also highly relevant. The aggressor may presume that there is relatively little threat of legal or other negative social consequences following an attack made in the home. And because family members differ in physical size and strength, reflecting differences of gender and generation, a more powerful member can also attack others with little fear of direct physical reprisal.

Thus the high frequency of family aggression can be seen as a consequence of the high frequency of annoying situations likely to arise within the family context, the relatively high probability of complaint, the high probability of conflict engagement and escalation, and the relatively low level of inhibitions against a transition from verbal aggression to physical attack. In the case of child abuse, the explanation focuses on the annoying situations that often arise in the context of child care and discipline, and the habitual use of physical means of control. The escalation of threats and punishments over the longer term increases the likelihood that when the child's behaviour proves especially annoying, and the parent's anger is uncontrolled, the child will be attacked. The discussion in this section has attempted to answer the question of why so much physical aggression is found within the family context. It will be recognized, however, that even in answering this question some clues have already been provided about how such violence might be prevented. In the chapters that follow, detailed examination will be made of the two classes of family violence that generally give rise to most concern, physical child abuse (Chapter 6) and marital abuse (Chapter 7). But first we briefly consider another class of family violence—elder abuse.

ELDER ABUSE

There has been relatively little research into what the popular press sometimes refers to as 'granny bashing', and what professionals now tend to refer to as 'elder abuse'. Like babies, old people are rather fragile. They bruise easily and their bones are easily broken, so that serious injury may result from even a relatively minor physical attack. Like babies and young children, older people are little able to defend themselves physically and are usually highly dependent upon those who abuse them.

'Granny bashing' is in many ways a singularly inappropriate label for elder abuse. For one thing, those who abuse old people are unlikely to be their grandchildren. In some cases the old person is attacked by their spouse, so that the elder abuse is a form of marital violence. Sometimes this is an extension of marital abuse which has continued over many years, but in some cases it represents a new problem within the marriage. Overall, it should be noted, the rate of marital violence *declines* sharply with the age of the couple (Straus, Gelles, and Steinmetz, 1980). More often the abuser is a son or daughter, or their spouse, and some reports suggest that the unmarried daughter, alone with the parent, is most at risk of abusing (Renvoize, 1978). In some such cases there will have been a long history of parental abuse but in most cases physical maltreatment will have begun only after the parent has become elderly.

Although the issue rarely receives public attention, it should be remembered that children (especially adolescents) sometimes abuse their parents. In one study (Cornell-Pedrick and Gelles, 1982), 9% of the parents of one or more adolescents had experienced severe violence at the hands of an adolescent child ('severe violence' here included being punched, kicked, bitten, or beaten up). Mothers were more likely to be the victims and boys were more frequently the perpetrators. These authors found that the risk of adolescent violence towards a parent was directly related to abuse of the child and also to marital violence. And although there is a tendency to think of the sons and daughters of old people as being in their 30s or 40s, many are considerably older and would themselves be considered elderly. Thus the son or daughter looking after an 85-year-old is likely to be over 60. And although old people living with relatives seem to be more at risk, it should not be forgotton that some elder abuse does take place in institutions (Pillemer, 1988). Neither is the term 'bashing' appropriate as a general term for the maltreatment of the elderly, because elder abuse takes many forms besides physical violence. Emotional abuse and neglect are quite common forms, and even the sexual abuse of the elderly is not unknown. As with the forms of abuse considered in the next two chapters, however, the focus will be primarily on those cases in which physical violence is involved.

For many old people, living with the younger family is a very favourable experience. The opportunity to be near their children and grandchildren, and to be part of a family once again, can bring a new 'lease of life' and prove very satisfying. For the relatives, too, being joined by an elderly relative may add more interest and enjoyment, and they may feel pleased that they are able to offer the old person a home. They may be relieved that they no longer need to make long journeys to visit, and reassured by the fact that they can now provide care and make sure that the elderly person is eating well, taking medication regularly and staying healthy. In many such cases there will be a feeling of satisfaction that everything that could reasonably be asked is being done for the old person, and family members may be uplifted by the old person's obvious appreciation of their efforts.

On the other hand, things do not always work out well. The old person may initially have been welcomed into the home, but chronic illness, progressive disability, incontinence, and a worsening cognitive and emotional state may have made the situation intolerable. The relatives, landed with much more than they bargained for, may feel frustrated and trapped. The old person, initially happy and grateful, may have come to take the situation for granted and may have developed a 'difficult' attitude. Thus after a 'honeymoon period' that may last for several months or years, the situation can become fraught and conflictual. In other cases the person will have been taken in with great reluctance, and a situation that started off rather badly may have further deteriorated over the years.

The incidence of elder abuse is unknown, and it is very difficult to obtain any realistic assessment of the frequency of the problem. Available estimates vary enormously, partly because they use quite different definitions of the problem, and partly because they rely on different sources of data. Figures for notified cases are very low, but gross under-reporting is to be expected since professionals have little opportunity to monitor the well-being of old people, and neither the perpetrators nor the victims are likely to disclose information about any attack. The victim's reticence about making the abuse known will reflect their family pride, feelings of shame about what their relatives have done to them, fear of reprisal, and their continuing dependency. Even if they live in fear of maltreatment in the home of relatives, old people may dread the imagined consequences of being admitted to a residential institution.

From the various surveys that have been carried out it is possible to make certain generalizations about the nature of the problem and to identify some of the factors associated with an especially high risk to old people. It seems that elder abuse is rarely an isolated incident, but is often recurrent and can become habitual. In addition to violent abuse, many old people are subjected to mental anguish as a result of emotional abuse. They are made to feel unwanted, hated and guilty. Sometimes their needs are totally neglected, including their medical needs, and in some cases they are confined to a small part of the house. Neglect may be passive—simply failing to attend to their needs—or active— food, medicine and privileges may be withheld. In addition, some old people are exploited financially by their families.

The two factors most clearly shown to be related to the risk of elder abuse are the age of the old person and the degree of dependency on their relatives. The older an elderly person is, the more likely he or she is to be abused (Bergman *et al.*, 1980). Those over 75 seem to be at an especially high risk of being abused and, because of their higher longevity, women are more at risk than men (Zdorkowski and Galbraith, 1985). The very old are likely to be physically frail, so that violent acts will prove more dangerous to them. The proportion of the elderly in the population is increasing at an alarming rate, as more people live to an advanced age and the sharp fall in family size reduces the relative number of younger people. Estimates suggest that in the 25 years between 1970 and 1995 the number of people aged 85 and over will have increased by 50%. Obviously many of these will continue to lead independent lives (as about one-third of old people do now), and some will be cared for in residential homes. But it is likely that a high proportion will be cared for by relatives. This suggests that the number of cases of elder abuse may be higher now than in previous times, and can be expected to increase further.

Steinmetz (1984) found that the risk of a caregiver being violent was highly correlated with the stress experienced as a result of performing 'dependency' tasks. Those who regarded caring as very stressful were far more likely to abuse the elder relative than those who did not. She also found that risk was related to the presence of other family stresses (for example, illness, marital instability, and financial hardship), and so it seems that the total amount of stress experienced by the relative may be as important as the stress generated specifically as a result of caring for the elderly person. Families that are socially isolated may be at increased risk of perpetrating elder abuse as well as other forms of family violence (Pillemer and Suitor, 1988).

It is not difficult to see why, for some families, taking in an elderly relative proves very costly and very stressful, and why families may frequently feel anger. Accommodating an elderly relative necessitates a major structural change to the family system, and some families will have evolved a structure, rules, and ways of doing things over the years that they are very reluctant to change. In such a situation, a number of special tensions are likely to make an impact. For one thing, there may be some difference of attitude between the old person and their younger relatives about what their role in the family should be. Many sons and daughters remark that their parents never treat them as independent adults, but this may be regarded as a mere foible until the elderly person who has moved into the home starts to adopt a 'parent' role and tries to exert parental responsibilities and parental power. There will often be an initial contest for power, and the older person may find it very difficult to accept that their advice and their demands are sometimes disregarded. Such a power struggle may develop into a chronic problem, with the older person continually reluctant to accept a dependent role. They may try to exert an influence that is resented by other members of the family, and this is likely to result in frequent arguments relating to the old person's rights and duties.

The power structure in the family will reflect such factors as the relative age of the elderly person and other family members, the 'blood' or 'in-law' nature of relationships, the ownership of the home, and the degree and direction of financial dependency. Although there would seem to be an added risk of abuse if the old person proves a financial drain on the family, financial dependency in the other direction is also a risk factor (Wolf, Strugnell and Godkin, 1982). The old person who has more resources than the rest of the family may use this as a means of exerting influence and authority, and the family may resent their dependency and perceive the older relative's attitude as overbearing and patronizing.

The situations that tend to generate anger and sometimes violence by those caring for the elderly can be seen, as with other forms of family violence, in terms of irritants, costs, and transgressions. Several aspects of the old person's behaviour are likely to prove irritating to other members of the family. Their standards of personal hygiene might have deteriorated with age, for example, or intellectual and memory difficulties may lead them to repeat the same request or story many times, to need constant prompting, and to lose things with great regularity. Hearing difficulties may require family members to shout to communicate with them or to repeat statements many times, and radio and television may have to be played at a high volume that other people find intrusive and annoying. Sometimes the older person will be bored, and will be seen as constantly 'getting in the way'; in other cases they may sit, staring before them silently for long periods, so that their mere presence becomes an irritation. Older people often need less sleep, and their waking pattern may be erratic. They may stay up very late at night and be up again first thing in the morning, so that the younger people will seldom have an opportunity to be alone together.

Numerous financial and other 'costs' may be involved in having an elderly relative living in the home. If the old person has few means of contributing to the family budget the cost of feeding and clothing them has to be borne by the rest of the family. Because older people are especially susceptible to discomfort from cold, the house may have to be heated to a higher temperature than normal, and heating provided for extra weeks or months throughout the year. In some cases expensive modifications will have to be made to the house, or special equipment will need to be bought to aid the mobility and toileting needs of the elderly person. There may be recurrent costs for special clothing or for foods to meet particular dietary needs, and if the old person has acute memory problems or is unsteady in their gait then this may lead to accidents that prove costly. An additional major economic burden will be placed on the family if the old person's need for continual care prevents one of the family from working. Such costs are likely to be resented by family members, particularly if they are constantly mindful of the fact that what is being spent on the older relative is depriving other members of the family in some way. Thus whenever additional money has to be spent on the old person great annoyance may be felt.

Apart from the many financial costs, the family may regret the loss of space and the lack of privacy that this brings. Families that are less well off are likely to have limited space, and they may therefore experience such costs acutely. But undoubtedly the major 'cost' involved in living with an older person is the time and effort involved in their care. This is unlikely to fall evenly on family members, and in the majority of cases it is the younger woman who takes on most of the extra burden. She is therefore more likely than other family members to feel stressed, and if she has had to give up working outside the home she may feel that the presence of the older person is costing her dearly. The care that she gives might need to include toileting, and additional washing and cooking chores may prove highly demanding. The constant presence of the old person might also be experienced as irritating and 'costly', with the woman having little time to herself and few chances to leave the home. For all of the family, the presence of the old person may reduce the opportunities to make outings or to take holidays, either because the old person needs frequent attention or because of reduced financial resources.

As well as being annoyed by the personal costs imposed by the presence of the elder relative, family members may feel angry about the effects they see on other members of the family. There may be anxiety about how the children are being affected, or the older person may be blamed for causing difficulties within the marriage. In many cases the added stress *will* contribute to marital disharmony, and the issue of family duty may prove especially contentious because the old person will be a blood relative of only one of the couple. This may cause particular resentment if the relative most involved in the day-to-day management is an in-law, and feels less obligation to the elderly person. In some cases the older person will be scapegoated and held to blame for all manner of family problems for which they are not responsible, and the anger that one individual directs towards the old person may be rationalized in terms of the impositions made on the children or the spouse.

There are also likely to be many occasions when the old person angers a family member by 'transgressing' a rule or expectation. They may be seen as attempting to take too much part, or too little, in family affairs, as trying to influence the children in ways the parents find unacceptable, or as being untidy, 'interfering', or 'careless'. They may be regarded as deliberately avoiding contributing to the family budget, or withholding resources that might benefit the family as a whole. They may have conservative attitudes and openly express their disapproval of such matters as the food that is served, how the children dress, the music they play, or the content of television programmes. There may be a particular difficulty when the adult children have surpassed their parents educationally so that there is a wide difference between the social status, interests, values and lifestyle of the elderly person and the rest of the family. The old person may belittle what they regard as the affectation and excesses of the younger family's lifestyle, while other members may consider that the old person's values are mean and archaic. Some old people become cantankerous, or 'childish', due to the psychological effects of neurological deterioration, and many become frustrated by their failing health or mental powers. Such effects may make them less inhibited and controlled in their behaviour, and they may speak their mind openly about matters they do not like. Any frank or implied criticism of the family is likely to be greatly resented and may lead to conflict. Other people may find it difficult to make due allowance for the old person's physical and mental condition and judge all such comments and actions as deliberate or 'unthinking', and as unforgivable in the context of the extra burden being placed on the family.

While it can be seen that there will often be numerous triggers to anger in those who care for the elderly, we need to keep such issues in perspective. In Chapter 3, when considering the impact of caring for the chronically ill (including those suffering from senile dementia), it was seen that studies of caregiver populations generally provide much more evidence of anxiety and depression among such people than of anger. Different people have different styles of responding to stress. Some react by developing a somatic complaint, some become depressed, and some become angry (and many, it should be remembered, manage to cope without any of these negative effects). Anger is more likely to occur for some people than for others, but it is also more likely where the caregiver judges that the older person is fully responsible for their actions and is deliberately being difficult or has no concern for the feelings of others. Some will vent their anger by constantly reminding the old person of the costs they are inflicting or by withholding any expression of care or concern. Such actions may be preferable to the use of physical violence, but they are designed to make the old person feel guilty, ashamed, and disregarded, and might therefore be considered as a form of emotional abuse.

Sometimes the anger felt by a relative will not be expressed verbally but will result in physical violence, and in some cases anger generated in other contexts (for example, marital, or work-based) will be vented on the old person following some slight mishap or transgression. It is often considered particularly shocking that someone would deliberately aim to inflict hurt and injury on an old person but, as with child abuse and marital abuse, the violence is often justified by the assailant in terms of being 'the only thing that works' as a means of exercising power and discipline over the victim. It is therefore most likely to be used by those who feel that they have no alternative means of effective influence. Physical violence generally starts on one occasion with a push or a fretful slap but may then escalate over successive weeks and months until it becomes severe and habitual. As this happens, any inhibitions about hitting the old person that may have been present initially will gradually be eroded. Even when the physical abuse has become habitual, however, attacks will not be spontaneous or 'unprovoked'. Invariably they will occur in response to some action that incites intense annoyance in the caregiver and, as we have seen, there are many potential triggers to such aggravation.

Thus some old people are in danger because they are difficult to care for and because those who care for them resort to aggression rather easily. In some cases the caregiver's tendency to be aggressive will reflect their own treatment as children, and therefore in some instances they will be abusing a parent who abused them many years ago. But the perpetrator's appraisal of the victim's actions is crucial to the generation of anger. Those who engage in elder abuse may have little understanding of their victim, and little empathy. They are likely to be unskilled in managing the person, they may use ineffective ways of trying to gain compliance, and they may be uncharitable in their judgement of whether an action is 'accidentally' or deliberately provocative. Some people have little understanding and appreciation of old people just as some have little understanding and appreciation of young children.

There are clear implications from what is known about elder abuse for prevention and treatment. One possible intervention, suggested by the account given here, is that caregivers might be helped to better understand some of the reasons why old people may prove difficult. The more that family members understand any medical condition that may be giving rise to psychological problems (including changes of mood, difficulties of memory, confusion, and disorientation) the more likely they will be to take a charitable view of that person's behaviour and the safer the old person is likely to be. Health professionals therefore have an important role to play in informing the family about the likely effects of any such condition and advising them of any steps they may take to make the old person's behaviour less disruptive. Through their own interaction with the old person, professionals may be able to provide the family with a model of how they might best deal with difficulties.

Sometimes, of course, there is no diagnosed organic pathology that can be used by the family to 'excuse' disruptive behaviour, but a knowledge of how old people generally strive to cope with their limited capacities and their constrained lifestyle may aid charitable appraisal. In providing any such explanation of the old person's behaviour, however, care must be taken not to undermine that person's integrity. And it is not always the case that the old person *is* especially difficult to care for. In many cases it is simply that the additional presence of the old person stretches resources and patience. Ideally, steps would be taken to monitor families that might be at risk, and to provide easy access to advice and help. Following the recognition that a particular family caring for an elderly relative is under stress, various forms of practical help might be provided. Some of the stress of constant caring can be relieved by providing a visiting nurse or home-help, by using resources such as day centres, and by arranging holiday placements. A study by Walker (1985) found that elder abuse and neglect usually ceased when some of the burden of caring was lifted from the family. Another very practical way of reducing the risk involves providing aid with accommodation. Families striving to care for an elderly relative in very crowded rented accommodation could be helped to find and pay for more suitable housing. The danger of violence is likely to be considerably reduced if the old person has at least a room of their own and can withdraw to a pleasant, reasonably spacious and private environment for some part of the day.

Increased monitoring of families at risk, and the provision of information about the effects of certain medical conditions, suitable accommodation, and some relief from constant caring, would therefore seem likely to considerably reduce the danger to old people. However, such interventions will not be feasible, or effective, in every case, and where the situation continues to be dangerous the best solution will often be for the elderly person to leave the family home and to enter sheltered residential accommodation. Such a change has to be handled sensitively to prevent the old person feeling traumatized and 'thrown out' by the family and to prevent the family feeling unduly guilty. In some cases, however, such a change will allow the old person and the family to renew the positive aspects of their relationship. The increased distance between them, and the greatly reduced dependence of the elderly person, may encourage an optimal degree of sharing and intimacy. The intense pressures that have arisen from living closely together may have threatened to destroy all love and respect between the generations, but when interdependence is reduced and their contact is more restricted they may discover that there is a good deal of underlying concern and commitment.

REFERENCES

Argyle, M. and Henderson, M. (1985) *The Anatomy of Relationships*. Harmondsworth: Penguin.

Bergman, J. A., O'Malley, H. and Segars, H. (1980) Legal research and services for the elderly. In: *Select Committee on Aging, Elder Abuse: The Hidden Problems*. Washington, DC: US Government Printing Office.

Bornstein, P. H. and Bornstein, M. T. (1985) *Marital Therapy: A Behavioral-Communications Approach*. New York: Pergamon Press.

Cooper, C. R. and Ayers-Lopez, S. (1985) Family and peer systems in early adolescence: new models of the role of relationships in development. *Journal of Early Adolescence*, **5**, 9–21.

Cornell-Pedrick, C. P. and Gelles, R. J. (1982) Adolescent to parent violence. *Urban and Social Change Review*, **15**, 8–14.

Dobash, R. E. and Dobash, R. (1979) *Violence against Wives*. New York: Free Press.

Epstein, N. and Eidelson, R. J. (1981) Unrealistic beliefs of clinical couples: their relationship to expectations, goals and satisfaction. *American Journal of Family Therapy*, **9**, 13–22.

Fincham, F. D. and Bradbury, T. N. (1987) The impact of attributions in marriage: a longitudinal analysis. *Journal of Personality and Social Psychology*, **53**, 510–517.

Fincham, F. D., Beach, S. and Baucom, D. (1987) Attribution processes in distressed and non-distressed couples: 4. Self–partner attribution differences. *Journal of Personality and Social Psychology*, **52**, 739–748.

Frude, N. J. (1980) Child abuse as aggression. In N. Frude (ed.), *Psychological Approaches to Child Abuse*. London: Batsford.

Frude, N. J. (1989) The physical abuse of children. In: K. Howells and C. Hollin (eds.), *Clinical Approaches to Violence*. Chichester: Wiley.

Gelles, R. J. (1987) *The Violent Home: Updated Edition*. Beverly Hills, CA: Sage.

Gottman, G. M., Notarius, C., Gonso, J. and Markman, H. (1976) *A Couple's Guide to Communication*. Champaign, IL: Research Press.

Jacobson, N. S. (1981) Behavioural marital therapy. In: A. S. Gurman and D. P. Kniskern (eds.), *Handbook of Family Therapy*. New York: Brunner/Mazel.

Jacobson, N. S., McDonald, D. W., Follete, W. C. and Berley, R. A. (1985) Attributional processes in distressed and non-distressed married couples. *Cognitive Therapy and Research*, **9**, 35–50.

Jessop, D. J. (1981) Family relationships as viewed by parents and adolescents: a specification. *Journal of Marriage and the Family*, **43**, 95–107.

Nye, F. I. and McLaughlin, S. (1982) Role competence and marital satisfaction. In: F. I. Nye (ed.), *Family Relationships: Rewards and Costs*. Beverly Hills, CA: Sage.

Olson, D. H., McCubbin, H. I., Barnes, H. L., Larsen, A. S., Muxen, M. J. and Wilson, M. A. (1983) *Families: What Makes them Work?* Beverly Hills, CA: Sage.

Patterson, G. R., Hops, H. and Weiss, E. L. (1975) Interpersonal skills training for couples in early stages of conflict. *Journal of Marriage and the Family*, **37**, 295–302.

Pillemer, K. (1988) Maltreatment of patients in nursing homes: overview and research agenda. *Journal of Health and Social Behaviour*, **29**, 227–238.

Pillemer, K. and Suitor, J. J. (1988) Elder abuse. In: V. B. Van Hasselt, R. L. Morrison, A. S. Bellack and M. Hersen (eds.), *Handbook of Family Violence*. New York: Plenum.

Renvoize (1978) *Violence in Families*. London: Routledge and Kegan Paul.

Steinmetz, S. K. (1984) Family violence towards elders. In: S. Saunders, A. Anderson, C. Hart and G. Rubenstein (eds.), *Violent Individuals and Families: A Handbook for Practitioners*. Springfield, IL: Charles C. Thomas.

Straus, M. A., Gelles, R. J. and Steinmetz, S. K. (1980) *Behind Closed Doors: Violence in American Families*. New York: Doubleday.

Walker, J. C. (1985) Protective services for the elderly. In: J. J. Kosberg (ed.), *Abuse and Maltreatment of the Elderly: Causes and Interventions*. Littleton, MA: John Wright PSG.

Wolf, R., Strugnell, C. and Godkin, M. (1982) *Preliminary Findings from Three Model Projects on Elderly Abuse*. Worcester, MA: University of Massachusetts Medical Center.

Zdorkowski, R. T. and Galbraith, M. W. (1985) An inductive approach to the investigation of elder abuse. *Ageing and Society*, **5**, 413–429.

6
Physical Child Abuse

CHILD ABUSE

The term 'child abuse' covers several different forms of maltreatment. At least four types are commonly distinguished—physical (or 'injurious') abuse, sexual abuse, neglect, and emotional abuse. Although some people, including a number of professionals who deal with problem families, make little distinction between these various types of maltreatment, they *are* different in many respects and it is appropriate to regard them as distinct problems requiring different forms of intervention. Although two or more forms of abuse are sometimes directed at a particular child, this is by no means always the case.

Child sexual abuse differs from physical child abuse in many ways. The two forms of abuse differ in terms of the gender of the children and the perpetrators, the age of the victims, and the social and educational level of the parents. Thus statistics on the type of maltreatment and the age of the child involved, based on over a third of a million children (American Association for Protecting Children, 1985) show that sexual maltreatment is more likely in the older age range (12 to 17 years) whereas physical maltreatment (and especially cases of major attack and injury) are more likely in the youngest age range (from birth to five years). More crucially, the nature and causes of the two problems are quite different and they have different effects on the victims (Frude, 1980, 1985). Only a minority of sexually abused children are also physically abused, and although a high proportion of sexual abuse is intra-familial, many perpetrators of sexual abuse are not related to the victim. In contrast, it is very rare indeed for a child to be physically abused by an adult who is not in a caretaking role. Thus a number of strong arguments can be made for distinguishing between sexual abuse and physical abuse (Bousha and Twentyman, 1984; Herrenkohl, Herrenkohl and Egolf, 1983).

Similarly, there are a number of reasons for distinguishing physical abuse from emotional abuse, and from neglect. For example, Herzeberger, Potts and Dillon (1981) found that although emotional abuse (including emotional neglect and name-calling) was sometimes associated with physical abuse, a substantial number of physically abused children did not appear to have been emotionally abused. The authors therefore suggest (along with Kinard, 1979, and others) that physical and emotional abuse should be regarded as two distinct phenomena. Finally, physical abuse should be distinguished from neglect. Bauer and Twentyman (1985) are among those who have found highly significant differences between physically abusive and neglecting parents, and they argue, along with others (e.g. Bousha and Twentyman, 1984; Larrance *et al.*, 1982) that neglecting parents are a definite subgroup, with behavioural and cognitive patterns that differentiate them from aggressively abusing parents. Most physically abused children are not neglected, and most neglected children are not subjected to serious physical abuse. Since the causes and effects of the different forms of child abuse seem to be different, and since the interventions that will be appropriate differ in several important respects, there are very good reasons for considering each problem separately. This chapter will be concerned only with physical child abuse.

DEFINITION AND INCIDENCE

It is difficult to gauge the incidence of physical abuse. Estimates vary enormously, reflecting the source of the data used and, most importantly, the criteria used to define 'a case'. Thus if estimates are based on children who receive medical attention for injuries known to have been inflicted by a parent or other caregiver they will certainly be too low, for it is clear that only a proportion of the children injured in this way will be presented for treatment. We do not know what proportion this is, but since cases identified by emergency medical services are likely to be particularly serious, and most injuries caused by parents will be less serious, it is reasonable to assume that the proportion of injuries receiving medical treatment (and known to have been inflicted as a result of a parental assault) is low. Using this criterion, an annual incidence figure would certainly be well under 1%.

The two major problems with this approach to estimating incidence are the 'diagnostic problem' (not all cases of child injury by a parent will be identified) and the 'definitional problem'. The definitional issue raises the questions: 'what constitutes injury?' and 'is the infliction of injury a necessary condition of abuse having taken place?' The first of these questions concerns whether a minor bruise, for example, constitutes injury. This question is important because the most common physical consequence of parental attack on a child is likely to be a minor bruise. The second question is also crucial. In most cases in which an enraged parent assaults a child, injury will be avoided (often by luck, and sometimes by design). Are only cases resulting in injury to be included in 'child abuse' estimates, or all parental assaults (and if so, what constitutes an 'assault', as against an 'appropriate' administration of punishment)? If all occasions of the use of porporal punishment are characterized as assaults, for example, then the annual incidence appears to be over 60% (Straus and Gelles, 1986). Indeed, Gelles (1979) pointed out that physical methods of discipline are used in most homes and that the average child is subjected to literally thousands of hits during the period of development. The question is whether all of the children disciplined in this way should be regarded as 'abused'.

There are no right and wrong answers to these definitional questions. It is for the person who makes the estimate to choose a definition that they consider to be 'appropriate'. But it is essential to realize that the definition used (and thus the criteria used to identify a 'case') will have profound effects on the estimate given. The point is well illustrated by the work of those who carried out national surveys in the United States in 1975 and 1985 (Straus, Gelles and Steinmetz, 1980; Straus and Gelles, 1986). The total number of families who participated in these studies was over 5000. In the 1975 survey, using a 'lenient' set of criteria (so that slapping and spanking were included as 'acts of minor violence'), 63% of the respondents who had at least one child between the ages of three and 17 living at home reported one or more violent episodes during the survey year. Using a stricter set of criteria (in which pushing, grabbing, slapping and spanking were excluded) the figure for 'acts of severe violence' was 14%. And when even more restricted criteria were used (so that only kicking, bitting, hitting with a fist, beating up, and threatening with or using a knife or a gun were included) then the figure dropped to 3.6%. The authors decided to count only cases that met the strictest of these sets of criteria as cases of 'child abuse' (following the above discussion on the different types of child abuse, it should be noted that they were concerned only with 'physical abuse'—not with sexual abuse, emotional abuse or neglect). It must be remembered that these figures represent an *annual* incidence; the proportion of children subjected to abuse at some time in their early lives would obviously be somewhat higher.

In the follow-up survey, 10 years later, the researchers used the same sets of criteria. Although there was little change in the number of cases of 'overall violence', there was a significant drop in 'severe violence' (from 14% to 10.7%) and a massive 47% drop (from 3.6% to 1.9%) in 'very severe violence' (i.e. by the authors' criteria, 'child abuse'). According to Straus and Gelles (1986) this drop reflects the success of the considerable growth in public awareness, education, services and intervention programmes. It is unfortunate that national surveys of the size and sophistication of those conducted by Murray Straus and his team have not been carried out in other countries.

DEMOGRAPHIC PATTERNS

The overall picture to emerge from studies that have examined the gender of the victims and perpetrators of physical child abuse is that roughly equal numbers of boys and girls are victims of attacks made by a parent or caregiver (a 'caregiver' who is not related to the child is most likely to be the mother's or father's cohabitee) and that the attacker is equally likely to be a man or a woman. This pattern is strikingly different from that found for sexual abuse, in which many more victims are female and the vast majority of perpetrators are male. The finding that men and women are equally likely to attack a child is somewhat at odds with the very strong tendency for perpetrators of most other forms of physical violence to be male, but the effect of a higher general aggressiveness may be balanced by the fact that mothers usually spend much more time with children and are usually more involved in their care. Having noted that equal numbers of men and women abuse their children, it needs to be acknowledged that most of the studies of abusive parents (including most of those reviewed in this chapter) have been conducted using only women subjects. The main reasons for this are probably that women are more often available for studies that are carried out during the day, and that they may be less reluctant to take part in studies relating to child abuse, but it is nevertheless regrettable and obviously raises a question concerning the applicability of the findings to male abusers.

The age of the child is also an important predictor of abuse risk. Babies and young children are much more likely to be injured by their parents than are older children (hence the term 'baby battering' used by the popular press). Undoubtedly part of the reason for this is that the very young are physically more vulnerable. It takes much less force to injure a baby than to injure a 10-year-old. But part of the explanation may also relate to the fact that babies are very demanding and need continuous care. They cry a lot, the reason for their crying is not always easy to judge, and it is impossible to 'reason' with them or to cajole, beg, or threaten in order to get them to comply. The age of the parent is also a relevant factor. It has been found repeatedly that very young parents (and especially those still in their teens) are especially likely to abuse (Creighton, 1988). The main reasons normally given for this are that the pregnancy is likely to have been unwanted, and that young parents are often poor, unprepared for parenthood, immature and lacking confidence regarding the treatment of the baby, and that they may resent the many restrictions imposed by the child's presence.

A cluster of variables relating to social status, including social class, living conditions, financial security, employment status and educational level, have also been shown to be associated with family violence. Those of lower social class, and those who are poor, badly housed, unemployed and have had relatively little education are at considerably higher risk of abusing their children. Although doubts have been raised about whether this pattern simply reflects a bias in identifying or reporting cases, it is now generally agreed that even allowing for the distortions generated by such effects there are real associations between the risk of physical abuse and these social indicators.

There are a number of possible reasons for these associations. Steinmetz (1987) suggests that those of lower social status may have fewer verbal resources to call upon when attempting to deal with conflict and stress, but it is also likely that parents who are disadvantaged will experience more stressors (including those generated by poverty, unemployment, and overcrowding) and will lack resources that other parents may use to help relieve some of the burden of childcare (for example, nurseries and baby-sitters). It is also likely that part of the association with social class and with educational level can be explained by reference to different attitudes to children, to parenting, and to discipline, that are found among the different groups (Newson and Newson, 1980). Single mothers are also at greatly increased risk of abusing their infants (Sack, Mason and Higgins, 1985). This may be because they often face considerable economic hardship and many are young. In addition, the single mother may have no intimate to confide in or to turn to for help, and may be isolated from neighbours and relatives.

To examine the causes of child abuse a particular model will be employed. This suggests that certain demographic factors are associated with an increased risk of child abuse because of particular effects that they have on the individual who carries out the attack. Thus social class, for example, is seen as a distal causal factor, and its effect is explained by the stress it produces for the individual and the effects it has (by various indirect routes) on an individual's attitudes, perceptions and behavioural patterns. A person categorized as being of 'lower socio-economic status' may have been raised in a poor family in which certain 'pro-aggressive' attitudes were taught, may be in regular contact with people who hold such views, and may have had relatively little exposure to people who hold different opinions, or to magazine articles and television programmes that challenge their beliefs about how children should be raised. In such circumstances the person *may* subscribe to authoritarian views, and if this is the case it *may* affect how he or she treats children and *may* therefore increase the risk of a child being abused.

Thus the distal variable, social class, can be translated into a proximal variable, a parental attitude, that would help to explain why a particular child is injured. An examination of tens or hundreds of such cases would then disclose a general relationship between social class and child abuse, although this alone would not tell us *why* social class was related to abuse. Needless to say, there are numerous possible pathways such as that outlined in the above example. The relationship between the more distant variable (in this case, social class) and more proximal variables (such as parental attitudes to punishment) must always be seen in probabilistic terms. We lose precision in our explanation by 'moving out' to variables such as 'isolation' and 'educational level' and we gain precision and explanatory power by moving in closer to examine the immediate psychological precursors of an attack. But we can see from the example given that to give an account of abuse in terms of proximal causes (for example, in terms of the parent's perception of the child's behaviour, and the emotional response to this perception) is not to deny the relevance of more distal factors such as educational level or social class.

Two other general factors that have commonly been found to be related to the risk of child abuse are marital instability and social isolation. The level of marital conflict in abusing families is often high (Wolfe, 1985) and abusive parents often fail to develop supportive social networks. They are less involved in their neighbourhood, and have fewer friends with whom they keep in regular contact (Garbarino, 1977; Burgess, 1985; Salzinger, Kaplan and Artemyeff, 1983). On the other hand, although it has been supposed that the abuse of alcohol and other drugs may be strongly related to abuse, the evidence suggests that the effect played by these may be rather minor (Steinmetz, 1987). Similarly, the role played by mental illness appears to be relatively small. Although one popular view of those who assault their children is that 'they must be mentally unstable', research has consistently failed to identify a psychopathology of abusers. The evidence suggests that child abusers are no more and no less likely to be mentally ill or psychologically disturbed than other parents. However, as the review that follows clearly shows, comparisons between groups of abusing and non-abusing parents do reveal many differences in emotional, cognitive, and behavioural variables, and most of these differences are directly relevant to how the parent relates to the child.

AN EXPLANATION OF CHILD ABUSE—AN OVERVIEW

The explanation of child abuse to be presented in this chapter will follow the interactional approach (the distinction between this and the cultural approach was discussed in Chapter 5). The major premise is that physical abuse is best understood as a form of aggression, a hostile attack made by an angry parent who has been intensely annoyed by some action of the child victim. The child's behaviour instigates a high degree of parental anger so that, in the absence of effective inhibitions against attacking the child, an assault will occur. The model is essentially very simple, although the elaborations are somewhat complex. Although the model emphasizes the proximal causes of the attack, these are clearly linked to more distal variables such as the parent's general attitude to the child, the quality of the marital relationship, and the various cultural and demographic factors outlined above. The part played by such factors, however, will be explained in terms of the effect that they have on the parents as individuals. The model presented here is an elaboration of an earlier version (Frude, 1980).

Because the explanation given is essentially interactional, we will be considering not only the parent's role in the abuse, but also the role the victim plays in the events leading up to an attack. This does not mean, of course, that children are held to be responsible for the injuries that they suffer, but it will become clear that a consideration of the child's behaviour (and, especially, of the *interaction* between the parent and the child) is essential if we are to gain a reasonable understanding of physical child abuse. Although chance plays some part in determining whether a child is injured, it is clear that the probability of injury will be greatly increased if harsh aggression is frequently directed towards the child. The risk of serious injury will also be related to the particular form that such attacks normally take. If the parent habitually punches the child, for example, then the risk that serious injury will occur on one or more occasions will be much greater than if a typical attack involves only slaps.

The probability that the parent will engage in 'customary high-level aggression' against the child can be shown to be related to factors in the parent's background and personality, to aspects of the child's behaviour, and to the history of parent–child interactions during previous disciplinary encounters. If the parent finds it difficult to control the child's behaviour then serious disciplinary confrontations involving intense anger are likely to be frequent. Such anger is likely to lead to the use of harsh forms of discipline, and the more often that hostile episodes occur the more aggressive and assaultive the parent is likely to become.

To provide a more complete explanation we need to account for why discipline becomes so 'out-of-control' in some families and not in others. To answer this question we need to make reference both to the parent's attitudes, beliefs and behaviours and also to the child's behaviour, particularly in response to the disciplinary actions. Frequent and harsh discipline is more likely to be used if the child often engages in serious 'bad behaviour', and especially if this includes aggression and non-compliance. But it will also develop if the parent is critical, has a strong tendency to blame the child, and lacks effective child-management skills. Similarly, to answer the question of *why* certain children are judged to behave badly, we need to consider the general quality of the relationship between the parent and the child. If the child is unloved and unloving then a distant and mutually antagonistic relationship can develop (although if the child is very young it is not appropriate to speak of '*mutual* antagonism').

Thus, in summary, certain aspects of the parent–child relationship are likely to lead to disciplinary problems. Frequent and badly handled disciplinary encounters are likely to escalate in seriousness and may lead to the customary use of dangerous forms of aggression, and if this happens then on one or more occasions such aggression is likely to lead to the child being injured.

ARE ABUSIVE PARENTS AND ABUSED CHILDREN 'ABNORMAL'?

Studies comparing abusing and non-abusing parents, abused and non-abused children, and parent–child relationships in abusive and non-abusive families have identified an impressive array of differences between the groups. Before reviewing some of the findings, however, we need to consider what such results imply. Characteristics identified as differentiating abusive (or 'at risk for abuse') from non-abusive *groups* will rarely be found in *all* of the abusing families and *none* of the non-abusing families. And none of the abusing parents or abused children are likely to have *all* of the 'risk characteristics' reported. An unfortunate effect of reporting group differences is that this tends to reinforce the notion that all abusive families conform to a special 'type', and that they are qualitatively different from 'normal' families. We should guard against thinking of abusive parents or their children as 'a breed apart' (Main and Goldwyn, 1984). They differ from other families only in some respects, and these differences are quantitative rather than qualitative.

Thus we do not need to create a battery of unfamiliar psychological principles to explain why abuse occurs. Abusing parents are angered by their children for much the same reasons that most other parents are angered by their children, and abusive aggression can be seen as a more extreme form of the aggression that many parents direct towards their offspring. Belsky (1988) suggests that: 'child abuse and neglect should not be regarded as distinct entities but rather as cases of parenting gone awry which are lawfully related to relationship processes in nondysfunctional families', and Straus (1983) emphasized that the same factors are involved in child abuse and 'ordinary physical punishment'. Thus all families may be seen as ranged along a continuum of abuse risk. Since the associations between abuse and various parent and child attributes, although significant, are often rather small, they will be of limited value in identifying potentially abusive families. Only a minority of the parents who are found to have many high-risk attributes will ever severely injure a child, and a few of those who lack most of the risk characteristics *will* engage in serious abusive behaviour.

Finally, it should be remembered that characteristics found to differentiate between groups of abusive and non-abusive families are merely *associated* with abuse. The fact that they are 'risk factors' does not mean that they are necessarily 'causes', and it is often impossible to say whether the correlation does represent a causal relationship. The association between abuse and a particular child- or parent-variable may not reflect a direct causal link. Thus if prematurity is identified as a risk factor, for example, the association might reflect the fact that both prematurity and child abuse are correlated with social class, and might not reflect a direct causal link between prematurity and abuse. In many cases, also, an association may be as well explained by suggesting that the attribute has developed as a *result* of abusive, 'quasi-abusive' or 'pre-abusive' actions as to suggest that the characteristic or interactional style has caused the abuse.

The difficulties involved in disentangling causes and effects are even greater than the discussion so far suggests, because an effect of one abusive episode may contribute to the onset of subsequent abusive acts. The relationship that develops between the parent and child emerges in a highly dynamic and interactive way, with each individual constantly changing in response to the other's behaviour. Thus the parenting style of any parent will reflect their experience of the individual child, and the child's behaviour will reflect the parent's actions. The account of physical child abuse to be presented here reflects this mutual contingency. Nevertheless it is useful to consider the contributory factors by distinguishing between 'parent variables', 'child variables' and 'interactional variables'. An abusing parent's style of parenting, for example, will not have developed solely in response to the particular child, but will also reflect the parent's own background, established attitudes and marital history, etc. (Belsky, 1988).

PARENT CHARACTERISTICS

Among the parent characteristics found to be associated with child abuse are low levels of warmth and positive responding to the child, the infrequent use of positive responses, a negative bias in judging the child, and a lack of empathy. In addition, parents often find many of the child's behaviours particularly aversive. They tend to have very low criteria for judging that a behaviour is 'bad' or 'naughty', they may have unrealistic standards regarding children's behaviour, and they often attribute a child's annoying behaviours to internal factors such as the child's personality, or defiance, and make few allowances for situational circumstances (such as the child's excitement at the time, or accidental factors).

Both interview studies with parents and observational studies reveal that the general atmosphere in abusive families is often seriously lacking in warmth. Those who have observed abusive and non-abusive parents in interaction with their children (and who are not aware of which families are abusive) judge that abusive parents derive little enjoyment from such contact (Reid, 1983), that they give the child little positive attention or affection (for example, they rarely look at or touch the child), and that they seldom give praise for good behaviour. The responses that these parents do make are often negative and inappropriate. They tend to make more complaints and issue more threats than non-abusive parents, and they express more dislikes about their child (Burgess and Conger, 1978). In their attempts to control the behaviour they seem to take little account of the child's own wishes and feelings and often ignore initiatives. Instead they tend to bombard the child with questions, demands and orders (Fontana and Robison, 1984). Hyman, Parr and Browne (1979) reported that abusive parents had an 'intrusive' style of interaction with their children, and Crittenden and Bonvillian (1984) found that abusive mothers were often extremely insensitive to their children's cues. They reported that such mothers frequently provided inappropriate stimulation, for example by interfering when the child was playing happily.

One reason why abusive parents fail to respond positively to the child may be a lack of empathy or insight into the child's feelings (Letourneau, 1981), but abusive parents frequently also have a pronounced bias against the child (Mash, Johnson and Kovitz, 1983). It has been found, for example, that abusive parents attribute negative characteristics to their children even when there is no valid basis for such judgements (Larrance and Twentyman, 1983; Richman, Stevenson, and Graham, 1982). Thus it is likely that many of the child's actions will be disapproved of, and that some will prove especially aversive to the parent. Dale *et al.* (1986) noted that: 'In child-abusing families, children's *normal* patterns of eating (including experiments with self-assertion through food refusal) provoke disproportionately intense negative reactions in parents'. Studies have shown that abusing parents tend to become physiologically aroused and report feeling stressed when viewing videotapes of even quite innocuous child and infant behaviour (Disbrow, Doerr and Caulfield, 1977; Frodi and Lamb, 1980; Wolfe *et al.*, 1983). Abusive parents frequently dislike all children, but they often dislike their own children more than most, and the child who is abused is generally seen in a more negative light than other children in the family (Herrenkohl and Herrenkohl, 1979).

Bauer and Twentyman (1985) compared groups of abusive, neglecting and control mothers on an experimental task. The mothers were asked to picture a situation with their own child while they listened to an audiotape that included a description of a parent–child interaction. Each description was followed by a one-minute recording of a young child crying. The episodes described included one in which a child was hurt, one in which a child was angry with the parent, and another in which a child did something that was forbidden. Two additional tapes provided descriptions of stressful situations not involving a child, and each of these was followed by one minute of the sound of a fire alarm or of car horns honking. The mothers were asked to rate their level of annoyance during each tape presentation and the analysis of these ratings revealed that abusive mothers experienced more annoyance than those in either of the other two groups. It is particularly interesting that this difference was also found for the non–child situations, suggesting that abusive mothers may have a low irritation threshold that applies across a broad range of conditions.

Most parents find it relatively easy to distinguish between 'good' and 'bad' behaviour by a child, but many abusive parents seem to have great difficulty in making this distinction. In one study (Wood-Shuman and Cone, 1986) in which abusive, at-risk and control mothers were asked to rate videotapes of children behaving in various ways (e.g. playing quietly, or refusing to go to bed), it was found that abusive mothers were 'blame-oriented' and tended to rate even innocuous behaviours as blameworthy. The authors suggested that because a number of the abusers had themselves been ill-treated as children they might have learned to classify a wide range of behaviours as 'bad'. Furthermore, parents who are relatively isolated will have little opportunity to learn from other parents that their judgements are unusually demanding and harsh. One of the consequences of labelling many behaviours as 'bad' is that a great many situations will be judged as calling for disciplinary intervention (Wolfe *et al.*, 1983).

The tendency to categorize many of the child's actions as bad may reflect the parents' inappropriately high standards and their unrealistic judgements of how children of a particular age normally behave. Thus a parent who believes that young children should be tidy, careful, and never disobedient will judge their own child's normal behaviour as problematic and naughty (Rosenberg and Repucci, 1983; Twentyman and Plotkin, 1982). Azar *et al.* (1984) found that abusive parents frequently had highly unrealistic expectations of children. Thus they often agreed with such statements as: 'There is nothing wrong with punishing a 9-month-old for crying too much' and 'Most often a 3-year-old will know how to play quietly for long periods of time when his or her mother is not feeling too well.' The way in which parents interpret 'bad' behaviour (for example, why it happened, and whether the child was being *deliberately* naughty) is also very important in determining their emotional response. In the study by Bauer and Twentyman (1985), described above, mothers were asked to indicate, after each of the child-related stories, whether they thought that the child had acted deliberately to annoy the mother. It was found that, overall, the abusive mothers were much more inclined to judge that there had been a deliberate intention to annoy. Similarly, Golub (1984) found that abusive mothers were more likely to see misbehaviour as intentional, defiant, and as the result of the child's personality, rather than as caused by accidental and unstable factors. Abusive parents may even interpret a young baby's crying in negative ways, as a sign of defiance, greed, or stubbornness, long before such judgements can realistically be applied to an infant's psychological state (Steele, 1970; Call, 1984).

It is not difficult to understand how each of the parent characteristics reviewed here may contribute to the risk to the child. They all predispose the parent to become angered by the child's behaviour, or increase the likelihood of a disciplinary response. If normal, innocuous, and age-appropriate behaviours prove aversive, and are judged to be deviant or regressive, then these benign behaviours, as well as acts that other parents would also judge to be naughty, will cause annoyance and provoke a disciplinary response. And if discipline is frequent it is likely to lose its effect, so that it may escalate in severity over time. In addition, the overall atmosphere in the potentially abusive relationship appears to be fraught and joyless, and thus does not foster the goodwill that helps many parents to cope with their child during times of special provocation.

The view that the parenting behaviour of most people who abuse a child is not qualitatively different from that of other parents suggests that studies of the influences on 'normal' parenting behaviour may help us to understand why things sometimes go disastrously wrong. In their extensive review of the factors that are known to affect parenting, Belsky and Vondra (1987) suggest that parental behaviour is determined by three principal sources of influence— the parent's psychological well-being, the child's unique characteristics, and contextual sources of stress and support. It is clear that a parent who is under considerable stress and is experiencing psychological problems is likely to be preoccupied with their own difficulties and may be functioning generally at a low level of effectiveness. They are therefore likely to face special hardship in coping with the demands of parenting. Patterson (1982) showed, for example, that depression and other emotional problems decreased parents' ability to handle discipline problems effectively.

The social context also affects parenting. In a study of the mothers of four-month-old infants, Crnic et al. (1983) found that intimate support from the husband, and the mother's attitude to this support, had a highly significant effect on her attitude to parenting, and that support from other relatives and from friends also provided important benefits. Reviewing the literature on the relationship between social support and child maltreatment, Seagull (1987) concluded that the quality of the support was more important than the amount of support. In his overview, Belsky (1988) noted a consistent finding that those in happier marriages, and those with a supportive network of family and friends, are less punitive and more nurturant towards their children. In addition to the degree and quality of current social provisions, a person's childhood history is also relevant to how well they cope as parents. Belsky and Isabella (1985) found that adjustment to parenthood was significantly related to both husbands' and wives' reports of aspects of their own childhood, and Main and Weston (1982) found that if a mother had been rejected by her own mother in childhood she was likely to reject her infant. There is of course a well-documented link between a parent's history of having been abused in childhood and the risk that they will abuse their own children (Egeland, 1988). Thus the parent's current level of psychological functioning, current relationships, and previous life history, all influence parenting style, and this is no less true of abusive parents than of others.

CHILD CHARACTERISTICS

Although it is clear that abusive parents tend to have negative judgements of their children, we cannot simply assume that the children's behaviour is no more problematic than the behaviour of other children of the same age. We have to allow the possibility that abused and 'at-risk' children are 'objectively' less appealing, that they *are* naughtier, and that aspects of their behaviour *are* more aversive. The evidence indicates that many abused children do behave in a disturbed and disturbing way. The fact that some or all of the disturbance may be the result of a history of parental mishandling and abuse must be acknowledged, but the point is only of limited relevance. Whatever the origin of the disturbance, in the 'here and now' it is likely to prove annoying to the parent, and may thus trigger an incident that results in an aggressive attack on the child.

The characteristics shown to differentiate between groups of abused and non-abused children include developmental difficulties and delays (including those resulting from handicap), a number of behavioural symptoms, and high levels of aggression. Thus babies who are awkward, 'floppy', or socially unresponsive, those who cry more than the average baby, and those who are particularly difficult to soothe, would seem especially likely to attract parental wrath (Heinicke, 1984). Prematurity and low birth weight are also related to abuse (Martin et al., 1974; Browne and Saqi, 1988), possibly because such babies are likely to cry in ways that their parents find particularly annoying. Frodi et al. (1978) showed that people feel less sympathy for videotaped presentations of crying premature babies than they did for full-term babies, and that the cries were judged to be more aversive. The fact that such babies also tend to be less responsive and are frequently more difficult to care for (Goldberg, 1978) may also help to account for their increased risk of maltreatment. At-risk infants have a tendency to be less healthy than other children, and have more illnesses in the first year of life (Lynch, 1975; Martin, 1979); they often have poor muscle tone and may be slow to acquire such skills as crawling, walking, and self-feeding (Oates et al., 1979; Schilling and Schinke, 1984).

A relatively high number of older abused children are enuretic and have frequent tantrums. Many are also non-conforming, show 'oppositional behaviour', and are low in compliance (Martin and Beezley, 1977; Kinard, 1980; Bousha and Twentyman, 1984). It has also been shown that these children often have a very low tolerance for situations in which they cannot get their own way (Herrenkohl and Herrenkohl, 1981). On the other hand, Crittenden (1988) has observed that some abused children become excessively compliant, and use total conformity as a strategy for avoiding parental anger and consequent maltreatment. In addition, many are socially anxious, having a tendency to isolate themselves from other people, and some show an aversive and unsympathetic response to the distress of others (Perry and Doran, 1983; Main and Goldwyn, 1984). A lack of empathy towards other children and adults has been noted both in observational studies and in more structured tests of empathy (Straker and Jacobson, 1981).

The child who is mentally or physically handicapped is at relatively high risk (Starr et al., 1984; Morgan, 1987; White et al., 1987). In considering the relationship between physical child abuse and mental retardation, however, it is particularly difficult to disentangle cause and effect (Sandgrund, Gaines and Green, 1983; Jaudes and Diamond, 1987). In some cases it is highly probable that assaults on the child have contributed to the retardation, particularly where direct blows have been administered to the child's head. On the other hand, a child who is handicapped (whether congenitally or as a result of abuse) is likely to be at special risk of parental maltreatment for a number of reasons. The child may be less competent than other children because of the handicap, and if due allowance for the condition is not made then the child will be judged more frequently as 'failing' and as 'not trying'. Some aspects of the handicapped child's appearance and behaviour (including gait, attempts at self-feeding, and 'stereotyped behaviours') are likely to prove especially irritating. Furthermore the costs of caring, in terms of effort, time, and money, will be higher than for other children, and the 'returns' in terms of the child's achievements, and the pride that the parent can take in the child, will be less. As shown in Chapter 4, most parents of handicapped children soon make adjustments in their expectations, the demands they make, and the costs they anticipate in caring for the child. But whereas the majority of parents are able to accommodate to the child's special difficulties, it is not difficult to understand why those who do not are at a relatively high risk of abusing their disabled child.

One of the strongest and most frequently reported characteristics of abused (and 'at risk of abuse') children is their high level of aggression. Thus they tend to fight more with siblings (Burgess and Conger, 1977; Straus, 1983), they often show aggression at school (Sroufe, 1983), and in home- and clinic-based observational studies they have been found to exhibit high levels of aggression towards their parents (Patterson, 1982; Main and Goldwyn, 1984; Reid, 1986). Reid, Taplin and Lorber (1981) reported that many vulnerable children frequently display both very aversive behaviours (including hitting others, and issuing verbal threats) and 'mildly obnoxious' behaviours such as whining and teasing. George and Main (1979) concluded from their study that abused children often 'harass' their peers and their parents. During the experimental observation period, battered children were seen to harass their caregivers eight times as frequently as non-abused children, and they were also found to be highly avoidant of friendly gestures made by parents and peers. When a peer became distressed, the abused children failed to show the usual concern or sadness. They tended to respond instead with fear or anger, and in some cases they actually hit the child who was distressed.

It is important to remember that the characteristics reported in these studies have been found in experimental or observational studies of the children themselves, and are not based on parents' reports. Thus, according to objective criteria, these children are often different from other children in a number of respects, and in ways that are likely to make them less attractive and 'lovable', more annoying to their parents, and more difficult to control. Belsky and Vondra (1987) suggest that: 'Certain children ... in and of themselves are at greater risk of maltreatment by their parents.' The fact that many of these characteristics may be the result of previous maltreatment is not directly relevant for an explanation of how abuse incidents arise. In attempting to explain the parent's 'here and now' response to the difficult, annoying, or aggressive child, the actual cause of the child's behaviour is much less important than how the parent understands that behaviour (and abusive parents, as we have seen, are not likely to 'excuse' problematic behaviour by holding themselves responsible for it).

PARENT–CHILD INTERACTION

The Parent–Child Relationship

Child abuse is not something that often occurs in the context of a 'good' parent–child relationship; the relationships between abusing parents and their children are often chronically and seriously disturbed. The problems that we have identified as the 'parent contribution' and the 'child contribution' are not independent but are inextricably entwined. Gaensbauer, Mrazek and Harmon (1980) speak of a 'lack of sensitive and contingent reciprocity between mother and infant'. Both parent and child bring to the relationship their own characteristics (in the case of the parent, reflecting constitution, past experience and current circumstances; in the case of the child, reflecting just innate constitution), but from the moment of birth there is a mutual influence and a high level of interdependence.

Main and Weston (1982) found that a mother's rejection of her child was related to the child's response to her following a brief separation in an experimental setting. Children who avoided their mother when she returned to the room tended to have mothers who rejected them. This is a good example of an association that could be interpreted in a number of different ways. An avoidant child might lead the mother to be rejecting, or a rejecting mother might lead the child to develop what Main and Weston describe as a syndrome of avoidance, hostility and lack of feeling for others. But both of these accounts are probably too simplistic, because they fail to acknowledge the continuing interaction between child avoidance and parent rejection. A vicious circle involving avoidance and rejection is likely to develop and, like the proverbial chicken and egg problem, it may be impossible to say 'which came first'. But establishing the root cause of the situation may be less important than recognizing the cycle and trying to break it. Thus if a mother is encouraged to show more acceptance of her child, the child's avoidance might decrease, and this is likely to encourage further maternal acceptance, etc., so that the vicious cycle may be replaced by a 'virtuous' counterpart.

The Instigation of Anger

Children who are 'at risk' or have been abused often present their parents with more problems than the average child, but it seems that in many cases there is a multiplicative effect of the child's difficult behaviour *and* the parent's negative perception that together provoke frequent and intense parental anger. In terms of the model outlined in Chapter 5, both the child behaviours and the parental sensitivities and perceptual styles seem tailored to lead to irritation, to provoke high 'cost' evaluations, and to incite judgements of transgression. Given such conditions, the parent is likely to become annoyed and angry very frequently. Thus we have seen that many of these children tend to cry a lot, to whine and tease, and to engage in behaviours that are objectively rated as 'harassing'. Several of the behaviours shown by groups of the vulnerable children are likely to make extra demands on time, effort, and money (and since the parents may be poor, and have few resources to make life easier, these may prove especially 'costly'). Belsky and Vondra (1970) also make the point that extra caretaking demands translate into additional stress on the parents. In addition, many of the behaviours engaged in by these children are clear transgressions. For example, they behave in aggressive ways towards peers, siblings, and parents, and they are often non-compliant.

The model discussed in Chapter 5, however, suggests that it is the impact or judgement of certain actions by other people, rather than the actions themselves, that cause a person to become angry. Studies of abusive parents suggest that their sensitivities and judgement styles are such that they often experience rage in response to a child's behaviour. Some have a very low threshold to a range of irritants, they often exaggerate the 'costs' of their care of the child, and they have a tendency to judge harshly and uncharitably, so that they consider many child actions to be inadequate, incorrect, wicked, or deliberately provocative.

The evidence that many of these parents find many of the child's behaviours especially irritating comes from a number of sources. Even when they are exposed to videotapes of children behaving in innocuous ways they often respond with an aversion that is evident in their physiological responses and in their verbal reports. It has also been suggested that some of the parents who batter very young infants are especially sensitive to the particular sound frequencies emitted by some babies when they cry. There is also another reason why we might expect these parents to be more easily irritated by their children. People are rarely irritated by the actions of those they like and are getting on well with, and are frequently irritated by even very minor behaviours of those whom they detest and reject. The parent–child relationship in many abusive families is hostile, and the parents in such families are often especially sensitive to potentially irritating child behaviours.

The quality of the relationship also influences how people judge the 'costs' arising from their interaction with others. Abusing parents seem prone to exaggerate the costs they incur in child care, and to minimize the benefits. Indeed, they may experience very few benefits, since they seem to derive little pleasure from their interaction with the child. The fact that the child rarely invites or returns affection, and that the parents may have less to feel proud about, is likely to mean that the child will be seen as providing few 'rewards' and that the parents will therefore judge that there are few benefits to offset the costs involved in caring for and controlling the child.

With respect to parental judgements of transgressions, there is ample evidence to suggest that abusive parents apply inappropriately high standards in judging their children's behaviour, that they are 'blame-oriented', and that they attribute many actions to the child's conscious decision to be naughty or defiant. They are therefore likely to register many 'offences'. When they are faced with the child's aggression towards them they are likely to become very angry, especially if they judge this to be a deliberate infringement and a direct challenge to their authority. There is also a tendency of 'behavioural reciprocity'—people tend to respond to hostility with hostility. The child's aggression is likely to be judged as requiring harsh disciplinary intervention, and it may also be seen as justifying a physically aggressive response.

Thus the abused child's behaviour is often problematic, and the abusing parent's perception of the child's behaviour also tends to focus on and exaggerate problem aspects. And there is a general absence of the parent–child warmth that might serve to minimize any adverse emotional and behavioural response to problems experienced with the child's behaviour. In high-risk families the child's difficulties are less likely to generate emotions such as anxiety, depression or guilt, and more likely to generate anger. The nature of the child's special characteristics, and the way that the parent perceives and judges them, conspire to increase the frequency of frustration and rage.

Discipline

The parent and child characteristics found to be relatively common in abusive parent–child relationships will affect not only the frequency and severity of the initial annoyance, but also the course of the disciplinary confrontation that this is likely to trigger. A parent–child relationship in which there is little love, little mutual respect, and little understanding would be expected to create special problems when the parent attempts to control and discipline the child. It is very important to understand the dynamics of these interactions because many serious aggressive and abusive incidents do arise in the context of disciplinary confrontations (Wolfe, 1987). Even before we review the evidence that bears directly on disciplinary encounters in abusive families, the facts about parent and child characteristics described above provide a number of reasons for expecting there to be special difficulties in the context of discipline. It is not surprising, therefore, that disciplinary encounters have been found to be far more frequent in abusive families than in other families (Reid, Taplin and Lorber, 1981) and that they tend to last longer and to escalate in severity.

A major reason for such prolongation and escalation is that abusive parents tend to have poorly developed skills of discipline management. The parents often fail to notice the child's good behaviour, threaten punishment too frequently and too easily, issue ambiguous and inconsistent commands, and fail to positively reinforce compliance when it occurs (Kadushin and Martin, 1981; Reid, Taplin and Lorber, 1981; Herrenkohl, Herrenkohl, and Egolf, 1983; Schindler and Arkowitz, 1986). Another reason why discipline is often ineffective and gets out of hand, however, is that abused children tend to be less responsive to parental attempts at control. They are often non-compliant and little affected by normal disciplinary sanctions (Trickett and Kuczynski, 1986). Indeed, parental responses such as shouting and threatening punishment that are meant to stop the child's behaviour may actually encourage it by providing the attention that would otherwise be lacking. It has been demonstrated many times that, for children who are especially aggressive, parental attempts at discipline may increase the probability of continued and escalating disruption (Patterson, 1982).

There is evidence, too, that abusive parents fail to adjust their punishment to fit the child's 'crime', so that their response is not contingent upon the child's behaviour. Trickett and Kuczynski (1986) analysed 'conflict diaries' that they had asked parents to keep. Whereas the levels of discipline used by non-abusive parents reflected the seriousness of particular misbehaviours, abusive parents reported using more punitive approaches regardless of the type of child misdemeanour.

Parents normally develop their disciplinary skills as they observe how the child responds to various control strategies. In a way, therefore, children train their parents to use disciplinary behaviours that are effective. The fact that abused children are often non-compliant and may be rather erratic in their response to threats and punishments, suggests that they give their parents poor feedback and may thus prevent them from learning effective disciplinary skills. Indeed, such children may respond predictably in the desired way only when the parental action is particularly harsh. Thus it could even be claimed that the behaviour of these children actually trains or encourages the parents to use severe punishment methods (needless to say, this is not to imply that such children are to blame for the attacks made on them). Failure is often frustrating, and failure to control a child who is behaving in an annoying way may cause intense frustration to a parent who is already very angry and lacks confidence about parenting skills. It is not surprising, therefore, that abusive parents tend to experience more anger than other parents during disciplinary encounters (Frodi and Lamb, 1980; Altemeir et al., 1982; Reid, 1983).

If such clashes are very frequent it is likely that the severity of the punishments used will quickly escalate. Evidence of a positive association between frequency and severity comes from observational studies (Reid, 1986) and from parent interview studies (Straus, Gelles and Steinmetz, 1978). There is even confirmatory evidence from reports by victims themselves. Herzeberger, Potts and Dillon (1981) found that children who had not been abused reported an average frequency of spanking of approximately once a week, those who had been bruised on at least one occasion reported a 'normal' spanking rate of a few times a week, and those who had actually been injured as the result of a parental attack reported spankings on a near-daily basis.

For whatever reason, it is clear that many abusive parents do use harsh punishments in the course of their normal disciplining and that they attempt to control the child by relying on the direct assertion of power (Reid, 1978; Patterson, 1982; Oldershaw, Walters and Hall, 1986; Trickett and Kuczynski, 1986). Thus many abusive families show a *customary* high level of physical aggression (Burgess and Conger, 1978; Bousha and Twentyman, 1984; Lahey *et al.*, 1984). Reid (1986) reported that abusive mothers engaged in aversive interchanges with their children over three times as frequently as other mothers, and that their rate of 'quasi-abusive' behaviours during such interchanges was five times that of non-abusive parents. Such constant use of harsh discipline both contributes to and reflects the abusing parent's attitude to child control. These parents often subscribe to the belief that strong disciplinary methods are necessary and justified. 'Spare the rod and spoil the child' is an epithet they often adopt, and in many cases this will reflect their own parents' attitudes when they were children. Parents who were themselves abused as children often use severe methods of discipline (Herrenkohl, Herrenkohl and Toedter, 1983).

THE ABUSIVE INCIDENT

Incidents that result in a child being seriously injured usually begin as disciplinary encounters (Schindler and Arkowitz, 1986; Wolfe, 1987). Parents who normally rely on harsh physical methods of discipline are likely, when they are intensely angry and have lost control, to land a series of blows that threaten the child's safety. On some such occasions, either by chance or by design, the child will be seriously hurt. However, it is not simply a matter of chance whether injury occurs. There are often special circumstances that lead to a particularly devastating assault (Frude, 1980, 1989). Typically the trigger is prolonged crying or screaming, in the case of babies, or, with older children, some act of particular 'naughtiness'. Following a detailed analysis of incidents leading to child injury, Kadushin and Martin (1981) concluded that in every case the sequence of events began with a behaviour by the child that was perceived as aversive by the parent. In their analysis of over 300 families, Herrenkohl, Herrenkohl and Egolf (1983) found similarly that physical abuse was associated with the child's behaviour at the the time. Among the triggers they identified were the child lying, stealing and behaving aggressively. Thomson *et al.* (1971) also maintained that most abusive incidents were 'provoked' by the child, and they provided a list of provoking behaviours that includes crying, wetting, refusing to eat, and stealing. It is clear that the examples supplied by those who have examined such triggers all have at least one of the elements of irritant, cost, and transgression. In his interviews with fathers whose attack had actually led to the death of a child, Scott (1973) also found that in every case the fatal incident had been precipitated by a behaviour that the father had found especially annoying.

An attack does not automatically follow provocation by the child, but depends critically on the psychological response of the attacker. The attacker first appraises, or judges, the child's behaviour. If the appraisal generates extreme anger (cases of children being attacked 'coldly' are very rare indeed), this will lead to a dangerous assault only if the parent lacks effective inhibitions against attacking the child. An analysis of each part of this sequence is necessary to gain an understanding of how abuse incidents arise.

The way in which a situation is judged determines its emotional impact. We know that abusive parents tend to be negative and 'blame-oriented', and case reports of abusive incidents provide many examples of how a particularly negative interpretation of a child's behaviour can lead to a vicious attack (Frude, 1989). In one example a mother reported of her baby: 'He looks at me as if to say "Just you try and feed me"' (Brandon, 1976), and in another a mother explained: 'when he cried all the time, it meant he didn't love me, so I hit him' (Steele and Pollock, 1968). Such extreme negative appraisals would be likely to provoke intense anger in any parent, but those who are abusive also have a tendency to flare up easily (Reid, 1983). Anger often accumulates over successive incidents, and there is evidence that injuries are more likely to occur when the parent has experienced a particularly harrowing day. In some cases the child will have been particularly annoying and uncontrollable, so that a final act that is perceived as defiant or evil will be 'the last straw' and provoke an assaultive outburst. In other cases a high level of ambient anger may have been instigated by events not directly connected with the child. For example, it has been found that fierce arguments between the parents sometimes immediately precede the physical abuse of the child (Straus, 1980; Reid, Taplin and Lorber, 1981). When people are very angry they have a low threshold for annoyance and may take great exception to things that they would not normally notice. It is also possible that a parent who is angry will tend to bring to mind particular thoughts and memories that serve to further fuel the anger (Bower, 1981). Thus, for a number of reasons, when a parent is already in an angry mood it will take very little on the part of the child to generate extreme rage.

Even when a person has been roused to a state of extreme anger, physical aggression is by no means inevitable. Thus if anger is generated by someone in a position of authority or, to take an extreme example, by someone holding a gun, the angry person will not generally attack. Fear of reprisal is not the only source of inhibition. Angry people are often inhibited from open aggression because they believe aggression to be immoral or unsophisticated, or because they do not wish to hurt the victim. Many parents admit that there are times when they have been so angry with the child that they have felt tempted to launch an attack. When asked how they managed to control themselves on such occasions, they report a wide range of cognitive strategies (Frude and Goss, 1979). Most parents, then, have inhibitions and skills that are sufficient to enable them to control their aggression. Abusive parents, however, lack such control. One of the most consistent findings to emerge from studies of abusive parents is that many of them have a general difficulty in controlling aggression (Parke and Collmer, 1975). In part this may reflect their belief that strong discipline (which is how they often regard the abuse) is necessary to prevent the child from becoming uncontrollable. Whereas most parents use self-talk at times of extreme provocation to inhibit their actions, abusive parents may employ covert statements to incite their aggressive behaviour; and whereas most parents are able to refrain from attacking because they empathize with the hurt that the child will feel, abusive parents, as we have seen, often lack such empathy.

Because abusive parents tend to use harsh methods in their routine disciplining they may become desensitized to the intensity of aggressive actions, and this may lower their inhibitions against launching an 'all-out' attack. The escalation from low-level punishments to very harsh punishment is likely to be gradual, and each step might seem rather insignificant. In a series of experiments on obedience (using an 'administration of punishment' paradigm), Milgram (1974) was able to demonstrate that many people will eventually administer very severe punishments if they start from an initial lenient action and if each subsequent step is only slightly more severe than the previous one. In the context of child discipline, such a process of escalation has been reported by Patterson (1982) and others, and some abusing parents have provided first-hand accounts of how the process occurred in their own case (Renvoize, 1978).

Finally, when the parent does attack the child, the precise form of the attack is crucially important. If it involves a very hard slap to the buttocks, for example, there is little danger that serious physical injury will be caused, but if it takes the form of a punch to the head or a pillow held over the face then it may prove very dangerous indeed. The form of aggression used will largely reflect the degree of anger and any specific inhibitions the parent has against the use of particular actions. As the level of anger rises, control will tend to lessen and the attack is likely to take a more dangerous form (Engfer and Schneewind, 1982; Golub, 1984). Slaps will be harder, and there may be a point where the slaps become punches, kicks or bites. There are many ways of hurting a child, and different parents use different methods to inflict pain and injury. The particular form the aggression takes is likely to reflect aspects of the person's childhood experience, the methods of punishment they have evolved during their interactions with the child, and the 'purpose' of the attack. Thus some parents appear to copy the methods that were used to punish them when they were children (Gelles, 1987). Parents also develop *habits* in their normal punishment routines, and these may shape their actions during an all-out attack. Thus a parent who usually chastises the child with a belt or a strap may use this weapon in an unrestrained way during an assault intended to cause very severe hurt or injury.

Other elements that play some part in shaping the action used during an assault have been discussed by Frude (1989). For example, some abusive acts take the form of an exaggerated *instrumental* response. Thus a parent who smothers a screaming child is using an extreme form of an action directed at stifling the child's screams. A child who refuses to eat may be subjected to abuse that takes the form of very aggressive force-feeding. The majority of parents interviewed by Kadushin and Martin (1981) about their abusive attack reported an instrumental intent; they maintained that their action represented an attempt to control some aspect of the child's behaviour. Sometimes the action can be seen as *symbolic*, as when a parent throttles a child who will not eat, or forces caustic liquid into the child's mouth as an 'act of purification' following the utterance of some profanity (this is an exaggerated form of the 'traditional' punishment for such a transgression—washing the child's mouth out with soap).

Some attacks represent an action 'promised' by a previous verbal threat. Such *threat execution* explains some of the more bizarre forms of abuse. Thus a parent who uses the extreme verbal threat 'One day I'll push you through that window' might attempt to carry out this threat, rather than using another form of attack, when in a state of extreme rage. The verbal formula acts as a cue that prompts the behaviour. Another element that helps to steer the assaultive action is *retaliation*. In line with the general tendency of 'behavioural reciprocity', the abuse may involve a more extreme form of an aggressive action carried out by the child. Thus a child who has pulled at another child's hair (or the parent's hair) may have bunches of hair pulled out. The parent may be prompted by ideas of 'justice', and self-statements that cue and accompany the action are likely to include such formulations as: 'I'll show you'; 'See how it feels'; and 'So that's the game you want to play'. Finally, the nature of the attack sometimes reflects an *opportunism* on the part of the parent. He or she may use as a weapon any device that happens to be at hand. Thus a mother who is enraged when ironing may burn the child with the iron, or a father who is working with a knife when provoked may stab the child.

THE EFFECTS OF PHYSICAL ABUSE ON THE VICTIM

A small proportion of children who are abused die as a result of a parental attack. It is estimated that the annual incidence of such deaths is between 50 and 100 in the UK and 1000–1200 in the US, although these figures are often disputed (many feel that they are gross under-estimates). Some abused children are permanently scarred or disabled, some sustain serious brain damage and, even where there are no external injuries, neurological impairment may follow such actions as the parent shaking the child severely. Blows to the head can also result in permanent visual impairments, and intraocular bleeding can lead to retinal scarring, squints and a loss in visual acuity (Lynch, 1988). As well as the direct physical effects of abuse, some somatic effects may result from the stress associated with attacks or with the effects of constantly living in a hostile environment. Thus some abused children show a failure of growth and development that is now recognized as the 'failure to thrive' syndrome, although this is more often associated with emotional abuse than with physical abuse (Iwaniec, Herbert and Sluckin, 1988).

The issue of the psychological effects of physical abuse is somewhat complex. It would certainly be anticipated that the experience of being physically abused would interfere dramatically with a child's behavioural, emotional and social development, and many children who have been abused do show a number of psychological symptoms. However, there is often a problem of interpreting the meaning of the association between the evident symptoms and the history of abuse. Many of the child attributes cited earlier in this chapter as possibly increasing the child's vulnerability to abuse, for example, might also result from previous episodes of abuse, or from a general parental mishandling of the child.

Thus the relatively high incidence of enuresis found in the abused population; the increased frequency of whining, teasing, tantrums, aggression, and 'oppositional behaviour'; the social withdrawal and lack of empathy; the extremes of compliant behaviour; and the lack of response to normal disciplinary sanctions—as well as abnormalities in attachment behaviour—might all be consequences of physical abuse. Following the earlier analysis, in which such characteristics were identified as possible precursors of abuse, we are therefore left with the conclusion that such symptoms might be either the *causes* or the *effects* of abuse (or both). Some other characteristics (such as prematurity) clearly cannot be the effects of abuse, whereas a number of symptoms would seem much more likely to result from abuse than to trigger hostile attacks. Symptoms that could be considered as falling into this category would include depression and low self-esteem (Kinard, 1980; Kazden *et al.*, 1985), self-destructive behaviour, including head-banging and self-mutilation, and suicide attempts (Martin, 1976; Green, 1983).

It may not be important whether a symptom is the specific result of violent attacks or whether it results from some more enduring aspect of the high-risk family, but it is clear that in many cases the relationship between a history of abuse and the presence of a problem with the child can be accounted for in a number of different ways. One kind of explanation suggests that the observed characteristic is indeed an effect of an abusive episode. The symptoms to which such an explanation most clearly applies are those that result from neurological damage brought about by an attack. Thus there can be little doubt that some part of the association between a history of abuse and intellectual retardation is explicable in terms of neurological damage sustained during abusive episodes (Jaudes and Diamond, 1985).

The second type of explanation suggests that an observed characteristic reflects other features of 'high-risk' homes (including low parental warmth, the general high level of hostility, marital conflict, and social deprivation). Thus the fact that some abused babies have been found to be relatively unresponsive and are slow to acquire such skills as crawling, walking, and self-feeding, may reflect the fact that abusive parents tend to interact with their infants very little and give them little encouragement. Similarly, the extremes of high and low compliance might result from parental inconsistency in the administration of discipline, and high levels of aggression might reflect the parents' frequent use of harsh punishment methods (leading the child to become extremely frustrated or providing a model for the child's aggression). This type of explanation might also apply to the difficulties abused children often have in relating to other people. Parental hostility might have led the child to develop an antipathy to the parents that has generalized to other adults and peers.

A third possible type of explanation suggests that the child characteristic may reflect stresses that have arisen since the abusive incident. The injury may have led to internal changes in the family dynamics, perhaps reflecting guilt and recrimination, and may also have brought the family into contact with 'threatening' external agencies. The child may have been removed from the home and placed in foster care, and a number of professionals, including the police, might have become involved with the family. It is likely that considerable parental anxiety or anger may have been generated in response to such 'interference' and all of this is likely to have placed the child under great strain. Thus stresses following the abuse, rather than the abusive episode itself, might explain why children from abusive homes show relatively high rates of such symptoms as enuresis, withdrawal and depression.

The fourth possibility is that a characteristic may have developed independently of the abuse and that the association reflects the inability or unwillingness of abusing parents to help the child to cope with difficulties. Thus the observed symptom could reflect the omission of parental support rather than the commission of abusive acts. Children have a natural tendency to behave in disruptive and antisocial ways, but whereas most soon attain some degree of self-control as a result of their parents' guidance, limit-setting, and effective discipline, those whose parents are ineffective in such training may continue to behave in a disruptive fashion. In addition, most parents are able to help their children in times of stress. They give comfort and encouragement, offer a coping model, and provide security. Children whose parents fail to give such support would be expected to be vulnerable to a range of emotional disorders.

Finally, there is the possibility that some of the characteristics observed to be relatively frequent in an abused population are not consequences of abuse or of any parental act of omission or commission, but are features of the child's biological make-up, or problems that the child would have developed no matter how the parents behaved. The association between the symptom and the abuse would then be explained by the effect of the characteristic in making the child more vulnerable to parental attacks. Such an explanation would account for the relationship between abuse and such factors as congenital handicap, prematurity and low birth weight.

Although we can sometimes say which type of explanation is most likely to provide a valid account of why abused children show a particular symptom, it is often the case that a number of alternative explanations are equally plausible. Few studies have examined the same children before and after abuse, and even if it were shown that a particular symptom only emerged following abuse it still would not be clear whether this was due to the abuse itself or to the repercussions that followed. Similarly, if a symptom was shown to be present both before and after a particular abusive incident this would not rule out the possibility that it had resulted from some previous aggressive episode or from general mishandling by the parent. Thus we are rarely in a position to conclude that a symptom shown by a child is or is not the result of abuse.

Certainly there is no symptom or syndrome which inevitably follows abuse, and some children who are abused, including some who suffer serious injuries, appear not to show any adverse psychological effects. Thus, contrary to expectation, it seems that some victims emerge from abusive episodes relatively unscathed. Wolfe (1987) notes that: 'a remarkable number of children seem capable of adapting successfully to extremely traumatic and stressful situations'. The results of many studies on a range of problems indicate that great resilience is shown by many children following accidents, serious illnesses, physical abuse, sexual abuse and other potentially devastating occurrences. It has even been suggested that for almost all physically abused children the impact of abuse fades into insignificance when compared to the adverse effects of a deprived family background. Thus in a follow-up study Elmer (1977) found very few differences between abused, accidentally injured, and control children. Indeed, very few of the children were faring well, and Elmer concluded that the lower social class status of all of the families in her study was a more important determinant of child development than the experience of having been abused. These results were later supported by the findings of Starr (1982).

But while it may be true that not all abused children suffer trauma, case studies do indicate that at least some appear to show extreme adverse effects of

the beatings they have suffered. It is obviously very important to try to understand why some children are more affected than others. The degree of disturbance caused by physical abuse would be expected to depend on such factors as
the severity and nature of the attack(s), the age of the child, the context and
'meaning' of the assault(s), and the quality of the everyday relationship
between the parents and the child. Lynch (1988) found that those who were
faring well were more likely to have been young when abused and to have
escaped neurological damage. In addition, they were less likely to have been
involved in protracted legal proceedings or to have had a history of frequent
placement changes. Lynch also suggests that the possession of above-average
intelligence may be a protective factor, and she reports her clinical impression
that children who manage to escape negative consequences are friendly, likeable
children who seem to have been able, despite their history of maltreatment, to
develop a basic trust of adults and peers. Wolfe (1987) suggests that the child's
own coping abilities and the impact of supportive relatives are particularly
important.

If it seems extraordinary that not all abused children suffer severe
psychological affliction as a result of parental violence, it is equally remarkable
that many children maintain a positive view of their abusive parents. In the
study by Herzeberger, Potts and Dillon (1981), abused boys between the ages
of eight and 14 years who had been removed from the family and were living in
residential homes were asked about their attitudes to their parents and their
parents' use of punishment. Abused children described their parents in more
negative terms than did a comparison group of non-abused boys, and abusive
mothers, especially, were often described as emotionally neglecting, insulting,
and critical. However, the majority of abused children still felt loved, wanted
and cared for by the abusive parent. When they were asked why the parents
punished them, both groups of boys attributed much of the responsibility to
themselves, although children who had been abused by their father also judged
that the punishment reflected the father's 'mean character'.

Infants do not make attributions of responsibility, but the attributions made
by older victims would seem to be an important factor in determining the
nature of any psychological effects following abuse. Those who attribute an
attack to the parent's personality, or to particular stresses acting on the parent
at the time, would seem less likely to suffer a loss of self-esteem than those
victims who see the attack as reflecting outright parental rejection.
Furthermore, if aggression is seen by the child as a legitimate way of resolving
conflicts then this may increase the risk that one day the victim will imitate
such behaviour and become the perpetrator of some serious act of violence.
Thus abused children might be helped to adjust positively by encouraging
them to avoid self-blame and persuading them that violence is a totally
unacceptable way of responding to annoyance.

The evidence reviewed here has significant implications for professionals who deal with the victims of physical abuse. They should not *assume* that an abused child will be psychologically damaged but should make a careful assessment to determine whether there are any symptoms that need attention. And they should certainly not communicate to the victim or the parents (or to foster parents or prospective adoptive parents) the suggestion that a child who appears to be coping well 'must be' psychologically damaged and that symptoms should be expected to emerge in the future.

So far we have considered the possible consequences of abuse while the victim is still a child, but it is also important to consider whether there might be effects later in life. The view is often expressed that children who have been abused are likely to be psychologically scarred for the rest of their lives, and studies of former victims in their adolescent and adult years do reveal relatively high rates of a number of problems. But once again there are considerable difficulties in interpreting the meaning of such associations. With some slight adaptation, all of the explanations discussed above could apply equally well to the links between a history of abuse and later adversities or behavioural dysfunctions.

Those who were subjected to abuse during childhood have a relatively high rate of delinquency and a high rate of convictions for violent crimes (including murder and rape) as well as being at increased risk of committing suicide (Tarter *et al.*, 1984; Steinmetz, 1987). It needs to be emphasized, however, that only a minority of abused children become involved in violent transgressions, and it is therefore important to avoid any suggestion that abused children are somehow destined to lead a life of assaultive lawbreaking. And although it has repeatedly been found that those who engage in marital abuse and child abuse have often been abused in their childhood this does not mean that the majority of abused children will later become perpetrators of family assaults. Most abused children do *not* grow up to become abusive parents or abusive partners. For example, in a prospective study, Hunter and Kilstrom (1979) found that more than 80% of parents who had been victims did not abuse their own children. Indeed, some of those who suffered abuse during their childhood may develop particularly strong inhibitions against the use of harsh punishment methods.

THERAPY FOR VICTIMS

Because there is no 'typical' psychological aftermath of physical abuse, and since not all victims appear to be seriously adversely affected, there can be no standard treatment for children who have been subjected to hostile attacks by their parents. Plainly, any physical injuries must receive immediate attention, and it may be necessary to closely monitor the child's physical and psychological development to determine whether there is any evidence of a physical 'failure to thrive', any delay in the acquisition of developmental competencies, or any sensory or intellectual sequelae of neurological damage inflicted during attacks. Careful assessment should also be made of how the child is functioning emotionally and is coping with the plight of having been subjected to a vicious attack by a parent. Such investigations must be handled very sensitively so that the child is not distressed or tormented by unhappy memories.

When emotional or behavioural problems are identified it is usually appropriate to treat them with established forms of therapy. Children who are anxious or depressed are likely to benefit from sensitive counselling about the causes of their distress, and those who show pronounced aggression may be schooled in alternative ways of dealing with their frustrations. Although parents are often used as 'therapists' in the treatment of childhood behavioural problems, and although this *might* prove extremely constructive in some of these cases, it can easily be seen that many formerly abusive parents will be particularly ill-equipped to participate in the child's treatment. This will be the case if they lack skill in handling the child, if they have a poor understanding of the child's behaviour, or if they focus on failure and negative matters rather than on success and positive aspects. They are also likely to be unsuitable as therapists because their interaction with the child will be tense rather than relaxed, and because they are likely to view any minor setback as indicating failure. With very young victims, individual work may involve such techniques as play therapy and art therapy. Through playing and drawing, the child's current anxieties and fears may be disclosed, and the therapist may be able to encourage the child to work through these and to develop effective psychological coping strategies. Group sessions for victims, including role-play and structured games, may also prove very useful.

The older abused child may have developed a number of 'safety strategies' (for example, high compliance, or social avoidance) that will prove maladaptive in the long run. If such strategies are no longer needed, because the danger has passed, then steps should be taken to replace them with more adaptive and enterprising behaviours. Some abused children have learned to attribute stressful uncontrollable events in an internal, stable, and global way. They may blame themselves for the attacks made on them and may have taken to heart the many cruel gibes and insults hurled at them by a parent. Such children need to be helped to build their self-confidence and self-esteem, to regard themselves positively, and to develop a realistic appreciation of their talents and limitations. It is especially useful if programmes designed to increase their confidence are implemented in the school as well as in the clinic setting. Teachers are especially well placed to play an active role in helping the child to relate to other children empathically and amicably, without engaging in aggressive and bullying behaviour, and to convey the belief that violence is not an acceptable way of dealing with difficult situations.

CASE MANAGEMENT

Sometimes a professional, a family friend or a relative becomes alarmed by their observation of the parent's interaction with the child or the parent's expression of a profoundly negative attitude. They may make their anxiety about the child's safety known to an agency. In other cases a parent who feels in danger of injuring the child will call for help. Thus in some cases an alarm is sounded before there has been serious abuse, and in some cases intervention will prevent the child from being injured. In other cases, however, there has been no forewarning and the child's ordeal becomes evident only when a bruise or other wound is noticed, for example during a routine medical examination or at school. And sometimes abuse is not suspected until the parent presents a child for emergency treatment at a casualty unit.

Parents rarely admit that an injury is the result of a deliberate attack. Very often they give an account of some accident. There must be many cases of abuse where, because the story is plausible and consistent with the pattern of injuries, and where there is no circumstantial evidence to suggest that the injuries are the result of violence, an abusive injury is mistakenly attributed by health professionals to accidental causes. If the story is implausible, however (for example, if it is inconsistent with the profile of the injuries or includes a description of some action that would be impossible for a child of that age), this will raise the suspicion that the parent is attempting to cover up an abusive episode. The child may be too young to present his or her own version of what happened, and older children may have been 'schooled' by the parent to present a story that will allay suspicion.

Since many accidents do happen to children, it can be very difficult for a physician examining a child to make a decision about whether particular injuries do or do not have their origin in an abusive attack. The physician needs to take into account the family history and background, details of other recently reported 'accidents' involving the child, and the precise nature and pattern of physical injuries. Certain signs such as bite marks, repeated cigarette burns, and bruises or burns that take the shape of a weapon, may provide fairly conclusive evidence of abuse, but in many cases the pattern of injury does not permit an unequivocal judgement about how the injury was sustained. The paediatric examination of the injured child in cases where abuse is suspected is described by Kessler (1985).

In many cities 'at-risk registers' are kept. These are lists of children in the area who are considered to be in danger of physical abuse or some other form of maltreatment. The criteria for placing a child's name on such a register differ somewhat from place to place, but a history of violence by one or both parents, anxiety expressed by a health visitor or physician about the standard of care provided for the child, or a child's apparent failure to develop well, are typical reasons for placing a child's name on the register. It is common practice for copies of the register to be made available to paediatricians, and especially to health professionals who provide emergency cover. Obviously, finding that a child presented as an accident victim is listed on the register will greatly increase the suspicion that the injury may be the result of abuse.

If there is medical evidence or some other reason for suspecting that the child may be in immediate danger, a decision has to be made about whether it is safe for the child to remain at home or whether he or she (and possibly siblings, too) should be taken into care. The need to make such a decision places considerable pressure on professionals. If a 'false positive' error is made then a child who is distressed by injury but has not been abused will be separated from the parents and taken from the home environment at a time when parental comfort and support are crucial. On the other hand, if a 'false negative' error is made then the child may be returned to a dangerous situation and may face further brutality. Some such errors have resulted in the death of the child and the denunciation of the professionals responsible. Dale *et al.* (1986) have examined the pressures that social workers and others face when they are dealing with such aspects of child abuse cases. These authors emphasize the need for members of different professions and agencies to work together as an integrated team, to share the responsibilities and decision-making, and to provide mutual support.

One widely used procedure that has evolved for considering the diagnosis and management of child abuse cases is the 'case conference'. The paediatrician, social worker(s), psychologist, and a police officer, as well as any other professionals who are involved in the case (such as the health visitor or the child's teacher) gather to consider all of the information available regarding the family and the child's condition. An initial conference will consider whether the case justifies the initial misgivings and whether it warrants any immediate legal or supervisory action. Later conferences may focus on the progress being made by the parents in therapy and issues relating to the longer-term welfare of the child.

In the US the legal process relating to the removal of a child from the home differs from State to State. The relevant legal system in the UK is rather complex and provides a number of options allowing agencies and individuals other than the parents to have some legal rights and duties with regard to care and protection. When the child is believed to be in immediate danger the police or a social worker can apply for a 'place of safety order' which allows the child to be removed from the parents for a period of up to 28 days. This may be extended for another 28 days following the granting of an 'interim care order'. After this, if it is still considered that the child is in danger, the matter can be brought before a court that has the power to issue a care order that will commit the child to the care of the local authority until s/he is 18 or until the order is revoked. Care orders do not *oblige* the local authority to keep the child away from the family home, but they give the authority *discretion* to do so. The agency then has the power to dictate certain conditions that the parents must fulfil if they wish the child to be returned to them. One such condition is likely to be that they cooperate fully in any assessment and treatment programme.

Besides granting a care order, several other options are open to the court. It may dismiss the authority's application, it may require that the parent(s) undertake to provide proper care and control of the child, it may place the child under the guardianship of the local authority, or it may issue a 'supervision order'. The last of these options requires the agency to appoint a person to 'advise, assist, and befriend' the child. It provides some increased rights of surveillance and imposes certain protection responsibilities, but is far less powerful than a care order. Despite repeated calls for special 'family courts', matters relating to cases of child abuse are still dealt with in civil and criminal proceedings brought before the customary juvenile and other courts. This means that they are subject to the adversarial nature of the legal process. The wrangle that often develops between the local authority and the parents, with both claiming that they have the child's best interests at heart, can make it difficult for the court to come to an equitable decision. To help in this task, the court may appoint a 'guardian *ad litem*' to safeguard the child's interests. Those who take on this role are generally experienced social workers. They act as officers of the court, taking on a special responsibility for the child's welfare. They are able to interview all of the principals in the case, to advise the court on the best option available, and to appeal against any court decision that they consider undesirable.

When a child has been temporarily removed from the home the situation will be constantly monitored and a thorough assessment will be made of the family's problems, resources, and needs. Following removal, the major question is when (or if) it will be safe for the child to return home. In the past there was often a considerable interval between a child's removal and a final decision about whether rehabilitation would be possible. This delay in the decision-making process reflected the professionals' objective of gaining as much information as possible, including details concerning the role of the 'other parent' and the progress of any therapeutic endeavour. Recently, however, there has been a move towards 'permanency planning', and it is often considered that a decision to return the child to the parents or to arrange an alternative permanent placement should be made sooner rather than later. Thus there is now greater emphasis on the need to make on urgent assessment of the situation and to come to an early decision. Child abuse management teams are not only concerned with children who may be in immediate danger. Some of their decisions relate to the siblings of a child whose safety is causing concern. Or, if there is a history of abuse in a family, the team may need to consider whether it would be safe for a woman who is pregnant to keep the new baby.

Different teams report widely disparate rates for the number of children who are eventually returned to the family home. This may reflect differences in the seriousness of the cases monitored by the various agencies or different policies concerning the basis on which children should be returned or withdrawn. In some cases it is quite clear that it would be dangerous for the child to go back to the parents, and alternative arrangements have to be made. Many of the children who are not returned are placed in long-term foster care, and eventually many of them will be adopted. In other cases detailed assessment reveals that the incident responsible for precipitating the intervention was not in fact abusive or is most unlikely ever to be repeated, and it is agreed that the child should return home. But the situation is often not clear-cut, and there is often a combination of positive and negative features. The team will then become involved in the formidable task of weighing probabilities, and a number of very different views about the best course of action may be expressed.

The decision about whether the child should return is not based solely on the question of physical safety. The quality of life in the home is also a major consideration. Even if no further injury is likely to occur, there may be good reasons for placing the child in an alternative home. A surprising number of parents are actually ambivalent about whether they want their child to return, and some frankly reject the youngster or admit that a return would prove dangerous. Dale *et al.* (1986) report that, in a number of the cases they have dealt with, a permanent separation has been arranged with the full consent of the parents. Even in such cases, however, the team would not rule out the possibility that the couple might be allowed to keep, and would successfully parent, a child born at some future time. Where rehabilitation is not considered advisable, the best possible provision needs to be made for the child and s/he may need therapeutic help in making the transition to a new family.

Where rehabilitation does occur, the process must be handled with great care. The return may be 'phased', or a 'rehabilitation contract' may be drawn up, outlining a number of special conditions. Such a contract will certainly include provision for professionals to make unannounced visits to the home, and on such occasions is it essential that the child is seen by the professional—a doorstep visit and the parent's verbal assurance that all is well are clearly not sufficient. Other clauses may include promises by the parents to contact the agency if any crisis arises, and to abstain from illegal drugs. When there is a 'phased return', the child will first make short visits to the family home accompanied by a social worker. If these are successful and increase the professionals' confidence in the parents' capacity for handling the child safely, then progressively longer stays will be introduced, until eventually the child returns to live at home.

Some agencies favour a well-planned single-step return, although they may insist that the child regularly attends a day nursery during the months that follow. This has the dual function of relieving some of the day-to-day stresses of childcare for the parent and allowing close monitoring of the child's emotional well-being and physical condition. Once the child is home again, many parents consider that they have been 'approved' and that the agency will play no further role, but the period following return is always marked by the close involvement of the therapeutic or management team and it may be many months or even years before monitoring and therapy are reduced to a minimum. Whether or not the point is made explicitly, the stage following return is essentially a 'trial period', and if there are further danger signs, or if abuse reoccurs, the rehabilitation will be considered to have failed and the child will once again be admitted to care.

THERAPY FOR ABUSIVE FAMILIES

Many different types of treatment have been offered to abusive and high-risk families. Therapy given to a parent, or to the family, must be focused on elements that are judged as contributing to the risk to the child, and since there are likely to be many such elements many different points of intervention might provide a suitable focus for treatment. There are also many different ways of bringing about effective change at any of these points. A simplified example will illustrate this. Suppose that a comprehensive assessment of the family, and particularly of hostile incidents, has revealed that the child is sometimes punished in a particularly dangerous way, but that this only happens following a bitter argument between the parents about the alcoholic father's drinking. Possible focal points for intervention might be the father's alcoholism, the style of marital conflict, or the dangerous method used to punish the child. Obviously more than one of these could be targeted, and such variables as the parents' reaction when angry, and their appraisal of the child's annoying behaviours, might also be useful focal points. Furthermore, a number of different *methods* could be used to bring about change at any of these points. There are a number of alternative ways of changing marital conflict styles, for example, and of persuading parents to change their punishment methods.

It cannot be expected that all abusive parents will readily agree to participate in therapy, and a proportion of clients will accept treatment only under duress. Their agreement to cooperate may be based on the knowledge that a failure to collaborate is likely to lead to a recommendation that the child should be removed from the home or should not be returned. The resistance shown by some parents to attending therapeutic sessions, cooperating with the therapist, and accepting the possibility of therapeutic change, is evident from a number of examples given by Dale *et al.* (1986). They provide graphic illustrations of clients' manipulative and obstructive skills. Sometimes the anger that clients feel towards the therapists is openly expressed, but sometimes it remains covert. The need to 'engage' the parents, and the importance of achieving their full cooperation and maintaining their motivation, is also emphasized by Nicol (1988).

Dale *et al.* (1986) provide a number of guidelines that they have found useful in dealing with their clients. They insist that the parents admit their responsibility for previous maltreatment and are fully aware of the influence that the therapeutic team has on decisions concerning the future welfare of the child. Following an exploratory session, the team draws up a written contract in which it undertakes to honour certain commitments provided that the parents undertake to fulfil certain conditions. Thus the parents agree to attend regularly for therapy and to allow all aspects of their personal history and current relationship to be examined in detail, and the therapists specify the degree of contact that the parents will be allowed to have with children who have been removed. This team also emphasizes the need for parents to remain fully engaged in the therapeutic process for as long as the therapists feel is necessary. Thus parents must be discouraged from the belief that once the child has been returned to them, or once they have completed a term of probation or imprisonment, they will be free from monitoring or the need to continue with therapy.

In Nicol's (1988) description of a programme for home intervention in high-risk families, emphasis is placed on the need for the therapist to develop a close and warm relationship with the parents, and to provide a high level of social reinforcement for positive aspects of their behaviour. Nicol also warns of the danger of alienating parents by prescribing strategies that are too complex for them to understand. Thus a variety of 'carrot' and 'stick' strategies are used to encourage parents to take the therapy seriously, to cooperate, and to maintain an optimistic view of the likely outcome.

ASSESSMENT

Detailed assessment of the individual case is necessary to establish the nature of the difficulties and to determine which factors might be suitable points of intervention with the family. Assessment methods include interviews with parents and caseworkers, casual and structured observations of parent–child interaction, and questionnaires and psychological tests that examine aspects of the child's behaviour and the parents' attitudes and knowledge concerning children. It is especially useful to gather accounts of previous abusive or near-abusive incidents, and the parents may be asked to keep a diary in which they record details of particular occasions of anger and their reactions during difficult confrontations with the child. The point of the extensive assessment is to allow the therapist, or the therapeutic team, to construct a model of why abuse is occurring, or may soon occur, and then to facilitate the selection of suitable targets for intervention.

A comprehensive assessment of the abusive family will include information on a whole range of issues including the parents' background (especially any history of victimization), their current lifestyle (with special emphasis on stresses stemming from poverty, poor accommodation, unemployment, etc.); their relationship with friends, neighbours and kin; and their degree of integration with or isolation from the local community. Another focus will be on the marital relationship, and particularly on the degree of disharmony and any long-term or recurrent issues of conflict. In addition to such 'distal' factors, there will be extensive investigation of elements more directly related to the parents' treatment of the child, including their attitude to children generally, and areas of dissatisfaction or frustration with the behaviour of the child who is at risk.

Of particular interest in this regard will be unrealistic parental expectations or perceptions of the child, features of the child's behaviour that the parents find especially annoying, the frequency of disciplinary encounters, the parents' normal methods of discipline, and the ways in which they recognize and deal with their own anger.

PARENT, FAMILY, AND MARITAL VARIABLES

The choice of suitable targets for intervention will be guided by a number of questions, including whether the variable under consideration is 'distal' or 'proximal' to the aggression problem, whether it is salient and central to the continuation of the abuse, and whether available methods are likely to bring about effective change. Although 'distal' targets are often the focus for *prevention* programmes, they are generally less useful in therapy aimed at families where abuse has already taken place or where there is a very high risk of the child being injured. In such cases it is more usual for treatment to focus on proximal variables such as attitudes to children, parenting skills, or anger control, although there may well be some additional attempt to tackle such 'background' variables as a parent's heavy drinking or the couple's marital dysfunction. Some elements, such as social class and unemployment, are so distant from the problem at hand, and so difficult to modify, that they would not usually be prime targets for intervention. Nevertheless, it may be possible and useful to reduce the overall stress on the parents by providing practical help on such matters as poor accommodation and financial difficulties.

Attempts may be made to relieve economic stress by arranging access to available welfare resources, by enrolling the parent for vocational training, or by providing instruction in job-finding skills. The problem of the social isolation of the family may be tackled by encouraging the use of available resources such as day-care facilities and 'mother and toddler groups', and, if necessary, by providing social skills training. In some cases one or both parents will be diagnosed as suffering from a specific psychiatric disorder and it will be necessary to provide specialist help. Where drug addiction or alcohol abuse is identified as an important risk factor this may also provide a useful focus for intervention.

Help can be provided, too, for parents who have not resolved important issues from their past lives (Dale *et al.*, 1986), and marital therapy may be a useful secondary treatment focus for couples whose extreme marital discord frequently provokes conditions that threaten the safety of the children. For many of these problems a wide range of intervention methods is available. In some cases, as with parental alcoholism and marital conflict, it is appropriate to speak of the intervention as 'therapy', whereas in others (such as making sure that the family are receiving the state benefits to which they are entitled) the term 'case management' is more suitable.

THE PARENT–CHILD RELATIONSHIP

The quality of the parent–child relationship in abusive families is frequently very poor, and abusive parents often seem to be highly stressed by the demands of parenting. In addition, many such parents exhibit low rates of positive and appropriate behaviour, such as praising desirable child conduct, showing physical affection, and conveying requests clearly. As a result, there is often a general lack of good-natured interaction and an atmosphere of unconcern or irritation may prevail.

If the assessment process reveals that the quality of day-to-day parent–child interaction is very poor then the improvement and enrichment of the relationship may be regarded as a prime goal for therapy. Family therapy might be used to explore the dynamics of the family system, and of inter-generational relationships in particular, and to provoke changes that will improve the general level of functioning (Dale *et al.*, 1986). Alternatively, a behavioural approach may be used, for example to encourage the parents to increase the frequency of their positive behaviours towards the child or to teach them constructive ways of engaging with the child in play. (An excellent overview of behavioural approaches to intervention with abuse-prone families has been provided by Kelly, 1983.) The therapist may attempt to shape the parent's perception and understanding of the child, correcting any faulty understanding of child development and any unreasonable performance expectations, and helping the parent to identify the child's achievements and positive qualities. By providing a model of 'reasonable interpretations' the therapist may be able to change the parents' negative attributions regarding the child's behaviour, and to increase their sensitivity to the child's feelings and needs.

Another approach to improving the quality of the parent–child relationship involves reducing the stress of childcare. This may be accomplished by a number of practical management strategies including the provision of subsidized day-care, drop-in centres, or residential facilities. The stress of childcare will also be reduced as a result of increasing parenting skills (so that the child's behaviour *becomes* less problematic) and by helping the parent to develop a more positive attitude towards the child (so that the child's behaviour is *seen* as less problematic).

In some cases the assessment process will reveal that, in objective terms, the child's behaviour is particularly irksome or difficult. Sometimes a psychiatric condition will be diagnosed, but in many other cases a more specific behavioural difficulty will be identified. It may be appropriate for a therapist to work with the child directly to try to tackle the identified problem. Dealing with child symptoms that appear to function as triggers for abusive incidents provides useful therapy for the child's problem and may also help to prevent further abuse. A whole range of intervention methods have been shown to be effective in treating child behaviour problems. Among the potentially annoying behaviours that have been effectively modified using behavioural methods such as contingent attention and attention-removal techniques are fighting, 'hyperactivity', non-compliance, and tantrums (Kelly, 1983). Eventually the parents must learn to deal with the child who is engaging in offensive or disturbing behaviour, but at an early stage they may find this particularly difficult. The therapist's intervention with the child provides the parents with a model of how the child can be controlled without resorting to violence.

PARENT–CHILD INTERACTION DURING DISCIPLINE

Abusive parents often have special problems in dealing with disciplinary situations. Studies show that they tend to identify more situations as calling for disciplinary intervention, that they are often deficient in child-management skills, and that they are liable to use ineffective and dangerous methods in their bid to control the child's behaviour. In an attempt to reduce the overall frequency of disciplinary confrontations, and to 'normalize' the parents' judgements, training may be given in the classification of behaviours as 'good' or 'bad'. Thus numerous situations involving child behaviour might be described, and the parent invited to discuss with the therapist or with other parents whether such behaviour is 'normal', 'customary', 'malevolent', and 'harmful', and whether it would merit correction or punishment.

An examination of abusive or near-abusive incidents may reveal that parental tensions not provoked by the child often precede an attack, and that the child is frequently the victim of displaced aggression. If a parent who has lost money gambling is in a bad mood, for example, some slight irritation by the child may lead to an uncontrolled attack. Similarly, those who feel slighted by the partner may easily lose their temper with the child. It may help parents who are abusive in such circumstances to be made aware of the true source of their rage and of the fact that they are using the child as a sponge to soak up their hostility. The therapeutic task in such a case would involve identifying the pattern for the parents, pointing out the particular unfairness of their abusive behaviour, and teaching them ways of controlling their anger or of venting their hostility without victimizing the child. The parents might also be given treatment (e.g. marital therapy, or treatment for compulsive gambling) that would help them to avoid the situations that commonly provoke their intense anger.

Some interventions for abusive parents provide specific training in disciplinary skills. The aims are to teach them how to control the child's behaviour more effectively, and to make disciplinary encounters less prolonged and less prone to escalation. Abusive parents often fail to notice or reinforce the child's good behaviour, they may repeatedly threaten punishment, and they may make unclear and inconsistent commands. A detailed assessment of a number of recent confrontations may allow the therapist to identify errors that frequently recur and to suggest and demonstrate alternative and effective means of control. Thus training might be given in techniques such as 'time out' and the use of response-contingent attention and attention-withdrawal. 'Time-out' involves removing the child from sources of reinforcement for a set period, and is often used in the course of normal parenting (for example, parents may send a child who is misbehaving to a bedroom for a few minutes). Those who have not used the technique, or who use it ineffectively (for example, not matching the length of the 'time-out' to the severity of the 'offence') may benefit from the prescription of a simple routine to be followed.

Many abusive parents inadvertently reinforce their children's continued misbehaviour by providing attention only when the child is 'playing up' or being naughty. They can be taught that the withdrawal of attention is usually much more effective in reducing the undesirable behaviour than the use of such 'attentive' behaviours as shouting and hitting (Patterson, 1982). Ignoring misbehaviour is an important parenting skill that many abusive parents have not developed. It needs to be emphasized to parents that all of these techniques require consistent application, and that strategies for reducing or eliminating 'bad behaviour' should be accompanied by the use of frequent rewards (in the form of praise and positive attention) whenever the child engages in 'good behaviour'. The therapist may demonstrate the use of specific procedures by incorporating them in role-plays that have a particular relevance to problems that the parents commonly face.

Sometimes the parents will have very strong pro-punishment attitudes and these may need to be confronted directly by the therapist. It should be recognized that in many cases such an attitude will have been influenced by the parent's own treatment as a child, and it may be helpful for them to talk through their experience as a victim (this may also be useful in developing the parent's empathy for the child). In some cases the attitude favouring harsh punishment will stem from strong religious fundamentalist views, and these may need to be challenged by a philosophical dispute on the virtues of charity and forgiveness. Parents who fear that if a transgression is not dealt with harshly the child will 'run amok' can be assured that 'sparing the rod' will not, in fact, 'spoil the child'. They need to learn the distinction between severe punishments and effective control methods, and to appreciate that positive strategies (such as the use of rewards for good behaviour) are often much more effective than those that rely on punishment.

Parents who frequently use severe and dangerous methods of control also need to be made aware that more refined techniques are not only more appropriate but can also be more effective. Different therapists have different ideas about whether it is feasible or desirable to try to eliminate all forms of corporal punishment, but many parents need to be told which forms of punishment are reasonable and which are unacceptable and dangerous. Thus if it is agreed that it might sometimes be appropriate to slap a child who is behaving in a dangerous way, it would also be emphasized that such a slap should only be administered to the buttocks, and with an open palm. Slaps to the head would certainly be 'outlawed', as would biting, hair-pulling, punching and shaking. The parent who habitually shakes a child needs to be informed that this can result in diffuse brain damage. Parents can be told, too, about the many disadvantages of the frequent use of corporal punishment— that it disturbs the general atmosphere in the home, that it fails to guide the child towards behaving in an acceptable way, that any control gained in this way is likely to be temporary, and that children soon harden to physical punishment, thus making future escalation likely.

AGGRESSION MODIFICATION

Some interventions focus directly on increasing the parent's control during potentially catastrophic incidents, for example when a disciplinary encounter has escalated and is out of control. Thus the parent may be taught anger control methods and stress-management skills. Following the analysis of abuse incidents developed earlier in this chapter, interventions that focus directly on aspects of 'critical incidents' can be categorized in terms of whether they are aimed at changing (a) the provoking situation, (b) the parent's appraisal of the child's behaviour, (c) the experience of anger, (d) parental inhibitions, or (e) the form of aggressive behaviour.

If it is found at the assessment stage that a specific child behaviour proves exceptionally annoying or aversive to the parent, then the child's behaviour may be changed by the therapist (if it is genuinely problematic), or the parent might be desensitized to the particular *situation* that produces intense irritation. Situations that commonly give rise to such 'visceral' reactions include those of a child screaming or eating in a manner that is found repulsive. Desensitization procedures involve gradually presenting a hierarchy of the irritating cues (for example a tape of the child screaming, played over several sessions at progressively higher volumes) while the parent is in a state of deep relaxation (Doctor and Singer, 1978). Teaching the parents how to gain control over the child's behaviour will give them some power to curtail irritating, 'costly', and 'transgressive' actions, but they may also need to learn the 'emergency procedure' of placing themselves at a safe distance from the child whenever a serious crisis situation arises.

Parents can also be taught to change their judgement or *appraisal* of the child's behaviour, for example by using powerful imagery or a pre-taught formula of self-statements, in a bid to 'defuse' the situation. Thus the parent might be able to call to mind the fact that all children are naughty sometimes, that the child does not understand the impact of the annoying action, or that childhood problems do not last forever. There are also a number of effective strategies for reducing the level of *anger*, including relaxation, deep breathing, and the use of pleasant imagery or calming self-talk (Novaco, 1975). Parents may learn how to recognize the various physiological, cognitive and behavioural symptoms of anger and then master skills of 'dissolving' their fury.

Another useful focus for self-control involves the person calling to mind specific *inhibitions*, thus reducing the danger that anger will be expressed in the form of an explosive assault. Among the techniques used for increasing inhibitions are some that seek to intensify the awareness of the potential 'costs' of aggression. Thus the parent may be trained to recall, at times of special provocation, that an attack on the child may bring serious injury, heavy legal penalties, the child's removal from the home, and the scorn of neighbours and relatives. Parents will respond to each of these alternatives with varying degrees of alarm, and it is important to determine which 'possible consequence' is likely to prove the most effective in restraining the parents' action. Inhibitions may also be increased by encouraging the parent to feel empathy for the victim's suffering and by indicating the dangers associated with particular methods of punishment such as severe shaking or the use of weapons. This is also a method of confining the form of *aggression* within reasonably safe limits.

An additional technique for increasing inhibitions involves modifying any parental self-statements that are used to 'justify' the aggression. Thus a parent who covertly recites the statement 'he deserves this', when attacking the child, can be trained to change this to 'he's only a young child, if I attack him he may be seriously hurt'. There is evidence that many non-abusing parents use such strategies to good effect when they are tempted to attack the child (Frude and Goss, 1979). One final strategy that will have a marked effect on raising inhibitions involves the parent 'going public' at times of special stress. If they place themselves in a situation where other people can witness their behaviour (such as a neighbour's house, a supermarket, or even when someone is 'present' on the telephone) it will be most unlikely that they will launch a full-scale attack on the child.

THE THERAPEUTIC SETTING

The various treatment methods outlined above should not be regarded as alternatives, but rather as a range of elements many of which can be combined to form a comprehensive and multi-faceted therapeutic programme. Single-focus therapies are far less likely to be effective than those which simultaneously address a number of problematic issues. The elements incorporated into the programme should be tailored to the particular needs of the family. Many of these will have been identified at the initial assessment stage, but others may become apparent during the course of treatment.

The techniques described have been incorporated into many different intervention programmes. These have been implemented in a number of settings and are presented in a variety of ways. The therapeutic programme described by Dale *et al.* (1986), for example, focuses on the parents' histories (especially on 'unresolved conflicts') and on the family systems pressures that make abuse more likely, but the team also conducts role-play sessions in which family members act out situations relating to difficulties that they are likely to face in the future. The therapists model alternative adaptive ways of responding in potentially dangerous situations. The authors make the point that such enactment is far more powerful than merely describing what might happen and how a situation should be handled. Thus in this programme behavioural components are incorporated, although the approach is guided primarily by 'family systems' thinking.

Kelly (1983) describes a wide range of behavioural techniques that can be used by professional psychologists in the normal clinical context, and Nicol (1988) discusses how such methods may be adapted for use by nurses working within the home. This programme includes a number of familiar elements, including confrontation over the parent's attitudes to corporal punishment, the teaching of 'time-out', training in attention withdrawal and positive reinforcement procedures, and instruction in anger management techniques. Nicol emphasizes that the methods used should be simple enough for the parents to grasp easily, and that parents may benefit from being prescribed one or two simple control routines that they can use across a wide range of situations. A programme devised by Wolfe, Sandler, and Kaufman (1981) focuses on child management skills, relaxation and the self-control of anger, and takes the form of weekly group discussions and training sessions supplemented by films and reading materials.

A multidimensional programme incorporating some of the ideas and techniques described above is also provided by a US self-help organization, 'Parents Anonymous'. In an atmosphere of shared concern and cooperation, parents meet to develop new habits and skills in dealing with their children. They learn from each other what control methods are safe and effective and they evolve new ways of responding to stressful events. The groups also put parents in touch with agencies that might be of benefit—including child care, marital counselling and psychological services—and through their regular meetings the parents make new social contacts and become involved in existing community networks.

A number of studies have now examined the effectiveness of various programmes incorporating the kinds of strategies described above. Several of these have reported favourable results (e.g. Egan, 1983; Wolfe, Sandler and Kaufman, 1981; Nicol, 1988) while others have produced inconclusive or mixed results (e.g. Berkeley Planning Associates, 1977; Smith and Rachman, 1984). Several programmes have reported a high drop-out from treatment among those parents who 'voluntarily' attend for therapy. It is often difficult to achieve continued participation and enthusiasm for the programmes, but if therapists are in a position to influence the use of legal sanctions then it is often possible to ensure that parents remain fully 'engaged' and highly motivated until the therapeutic goals have been achieved.

THE PREVENTION OF PHYSICAL ABUSE

'Primary prevention' refers to an endeavour that pre-empts a problem before it occurs. It is therefore provided for cases where the particular disease or difficulty is not evident, although it may be targeted at specific groups that are known to have an especially high risk of developing the problem. 'Secondary prevention' refers to some activity that is designed to eradicate the affliction at a very early stage, and 'tertiary prevention' aims to arrest a problem once it has developed. Thus many of the treatment programmes discussed above could also be seen as forms of secondary or tertiary prevention. And just as treatment can be directed at a very wide range of 'distal' and 'proximal' factors, so prevention programmes may be aimed at modifying any factor that is suspected of being immediately or more remotely implicated in the causation of the problem. Thus measures designed to prevent child abuse may aim to promote parental competence and foster 'safe' attitudes to children, to reduce child characteristics that may provoke abuse, or to improve the parent's ability to cope with stress. They may also be designed to reduce marital conflict, unemployment, or social isolation, to increase the community resources available to families, or to outlaw the use of physical punishment by parents. In an example of a scheme aimed at reducing the risk of child abuse by tackling more distal elements, Lutzer, Wesch and Rice (1984) devised a programme that included training in home safety and a strategy for teaching parents skills useful in finding jobs, maintaining health and planning a nutritious diet for the family. This approach contrasts with programmes that aim to modify 'proximal' variables such as the parents' disciplinary attitudes or behaviours.

TARGETING PREVENTIVE MEASURES

Whereas some child abuse prevention programmes are 'universal', being directed at 'all parents', others are directed at more discrete target populations. Such targeted groups include particular local communities with an established high incidence of abuse; individuals who fall into a particular 'risk category', such as single parents, the parents of premature babies, and those of low socio-economic status; and families who have been shown to have high scores on multivariate measures designed to screen for 'abuse risk'. In the section on case management, earlier in this chapter, it was noted that many authorities maintain 'at-risk registers' listing children who are suspected of being in danger of serious maltreatment. The purpose of such registers is to identify children who might benefit from special surveillance or protection measures. Children's names are entered on such lists according to a number of different criteria, but in most cases these amount to the fact that some professional feels especially anxious about the child. Obviously only a small proportion of vulnerable children are likely to be noticed in this way and the process is therefore somewhat haphazard. It has long been hoped that an effective method might be found of screening all families (perhaps at the time of the birth of a child) so that all children at special risk could be identified.

A number of measures designed to identify especially vulnerable children have been developed over the years. They generally take the form of a checklist of factors known to be associated with physical abuse, including many of those discussed earlier in this chapter. Thus such inventories usually include a number of demographic variables (social class, mother's age, marital status), parent background items (history of family violence, previous or current drug abuse or mental illness), and child variables (low birth weight, prematurity). They may also include observational data regarding the parent–child interaction, and psychological measures of parent attitudes or beliefs. This information is gathered for all families within a 'prevention project' area, and those with a high composite score on the screening measure are labelled 'high risk'. The purpose of the procedure is to identify families that would especially benefit from intervention, so that limited resources can be deployed most effectively (Pringle, 1980).

Although the logic of the exercise is sound there is a major problem, namely that the vast majority of those who obtain high scores on such measures will not in fact abuse their children even if special help is not made available to them. In other words, such screening procedures yield a very high number of 'false positives'. Thus, in their follow-up of 949 families that had been identified as 'high risk', Browne and Saqi (1988) found that 893 fell into the 'false positive' category. If an intensive prevention scheme had been made available for all of the 'high-risk' families then, in terms of the single criterion of preventing physical abuse, it would have been 'unnecessary' in about 94% of cases. Such results indicate the low overall efficiency of intensive prevention schemes directed at families identified as 'high risk' following the birth of a child. They also indicate that such schemes are likely to incorrectly label many families as 'potential abusers', and it is evident that this could have a very damaging effect on the self-confidence and self-esteem of these new parents.

INTERVENTIONS WITH HIGH-RISK FAMILIES

On the other hand, it may be that interventions directed at specially targeted families will have a number of beneficial effects apart from any reduction in the number of children who are seriously injured. When resources for helping parents are very scarce it certainly makes more sense to allocate them to those who have some special difficulty, rather than to a random sub-group of the population. A number of prevention programmes have provided self-help groups, home help, regular calls by lay 'visitors', or special interventions by health visitors, for such groups as single parents or those with a handicapped or premature child. In one of the earliest 'visitation programmes', Kempe (1973) recruited a number of senior citizens to visit families that might be experiencing difficulties. These volunteers were carefully selected and trained, and were then assigned to one or two families whom they visited once a week. In other programmes nurses have been enlisted to provide support and act as parent role models. They have been particularly concerned to reinforce positive aspects of the parents' interaction with the child, to boost the parents' self-confidence, and to correct any unrealistic beliefs or expectations, or any unreasonable attributions that the parent might make about the infant's behaviour.

The results of such intervention schemes have been somewhat mixed. Thus in one study, Olds (1984) found that mothers who were 'visited' viewed their infants more positively, reported fewer instances of 'conflict' with the baby, and punished their infants less frequently than high-risk mothers who had not received such visits. The incidence of child abuse and neglect was also significantly lower in this group than in a high-risk comparison group. Minde et al. (1980) found that mothers of pre-term babies who were randomly assigned to a self-help group coped more effectively with their infants. Three months after their discharge from the maternity hospital they showed more involvement, more interaction, and more concern for the child, and at one year they provided more freedom and stimulation. The infants of mothers in the intervention group also displayed higher levels of exploratory behaviour and self-feeding than the infants of mothers in the control group. On the other hand, Stevenson, Bailey and Simpson (1988) used health visitors to screen and intervene in cases of high risk, but found little evidence that the programme had produced positive results in terms of the mother's psychological well-being, the child's behaviour problems, or parenting style.

The intervention schemes described so far depend for the most part on personal contact between a professional or lay person and the family. The visitor is usually given a broad remit to help in any way that seems suitable and is within their competence, and to refer the family to a specialist if additional help is required. The visitor and back-up team may help the parents to evolve appropriate routines of childcare and suitable methods of discipline, and they will also increase the parents' knowledge about child development, correct misattributions, and provide advice on ways on controlling anger. Where it seems appropriate they may attempt to modify a child's 'difficult' behaviour. They are also likely to provide informal counselling for other stresses and problems that a parent confides in them. The main problem with schemes that rely on personal contact, however, is that they are generally very costly. Recent innovations in this area involve the use of books, pamphlets and games, and at least one team has developed video-cassettes that educate parents about methods of coping when faced with problems concerning the child's behaviour (Wolfe, 1987).

Most of the schemes described are backed up with a 'telephone hotline' or similar facility to enable the parents to make contact with their special helper, or with some suitable professional, at times of special crisis. This type of resource provides a valuable safety net, although typically it is found that parents need to make very little use of such emergency services.

INTERVENTIONS WITH HIGH-RISK COMMUNITIES

Some prevention programmes are directed at particular 'high-risk communities', and many such interventions have now been described and evaluated (Gray, 1983; Rosenberg and Repucci, 1985). Some of these have attracted substantial additional funds and an increase in professional involvement in the community, so that extra resources are provided in the form of day-care facilities, drop-in centres, nurseries, 'parent–toddler groups', parent education classes, and crisis services. But many programmes are designed to make a more effective use of the resources that already exist in the community and they draw principally on volunteers from within the neighbourhood. Even if it is not possible to increase resources, much can often be done to make them more accessible and more effective. One important aspect of many such programmes is the effort they make towards 'networking'—increasing the level of informal contact between neighbours and community members by organizing such functions as toy swaps, children's tea parties, and 'look in on your neighbour' days. Many of the programmes also include a strong information component. Some have launched local media campaigns designed to promote parents' positive attitudes towards their children, and to increase their knowledge about child behaviour, while other programmes have directed publicity efforts (ranging from notices in supermarkets to TV advertisements and features), more towards increasing parents' knowledge of available resources and strengthening their motivation to make use of them.

It is essential that professionals working in a community should have a comprehensive knowledge of what resources are available, and should be familiar with the work of other professionals and of volunteers who are willing to provide practical help and support. Thus important and highly cost-effective elements of a community-based programme might involve drawing up an inventory of the community's assets and services, and providing every relevant professional with the comprehensive list. In addition, it is useful to encourage increased communication between those who are in a position to act as advisors to parents, and programmes can help to increase the level of awareness of professionals and the public concerning the issue of child abuse. There is a need for all those who come into regular contact with children and their families (such as teachers, physicians, and health visitors) to remain vigilant regarding the problem and to be fully aware of any resources that can be mobilized to help families in distress.

One example of a comprehensive community programme aimed at decreasing child abuse (and also at improving children's performance at school) is 'Project C.A.N. Prevent'. This was targeted on low-income Hispanic families in the United States and included parent education classes, toy-making classes, a day centre, and a home visiting programme with regular filming of parent–child interaction. The results from this study showed that parents who participated significantly increased their knowledge about children and about local resources. Programmes that have focused on efforts to strengthen formal and informal helping networks include 'Project Network' in Atlanta, Georgia, and 'Primary Prevention Partnership' in Washington State. In England the 'Homestart' programme (Van der Eyken, 1982) and the comprehensive 'Newpin' project (Pound and Mills, 1985) reflect the view that by fostering close relationships within the community parents can be provided with emotional support and help with practical tasks, thus allowing them to cope more effectively with their problems. Like several of the US programmes, 'Newpin' makes extensive use of volunteers who are recruited from within the community.

One of the special difficulties faced by programmes targeted on communities, rather than on individual families or on the wider population, is the likelihood that the parents who would be likely to derive the most benefit from these schemes may be the least enthusiastic about participating. Such parents may not recognize that they need help, or may have a profound wariness of the professionals involved.

Several programmes include a 'crisis hotline' as an additional community resource, and national organizations in several countries also offer such a service for parents who feel that they need emergency help. Although this would seem a useful innovation, however, many parents who might benefit from the facility either do not know about the service or are very reluctant to make use of it. Typically, such lines rarely attract crisis calls (only about 1% of calls are of this nature). The vast majority of callers ask for or provide information, although the fact that many report alleged cases of abuse or neglect does demonstrate another useful function of such lines.

'UNIVERSAL' SCHEMES

It can be argued that there is a universal need to enhance the nurturing and protection of children and that the most effective schemes for reducing the incidence of child abuse might actually be those that are targeted on *all* parents and are designed to increase the general level of parenting skills and to promote a positive attitude towards children. Thus Belsky and Vondra (1987) argue that broad-based interventions designed to increase the general quality of parenting will have many benefits, including that of reducing the rate of physical abuse. They suggest a range of schemes, including some that are directly focused on parenting knowledge and skills, and some that are aimed at improving parents' general well-being (including efforts directed at 'making marriages more harmonious, social networks more supportive, and children more agreeable'). A special advantage of directing intervention at all families, they suggest, is that problem families will not regard themselves as special targets for the support being offered. To some extent, therefore, such programmes would side-step the motivational issue identified as a particular problem in the case of interventions addressed to particular communities.

Belsky and Vondra (1987) propose a number of 'mini-interventions' that make use of existing social structures. These are designed to have a cumulative and collective impact. Thus the school system could be used to provide parenting education for children. If this were introduced into the normal school curriculum (in the form of regular lessons and opportunities for supervised caregiving), children would form more realistic expectations about the satisfactions and frustrations of parenting, and those whose own parents had provided an especially poor model would gain a particularly valuable insight into more orthodox and sensitive ways of dealing with children.

Current pre-natal classes provide another 'ideal community structure' for a mini-intervention. The present focus of such classes is on childbirth and the physical care of the newborn baby but this could be broadened, so that expectant mothers (and fathers) would be provided with an opportunity to discuss how the birth of the child is likely to influence their lives. This would help them to foresee certain difficulties and to develop an 'anticipatory coping plan' for many of the problems they are likely to face. It would also encourage the development of long-term relationships between couples who live in the same neighbourhood and are at the same stage in their lives. The employment environment is suggested as another context in which 'parent-enhancement' schemes could be launched. Thus a 'family bulletin board' might be provided in the office or factory, with sign-up sheets for baby-sitting services, a children's clothing and furniture exchange, and space for announcements of births and birthdays. This would help to foster a mutual interest between colleagues in their families and would enhance their sense of pride about parenthood. It would also facilitate the offering and sharing of services and might therefore do much to reduce social isolation.

It can be seen that the introduction of broadly based interventions would be greatly accelerated by support and directives emanating from central government. Several prime examples of political initiatives that might help to reduce the incidence of physical abuse have been introduced in Sweden. Thus there are national 'Children's Days', on which the delights of children and childhood are celebrated, 'parenting' has been introduced into the curriculum as a basic subject at all levels of education and in 1979 the Swedish Government banned the use of corporal punishment by parents (Zeigart, 1983). The introduction of the relevant clause in the legislation was accompanied by a mass-media campaign and the distribution of pamphlets that were intended to increase public awareness of the problem of physical abuse and to guide parents towards using alternative methods of controlling their children. Opinion polls showed that the proportion of Swedish citizens who supported the use of corporal punishment fell after the introduction of the new clause, so that in 1980 two-thirds of those polled stated that parents should bring up their children without using corporal punishment. The government also supported forms of intervention for parents who were having special difficulties, and recognized that there would be particular problems to be faced in convincing immigrant parents and those from certain religious minorities of the rightness and feasibility of the ban.

REFERENCES

Altemeir, W. A., O'Connor, S., Vietze, P., Sandler, H. and Sherrod, K. (1982) Antecedents of child abuse. *Journal of Pediatrics*, **100**, 823–829.
American Association for Protecting Children (1985) *Highlights of Official Child Abuse and Neglect Reporting, 1983*. Denver, CO: American Humane Association.
Azar, S., Robinson, D., Hekimian, E. and Twentyman, C. T. (1984) Unrealistic expectations and problem-solving ability in maltreating and comparison mothers. *Journal of Consulting and Clinical Psychology*, **52**, 687–691.

Bauer, W. D. and Twentyman, C. T. (1985) Abusing, neglectful and comparison mothers' responses to child-related and non-child-related stressors. *Journal of Consulting and Clinical Psychology*, **53**, 335–343.

Belsky, J. (1988) Child maltreatment and the emergent family system. In K. Browne, C. Davies and P. Stratton (eds.), *Early Prediction and Prevention of Child Abuse.* Chichester: Wiley.

Belsky, J. and Isabella, R. A. (1985) Marital and parent–child relationships in family of origin and marital change following the birth of a baby: a retrospective analysis. *Child Development*, **56**, 361–375.

Belsky, J. and Vondra, J. (1987) Child maltreatment: prevalence, consequences, causes and prevention. In: D. H. Crowell, I. M. Evans, and C. R. O'Donnell (eds.), *Childhood Aggression and Violence: Sources of Influence, Prevention and Control.* New York: Plenum.

Berkeley Planning Associates (1977) *Evaluation of Child Abuse and Neglect Demonstration Projects 1974–1977*, Vol. 3: *Adult Client Impact.* Hyatsville, MD: National Center for Health Service Research.

Bousha, D. M. and Twentyman, C. T. (1984) Mother–child interactional style in abuse, neglect and control groups: naturalistic observations in the home. *Journal of Abnormal Psychology*, **93**, 106–114.

Bower, G. H. (1981) Mood and memory. *American Psychologist*, **36**, 129–148.

Brandon, S. (1976) Physical violence in the family: an overview, In: M. Borland (ed.), *Violence in the Family.* Manchester: Manchester University Press.

Browne, K. and Saqi, S. (1988) Approaches to screening for child abuse and neglect. In: K. Browne, C. Davies and P. Stratton (eds.), *Early Prediction and Prevention of Child Abuse.* Chichester: Wiley.

Burgess, R. L. (1985) Social incompetence as a precipitant to and consequence of child maltreatment. *Victimology: An International Journal*, **10**, 72–86.

Burgess, R. L. and Conger, R. D. (1977) Family interaction patterns related to child abuse and neglect: Some preliminary findings. *Child Abuse and Neglect*, **1**, 269–277.

Burgess, R. L. and Conger, R. D. (1978) Family interaction in abusive, neglectful and normal families. *Child Development*, **49**, 1163–1173.

Call, J. D. (1984) Child abuse and neglect in infancy: sources of hostility within the parent–infant dyad and disorders of attachment in infancy. *Child Abuse and Neglect*, **8**, 185–202.

Creighton, S. J. (1988) The incidence of child abuse and neglect. In: K. Browne, C. Davies and P. Stratton (eds.), *Early Prediction and Prevention of Child Abuse.* Chichester: Wiley.

Crittenden, P. M. (1988) Family and dyadic patterns of functioning in maltreating families. In: K. Browne, C. Davies and P. Stratton (eds.), *Early Prediction and Prevention of Child Abuse.* Chichester: Wiley.

Crittenden, P. M. and Bonvillian, J. D. (1984) The relationship between maternal risk status and maternal sensitivity. *American Journal of Orthopsychiatry*, **54**, 250–262.

Crnic, K. A., Greenberg, M. R., Ragozin, A. S., Robinson, N. M. and Basham, R. (1983) Effects of stress and social support on mothers and premature and full-term infants. *Child Development*, **54**, 1199–1210.

Dale, P., Davies, M., Morrison, A. and Waters, J. (1986) *Dangerous Families: Assessment and Treatment of Child Abuse.* London: Tavistock.

Disbrow, M. A., Doerr, H. and Caulfield, C. (1977) Measures to predict child abuse. Paper presented at the Biennial Meeting of the Society for Research in Child Development, San Francisco, CA, March 1977.

Doctor, R. M. and Singer, E. M. (1978) Behavioral intervention strategies with child abusive parents. *Child Abuse and Neglect*, 2, 57–68.

Egan, K. J. (1983) Stress management and child management with abusive parents. *Journal of Clinical Child Psychology*, 12, 292–299.

Egeland, B. (1988) Breaking the cycle of abuse: Implications for prediction and intervention. In: K. Browne, C. Davies and P. Stratton (eds.), *Early Prediction and Prevention of Child Abuse*. Chichester: Wiley.

Elmer, E. (1977) *Fragile Families, Troubled Children: The Aftermath of Infant Trauma*. Pittsburgh, PA: Pittsburgh University Press.

Engfer, A. and Schneewind, K. D. (1982) Causes and consequences of harsh parental punishment: An empirical investigation in a representative sample of 570 German families. *Child Abuse and Neglect*, 6, 129–139.

Fontana, V. J. and Robison, E. (1984) Observing child abuse. *Journal of Pediatrics*, 105, 655–660.

Frodi, A. M. and Lamb, M. E. (1980) Child abusers' responses to infant smiles and cries. *Child Development*, 51, 238–241.

Frodi, A., Lamb, M., Leavitt, C., Donovan, W., Neff, C. and Sherry, D. (1978) Fathers' and mothers' responses to the faces and cries of normal and premature infants. *Developmental Psychology*, 14, 490–498.

Frude, N. J. (1980) Child abuse as aggression. In: N. Frude (ed.), *Psychological Approaches to Child Abuse*. London: Batsford.

Frude, N. J. (1985) The sexual abuse of children within the family. *Medicine and Law*, 4, 463–472.

Frude, N. J. (1989) The physical abuse of children. In: K. Howells and C. Hollin (eds.), *Clinical Approaches to Violence*. Chichester: Wiley.

Frude, N. J. and Goss, A. (1979) Parental anger: a general population survey. *Child Abuse and Neglect*, 3, 331–333.

Gaensbauer, T. J., Mrazek, D. A. and Harmon, R. J. (1980) Emotional expression in abused and neglected infants In: N. J. Frude (ed.), *Psychological Approaches to Child Abuse*. London: Batsford.

Garbarino, J. (1977) The price of privacy in the social dynamics of child abuse. *Child Welfare*, 56, 565–575.

Gelles, R. J. (1979) *Family Violence*. Beverly Hills, CA: Sage.

Gelles, R. J. (1987) *The Violent Home: Updated Edition*. Beverly Hills, CA: Sage.

George, C. and Main, M. (1979) Social interactions of young abused children: approach, avoidance and aggression. *Child Development*, 50, 306–318.

Goldberg, S. (1978) Prematurity: effects on parent–child interaction. *Journal of Pediatric Psychology*, 3, 137–144.

Golub, J. S. (1984) Abusive and nonabusive parents' perceptions of their children's behaviour: an attributional analysis. Unpublished Ph.D. dissertation. University of Los Angeles, California.

Gray, E. B. (1983) *Collaborative Research of Community and Minority Group Action to Prevent Child Abuse and Neglect*, Vols I–IV. Chicago, IL: National Committee for Prevention of Child Abuse.

Green, A. H. (1983) Dimensions of psychological trauma in abused children. *Journal of the American Academy of Child Psychiatry*, **22**, 231–237.

Heinicke, C. M. (1984) The role of pre-birth parent characteristics in early family development. *Child Abuse and Neglect*, **8**, 169–181.

Herrenkohl, E. C. and Herrenkohl, R. (1979) A comparison of abused children and their non-abused siblings. *Journal of the Academy of Child Psychiatry*, **18**, 260–269.

Herrenkohl, R. C. and Herrenkohl, E. C. (1981) Some antecedents and developmental consequences of child maltreatment. In: R. Rizley and D. Cichitti (eds.), *New Directions for Child Development*. San Francisco, CA: Jossey-Bass.

Herrenkohl, R., Herrenkohl, E. C. and Egolf, B. P. (1983) Circumstances surrounding the occurrence of child maltreatment. *Journal of Consulting and Clinical Psychology*, **51**, 424–431.

Herrenkohl, E. C., Herrenkohl, R. C. and Toedter, L. J. (1983) Perspectives on the intergenerational transmission of abuse. In: D. Finkelhor, R. J. Gelles, G. T. Hotaling and M. A. Straus (eds.), *The Dark Side of Families*. Beverly Hills, CA: Sage.

Herzeberger, S. D., Potts, D. A. and Dillon, M. (1981) Abusive and nonabusive parental treatment from the child's perspective. *Journal of Consulting and Clinical Psychology*, **49**, 81–90.

Hunter, R. S. and Kilstrom, N. (1979) Breaking the cycle in abusive families. *American Journal of Psychiatry*, **136**, 1320–1322.

Hyman, C., Parr, R. and Browne, K. (1979) An observational study of mother–child interaction in abusing families. *Child Abuse and Neglect*, **3**, 251–256.

Iwaniec, D., Herbert, M. and Sluckin, A. (1988) Helping emotionally abused children who fail to thrive. In: K. Browne, C. Davies and P. Stratton (eds.), *Early Prediction and Prevention of Child Abuse*. Chichester: Wiley.

Jaudes, P. K. and Diamond, L. J. (1985) The handicapped child and child abuse. *Child Abuse and Neglect*, **9**, 341–347.

Kadushin, A. and Martin, J. A. (1981) *Child Abuse: An Interactional Event*. New York: Columbia University Press.

Kazden, A. E., Moser, J., Colbus, D. and Bell, R. (1985) Depressive symptoms among physically abused and psychiatrically disturbed children. *Journal of Abnormal Psychology*, **94**, 298–307.

Kelly, J. A. (1983) *Treating Child-Abusive Families: Intervention based on Skills-Training Principles*. New York: Plenum.

Kempe, C. H. (1973) A practical approach to the protection of the abused child and the rehabilitation of the abusing parent. *Pediatrics*, **51**, 804–812.

Kessler, D. B. (1985) Pediatric assessment and differential diagnosis of child abuse. In: E. H. Newberger and R. Bourne (eds.), *Unhappy Families: Clinical and Research Perspectives on Family Violence*. Littleton, MA: PSG Publishing Co.

Kinard, E. M. (1979) The psychological consequences of abuse for the child. *Journal of Social Issues*, **35**, 82–100.

Kinard, E. M. (1980) Emotional development in physically abused children. *American Journal of Orthopsychiatry*, **50**, 686–696.

Lahey, B. B., Conger, R. D., Atkeson, B. M. and Treiber, F. A. (1984) Parenting behaviour and emotional status of physically abusive mothers. *Journal of Consulting and Clinical Psychology*, **52**, 1062–1071.

Larrance, D. T. and Twentyman, C. T. (1983) Maternal attributions and child abuse. *Journal of Abnormal Psychology*, **92**, 449–457.

Larrance, D. L., Amish, P. L., Twentyman, C. T. and Plotkin, R. C. (1982) Attribution theory and child abuse. *Selected Procedings of the Third International Congress on Child Abuse and Neglect*. Amsterdam: Free University Press.

Letourneau, C. (1981) Empathy and stress: how they affect parental aggression. *Social Work*, **26**, 383–389.

Lutzer, J. R., Wesch, D. and Rice, J. M. (1984) A review of 'Project 12-ways': an ecobehavioural approach to the treatment and prevention of child abuse and neglect. *Advances in Behaviour Research and Therapy*, **6**, 63–73.

Lynch, M. (1975) Ill health and child abuse. *Lancet*, **2**, 317–319.

Lynch, M. (1988) The consequences of child abuse. In: K. Browne, C. Davies and P. Stratton (eds.), *Early Prediction and Prevention of Child Abuse*. Chichester: Wiley.

Main, M. and Goldwyn, R. (1984) Predicting rejection of her infant from mother's representation of her own experience: implications for the abused–abusing intergenerational cycle. *Child Abuse and Neglect*, **8**, 203–217.

Main, M. and Weston, D. (1982) Avoidance of the attachment figure in infancy. In: C. M. Parkes and J. Stevenson-Hinde (eds.), *The Place of Attachment in Human Behaviour*. New York: Basic Books.

Martin, H. P. (1976) Which children get abused: high risk factors in the child. In: H. P. Martin (ed.), *The Abused Child: A Multidisciplinary Approach to Developmental Issues and Treatment*. Cambridge, MA: Ballinger.

Martin, H. P. (1979) *Treatment for Abused and Neglected Children*. DHEW Publications (OHDS) 79-30199, Washington, DC, August.

Martin, H. P. and Beezley, P. (1977) Behavioural observation of abused children. *Developmental Medicine and Child Neurology*, **19**, 373–387.

Martin, H. P., Conway, E., Beezley, P. and Kempe, H. C. (1974) The development of abused children. Part 1: A review of the literature. *Advances in Pediatrics*, **21**, 43–58.

Mash, E. J., Johnson, C., and Kovitz, K. (1983) A comparison of the mother–child interactions of physically abused and non-abused children during play and task situations. *Journal of Clinical Child Psychology*, **12**, 337–346.

Milgram, S. (1974) *Obedience to Authority*. New York: Harper and Row.

Minde, K. Shosenberg, N. E., Marton, P., Thompson, J., Ripley, J. and Burns, S. (1980) Self-help groups in a premature nursery: a controlled evaluation. *Journal of Pediatrics*, **96**, 933–940.

Morgan, S. R. (1987) *Abuse and Neglect of Handicapped Children*. New York: Plenum.

Newson, J. and Newson, E. (1980) Parental punishment strategies with eleven-year-old children. In: N. J. Frude (ed.), *Psychological Approaches to Child Abuse*. London: Batsford.

Nicol, R. (1988) The treatment of child abuse in the home environment. In: K. Browne, C. Davies and P. Stratton (eds.), *Early Prediction and Prevention of Child Abuse*. Chichester: Wiley.

Novaco, R. W. (1975) *Anger Control: The Development and Evaluation of an Experimental Treatment*. Lexington. DC: Heath Lexington Books.

Oates, R. K., Davis, A. A., Ryan, M. G. and Stewart, L. F. (1979) Risk factors associated with child abuse. *Child Abuse and Neglect*, **3**, 547–554.

Oldershaw, L., Walters, G. C. and Hall, D. K. (1986) Control strategies and noncompliance in abusive mother–child dyads: an observational study. *Child Development*, 57, 722–732.

Olds, D. L. (1984) *Final Report: Prenatal/Early Infancy Project*. Washington, DC: Maternal Health and Child Care Research, National Institute of Health.

Parke, R. D. and Collmer, C. W. (1975) Child abuse: An interdisciplinary analysis. In: E. M. Hetherington (ed.), *Review of Child Research and Development*, Vol. 5. Chicago: University of Chicago Press.

Patterson, G. R. (1982) *Coercive Family Process*. Eugene, OR: Castalia.

Perry, M. A. and Doran, L. D. (1983) Developmental and behavioural characteristics of the physically abused child. *Journal of Clinical Child Psychology*, 12, 320–324.

Pound, A. and Mills, M. (1985) A pilot evaluation of Newpin. *ACPP Newsletter*, 7, 13.

Pringle, M. K. (1980) Towards the prediction of child abuse. In: N. Frude (ed.), *Psychological Approaches to Child Abuse*. London: Batsford.

Reid, J. B. (ed.) (1978) *A Social Learning Approach to Family Intervention*, Vol. II: Observation in Home Settings. Eugene, OR: Castalia.

Reid, J. B. (1983) *Final Report: Child Abuse: Developmental Factors and Treatment*. Grant No. 7 ROI MH37938, NIMH, USPHS.

Reid, J. B. (1986) Social interactional patterns in families of abused and non-abused children. In: C. Zahn-Waxler, E. M. Cummings and R. Ianotti (eds.), *Altruism and Aggression: Biological and Social Origins*. Cambridge: Cambridge University Press.

Reid, J. B., Taplin, P. S. and Lorber, R. (1981) An interactional approach to the treatment of abusive families. In: R. Stuart (ed.), *Violent Behaviour: Social Learning Approaches to Prediction, Management and Treatment*. New York: Brunner/Mazel.

Renvoize, (1978) *Violence in Families*. London: Routledge and Kegan Paul.

Richman, N., Stevenson, J. and Graham, P. (1982) *Preschool to School: A Behavioural Study*. London: Academic Press.

Rosenberg, M. S. and Repucci, N. D. (1983) Abusive mothers: Perceptions of their own and their children's behaviour. *Journal of Consulting and Clinical Psychology*, 51, 674–682.

Rosenberg, M. S. and Repucci, N. D. (1985) Primary prevention of child abuse. *Journal of Consulting and Clinical Psychology*, 53, 576–585.

Sack, W. H., Mason, R. and Higgins, J. E. (1985) The single-parent family and abusive child punishment. *American Journal of Orthopsychiatry*, 55, 252–259.

Salzinger, S., Kaplan, S. and Artemyeff, C. (1983) Mothers' personal social networks and child maltreatment. *Journal of Abnormal Psychology*, 92, 68–76.

Sandgrund, R. W., Gaines, R. W., and Green, A. H. (1983) Child abuse and mental retardation: A problem of cause and effect. *Journal of Mental Deficiency*, 19, 327–330.

Schilling, R. F. and Schinke, S. P. (1984) Maltreatment and mental retardation. In: J. M. Berg (ed.), *Perspectives and Progress in Mental Retardation*, Vol. 1. Baltimore MD: University Park Press.

Schindler, F. and Arkowitz, H. (1986) The assessment of mother–child interactions in physically abusive and nonabusive families. *Journal of Family Violence*, 1, 247–257.

Scott, P. D. (1973) Parents who kill their children. *Medicine, Science and the Law*, 13, 120–126.

Seagull, E. A. W. (1987) Social support and child maltreatment: a review of evidence. *Child Abuse and Neglect*, 11, 41–52.

Smith, J. and Rachman, S. J. (1984) Non-accidental injury to children. II: A controlled evaluation of a behavioural management programme. *Behaviour Research and Therapy*, **22**, 349–366.

Sroufe, L. A. (1983) Infant–caregiver attachment and patterns of adaptation in preschool: The roots of maladaptation and competence. In: M. Perlmutter (ed.) *Minnesota Symposium on Child Psychology:* Vol. 16. Hillsdale, NJ: Erlbaum Associates.

Starr, R. H., Jr (1982) A research-based approach to the prediction of child abuse. In: R. H. Starr, Jr (ed.), *Child Abuse Prediction: Policy Implications*. Cambridge, MA: Ballinger.

Starr, R. H., Dietrich, K. N., Fischoff, J., Ceresnie, S., and Zweier, D. (1984) The contribution of handicapping conditions to child abuse. *Topics in Early Childhood and Special Education*, **4**, 55–69.

Steele, B. B. (1970) Parental abuse of infants and small children. In: E. J. Anthony and T. Benedeck (eds.), *Parenthood: Its Psychology and Psychopathology*. Boston, MA: Little, Brown.

Steele, B. B. and Pollock, D. (1968) A psychiatric study of parents who abuse small children. In: C. H. Kempe and R. E. Helfer (eds.), *The Battered Child*. Chicago, IL: Chicago University Press.

Steinmetz, S. K. (1987) Family violence: past, present and future: In: M. B. Sussman and S. K. Steinmetz (eds.), *Handbook of the Marriage and the Family*. New York: Plenum Press.

Stevenson, J., Bailey, V. and Simpson, J. (1988) Feasible intervention in families with parenting difficulties: A primary prevention perspective on child abuse. In: K. Browne, C. Davies and P. Stratton (eds.), *Early Prediction and Prevention of Child Abuse*. Chichester: Wiley.

Straker, G. and Jacobson, R. (1981) Aggression, emotional maladjustment, and empathy in the abused child. *Developmental Psychology*, **17**, 762–765.

Straus, M. A. (1980) Social stress and marital violence in a national sample of American families. In: F. Wright, C. Bain and R. W. Bieber (eds.), *Forensic Psychology and Psychiatry: Annals of the New York Academy of Science*, 347–358.

Straus, M. A. (1983) Oridinary violence, child abuse and wife beating: what do they have in common? In: D. Finkelhor, R. J. Gelles, G. T. Hotaling and M. A. Straus (eds), *The Dark Side of Families*. Beverly Hills, CA: Sage.

Straus, M. A. and Gelles, R. J. (1986) Societal change and family violence from 1975 to 1985 as revealed by two national surveys. *Journal of Marriage and the Family*, **48**, 445–479.

Straus, M. A., Gelles, R. J. and Steinmetz, S. K. (1980) *Behind Closed Doors: Violence in American Families*. New York: Doubleday.

Tarter, R. E., Hegedus, A. E., Winsten, N. E. and Alterman, A. I. (1984) Neuropsychological, personality and familial characteristics of physically abused delinquents. *Journal of the American Academy of Child Psychiatry*, **23**, 668–674.

Thomson, E. M., Paget, N. W., Bates, D. W., Mesch, M., and Putnam, T. I. (1971) *Child Abuse: A Community Challenge*. New York: Henry Stewart and Children's Aid and Society for the Prevention of Cruelty to Children.

Trickett, P. K. and Kuczynski, L. (1986) Children's misbehaviors and parental discipline strategies in abusive and nonabusive families. *Developmental Psychology*, **22**, 115–123.

Twentyman, C. T., and Plotkin, R. C. (1982) Unrealistic expectations of parents who maltreat their children: An educational deficit that pertains to child development. *Journal of Clinical Psychology*, **38**, 497–503.

Van der Eyken, W. (1982) *Home Start: A Four Year Evaluation*. Leicester: Home Start Consultancy.

White, R., Benedict, M., Wulff, L. and Kelly, M. (1987) Physical disabilities as risk factors for child maltreatment: a selected review. *American Journal of Orthopsychiatry*, **57**, 93–101.

Wolfe, D. A. (1985) Child abusive parents: an empirical review and analysis. *Psychological Bulletin*, **97**, 462–482.

Wolfe, D. A. (1987) *Child Abuse: Implications for Child Development and Psychopathology*. Beverly Hills, CA: Sage.

Wolfe, D. A., Fairbank, J. A., Kelly, J. A. and Bradlyn, A. S. (1983) Child abusive parents' physiological responses to stressful and non-stressful behaviour in children. *Behavioural Assessment*, **5**, 363–371.

Wolfe, D. A., Sandler, J. and Kaufman, K. (1981) A competency-based parent training program for child abusers. *Journal of Consulting and Clinical Psychology*, **49**, 633–640.

Wood-Shuman, S. and Cone, J. W. (1986) Differences in abusive, at-risk for abuse, and control mothers' descriptions of normal child behaviour. *Child Abuse and Neglect*, **10**, 397–405.

Zeigart, K. A. (1983) The Swedish prohibition of corporal punishment: a preliminary report. *Journal of Marriage and the Family*, **45**, 917–926.

7

Marital Abuse

INCIDENCE

Estimates of the incidence of violence within marital and cohabiting relationships vary greatly, and as with all other forms of family abuse the variation reported between studies mostly reflects the criteria used to define 'violence'. Thus, according to the two national US surveys conducted by Straus and his colleagues (Straus, Gelles and Steinmetz, 1980; Straus and Gelles, 1986), if slapping, pushing and grabbing (as well as more serious forms of attack) are included, then the yearly incidence figure is 16% of couples. If minor forms are excluded, however, then the one-year incidence (for both the 1975 and the 1985 surveys) is in the region of 6%. Thus for 6% of couples at least one act of serious violence was perpetrated by one or both partners at least once during the year studied. In some cases there will have been just a single serious assault, but in many cases serious violence will have recurred frequently. It should be noted that these surveys were concerned exclusively with violent attacks and did not include data on other forms of marital abuse such as emotional abuse (or 'mental cruelty'), neglect, and marital rape. The discussion in this chapter will also be confined to physical violence, although this is not to deny that other types of marital abuse may be very common and have a devastating impact on the victim. In one US study it was found that 14% of wives had been raped by their husband or ex-husband (Russell, 1982). Forced sex in marriage is probably the most common form of sexual assault, although it should be recognized that in many of these cases the victims themselves do not label their experience as 'rape'.

As with other forms of family violence, the growing awareness of the problem of marital abuse in recent decades has led to a significant increase in the number of cases reported, and this can give the impression that there is a new epidemic. In fact both historical research and studies that have examined changes over recent years suggest that, if anything, the problem may be declining. The term 'rule of thumb' originated from an old English law that held that a man might legitimately chastise his wife using a whip, provided that the whip was no thicker than his thumb. It was generally held that a degree of what would now be labelled 'serious violence' was to be expected in a marriage and was acceptable. Perhaps things have not changed too dramatically. A few years ago in an English court, the witness of an incident in which a man attacked a woman in the street was asked why he had not intervened. He explained: 'I thought she was his wife'. It *is* a sign of changing attitudes, however, that most people are now horrified by the implication of this statement. Unlike the witness, they do not think that being married to a woman gives a man the right to beat her up. There is less tolerance for marital aggression than there was in the historical past, and it seems likely that there are now fewer acts of marital violence. The incidence of severe violence by men towards their partners (but *not* by women towards their partners) may also have declined sharply in recent years. The national surveys quoted above found a 27% drop in the rate of wife abuse between 1975 and 1985, the authors attributing this to heightened public awareness and an increased professional response.

Such evidence of a decline in wife abuse is certainly encouraging but provides no room for complacency. Many women are severely beaten by their husbands and are in desperate need of rescue. Stark and Flitcraft (1988) suggest that battering is the single most common source of serious injury to women and is responsible for more injuries than road accidents, muggings and rape combined. Everything possible must be done to protect women who are at risk of such abuse, and understanding why brutal attacks occur is likely to suggest a number of ways in which assaults can be prevented. In trying to develop such an understanding, however, we must avoid the temptation of using too wide a definition of 'violence' so that we fail to distinguish adequately between marriages in which there are occasional pushes and pulls and those in which serious beatings occur.

The failure to make such a distinction is not uncommon, particularly among feminist writers, and it has allowed some to draw the conclusion that wife-beating is universal, or nearly universal, and that assaults on wives are a necessary consequence of the institution of marriage and of society as it is currently organized. Such writers may even draw the depressing conclusion that 'wife-beating will remain "the norm" until there are fundamental changes in society'. The contrasting view, that domestic violence is not common and 'ordinary', but is out of line with cultural standards ('deviant'), suggests that the behaviour of men who attack their wives might be changed to bring it *in line with* the prevailing order. This is not, of course, to argue against the need for social change, or to reject the view that a general re-orientation of male and female roles would bring many benefits, including favourable changes in marital relationships, and would help to reduce the number of husbands who brutally attack their wives. However, it is a counsel of despair to suggest that a societal revolution and the end of patriarchy is the *only* way in which marital abuse can be prevented or 'treated'.

Steinmetz (1987) remarks that some feminist writers have also tended to de-emphasize the use of violence by women and speaks of a 'conspiracy of silence' on this issue. She notes that there is in fact overwhelming evidence showing that many women are violent towards their husbands. US homicide figures show that of the cases in which one partner kills the other, women are the perpetrators in about 40% of cases. For less serious violence there is also evidence of a high rate of abuse by female perpetrators. The US national surveys reported that there were as many cases of wife-to-husband violence as there were of husband-to-wife violence. The figures were fairly stable for 'overall violence' over the two years sampled, but whereas the rate of 'severe' husband-to-wife violence fell considerably, the rate of 'severe' wife-to-husband violence did not, so that in 1985 there were actually *more* cases of 'husband abuse' than of 'wife abuse' (Straus and Gelles, 1986). It is not surprising that these results have proved highly controversial and that other authors have produced very different estimates. Thus Steinmetz (1987) suggests that the ratio of physically abused wives to physically abused husbands is probably in the region of 12:1.

Because men are usually physically stronger and more resilient than women, they may sustain fewer injuries as a result of the attacks made on them, and this would explain why so few men actually appear to be 'battered'. It also needs to be noted that much of the female violence that occurs may be retaliatory or defensive. On the other hand, whatever data source is used, and whatever criteria are used to define 'violence', it is clear that marital violence by females is not rare or non-existent, as some feminists have tried to maintain. Having made a number of critical points about the role of feminist writers in misrepresenting the realities of marital abuse, it is appropriate to acknowledge the substantial and important contributions that such commentators have made to research and debate on the issue. Feminist workers have also been at the forefront of developments in providing residential shelters for women who are in acute danger.

RISK FACTORS

A number of variables have been consistently shown to increase the risk of marital abuse. These can be grouped into (a) stress factors, (b) marital factors and (c) personality factors.

STRESS FACTORS

Social factors that are presumed to have their influence through the stress they impose include crowded living conditions, poverty, and unemployment. Each of these, it will be noted, is related to social class. Since 'social class' is not a psychological variable, however, to give a psychological account of why those from one social class are more likely to abuse we need to translate this 'distal' variable into more 'proximal' variables such as an individual's attitudes, expectations, judgements or habits. Couples facing economic and environmental stresses are likely to become frustrated and may engage in frequent struggles over the allocation of their limited resources. Unemployment not only brings loss of income and status but also increases the partners' isolation and brings them into close contact for prolonged periods. This can produce chronic irritation, particularly if the living conditions are cramped. With few resources available to break up the day, and with little to look forward to, both partners may become bored and irritable, and one person's anger about problems and privation may be vented on the unfortunate partner. Although couples from lower socio-economic groups are more at risk of marital abuse, the problem is by no means restricted to those with lower incomes. Marital violence occurs in all sections of society. Frustration, conflict and aggression reflect not only unfavourable environmental and financial conditions, but also many other problems that arise for individuals and between couples.

Another demographic factor that has been shown to relate to the risk of marital violence (again related to social class) is the educational level of the partners. The more education a man has had, the less likely he is to abuse his wife, and wives with more education are less likely to be abused by their husbands (Steinmetz, 1977). These associations between educational level and abuse risk could be explained in a number of ways. For one thing, those who have benefited from higher education are more likely to be in stable employment, to have a good income and to live in favourable conditions. Thus they will escape many of the stresses likely to affect the less educated. But those with more education may also have different attitudes to marriage and to violence, perhaps because they come from more favourable backgrounds where they are less likely to have been subjected to abusive behaviour in childhood, or because they are more often exposed to anti-aggressive attitudes and models. The better educated may also make more use of negotiation and problem-solving strategies in dealing with conflicts, making it less likely that intense anger will be elicited. Studies of marital conflict do support this view. Thus it has been shown that those with more education are less likely to engage in violent quarrels (Komarovsky, 1967).

The overall picture of the relationship between education and marital violence is somewhat complicated, however, by the fact that although highly educated women suffer less marital abuse, they are more likely than other women to be the perpetrators of such abuse (Straus *et al.*, 1980). Steinmetz (1987) suggests that within the more egalitarian relationship assumed to exist between college-educated couples, women will tend to be assertive, and that in some cases one result of this will be an increased use of physical aggression. The importance of the *relative* educational and work status of the husband and wife will be discussed later.

Social isolation is another factor that increases the risk of marital violence. Straus (1980) found that the extent of social integration or isolation significantly influenced the risk of violence between husbands and wives. Gelles (1987) reported that many couples involved in marital abuse were almost completely cut off from their neighbours and had few friends. Loneliness creates tension, and those who are isolated have few opportunities for talking to other people or calling upon them for advice and practical help. Isolation from neighbours and relatives (and from work colleagues, due to unemployment) markedly reduces the social support that has been shown to be a highly effective buffer in times of stress. People may be isolated because they live in an environment that provides little chance of meeting neighbours, or because they have little social interest or lack social skills. Gelles pointed out, however, that some violent families appear to isolate themselves deliberately so that other people will not find out about the abusive behaviour.

Change (especially if it is threatening and uncontrollable) often produces tension, and some families are better at coping with this than others. Some traumatic changes (for example, the birth of a handicapped child, or the imminent death of a member of the family) generally seem to increase family cohesion, and any hostility may be directed at fate or some other external target. Thus some stressful changes may actually reduce the risk of marital conflict, at least temporarily. When certain other changes occur, however, such as an adolescent leaving home or an elderly relative coming to live, the effects on marital conflict are less predictable. Sometimes the couple will unite to face the common stress and their interaction will be cooperative and subdued. In other cases the same 'threat' will generate bitter strife. Individuals sometimes vent their personal frustration about a difficult situation by blaming their partner for causing the predicament, or for not doing enough to prevent it. Pregnancy, moving house and being made redundant at work are transitions that often demand considerable readjustment and may lead to overwhelming tension and conflict.

MARITAL FACTORS

Certain aspects of the marital relationship are strongly associated with the risk of violence. As would be expected, unstable and disorganized marriages, those in which there is a low level of marital satisfaction, and those in which conflict is dealt with in an aggressive and uncontrolled way, are especially likely to be physically violent.

Marital Instability

Those involved in marital abuse are less likely to have happy and stable marriages. Such couples have often had a number of separations and express low satisfaction with their relationship (Rosenbaum and O'Leary, 1981). In many cases, of course, instability and low satisfaction may be a *consequence* of previous violent incidents, but the tension within unstable relationships increases the risk that a minor conflict will produce an explosive response. The rate of abuse is also significantly higher if the couple are living together but not married. Yllo and Straus (1981) reported that women in cohabiting relationships were four times as likely to suffer severe violence as those who were married.

Family Structure and Communication

Marital violence asserts the aggressor's power over the victim and may therefore be used to establish control or to reassert authority that is judged to be under threat. One prediction that might be derived from this is that abuse will be particularly prevalent where the woman has a higher status than the man (in terms of income or employment status, for example), particularly if the man has conservative or sexist views. In his examination of the impact of family variables upon the relationship between stress and spousal abuse, Straus (1980) found that unequal power was related to the risk of marital abuse, and Hornung, McCullough and Sugimoto (1981) also found that a wide status difference between the partners was associated with a higher frequency of violence. They further reported that the risk was especially high if the man had lower status than his wife. One explanation of why physical violence might be used to assert power in such a situation comes from 'resource theory' (Goode, 1971). This suggests that when people have few resources or little capacity to exert control in other ways they will tend to resort to physical violence as a means of influencing others. Thus the man who has little prestige, social rank or earning power compared to his wife cannot draw upon these as sources of strength in an argument and may therefore use brute force as a means of 'persuasion'.

Marital violence also reflects the way in which the family normally communicates. Olson *et al.* (1983) suggest that healthy families are open in their communication, that they use negotiation often, and that they have relatively few implicit rules. Olson also suggested that well-adjusted families usually have an egalitarian marital relationship. Some support for an association between the general level of functioning of the family and the level of physical violence comes from a study by Resick and Reese (1986). They asked a large group of students to disclose whether their parents' relationship had been physically violent and to rate the general family atmosphere on a number of dimensions. They found that families with a history of marital violence were also reported as having a high level of general conflict, with openly expressed anger, disorganization, and a clear dominance hierarchy. Maritally violent families engaged less often in pleasant communal activities and were less tolerant of independent initiatives by individual members.

Marital Conflict Styles

In the discussion of marital conflict, in Chapter 5, it was noted that many couples develop characteristic styles of fighting and evolve particular conflict 'habits'. Some of these involve serious escalation, 'dirty tactics', and a rapid transition from the verbal to the physical. It is plain that the habitual style of conflict engagement and conflict development is likely to have a major effect on the risk of dangerous physical assault. It has already been noted that marital abuse is related to the general communication style of the family, and the way in which problematic issues are dealt with, and Straus (1974) found that physical violence was more likely to occur in homes that rarely employed rational problem-solving strategies.

Margolin, John and Gleberman (1988) compared the behavioural and emotional responses of physically abusive couples and non-violent couples in a laboratory-based conflict situation. Observers who viewed videotapes of the couples' discussions rated physically abusive husbands as showing more offensive behaviours. The authors suggest that this might indicate a general destructive style of conflict engagement that could periodically escalate to extreme aggression. The abusive men were found to use more hostile gestures (including pointing, arm-waving and threatening actions) and more hostile verbal behaviours (including angry vocalizations, sarcasm, nagging and accusations). They reported more anger and anxiety, and were more likely to feel under attack than men in the other groups. Furthermore, they experienced somewhat more physiological arousal. The physically abused wives were more offensive than other wives in their verbal behaviour and showed a rapid pattern of escalation and de-escalation of overt negative behaviours. It should be noted that the 'abusive' couples who participated in this study had not been involved in severe violence (the authors remark that 'the women did not perceive themselves as "battered wives"') but it is remarkable that consistent differences between the groups were demonstrated in the 'public' laboratory setting.

Many efforts at treating marital abuse focus on trying to change the couple's conflict style. They often attempt to alert the couple to the dangers of rapid escalation, of attacks against the partner's self-esteem or personality, and of steering an argument towards particularly dangerous areas (referred to by Gelles, 1987, as 'incendiary topics'). In some cases physical violence almost always follows an explosive confrontation in which both partners engage in unrestrained verbal attacks before the first blow is dealt. Steinmetz (1987) labelled such couples 'Saturday night brawlers'. She was careful to point out, however, that not all cases of marital abuse follow this pattern and that there are some 'chronic battered women' who are passive victims of their partner's assaults.

PERSONALITY FACTORS

'Aggressiveness' is a measurable and relatively stable aspect of personality (aggressive children tend to become aggressive adults; Eron *et al.*, 1987). Thus it would be expected that those who engage in serious violence towards their spouse will also be aggressive in other aspects of their lives. It is well established, for example, that those who assault their partner are also likely to attack their children. As for any other personality trait, the issue of why some people are more aggressive than others is complex. There is strong evidence of an hereditary component in aggressiveness (Rushton *et al.*, 1987), but it is also well established that early and later environmental influences play a very important part. It is of particular interest that men who batter (and, to a somewhat lesser extent, wives who are battered) are likely to have been physically abused as children (Rosenbaum and O'Leary, 1981; Telch and Lindquist, 1984).

Maiuro *et al.* (1988) studied men who were participating in a specialized treatment programme for problems of anger and violence. Some of the men were involved in domestic violence and others were involved in attacks beyond the home, and both of these groups were compared with a control sample of 'non-violent' men. It was found that men in each of the violent groups scored higher on personality measures of overt and covert aggression, assault, irritability, resentment, and suspiciousness. Violent men also had higher scores for 'guilt' and were likely to be depressed. Those involved in domestic violence were significantly more depressed than those in either of the other groups. The authors note that their results are consistent with the idea that anger is a key emotion in the psychological profile of the domestic batterer. They also suggest that the similarity of the personalities of men involved in marital violence and those involved in non-domestic violence supports the view that marital abuse is similar to other forms of violence and fails to endorse the 'ideological separation' of marital abuse from other types of assaultive behaviour.

Besides aggressiveness and a potential for anger, a number of other personality characteristics seem to make marital assault more likely. Thus men who assault their wives tend to have low self-esteem (Telch and Lindquist, 1984; Goldstein and Rosenbaum, 1985). This may produce a general frustration that will generate aggression towards a suitable victim. Such men are likely to react angrily to anybody who affronts them. Those who are critical or seem to be treating them with disdain threaten their fragile self-esteem. This will generate indignation and rage, but overt aggression is more likely to be directed at those who are incapable of retaliating. The family situation provides a relatively safe context in which such men can vent their aggression, and the partner and children are therefore likely to become scapegoats.

A few of those who violently attack their partner are suffering from some severe psychopathological condition, so that their judgement and self-control are seriously impaired. But such cases are rare. In many more cases, aspects of the individual's personality establish an appraisal style that produces a profound over-sensitivity to irritation, a tendency to exaggerate the degree to which other people's actions inflict personal 'costs', and a general proclivity for judging behaviour as 'transgressive'. Thus just as some abusing parents are 'blame-oriented' and interpret their children's normal behaviour as 'naughty' or 'malicious', so some individuals interpret their partner's actions as despicable and deliberately provocative.

A clear example of such a tendency can be found in the case of the suspicious and distrustful husband (support for the idea that violent men are unusually suspicious comes from the Maiuro *et al.* study described above). A man who is 'a profoundly jealous type' is likely to judge many of his wife's actions as evidence of an affair or her desire to be unfaithful. Her protests that his suspicions are unfounded are not likely to satisfy him, and it will be difficult for him to be reassured that she has not been unfaithful. In many cases the man's unease with his role in the relationship (and his unease with himself) will contribute to his distrust. Jealousy is just one way in which a person's attitudes and beliefs can contribute to the danger of violence. Some men have very ruthless and repressive attitudes to marriage and child discipline so that their partner is often judged to be 'stepping out of line' (of showing too little interest in the home, for example, or failing to exert enough control over the children). Such 'offences' are likely to be seen as meriting strong chastisement. Men who hold strong sexist views will more readily judge that their partner's behaviour is transgressing 'proper' norms, and they may attempt to ensure compliance by means of threats or a physical attack. Thus those who reject an egalitarian view of marriage are more likely to be violent towards their partner. Rosenbaum and O'Leary (1981) found that abusive men were highly conservative in their attitudes to women, and in a study based in Northern Ireland, Evason (1982) found that 66% of violent husbands favoured the traditional male-dominated model of marriage, compared with just 34% of non-violent husbands. Rosenbaum and O'Leary (1981) also found that those who abuse their partner often have a high 'need for power', and additional support for the relevance of this personality variable comes from a study of college students' violence towards their (marital or dating) partners. Mason and Blankenship (1987) found that male students who had high scores on a 'need for power' measure were more likely to have been violent towards their partner than those who had low scores on this variable.

The personality of the victim may also help to predict marital abuse. Partners who are highly critical, engage in frequent complaining, fight 'below the belt', use physical aggression themselves and behave in ways that are likely to encourage jealousy, are more likely to become victims. A jealous wife or husband may engage in compulsive and insistent cross-examination of their partner, provoking the partner to an indignant fury. Thus aspects of the victim's personality and appraisal style may play an important part in initiating conflicts that eventually become violent. Their style of conflict engagement is then likely to contribute to the way in which the altercation develops, and whether it becomes vicious and out of control. In the study by Margolin and her colleagues discussed above (Margolin, John and Gleberman, 1988) it was found that wives in physically abusive relationships were more frequently critical and verbally offensive than other wives, and that their level of overt negative behaviours rapidly changed throughout the course of the (laboratory-based) conflict. The victim's personality will also guide the strategy she chooses in a bid to avoid a violent attack. Some victims respond passively to the mounting tension, and some try to counter the threat of aggression by making a 'pre-emptive strike'. They may be physically violent or verbally aggressive, or threaten to leave, to call the police, or to tell relatives. Sometimes such 'defensive' moves have the opposite effect of that intended. Rather than inhibiting the aggressor, they may generate intense anger and increase the risk that the confrontation will end in a violent attack. Thus the part the victim *sometimes* plays in provoking and escalating the conflict and in using unsuitable self-defence tactics needs to be taken into account when attempting to clarify the nature and course of marital violence, although it should be emphasized — once again — that this does not shift the blame for the violence from the aggressor.

INCIDENT DYNAMICS

It has been argued that the most suitable approach to understanding how incidents of family violence arise involves focusing on the interaction between the assailant and the victim. We need to consider how incidents of marital abuse arise, and to illustrate how risk factors such as poverty and unemployment, marital conflict style, and the assailant's personality, come to be associated with violent incidents.

The account to be given suggests that in most cases marital violence is the result of a conflict that escalates until one partner administers a blow. A similar analysis was provided by Patterson and Hops (1972). They found that victims and aggressors usually exchanged a series of preliminary verbal attacks and counterattacks (which the authors refer to as 'coercion spirals'), before physical violence erupted. The conflict episode need not be prolonged, and on some occasions aggression may follow from a single comment or action that the assailant finds 'irritating' or 'costly', or judges to be a 'transgression' (or some combination of these). But the assailant's action is almost always 'spontaneous'—it is rarely planned or strategic. It is almost always 'rational' from the abuser's perspective. And it is almost always 'interactional', generally arising as a reaction to some action by the victim or from an initial non-violent interaction between the perpetrator and the victim.

Evidence from the study by Gelles (1987) supports the claims that marital abuse is typically spontaneous, 'rational', and reactive. Because the attack invariably follows some annoying action by the victim, Gelles suggests, victims are not 'whipping boys' or 'hostility sponges', but play a major role in precipitating the attack. This does not mean that the victim is *responsible* for the violence, however, as expressed in the statement 'she has only herself to blame'. Thus a woman who refuses to have intercourse with her husband plainly does not 'deserve' an attack and is certainly not 'asking to be beaten', but her refusal to have sex is nonetheless the action that gives rise to the assault. It is a necessary but not sufficient condition for the abusive reaction. Other necessary conditions include the man's negative interpretation of the refusal, his anger and annoyance (it may irritate him, it 'costs' him sexual satisfaction, and it may be seen by him as a 'transgression'—an unfair deprivation of his rights). And an aggressive action also reflects the man's lack of inhibition about hitting his wife. This analysis, with its emphasis on the assailant's psychological processes, indicates how important it may be for those involved in treating abusive men to challenge inappropriate perceptions of the victim's behaviour and the attitudes that help to shape these judgements.

The understanding of marital abuse can be increased by a knowledge of *when* and *where* attacks take place. Most family violence takes place in the home when only the family is present (Gelles, 1987). People are much less inhibited about assaulting a family member in the privacy of their home. Goffman (1959) characterized the home as 'backstage'—a domain where people are relaxed and uninhibited and behave in less restrained and less controlled ways than they would in other social contexts. And when family members are at home together they may feel little necessity to 'keep up the appearance' of being united and civil to one another. The most likely time for violence to occur is the evening. This is when the couple are most likely to be alone, to get into discussions, and to think about sex. It is also the time when drinking is most likely to occur. Possibly for many of the same reasons, weekends are associated with a relatively high frequency of marital abuse. The Christmas and New Year periods (associated with increased financial spending, increased time spent together, and increased drinking) also seem to be especially dangerous for many couples.

The next question is *how* particular incidents arise. In the discussion on marital conflict, in Chapter 5, it was noted that marital rows often start when one partner makes a complaint about the other not living up to an expectation, or breaking a 'rule of marriage'. The breaking of some rules (such as forgetting an anniversary) is likely to lead to a quietly expressed disappointment, but some transgressions (such as infidelity or being disloyal to the partner in front of other people) are likely to produce stinging complaints. Gelles found that marital abuse was generally triggered by some verbal behaviour of the victim, including nagging, criticizing, name-calling, and gibes about status or sexual performance. Needless to say, many such criticisms might be justified, and the gibes might be accurate, but they will be experienced as irritating, costly or transgressive for all that, and are therefore likely to incite extreme anger. Sometimes the criticism touches a particularly sore point, as when a woman berates her husband for his unemployment or his lack of sexual stamina, and the emotional response is all the more likely to produce excessive anger. Verbal triggers will often reflect the victim's own stress, anxiety, disappointment and harassment, and the style of the complaint will often be affected by her emotional state. Partners become experts at attacking the other's weaknesses, and when they are angry they are liable to 'go for the jugular' and to 'punch below the belt'. Such 'unfairness' is likely to be seen by the partner as outrageous and offensive and may thus be taken by the assailant as a justification for his violent attack.

THEMES OF VIOLENT MARITAL ENCOUNTERS

Certain topics frequently recur as themes in episodes of marital violence. Arguments sometimes start over trivial issues and then escalate, or they digress into issues that concern major longstanding grievances or disputes. Sometimes the fundamental controversy is obvious from the content of the verbal battle, but in many cases the matters addressed in the argument will cover a deeper, implicit problem (such as concern over power or commitment). Complaints and disputes that eventually lead to violence often focus on such topics as child discipline, meals, chores, and alcohol, as well as two areas that we will examine in more detail—sexual issues and money (Roy, 1977, 1982; Dobash and Dobash, 1979; Pahl, 1985).

Sexual Issues

Sexual issues are often the source of quarrels that result in violence. Partners commonly have different expectations about sexual interaction (how frequently they should have sexual contact, for example, or what behaviours are exciting and permissible). Gelles (1987) found that complaints about frigidity or impotence and other arguments over sex frequently led to violent outbursts. A woman who is told that she is 'cold', or a man whose sexual prowess is called into question, is likely to respond in an exaggerated fashion. Stress may affect partners' sexual appetite in different ways, with some losing interest and some wishing for increased sexual contact. A general disaffection between the couple will often become most apparent in the context of sexual encounters or discussions of sexual matters, and such occasions may precipitate violent quarrels that actually reflect deeper problems in the relationship.

Accusations of infidelity are powerful triggers of aggression. Whether or not the accusation is justified, jealous arguments over suspected affairs or flirtation are likely to end up with spouses hitting each other. In many cases such violence follows from a prolonged interrogation of the partner who is suspected of cheating. In this area in particular, women may have the same potential for aggression as men (Gelles, 1987), and the person who becomes physically violent may be either the accuser (in response to an admission of the offence, or a continual denial) or the one who is accused (in response to what they see as the 'third-degree' tactic of the accuser). A jealous partner may be super-vigilant for signs of infidelity and draw conclusions of flirtatious behaviour or an affair from meagre cues. Thus a woman who dresses up for an evening out may be accused of trying to attract other men, or a man's reduced interest in sex may be taken as an indication that he is having an extramarital affair.

It is rare for victims to strategically precipitate violence, but such cases are sometimes reported. A few victims might actually welcome a low-level assault as providing them with a socially approved reason for leaving the relationship and powerful legal grounds for separation and divorce. One case of strategic provocation to violence is cited by Gelles (1987). A woman reported that she would sometimes provoke her husband to beat her so that he would leave the house and she would thus avoid having sex with him. It must be emphasized that such deliberate victim-provoked attacks are a rare exception, but such accounts do show that victims are sometimes *capable* of provoking a violent attack.

Money

Some conflicts can be seen primarily as fights over resources such as money or free time. Most couples have limited finances, and there are certain tasks and chores that have to be performed by one or the other. The benefits that one person derives from personal expenditure represent a cost to the other person, and there may be endless wrangles about the fair allocation of money, chores and privileges. It is within this framework that the impact of poverty can be understood as increasing the risk of violence. Poverty is likely to lead to numerous arguments over how the meagre finances are to be spent. The partners are likely to differ in their perception of priorities so that when one person spends money, and particularly if it is seen as wasted (on gambling, for example, or alcohol) the other partner is likely to complain about the transgression of squandering money. Any frustration and guilt that the 'culprit' has about having wasted resources (especially if a gambling loss is involved) will make him extremely aggravated, and in such circumstances a complaint, especially if it is 'undiplomatic' in tone, is likely to provoke extreme rage. Similarly, the situation may prove especially dangerous if a complaint is made about money spent on alcohol or other drugs while the 'offender' is still intoxicated.

The assailant's use of severe violence will have the long-term effect of increasing fear. The abuser may hope that, following an aggressive attack, the partner will not dare to complain again about such spending, thus leaving him free to use all of the joint resources as he wishes. Thus aggression not only expresses current feelings of anger but may also be instrumental in bringing about a 'reign of terror' that gives the aggressor power to have his own way. It seems unlikely that many people deliberately use violence in a cold-blooded way to establish such power, but the aggressor may well realize that the use of violence might grant him immunity from further complaints, and he may later reinforce the woman's fear by reminding her of the outcome of her previous accusation.

THE ROLE OF ALCOHOL

Many reports suggest that the consumption of alcohol greatly increases the risk of marital violence (Leonard and Jacob, 1988). There are a number of explanations of why alcohol tends to make situations dangerous. Intoxication reduces the accuracy of social judgement and leads to behaviour that is likely to attract complaints (a general condemnation of the drunkenness, for example, a criticism about the money wasted on drink, or a specific protest about some aspect of drunken behaviour). Some people seem to respond particularly badly to complaints when they have been drinking, and become intensely angry very quickly. The effect of alcohol in reducing inhibitions may also increase the likelihood that the angry person will attack in a violent and uncontrolled way. Gelles (1987) suggested that some men might deliberately use alcohol to provide an excuse, after the event, of why they beat up their wife. Alcohol, he claims, provides people with 'time out' from normal moral judgements and allows for 'deviance disavowal' by both the attacker and the victim ('it wasn't really me/him, it was the drink'). Thus he suggests that some individuals become intoxicated in order to carry out the violent act. Sedlak (1988) concluded that the use of alcohol by abusive men is often such an important factor that dealing with the drink problem can be a highly effective way of intervening in many cases of wife abuse.

THE FORM OF AGGRESSION

Physically aggressive attacks take many different forms, and although severe violence is always unacceptable, some types of attack are clearly much more dangerous than others. What, then, determines whether marital abuse takes the form of a slap, a kick, a punch to the stomach, a punch to the head, or an all-out battering with multiple blows to particularly vulnerable parts of the body? Following the analysis of the forms of aggression used in physical child abuse, in Chapter 6, a number of contributory factors can be identified. One principal determinant is likely to be the degree of anger that gives rise to the attack. Extreme anger may lead to an 'all-out' attack, while lower levels of anger may preserve some degree of control, so that the assault results in less serious injury. Some men follow their own idiosyncratic guidelines about what forms of aggression are 'legitimate' (examples of such rules are: 'never hit a woman in the chest' or 'only a coward kicks someone when they're down'), and others specifically avoid inflicting injuries, such as a black eye, that will later draw attention to their brutality.

The form of aggression sometimes follows previously uttered threats, as if the verbal threat provides a cue for the precise form of action used. Sometimes there is an instrumental aspect to the aggression, as when a woman who is screaming has a pillow held to her face, or instrumental and symbolic elements may be involved, as when a man hits a woman in the face so that 'no-one else will look at her'. Gelles (1987) suggested that specific techniques of family violence tend to be passed on from one generation to the next. Thus a man who was punched as a child, and witnessed his father punching the mother, would perhaps be more likely to punch his wife than to kick her. A particular form of aggressive action may become habitual, although the severity with which it is used will vary with the circumstances and the attacker's degree of anger.

THE AFTERMATH OF MARITAL ABUSE

THE VICTIM'S IMMEDIATE RESPONSE

Faced with the threat of a violent attack by her partner, how does the woman respond? Gelles (1987) and Bowker (1983) found that wives attempt to protect themselves from violence by using a number of strategies. Many of these involve threats—threats of calling the police, leaving, taking the children away, or withholding sexual favours. Many wives have learned through experience, however, that threatening physical violence, or using pre-emptive or retaliatory violence, often escalates conflict, and they therefore avoid hitting the man because they fear that this may increase the likelihood and severity of his attack. Straus and Gelles (1986) point out that this is relevant to the issue of whether it is advisable to promote karate and other martial arts as means of 'self-defence' for women at high risk of domestic violence. They suggest that in many cases such a 'self-defence' strategy might prove highly dangerous and counter-productive. Walker (1979) reported that some women learn to recognize when tension is mounting to a dangerous level and when an all-out attack is imminent, and develop the skill of preventing escalation to the acute battering stage by provoking a minor scene to relieve some of the hostility.

Many women who are under attack escape to a place in the house (usually the bathroom) where they can lock the door, while others manage to make a getaway and seek refuge with neighbours, or with relatives who live nearby. This provides an escape from the immediate danger, and perhaps a place to stay for some hours or days. Wives realize that even if the husband appears on the scene he is unlikely to use violence when other people are around. Sometimes the woman feels that she is not on sufficiently good terms with the neighbours, and no relatives live in the vicinity, and she will simply escape to a public space. Some women know of a shelter for battered wives and seek refuge there. Most battered women, however, do not seek refuge in such shelters; those who do are likely to have been subjected to more severe attacks and to have few family supports (Berk, Newton, and Berk, 1986). Wives also appear less likely to seek refuge if they have witnessed their mother as a marital abuse victim (Lerman, 1981). Some women are unable to escape, either because the husband forces them to stay, or because they are afraid to leave without the children in case harm should befall them.

Thus the decision about whether to escape depends on such factors as the severity of the beating, the immediate threat of further violence, and the accessibility of alternative accommodation. The aggressor's presumed response to an escape may also be important. If the woman believes that her leaving is likely to bring home to the man the seriousness of his attack and the possibility that she might end the relationship, this may prompt her to leave. If she believes that he will react angrily, however, she may decide to stay in a bid to pacify him. Many women are very reluctant to leave. They may consider that this will prolong and escalate the conflict, and prevent a hoped-for reconciliation. Going away entails leaving possessions and familiar surroundings and making the fact of the marital violence known to other people, and some women are particularly uneasy about being identified by relatives, friends and neighbours as a 'battered woman'.

In addition to the decision of whether to escape and seek refuge, the woman has to decide whether to call the police and whether to seek medical help. There may be considerable ambivalence about both of these issues. The woman's decision about whether to request help from the police is likely to reflect her general attitude to the police and her beliefs about whether their approach will be supportive or punitive. She may judge that the police are unlikely to be sympathetic to her, but such doubts and uncertainties will often be overcome if the abuse has been very severe and if there is an immediate threat of a further assault. Some women contact the police simply because they want immediate protection whereas others wish to bring charges, either in a bid to ensure longer-term protection or as a means of bringing their assailant to justice. Some wives are very hesitant about adding to the partner's stress and frustration by confronting him with a legal obstacle, and others fear that such action would lead to later reprisal. One woman told Gelles (1987) that she refrained from calling the police because she feared that an account of the attack would appear in the newspapers, and she didn't want the neighbours to know that her husband had assaulted her.

In the immediate aftermath of the attack the woman may be unclear about what she wants from the police and what options are open to her. Women are often unsure whether involving the forces of law will help them or add to their problems. Many initially bring charges and later, perhaps after a reconciliation, decide to drop the case. It is hardly surprising that police officers are often frustrated by 'domestics', and their general scepticism about the eventual outcome of cases may be apparent in their treatment of abused women. Many of the strategies proposed (and in some cases implemented) for the more effective management of cases involve changing legal procedures to make it clear to the woman just what her options are and to make her experience less formidable. Some of these innovations will be considered later in this chapter.

The woman may also be unsure about whether to seek medical help. Some injuries will clearly demand immediate attention in a hospital casualty ward. Others will require only first-aid measures. In many cases, however, the woman will be uncertain about the severity of her condition. Whether or not a woman attends for treatment will depend not only on the seriousness of the injuries, but also on a number of other factors. Thus attendance for medical care may provide a useful means of escaping from a home environment that still presents an acute threat, and it may be effective in making the man realize the serious effects of his attack. On the other hand, the woman may be reluctant to attend a clinic because she fears that her injuries will expose the man to legal action. Thus many women provide an alternative (though rarely convincing) account of how their injuries were sustained.

LONGER-TERM EFFECTS AND DECISIONS

In the longer term the woman has a number of further questions to consider. Will she try to conceal the abuse, or make it known to relatives, or to a lawyer? Will she leave the relationship (or, if she did escape, will she return)? And will she seek a formal separation or a divorce? She is likely to evaluate the costs and benefits of each of the alternatives. Central to her evaluation will be her perception of the overall quality of the relationship, her judgement of what the abuse 'means', her estimation of the future threat, and her experience of the man's response following the attack. The intermittent nature of the abuse, and the fact there are some positive aspects to the relationship, will often undermine any temptation to leave. It is likely to be crucial whether the woman perceives the abuse as becoming more or less severe, and more or less frequent.

The man's behaviour following the attack is often of key importance. Although some men maintain a hostile attitude, and strive to sustain their 'reign of terror', others enter into a long period of sullen silence. Many men, however, earnestly express regret, offer profound apologies and swear that such violence will not occur again. Pahl (1985) reported that some men showered their wives with lavish gifts in the period following a severe attack, sending bunches of red roses, buying expensive perfume or, in one case, promising the children new bikes for Christmas if they would persuade their mother to agree to a reconciliation. Some abusive husbands have been characterized as 'Jekyll and Hyde' characters who are calm, reasonable and loving between their occasional attacks. Such men may encourage the woman to stay by assuring her that their aggressive outburst was a temporary aberration and that they will never assault her again. In many cases the perpetrator's strategy for regaining the woman's confidence and her concern prove effective, and she agrees to a reconciliation (Walker, 1979).

'Making up' after an attack often has a remarkably powerful effect on restoring the woman's optimism and confidence in the relationship, so that it is almost as if nothing traumatic had occurred. Deschner and McNeil (1986) found that although the experience of quarrels, anger, and violence had the expected adverse effect on a woman's degree of satisfaction with her marriage, this effect was strikingly reduced after the couple had achieved a reconciliation. This study also indicated that incidents of physical violence had less impact on marital satisfaction than the verbal violence that occurred during arguments. The couples involved in this study had not been involved in severe violence (the authors note that all of the 'violence' reported by their subjects was of the 'minor slap' variety, and that much of it was committed by women), but the power of a reconciliation to counteract the woman's apprehensiveness about the relationship, and to make her 'forget' the abusive incident, has been described many times in accounts of the aftermath of very severe marital assaults (e.g. Walker, 1979).

The abused woman will make attributions about why the attack occurred, and it has become clear that many battered women blame themselves (Walker, 1979, 1984). If a battered wife explains the man's behaviour by making attributions that are external, unstable, and specific ('It was the drink that made him do it; he doesn't get drunk very often; he's not normally like that') it is improbable that she will decide to end the relationship. The husband usually attempts to shape the woman's attributions, providing a self-justificatory account of his actions and hoping that she will accept and adopt the explanation he gives.

Many people find it remarkable that the majority of women choose to remain in a violent relationship, even though they are likely to be further abused and may even face permanent injury or death. However, it is not difficult to understand some of the reasons why women stay. Although those who meet the woman immediately following an abusive episode may regard the couple simply as 'an aggressor and his victim' this is unlikely to be an accurate picture of their overall relationship. Some women are prepared to 'take the rough with the smooth', and even a 'battering relationship' can at times be rewarding and loving. Thus some women stay simply because they value the relationship overall and have a high commitment to it. In many cases a period of special calmness and civility follows a serious assault ('a lull after the storm'), and at this time of heightened security and freedom from danger the woman is unlikely to experience any urgency about leaving. Indeed, it may be to avoid the threat of her departure that the man ensures that this is a time of special peace and harmony. Many abused women stay because of inertia—they are hesitant about change—or because they fear the unknown (they might express this feeling as 'better the devil you know than the devil you don't'). However strong a woman's intention to leave in the immediate aftermath of an abusive episode, she may find the prospect of remaining in the home less formidable than the thought of leaving the relationship and venturing into the unknown.

A number of other perceptions and realities are also likely to make the option of leaving seem unattractive or impossible. One major consideration for many women is the sheer economic non-viability of a departure from the family home. A woman may be totally dependent on her husband for income to support herself and her children, and judge that if she left she would become destitute. The prospect of finding suitable accommodation might be especially daunting, and many women see no possibility of being able to feed and clothe their children without their partner's financial support. Such judgements may be somewhat over-pessimistic, and may fail to take into account certain State benefits that would be available, but a woman's decision will reflect her own appraisal of the situation. Thus some women decide with great reluctance that there is no option but to stay, because they assume that a life apart from their husband would not be financially viable.

The imagined or experienced attitudes of other people are also likely to play a role in the woman's decision to remain with the abusive partner. Although some relatives and friends may encourage the woman to leave, others are likely to urge her to stay 'to try to mend the relationship'. She may fear the stigma of divorce and, especially, of being identified as a 'battered woman'. Thus love, commitment, inertia, economic forces, and the attitudes of friends and relatives may all conspire to prevent the woman from leaving the relationship. And even if she left the home following an assault, these factors may induce her to return. For most women, even escape to a shelter does not mark the end of the relationship with the assailant. Giles-Sims (1983) and Stone (1984) found that nearly half of the women who sought refuge in a shelter later returned to continue their relationship with the abuser, and that over half of these experienced further violence in the six months following discharge. Many of those who went back did so despite the fact that during their stay in the refuge they implied that they had no intention of returning.

A number of studies (Rounsaville, 1978; Snyder and Scheer, 1981; Snyder and Fruchtman, 1981; Binney, Harkell and Nixon, 1981) have attempted to identify factors that predict whether or not a woman will return to the relationship following a stay in a shelter. The results suggest that those who return are more likely to be married to the assailant, rather than cohabiting with him, are less likely to have had previous separations, and are more likely to have expressed the intention of returning. Women who do not return are more likely to have retaliated against the abuser, to have been severely beaten, to fear being killed, and to have contacted the police following an assault. If the husband has abused the children as well as the wife then the woman is more likely to end the relationship. Strube and Barbour (1983, 1984) found that women who were highly dependent on the husband economically, and those who had a high psychological commitment to the relationship, were more likely to return. Commitment was measured in terms of the length of the relationship and the woman's rating of how much she loved her partner. The most important single predictor of return was employment status (women not in paid employment were more likely to return), followed by the length of the relationship. These researchers also found that women who ended the relationship were more likely to have brought assault charges against their partner or to have obtained a protection order, and they were less likely to have said on entering the shelter that they were seeking refuge because they had nowhere else to go. Sedlak (1988) reported that the longer a woman stayed in the shelter the less likely she was to return.

Strube (1988) considered a number of models that could be used to explain why women return. He makes the basic assumption that the decision to leave or to remain in the relationship is 'rational' from the woman's perspective. Although he was specifically concerned to explain why a woman returns following a period in a shelter, his analysis is also relevant to the issue of whether the woman leaves home and seeks refuge following abuse. The first model he considers is that of 'entrapment'. Psychological entrapment is a decision process whereby individuals escalate their commitment to a problematic course of action (in this case staying with the man who has abused them) in order to justify or 'make good' prior investments. This analysis therefore suggests that women who stay might have suffered so severely in the past that they feel they have invested too much in the relationship to bring it to an end. The more time and effort the woman invests, the more difficult it will be for her to leave the relationship. The fact that the abuse is intermittent is also likely to periodically reinforce her hope that a good and non-violent relationship with her partner might be attainable. According to the second formulation considered by Strube, the battered woman who returns to the relationship is in a state of 'learned helplessness' that saps her motivation to change her lifestyle.

The third formulation focuses on the woman's perception of the relative costs and benefits of the current relationship compared with those of alternatives. If both the existing and alternative relationships seem costly (if, for example, she imagines that any other partner will probably be violent) then she will be unlikely to leave. Ties to the neighbourhood, the house, and possessions will add to her reluctance to go. She will also stay if the perceived rewards of the current relationship exceed the judged costs. This might happen, for example, if the woman plays down the severity, frequency or significance of the beatings, or regards 'the good times' as making everything worthwhile. It is only when the current relationship is seen as costly, and when the rewards of other possible relationships (or independent living) are judged as likely to be rewarding that she is likely to leave. According to the final model considered by Strube (based on the 'reasoned action' model; Ajzen and Fishbein, 1980), the decision to stay will reflect the woman's 'behavioural intention', a product of her attitudes towards leaving and staying and her beliefs about what other people would expect her to do. According to this model the woman will assess all of the possible consequences of leaving and make an overall evaluation. She will then be influenced by her judgement of what other people would expect her to do in the circumstances, and will form an intention either to leave or to stay.

Several of these models suggest ways in which the woman's decision can be influenced. Those most concerned to exert such influence will be the husband, who will probably wish her to stay, relatives, who may either try to persuade her to stay or to leave, and social workers or refuge workers, who are likely to consider that it would be in her best interests for her to leave the abusive relationship. Thus the husband may attempt to influence her decision by persuading her that it is very unlikely that she will be able to support herself or to find suitable accommodation, while assuring her that if she stays she will be better off materially and emotionally and need have no fear of further violence. On the other hand, shelter workers may be able to point to currently available accommodation and to cite cases of women who have managed well on their own, and they may warn the woman that further attacks are likely if she does return. Whatever decision is finally reached, the fact that a woman considers a number of alternatives may help her to recognize that she has the power to choose between courses of action and is not totally constrained. A heightened sense of control may enable her to reach the optimal solution, and one that is in her own best interests and those of her children.

The woman who has frequent contact with her partner is especially likely to return, particularly if the husband pleads, flatters her and makes extravagant promises. Throughout what may be days or weeks of constant pressure to return, the woman only has to weaken once in her resolve and she is likely to re-enter the home. The chances of this happening are particularly high if going back appears to be 'an easy way out' of a currently unfavourable situation. Once she is back in the home it will take a considerable effort of will for her to leave again, and the fact that she has returned may well have the effect of further increasing her commitment to the relationship.

Many women who return to an abusive relationship are subjected to further episodes of physical aggression and sustain further injuries. Eventually their cumulative experience of violence may bring about a shift from the attitudes and beliefs that led them to return previously, and they may decide to make a permanent break. Some stay and endure the fate of the chronically battered woman at the hands of a man for whom abuse has become habitual. Between the aggressive episodes there may be long periods of respite, and even times when the husband is agreeable and supportive, but both partners are likely to recognize that it is only a matter of time before the next attack. It is hardly surprising that many battered women suffer from stress-related physical illnesses and severe problems of depression and anxiety (Hofeller, 1982). Such women are also at high risk of alcoholism, drug abuse, and suicidal behaviour (Stark and Flitcraft, 1988; Sedlak, 1988).

Despite this generally gloomy picture, it must be acknowledged that not all abusive men continue with their violent behaviour. Some come to realize that their actions threaten the loss of their partner, or serious legal consequences, and manage to control their aggression. Some are influenced by powerful sanctions and persuasion by relatives or friends, and others are helped by therapy or special intervention programmes. Thus the eventual outcome of a battering relationship *is* often uncertain and many of the women who stay with a violent man in the hope that the abuse will come to an end are not being totally unrealistic in their expectations. Their optimism and their aspirations for the relationship reflect both their commitment to the partner and their adverse perception of alternative lifestyles or other potential partners.

EFFECTS ON CHILDREN

In the vast majority of cases of marital abuse children are present in the home (Pahl, 1985). Witnessing scenes of violence between parents, especially if they are brutal and frequent, would be expected to have serious detrimental effects on children. Sometimes they will not see the actual attack because it takes place late at night, or because the assailant is inhibited about hitting his wife when the children are present, but they are likely to hear the shouts and screams and may later see signs of injury. They will also be affected by the general air of tension and the victim's misery in the aftermath of an assault. Many children in maritally abusive homes are emotionally torn by a divided loyalty towards the parents, and anxiously avoid taking sides. They may also fear for their own physical safety and imagine horrendous possible consequences of further attacks (being taken away from the home, the police becoming involved, the father being taken away, or the mother being killed). Many children in these circumstances also feel that they are in some way to blame for the violence.

Even if the conflicts leading to the assaults do not focus on matters concerning the children, there are likely to be some issues of discord regarding their behaviour, care and discipline. Children have a natural tendency to focus on matters that directly concern them, and are therefore likely to imagine that these are provoking the violent attacks. Thus the child who does not directly witness the assaults, but who sees the effects, is likely to feel personally responsible. Older children may also feel guilty about their inability to protect the mother from injury.

Children of women who enter shelters for victims of marital violence have been shown to be at relatively high risk of health problems (including asthma, headaches, enuresis and bowel disorders) and psychological problems such as excessive crying, intense fear, aggressiveness, and extreme passivity and withdrawal. Boys are more likely to be aggressive, and girls to be anxious or clinging, and younger children are the most likely to suffer from physical disorders (Hilberman and Munson, 1978). However, a difficulty with most studies in this area is that they fail to differentiate between children who have merely witnessed marital abuse and those who have also been abused themselves. Two studies that have attempted to control for this suggest that while there are often strong negative effects of observing abuse, the effects of also having been abused are somewhat greater. Jaffe et al. (1986b) compared the psychological adjustment of three groups of boys. One group had been abused and had also witnessed severe marital violence; the second group had witnessed severe marital violence but had not been abused themselves; and the third group had neither been subjected to nor witnessed abuse. They found that, compared to those in the control group, boys in both of the groups exposed to violence had more behavioural problems and were more likely to be depressed and clingy. They were also more likely to be disobedient and aggressive.

Davis and Carlson (1987) replicated these findings, and found a broadly similar pattern for girls. They reported that the boys who appeared to be most affected were those of pre-school age, whereas the girls who showed the most evidence of adverse effects tended to be of school age. At least half of the children in these specially vulnerable sex- and age-groups were found to be severely aggressive or clinically depressed. Each of the studies cited examined the children of women who were in shelters, and they were therefore likely to have witnessed very serious violent incidents in the recent past. It is possible that some of the symptoms reported are not directly due to having witnessed violence, but to changes following marital abuse, including the mother's tension, the acute uncertainty about the future, and the disturbance involved in being removed from the home environment to a strange and perhaps somewhat disturbing life in the shelter (Wolfe et al., 1985). A consistent finding in the field of marital abuse is that boys who witness parental abuse in their early years are more likely to be the perpetrators of marital abuse in their adult years

(Egeland, 1988). Thus in considering the effects of children's exposure to marital abuse both the short-term and the longer-term effects need to be taken into account.

Alessi and Hearn (1984) described an intervention designed to prevent serious adjustment problems among children from families in which there is severe marital abuse. The programme includes a number of crisis management strategies (for example, having the children attend their normal school, and discussing with the child the nature of the violence and who is responsible for it) as well as longer-term intervention. There is a particular focus on helping the family to build a social support network, so that the mother can contact people in times of crisis, thereby reducing the risk of serious abuse and so protecting the children from adverse reactions.

INTERVENTION AND TREATMENT

Help for women who are under threat of marital abuse, or have experienced physical assaults, takes many different forms. Among the interventions that have been implemented are changes in legal procedures, the provision of shelters or refuges for battered women and their children, and the introduction of therapeutic programmes aimed at reducing the intensity of marital conflict or, more specifically, reducing the abuser's anger and aggression. In some cases it is quite apparent that the most suitable intervention would be to encourage the woman to leave the abusive relationship, but many victims repeatedly express a strong desire to stay with their partner, although they are very concerned that the violence should end. Such women often express frustration over the non-availability or failure of counselling and other intervention strategies (Brygger and Edelson, 1987). In this section we review some of the strategies and programmes that have been shown to reduce the frequency and severity of marital assaults. Because they appear to be effective in increasing the safety of women under threat, it is very unfortunate that so few of them are widely available.

COMMUNITY RESPONSES

Violence is associated with general stressors including poor housing, unemployment, and poverty. To some extent, therefore, suitable intervention might be directed towards reducing such sources of stress for the family, and increasing family provision and family support services (Farrington, 1986). Jaffe et al. (1986a) identified a number of community responses that might be useful in reducing the incidence of battering and in reducing the likelihood of further violence by current perpetrators. These include implementing policy changes so that the police, rather than victims, are expected to lay charges in cases of domestic assault, providing victim advocate services, and increasing public awareness and professional education on the subject of family violence.

Changes in Legal Procedures

A number of writers (e.g. Jaffe *et al.*, 1986a; Brygger and Edelson, 1987) have documented the very low frequency with which police normally lay charges against the perpetrator in cases of marital abuse. The police decision reflects the strength of the evidence, their judgement about whether the victim will testify, and assessments of whether prosecution and conviction are likely. In the US a widely used training manual for police officers that was in operation before 1976 recommended that in cases of marital abuse the best course of action was to separate the partners and then leave the scene. The 1976 revision, however, recommended that marital assaults should be dealt with in the same way as other assaults (Straus and Gelles, 1986). In practice, police often avoid arresting the perpetrator, and prosecutors often discourage court action. Many cases that do proceed are eventually withdrawn or dismissed. A police policy of minimal intervention is particularly lamentable because there is evidence that the experience of being arrested often has a strong deterrent effect on men involved in marital abuse (Berk and Newton, 1985; Jaffe *et al.*, 1986a). Sherman and Berk (1984) reported that a police intervention that included arrest was twice as effective in reducing violence in the following six months as one that did not (for example, where the police merely gave advice or a warning, or separated the couple for a short time).

Jaffe *et al.* (1986a) examined the impact of a change in police policy in London, Ontario. The new policy placed the responsibility on the police for laying charges in cases of wife abuse. Despite the fact that the same number of cases were brought to police attention two years before the policy was introduced and two years after, the number of charges made by the police increased from 12 to 298 (an increase from 2.7% to 67.3%). Furthermore, the proportion of cases heard in criminal court rose from a very small minority to three-quarters of cases, so that the new procedure appeared to dramatically reduce the risk that charges would be withdrawn or dismissed. Victims who had involved the police since the change of policy were contacted over a year later and asked about the perpetrator's aggressive behaviour in the year before and in the year following the reported incident. There had been a significant reduction in the occurrence of many forms of violence. The rate of 'beating', for example, decreased from 63% to 25%, and the rate of 'kicking, biting or hitting with a fist' decreased from 57% to 23%.

Thus although many of these men were still very violent towards their spouse, there was a clear overall reduction in the number and severity of attacks. A comparison of victims' satisfaction with police action before and after the introduction of the new policy showed that dissatisfaction had fallen from 47% to 6%. The majority of victims felt that the police and the court had played an important role in reducing or terminating the violence. And although some victims had feared retaliation following police charges, it appeared that perpetrators who were *not* charged were more likely to threaten or assault their wife following their interaction with the police.

In a further part of this study the research team examined police officers' attitudes to the new 'charging' policy. They found little consensus in their opinions of whether the policy was effective in helping battered women or whether it had negative effects such as discouraging women from calling the police. There was considerable agreement, however, that the policy conveyed an important message to the community, that it was unlikely to lead husbands to become more dangerous, and that the courts did little to support the policy. The study by Jaffe and his colleagues provides just one illustration of how a change at the community level can reduce the incidence of marital violence. It suggests that even a single policy change may have a fairly dramatic effect on the level of abuse, but it also indicates that clear evidence of effectiveness may be needed to convince policy-controllers that a change in procedure would be beneficial, and to persuade those who have implemented new policies that their actions have become more effective. There is often considerable resistance to change, and an innovation at one level (for example, at the level of police policy) may have limited impact due to resistance at another level (for example, at the court level).

In the UK an Act was passed in 1976 allowing a woman to take out an injunction against her husband even if she was not seeking a divorce or legal separation. The new Act permitted a county court to grant orders restraining the husband (or cohabitee) from molesting the woman and children living with her, excluding him from the home or neighbourhood area, or requiring him to allow the woman back into the home. Judges were also able to attach a power of arrest to any of these orders. Two years later another Act permitted magistrates to grant a 'personal protection order', again with the option of a power of arrest. Injunctions and protection orders may be useful in alerting husbands to the fact that their violent behaviour has been recognized in a court of law. They also identify the woman to the police as someone who is under serious threat, and they provide the police with the power to arrest without special warrant if the violence recurs. Thus these measures do offer women some added protection, although they are not without their critics (e.g. Parker, 1985).

Shelters

One form of community intervention that has now become very widespread is the provision of public 'shelters' or 'refuges' for battered women and their children. The first such shelter was set up in the UK in 1971 (in Chiswick, London), primarily as an advice centre. Now there are some 300 shelters in the UK (in any one year they accommodate 12,000 women and 21,000 children) and over 700 in the US. Although they are usually regarded primarily as temporary accommodation, and as a place of safety for women in immediate danger of being attacked by their partner, they also have a number of other important functions. Thus they offer emotional support to the woman at a crisis point in her life and an opportunity to share her experiences with other women who have faced similar situations. The sense of community may be especially important for women who have lived for a long time in relative isolation. Many shelters are also able to help in obtaining social service support and in liaising with the police, and some provide an advocacy service and professional counselling. Special provisions are made for children, and the woman is helped to think through the important decisions she must make. Women who wish to leave their partner are often helped to find long-term accommodation, to claim appropriate public benefits, and to establish a new and supportive social network (Pahl, 1985).

The protection function alone would be enough reason to welcome the continued expansion of shelters, but the many other resources and services these centres provide make them the most important innovation in the field of family violence and an indispensable aid to the protection of women. The fact that many women return to live with their assailant after their stay in the shelter does not mean that shelters have failed in these cases. Some women simply need a refuge from a danger that is essentially temporary, and the short-term stay often has a number of additional beneficial effects. Pahl (1985) suggested that involvement in a refuge improves women's self-confidence and personal autonomy, and Sedlak (1988) found that a shelter stay helped to make many women much less depressed and increased their sense of power over their lives.

The fact that a woman has taken refuge in a shelter may also reduce the partner's use of violence. Berk, Newton and Berk (1986) found support for their hypothesis that a stay in a shelter would reduce the frequency and intensity of violence after the woman's return home, although they found that the effect was considerably greater if the woman had also begun to take control over her life in other ways (for example, by seeking additional help from other sources). In some cases a shelter stay was regarded by the husband as an act of disobedience and actually triggered retaliatory violence, but men who recognized the stay as a step towards independence were likely to appreciate that the next step might be for the partner to opt out of the relationship. This often had a powerful deterrent effect and thus reduced the use of violence.

THERAPY FOR AGGRESSION

Couple-based Approaches

Some forms of intervention focus on long-standing problems within the marital relationship or the family in general, following the rationale that if a relationship is relatively free of serious problems, and a couple learns to deal with contentious issues in a constructive and problem-solving way, violence will be unlikely to occur. Thus general strategies of marital therapy or family therapy are employed to tackle dysfunctional aspects of the couple's relationship or the family system. Other interventions deal more specifically with the interactions that occur during marital conflict. They use a variety of strategies, including many that were outlined in Chapter 5. The goals of conflict training with couples include teaching them effective skills for listening to and understanding one another, generating constructive ways of dealing with clashes of interest and opinions, preventing escalation, and avoiding the use of inflammatory statements and highly provocative fight tactics. Programmes that focus on the quality of the couple's relationship may include a number of 'relationship enhancement' techniques such as training partners to increase their rate of giving approval and support. A useful review of behavioural approaches for reducing the frequency of marital conflict and helping couples to confine their conflictual interactions to safe limits is provided by Bornstein and Bornstein (1985).

Some interventions for couples focus more specifically on potentially violent situations. Thus both partners may be trained to recognize situations that are becoming out of control. The aggressor may be trained to calm himself in such situations, while the potential victim is taught how to recognize signs of the man's mounting anger and to reduce the danger of an attack by 'talking the situation down', 'taking time out', or using other defensive measures. Deschner and McNeil (1986) describe a 10-week anger control programme for victims and aggressors. They subscribe to the view that victims as well as aggressors must change their input into 'coercion spirals' if rage and violence are to be effectively controlled. They suggest that just as it takes two to make an argument so it takes two to make peace. Indeed, in diaries kept by participants during the course of the treatment it was found that the women victims were often *more* angry than their partners during arguments.

In the programme described by Deschner and McNeil, men and women participate in separate groups. Initial discussion concerns the nature of marital abuse, and then in the training phase individuals learn to recognize times of special danger and to take 'time out' (this usually involves leaving the situation), to distract themselves from the situation by calling pleasant thoughts to mind, and to openly admit to 'a 1% technical error' in their previous interaction (for example: 'I shouldn't have said what I said about your mother'). They are also taught to recognize sources of stress and anger, to use relaxation, and to modify their 'self-talk' so that anger is reduced rather than increased. Another component of the programme involves training in 'listening skills', and individuals also learn how to use assertive, but non-provoking, methods of responding to another person's anger (for example, by using diplomatic correction).

In their evaluation of the effectiveness of the programme the authors report that after training clients judged themselves to be less angry, less depressed and less aggressive. In addition, the number of arguments, the anger experienced during arguments, and the number of incidents of physical violence all declined, and at follow-up eight months later it was found that such improvements had been maintained. An analysis of the effectiveness of particular treatment components suggested that the 'time out' technique had proved very useful and that the 'admission of a 1% error' strategy was especially powerful. In the few cases in which violence had recurred, one partner had consistently refused to 'back down' or admit to having acted unfairly. The authors suggest that receiving a mature and caring gesture such as an admission that a reaction was partly unjustified or an expression of regret is likely to change the individual's judgement of their partner. They will tend to regard the person as a 'reasonable and trustworthy friend' rather than as an 'unreasonable enemy' and the warm feelings that emerge as a consequence are likely to reduce feelings of hostility. The person is therefore likely to respond generously and a 'virtuous circle' may be initiated, so that conflict is resolved and reconciliation achieved.

Individual-based Approaches

Sometimes marital abusiveness is just one part of a much more general problem of the individual. If a psychopathological condition (for example, paranoia) is recognized as being responsible for the violent attacks, then effective treatment for that disorder is likely to help reduce the abuse as well as many other problems in the person's life. In many more cases the abuse of alcohol or drugs will be seen as playing a major part in the domestic violence, and again the most successful approach may be to deal with the more global problem. But in the majority of cases there will be no evidence of psychological disorder other than the tendency to become violent, and alcohol or drug abuse will not be identified as the 'major cause' of the attacks on the partner. Many forms of intervention for marital abuse attempt to train the abusive individual to avoid the generation of anger, to control anger when it does occur, and to inhibit aggression or to express it in non-violent ways. There is very convincing evidence that individuals *can* learn to control their aggression (Novaco, 1975).

An analysis of occasions when extreme anger has been generated and followed by an assault may point to a major contribution of certain attitudes, beliefs or expectations. Counselling may then be valuable in allowing the client to identify, critically examine, and revise such precursors to anger and violence. In some cases the counsellor will need to be didactic, prescribing and directing changes in values or beliefs, but in other cases a detailed analysis of the psychological processes that lead up to attacks will allow the client to recognize the inappropriateness of particular negative attitudes and beliefs.

Ellis (1977) has provided a self-help guide for implementing such revisions in outlook, using his framework of 'rational-emotive therapy'. Thus suspiciousness and jealousy; restrictive and sexist attitudes towards women; and beliefs about the morality, normality, and usefulness of violence may be effectively altered. By changing relevant aspects of the assailant's general approach to judging social actions, and especially those of his partner, it is expected that he will become annoyed on fewer occasions, that his anger will be reduced, and that he will become much more inhibited about expressing anger in the form of assaultive aggression.

Other approaches have similar goals. They often involve training the individual to judge situations in ways that are unlikely to provoke anger, teaching him methods by which he can gain control over his anger, and encouraging him to behave in ways that are incompatible with physical aggression. Thus the person might be taught to use the cognitive strategies of distraction and reframing, so that potentially annoying events are ignored or take on a relatively benign meaning. As a result of changes in his interpretations of other people's actions, the individual may come to attribute annoying actions not to internal factors such as the partner's personality or defiance, but to 'external' factors such as an accident, misunderstanding or confusion. Thus by learning to provide 'excuses' for the other person's potentially provoking action, and calling possible 'mitigating circumstances' to mind, the risk of intense anger is likely to be considerably reduced.

Even when anger does occur, it is usually amenable to control, although self-control is much more easily achieved when anger is at a low level than when the person is at the height of rage. One important aspect of gaining control, therefore, is for the person to learn to recognize when he is becoming angry. This may involve learning to identify physiological cues such as increased tension in the muscles, or a rapidly beating heart, and cognitive signs, such as negative self-statements (e.g. 'who does she think she is?'; 'I'm not going to be treated like this'). Anger reduction techniques include the use of relaxation or meditation, and the use of calming self-statements ('slow down'; 'just relax'; 'let it pass'). More controversial is the use of the catharsis strategy, based on the idea that by venting anger in non-abusive ways it will effectively 'drain away'. Thus some therapists encourage clients to yell loudly or punch cushions when they are in a rage. Another suggestion is that catharsis can be achieved by using fantasy, and thus the angry individual may be encouraged to *imagine* 'evening the score' by hurting the victim. Many doubt whether cathartic techniques are ever really successful, and the use of fantasy aggression, in particular, could easily prove dangerous (by acting as a cue for a real attack), so this method is rarely high on the agenda of promising therapeutic interventions for abusive men.

Not all anger is expressed in the form of aggressive action, so an additional focus of intervention involves the specific control of aggressive behaviour

(Steinfield, 1986). One useful technique is to increase inhibitions against assault, for example by encouraging the person to call to mind the possible damaging consequences of abuse—including serious injury, a respected relative's reaction to learning of the assault, arrest and court action, the wife leaving, and possible effects on the children. Other techniques include helping the person to devise strict rules of behaviour to be resolutely followed at times of intense anger, and specifying actions to be carried out instead of an attack. Such behaviours should be incompatible with aggressive action and might include alternative ways of achieving a positive response from the partner. Therapists often model alternative, non-aggressive, responses to conflictual and annoying situations, and in a group therapy context members may generate a number of such strategies. Alternatively, the individual might be able to imagine how a particular admired and non-aggressive person would behave when faced with the specific situation, and use this as a prescription for his own response.

COMPREHENSIVE PROGRAMMES

The approaches to intervention discussed so far are by no means mutually exclusive, and it seems probable that the most effective programmes will involve many of the elements described. Such a programme should be not only comprehensive, but also well-coordinated, so that if several professionals are involved they work together as a team, each one knowing what the others are doing at any time. It is also essential that family members understand the function of each of the components of the intervention and how they relate to one another.

One of the most innovative and comprehensive programmes for dealing with marital abuse is the Minneapolis 'Domestic Abuse Project' (DAP) (Edelson and Brygger, 1986; Brygger and Edelson, 1987). Shelters are provided for abused women and their children, offering immediate protection, a high level of emotional support, and practical help to enable the woman to negotiate the legal process. As expressed in their literature, those involved in the DAP subscribe to a cultural model of abuse. Thus they define male violence primarily as 'criminal behaviour', they avoid 'family systems' formulations, and they reject the notion of 'provocation'. Despite this avowed philosophy, however, many of their specific strategies for change do focus on a detailed analysis of patterns of events that precede aggressive attacks.

Education and treatment programmes are provided for the aggressor, the victim, and the children, and a strong legal presence is maintained throughout the clients' involvement with the project. The active cooperation of police officers, judges and probation officers is essential, and project team members have played an active role in persauding those responsible for administering the law to change their customary practices in a number of ways. The police now follow the policy of arresting the suspect if it is considered probable that a domestic assault has occurred. Following the man's arrest, trained volunteers immediately contact both the victim and the assailant. The man is offered a range of treatment options and support through the legal process, while the woman is offered advice, shelter and legal advocacy. The close relationship between the law enforcement agency and those who operate the therapeutic part of the project means that there is some power to control legal sanctions in such a way that men who are initially reluctant to join treatment groups have a special incentive for participating.

In addition to the main therapeutic approach, involving separate self-help groups for victims and assailants, some individual treatment is provided and, in a few cases, family therapy. The 'men's group' is facilitated by a professional counsellor and meets on two nights a week for 16 weeks—a total of 80 hours. One important element of the therapeutic process is the development of a detailed violence control plan. This requires the man to identify cues that signal an escalation towards violence and to design a series of steps that will inhibit such escalation. Each man in the group presents an analysis of his most violent incident, with special attention being paid to the 'self-statements' made during that episode. The advantage of using a group-based approach is that each participant is able to benefit from the experience of a number of others. He will hear about the situations that have made other abusing husbands angry and how they judge that their anger is increasing. He will also learn about their aggression and how they propose to control it. Each person in the group therefore acts as a model for the others and each is helped to evolve a number of control strategies. The group leader's role is to support changes in the men's behaviour and attitudes while actively confronting any attempts they might make to deny or minimize the severity or effects of their violent behaviour.

A principal task for the woman is to develop a detailed protection plan. Women are helped to identify cues that precede their partner's violence and to devise a number of strategies they could use to protect themselves and their children in times of danger. Group discussion is aimed at increasing women's understanding of domestic violence (including cues to anger and escalation), and of their legal rights. Each woman discusses her protection plan with the group so that she can modify it as a result of other women's suggestions. The issues of shame and guilt following abuse are directly addressed, and any other relevant matters (including, for example, those relating to sexuality and parenting) are dealt with as they emerge. The dangers associated with isolation are also examined and the women are encouraged to build new and effective social networks.

The DAP also organizes child–parent groups designed to alleviate the problems that children may experience as a result of living with marital violence. Through the use of role-play, mime, art and dance therapy they are encouraged to give expression to any feelings of personal responsibility for the violence, to rebuild their self-esteem and to develop their own self-protection skills. Couple therapy or family therapy is provided if all of the members who would be involved in the therapy request it, and if there is no suspicion that the woman and children will be inhibited through fear of violence or retaliation by the man. The therapists who run this component of the project often have to address longstanding difficulties between the couple or within the family, and in some cases the principal task may be to facilitate an orderly dissolution of the marital relationship. But although certain general problems are recognized as contributing to the stress within the family, care is taken not to diffuse the focus on violence.

A further feature of the DAP is that support for families continues over a long time-span. Family members are encouraged to keep closely in touch with the project (including, in times of crisis, via a telephone hot-line), to maintain contacts with the other clients in their group, and to continue building their own support networks. The data now available on several hundred families that have participated in the project indicate that two-thirds of the men who finish the programme remain non-violent six months after the completion of their treatment.

REFERENCES

Ajzen, I. and Fishbein, M. (1980) *Understanding Attitudes and Predicting Social Behaviour*. Englewood Cliffs, NJ: Prentice-Hall.

Alessi, J. J. and Hearn, K. (1984) Group treatment of children in shelters for battered women. In: A. R. Roberts (ed.), *Battered Women and their Families*. New York: Springer.

Berk, R. A. and Newton, P. J. (1985) Does arrest really deter wife battery? An effort to replicate the findings of the Minneapolis spouse abuse experiment. *American Sociological Review*, **50**, 253–262.

Berk, R. A., Newton, P. J. and Berk, S. F. (1986) What a difference a day makes: An empirical study of the impact of shelters for battered women. *Journal of Marriage and the Family*, **48**, 481–490.

Binney, V., Harkell, G. and Nixon, J. (1981) *Leaving Violent Men*. London: National Women's Aid Federation.

Bornstein, P. H. and Bornstein, M. T. (1985) *Marital Therapy: A Behavioral-Communications Approach*. New York: Pergamon Press.

Bowker, L. H. (1983) *Beating Wife-Beating*. Lexington, MA: Lexington Books.

Brygger, M. P. and Edelson, J. L. (1987) The Domestic Abuse Project: A multi-systems intervention in woman battering. *Journal of Interpersonal Violence*, **2**, 324–336.

Davis, L. V. and Carlson, B. E. (1987) Observation of spouse abuse: what happens to the children? *Journal of Interpersonal Violence*, **2**, 278–291.

Deschner, J. P. and McNeil, J. S. (1986) Results of anger control training for battering couples. *Journal of Family Violence*, **1**, 111–120.

Dobash, R. E. and Dobash, R. (1979) *Violence against Wives*. New York: Free Press.

Edelson, J. L. and Brygger, M. P. (1986) Gender differences in reporting on battering incidences. *Family Relations*, 35, 377–382.

Egeland, B. (1988) Breaking the cycle of abuse: Implications for prediction and intervention. In: K. Browne, C. Davies and P. Stratton (eds.), *Early Prediction and Prevention of Child Abuse*. Chichester: Wiley.

Ellis, A. (1977) *How to Live With and Without Anger*. New York: Readers Digest Press.

Eron, L. D., Huesmann, L. R., Dubow, E., Romanoff, R. and Yarmel, P. W. (1987) Aggression and its correlates over 22 years. In: D. H. Crowell, I. M. Evans, and C. R. O'Donnell (eds.), *Childhood Aggression and Violence: Sources of Influence, Prevention and Control*. New York: Plenum.

Evason, E. (1982) *Hidden Violence*. Belfast: Farset Press.

Farrington, K. (1986) The application of stress theory to the study of family violence: Principles, problems and prospects. *Journal of Family Violence*, 1, 131–147.

Gelles, R. J. (1987) *The Violent Home: Updated Edition*. Beverly Hills, CA: Sage.

Giles-Sims, J. (1983) *Wife Battering: A Systems Theory Approach*. New York: Guilford Press.

Goffman, E. (1959) *The Presentation of Self in Everyday Life*. Garden City, New York: Anchor Books.

Goldstein, D. and Rosenbaum, A. (1985) An evaluation of the self-esteem of maritally violent men. *Family Relations*, 34, 425–428.

Goode, W. J. (1971) Force and violence in the family. *Journal of Marriage and the Family*, 33, 624–657.

Hilberman, E. and Munson, K. (1978) Sixty battered women. *Victimology: An International Journal*, 3–4, 460–470.

Hofeller, K. H. (1982) *Social, Psychological and Situational Factors in Wife Abuse*. Palo Alto, CA: R&E Research Associates.

Hornung, C., McCullough, B. and Sugimoto, T. (1981) Status relationships in marriage: risk factors in spouse abuse. *Journal of Marriage and the Family*, 43, 675–692.

Jaffe, P., Wolfe, D., Telford, A. and Austin, G. (1986a) The impact of police charges in incidents of wife abuse. *Journal of Family Violence*, 1, 37–49.

Jaffe, P., Wolfe, D., Wilson, S. K. and Zak, L. (1986b) Similarities in behavioural and social maladjustment among child victims and witnesses of family violence. *American Journal of Orthopsychiatry*, 56, 142–146.

Komarovsky, M. (1967) *Blue Collar Marriage*. New York: Vintage Books.

Leonard, K. E. and Jacob, T. (1988) Alcohol, alcoholism and family violence. In: V. B. Van Hasselt, R., L. Morrison, A. S. Bellack and M. Hersen (eds.) *Handbook of Family Violence*. New York: Plenum.

Lerman, L. G. (1981) *Prosecution for Spouse Abuse: Innovations in Criminal Justice Response*. Washington, DC: Center for Women Policy Studies.

Maiuro, R. D., Cohn, T. S., Vitaliano, P. P., Wanger, B. C. and Zegree, J. B. (1988) Anger, hostility and depression in domestically violent versus generally assaultive men and nonviolent control subjects. *Journal of Consulting and Clinical Psychology*, 56, 17–23.

Margolin, G., John, R. S. and Gleberman, L. (1988) Affective responses to conflictual discussion in violent and nonviolent couples. *Journal of Consulting and Clinical Psychology*, **56**, 24–33.

Mason, A. and Blankenship, V. (1987) Power and affiliation motivation, stress and abuse in intimate relationships. *Journal of Personality and Social Psychology*, **52**, 203–210.

Novaco, R. W. (1975) *Anger Control: The Development and Evaluation of an Experimental Treatment.* Lexington, MA: Lexington Books.

Olson, D. H., McCubbin, H. I., Barners, H. L., Larsen, A. S., Muxen, M. J. and Wilson, M. A. (1983) *Families: What Makes them Work?* Beverly Hills, CA: Sage.

Pahl, J. (ed.) (1985) *Private Violence and Public Policy: The Needs of Battered Women and the Response of the Public Services.* London: Routledge and Kegan Paul.

Parker, S. (1985) The legal background. In: J. Pahl (ed.), *Private Violence and Public Policy: The Needs of Battered Women and the Response of the Public Services.* London: Routledge and Kegan Paul.

Patterson, G. R. and Hops, H. (1972) Coercion, a game for two: intervention techniques for marital conflict. In: R. E. Ulrich and P. T. Mountjoy (eds.), *The Experimental Analysis of Social Behavior.* New York: Appleton-Century-Crofts.

Resick, P. A. and Reese, D. (1986) Perception of family social climate and physical aggression in the home. *Journal of Family Violence*, **1**, 71–83.

Rosenbaum, A. and O'Leary, K. D. (1981) Marital violence: characteristics of abusive couples. *Journal of Consulting and Clinical Psychology*, **49**, 63–71.

Rounsaville, B. J. (1978) Battered wives: barriers to identification and treatment. *American Journal of Orthopsychiatry*, **48**, 487–494.

Roy, M. (1977) *Battered Women: Psycho-sociological Study of Domestic Violence.* New York: Van Nostrand Reinhold.

Roy, M. (Ed.) (1982) *The Abusing Partner: An Analysis of Domestic Battering.* New York: Van Nostrand Reinhold.

Rushton, J. P., Fulker, D. W., Neale, M. C., Nias, D. K. B. and Eysenck, H. J. (1987) Altruism and aggression: the heritability of individual differences. *Journal of Personality and Social Psychology*, **50**, 1192–1198.

Russell, D. E. H. (1982) *Rape in Marriage.* New York: Macmillan.

Sedlak, A. J. (1988) Prevention of wife abuse. In: V. B. Van Hasselt, R. L. Morrison, A. S. Bellack and M. Hersen (eds.), *Handbook of Family Violence.* New York: Plenum.

Sherman, L. W. and Berk, R. A. (1984) The specific deterrents of arrest for domestic assault. *American Sociological Review*, **49**, 261–272.

Snyder, D. K. and Fruchtman, L. A. (1981) Differential patterns of wife abuse: a data-based typology. *Journal of Consulting and Clinical Psychology*, **49**, 878–885.

Snyder, D. K. and Scheer, N. S. (1981) Predicting disposition following brief residence at a shelter for battered women. *American Journal of Community Psychology*, **9**, 559–566.

Stark, E. and Flitcraft, A. (1988) Violence among intimates: An epidemiological review. In: V. B. Van Hasselt, R. L. Morrison, A. S. Bellack and M. Hersen (eds.), *Handbook of Family Violence.* New York: Plenum.

Steinfield, G. J. (1986) Spouse abuse: clinical implications of research on the control of aggression. *Journal of Family Violence*, **1**, 111–120.

Steinmetz, S. K. (1977) *The Cycle of Violence: Assertive, Aggressive and Abusive Family Interaction.* New York: Praeger.

Steinmetz, S. K. (1987) Family violence: past, present and future. In: M. B. Sussman and S. K. Steinmetz (eds.), *Handbook of the Marriage and the Family.* New York: Plenum Press.

Stone, L. H. (1984) Shelters for battered women: a temporary escape from danger or the first step to divorce? *Victimology: An International Journal,* 9, 284–289.

Straus, M. A. (1974) Leveling, civility, and violence in the family. *Journal of Marriage and the Family,* 36, 13–29.

Straus, M. A. (1980) Social stress and marital violence in a national sample of American families. In: F. Wright, C. Bahn, and R. W. Reiber (eds.), *Forensic Psychology and Psychiatry. Annals of the New York Academy of Science,* 347, 229–250.

Straus, M. A. and Gelles, R. J. (1986) Societal change and family violence from 1975 to 1985 as revealed by two national surveys. *Journal of Marriage and the Family,* 48, 445–479.

Straus, M. A., Gelles, R. J. and Steinmetz, S. K. (1980) *Behind Closed Doors: Violence in American Families.* New York: Doubleday.

Strube, M. J. (1988) The decision to leave an abusive relationship: Empirical evidence and theoretical issues. *Psychological Bulletin,* 104, 236–250.

Strube, M. J. and Barbour, L. S. (1983) The decision to leave an abusive relationship: Economic dependence and psychological commitment. *Journal of Marriage and the Family,* 45, 785–793.

Strube, M. J. and Barbour, L. S. (1984) Factors relating to the decision to leave an abusive relationship. *Journal of Marriage and the Family,* 46, 837–844.

Telch, C. F. and Lindquist, C. U. (1984) Violent versus nonviolent couples: A comparison of patterns. *Psychotherapy,* 21, 242–248.

Walker, L. E. (1979) *The Battered Woman.* New York: Harper and Row.

Walker, L. E. (1984) *The Battered Woman Syndrome.* New York: Springer.

Wolfe, D. A., Jaffe, P., Wilson, S. and Zak, L. (1985) Children of battered women: The relation of child behavior to family violence and maternal stress. *Journal of Consulting and Clinical Psychology,* 53, 657–665.

Yllo, K. and Straus, M. A. (1981) Interpersonal violence among married and divorced persons. *Family Relations,* 30, 339–347.

8

Separation and Divorce

DIVORCE 'RISK'

It is estimated that about a third of all marriages that now take place in the UK and half of marriages that take place in the US will end in divorce. Approximately 165,000 couples in the UK and 1.25 million in the US, get divorced each year, and about half of the individuals involved in these divorces get married again within four years. The rate of divorce for a second marriage, however, is somewhat higher than that for a first marriage, so that there is a relatively high probability that those who remarry will get divorced for a second time. Thus one factor associated with 'divorce risk' is having been divorced previously. This chapter first considers the broad range of risk factors (including demographic variables, the partners' personalities, and aspects of the marital relationship) before discussing the course of marital breakdown, separation, and legal divorce. The effects of marital dissolution on adults and children are then examined, and the chapter concludes with a discussion of issues relating to custody, access to children, remarriage, and the formation of 'stepfamilies'.

A number of demographic factors, including age at marriage, social class, and occupation, are associated with the 'risk' that a married couple will divorce. Thus couples who marry when one or both partners is a teenager, those who marry when the woman is already pregnant, and those who had a brief courtship,| are more likely than others to experience marital breakdown (Thornes and Collard, 1979). Lower social class is also a risk factor. If the husband is an unskilled manual worker then the couple is about four times as likely to get divorced as a couple in which the husband has a professional occupation (Haskey, 1984). The specific nature of the man's work is also relevant. Men in the armed forces have a high divorce rate, for example, as do professional entertainers. This is partly explained by the detrimental effects of a couple living apart frequently or for prolonged periods. Among male academics there are sharp disparities in divorce rate between those from different disciplines, with engineers and those in the physical sciences having much more stable marital careers than those in the arts and social sciences. The high divorce-proneness of those in the humanities may reflect their more liberal outlook and their failure to subscribe to traditional family values, although some have explained it by referring to the fact that these disciplines typically attract more female students and increase the opportunities for male academics to engage in extramarital liaisons.

The divorce rate of unemployed men is exceptionally high (Haskey, 1982). Unemployment not only brings a loss of status and financial hardship, thus placing considerable strain on the marriage, but may also bring the couple into close contact for prolonged periods. In the context of an unfavourable and frustrating set of social and economic conditions, such sustained proximity may produce repeated conflict that contributes to a rapid deterioration of the relationship. The association between a woman's employment status and the probability that she will get divorced is quite different from that described for males. Employed women are more likely than unemployed women to consider divorce (Huber and Spitze, 1980), and marriages in which the woman has a higher occupational status than the man are especially vulnerable to breakdown (Thornes and Collard, 1979).

People who marry tend to share many characteristics. They are usually of approximately the same age, they are generally from the same race, and they often have the same religious beliefs. The phenomenon whereby 'like tends to marry like' is known as 'homogamy', and marriages between partners who match on such attributes are more likely to survive than those in which the partners are markedly dissimilar. Thus 'mixed marriages', in terms of race or religion, more often end in divorce than those that are homogamous with respect to these variables, and a wide age difference between the partners similarly increases the risk of marital breakdown.

Marital unhappiness and instability also appear to be related to the partners' personalities. In a review of the relevant research, Newcomb and Bentler (1981) found that those who were highly autonomous, had a high level of personal drive, and were very ambitious and competitive, had relatively high rates of divorce. They suggested that extreme individualism may lower the person's commitment to the marriage, and that when two independent and assertive people get married they are likely to engage in frequent conflict. Divorce risk is also related to the psychological adjustment of the partners. If either suffers from an emotional disorder the level of marital satisfaction of both partners tends to be low, and the chances that the relationship will break down are significantly increased (Kitson and Sussman, 1982). However, because an unfavourable relationship with the marital partner is likely to contribute to psychological distress, the association between emotional well-being and divorce risk may be the result of a number of different effects.

Certain aspects of an individual's personal and family history are also related to the probability that they will get divorced. It has already been noted that a previous divorce adds to the risk. Those who had a large number of sexual partners before getting married are at increased risk of divorce, possibly because they are more likely to engage in extramarital affairs than those who have had less extensive sexual experience. On the other hand, whether the partners did or not did not cohabit together before marriage does not appear to alter the probability that their relationship will end in annulment. A history of divorce in an individual's family increases the chances that their own relationship will also end in divorce. Thus those whose parents or siblings have been divorced are more likely than other people to get divorced themselves. Some explain the inter-generational association in terms of an overlap of personality or demographic characteristics between parents and children, whereas others suggest that there may be a transmission of permissive or pro-divorce attitudes. It has also been hypothesized that divorce occurs more frequently among the children of divorced parents because they have had little opportunity to learn about conventional and positive styles of marital interaction (Pope and Mueller, 1976).

REASONS FOR DIVORCE

In recent decades the divorce rate in many countries has increased at a very rapid rate. Thus in 1913 there were only 7000 divorces in England and Wales (compared with a current annual rate of over 150,000), and in the US in the 1920s one in seven marriages were dissolved (compared to over one-third in the 1980s). Some authors have suggested that these striking increases reflect the rise of individualism. It is implied that people constantly monitor whether they are getting the best out of life, and that when they feel their marital situation is less than optimal they seek change. For a number of reasons, opting out of the relationship is now much easier than it once was. For one thing, the legal system in many countries has been changed to reduce many of the obstructions once placed before those who wished to annul their marriage. The 'no-fault' divorce and the introduction of 'irretrievable breakdown' of the relationship as a sufficient reason for dissolving the marriage have done much to reduce the traumatic and adversarial nature of the legal procedures pertaining to divorce. And as more people end their marriages, the role of 'divorcee' and the process of becoming divorced are seen as less aberrant and less 'shameful', so that individuals contemplating divorce are less likely to be inhibited by the thought that if their marriage ends they will be socially stigmatized.

There is clearly a need to make a distinction between 'marital unhappiness' and the legal event of divorce. Many unhappy marriages continue without divorce being contemplated by either partner. People differ considerably in their 'divorce threshold'. Whereas some begin to think in terms of separation and divorce as soon as they realize that their relationship is less than perfect, many who find their marriage unbearable still consider divorce to be 'unthinkable'. The divorce threshold has become much lower in most Western cultures in recent decades, but individuals still differ widely in the degree to which they are prepared to consider this as a solution to a difficult marital relationship. The variation reflects the considerable differences in people's personal values, and in the relevance they assign to the various religious and social attitudes to marriage and divorce. The sharp disparity between the divorce rates of Catholics and Protestants appears to be more a function of the Catholic attitude to divorce than testimony to the greater happiness of Catholic marriages.

The way people feel about divorce will also reflect their family history. If they have experienced the divorce of close relatives, and particularly if their own parents' marriage was dissolved, they are likely to find it easier to contemplate the dissolution of their own marriage. Where there is a strong aversion to the idea of divorce, a couple may devise alternative ways of disengaging from their deteriorated relationship. Thus by suitably arranging their work-patterns and their leisure activities, and perhaps their living arrangements, they may contrive to spend very little time together. The desolate relationship can then continue as long as the couple are able to maintain their rather autonomous lifestyles.

Marital breakdown tends to occur early in a marriage. Many couples separate within the first year or two, and over a third of marriages that end in divorce last less than four years. The largest number of separations occur between one and three years after the wedding. Some individuals appear to have a very low threshold for 'calling it off' and move towards separation as soon as any serious problem becomes evident. Typically, following the brief 'honeymoon period', the early stage of a marriage is especially problematic as the partners struggle to establish a new lifestyle, to make mutual adjustments, and to become 'a couple'. Some individuals are unable or unwilling to adapt, so that they are never able to negotiate with their partner the foundation of a stable marriage. Others may regard an early problem not as a hurdle to be overcome but as proof that the relationship is ill-fated, and decide to opt out before they have invested too much and become too involved. They may feel that securing a divorce as early as possible will limit the distress, and fear that a pregnancy will prevent them from leaving the relationship. They may judge that such a misfortune would trap them into staying with the partner, or would mean that they would have to obtain an abortion, abandon the child, or opt for the difficult role of a single parent. Thus it seems that some marriages hardly get off the ground before they fail. The couple may never work out a way of living happily together, and one partner may decide to escape from the relationship before the repercussions of a divorce are too damaging.

The level of marital satisfaction is often particularly low during the period when a couple have young children, and this would suggest that the divorce rate at this stage would be high. However, it seems that the presence of children also raises the divorce threshold, so that couples facing difficulties at this stage are often very hesitant about separating and getting a divorce. Thus the frequency of separation is low when a child under two is present in the family (Waite *et al.*, 1985), although the prescription that couples should stay together 'for the sake of the children' has decreased significantly in recent decades (Thornton, 1985). When the couple have passed through the stage where the children are very young, their satisfaction with the relationship tends to increase somewhat. Divorce then becomes less likely the longer a couple remain married, although it is by no means rare for couples to divorce after 10 or 20 years together.

In some cases marital breakdown stems not from an intrinsically problematic marriage, but from the fact that one or other spouse finds an alternative lifestyle or partner more attractive. Thus while some people may be 'pushed' from a marriage by the negative qualities of the relationship, others are 'pulled' from the relationship by external attractions. There is little consensus about how far the presence of an alternative potential partner does in fact threaten marriages. It is probably true that those who are confident about forming a new relationship are less willing to endure an unsatisfactory marriage, but relatively few of those who decide to separate have already established another partnership. Nevertheless, Udry (1981) found that the availability of another partner predicted separation more accurately than did marital unhappiness.

The discovery that the partner has been involved in an adulterous affair rarely leads an individual to wish to end an otherwise satisfactory marriage, but it may prove 'the last straw' if there are other serious difficulties with the relationship. Adultery appears to have a more important effect on the partner who actually has the affair, often 'pulling' them away from the marriage. Sometimes the new relationship is highly valued and assumed to be durable, so that the new lover is expected to supersede the current partner. In other cases the effects of having an affair are less specific. The experience of a romantic or sexual liaison may simply persuade the individual that other and 'better' partners are available. It is often very difficult to determine how far an affair has damaged and detracted from the existing marriage and how far dissatisfaction with the marriage had led one partner to seek another relationship. As on-going affair may incite a partner to deliberately 'sabotage' an otherwise good marriage, and the discovery that the partner is having an affair is certainly likely to increase the level of marital conflict, but the fact that a marriage has become tedious or hostile may also contribute to the initial temptation to indulge in an affair.

It is very unusual for a relationship to suddenly turn sour. Usually there is a 'slow distancing' and a gradual process of degeneration. Certain changes in the couple's interaction act as indicators of the erosion that is occurring. Thus there may be a decline in the partners' participation together in leisure activities or in their degree of sexual contact, or conflict may become more frequent and more intense. As disillusionment sets in, partners tend to make fewer positive remarks to one another and to make critical statements or cynical gibes. Thus reproachful comments become routine, praise is rarely given, and conflict often escalates. Less effort is expended in trying to resolve difficulties, loving gestures are rarely made, and feelings are seldom discussed. Each partner may set out a badger, blame, and belittle the other until, after many put-downs and unresolved fights, a hostile silence may be maintained. As the relationship further declines one partner may 'betray' the other, by humiliating them in public, for example, or by being unfaithful. Civility often vanishes, the normal 'rules of marriage' (Argyle and Henderson, 1985) are repeatedly broken, and it becomes increasingly clear that the damage to the relationship will almost certainly be permanent. Each partner may reconstruct the history of the marriage and judge that the relationship was doomed from the start, while alternative partners or lifestyles may be idealized.

In the highly charged atmosphere of the marriage under threat, judgements are likely to be impaired and it will be difficult for either partner to maintain a reasonable perspective on the relationship. Each will try to make sense of what is happening, and will construct a picture that is coloured by their personal feelings and their need to maintain self-respect. There is an understandable tendency to blame the other partner and rarely will there be agreement about which of them is most responsible for the difficulties they face. They are also likely to disagree about which issues are fundamental to the serious disruption in their relationship. The process of reframing and reinterpreting the situation continues throughout the term of the marital breakdown and may persist long after a divorce has been finalized. Thus partners' accounts of 'what went wrong' can rarely be taken at face value.

When asked to reveal what grievances they have about their relationship, estranged husbands are more likely than their wives to complain about sexual incompatibility, whereas wives are more likely to complain about financial problems, physical and verbal abuse, excessive use of alcohol, and mental cruelty (Levinger, 1966). Such issues are likely to have been the themes of recurring conflicts before the separation, but the husband and wife may disagree about whether they were critical or merely secondary to a general hostility and disenchantment. Asked about the fundamental difficulties that have caused the relationship to degenerate, those who have separated and are about to be divorced cite such insidious factors as communication difficulties, differences in values, and lack of love (Bloom, Hodges and Caldwell, 1983). In some cases individuals will have arrived at an accurate diagnosis of the difficulties with their relationship, but most people at this stage have such strong feelings of resentment, anger, jealousy, and vulnerability that their perception is distorted and they lack insight into the real reasons for their predicament.

Divorce petitions citing the 'grounds for divorce' are even less reliable as indicators of the real reasons behind the breakdown of relationships. If a divorce is contested, the legal advisor will guide the person seeking the divorce to formulate a rationale that will persuade the court, and this may bear little or no relationship to the reasons why the divorce is being sought. Until recent changes in the law (making 'no grounds' divorce possible), citing adultery was simply more expedient than presenting a complex account of interpersonal difficulties, or trying to persuade a court that hatred of the spouse was an adequate reason for granting a decree. But despite the frequency with which adultery is cited, it is hardly ever the solitary or principal cause of a person seeking a divorce.

THE DIVORCE PROCESS

It is rare for a partner to announce an intention to petition for divorce 'out of the blue'. The process by which couples in conflict become divorced proceeds through a number of stages. Typically, after a period when both partners recognize that there are severe problems with the relationship, one partner will suggest that they live separately, at least until they can decide whether or not the marriage should continue. If they fail to resolve their difficulties at this stage then one or other partner, and not necessarily the one who first suggested a separation, will take the crucial step of actively seeking a divorce.

SEPARATION

Few divorces take place when both partners are still living in the marital home, so that most divorces are preceded by a period of separation. Sometimes it is agreed that there will be a 'trial separation' and that they will reconsider the long-term future of their relationship at some later date. In many cases one or more reunions will take place before the final separation and divorce, and in some cases, of course, a period of separation is followed by a successful reconciliation, so that the immediate threat of divorce is removed. Reconciliation at this stage is more likely if the period of separation has been short and if there are few areas of fundamental conflict. The relationship is also more likely to be re-established if the couple have no children, and if divorce would leave the woman in a state of severe financial hardship (Kitson and Langlie, 1984). But the chances of a successful reunion are also influenced by how well the partners have fared during their time apart. Those who experience a lonely and uncomfortable existence are more amenable to a reconciliation that those who cope well, make new friends, and enjoy their time away from the marital strife.

Even after separation, some individuals and couples contact counselling agencies in a bid to save their marriage. However, it seems that the effectiveness of marital therapy at this stage is very limited. Very few partners of those who ask for professional help at this stage are willing to attend for counselling, and it is almost impossible to facilitate a marital reconciliation when working with just one person. Many marital problems arise from misunderstandings and communication difficulties, and these cannot be adequately recognized and dealt with unless both partners are willing to participate. When the couple are seen together the therapist can ascertain the viewpoints of both partners, observe their interaction together and involve them in discussions about possible solutions to their problems. Partners who examine their situation together are more likely to recognize ambivalent attitudes and are able to express hostile feelings towards their spouse in a relatively 'safe' and 'refereed' environment (Parkinson, 1987).

There is usually a period of between six months and two years from the final separation to the legal divorce, and during this time most individuals suffer great distress. Indeed, many of those who have been through the divorce process report that the time of separation was the most traumatic and critical they experienced (Chiriboga and Cutler, 1977). In a study of people who had been separated from their partners for around two months, Bloom, Hodges and Caldwell (1983) found that at least half complained of weight loss, an upset stomach, aches and pains, loss of appetite, headaches, difficulty sleeping, and the feeling that they were about to have a nervous breakdown. These researchers also reported that there had been little change in the frequency of these symptoms some six months later.

Those who have been rejected by their partner are particularly likely to experience adverse psychological effects. Such people often feel abandoned, helpless, angry, and inadequate (Kessler, 1975), and their distress is likely to be particularly acute if the partner's leaving was sudden and unexpected (Spanier and Casto, 1979). Those who initiate the separation are usually somewhat better off, either because they have already formed another relationship or because they have taken control of the situation, although they sometimes regret having broken up the marriage and feel guilty about having deserted their partner.

Many people are relieved when the separation finally occurs. They may look forward to a respite from the constant battles and indignities they have had to contend with in recent weeks and months. They welcome an end to the ambiguity and a chance to make plans for a new future. One critical factor in determining how well the individual will cope with the change is their analysis of why the separation has occurred. If they assume that the marital breakdown reflects their own inadequacy or shortcomings they are likely to be profoundly tormented, whereas if they attribute the failure of their relationship to some aspect of their partner's behaviour or to a mutual incompatibility they are more likely to be able to cope well with the separation (Kitson, 1985). The account an individual constructs of 'what went wrong' affects not only their own well-being but also their subsequent interactions with friends and relatives. Many find it very embarrassing and distressing to have to inform others about the separation, and they will be all the more embarrassed if they have to admit that their partner rejected them.

Those who receive news of a friend's or a relative's separation react in a variety of ways. Some pledge their unconditional support for the person, some are embarrassed and appear to want to ignore the revelation, and others are prepared to make instant judgements that lead them to condemn one or other party. In attempting to construct some coherent explanation about what happened between the couple, people frequently opt for a conventional rationale such as cruelty or adultery rather than for a less tangible explanation focusing on 'irreconcilable attitudes' or 'incompatibility'. If they hear accounts from both partners they may be struck by the profound differences between the two reports, and find it difficult to decide which partner most deserves their continued loyalty.

In an analysis of friends' responses following a couple's separation, Weiss (1975) found that in the initial stage considerable support is often given to one or other partner and a high level of contact is generally maintained. Later, a number of 'idiosyncratic reactions' may become evident, including fear, admiration, envy, and curiosity, and following this there is often a stage of 'mutual withdrawal'. At this point the separated individuals are likely to have progressively less involvement and less interaction with those whom they initially relied on for support. Finally there may come a stage when the separated person establishes a new circle of associates, including some whose circumstances are similar to their own, and loses contact with most of their former friends.

In many cases the parents of the separating couple are particularly distressed by news of the marital breakdown (Johnson and Vinick, 1981). They may blame themselves for 'not doing more to help' and may feel despondent about the loss of a son-in-law or daughter-in-law to whom they have become very attached. They are likely to worry about how their son or daughter will cope in the following months and years and will often offer practical help in the form of finance, childcare, companionship, or shelter. Bloom, Hodges and Caldwell (1983) reported that those who had separated often turned to family and friends, as well as to professionals, for help and felt that they had benefited from their assistance. More women than men, however, indicated that they had received a high level of support from friends and relatives. Those who experience difficulties following separation or divorce are generally more prepared to accept aid from relatives than from friends, and where support is offered and accepted, individuals tend to experience less distress (Raschke, 1977).

The time of separation before divorce is a period of transition, when the person must try to adapt to a new lifestyle that is likely to be maintained for some time. The separated individuals studied by Bloom, Hodges and Caldwell

(1983) reported a number of serious difficulties following separation, in addition to the persistent problem of their relationship with the spouse. When asked about their lives two months and eight months after their separation, many people disclosed that they were very lonely and that they were having a number of psychological problems. Some felt a sense of personal failure, many indulged in self-blame, and some had developed feelings of incompetence. Many also experienced problems in dealing with their children, and such difficulties increased in severity between the two stages of the study.

The realities of financial hardship may also prove more daunting than was envisaged, and the individual may find it difficult to contend with chores and tasks that were previously undertaken by the partner. The non-custodial parent is likely to be concerned about whether he (or more rarely, she) will be able to maintain a close and rewarding relationship with the children. Thus many important personal and interpersonal tasks need to be accomplished during the difficult period before the divorce is finalized. Agreements must be negotiated, a viable lifestyle must be planned, anxieties must be conquered, the children must be handled with particular care, and any remaining attachment to the spouse must be subdued. A partner who is still in love with the spouse must systematically and strategically attempt to overcome their affection and any lingering feelings of commitment. All of this adds up to a daunting agenda, and some of the tasks may not have been satisfactorily completed by the time the legal divorce becomes absolute.

THE LEGAL PROCESS

Despite the fact that the majority of divorces are undefended, the decision to end a marriage is not generally arrived at by mutual agreement. Typically one person wants the divorce and the other does not, or at least the partners have markedly different views about whether the divorce is desirable. Hart (1976) found that only 5% of her sample had taken a mutual decision to separate. The partner who begins divorce proceedings is the 'petitioner', and the other partner is the 'respondent'. In about three-quarters of cases the petitioner is the wife. When the decision has finally been made, legal advice is sought and the couple will attempt to negotiate over such difficult matters as residence, child custody, and financial arrangements. Fights over resources, children, and the 'moral ground', may produce a bitterness and hatred that prevents the couple from arriving at a rational and equitable solution to their joint problems. Having been intimately involved for some time, and having engaged together in many conflicts, each partner will know the other's principal concerns and weaknesses, and may fight 'below the belt'. At this stage many individuals become very selfish and niggardly. Not only are they tactless and inconsiderate, but they may also show intense bitterness and resentment, so that they seek to impose maximum hardship on their partner and to cause them extreme distress.

There are 'civilized' divorces. Sometimes both partners agree at more or less the same time that the relationship has lost its attractions, and they make a joint decision that each should go their own way. They may agree to be mutually supportive throughout the divorce process, and hope to remain good friends for a long time afterwards. It is evident, however, that even some of the divorces that begin in a spirit of acceptance and compromise eventually turn into bitter wrangles. In some of these cases lawyers can be held to blame. Their intervention can cause a divorce that might have remained cordial and dignified to become sour and unseemly. In their attempts to achieve the best long-term outcome for their own client, each partner's legal advisor may encourage the disputing of contentious issues, so that one partner is effectively set against the other. Lawyers are often highly effective in protecting their client's material interests, but they sometimes initiate a battle that the couple themselves had managed to avoid, thereby generating considerable tension and distress.

Hagestad and Smyer (1982) made the distinction between 'orderly' and 'disorderly' divorces. They describe the orderly divorce as one in which there has been a gradual breakdown of the marriage and in which both partners have been successful in withdrawing their emotional investment in the relationship. Thus by the time the divorce is legally established each partner will have adjusted and made plans for their new life as a single person. In disorderly marriages, on the other hand, emotional attachment continues, the couple still feel that they are partners, and they fail to develop the emotional separateness and autonomy of lifestyle that would allow them to form new and satisfactory relationships.

This analysis recognizes that divorce involves progressive disconnection in a number of different domains and that individuals differ markedly in their ability and willingness to disengage. In an earlier account of the processes involved in withdrawal from a failed relationship, Bohannan (1970) identified six dimensions—the emotional divorce, the legal divorce, the economic divorce, the co-parental divorce, the community divorce (disengaging from joint social activities and shared friendships), and the 'psychic divorce' (arranging and engaging in an independent lifestyle). He suggested that at any one time the position of the partners on each of these dimensions may diverge widely, and that an individual's progress on the various dimensions may be drastically out of step. Thus the task of emotional divorce, for example, may be accomplished some considerable time before the legal divorce or may be only partially achieved for a long time following that event.

CONCILIATION, OR 'MEDIATION'

Most divorces are not legally contested, but various difficulties often threaten to prevent the legal process from being smooth and trouble-free. Generally speaking, if both partners agree on an issue then the court will concur with their consensus about such matters as finance, residence, and custody of the children. But there is often profound disagreement over such questions. The basic adversarial system of the court, and the approach traditionally taken by divorce lawyers, can lead to lengthy, costly, and bitter litigation, and there is good evidence that distress and resentment arising from the legal contest can have negative effects on the partners and on their children. There are therefore clear advantages in settling matters, as far as possible, out of court, and by negotiation rather than confrontation. Compromise and cooperation may produce a more equitable solution to a problem and reduce the emotional trauma involved in settling matters. Recognition of this has led in recent years to a substantial growth in the field of marital conciliation (sometimes referred to as 'mediation' or 'divorce mediation'). In Britain a major report commissioned by the government (Finer, 1974) recognized the potential value of such intervention and recommended that it should be made widely available.

Conciliation is an alternative to litigation. The partners agree to meet together with impartial conciliators (usually social workers, probation officers, or marriage counsellors) in order to reach a mutually acceptable solution to outstanding issues of conflict. The process of conciliation was used extensively in ancient civilizations and in tribal societies to settle differences, and it is currently used as a means of intervention in industrial disputes. Conciliation should not be confused with reconciliation, for the aim is not to reunite the couple. Neither should it be confused with divorce therapy, in which the principal goal is to moderate an individual's adverse response to an impending or recent divorce. Parkinson (1986) has made the point that although conciliation may be therapeutic in its effect, it is not intended as a form of therapy. Conciliation focuses on practical issues rather than on emotional problems, it deals with interpersonal rather than with personal issues, and the tasks and methods of the conciliator are quite different from those of the therapist.

Various agencies have evolved a number of strategies for promoting conciliation, and have developed different methods of working. A variety of theoretical frameworks form the basis of these practices, including family systems theory, communication theory, and conflict management theory. The techniques used by conciliators reflect their own theoretical orientation and skills as well as the traditions and practices of the agencies they work for. But the issues that are usually the focus of conciliation differ very little. The principal matters dealt with by conciliators concern custody and access to children, and financial arrangements. Conciliation typically involves just a few meetings between the partners and one or two conciliators. In an informal atmosphere, after each party has been assured that confidentiality will be maintained, the conciliators gather information about matters of dispute and gauge the opinions and interests of each partner before making suggestions about how such issues might be resolved and comprises achieved.

Some controversies may be seen as open to resolution, because the interests and wishes of the two partners are not fundamentally incompatible. The conciliator will then attempt to handle the negotiation between the partners so that a mutually satisfactory solution to the problem can be found. This process involves suggesting a range of alternatives and helping the partners to compromise and reach agreement. Conciliators can often encourage 'fair play' in situations where the partners have very different degrees of bargaining power, and they must be able to formulate alternative solutions quickly and to express them clearly and unambiguously. If two conciliators work together, and particularly if one is male and the other female, their own style of communication may act as a model for the estranged couple.

Participation in conciliation is entirely voluntary and the conciliators have no power to force decisions. They have a specialized knowledge of relevant legal matters and are particularly familiar with the attitudes and responses of adults and children involved in separation and divorce. The conciliator needs to have a keen appreciation of the motives of each of the partners and to recognize that an agreement to participate in a conciliation session may not reflect a genuine desire to reach a settlement. Some individuals consent to take part because they feel that they will be able to use the situation to force their partner to yield to their demands, and others become involved because they hope that the conciliator will be able to bring about a reconciliation.

Conciliators need to be able to handle situations in which feelings run high, for intense anger, resentment, yearning or grief will often prevent a reasonable exchange of ideas. Sometimes the bitterness is so severe that the parties will refuse to negotiate face-to-face, and in such circumstances the conciliator may act as a go-between, visiting first one and then the other in a kind of 'shuttle diplomacy'. This strategy is less than ideal, however, for it may produce problems with respect to confidentiality and it increases the chances that the conciliator will develop a partisan relationship with one or other of the partners.

Some conciliation services (known as 'out-of-court' services) are totally independent of the court and take self-referrals, and referrals from lawyers and voluntary agencies. Other conciliation work is undertaken at the suggestion of the court. This can lead to difficulties over confidentiality, and is likely to change the atmosphere during negotiation, principally because clients may confuse the conciliation process with that of adjudication. When 'in-court' conciliation is undertaken the outcome is conveyed to the court, but details of the sessions are not disclosed. Conciliation has proved very successful in decreasing the number of defended divorces, and results from agencies that record the outcome of cases suggest that for about three-quarters of couples one or more major conflictual issues are fully or partially settled as a result of the conciliation process (Parkinson, 1986). It has to be acknowledged, however, that in a proportion of cases attempts at conciliation may actually make matters worse.

Conciliation has the potential to increase the well-being of family members in a number of ways. It saves time and money, and often reduces bitterness. A lessening of tension during the pre-divorce phase appears to increase individuals' ability to cope after the divorce. Those who have experienced a relatively peaceful and cooperative divorce appear to suffer less post-divorce distress than those for whom the divorce was a turbulent and desperate episode. If a conciliation service has managed to help the couple achieve an orderly divorce, practical issues concerning custody, access, finance, and residence are likely to have been resolved equitably, so that the divorced person who would otherwise have been disadvantaged will have fewer problems to cope with. In addition, the emotional climate during a more mannerly divorce is likely to produce far less trauma at the time and may also reduce the psychological suffering in the months that follow. Children are likely to benefit from their parents' involvement in conciliation because questions relating to their residence and care are likely to have been resolved more satisfactorily, thus reducing the chance that they will be pawns in a bitter feud over custody and access. Furthermore, it is clear that when the custodial partner copes well after the divorce, and when the parents are able to maintain a civil mode of communication, the children experience less stress. Thus by helping the parents to cope practically and emotionally, conciliation can play an important role in protecting children from the possible adverse consequences of divorce.

THE EFFECTS OF MARITAL BREAKDOWN ON ADULTS

THE READJUSTMENT PROCESS

For some people the legal event of divorce comes as something of a relief. After many months or even several years of ambiguity and ambivalence the decree marks the end of an unhappy chapter. They may be optimistic about beginning a new phase of their life and experience renewed feelings of competence and control. About a quarter of newly divorced people describe their divorce as a relatively painless event and say that it did not result in appreciable psychological disturbance (Albrecht, 1980). In dealing with people who have recently become divorced, therefore, it is wrong simply to assume that they will be in a disturbed and vulnerable state. Some are cheerful and untroubled, although many are not. How the individual reacts to the divorce will depend on their personality characteristics, on the nature of the marital breakdown, and on their current situation. Such factors as the duration and nature of the former marriage, the length of separation from the partner, and whether they were the petitioner or the respondent in the legal proceedings, will influence their reaction. But the response will also reflect their general attitude to divorce, and this will be a function of such elements as their religious beliefs and the attitudes and marital histories of their friends and relatives.

Many newly divorced people remain emotionally attached to their ex-partner, and contact in the early post-divorce stage, whether civil or aggressive, may generate feelings of love or closeness and cause severe emotional upset. Although co-parental responsibilities are usually the main reason for remaining in contact, it is clear that many divorced people find that any interchange with the ex-partner reawakens both positive and negative feelings associated with their previous relationship. Rapidly changing attitudes towards the former partner may cause drastic mood swings. Following their study of the persistent attachment of divorced people to their ex-partners, Kitson (1982) suggested that the strength of such feelings could be gauged from four reactions. Those who were still closely attached tended to spend a lot of time thinking about the former relationship; they often wondered what the ex-partner was doing; they 'doubted' at times that the divorce had really happened; and they often felt that they would never recover from the marital breakdown. Almost all the divorced individuals they studied recognized some degree of continued attachment and, although such sentiments usually faded after some time, in many cases a feeling of special affinity with the former partner was still evident some four years after the separation.

Most meetings between former partners occur when the non-custodial parent makes access visits to the children. Initially such meetings may be awkward and both parents may feel embarrassed. Residual hostility may be difficult to conceal and some encounters become contentious and heated. At a later stage, however, if the access arrangements prove satisfactory, and if both parents have established new satisfactory lifestyles, a cordiality may develop. The former partners may be able to relax in each other's company, to enjoy the children together, and to recall some of the more positive aspects of their former relationship. Divorced parents may be the most important supports for each other in dealing with childcare problems. Hetherington, Cox and Cox (1978) found that a mother's continued positive relationship with her ex-husband often helped her to deal effectively with the children. They showed that when the post-divorce relationship was agreeable and supportive there was less disturbance in family functioning and new stable patterns were soon achieved.

Ahrons and Rodgers (1987) developed a typology of the kinds of relationships maintained between former spouses. They distinguished between 'perfect pals', who maintain frequent and pleasant contact and share activities; 'cooperative colleagues', who get on well, but in a somewhat distant way; 'angry associates', who communicate only when absolutely necessary, and usually fight on such occasions; and 'fiery foes', who avoid each other at all costs. It is not uncommon for former partners to lose touch with one another, particularly if there are no children. But one or other may be keen to re-establish contact at some later stage, and it seems that men are more motivated than women to maintain some association with the former partner (Goetting, 1979).

Divorce leaves some individuals in a state of shock and completely undermines their self-confidence. Criticisms levelled at them by the former spouse may be frequently recalled and continue to provoke their misery or anger, or they may simply feel rejected. The process of readjustment is often gradual and painful, but most divorced people are aware of the need to work out a viable new lifestyle, and make strenuous efforts to do this. These endeavours may be hampered by severe financial hardship and the worries that this creates. In addition, certain benefits of the former marriage may become apparent only after the divorce. While they are still in a relationship, people are often more aware of problems than of positive aspects (Weiss, Hops and Patterson, 1973). Thus it is only after the divorce has been finalized that some people realize the full extent of what has been lost, and they may then come to the conclusion that they seriously undervalued their marriage and misjudged their former partner. Some conclude, too late, that their resolution to end the relationship was a momentous mistake.

For the custodial parent and the children, the dramatic changes of circumstances will necessitate a realignment of family roles. The need to act as both 'mother and father' to the children may prove highly stressful, and the situation may be especially difficult because many children exhibit behavioural problems during the period following their parents' divorce. Newly separated and divorced mothers have been shown to be somewhat harsh and erratic in disciplining their children, whereas fathers who have custody of the children are often over-indulgent (Hetherington, Cox and Cox, 1978; Walczak and Burns, 1984). Things often improve in this regard after the first post-divorce year, although relationships between mothers and their sons often continue to be difficult and antagonistic. On the other hand, the children's presence may reduce loneliness and help the custodial parent to maintain a structured lifestyle and a sense of purpose. Older children may also help to relieve the day-to-day burden by taking on some of the tasks and roles of the absent parent. For the non-custodial parent, being separated from the children may prove more painful than expected. Divorced men, who are more likely to move away from the former marital home and away from the children, tend to feel rootless and lonely, and they often report that their lives lack structure and purpose. Research on how well divorced people cope has failed to provide any consensus about whether those who have children find it easier or more difficult to make a good adjustment.

Substantial difficulty may be experienced in assuming the new identity of 'divorced person' and in readjusting to single status. Although divorce does not carry the same degree of stigma as it did some decades ago, Hart (1976) found that many newly divorced people were acutely aware of their minority position and felt that other people regarded them as in some way 'unnatural', 'abnormal' or 'freakish'. After being close to a partner for several years, and sharing interests, chores and plans, some people found it very difficult to function independently. Those who have become accustomed to thinking and planning exclusively in terms of 'we' and 'us' may find it difficult to revert to the use of 'I' and 'me'. Women have the added problem that they may still be referred to, and may think of themselves as, 'Mrs Wilson' long after they have been divorced from Mr Wilson.

Many divorced people feel socially isolated and are very lonely. Some former friends will probably have aligned with the other partner, and the divorcee may be seen by certain couples as threatening their own marital stability. Divorced women, in particular, may feel uncomfortable in venturing out alone to make new friends, and financial problems and the need to provide constant care for the children may limit their opportunities for developing new social contacts. Those with infants or young children are often unable to find a suitable baby-sitter, or cannot afford to pay for one, while those who live alone may be too depressed to take an interest in new topics or to pursue new friendships (Ambrose, Harper and Pemberton, 1983). Divorced people who fail to develop a rich and fulfilling new lifestyle are especially likely to make a poor adjustment. A favourable psychological outcome has been shown to be associated with the degree of involvement in social activities; the expression of feelings about the former relationship and the divorce; and an increasing sense of autonomy (Berman and Turk, 1981). Those who are able to build an extensive social network are not only able to lead fuller lives as a result, but are also more likely to meet someone with whom they can develop an especially close and intimate relationship. Many divorced people identify their major problem as the lack of intimate contact with a 'special' adult. Several studies have identified the important benefits that people gain from a close partnership, and it is clear that the formerly married often feel deprived of such rewards and support (Weiss, 1975).

ADVERSE EFFECTS

Divorce is a critical life change and a major stressor, and like other such stressors it often has serious adverse effects on an individual's physical and psychological health. Compared with the married population, divorced people are at higher risk of premature death, and have a higher incidence of pneumonia, strokes, cancer, and coronaries. Partly because they drink and smoke more, the rates of cirrhosis and of mouth and throat cancer are also high, and many recently divorced people have serious psychological problems (Bloom, Asher and White, 1978). A high proportion consult their doctor about stress-related symptoms and many are prescribed tranquillizers and antidepressant medication. Studies in many countries have shown that the risk of a person being admitted to a psychiatric institution increases significantly following divorce, this effect being stronger for males than for females. Rates for depression, in particular, show a significant increase, and divorced people are more likely to attempt suicide. The rate of death by suicide among the divorced is about three times that of the married population.

Those who have recently divorced often engage in unhealthy and dangerous behaviours, lead disorganized lives, and take less care of themselves. They drink more alcohol, smoke more, have low work efficiency, experience sleep difficulties, and have disorganized eating patterns (Price and McKenry, 1988). Those who are divorced are also involved more frequently than others in motor vehicle accidents. US national statistics show that the automobile accident fatality rate for divorced people is about three times that of married people, and studies in the US and UK have shown that around the time of their divorce people are twice as likely to be involved in a broad range of accidents as they are at other times in their lives.

Before drawing the conclusion that divorce often makes people ill, however, possible alternative explanations for these statistics should be considered. For one thing, problems with physical and mental health (as well as certain injurious behaviours such as excessive drinking) are likely to increase marital tension and prompt the partner to seek a divorce (Menaghan, 1985). Thus at least part of the association between being divorced and being in a poor state of health might be the result of illness making divorce more likely, rather than of the condition being the consequence of the marital breakdown. In addition, it is possible that the poor health of the divorced is not an effect of the divorce itself but is a result of having endured what might have been several years of severe marital conflict. Or the increased risk of physical or mental disorder might reflect the hardship and upheaval that so often follows a divorce. Finally, comparisons showing the relatively poor health of divorced people might be explicable by reference to other differences between the groups. For example, it has been suggested that women who get divorced, and stay divorced, may be older, less well educated, less attractive, and less socially outgoing than women who either stay married or remarry soon after divorce (Glass, McLanahan and Sørensen, 1985). Characteristics such as these, rather than the experience of divorce, might increase the individual's vulnerability to illness.

Research has shed some light on these various hypotheses. For example, studies that have examined the physical health of unhappily married people suggest that they actually suffer more physical ill-health than those who have been divorced for some years. This suggests that for some people divorce provides an escape from an unhealthy situation and that divorce may actually reduce their susceptibility to illness. Although we might therefore conclude that divorce offers health protection to some people, at least in the longer term, this should not be allowed to eclipse the fact that many people experience severe disturbance during separation and immediately after their divorce, and are vulnerable to a range of serious afflictions. The evidence suggests that people undergoing divorce are most disturbed at the time of the initial separation, and that they often remain in a poor physical and psychological condition until some time after the divorce. Eventually things tend to improve, with some divorced people adjusting, or recovering, more rapidly than others. Those who soon enter into a new relationship fare particularly well, but even those who remain on their own tend to be in somewhat better shape some years after the divorce.

Although the recently divorced are generally more at risk of mental and physical illness than those who are married or who remain single (and even, in some respects, than those who are widowed), divorce seems to have a much more detrimental effect on some people than on others. There is not total agreement regarding the association between gender and vulnerability, but the results of a number of studies do suggest that more men than women show serious adverse effects following divorce. Older divorced people are more likely to suffer severe disturbance than their younger counterparts, and the degree of physical or psychological disorder is also associated with various personality factors. Thus those who attain low scores on long-term measures of emotional stability and self-esteem seem especially vulnerable to a number of afflictions following divorce.

Features of the divorce itself are also linked to the risk of post-divorce symptomatology. Those who are ambivalent about their divorce, or who regard it as a unilateral rejection by their partner, are less likely to have a favourable outcome. Those who feel that the divorce was imposed upon them may regard their life as largely beyond their control. Feelings of powerlessness may lead to a profound loss of self-confidence and cause the individual to become depressed. On the other hand, those who played an active part in bringing the relationship to an end appear to fare relatively well. They may have judged accurately that the termination of the marriage would be beneficial, or the fact that they remained in control of events may have made the divorce process much less threatening. While some people place all of the responsibility for the marital breakdown on their ex-partner, or on themselves, others opt for an interpersonal explanation and accept that the relationship failed due to some weakness or a mutual incompatibility. A study focusing on recently divorced women found that those who assigned joint responsibility for the end of the partnership were generally happier and more optimistic about the future than those who placed the sole blame either on themselves or on their partner (Newman and Langer, 1981).

A divorce that is mutually agreed, and in which problem issues have been satisfactorily negotiated and resolved, seems to produce relatively good post-divorce adjustment in both partners. This therefore illustrates a substantial benefit that might follow from successful conciliation. As would be expected, the presence of supportive friends and relatives after the divorce can also act as an effective buffer against trauma. Those who have close friends and whose relatives are sympathetic are at lower risk of illness following divorce than those who lack such support (Colletta, 1979). Contact with other people will provide emotional comfort and enrich the social life of the newly divorced. Although the maintenance of a diverse friendship network is very valuable, however, the single most important protective factor seems to be the presence of an intimate (Hetherington, Cox, and Cox, 1978). Those who have already established, or soon manage to establish, an alternative and satisfactory intimate relationship seem relatively well protected from disorder (Hunt and Hunt, 1977). Although it is particularly useful if such a relationship takes the form of a stable partnership, however, it does not appear to be particularly important whether or not it involves marriage (Spanier and Furstenberg, 1982).

Thus we can conclude that some part of the association between illness and the state of being divorced may be due to the fact that ill-health sometimes aggravates marital tension. But there can be little doubt that the principal reason for the association is that marital disruption, divorce, and the aftermath of divorce are often highly stressful. Exposure to such stress directly increases an individual's vulnerability to psychological and physical illness and may lead them to adopt an unhealthy lifestyle and to engage in hazardous behaviours. Thus they may drink excessively, eat poorly, and drive dangerously. Poor health is particularly apparent during the separation phase and immediately after the divorce. The legal process can be distressing, but the divorce itself rarely acts as the trigger that precipitates ill-health. Some part of the distress of the newly divorced may be due to the long-term effects of a disordered and conflictual marriage and the various difficulties that they have encountered since the separation. These problems include loneliness, unresolved identity problems, difficulties relating to children, and various financial and practical adversities. The loss of a partner not only imposes a considerable stress but also removes the person who may in previous times have played a major role in helping the individual to cope with unpleasant life changes.

As with so many other important life changes, the adverse effects of divorce tend to fade with time. However, it may be several years before a divorced individual feels that they have successfully recovered from the stress imposed by the ending of the marital relationship. Wallerstein and Kelly (1980) followed their sample of divorcing parents for five years and found that, on average, it took women over three years after separation, and men over two years, to feel that their lives had resumed coherence and stability. Eventually, even those who suffered most from the ending of their marriage may be better off than those who have remained in a highly conflictual relationship. For some, therefore, divorce is a rather painful but ultimately effective remedy for a chronic, unbearable, and damaging life situation.

CHILDREN AND DIVORCE

On current trends it is estimated that about one in three children in the US and about one in five children in the UK will experience parental divorce before they reach the age of 16. This means that each year about 170,000 British children experience their parents' divorce. Two-thirds of these children are under the age of 11, and one-quarter are under five. It is therefore very important to understand how children are affected by the dissolution of the parents' marriage, both in the short term and in the longer term, and to consider how any potential adverse effects may be prevented or limited.

COMMUNICATION

When a marriage is under serious threat there is often a breakdown in communication between the generations. Mitchell (1985) interviewed parents and children in Scotland some five years after the divorce, and found that about one-third of the children could not remember ever being told that their parents were separating or had already been divorced. In many other cases little explanation had been given about what was happening or why one of the parents suddenly left the home.

Parents who are in emotional turmoil may be so preoccupied with their own concerns that they simply ignore the children's need to be kept informed. Those who believe that the children are aware of the threat to the marital relationship may also assume that they are coping adequately with the situation and have no need of further information or special emotional support. They are often unaware of the child's bewilderment, insecurity, and anxiety at this time. Many parents feel profoundly uneasy and embarrassed about discussing a situation that is highly stressful, uncertain in its outcome, and very difficult for the young child to interpret. Murch (1980) found that some parents reported that communicating news of the impending breakup to the children was the single most difficult task experienced during the entire separation and divorce process. Children often contribute to the conspiracy of silence by failing to ask questions. Sensing that the marital predicament is a taboo subject they may deliberately avoid raising issues that they feel would be difficult or painful for the parents to discuss.

Despite the lack of communication, almost all children whose parents are on the point of separation are well aware that their parents are not happy together. Nevertheless, only about half of the children interviewed by Mitchell actually recalled any serious incident of parental conflict, so some parents are clearly very effective in keeping their fights concealed from the children. Many of those who did recall parental arguments still had vivid and unhappy memories of these. Sometimes the parents quarrelled late at night when the children were in bed listening, feeling frightened and helpless. In the absence of any adequate explanation for the tense atmosphere, and the parents' secretiveness, many children imagine that they are the cause of the unhappiness and aggravation in the home. Such self-blame has been reported in many studies (e.g. Wallerstein and Kelly, 1980; Weiss, 1975; Mitchell, 1985) and seems to be more commonly assumed by younger children than by those who are older.

Many parents fail to realize that avoiding discussion of the issue, or denying that the relationship is under threat, often leaves children very confused and distressed. Children need to be reassured that they are not responsible for the disharmony and that they will continue to be supported. They need to understand that what is happening between the parents is separate from their own relationship with each of the parents. Explanations about such matters need to be given in terms that the children will readily understand. Younger children, especially, have little appreciation of the nature of adult relationships, and they therefore have few resources for constructing reasonable accounts of what is happening or for dealing with the emotions generated by the situation. They may feel that their circumstances are unique and fear that many dreadful repercussions will follow. In reality, much of what they have taken for granted will be threatened by the ending of the parents' marriage, but their fantasies about what might happen are likely to be more terrifying. Older siblings and peers may help to explain things and to allay certain anxieties, but children are highly dependent on trusted adults to clarify the situation and to provide reliable explanations. Grandparents may be in a specially good position to help support the child at the time of parental divorce, and in some cases they will find it easier than the parents to explain developments and to present a positive but realistic view of what the future is likely to hold.

REACTIONS TO THE SEPARATION

When one of the parents does finally leave the home, children respond in different ways. Some feel relieved, hoping that there will now be an end to the chaos and bitterness that has reigned in the household. A majority, however, are distressed by the separation. In Mitchell's study, two-thirds of the children reported that they had been upset. In contrast, only one-third of the parents felt that their child has been upset at the time. Some children become very angry when a parent leaves, while others feel acutely threatened. Many children are concerned for their parents' well-being, and become very worried when the custodial parent shows distress. They also worry about the happiness, health, and safety of the other parent and wonder how he will cope on his own. Warshak and Santrock (1983) found that the event of separation was distressing whichever parent left the house. At this time, children tended to demand more parental attention, to become highly anxious, and to fear total abandonment. They also cried more, showed more anger towards the custodial parent, and sometimes became withdrawn or irritable. Sleep disturbances and physical complaints were also evident. Some adverse reaction was almost universal, but parents also reported a number of positive changes. Thus some described their child as suddenly behaving in a more mature way or becoming more self-controlled.

Children often worry about whether they will ever see the other parent again, and they experience renewed anxiety when they hear one parent blamed and denounced by the other. The accusations and counter-accusations that often arise during the breakup can produce intense conflicts of loyalty for the children and they may feel very stressed as a consequence. Wallerstein and Kelly (1980) found that when unresolved conflict drove parents apart, children aged between 9 and 12 were particularly likely to form an alliance with one parent against the other. Overall, however, very few children reject either parent. They generally seek to maintain an affectionate relationship with both, and hope that they will both continue to be 'real parents'.

Few children, in retrospect, say that they welcomed the departure of a parent, and despite the tension that may have been apparent in the home before the separation a high proportion of children claim that they were happy while their parents were together. Many long for the absent parent to return and have fantasies, even after the divorce, about a reconciliation. In addition to reduced contact with the non-custodial parent, separation may bring a number of other alterations to the child's life. Some move to different accommodation and a different school, and may thus lose contact with many of their friends. Such changes may bring additional upheaval, more uncertainty and more stress. Some children feel stigmatized as a result of their altered circumstances, and many find it difficult to talk to their peers about what has happened. At a time when life at home is chaotic and less secure, the school and friend's homes may be relative havens. Mitchell (1985) found that some children gained support and helpful information from an older sibling and that girls, especially, tend to use their friends as a means of emotional support. Boys were more 'ashamed' about the separation and tended not to discuss their home affairs with other people.

As with any other major life event, children construct a personal account of the meaning and implications of the separation, and in many cases they do this with a very limited understanding of the concepts involved. Thus younger children, especially, have little appreciation of the legal nature of separation and divorce, and the terms that are used often confuse them. One of the children interviewed by Walczak and Burns (1984) said: 'My Mum and Dad were divorced twice, once when Dad left and then when they went to court', and a child in Mitchell's (1985) sample thought that 'divorce' meant that his father had been replaced. When told that the parents were divorced he went to different rooms in the house looking for 'my new Daddy'. Conversations with other children at school may promote various myths about the nature of separation and divorce.

Children who have been through the experience of a parental divorce are, in the end, likely to have been exposed to more discussion by relatives and friends about relationships and transitions than those whose families have remained intact. They are also likely to have spent more time thinking about relevant issues and actively developing their understanding of such matters. McGurk and Glachan (1987) systematically investigated children's concepts of parent-hood using structured doll-play. They compared the understanding of children from broken homes and those from intact homes. It was found that whereas very young children believed in the permanency of parenthood despite a long absence of one parent, older children understood the continuity of parenthood to depend on such factors as where the parent lived, whether there was still affection, and the subsequent marital and stepparent situation. From the age of 11 or 12, however, children again believed in the permanency of parenthood, but they now took the biological factor into account and thus distinguished between a parent's marital and parental roles. Although the overall developmental pattern was the same for both groups, McGurk and Glachan found that children whose parents were divorced tended to show more mature levels of understanding than children from intact families.

CUSTODY

Custody is usually awarded to one parent although in a minority of cases joint custody may be determined by the court. Sometimes there is 'divided custody', such that one child lives with one parent and another lives with the other. In the UK this happens in about 6% of cases. About 90% of sole custody orders are made in favour of the mother, although if the child is living with the father at the time of the proceedings then he will often be awarded custody. Fathers are also more likely to obtain custody of boys than of girls. Many fathers do not apply for custody because they imagine that they have no chance of being successful—they feel it to be foregone conclusion that the court will favour the mother's application rather than their own.

Warshak and Santrock (1983) claim that the mother's traditional advantage over the father in the matter of custody is based on the presumption that mothers are uniquely suited to care for children, and that young children, especially, will suffer irreparable damage if they are separated from the mother. These authors point out that the 'tender years doctrine' and the 'motherhood mystique' that have been so influential in guiding legal decision-making in past decades have been increasingly challenged by research findings. It is now more difficult to justify the view that unless the mother is exceptionally unfit to look after the child she is uniquely able to provide the best care. Sometimes, of course, there are prolonged fights over custody (the so-called 'tug-of-love' situation), and unless there is a successful attempt at conciliation a bitter court battle might ensue. In such cases all kinds of accusations and counter-accusations may be made in a bid to gain the 'prize' of custody. For example, one parent may try to disqualify the other's claim by accusing the partner of drug abuse, sexual abuse, promiscuity, or homosexuality.

It is much more common for couples simply to assume that the mother will care for the children, and in many cases the issue of custody is never seriously discussed. In the less typical situation where the father gains custody there is much more likely to have been some dialogue between the partners about the care and protection of the children. In such cases the children are also more likely to have been asked which parent they would prefer to live with. When the mother gains custody the children are unlikely to have been consulted about any preference they have about living with one parent or the other, and they are unlikely to have been involved in discussions about how they will later maintain contact with the father. But even when both partners agree that the mother should have custody, it seems that they are often mistaken in believing that the child has the same preference. Some children strongly disagree with the parents' decision, but their opinion is never solicited or is paid little heed (Mitchell, 1985).

Even in the small percentage of cases in which the court calls for a welfare report, the child's own wishes may not be ascertained. Indeed, getting a child to state a clear preference may not be easy. The phrase 'the wishes of the child' is frequently used, but this suggests that children have well-formulated and straightforward views on their continuing care. In fact, they are often unaware of the various options and may be confused when asked to state a preference. They may feel considerable pressure from one or both parents, and fear that choosing to live with one will be taken as a rejection of the other. When the custody issue is raised with a child, the various options need to be clearly and fairly stated. Children need to be protected from any emotional charge imposed by their parent, and they need to be reassured that, whichever way they choose, frequent contact with the non-custodial parent will still be possible.

There has been much more experience of the option of joint custody in the US than in the UK. The week may be split into two, or the duration of the child's stay with each parent may be a week, a month, or longer. In one case reported by Clingempeel and Repucci (1982) a child in California, whose parents lived nearly 200 miles apart, had been the subject of a joint custody arrangement whereby he changed home and school every two weeks. Evidence that continued contact with both parents is beneficial for children following divorce immediately suggests one advantage of a joint custody arrangement, but it will readily be appreciated that some agreements might prove severely disadvantageous for many children who would find great difficulty in adapting to the endless disturbance of residence and routine.

ADJUSTMENT PROBLEMS

The turmoil that often occurs at the time of marital breakup causes many children substantial emotional distress. Hetherington, Cox and Cox (1978) showed that only the death of a parent was a more stressful event in the lives of children than separation and divorce. Adverse effects are not universal, however, and many children soon settle into a new routine following the marital dissolution. Some respond very positively to the dramatic reduction of tension in the home, and show a decrease rather than an increase in symptoms (Lowery and Settle, 1985). For many, the stress of parental divorce does precipitate at least a temporary disruption of their development and social adjustment. Many studies have found a higher incidence of emotional and behavioural problems among children of divorce, and such children are over-represented in clinic populations (Warshak and Santrock, 1983).

Frequently noted reactions include denial, regression, helplessness and depression, abandonment fears, anxiety, and lowered self-esteem. Many young children feel that they are in some way responsible for the divorce, and others are preoccupied with fantasies of reconciliation. In her study sample, Mitchell (1985) reported high levels of truanting, clinging behaviour, withdrawal, moodiness, and aggressiveness. Adverse changes in the child's relationships with peers, parents and teachers have also been reported across a wide age-range. Hetherington, Cox and Cox (1979a) found that four-year-old children who had recently experienced parental divorce showed marked differences in their play and peer relationships when compared with children from intact families. Their play was less imaginative and they got on less well with peers. They were also more likely than other children to be aggressive or socially anxious, and were less frequently chosen as playmates.

In the light of this evidence it is tempting to draw the general conclusion that 'divorce is bad for children'. However, a number of further considerations need to be made in order to gain a sensible perspective on the evidence regarding adverse consequences. Some of the early research that supported the widely accepted belief that divorce has serious detrimental effects for children can be criticized for the way in which the children were selected for the studies. Clinic populations, and samples of particularly disadvantaged children, might be totally unrepresentative of the general population of 'children of divorce'. More recent studies have avoided such methodological shortcomings, and the picture that has emerged is considerably less gloomy. Given that some studies have continued to show apparent adverse effects, it is necessary to consider (1) whether there might be other reasons for the association between parental divorce and child symptoms, (2) the probable fate of the children had they remained in a highly conflictual family situation, and (3) how children who experience parental divorce fare in the longer term.

The events of a parent leaving and the legal divorce are preceded and followed by many longer-term circumstances that may contribute to any symptoms or adverse effects on development or progress at school. Thus Ferri (1976) reported the relatively poor educational achievement of the children of divorced parents in her sample, but suggested a number of alternative factors that might help to explain her results, including the relatively poor housing and poverty of the divorced families, and the fact that teachers may have had lower expectations of the children who were seen as coming from 'problem families'.

Any adverse changes found in children's health or adjustment following their parents' divorce may reflect changes in the parents' well-being, rather than being direct effects of the divorce. Parents may be depressed, extremely preoccupied with their own problems, and highly stressed. As a result they tend to be less considerate, less affectionate and less able to control the children. Walczak and Burns (1984) found that mothers tend to become inconsistent in matters of discipline and that, with boys especially, their treatment is often rather harsh. Hetherington, Cox and Cox (1978) also found that divorced mothers were less likely to reason with their children, were inconsistent in disciplining, and showed them less affection. In part these changes appeared to be a reaction to the children's difficult behaviour. In many cases the children had become aggressive, they frequently showed a high degree of dependence, and they were non-compliant. Such difficulties with discipline were most pronounced in the year following the divorce, and after this things tended to improve. Custodial fathers have also been shown to be less effective in their disciplinary actions following divorce, but they tend to err on the side of indulgence (Walczak and Burns, 1984). The parents' relatively poor well-being following the marital breakdown, and their less competent disciplining, would be expected to have adverse consequences for the child.

If divorce had not occurred then most of those who are now 'children of divorce' would remain 'children of marital conflict', and in many instances the adverse effects of living in an atmosphere of chronic discord might be considerably worse than those found some time after the divorce. In a review of the effects of severe marital conflict, Rutter (1975) showed that children often suffer as a result of hostility and feuding between the parents, and that the situation is particularly damaging if the child becomes directly involved in parental disputes or if the conflict persists over a very long time. Warshak and Santrock (1983) later suggested that there was consistent evidence showing that children who had lived through their parents' divorce had fewer problems than children who remained in unhappy and conflictual families. They therefore suggested that divorce is a complex transitional process which may initially trigger stressful reactions and may necessitate a period of recovery, but that eventually a new pattern of equilibrium is usually established so that the negative effects disappear.

Based on their own work, Hetherington, Cox and Cox (1979b) similarly concluded that although divorce may produce negative effects for many children in the short term, these tend to diminish in time, so that children who experience divorce are eventually better adjusted than those who remain within a discordant family. Their data suggest that restabilization is usually achieved between one and a half and two years after the divorce. Thus the stressful period of disorganization may be offset by the emergence of a new equilibrium that is apparently less damaging in the long run that the atmosphere of tension and conflict that might otherwise prevail. For children, as for the parents themselves, divorce may therefore be regarded as an effective, though sometimes 'painful', remedy for a chronic and highly disturbing problem.

Risk Factors

There are substantial individual differences in how children respond to the stress of divorce and its aftermath, and several factors associated with children's vulnerability have been identified. These include the children's age and sex, their understanding of the divorce, and the quality of their relationships with both parents after the separation. It can be argued on the basis of general developmental psychology that children of pre-school age are likely to be most affected by parental divorce. At this age children have little appreciation of the world beyond the home and the family, and they are rapidly developing a basic understanding of relationships, as well as evolving their own identity. Children become attached to a primary caregiver towards the end of their first year, but they do not sustain attachments over long absences until they are over three years old. Thus the young baby would not 'miss' a parent, but between infancy and school-age the child who suddenly becomes aware of the prolonged absence of a parent may feel abandoned and highly distressed. Older children are able to maintain an affection for the non-custodial parent despite frequent and lengthy absences, and adolescents are generally more independent, and thus less influenced by events happening in the home.

The hypothesis that the greatest disruption will occur when the child is between one and four years old at the time of the separation is supported by the findings of a number of studies. There is in fact a clear consensus that young children show more adverse effects than those who are older. Wallerstein and Kelly (1980), for example, found that pre-school children were most affected, tending to regress, to become clinging, and to be excessively anxious about the possibility of losing both parents. They found that the effects declined somewhat with age and that, as a group, adolescents were least affected. Lowery and Settle (1985) also showed that younger children display more anxiety and are at especially heightened risk of suffering from stress-induced physical illness. The age factor is one reason why two children in the same family may respond to the divorce of their parents in quite different ways.

Most studies have found that boys suffer more adverse effects than girls.

Boys often show more behavioural difficulties and seem to take longer to adjust to the changes in family structure. They tend to miss their father more than girls, and may have problems in adapting to the mother's changed role. One reason why boys may have more adjustment problems is that, since many more mothers retain custody of the children, more boys than girls live with the 'opposite-sex parent'. In a series of studies, Santrock and Warshak (1979; Warshak and Santrock, 1983) have found that children who live with the opposite-sex parent tend to experience more difficulties than those who continue to live with the same-sex parent.

Warshak and Santrock (1983) compared the interactions between the custodial parent and the child in custodial-father and custodial-mother families. On average, just over three years had elapsed since the marital breakup. Parent–child pairs from intact families were also observed. The pairs were videotaped in structured interaction situations and both the custodial parent and the child were interviewed. The videotaped child behaviour was then rated on a number of dimensions. The global pattern to emerge from the data was that children living with the same-sex parent often fared better than children living with the opposite-sex parent. Thus, boys in father-custody homes were less demanding than girls from such homes, whereas in mother-custody homes girls were less demanding than boys. A similar pattern emerged for the dimensions of maturity, sociability, and independence. Those who interviewed the children (and who were blind to their family situation) also rated them on a number of dimensions, and the same pattern emerged. Thus boys from father-custody homes were rated as more 'appealing' than girls from such homes, whereas girls from mother-custody homes were rated as more appealing than boys who lived with their mother. The same configuration was found for ratings of honesty, cooperativeness, and 'ease of rapport'.

Boys who live with their divorced mother tend to show various atypicalities in their sex-role behaviour. Those whose fathers have left the home, and are without a male parental figure, tend to be less independent than other boys and in a number of other ways their behaviour conforms less to the masculine stereotype (Clingempeel and Repucci, 1982). However, such effects on the boy's developing personality should not necessarily be judged as problematic or 'symptomatic'. If being reared by a divorced mother makes boys more caring, more nurturant, and less aggressive in their manner, then these effects, at least, would seem to be positive rather than negative. The child's personality, adaptiveness and resilience would also be expected to play a major part in determining how well they respond following parental divorce. Rutter (1978) found that children who are less adaptable are more vulnerable to a range of life changes and stressors, and Hetherington, Cox and Cox (1977) found that children who had the most difficulty in adjusting following divorce were often described by their mothers as having been difficult as infants.

Several reports (e.g. Wallerstein and Kelly, 1980; Walczak and Burns, 1984) suggest that a crucial factor affecting a child's response is the way that decisions about separation, divorce and custody are taken and explained. The breakdown of parent–child communication that often occurs around the time of separation and divorce is particularly unfortunate because the effects appear to be long-lasting. Walczak and Burns (1984) found that the quality of communication at the time of the separation was of vital importance in determining how well children coped at the time and for many years afterwards. They also found that good communication at this time helped to improve the quality of the relationship between the parents and the children during the period following the separation. Krantz *et al.* (1985) examined the question of whether children's understanding of their parents' divorce was related to their level of post-divorce functioning. These authors found that children who were poorly adjusted and displayed difficult behaviour in the home often had maladaptive appraisals of the divorce. They more often denied the reality of the separation, fantasized about reconciliation, and generalized from the parents' unsatisfactory relationship to all marriages.

Although it is important that the child achieves a realistic view of the divorce, the reality is sometimes very painful, particularly if the parents' relationship remains intemperate. If the parents manage to cooperate, and continue to communicate, then the child is less likely to develop emotional problems, but the continuation of parental feuding after separation and divorce is likely to be markedly traumatic for the child (Emery, 1982). Children whose parents continue to fight after the divorce, or who feel rejected by the non-custodial parent, are liable to develop stress-related physical illness, behaviour problems or depression, or may experience difficulties in keeping up with the work at school. Parents who remain civil to one another are likely to have fewer emotional problems themselves, and the custodial parent, in particular, will then be better able to provide good and consistent parenting for the child. If the parents are psychologically healthy, have positive attitudes, and maintain an open communication, then their children are likely to remain well adjusted.

A good relationship with *both* parents appears to act as a highly effective buffer against negative effects of divorce, and the degree of contact maintained with the absent parent is predictive of the child's level of well-being. Those who are frequently visited by the non-custodial parent show fewer signs of stress, are less aggressive, and maintain better relationships with their peers. Boys and pre-school children seem especially likely to benefit from regular visits by the absent father (Clingempeel and Repucci, 1982). However, the association demonstrated between the occurrence of such contact and the child's adjustment is open to a number of interpretations, because custodial parents who have the most difficulty adjusting, and whose problems may therefore contribute to the child's difficulties, may deny the former partner access to the children.

This analysis of the factors known to increase the risk of a child's adverse reaction to parental divorce allows certain suggestions to be offered about how parents may help to reduce children's distress and to attenuate any symptomatic effects. Children should be kept informed about what is happening and should be reassured that they are not to blame for the marital problems. It should be emphasized that they are still loved by both parents and that they will continue to be loved and cared for. Adequate contact between the child and the non-custodial parent should be arranged, and contact with a wider social network (particularly grandparents) should also be promoted. The divorce should be as orderly and good-natured as possible, and the parents should keep in regular contact and try to remain on reasonably good terms after the divorce. If the parents are able to tackle difficult issues rationally and to approach the divorce and post-divorce phases in a conciliatory rather than a confrontational frame of mind, then the effects for the children (as well as for the parents themselves) will be less traumatic. Trained conciliators can help to make the divorce process less chaotic and less turbulent, and any means of supporting the parents and improving their own adjustment is likely to reduce the severity of adverse effects on the children.

In recent years several intervention programmes have been described to help prevent and treat adverse effects following parental divorce. Ceborello, Cruise, and Stollak (1986) arranged group discussion and play sessions for mothers and children, and Pedro-Carroll and Cowen (1985) focused on encouraging schoolchildren to identify and express the feelings generated by their parents' divorce. In a group-based project with pre-school children, Rossiter (1988) used a series of structured play sessions involving activities, films and stories. These were designed to reduce any feelings of guilt that the children had, to build their vocabulary so that they were better able to express their feelings and to explain their current situation to other people, and to deal with fears of abandonment. Reconciliation fantasies were tackled by teaching the children to distinguish between hopes and wishes, and the children were also helped to understand the continuity of parenthood despite divorce. Those who conduct such intervention programmes are aware that the expression of significant emotions can evoke high anxiety, and the sessions are therefore structured so that the issues are tackled indirectly. Thus the intervention described by Rossiter involves sessions that begin with the children eating doughnuts and drinking juice, and a toy porcupine ('whose parents have recently been divorced') is used throughout as a 'carrier' of emotions. Feelings are identified by the use of masks and pictures.

THE LONGER TERM

In the longer term some children continue to suffer as a result of their parents' divorce. A number find it difficult to make satisfactory relationships, some lack self-confidence, and others remain sad and insecure. As when the more immediate effects of parental divorce were considered, however, such consequences should be judged against the possible consequences of the child's endurance of chronic marital conflict. Thus, although relatively high rates of delinquency have been found among children from broken homes, Rutter (1975) concluded that a higher rate of delinquency is associated with the child living in an atmosphere of continual marital discord.

Although some of the persistent adverse conditions observed following parental divorce may be the result of the stress associated with the marital breakup itself, they are more likely to reflect the continuing unhappiness of the custodial parent, or a deterioration in the family's financial, residential and social situation. In addition, the child's yearning for the other parent often continues to be a particular problem. The adage 'Out of sight, out of mind' is seldom an accurate reflection of how children respond to the absence of the non-custodial parent. Wallerstein and Kelly (1980) found that the importance of the absent parent did not diminish for the children they studied over the five years of their research. Although 40% of the custodial parents studied by Warshak and Santrock (1983) believed that the child still harboured a desire for parental reconciliation, when the children themselves were asked, no fewer than 84% expressed such feelings. These researchers asked children about the costs and benefits that followed as a consequence of their parent's divorce. The main advantage mentioned was the cessation of parental conflict, but the main disadvantage reported was the reduction of contact with the absent parent.

The children of divorced parents tend to become mature and responsible at a relatively early age (Weiss, 1979). They often report being given extra work after the separation, as family chores and roles are reassigned. Some, in retrospect, claim that the experience of their parents' divorce provided them with a better understanding of people and relationships (Walczak and Burns, 1987). Such attitudes may affect the course of their own relationships in later life, but they are also likely to make the child sceptical about any new relationship entered into by the custodial parent. An older child may be surprised and irritated at how a parent recovering from one apparently disastrous relationship appears to be eager to seek a new partnership. The child may find it especially difficult to come to terms with the fact that a parent is involved in a sexual relationship or is contemplating remarriage (Walczak and Burns, 1984). Having managed to adjust to the substantial changes following the divorce, and having successfully adapted to a major transformation of the family, the child is likely to feel highly threatened by any development that might demand another fundamental change of lifestyle.

'ACCESS' OR 'VISITATION'

In about half of the divorces in the UK some formal legal provision is made for regular access, although in many of these cases the specific arrangements for contact between the children and the non-custodial parent are left to be decided by the parents. The pattern of access immediately after the separation is predictive of the degree of contact later on, although there is a general decline in the frequency of access visits made. Warshak and Santrock (1983) found that over 60% of the children in their sample said that they would prefer to meet with the non-custodial parent more frequently. Because it appears to be very beneficial for the child to maintain contact with the absent parent, it is particularly unfortunate that up to a third of children lose contact with one of their parents (usually the father) soon after the parental separation (Mitchell, 1985).

In some cases the non-custodial parent is still very hostile towards the former partner, and access visits may then have serious adverse effects. These occasions may be marked by extreme conflict and fights that further damage the parents' relationships and leave the child in a highly distressed state (Clingempeel and Repucci, 1982). A problem that may arise in these and certain other circumstances is that the child becomes reluctant to meet with the non-custodial parent. Such a delicate situation needs to be handled very sensitively, for the parent may insist on his legal right to see the child, and forcing the child to undertake such visits may prove highly traumatic and lead to the development of physical illness or serious behavioural problems (James and Watson, 1984).

Richards (1982) examined the reasons why non-custodial fathers sometimes disappeared from their children's lives. In many cases it appears that they take a conscious decision not to make further visits or to remain in contact. This often reflects a belief that continued contact would produce more harm than good. Some fathers emphasize the pain that they themselves would feel, while others stress the disturbance that further meetings might cause to the child. Some fathers also mention that their new partner experienced distress when they made visits to their former home. As non-custodial parents become more involved in a new relationship, and especially if they remarry, the degree of contact with the children tends to decline.

Because meetings are typically infrequent, of short duration, and take the form of 'special occasions' rather than being part of a normal parent–child relationship, they often feel contrived and artificial, and this may limit the satisfaction they bring. Things may become especially tense when it is nearly time to part. To make meetings enjoyable and memorable for the child the father may provide elaborate treats of gifts, with the result that each meeting turns into something of a festive event (this has been labelled the 'every day is Christmas' syndrome). Such extravagance is likely to be greatly resented by the custodial parent, who may be struggling to manage on meagre resources and may regard the various presents and excursions provided by the father as blatant attempts to buy the child's affection and loyalty.

Sometimes the pain associated with previous visits will produce an ambivalence leading to postponements and cancellations of planned meetings, and custodial parents frequently complain about the unreliability of their former spouse in keeping to arrangements. A number of studies indicate that mothers and fathers differ in their judgement of whether the co-parenting arrangement is working out fairly and successfully. Non-custodial fathers commonly regard themselves as highly involved in the child's development and welfare, whereas their former wives often feel that they play a very tangential role and that their influence has mixed effects on the child. Arguments about the father's role and his degree of participation can lead to bad-tempered squabbles (Ahrons, 1980; Goldsmith, 1980). In an attempt to avoid such confrontations, and to ease the strain between children and their absent parent, some agencies provide 'access centres' that serve as a 'neutral ground' for meetings. Any such strategy is to be welcomed, for children often place great value on their continued contact. It is hardly surprising that many children report that after the divorce they come to feel much closer to the custodial parent than to the parent who is absent, but the large majority still insist that both parents remain very important in their lives.

REMARRIAGE

In the UK about two out of three divorced people eventually remarry, while in the US the figure is even higher (about four out of five). Remarriage usually takes place within five years of the divorce, and in a substantial proportion it happens within the first two years. Remarriage rates are higher for men than for women, and higher for younger people. The frequency and rapidity of remarriage indicates that the experience of an unhappy relationship that ends in divorce does little to persuade people that marriage is something to be avoided. Many individuals, however, remarry not because of the intrinsic attractions of the new partner or of the married state but because they find it difficult to cope with a lone existence. Compared with those who are due to marry for the first time, those about to remarry place less emphasis on romantic love and more on the practical benefits that they judge will be gained by being involved once again in a close relationship (Burgoyne and Clark, 1984). Remarriage may offer an escape from the loneliness, increased workload and financial hardship thay may have characterized life since the separation. Some individuals hasten into marriage as soon as a convenient partner is found, but many maintain a degree of caution. Over half of the divorced women who eventually remarry cohabit first, while some divorcees come to value an independent lifestyle and choose to enjoy this rather than opting for an early remarriage.

Although personal motives for remarriage are usually more important, a custodial parent may regard a new relationship as a way of providing a second 'resident parent' for the children and thus forming what is sometimes referred to as 'a reconstituted family', 'a reconstructed family' or 'a blended family'. The new partner may regard the parenting role as a central feature, or as a minor and incidental consequence of the relationship with the divorcee. The presence of the children may be considered an added bonus or a liability. For the custodial parent, how well the new partner gets on with the children, whether they appear to have the potential to be an effective stepparent, and whether the children accept them, are likely to be matters of crucial importance. Typically, parents in this situation will introduce the new acquaintance gradually, encouraging enjoyable interaction and keenly observing how the relationships progress. If the children accept their possible future stepparent enthusiastically, the parent may be hopeful that a lasting partnership will develop and that they will all live happily together. But if the relationship between the children and the parent's new companion is distant or hostile then the custodial parent may decide to end the relationship or at least to avoid committing themselves by remarrying. Thus some parents adopt a rather democratic policy when considering whether they should introduce a stepparent into the home, and they allow the children's opinions and preferences to exert a critical influence on their decision concerning remarriage. This might help to explain why, overall, those with children are somewhat less likely to remarry than those without children (Spanier and Glick, 1980).

At the beginning of this chapter it was noted that the rate of divorce following remarriage is higher than that of first marriages. The magnitude of this difference is not great, but the pattern has been demonstrated many times. A number of factors probably contribute to the relatively high rate of divorce in second and subsequent marriages. Individuals who are 'divorce-prone' because their personality, mental health, or family history makes it difficult for them to adjust to a stable relationship, or difficult for a partner to tolerate them, will become selectively available for remarriage. Thus those who 'come on to the market' for the second time, and are therefore eligible for remarriage, are not a random selection of individuals, but include a relatively high proportion of those who are likely to fail in any relationship they enter into.

The choice of a partner is likely to be much more restricted at this stage than it was before the original marriage. Age is one factor that contributes to this. A high proportion of the age-mates of those who are in their early twenties, for example, will still be single, whereas following a divorce at the age of, say, thirty, most contemporaries will be in stable relationships. Also, divorcees may be less attractive potential partners because they are older, have children, and already have a history of one failed relationship. Furthermore, many divorced people lead restricted social lives, so that they get few opportunities for meeting new partners. Because of their restricted choice, some people will enter into a relationship that seems less than ideal from the outset and ultimately proves unsuccessful. Faced with a very limited 'field of eligibles', an individual's enthusiasm for forming a close relationship may lead them to enter into an unwise partnership.

Experience of one divorce may lower an individual's 'divorce threshold', so that the decision to end a subsequent relationship will be made more easily when things begin to go wrong. Having managed for a while on their own they may have established that independent living is a viable or even an attractive alternative to living with a partner. In addition, the remarried person may feel wary and pessimistic about the likely outcome of their current marriage, and their constant anxiety about a possible breakup may place a strain on the relationship. Furstenberg and Spanier (1984) showed that fear of divorce was often present in those who had remarried. Some may feel that history will repeat itself and that any marriage in which they are involved is bound to fail.

Special stresses associated with a second marriage may result from the complex patterns of family relationships that are often entailed, from comparisons made between the current relationship and the previous one, and from difficulties with stepchild–stepparent relationships. During the first marriage certain habits and expectations will have been formed, and although the remarried person may be mindful of the danger, he or she is likely to use the original marriage as a kind of baseline against which to judge the second (Furstenberg, 1982). Spanier and Furstenberg (1987) remark that 'second marriages bear the continuing imprint of the previous relationship'. The presence of children may also place a special strain on the second marriage. White and Booth (1985) concluded from their study that difficulties in remarriage are principally caused by the presence of stepchildren, and they found no significant difference between first marriages and second marriages when the children lived elsewhere. Although it is commonly believed that if a remarried couple have a child of their own this will serve to 'cement' the relationship and to strengthen it, there is little evidence to support this hypothesis. Ganong and Coleman (1988) compared reconstituted families in which couples did and did not have children of their own, and found no difference between these in terms of the partners' satisfaction with the relationship.

STEP-RELATIONSHIPS

About one in 14 children in the UK, and one in six in the US, live with a stepparent, so 'reconstituted' or 'blended' families are no longer rare. In most cases it is the woman, the custodial mother, who brings children into the new marriage, so that there are more stepfathers than stepmothers. When remarriage occurs, both partners may previously have been married, and both may have children from their previous marriage. Later, the couple may have children together, so that there will be three sets of children, although it is unusual for all of them to be resident in the same household. But whether all of the children are 'on site', or whether contact with some of them is made only by one partner during access visits, the pattern of relationships associated with reconstituted families is often very complex. Hobart (1987) collected information on parents' relationships with their children and stepchildren and suggested that there are 'first-class' children—those who are shared, 'second-class children'—the wife's unshared children (who often live with the couple), and 'third-class children'—the husband's unshared children (who usually do not live with the family).

The formation of blended families leads to a greatly expanded 'extended family'. The children may gain a set of stepgrandparents and may meet many other blood relatives of their new stepparent. They may also become acquainted with the stepparent's own children. The term 'quasi-kin' was used by Bohannon (1970) to refer to former spouses and the husbands, wives, and blood relatives of former spouses. In terms of alliances, boundaries, and sub-groupings it can be seen that very intricate and elaborate structures may be information on parents' relationships with their children and stepchildren and suggested that there are 'first-class' children—those who are shared, 'second-class children'—the wife's unshared children (who often live with the couple), and 'third-class children'—the husband's unshared children (who usually do not live with the family).

While it has long been established that remarriage is, on the whole, good for the readjustment and psychological well-being of the divorced adult (Spanier and Furstenberg, 1987), it is not nearly as clear whether remarriage produces beneficial effects for children's happiness and well-being. Studies that have compared children's adjustment in cases where the custodial parent has or has not remarried have produced mixed results. Traditionally it has been acknowledged that the stepparent–stepchild relationship is a difficult one, and countless folk tales depict a stepparent (usually the stepmother) in a highly negative light. The stepmother role is likely to be more crucial than that of the stepfather, because mothers typically engage in more day-to-day parenting tasks than fathers. As a consequence of this closer involvement, a relationship of high emotional intensity would be expected to develop between stepchildren and their stepmother. This does often happen, but children still tend to rate their relationship with their natural (custodial) father as more important to them than their relationship with their stepmother.

Although the custodial parent who remarries may wish to reproduce the role structure of the original family, it is clear that the dynamics of the blended family are very different from those of the natural family. In an intact family the parents may be keenly sensitive of their biological relationship with the child, and they will both have played an active part in socializing the child from infancy. They come to know the child gradually, and their affection reflects an intimate knowledge of the child's history. The stepparent comes on to the scene some time later, probably when the child's socialization is well under way and when many interaction patterns and rules of behaviour have become well established. It may take some time for the stepparent to become acquainted with the child, to adopt the customary style of family interaction, and to develop a genuine and deep affection for the child. Especially with older children, the stepparent may choose to act more like an adult friend, or an uncle, than an 'acquired parent'.

The remarriage of the custodial parent is a highly significant event in the child's life and will demand further readjustment after the changes relating to the separation and divorce. Remarriage may upset a stable pattern and reduce the attention that the custodial parent gives to the child. The further radical change brought about by remarriage, therefore, may prove disruptive and lead to a further period of stress. In his analysis of data from an extensive longitudinal study of British children, Douglas (1970) found that divorce increased the rate of enuresis in children, but that while the incidence of this symptom returned to normal levels for children whose mothers remained unmarried, it remained comparatively high (even at the age of 15) for those whose mothers remarried. A more recent longitudinal study (Wadsworth *et al.*, 1983) showed that five-year-old children in stepfamilies had more accidents and higher rates of behavioural disturbance than those who remained with a single divorced parent.

There is no evidence to suggest that boys fare better or worse as stepchildren than girls, but there is some consensus that the age of the child is an important factor. It appears that younger children adjust relatively easily to the stepparent, and that adolescents have the most difficulty in accepting the changes brought about by remarriage. This pattern has been demonstrated for various measures of adjustment and is also evident in stepparents' reports of the difficulties they experience in their new role. Ferri (1984) compared stepchildren, children who remained with a lone parent, and children who lived with both natural parents. She found that in stepfather families (but not in stepmother families) children were significantly more likely to show behaviour problems and enuresis, to have problems with non-attendance at school, and to come into contact with the police and courts. Despite the higher incidence of such difficulties, however, it should be emphasized that only a minority of the stepchildren displayed any significant problem. Parent–child relationships were found to be more difficult in stepfamilies than in natural families, with the greatest complications occurring between girls and their stepmothers. A quarter of such girls stated explicitly that they did not get on well with their stepmothers.

Although older children are less likely to accept the changed family situation and may present special difficulties for the newly acquired stepparent, many of them will have developed important relationships with their peers and they may therefore have less contact and be less involved with the family. Some studies have identified a number of special difficulties that can sometimes occur between teenage girls and their stepfathers. When, in their early teens, girls develop an awareness of their sexuality, they may see themselves as being in competition with their mother for the love and attention of the new man in the house. Some stepfathers also find themselves sexually attracted to their stepdaughter and some take advantage of their special situation. While it would be damaging and distorting to over-emphasize this aspect of the stepfather–stepdaughter relationship, it must be acknowledged that the risk of a stepfather sexually abusing his stepdaughter appears to be many times higher than that of a father abusing his natural daughter.

A controversial question that has received some attention is whether the establishment of a good stepparent–stepchild relationship is aided or hampered by the child's continued close association with the non-custodial natural parent. Some have claimed that such frequent contact might spoil the formation of a special relationship with the stepparent. However, the available evidence (Richards and Dyson, 1981) indicates that the reverse is true and that children who often see their non-resident parent typically have a better relationship with the stepparent. It seems that the most appropriate role for the stepparent might be that of a 'third parent'—an addition to the child's world—rather than a substitute or a replacement for the absent natural parent. A bid by the stepparent to take over the special role of the non-custodial parent may be resented by the child as well as by the absent parent. Step-relationships seem to be most successful, especially when the child is not very young, when it is recognized and accepted by all concerned that the step-relationship is different from the relationship between a child and his or her natural parents.

REFERENCES

Ahrons, C. R. (1980) Divorce: A crisis of family transition and change. *Family Relations*, **29**, 533–540.

Ahrons, C. R. and Rodgers, R. H. (1987) *Divorced Families: A Multidisciplinary Developmental View*. New York: Norton.

Albrecht, S. L. (1980) Reactions and adjustments to divorce: differences in the experience of males and females. *Family Relations*, **29**, 59–69.

Ambrose, P., Harper, J. and Pemberton, R. (1983) *Surviving Divorce—Men Beyond Marriage*. Brighton: Wheatsheaf Books.

Argyle, M. and Henderson, M. (1985) *The Anatomy of Relationships*. Harmondsworth: Penguin.

Berman, W. H. and Turk, D. C. (1981) Adaptation to divorce: problems and coping strategies. *Journal of Marriage and the Family*, **43**, 179–189.

Bloom, B. L., Asher, S. J. and White, S. W. (1978) Marital disruption as a stressor: a review and analysis. *Psychological Bulletin*, 85, 867–894.

Bloom, B. L., Hodges, W. F. and Caldwell, R. A. (1983) Marital separation: the first eight months. In: E. J. Callahan and K. A. McCluskey (eds.), *Life-span Developmental Psychology: Nonnormative Life Events*. New York: Academic Press.

Bohannan, P. (1970) *Divorce and After*. New York: Doubleday.

Burgoyne, J. and Clark, D. (1984) *Making a Go of It: A Study of Stepfamilies in Sheffield*. London: Routledge and Kegan Paul.

Cebollero, A. M., Cruise, K. and Stollak, G. (1986) The long-term effects of divorce: mothers and children in concurrent support groups. *Journal of Divorce*, 10, 219–228.

Chiriboga, D. A. and Cutler, L. (1977) Stress responses among divorcing men and women. *Journal of Divorce*, 1, 95–106.

Clarke-Stewart, A. (1977) *Child-care in the Family*. New York: Academic Press.

Clingempeel, W. G. and Repucci, N. D. (1982) Joint custody after divorce: major issues and goals for research. *Psychological Bulletin*, 91, 102–127.

Colletta, N. D. (1979) Support systems after divorce: incidence and impact. *Journal of Marriage and the Family*, 41, 837–846.

Douglas, J. W. B. (1970) Broken families and child behaviour. *Journal of the Royal College of Physicians*, 4, 203–210.

Emery, R. E. (1982) Interparental conflict and the child of discord and divorce. *Psychological Bulletin*, 92, 310–320.

Ferri, E. (1976) *Growing Up in a One-parent Family: A Long-term Study of Child Development*. Windsor: NFER.

Ferri, E. (1984) *Step-children: A National Study*. Windsor: NFER–Nelson.

Finer Report (1974) *Report of the Committe on One-Parent Families*, 2 vols. Department of Health and Social Security, London: HMSO.

Furstenberg, F. F. (1982) Conjugal succession: reentering marriage after divorce. In: P. B. Baltes and O. G. Brim (eds.), *Life Span Development and Behaviour*, Vol. IV. New York: Academic Press.

Furstenberg, F. F. and Spanier, G. B. (1984) *Recycling the Family: Marriage after Divorce*. Beverly Hills, CA: Sage.

Ganong, L. H. and Coleman, M. (1988) Do mutual children cement bonds in stepfamilies? *Journal of Marriage and the Family*, 50, 687–698.

Goetting, A. (1979) The normative integration of the former spouse relationship. *Journal of Divorce*, 2, 395–414.

Glass, J., McLanahan, S. S. and Sørensen, A. B. (1985) The consequences of divorce: effects of sample selection bias. In: G. H. Elder, Jr (ed.), *Life Course Dynamics: Trajectories and Transition*. Ithaca, NY: Cornell University Press.

Goldsmith, J. (1980) Relationships between former spouses: descriptive findings. *Journal of Divorce*, 4, 1–20.

Hagestad, G. and Smyer, M. (1982) Dissolving long-term relationships: Patterns of divorcing in middle age. In: S. Duck (ed.), *Personal Relationships. 4. Dissolving Personal Relationships*.

Hart, N. (1976) *When Marriage Ends*. London: Tavistock.

Haskey, J. (1982) The proportion of marriages ending in divorce. *Population Trends*, 27, 4–8.

Hetherington, E. M., Cox, M. and Cox, R. (1977) Beyond father absence: conceptualization of effects of divorce. In: E. M. Hetherington and R. D. Parke (eds.), *Contemporary Readings in Child Psychology*. New York: McGraw-Hill.

Hetherington, E. M., Cox, M. and Cox, R. (1978) The aftermath of divorce. In: J. H. Stevens, Jr and M. Mathews (eds.), *Mother–Child, Father–Child Relations*. Washington, DC: National Association for the Education of Young Children.

Hetherington, E. M., Cox, M. and Cox, R. (1979a) Play and social interaction in children following divorce. *Journal of Social Issues*, **35**, 26–49.

Hetherington, E. M., Cox, M. and Cox, R. (1979b) Family interactions and the social emotional and cognitive development of children following divorce. In: V. C. Vaughan and T. B. Brazelton (eds.), *The Family: Setting Priorities*. New York: Science and Medicine Publishers.

Hobart, C. (1987) Parent–child relations in remarried families. *Journal of Family Issues*, **8**, 259–277.

Huber, J. and Spitze, G. (1980) Considering divorce: an expansion of Becker's theory of marital instability. *American Journal of Sociology*, **86**, 75–89.

Hunt, M. W. and Hunt, B. (1977) *The Divorce Experience*. New York: McGraw-Hill.

James, A. and Watson, K. (1984) The trouble with access: a study of divorcing families. *British Journal of Social Work*, **14**, 487–506.

Johnson, E. S. and Vinick, B. H. (1981) Support of the parent when an adult child divorces. *Journal of Divorce*, **5**, 69–79.

Kessler, S. (1975) *The American Way of Divorce: Prescriptions for Change*. Chicago IL: Nelson-Hall.

Kitson, G. C. (1982) Attachment to the spouse in divorce: a scale and its application. *Journal of Marriage and the Family*, **44**, 87–101.

Kitson, G. C. (1985) Marital discord and marital separation: a county survey. *Journal of Marriage and the Family*, **47**, 693–700.

Kitson, G. C. and Langlie, J. K. (1984) Couples who file for divorce but change their minds. *American Journal of Orthopsychiatry*, **54**, 469–489.

Kitson, G. C. and Sussman, M. B. (1982) Marital complaints, demographic characteristics, and symptoms of mental distress in divorce. *Journal of Marriage and the Family*, **44**, 87–101.

Krantz, S. E., Clark, J., Pruyn, J. P. and Usher, M. (1985) Cognition and adjustment among children of separated or divorced parents. *Cognitive Therapy and Research*, **9**, 61–77.

Levinger, G. (1966) Sources of marital dissatisfaction among applicants for divorce. *American Journal of Orthopsychiatry*, **36**, 803–807.

Long, B. H. (1987) Perception of parental discord and parental separations in the United States: effects on daughters' attitudes to marriage and courtship. *Journal of Social Psychology*, **127**, 573–582.

Lowery, C. R. and Settle, S. A. (1985) Effects of divorce on children: differential impact of custody and visitation patterns. *Family Relations*, **50**, 687–698.

McGurk, H. and Glachan, M. (1987) Children's conception of the continuity of parenthood following divorce. *Journal of Child Psychology and Psychiatry*, **28**, 427–435.

Menaghan, E. G. (1985) Depressive affect and subsequent divorce. *Journal of Family Issues*, **6**, 295–306.

Mitchell, A. (1985) *Children in the Middle—Living Through Divorce*. London: Tavistock.

Murch, M. (1980) *Justice and Welfare in Divorce*. London: Sweet and Maxwell.

Newcomb, M. D. and Bentler, P. M. (1981) Marital breakdown. In: S. Duck and R. Gilmour (eds.), *Personal Relationships. 3. Personal Relationship in Disorder*. London: Academic Press.

Newman, H. M. and Langer, E. J. (1981) Post-divorce adaptation and the attribution of responsibility. *Sex Roles*, 7, 223–232.

Parkinson, L. (1986) *Conciliation in Separation and Divorce*. London: Croom Helm.

Parkinson, L. (1987) *Separation, Divorce and Families*. London: Macmillan.

Pedro-Carroll, J. and Cowen, E. (1985) The Children of Divorce Intervention Project: an investigation of the efficacy of a school-based prevention program. *Journal of Consulting and Clinical Psychology*, 53, 603–611.

Pope, H. and Mueller, C. W. (1976) The intergenerational transmission of marital instability: comparison by race and sex. *Journal of Social Issues*, 32, 49–66.

Price, S. J. and McKenry, P. C. (1988) *Divorce*. Beverly Hills, CA: Sage.

Raschke, H. J. (1977) The role of social participation in post-separation and post-divorce adjustment. *Journal of Divorce*, 1, 129–140.

Richards, M. P. M. (1982) Post-divorce arrangements for children: a psychological perspective. *Journal of Social Welfare Law*, 133–151.

Richards, M. P. M. and Dyson, M. (1982) *Separation, Divorce and the Development of Children: Report to the Department of Health and Social Security*. Cambridge: Cambridge University Press.

Rossiter, A. B. (1988) A model for group intervention with preschool children experiencing separation and divorce. *American Journal of Orthopsychiatry*, 58, 387–396.

Rutter, M. (1975) *Helping Troubled Children*. Harmondsworth: Penguin.

Rutter, M. (1978) Protective factors in children's responses to stress and disadvantage. In: M. W. Kent and J. E. Rolf (eds.), *Primary Prevention of Psychopathology*, Vol. 3: *Promoting Social Competence and Coping in Children*. Hanover, NH: University Press of New England.

Santrock, J. W. and Warshak, R. A. (1979) Father custody and social development in boys and girls. *Journal of Social Issues*, 35, 112–125.

Spanier, G. B. and Casto, R. F. (1979) Adjustment to separation and divorce: an analysis of 50 case studies. *Journal of Divorce*, 2, 241–253.

Spanier, G. B. and Furstenberg, F. F. (1982) Remarriage after divorce: a longitudinal analysis of well-being. *Journal of Marriage and the Family*, 43, 709–720.

Spanier, G. B. and Furstenberg, F. F. (1987) Remarriage and reconstituted families. In: M. B. Sussman and S. K. Steinmetz (eds.), *Handbook of Marriage and the Family*. New York: Plenum Press.

Spanier, G. B. and Glick, P. C. (1980) Paths to remarriage. *Journal of Divorce*, 3, 283–298.

Thornes, B. and Collard, J. (1979) *Who Divorces?* London: Routledge and Kegan Paul.

Thornton, A. (1985) Changing attitudes toward separation and divorce: causes and consequences. *American Journal of Sociology*, 90, 856–872.

Udry, J. R. (1981) Marital alternatives and marital disruption. *Journal of Marriage and the Family*, 43, 889–897.

Wadsworth, J., Burnell, I., Taylor, B. and Butler, N. (1983) Preliminary Report of Ten-Year Follow-Up.

Waite, L. J., Haggstrom, G. W. and Kanouse, D. E. (1985) The consequences of parenthood for the marital stability of young adults. *American Sociological Review*, **50**, 850–857.

Walczak, Y. and Burns, S. (1984) *Divorce: The Child's Point of View*. London: Harper and Row.

Wallerstein, J. S. and Kelly, J. B. (1980) *Surviving the Breakup—How Parents and Children Cope with Divorce*. London: Grant McIntyre.

Warshak, R. A. and Santrock, J. W. (1983) Children of divorce: Impact of custody disposition on social development. In: E. J. Callahan and K. A. McCluskey (eds.), *Life-span Developmental Psychology: Nonnormative Life Events*. New York: Academic Press.

Weiss, R. (1975) *Marital Separation*. New York: Basic Books.

Weiss, R. (1979) Growing up a little faster: the experience of growing up in a single parent household. *Journal of Social Issues*, **35**, 97–111.

Weiss, R. L., Hops, H. and Patterson, G. R. (1973) A framework for conceptualizing marital conflict: A technology for altering and some data for evaluating it. In: L. A. Hamerlynck, L. C. Handy and E. J. Mash (eds.), *Behaviour Change: Methodology, Concepts and Practice*. Champaign, IL: Research Press.

White, L. K. and Booth, A. (1985) The quality and stability of remarriages: the role of stepchildren. *American Sociological Review*, **50**, 689–698.

9

Dying

UNDERSTANDING DEATH

CHILDREN'S UNDERSTANDING OF DEATH

Before the age of two years, children have little or no understanding of the meaning of death. Although by the age of 10 months they have begun to form attachments and may show separation anxiety, they have a very meagre conception of time. Before the age of two years children can make little or no distinction between a temporary and a permanent loss. Between the ages of two and four years they begin to form concepts, but although they speak of things being 'alive' and 'dead' they have only a slight understanding of the real meanings of these words. Nagy (1948) identified three stages of death-related concepts. In the first stage 'life' is identified as movement, and thus clouds, cars, and streams are seen as living; death is regarded as a temporary state, and dead people are believed to be conscious. At a later stage the concepts of life and death change; to be alive is now seen as being capable of moving *voluntarily*. Death is personified but the state of being dead is now understood to be permanent. Later, children begin to achieve a more adult-like conception of death and come to regard it not only as irreversible but also as inevitable; they may also become concerned about the process of dying. Although early research on children's concepts of death suggested that they had only a meagre understanding before the age of nine or 10 years, more recent work has indicated that most five-year-olds do have a fairly good grasp of the concept (Lansdown and Benjamin, 1985).

Death-related experiences (such as the death of a close relation, a national figure, or a pet) help to develop children's understanding of death, and a bereavement response following the death of a family pet, worked through with the help of understanding parents, may help to 'immunize' the child against the potentially damaging effects of a later human bereavement (Lonetto, 1980). Some educationalists have maintained that schools should play an active role in developing children's understanding of death and dying, and several educational programmes have been devised with the aim of providing children with a better realization of the nature of death and preparing them emotionally for losses that they may experience in their early lives. Stories featuring children who have had to cope with the loss of a parent or a pet, for example, may portray coping strategies that children can imitate. Topics often covered in such courses include the life cycles of plants and animals, dying, grief and mourning, and funeral and burial customs (Gibson, Roberts and Buttery, 1982). However, parents sometimes feel that this 'fact of life', like others, is too personal and sensitive a matter to be handled in the school context and they often express a preference for the issue to be dealt with at home and in response to specific inquiries by the child. But, as with sex education, their own anxieties may lead parents to feel embarrassed when asked certain delicate questions.

ADULTS' UNDERSTANDING OF DEATH

For adults, death is often a taboo subject, something they would rather not talk about or think about. In most advanced cultures dying is a rather hidden affair and people are helped to avoid the issue rather than to confront it (Nisbet, 1984). At some time during adulthood, however, usually in middle age, the person is forced to acknowledge their own ageing and will start to think at least occasionally about their own death. Events such as the death of a parent or a friend will remind the older middle-aged person that they may already have passed the mid-point in their lives. There is evidence of a peak in concern about one's own death in the years around 50 (Bengston, Cuellar, and Ragan, 1977). Older people tend to be somewhat less fearful about their own death than the middle-aged. By the time people reach their 60s they will usually have confronted the death of many friends and relatives and may have made various preparations for their own death (such as making a will or talking to relatives about their preference for a certain type of funeral). By confronting such issues older people are likely to come to terms with an issue that many younger people avoid.

Such repression is likely to be detrimental in a number of ways. It may serve to maintain the person's dread about dying throughout their adult years and make it more difficult for them to achieve the favourable state of 'acceptance' at the end of their life. Repression may also detract from people's ability to cope with the plight of dying relatives. There is growing support for the view that talking more openly about death may have beneficial effects, and this has led to an increasing enthusiasm for what has become known as 'death education'. This aims to put death into perspective, to help people to overcome some of their fears and anxieties about death, and to help them to provide aid and comfort to the bereaved. Adult courses designed for lay adults and professionals generally cover the topics of dying, bereavement and funeral practices, but are also likely to include discussion of such issues as euthanasia and suicide. The diffusion of such courses has been matched by a simultaneous growth in the academic study of death and dying—'thanatology'.

THE CHANGING NATURE OF DYING

In the technologically advanced world, the past few decades have witnessed striking changes in the facts of death. There have been profound shifts in the ages at which people die, in the causes of their deaths, and in the location of their dying. During this period life expectancy has greatly increased. In the UK, for example, a male born in 1900 had a life expectancy of 44 years whereas a boy born now has a life expectancy of over 70 years. Over the same period the life expectancy for women has increased from 48 years to 78 years. And this change is only partly accounted for by the high level of infant and child mortality at the beginning of the century. Young adults can now expect to live far longer than could their counterparts some decades ago.

In the past, people tended to die from acute infectious diseases, but as these have become increasingly preventable and treatable the majority of people now die from illnesses associated with old age. Over three-quarters of people in advanced societies now die from cancer, cardiovascular disorders and respiratory diseases. Whereas a clear majority of people used to die at home, most people now die in hospital (two-thirds of people in the UK). This change has arisen partly from advances in medical technology (more help is now available for the seriously ill, so more intense efforts are made to prolong life), and partly from changes in the causes of death. But it also reflects, and contributes to, a profound change in our conception of what it is to 'die'. Increasingly, death has come to be regarded as a medical incident rather than as a 'social' or 'family' happening.

AWARENESS OF THE TERMINAL CONDITION

Although the majority of people with a terminal illness realize that their illness is very serious, not all are told that they will soon die. This is despite the fact that the majority of people, when asked, say that they would wish to know if their illness is likely to prove fatal. On the other hand, relatives and friends are almost always informed. Thus doctors, nurses and relatives may be involved in a conspiracy in which the true nature and seriousness of the disease is kept from the patient. Over-optimistic appraisals of the likely outcome may be given, and technical or euphemistic terms used to cover up the fact that the patient has cancer or another life-threatening disease. The patient may be willing to accept any hopeful account, and use denial as a strategy for coping with the stressful situation. Some patients would not wish to be told of their imminent demise, and since it is difficult to judge whether someone would wish to be told or not, the physician may face a very difficult dilemma. To tell someone who does not want to know may be seen as a greater evil than not telling someone who would wish to know, and this may be one reason why physicians are often reluctant to disclose the terminal nature of the illness to the patient. In the 1950s there was a widespread tendency not to tell patients, but practice has changed considerably in the intervening decades and the majority of patients are now informed (Klenow and Youngs, 1987).

Families frequently complain about how professionals communicate with them when they face the approaching death of one of their number. In one study, doctors and nurses were observed in interaction with such families and were shown to use a range of social manoeuvres that distanced them from the family and curtailed discussion (Maguire, 1985). In the face of such intimidating behaviour by professionals, families were reluctant to ask candid questions, so that in many cases the medical personnel successfully avoided pressure to provide forthright information. Being 'kept in the dark' may bring considerable distress to families. Another study suggested that limited disclosure of information, and a reticence in communication both between professionals and families and within the family, caused more anxiety than any other aspect of the situation except chronic pain (Stedeford, 1981).

The fact that some patients are not told that they are dying does not mean that they do not know, or at least suspect, that their condition will prove fatal. There are major difficulties in assessing how far a person is aware that their time of death is approaching. They may 'know' at one level while denying it at another; or they may know but collaborate in the 'conspiracy of silence' of family members and medical professionals. Sometimes they avoid discussion about the probable outcome of their illness because they wish to spare others the pain of having to acknowledge and confront their impending bereavement. In many cases, of course, the person will simply be unsure (as may the medical staff and the family members) whether death will occur. Undoubtedly, a number of those who are seriously ill believe that they are dying when their illness will not in fact prove fatal.

THE EXPERIENCE OF DYING

For people who die suddenly, for example in a road accident, there is no time to appreciate the imminence of death, to make requests or embrace friends and relatives, or to engage in the psychological process of coming to terms with one's fate. For other people, however, there may be many weeks or months before a fatal illness eventually takes its toll. During this time many personal and social changes take place. The person may experience the time as one of 'serious illness', failing to acknowledge the impending death, or they may be fully aware that they are dying. People respond to the experience of dying in very different ways. Feelings of anxiety, panic, bitterness and depression are common, but many people make a good adjustment to their condition and come to accept the dying phase as a time for reflection, reminiscence and acceptance. They may use the opportunity to reinforce their bonds with others and enjoy a period of heightened harmony and tenderness in their relationships. Some people also use the interval before death to make amends for past transgressions, to heal damaged friendships and to put their practical affairs in order.

We will first consider psychological aspects of the pain and distress of dying people, before discussing the social aspects of dying. Consideration will then be given to an account that describes the psychology of the dying person in terms of a series of stages.

PAIN

Pain is the symptom most feared by dying patients although, happily, in almost all cases it can be controlled if medication is administered with the utmost skill (Saunders and Baines, 1983). The experience of pain reflects psychological as well as physical factors, and there is good evidence that people who are able to maintain positive social relationships experience less pain and discomfort (Achterberg et al., 1977). Maintenance of positive family relationships may therefore be useful in alleviating pain, and there is an additional gain if others who are in day-to-day contact with the dying person engage them in warm and empathic interactions. It has been shown, for example, that people who die in a hospital tend to experience less pain when they have good relationships with nursing staff (Bond and Pilowsky, 1966). Such social support is hardly ever sufficient to produce the total alleviation of pain, but it can considerably reduce the level of medication needed to produce pain relief. Obviously, some terminal conditions are considerably more painful than others, and there are pronounced differences in individuals' susceptibility to pain. There is evidence that younger dying patients tend to experience more pain than those who are older (Hinton, 1963).

DISTRESS

The terminally ill person may be distressed by many of the physical signs of illness (including incontinence, nausea, noxious smells and external signs of tumours, etc.). Breathlessness and pain, however, appear to be the symptoms which are particularly strongly associated with distress (Hinton, 1963). The patient may also be upset by a progressive helplessness and dependency on others, and by the distress caused to other members of the family. A proportion of dying patients become clinically anxious or depressed as a consequence of their worsening physical state. The subsequent emotional debilitation can in turn produce a physical weakening that increases the difficulty of providing adequate care.

A number of factors have been shown to influence a person's susceptibility to anxiety during the period leading up to death. Younger terminally ill patients, and especially those with young children, tend to be significantly more anxious in the dying stage than older people (Hinton, 1972). There is also a rather complex association between anxiety and religious faith. Hinton (1972) found that those who had a strong religious creed suffered least anxiety. Those who had a moderate belief, or were unsure where they stood on religious issues, had the highest level of anxiety. And those who were confirmed non-believers had a moderate degree of anxiety. Hinton found no significant relationship between the anxiety experienced during the terminal period and how nervous the person had been throughout their life, and this implies that those who know the person well may be surprised at how calmly, or how anxiously, they react to the prospect of death. Depression tends to increase with a lengthening period of illness, and also reflects the degree of physical discomfort.

SOCIAL PROCESSES

Kastenbaum and Weisman (1972) distinguished between two groups of terminally ill patients. One group maintained an active involvement in family life and tended to carry on 'as normal' as far as possible, maintaining their social network and their normal activities. The other group withdrew from normal social contacts, and became inactive, as if wishing to die alone. There is some evidence that the first of these types of reaction is associated with fewer complaints about pain and with a longer survival. Patients tend to become depressed if the family seems to be withdrawing emotionally and becoming more distant from them (Kalish, 1966). Such pulling away may occur if family members find the poignancy of the situation unbearable, of if they are unable to cope with the patient's anger or distress. Sometimes such withdrawal indicates that the relatives are already engaging in 'anticipatory mourning'.

THE JOURNEY TOWARDS DEATH

Several authors with an extensive experience of people who are about to die have distinguished a number of common stages through which the dying person may progress. Others stress the individuality of people's psychological responses to their terminal illness.

STAGES

On the basis of interviews and observations of over 200 terminally ill patients, Elizabeth Kubler-Ross (1969) distinguished five stages of dying. She described the patients' psychological states during each of these stages and suggested how friends and relatives might help during different phases.

Denial and Isolation

People often react to the news that they are dying with shock and disbelief. They may question the diagnosis and 'shop around' for a physician who will provide a more favourable prognosis. Those who persist longest with denial are often those who have used the denial strategy to cope with other crisis periods in their life. Relatives can help at this stage, Kubler-Ross suggests, by trying to understand why the patient is grasping at straws, by showing extreme patience, and by demonstrating a willingness to talk about the dying person's anxieties.

Anger

At the next stage the person acts in a hostile and defiant manner, often asking 'Why me?'. Anger may be expressed towards fate, God, relatives, professionals, or self, and the dying person may show a resentment towards all those who will remain after they have died. Caregivers are often targets for anger, particularly if their attitude is perceived as 'unreasonable' or 'uncaring'. Relatives need to understand why the person is showing hostility and to realize that an angry response to the fear of death may be targeted towards those for whom the person cares most. They should avoid feeling hurt and should resist any temptation to return the hostility or to enter into bitter exchanges.

Bargaining

Some dying people then progress to a relatively short stage in which they try to bargain with fate. They may attempt to strike deals with God, with fate, or with the doctor, along the lines: 'Let me live until my next birthday and then I'll go willingly'. Relatives should accept that such bargaining is a desperate and short-lived phenomenon and they should not engage in confrontation about the bargain, or dismiss it as fanciful. There is in fact some intriguing evidence suggesting that people are able to 'hold on' to life until some important event like a festival or family wedding has passed.

Depression

At the stage when the dying person accepts the inevitability of their death, they often become very depressed. They become depressed about the changes they have already experienced in their physical condition (a 'reactive depression') and about the fact that they will soon lose their family and friends (a 'preparatory depression'). Relatives should allow the person to express feelings openly and should offer consolation and support. They should not, however, attempt to cheer the patient with heartening comments.

Acceptance

Eventually there may come a stage of resignation or 'acceptance'. Kubler-Ross speaks of a 'journey of acceptance', a calm coming to terms with the fateful outcome. It is a period almost devoid of feeling. The person may wish to see few people, valuing silence and detachment. The psychological struggle is now over, and the patient takes 'a final rest before a long journey'. Relatives should appreciate that the person may not wish to talk and will have little interest in the outside world. The presence of a few close relatives at the end may provide a final comfort. Kubler-Ross claims that, given time, most dying people can reach this favourable state, but she emphasizes that to achieve it a person needs to acknowledge that they are dying and to be willing to speak openly about it. She also claims that family acknowledgement and discussion will not only help the dying patient but will also help other members of the family to cope with their bereavement.

ALTERNATIVE VIEWS

Other workers who have a similarly wide experience of interacting with dying people present somewhat different accounts. Rather than an ordered progression from one emotional state to the next, for example, Shneidman (1984) portrays dying in terms of a series of rapidly changing emotional states, with a constant interplay between hope and surrender. Rage, envy, distrust and terror alternate in a general context of bewilderment and pain, and the precise pattern of any individual's course through the period of dying reflects both their individual personality and the events that happen to them.

Pattison (1977) also stresses individual differences in the progression towards death. He emphasizes the importance of sorrow, of a 'fear of the unknown', and of a number of experienced losses—loss of self-control, loss of identity and loss of body. Patients may respond to bodily changes with disgust and shame, and if they find that they are unable to think as clearly and swiftly as before, they may fear that they are becoming mentally unstable. Pattison provides a number of recommendations for relatives. They should acknowledge the terminal nature of the condition, continue to provide close contact and emotional support, and strive to maintain respect for the patient. They should also help the dying person to maintain self-respect, and encourage them to accept their situation with dignity. The immediate problem to be faced is not death itself but the patient's experience of dying, and relatives can provide considerable help and support in making this a far less daunting experience than it might otherwise be.

THE POINT OF DEATH

Most patients become extremely tired towards the very end, and their talk becomes brief and intermittent. They may say farewell to relatives. There is often a loss of sensation, the normal reflexes wane, the patient may sweat profusely and lose body heat, and some people slip into a coma (Gray, 1984). Those who have had a 'near-death experience'—for example those who have been 'clinically dead' but have then been resuscitated—report the 'dying experience' as one of calmness, and they often recollect such perceptions as entering a tunnel with a bright light at the end, or images of people coming towards them, smiling and beckoning (Sabom, 1982; Bates and Stanley, 1985).

DYING AT HOME

The majority of people express a preference for dying at home rather than in a hospital. Yet there are often problems in providing adequate medical care (particularly pain relief) within the home setting, and almost half of the terminally ill patients who remain at home are assessed by community nurses as having a poor quality of life (Wilkes, 1984). In some cases the major problem is lack of social support, but in others the main difficulty concerns symptom control. Sometimes it is difficult for the family to obtain immediate medical advice or help, and there may be long delays in obtaining such essential aids as commodes. Wilkes found that admission to hospital was more often precipitated by difficulties encountered by the family than by a change in the patient's medical condition. Many families of those who died in hospital, however, say that they would have preferred it if the patient had been able to remain at home (Hinton, 1979), and this frequently expressed preference of both patients and their families has recently led to a major growth in support for those who care for the dying at home. With improved aid and nursing support, patients and their families experience lower levels of depression, anxiety, and hostility (Lack and Buckingham, 1978). Furthermore, home care services can bring almost total relief from pain in the vast majority of cases (Doyle, 1980).

THE HOSPICE MOVEMENT

The hospice movement grew out of a desire to alleviate suffering during the final phase of life and to provide an environment in which the physical, psychological, social and spiritual needs of the dying patient could be met. St Christopher's Hospice was opened in London in 1967, and since then many hospices have been set up in a number of countries. The hospice is a resource used by different patients in different ways. Some people enter as in-patients and remain in the hospice until they die. Others attend as out-patients, although they may later enter the hospice for full-time care. Some hospices provide a base for nursing teams that offer home support for the terminally ill.

The strength of hospice care reflects two essential elements—an openness about death, with constant provision of expert and sensitive emotional support, and a very high level of expertise in pain control. Hospices have pioneered new techniques in pain relief and experimented with many different drug regimes. Dr Cicely Saunders, who founded St Christopher's, introduced 'The Brompton mix', containing heroin, cocaine and gin, to relieve the pain of terminal cancer. Hospice staff maintain a conviction that the terminal patient's pain is subject to alleviation, and strive to relieve the pain in such a way that consciousness and psychological functioning are minimally affected. The importance of continued family support for the dying patient is also fully recognized. Few restrictions are placed on visits by relatives, and family members are encouraged to get to know the staff and to participate in the patient's care. Such participation may help to bring about a good recovery after bereavement, and bereaved relatives are encouraged to remain in contact with hospice staff after the patient's death.

A number of studies have been conducted to evaluate aspects of hospice care. Hinton (1979) reported that, compared to those dying in an acute hospital or a special home for cancer patients, hospice in-patients were less anxious, depressed and angry. Hospice out-patients did not fare quite so well on these dimensions as the in-patients, but they expressed a preference for remaining at home. Hinton considered openness of communication to be the key feature responsible for such favourable results. He found that patients were able to speak openly about their life coming to an end, and that nurses and doctors were able to discuss freely issues of prognosis and treatment with their patients. It was clear that patients greatly appreciated the provision of information in a candid and forthright manner and were greatly heartened by the absence of dishonesty and evasion.

Despite their somewhat less favourable outcome on measures of emotional adjustment, the hospice out-patients in this study expressed a continuing preference to remain at home. Hinton noted that these people appeared to retain more of their former personality. Whereas many of those who entered the hospice seemed to develop a new tranquil temperament and were concerned to have a period of rest and contemplation away from normal day-to-day concerns, those who remained at home continued to play their part in the family drama. This difference, noted by Hinton, may parallel the distinction made by Kastenbaum and Weisman (1972) between those who strive to carry on 'as normal' and those who tend to retreat from their family and from worldly concerns.

Yet people who are dying in a hospice certainly do not withdraw entirely from their normal family contacts. Parkes (1979a, b) found that patients at St Christopher's Hospice spent more time with their husband or wife, and more time talking with staff, other patients, and visitors, than those dying of cancer in nearby hospitals. Thirteen months after their bereavement, Parkes interviewed the spouses of people who had died either in St Christopher's or in normal hospitals. Recollecting the experience of their husband or wife in the weeks before their death, the spouses of those who died in the hospice recalled less pain, less distress, greater mobility and less drug-induced confusion than did the spouses of those who had died in hospital. Although there appeared to be no difference in the reactions of these two groups of spouses immediately after the death, when they were interviewed 13 months later the spouses of hospice patients reported less anxiety.

When this study was replicated with patients who died 10 years later (Parkes and Parkes, 1984), the differences between the two types of institution were far less marked, and it seemed that training provided by the hospice to hospital staff had significantly reduced the distress of the hospital patients. Thus it would appear that optimal care for the terminal patient can be provided either in a hospice or in a traditional hospital, provided that the hospital has a specialist ward that adopts a 'hospice philosophy' and can provide effective pain relief. A number of such 'palliative care units' have now been set up within general hospitals in many countries.

RELATIVES' EXPERIENCES OF THE DYING PATIENT

The news that an illness is likely to prove fatal will often be imparted to a member of the patient's family rather than directly to the patient. Sometimes the news will have been half-expected because of the evident seriousness of the condition, but sometimes it will come as a shock. A decision will need to be made about whether to tell the patient, and then about how to broach the subject or how to fend off difficult questions. Often there will be no opportunity to discuss matters with other family members before the patient is confronted, and an individual may be in a state of shock as he or she faces the daunting task of presenting some account of what the physician has said. Some indication is likely to have been given of how long the patient has to live, and about how rapidly the physical condition is likely to deteriorate. Among the issues most likely to dominate the relative's thoughts at this time will be questions about where the patient will die, how the patient will cope with the likely pain and physical weakening, and how members of the family will cope with their crisis in the days or weeks ahead.

There may be some relief if circumstances do not allow the patient to remain at home, but admission into hospital may also produce feelings of guilt in relatives. If the patient can remain at home, and expresses a wish to do so, then the family face the unnerving task of providing physical care and remaining outwardly calm while they struggle to contain their feelings of depression and anxiety. Apart from the emotional strain that family members feel about the impending death and the discomfort and distress of their dying member, they may find some aspects of the person's appearance and behaviour aversive. The strain of caring intensively for a person who is in pain and incontinent, and who may be unable to take food, or may vomit frequently, is likely to produce feelings of frustration, anxiety, tiredness, and anger. The patient may sleep for long periods, or may have difficulties in sleeping. At times relatives may find themselves wishing that the death would come soon, and they may then feel guilty about having such thoughts. The strain may become evident in a decline in the quality of relationships between family members.

On the other hand, the period of caring for the person who is known to be terminally ill may be rewarding in many ways. Good relationships at that time will do much to help the dying person to cope psychologically with the pain and the fact of their approaching death. A loving intimacy with the dying person will also help family members to cope with their immediate emotional crisis, and may afterwards help them to cope more positively with their bereavement (Parkes and Weiss, 1983). A period in which the dying person and relatives acknowledge and accept that death will come soon offers a chance to be especially close and an opportunity for family members to 'do everything' for the dying person. This period can therefore be a precious time in which love and concern triumph over past difficulties and in which family members make their peace.

The dying patient may make it easier, or more difficult, for relatives to come to terms with the imminent death. A person who accepts their impending death calmly may reflect happily on their life and relationships, remembering especially good times and healing old interpersonal wounds. Such a person may thank relatives for their concern and care, and this will often do much to ease the burden of guilt that many people feel following bereavement. Some dying people, however, make things more difficult. Their anger dominates and they castigate relatives for their past transgressions or present shortcomings. Some dictate onerous and oppressive instructions about how family life should progress after their death, while others issue particular 'deathbed commissions' that will establish a long-term burden for one or more members of the bereaved family (Parkes and Weiss, 1983).

Those who witness the plight of a dying relative during the weeks before death frequently become depressed. Their misery is likely to reflect both a response to the dying person's present state and an anticipation of the death and its aftermath. The 'reactive depression' component will be exacerbated by the relative empathizing with the dying person's pain, discomfort and fears, and by any guilt they feel as a result of being unable to ease the distress. The physical demands of caring for the dying person may bring about a profound tiredness and irritability, and relatives may react badly to the dying person's anger, later feeling guilty about their lack of self-control. They may also suffer a 'preparatory depression' as they anticipate the loss that is to come. Some are plagued with frequent visions of the moment of death or of the funeral, or become preoccupied with anxiety about how they will survive with their loneliness after the death. Others live from day to day, repressing all thoughts about the future. Relatives may also become obsessional about minor issues and often find it very difficult to cope with the predicament of not knowing exactly when the person will die.

The impact of a relative's death is considerably less for those who have anticipated the event than for those who experience a sudden and unpredicted loss (Parkes and Weiss, 1983). One reason for this is that people who know that the loss of a partner, parent, child, or other family member is imminent engage in a process of preparation. They adjust their plans, they mentally rehearse future events, and they practise coping strategies that are likely to be of use to them in the coming weeks. Their assumptions about the future change, and they brace themselves in such a way that the event of the person's death does not come as a shock. In addition to these individual precautionary strategies, several constructive interpersonal processes are likely to take place. Family members tend to unite in the face of the common crisis, offering high levels of support and reassurance, and striving to avoid conflict. There may be a temporary realignment of roles, with those who normally play little part in household chores rallying round to aid with tasks and duties. With the knowledge that the emergency they face will soon pass, family members are likely to be especially tolerant of one another, especially tender, and especially helpful.

Thus the period of caring for the dying person is one in which relatives prepare themselves psychologically for the death and a particularly positive atmosphere may prevail in the household. Such personal and family adjustments often help to foster a special emotional closeness between family members and the person whose death is imminent, and all of these changes serve to protect the individual against the extreme emotional crisis that may otherwise be instigated by the death of a close relative. Indeed, individuals may be so well prepared for the death that after weeks or even months of anxious anticipation the death itself may come as something of a relief. If death does not occur 'on schedule' relatives may find it difficult to hold on to their emotions. If the death occurs as they had anticipated they will experience it not as a shock but as an end to the person's suffering. In such circumstances they are likely to be much more accepting of their loss and to regard it as 'a happy release' for the departed.

CHILDREN DYING

So far, we have considered what it is for an adult to die, but it is an unfortunate fact that some children also suffer from terminal illnesses. Thankfully, in advanced cultures death in childhood is now very rare, but in former times it was much more common. Of all deaths in the United States in 1900, for example, over half were those of children under the age of 15. For parents, the death of a child is the cruellest blow, and if they face a period of knowing that the child will die they must try to repress their intense distress in order not to provide further apprehension and anguish to the dying child. It would be difficult to imagine any more difficult task of parenting than that of trying to protect and cheerfully nurse a child who is known to have a short time to live.

There is a considerable body of evidence showing that the siblings of children who are dying fare badly. Early studies indicated that siblings experienced feelings of guilt, rejection, fear and depression, and were subject to physical problems including headaches and abdominal pain. Some clinicians reported that siblings often had physical complaints that mimicked those of the dying child. Spinetta (1981) found that siblings' needs were met significantly less well than those of the parents and the dying child. He found that siblings showed great sensitivity towards the sick child but developed a rather negative image of themselves.

Below the age of four, children who are dying are unable to have any accurate conception of what this means. They are more likely to be concerned with the immediate pain or discomfort of their condition, and with any immediate separation from their parents due to hospitalization, than with the possible longer-term outcome. Children of four or five years who are aware of their own impending death often develop an anticipatory form of separation anxiety. They may develop intense fears about being abandoned, being alone, and losing contact with their parents (Spinetta, 1974). From six onwards, children may also become very alarmed about future physical injury and pain, and some time before the age of nine they may develop an additional anxiety about the loss of bodily functions (Simeonsson, Buckley and Monson, 1979).

As in so many other aspects of their understanding, children depend largely on parental responses for their awareness of their condition, and their emotional responses will reflect the cues shown by parents and other relatives. Parents facing the impending death of their child often make brave efforts to conceal their despair and may distract the child, capturing their attention with a new story or a treat that allows them temporary respite from their discomfort and anxieties. Children who are aware that they are dying will often wish to talk through their fears, and they may take great comfort in accounts given to them of an eventual family reunion after death. One parent, describing Heaven to his dying daughter, proclaimed it to be 'a kind of Super Disneyland where the sun always shines and all the rides are free'.

Despite the fact that recent medical advances mean that the majority of children with cancer now recover, this disease is still one of the major causes of death in childhood. Most children who are terminally ill with cancer experience a period of symptom remission some time before their death, and this often allows the family to have a special time together. Knowing that the child will die within weeks or months, parents often arrange special outings and treats, and 'birthday' and 'Christmas' festivities may be held somewhat in advance of the normal dates for these celebrations (Lansdown and Goldman, 1988).

As for adults, death at home is generally preferred for the child , and this will be possible if specialist medical support is available to the family. If it is not, or if the parents cannot face the prospect of being 'alone' with the dying child, then the child will be admitted to a hospital or paediatric cancer centre. In recent years a few hospices for dying children have been established, although these usually function as supportive facilities for the family coping with the home-care of the child, rather than as a place for the child to die (Corr and Corr, 1985; Dominica, 1987).

REFERENCES

Achterberg, J., Lawlis, G. F., Simonton, O. C. and Matthews-Simonton, S. (1977) Psychological factors and blood chemistries as disease outcome predictors for cancer patients. *Multivariate Experimental Clinical Research*, 3, 107–122.

Bates, B. C. and Stanley, A. (1985) The epidemiology and differential diagnosis of near-death experience. *American Journal of Orthopsychiatry*, 55, 542–549.

Bengston, V., Cuellar, J. and Ragan, P. (1977) Stratum contrasts and similarities in attitudes towards death. *Journal of Gerontology*, 32, 76–88.

Bond, M. R. and Pilowsky, I. (1966) Subjective assessment of pain and its relationship to the administration of analgesics in patients with advanced cancer. *Journal of Psychosomatic Research*, 10, 203–210.

Corr, C. A. and Corr, D. M. (1985) Pediatric hospice care. *Pediatrics*, 76, 774–780.

Dominica, F. (1987) The role of the hospice for the dying child. *British Journal of Hospital Medicine*, 38, 334–342.

Doyle, D. (1980) Domiciliary terminal care. *Practitioner*, 224, 575–582.

Gibson, B., Roberts, P. and Buttery, T. (1982) *Death Education: A Concern for the Living*. Bloomington, IN: Phi Beta Kappa Foundation.

Gray, V. R. (1984) The psychological response of the dying patient. In: P. S. Chaney (ed.), *Dealing with Death and Dying*, 2nd edn. Springhouse, PA: International Communications/Nursing Skillbooks.

Hinton, J. M. (1963) The physical and mental distress of the dying. *Quarterly Journal of Medicine*, 32, 1–12.

Hinton, J. M. (1972) *Dying*, 2nd edn. Harmondsworth: Penguin.

Hinton, J. M. (1979) Comparison of places and policies for terminal care. *Lancet*, i, 29–32.

Kalish, R. A. (1966) Social distance and the dying. *Community Mental Health Journal*, 2, 152–155.

Kastenbaum, R. and Weisman, A. D. (1972) The psychological autopsy as a research procedure in gerontology. In: D. P. Kent, R. Kastenbaum and S. Sherwood (eds.), *Research Planning and Action for the Elderly*. New York: Behavioral Publications.

Klenow, D. J. and Youngs, G. A., Jr (1987) Changes in doctor/patient communication of a terminal prognosis: a selective review and critique. *Death Studies*, 11, 263–277.

Kubler-Ross, E. (1969) *On Death and Dying*. New York: Macmillan.

Lack, S. A. and Buckingham, R. W. (1978) *First American Hospice: Three Years of Home Care*. New Haven: Hospice, Inc.

Lansdown, R. and Benjamin, G. (1985) The development of the concept of death in children aged 5–9 years. *Child: Care, Health and Development*, 11, 13–20.

Lansdown, R. and Goldman, A. (1988) The psychological care of children with malignant disease. *Journal of Child Psychology and Psychiatry*, 29, 555–567.

Lonetto, R. (1980) *Children's Conceptions of Death*. New York: Springer.

Maguire, P. (1985) Barriers to psychological care of the dying. *British Medical Journal*, 291, 1711–1713.

Nagy, M. (1948) The child's theories concerning death. *Journal of Genetic Psychology*, 73, 3–27.

Nisbet, R. (1984) Death. In: E. S. Shneidman (ed.), *Death: Current Perspectives*, 3rd edn. Palo Alto, CA: Mayfield.

Parkes, C. M. (1979a) Terminal care: evaluation of in-patient services at St Christopher's Hospice. Part I: Views of surviving spouse on effects of the service on the patient. *Postgraduate Medical Journal*, 55, 517–522.

Parkes, C. M. (1979b) Terminal care: evaluation of in-patient services at St Christopher's Hospice. Part II: Self-assessment of effects of the service on surviving spouses. *Postgraduate Medical Journal*, 55, 523–527.

Parkes, C. M. and Parkes, J. (1984) 'Hospice' versus 'hospital' care: reevaluation after 10 years as seen by surviving spouse. *Postgraduate Medical Journal*, 60, 120–124.

Parkes, C. M. and Weiss, R. (1983) *Recovery from Bereavement*. New York: Basic Books.

Pattison, E. M. (1977) The experience of dying. In E. M. Pattison (ed.), *The Experience of Dying*. Englewood Cliffs, NJ: Prentice-Hall.

Sabom, M. B. (1982) *Recollections of Death: A Medical Investigation*. New York: Harper and Row.

Saunders, C. and Baines, M. (1983) *Living with Dying: The Management of Terminal Disease*. Oxford: Oxford University Press.

Shneidman, E. S. (ed.) (1984) *Death: Current Perspectives*, 3rd edn. Palo Alto, CA: Mayfield.

Simeonsson, R., Buckley, L. and Monson, L. (1979) Conceptions of illness causality in hospitalized children. *Journal of Paediatric Psychology*, 4, 77–84.

Spinetta, J. J. (1974) The dying child's awareness of death: a review. *Psychological Bulletin*, 81, 256–260.

Spinetta, J. J. (1981) The sibling of the child with cancer. In: J. J. Spinetta and P. Deasy-Spinetta (eds.), *Living with Childhood Cancer*. St Louis, MO: C. V. Mosby.

Stedeford, A. (1981) Couples facing death. II: Unsatisfactory communication. *British Medical Journal*, 283, 1098–1101.

Wilkes, E. (1984) Dying now. *Lancet*, i, 950–952.

10
Bereavement

GRIEF AND MOURNING

The loss of someone close is a major stressor. Typically it produces strong emotional and behavioural responses, and in many cases it has serious adverse effects on the survivor's mental and physical well-being. The term 'bereavement' refers to the state of loss; 'grief' is the emotional response to bereavement; and 'mourning' refers to certain culturally prescribed behaviours associated with the period following loss. The immediate response on learning of the death of a close friend or family member will largely depend on whether the news had been expected or has come as a shock. Those who were aware that the person's death was imminent will have had time to rehearse their emotional response, to devise coping stategies, and to brace themselves for the news. Where the death was completely unexpected, however, the person is suddenly faced with a situation that is highly distressing and in many ways threatening.

Symptoms of grief frequently experienced in the first hours and days following the loss include shock, numbness, denial, anger, guilt, withdrawal, fatigue, anxiety, loss of appetite, depression, and sleep disturbance. Weeping, tremor and an 'empty feeling' are also common. In one of the first structured studies of grief, Lindemann (1944) described the responses of 100 people who had lost family members in a tragic fire at the Coconut Grove restaurant in Boston. Among the common symptoms reported by Lindemann were a form of physical distress that came in waves and lasted for up to an hour, a tightness in the throat, shortness of breath, a loss of muscle power, a need to sigh, an empty feeling in the stomach, and intense feelings of despondency. Other observers have noted that absent-mindedness, obsessive rituals and problems with concentration and memory are also prevalent. More recent studies have directly examined the physiological changes produced by bereavement, and have shown that a major loss affects the functioning of the nervous system, the respiratory system and the hormonal system, as well as producing changes in the cardiovascular and immune systems (National Academy of Sciences, 1984).

The newly bereaved often ask for detailed information about the death, and those who were with the person during the last days or hours may repeatedly recall minute details of what the person said or did, and what seemed to affect their mood. Although such details may seem somewhat trivial to outsiders, it is clear that for many bereaved people the slightest incident takes on a profound significance. Some of their recollections will be positive, and will appear to ease their suffering, but sometimes the bereaved person will appear to ruminate on an aspect that makes them feel sorrowful or guilty.

The grief responses of elderly people appear to be somewhat different from those of younger people. Older people tend to accept loss more readily and are less likely to experience denial, guilt or numbness. On the other hand they are more likely to experience illusions and hallucinations involving the deceased person (Kosten, Jacobs and Kasl, 1985). It is probable that many of these apparent differences reflect the fact that older people are likely to face the loss of a spouse who was also quite old, who may have been ill for some time, and whose death was not as 'untimely' as the death of a young person.

EXPLANATIONS OF GRIEF

There are a number of ways of explaining why loss produces a grief reaction. It is common to regard grief either as a form of depression or as a response to the impact of a major life-stress. According to the depression model, grief is a form of depression triggered by loss. The emotional reaction of grief is seen as having much in common with clinical depression and the origins, nature and functions of grief are therefore explained by reference to general theories of depression. Low self-esteem, guilt and pessimism about the future are common features of clinical depression, and these are also much in evidence in grief. Bowlby (1981) regards depression as the emotional response to separation from an attachment figure, and grief is depicted as the aversive reaction to separation through death. This formulation is particularly useful in explaining why the bereaved person may 'search' for the dead person and feel anger at having been 'deserted'. Another model of depression, the learned helplessness formulation (Abramson, Seligman and Teasdale, 1978), would explain grief as the emotional response to loss of control over one's life. This model stresses the importance of the individual's interpretation of the meaning of the event, so that someone who feels responsible for the death, however unrealistically, is likely to experience guilt.

The stress model approaches grief in a somewhat different way. Bereavement is regarded principally as a stressful life event that taxes the survivor's resources. The effects of the stressor are seen to be largely determined by how the individual judges the event, and on the personal resources available for coping with it ('resilience'). It is well established that major stressors bring about emotional and physiological reactions, and grief is regarded as the stress response to bereavement. When the individual becomes unable to cope effectively with the stress this is likely to lead to serious physical and psychological problems. In a particular variation of the stress model of grief, the 'deficit model of partner loss', Stroebe and Stroebe (1985) suggest that a partner's death produces stress because it creates a number of deficiencies in the survivor's life. The loss of a spouse creates a state of sudden deprivation because the spouse is no longer present to provide the support that a marriage normally provides. Such support includes practical support, emotional support, social identity, and 'validational support'—the partner acts as a monitor, allowing the individual to verify the appropriateness of emotional reactions, particularly in novel situations.

Although the two models of grief differ somewhat in their focus and their emphasis, they are not 'at odds'. Most people do experience grief as a form of depression, and the loss of a spouse or other family member is certainly a major stressor. Both models highlight the importance of how the individual appraises the loss, and both are useful in explaining particular symptoms that commonly occur. Clearly, however, the two models of grief have somewhat different implications for the response to the bereaved and suggest rather different intervention strategies.

GRIEF WORK

A good deal of attention has been paid to the question of whether it is necessary for the bereaved person to grieve. In some cases there appears to be an absence of grieving, and this could be regarded either in a positive way—as the sign of extremely effective coping—or in a negative way—as a sign of denial and a failure to accept the loss. If absence of grieving is a negative sign then there is the danger that a bereaved person who fails to grieve will develop psychological and physical problems as a result of having 'bottled up' feelings about the loss. The consensus in the literature is that the absence of expressed grief is a dangerous sign that signifies avoidance of confrontation with the reality of the loss. It is suggested that people who have failed to confront and express their feelings are likely to continue to have problems until they have engaged in such 'grief work' (Ramsay, 1977; Parkes, 1987).

'Grief work' implies more than simply reflecting about the person's death. Mere reflection does not seem to help, and thinking about the death or the dead person in an obsessional way may actually hinder the bereaved person's recovery (Pennebaker and O'Heeron, 1984). Effective grief work involves probing for the meaning of the experience, attempting to regain mastery over one's life, and endeavouring to maintain a high level of self-esteem (Stroebe and Stroebe, 1987). Although it is principally an individual process, working through grief can be aided by friends and relatives and by professional or volunteer helpers.

The view that grief work aids recovery implies that great care should be taken in prescribing drugs for the newly bereaved. Although there may be some immediately palliative effects of sedative, tranquillizer and anti-depressant medication, there is a general consensus that drugs should not be given too freely (Osterweis, Solomon, and Green, 1984). People who were given sedatives immediately after their bereavement often report that the medication made them dazed and less able to come to terms with the loss. Antidepressants may inhibit the expression of grief and thus forestall the benefits that follow the ventilation of feelings. A short-term prescription for sleeping pills, however, may help those who are exhausted as a result of persistent insomnia.

MOURNING

A death in the family brings an immediate need to deal with a number of urgent practical matters. Relatives must be informed, there are certain legal aspects to attend to, and the funeral must be arranged. A decision might be needed about where the body is to be kept and whether some people should be encouraged to view the corpse. It is generally agreed that in most circumstances it is beneficial for the bereaved spouse and other members of the family to see the body, although there are exceptions when there has been an accidental death with obvious injuries, or where the bereaved person would find the experience especially harrowing. Similarly, it appears that attendance at the funeral is often useful in providing emotional relief and aiding later recovery (McNeill-Taylor, 1983).

Some bereaved people feel the need to provide an elaborate funeral as a gesture of respect and honour, and sometimes the family go to great lengths to make sure that the person's wishes regarding burial or cremation are precisely followed. They may also make plans for some permanent memorial to be established. Such 'details' may be of considerable importance in allowing the bereaved to feel that they have 'done their best' for the dead person and 'played their part' as the individual would have wished. As well as following the expressed or assumed wishes of the person who has died, they will generally comply with certain cultural norms prescribed for the period of mourning. Behaviours such as wearing black, fasting, drawing curtains, and so forth, vary greatly from culture to culture and from one historical period to another. There is usually a range of 'permitted' actions, but there are also strong injunctions about how relatives should and should not behave following a loss.

THE PATHWAY TO RECOVERY

For some people a bereavement is 'the beginning of the end'. They seem to lose their will to live. For others there is a slow and steady progress towards recovery, and it may be many months or years before they feel restored to a former level of health and well-being. Eventually they may come to regard the bereavement as marking the end of one chapter of their lives and the beginning of a new chapter. Bereaved people need to adapt to their new role and status, for example that of 'widow', and may struggle with issues of identity. They have to stop seeing themselves as part of a couple and come to accept that they are now single. Eventually some will go on to enjoy an entirely new lifestyle, perhaps with a new partner. Some of those who have lived through the pain of loss feel that they learned a great deal by the experience and that their lives have gained a new meaning as a result of their ordeal and subsequent recovery. In particular, the loss may endow them with a greater appreciation of their own mortality and may reduce their own fear of dying (Miles and Crandall, 1983).

STAGES OF GRIEF

Various authors have identified a number of stages in the pathway from the initial grief reaction to recovery from the bereavement. Parkes (1972), for example, outlined four such stages. The first stage occurs immediately after learning of the death. The initial reaction is often one of numbness, shock and disbelief, and the bereaved person may feel dizzy and oblivious to the world around. This state can last for a number of days, which means that some people remain in a dazed state at the time of the funeral. The second stage of grief is characterized by yearning and protest. The person may pine and weep, or become angry and irritable. Anxiety and restlessness are also common, and there is likely to be a great deal of concern about the future lifestyle. The bereaved person may lose confidence and struggle to make sense of things, while at the same time being preoccupied with memories of the person who has died. The length of the second stage varies considerably from person to person, but there may be many months over which yearning persists and extensive social support is called for.

There follows a third stage, characterized by disorganization and depression. At this time, especially, bereaved people may become very apathetic and neglect their health. They may also neglect to plan for the future. A loss of appetite is frequently reported, serious physical problems sometimes arise, and the mortality rate is somewhat higher than that of other people of the same age. Relatives of the bereaved often find this period especially difficult to deal with, particularly if they judge that the person is resistant to an improvement in their emotional state. The final stage is 'recovery', and this is marked by the person adjusting in a healthy way to the loss, accepting their new status and involving themselves in making plans for the future. During the recovery phase there is a tendency to renew former social relationships and to initiate new activities. For most people, recovery usually begins within two years of the loss.

Although it is useful to characterize the progress from the initial grief through to recovery in terms of such a series of stages, it would be inaccurate to think of the improvement in terms of a steady pathway with clearly demarcated phases. In reality, the day-to-day pattern is more complex and more unsettled. At any stage there are likely to be relatively good days and relatively poor days. Even when the symptoms of grief have mainly receded there may be temporary setbacks. Recurrences of symptoms often occur at significant times such as the dead person's birthday, the wedding anniversary, or Christmas, or when the survivor visits places, meets friends, or listens to pieces of music that bring back memories of the person they have lost. 'Anniversary reactions' also occur around the date of the death, and studies that follow the progress of the bereaved therefore usually avoid monitoring the person's state around the anniversary of the death, when the responses may be untypical of the general progress achieved by that time. Thus for a number a reasons the course of recovery for any one bereaved individual is likely to be considerably more erratic than the ordered progression depicted by general stage models.

INDIVIDUAL VARIATION IN RECOVERY

Whereas some people manage to recover from their loss within months, with relatively little disruption to their health, and with a reasonably optimistic view of the future, there are others for whom the grief is exaggerated, distorted and prolonged. It is obviously important to understand the factors that increase the chances that a bereaved person will respond badly following the death of a loved one. Some of these are self-evident. Thus the relationship between the dead person and the bereaved individual is important; we would hardly expect the death of a distant relative to have as much impact as the death of a child or spouse. Characteristics of the survivor associated with poor recovery include a previous history of mental illness, an 'insecure' personality, previous unresolved losses, and physical illness or disablement. Social circumstances also seem to be important. Those most at risk of poor recovery are those who lack an intimate confidant, those who have young children, those who are unemployed or are unhappy at work, and those of lower social class (Parkes, 1986).

Thus factors associated with the person's character and previous history, physical and mental health, and social circumstances all affect the degree and speed of recovery. Studies of post-bereavement adjustment and morale suggest that age and sex are also important variables. There is evidence that the elderly generally face bereavement with more forbearance (Kosten, Jacobs and Kasl, 1985), and one study (Ferraro, 1985) indicated that the 'old-old' (i.e. those over

74 years) were more optimistic about the future than those who were younger (between 65 and 74). This study also indicated that elderly bereaved widows were considerably more optimistic than widowers of the same age. Ferraro's research suggested that financial security was only marginally beneficial for psychological adjustment, whereas several other studies (for example, Scott and Kivett, 1985) indicate that wealth is associated with higher morale. Indeed, it has been argued by some authors (e.g. Bahr and Harvey, 1980) that poor adjustment to bereavement is largely attributable to economic hardships consequent to the loss. It is undeniable that for many people the death of a spouse entails a severe 'financial drop', and that this often brings an anxiety about 'making ends meet'. Financial hardship can certainly prevent the bereaved person from partaking of certain activities (such as visiting distant friends and relatives) that might well help in the later stages of bereavement recovery.

THE HARVARD BEREAVEMENT STUDY

A good deal of further valuable information on the factors associated with relatively good, and relatively poor, recovery has been gained from 'The Harvard Bereavement Study'. Relevant findings are reported by Colin Murray Parkes and Robert Weïss (1983) in their book *Recovery From Bereavement*. The study set out to identify major factors that affect the course of psychological recovery during the first years of bereavement. A sample of young widows and widowers (between 21 and 46 years old) were interviewed three weeks after the death of their partner, again some five weeks later, then 13 months after the loss, and finally shortly after the second, third or fourth anniversary of the death. Information was gathered about the nature of the marriage, the circumstances of the death, and the partner's health and lifestyle. 'Health checklists' were used to monitor the physical and psychological health of the bereaved at the time of each interview, and their coping styles and current circumstances were explored. Trained coders listened to tape-recordings of the interviews and rated the outcome on a number of dimensions including general level of functioning, the degree to which the bereaved seemed to have 'accepted' the loss, their attitude towards the future, and their level of anxiety and depression.

The widows' and widowers' physical and psychological states 13 months after the bereavement were compared to those of a matched control group of married men and women. The bereaved reported more symptoms of physical ill-health, especially autonomic nervous system symptoms such as trembling and twitching, sweating, and dizziness, and more of this group had had a recent hospital admission. They disclosed greater emotional distress (especially depression) and reported more consultations with professionals for help with psychological problems. The bereaved group had also had more sleep difficulties and eating problems, and as a group they had markedly increased their smoking and their consumption of alcohol and tranquillizers. Significantly more of the bereaved than of the control group were described as 'socially withdrawn'.

In a further analysis the bereaved group was divided roughly into three groups, comprising people who showed a 'good outcome', an 'intermediate outcome' or a 'bad outcome'. Several factors were found to distinguish these groups. Those who were showing a poor outcome 13 months after the spouse's death tended to have a high level of 'yearning' and had reacted to the death with anger and self-reproach. Those whose partner had died suddenly were more likely to be faring poorly, as were those whose marriage had been subject to a known infidelity. Adjustment at this stage was not related to the person's age or religious faith, or to the number of people living in the home. Looking back at the data concerning how individuals from the three groups had responded shortly after the death (at the time of the first interview) it was found that the immediate reaction was not predictive of the subsequent level of adjustment (at 13 months).

Unanticipated Grief

On the basis of the findings from this study, Parkes and Weiss identified three 'syndromes' that may be responsible for a poor longer-term recovery from bereavement. The first of these is 'the syndrome of unanticipated grief'. Many differences were found in the immediate responses, and the recovery patterns, of those who had been given a brief forewarning (three days or less) or no warning at all, and those who had been given a long forewarning (two weeks or more) of their partner's imminent death.

When interviewed just three weeks after the death, those in the long forewarning group were far less likely to appear upset or disturbed, and they were much less likely than those in the brief forewarning group to agree with the statement 'I wouldn't care if I died tomorrow'. At the time of the second interview, some four weeks later, those who had had a long forewarning were more likely to have responded to social invitations. And by the time of the third interview (13 months after the loss), 56% of the long forewarning group were judged to be showing a 'good outcome', compared with only 9% of those for whom there had been little or no warning about the loss. This much more positive picture for the long forewarning group was also maintained at the time of the final interview, two or three years later.

Parkes and Weiss explain these findings by noting that a bereavement is a form of transition. Each person maintains an internal 'assumptive world', a picture of the nature of things, and major changes can be accommodated only if they occur gradually and are anticipated. But a major unexpected loss is highly disturbing because it indicates that the world is unpredictable, and if there is no 'adequate' explanation of the death there is a great potential for the survivor to indulge in self-blame. Drawing upon the general field of 'attachment theory' that forms the basis of much of their theorizing, the authors point out that the marital partner is an important attachment figure who generally provides security. When this security suddenly disappears the survivor is left alone, beleaguered and vulnerable. Parkes and Weiss also point out that when a death is anticipated, the partner has a chance to 'serve' the dying person, so pre-empting feelings of guilt following the loss. The couple also have the opportunity to be especially close, and this can help the survivor to cope following the bereavement.

The clear importance of forewarning, and the evident poor recovery of those who had not been alerted to the imminent death of their partner, led Parkes and Weiss to identify 'the unexpected loss syndrome', a constellation of symptoms that tends to follow a major loss that is both unexpected and untimely. Those who suffer from this syndrome have great difficulty in coming to terms with the loss, they avoid confronting the issue of their own psychological survival and frequently suffer from feelings of self-reproach and despair. They may also remain socially withdrawn for a long time after the death of their partner. Parkes and Weiss suggest that in order to reduce the number of people affected by this syndrome, those who are in imminent danger of loss should be informed, and family members should be encouraged to take on some of the burden of nursing. The authors point out that 'There is a real danger that intensive care units and other inpatient facilities, to the extent that they take away from the family the opportunity to care for the dying individual, may create problems for the family in the future.'

Conflicted Grief

It is to be expected that the process of recovery from bereavement will be related to certain qualities of the marriage. Contrary to expectation, however, particular difficulties in recovery often seem to follow loss in marriages that were troubled and conflictual rather than in those that were 'perfect' and peaceful. The bereaved partners were asked whether their marriage had been a happy one, and whether there had been a high or low level of conflict. Analysis indicated a striking association between the degree of conflict and the reaction to bereavement at different points in the study. In the early stages (during the first and second interviews) partners who described the marriage as highly conflictual tended to display little emotional distress. Only 11%, for example, agreed with the statement: 'I don't seem to laugh any more', compared with 83% of those who described their marriage as having little conflict.

By the time of the third interview, however, things had changed significantly. The high-conflict group were judged as showing a much poorer recovery than those in the low-conflict group, and at the time of the final interview (between two and four years after the partner's death) those in the high-conflict group were more likely to appear depressed, to exhibit anxiety and guilt, and to be yearning for the return of the partner. The physical health of the people in this group was also judged to be poorer. Parkes and Weiss suggest that although high-conflict marriages produce high levels of anger, the partners in such relationships often have especially close attachments. They suggest that residual anger may be responsible for the initial lack of extreme grief reaction, but that this later subsides so that the effects of the loss of the powerful attachment figure become apparent. A further suggestion is that the loss of a partner in an ambivalent marriage may leave many causes for regret and self-reproach. The problematic adjustment of those who had been involved in such ambivalent relationships is labelled 'the conflicted grief syndrome'.

Chronic Grief

The Harvard study showed that the level and type of distress experienced in the early stages of bereavement correlated with features of the person's psychological state at later stages. In the first interview they assessed the bereaved person's degree of 'yearning'. Those who exhibited a high level of yearning tended to have little self-confidence and frequently felt helpless when they ruminated on their loss. Many found it difficult to concentrate and expressed a wish that 'someone would just take over'.

A high level of yearning at the time of the first assessment was associated with poor general outcome scores at later stages. At the 13-month stage those who had been assessed initially as 'high yearners' were more likely to be tearful during the interview and seemed to be constantly preoccupied by memories of the lost partner and their life together. At the time of the last interview these people were much more likely than those who had originally exhibited a low level of yearning to agree with the statement: 'Deep down I wouldn't care if I died tomorrow'. They also appeared much more anxious during the interview, and were less likely to be rated as progressing well with their recovery from the bereavement. Analysis of the results led Parkes and Weiss to conclude that a yearning response was much more common in those who had been highly dependent on the partner, or whose partner had been highly dependent on them.

Those who had experienced a close relationship with their partner but had also managed to remain somewhat autonomous generally recovered well from bereavement. One woman described her independence and recalled advice that her mother had once given to her: 'She said: "Never have a leaning post, because when the leaning post falls you fall with it." So we never did. And I think that's probably why I was able to face up to a lot of the problems I had over the past two years.' The authors emphasize the point that autonomy can coexist with genuine attachment. When a loss occurs, those who have remained somewhat autonomous are better able to cope. Those who became totally dependent on their partner, however, have few inner resources to call upon. Such people are prone to 'the chronic grief syndrome', the essential determinant of which is insecurity.

The Recovery Process

Parkes and Weiss suggest that people recovering from bereavement face three distinct tasks. They must learn to accept the loss both intellectually and emotionally (rather than distancing themselves, denying the reality of the loss, or engaging in 'displacement activities') and they must change their 'model of the world' to match the new reality. This in turn means that they must accept their new status and identity as 'single' or 'widowed'. An alternative to this, of course, is to seek a new partner, and the results of the study did indicate that many of the widows and widowers who had made an especially good recovery had formed a new close relationship by the time of the final interview.

Overall, the Parkes and Weiss study indicates that a good outcome following the loss of a marital partner is associated with a long forewarning of death, a marriage low in conflict, and a relationship in which a degree of independence had been maintained. The authors believe that these factors are important because they affect the tasks of grieving. They suggest that an absence of forewarning inhibits the ability to come to terms rationally with the loss, that a conflictual marriage leaves a legacy that impedes emotional adjustment, and that over-dependence prevents the bereaved person from achieving a new autonomy and identity. Having identified three important grief syndromes— 'the unexpected loss syndrome', 'the conflicted grief syndrome', and 'the dependent grief syndrome', Parkes and Weiss suggest that most people who develop psychiatric illnesses following bereavement suffer from one or more of these syndromes.

SOCIAL SUPPORT

Although the level of social support received by the bereaved did not emerge in the Harvard study as a clear predictor of how well a person would recover, other research has indicated that such support may be crucial. Thus Clayton (1975) found that, 13 months after the loss of their partner, widows who were living alone had significantly higher depression ratings than those who were living in a family. Lopata (1973) reported that widows who had adult children living locally recovered more successfully than those whose children lived further away, and Bahr and Harvey (1980) showed that social contacts increased the morale and life satisfaction of widows. A lack of intimate social contacts also seems to be particularly common among bereaved people who commit suicide (Stroebe and Stroebe, 1987). A study by Brown and Harris (1978) (concerned with depression in women, rather than with the specific effects of bereavement) suggested that a single 'special' confidant is more important in inhibiting a depressive response to stress than a large number of friends or acquaintances.

Intimacy is not the only variable affecting the 'quality' of social support. Some friends, acquaintances and relatives may be more effective than others in helping the bereaved. Some people are 'natural healers' and have the gift of being able to help others instinctively—to say the right thing at the right time, and maintain contact without being intrusive. In their study, Stroebe and Stroebe (1987) found that a number of widows reported that some friends and relatives had offered 'platitudes' and 'ungenuine offers of help'. Some individuals may be judged by the bereaved person as treating them too delicately and underestimating their resilience, and this is another source of potential irritation. Remarks that imply either extreme fortitude (such as 'I have no doubt that you will pull through') or extreme helplessness (such as 'You must try to keep going') may bring intense resentment. There is a tendency for people to offer support in the early days in the expectation that the person will soon recover. Often, however, recovery takes longer than they expected, and there may be some irritation and impatience, with the feeling that 'by now s/he should have got over it'.

Men generally suffer greater social disruption following bereavement than do women (Bock and Webber, 1972), probably because many men rely on the wife to maintain social relationships with relatives and friends. Men depend largely on the work situation for providing social contacts, and when widowers lose their occupational role through retirement or redundancy this markedly increases their social isolation (Berardo, 1970). Glick, Weiss, and Parkes (1974) found that few men were able and willing to talk about the death of their wives to family or friends and preferred to suffer in silence rather than showing their emotions openly.

THE EFFECTS OF PREVIOUS LOSSES

There are contrary expectations about how having experienced an earlier loss will affect recovery from a subsequent loss. On the one hand it might be supposed that a previous bereavement is likely to have left the individual vulnerable and may therefore hinder recovery. As we shall see later in this chapter, there is convincing evidence that loss during childhood often predisposes individuals to depression in adulthood. On the other hand it might be presumed that a previous experience of loss will strengthen the individual against subsequent losses. An individual who has coped with one bereavement, and recovered, may have developed effective coping strategies and therefore be 'prepared' for future losses, as if immunized against adverse effects.

Furthermore, having once succeeded in recovery, the person will understand that the grief will eventually end, and this may make the period of intense grief more tolerable. Although only limited evidence is available concerning the effects of previous bereavements, it appears that such earlier experiences may indeed facilitate good outcome following a later loss (Stroebe and Stroebe, 1987). It may be that whereas most adults eventually recover from a loss and 'gain' by the experience, many young children who lose a parent are chronically adversely affected and remain emotionally weakened by their experience.

BEREAVEMENT AND HEALTH

It was established in Chapter 1 that life events, especially those which have threatening implications for the individual, often have profound adverse effects on psychological and physical health. Bereavement is a major negative stressor and would therefore be expected to have such detrimental consequences. But as well as the direct stressor effect, bereavement is likely to bring a number of lifestyle changes that may endanger health. It may deprive the individual of support and companionship and produce changes in behaviour that increase the risk of psychological disturbance, accident, or disease. The bereaved may be so preoccupied with their loss that they fail to recognize or to take appropriate action following early signs of illness; they may take little care of themselves; and they may behave recklessly and expose themselves to hazards. It is well established that smoking, the intake of alcohol, and the use of prescribed and non-prescribed drugs, increase markedly following loss. Thus by maintaining a disorganized lifestyle and failing to protect themselves, bereaved individuals often increase the risk that they will suffer a serious physical or psychological illness, and they may even endanger their own life.

Although there has been little investigation of the association between serious health effects following bereavement and such factors as the suddenness of the loss and the coping strategies used by the bereaved, it is likely that the variables shown to aid the rate and degree of recovery also have positive effects in safeguarding health. Thus low conflict and low dependency in the marriage may well serve to protect bereaved individuals from death or serious disorder, and there may well be a beneficial buffering effect of adequate social support. Those who are able to express their grief, or are encouraged to do so, may benefit in terms of their health as well as their general mood and sense of well-being.

PSYCHOLOGICAL ILLNESS

There is a wealth of evidence supporting the common-sense notion that many bereaved people suffer from fairly long-term psychological problems.

Maddison and Viola (1968) compared the psychiatric health of widows and controls, and found much higher rates among the widowed of nervousness, fears of a nervous breakdown, other fears, nightmares, sleeping problems, trembling, and depression. Many bereaved people become dejected and pessimistic, and it seems that a fairly high proportion become clinically depressed. Studies of rates of psychiatric admission, and of out-patient attendance for psychiatric treatment, show that the widowed are over-represented (Gove, 1972; Parkes, 1964a) and that psychiatric disturbance is particularly common among the newly widowed (Stein and Susser, 1979). Although many of the major symptoms of grief decline in the months following bereavement, several studies show that depression may be maintained for a considerably longer period (Osterweis, Solomon and Green, 1984).

There is some confusion about whether a higher proportion of men or women become depressed. According to one recent review (Stroebe and Stroebe, 1987) more bereaved men suffer from depression, whereas Kosten, Jacobs and Kasl (1985) concluded from their review that women were at higher risk. There is less confusion about sex differences with respect to other forms of psychological disturbance. Women appear to be at higher risk of anxiety disorder, and men appear to be more at risk of chronic alcoholic abuse.

PHYSICAL ILLNESS

The post-bereavement phase is often a time of especially poor physical health. Minor symptoms such as insomnia, dizziness, weight loss and fatigue are very common in the newly bereaved, and they are also at high risk of contracting infectious diseases during the first year of bereavement. The study of bereaved women by Maddison and Viola (1968) indicated a relatively high rate of such physical symptoms as chest pains, difficulty in swallowing, headaches, and skin rashes. Some of the women said that they had developed excessive appetites but many more experienced a loss of appetite with consequent weight loss, and a high proportion complained of palpitations, chest pain and severe fatigue. In a study of over 3000 bereaved people, Ferraro (1985) found that there was an immediate fall in the level of physical health but that this effect did not last long. Parkes (1964b) found little change in the rate of consultation for acute physical conditions but did find a significant increase in widows' consultations for psychiatric problems and chronic conditions such as rheumatism.

INCREASED MORTALITY

It has long been claimed that some people die 'of a broken heart' following bereavement, and studies do indeed show a pattern of excess mortality in the widowed, especially in males (Kosten, Jacobs and Kasl, 1985). The peak of increased risk for men appears to be in the first six months following the loss, whereas for women the peak occurs during the second year. The degree of increased risk is higher for younger people. Although various studies have provided different estimates of the mortality of the recently bereaved, compared to same-age controls, several have reported at least a doubling of the risk of death, and a few studies suggest that the increased risk might be considerably higher than this (e.g. Rees and Lutkins, 1969).

Little is known about any particular aspects of the original death that especially increase the risk of a bereaved partner dying, but there is evidence suggesting that sudden bereavements may be associated with a particularly high mortality risk. Thus the particular vulnerability of younger bereaved partners may reflect the fact that their spouses were also probably young, and are therefore likely to have suffered an 'untimely' and unforeseen death. Further evidence comes from research by Rees and Lutkins (1969) which indicated that the site of death was an important determinant of additional risk. If the original death had happened in a public place (in a shop, for example, or on the road) there was a greater increase in mortality than where the death had occurred in a hospital or at home. The place of death is obviously linked to the expectedness or unexpectedness of the death. This study also examined the mortality risk following death in hospital and at home, and found the rate to be higher when the spouse had died in hospital. It is possible that the benefits known to be gained by the bereaved as a result of being given the opportunity to nurse and look after the dying person extend to providing some protection against their own death in the months that follow.

The increased mortality of the bereaved reflects a number of different causes of death, including disease, suicide and accident. It appears that much of the excess mortality due to disease can be attributed to coronary thrombosis and other cardiovascular problems. Studies by Parkes, Benjamin and Fitzgerald (1969) and Kaprio and Koskenvuo (1983) have found that the major cause of increased mortality for men during the first six months after bereavement is circulatory disorders. Other deaths through disease are caused by cirrhosis of the liver, cancer and infectious diseases (Stroebe et al., 1982).

There is also an increased rate of suicide during the first months after bereavement, and this is greater for men than for women (Stroebe and Stroebe, 1983). Overall, the suicide rate for those bereaved within the previous year is about twice that of an age-matched control group, and the time of highest risk is the period immediately following the loss. Kaprio and Koskenvuo (1983) showed that during the first week following the loss of a spouse the rate of suicide for men is 66 times the age-expected rate, and for women it is nearly 10 times the expected rate. The bereaved are also much more likely to be involved in serious accidents, and it has been suggested that this results from a combination of a 'suicidal mentality' and lack of care (Stroebe and Stroebe, 1987).

FAMILY ADJUSTMENT

As well as affecting individual members, a death in the family has profound effects on the family system. Different families have different styles of coping with crisis and some are a lot more vulnerable than others. Gleser, Green and Winget (1981) suggest that the degree of disruption caused to a family by the death of one of its members depends mostly on the timing and nature of the death, the family position of the dead family member, and the 'openness' of the family system. An 'open' family permits and encourages the free expression of emotions and welcomes some degree of influence and support from outside the family. 'Closed' families, by contrast, inhibit any display of feelings and maintain a determined isolation.

Although it is generally agreed that the open expression of grief is highly beneficial, some families steadfastly repress any verbalization or show of grief. This may reflect the general cultural taboo about death, but for many families it merely exemplifies a general proscription against showing distress. In other cases the pain caused to one or more individuals by the loss may lead the family to avoid discussion or any display of emotion, and the emphasis in such families is likely to be on practical matters. In more open families, and where the tension caused by the death is somewhat less, family members will help each other by talking about the person who has died, perhaps remembering their most endearing characteristics and the good times that they had together. Family tales will be re-told or re-invented and there is likely to be some idealization of the dead person.

As the family strives to readjust and gain a new long-term stability, a number of compensatory or 'homeostatic' manoeuvres are likely to come into play. There may be some re-ordering of priorities, some alliances may be strengthened, and there is likely to be a restructuring of roles. Tasks and responsibilities previously assigned to the person who has died will be undertaken by other family members. Thus a bereaved husband may be faced with new tasks such as cooking a family meal, or a bereaved wife may be forced by circumstance to proceed with legal matters that would formerly have been dealt with by the husband. The coalitions and sub-groupings within the family will also change, and there may be struggles over issues of power, control and independence. If the person had been seriously ill for some time before death then some of the re-adjustment may already have taken place. In some cases a particular family member may have maintained loyalty to the family as a whole because of a strong alliance with, or a sense of duty towards, the person who has died. Following the loss such a person may take the opportunity to break free from the family. In other cases the guilt and anger of family members following the bereavement can lead to scapegoating (Goldberg, 1973).

As well as the changes that occur within the immediate family, a death often changes the relationship between the family and other friends or relatives. The dead person may have been instrumental in maintaining particular links with other people, and the relationships between the family and these individuals or groups are likely to weaken following the death. In other cases friends and relatives will make a special effort to make regular contact, to offer support and practical help. They may invite one or more members of the immediate family to stay, to take a break from the home and to have some time to recover psychologically from the bereavement.

For some people the loss of a parent, the spouse, or a child literally means the end of their family and they are left to face a life alone. They may make efforts to build a new 'family' by contacting distant relatives or by increasing their contacts with old and new friends, but often such efforts prove fruitless and the person must try to come to terms with a solitary existence. Loneliness is a serious and chronic problem for many bereaved people, including many who have family members living with them or close by. For those who have little social contact the anguish of loneliness can become a permanent nightmare (Berardo, 1970).

Another source of radical family change involves new intimate relationships that may be forged some time after the death. Following the loss of their partner a proportion of widows and a substantially higher proportion of widowers eventually form a new close relationship. The introduction of a new person into a family that has re-adjusted following the death of a member will demand important new changes. Sometimes the new partner will simply slip into the role occupied by the person who has died, and the family may revert towards its former structure, but there may be considerable reluctance among some family members to accept such a solution, and a new order may need to be established.

HELP FOR THE BEREAVED

There are many ways in which the bereaved can be helped to come to terms with their loss and to adjust to a new lifestyle. Friends and relatives are able to help in the initial stages by providing practical and emotional support, by being careful not to intrude, and by avoiding platitudes. Later, help is given by maintaining contact after the crisis of bereavement has passed, and by remaining patient with the person who appears to be taking a long time to recover. Social support is also important in the longer term in helping the individual to establish a new lifestyle (Bankoff, 1983). Some bereaved people, however, lack close social contacts, or family and friends may not be able to provide sufficient help to bring about a full and timely recovery. Sometimes the individual's suffering is so intense and prolonged that additional aid is needed.

In such circumstances the bereaved person may benefit from help and therapy offered by professionals or voluntary organizations.

GRIEF COUNSELLING

Several research studies indicate that the provision of either individual counselling by professionals or group support can significantly reduce the adverse effects of bereavement, particularly for those who are at high risk because they lack supportive intimates. Thus Gerber and colleagues (1975) found that, compared with controls, a bereaved group who received telephone counselling received less medication and had fewer consultations with physicians. The positive effects of this counselling service were strongest around six months after the loss. Similar results were found in Raphael's (1977) evaluation of a face-to-face 'at-home' counselling service. Clients were counselled for between one and nine sessions, and were encouraged to express their feelings of anxiety, anger, and grief. When the effects of the service were evaluated 13 months after the bereavement it was found that those who had received counselling had consulted with doctors far less frequently than a non-counselled control group.

Parkes (1980) found that high-risk bereaved people benefited in a number of ways from participation in group discussions. The discussions took place during the first six months following bereavement and focused on issues relevant to loss. In this study the groups were led by a trained therapist, but other studies indicate that participation in self-help groups may also reduce adverse effects. Vachon *et al.* (1980) studied the effects of widows' interactions with other widows who had successfully resolved their grief. This was shown to have a modest favourable impact on the psychological health of the 'treated' widows, and those who were at especially high risk of serious adverse consequences seemed to benefit considerably from their conversations with a volunteer. Parkes (1987) suggests that volunteers probably need about a year of experience in supporting the bereaved before they attain a high level of competence, but he maintains that with such experience many volunteers rival professionals in their ability to provide advice, comfort, and support. He also stresses that the person's own home is the optimal environment for providing help, and that if circumstances permit then support should be initiated before the loss has actually occurred. Thus evidence and opinion support the view that voluntary organizations such as 'CRUSE' in the UK and 'Widow-to-Widow' in the US may have a great deal to offer to the newly bereaved and to those who are finding it difficult to adapt to a new lifestyle following the death of a spouse.

So far there has not been sufficient work in the area of grief counselling to permit a clear understanding of what aspects make it effective. It is, however, possible to identify a number of features that probably help. One of these is the expression of feelings, and this element is often stressed in existing counselling programmes. But counsellors may also help by giving advice, by reassuring the client that they have no reason to feel guilty, by instilling hope that the more intense features of the grief experience will eventually weaken, and by reassuring the client that much of what they are experiencing is normal and to be expected in the circumstances. By interpreting symptoms, and reassuring the individual that he or she is not 'going mad', the counsellor can thus provide 'validational support' for the client.

GRIEF THERAPY

It is useful to draw a distinction between the kind of 'grief counselling' already described, in which people are helped through their grief by the provision of support, comfort, and care, and 'grief therapy', in which special techniques are used to help people with highly disturbed grief reactions. For those with 'pathological grief' (grief that is profoundly distorted, inhibited, exaggerated or prolonged), counselling support may not be sufficient to help, and various therapeutic methods have been devised to ameliorate such conditions. The techniques used are often aimed at allowing clients to overcome their reluctance and resistance about facing their grief directly. Thus an individual, a couple or a whole family may be encouraged to express openly their inhibited feelings of grief while they are guided through a period of intensive mourning (Lieberman, 1978; Paul and Paul, 1982).

In one study of this type of therapy, individuals with pathological grief patterns were randomly assigned either to a control group or a 'guided-mourning' treatment group (Mawson et al., 1981). Those in the control group were requested to hold back all thoughts about their loss, while those in the treatment group were encouraged during the therapy sessions to think about all of the painful aspects of the bereavement. The psychological adjustment of those who experienced the guided mourning improved considerably after two weeks of treatment (there were three treatment sessions per week). These clients became less depressed and less anxious, their social adjustment improved, and many signs of pathological grieving disappeared. Furthermore, this progress was shown to be maintained up to six months after the completion of treatment, whereas the well-being of the control subjects did not improve during the period of the study and follow-up.

Two further points need to be emphasized. The first is that men, especially, may be highly reluctant to express their feelings openly. When they seek assistance following bereavement they often request help in controlling their feelings, rather than expressing them (Glick, Weiss and Parkes, 1974). Whether they are given the help they request or are encouraged to explore and display their emotions is clearly a matter calling for sensitive clinical judgement. The other point is that providing counselling or therapy for the bereaved is often highly stressful (Black and Urbanowicz, 1987; Raphael, 1982), and will frequently tax the emotional resources of the volunteer or the professional. It is essential that those involved in such work have adequate contact and back-up from others, so that they can examine and express their own emotional reactions to the grief of those they are helping.

SPECIAL CASES

So far we have dealt mainly with the effects of the death of a partner on the adult survivor, and the death has been assumed to be through illness or accident. This reflects the fact that the death of a spouse is a stress faced by many people (there are 4 million widows and widowers in the UK, and 20 million in the US), that most people now die after they have reached the age of 50, and that illnesses and accidents account for almost all deaths. Research on bereavement generally reflects these facts and has concentrated on the more common forms of loss. But some of the more exceptional cases deserve consideration, and this section examines first how young children react after the death of a parent and then how parents react after the death of a baby or a young child. Finally the responses of those who are bereaved as a result of someone committing suicide are considered.

THE DEATH OF A PARENT

Early writers suggested that children were more likely than adults to suffer from pathological grief reactions, including denial of the death, feelings of anger and blame, and fantasies concerning reunion. In many children the 'pathological sign' was said to be an apparent absence of grief. However, it may be that normal grief in children is somewhat different from that in adults, and that these early studies were describing normal, rather than abnormal, child grief.

In a study of children between two and eight years old who had recently lost a parent, Raphael (1982) found that over 90% showed evidence of behavioural disturbance, including clinging; high anxiety; aggression; excessive crying; and disturbances of sleep, eating and toileting. Van Eerdewegh, Clayton and Van Eerdewegh (1985) reported that many bereaved children were highly disturbed one month after the loss of a parent, and that these children were still showing more depressive symptoms and more withdrawn behaviour than a control group one year after the bereavement. The academic performance of these children at school had also frequently suffered. For some children, problems persist for considerably longer. Kaffman and Elizur (1983), for example, found that many bereaved children had adjustment difficulties over three years after the loss. Rutter (1966) found a relatively high incidence of bereaved children among those attending a psychiatric clinic, and in a study comparing bereaved and non-bereaved child-clinic attenders, Caplan and Douglas (1969) found higher frequencies of depression, school refusal and phobic disorders among the bereaved.

The results from these studies indicate a number of variables that appear to be associated with an especially adverse response to loss. Black (1978) reviewed the available evidence relating the bereaved child's age, sex, and ordinal position to adverse effects of the loss, and suggested that younger children are more affected, that girls may be somewhat more vulnerable to the stress of bereavement than boys, and that being the elder sibling increases the risk of disturbance. There is also evidence of an especially high level of disturbance in the children of a parent who has committed suicide, although this probably reflects the stresses of living with that parent prior to their death (Shepherd and Barraclough, 1976).

Raphael found that symptoms evident immediately after the loss were somewhat worse for children whose parent had died suddenly, and Van Eerdewegh, Clayton and Van Eerdewegh (1985) found that children with a widowed mother who was depressed were faring particularly badly 13 months after the loss. Similarly, Kaffman and Elizur (1983) reported that the mother's psychological state was the most important predictor of the bereaved child's adjustment some two to three years after the loss. As well as the loss itself, the death of a parent may bring many changes to the child's life, including several that might well cause difficulties. Thus the aftermath of the death may bring changes of home and school, and the child may feel stigmatized as a result of the parent having died. In some cases the bereavement will cause the child to be fostered, or placed in a home. Children who remain at home with the surviving parent may be the target for anger, or may be neglected by a parent who is failing to recover well following the partner's death. The home atmosphere may be dour and oppressive, or the parent may have frequent and intense mood swings and behave in unpredictable ways.

It is clear that effective intervention with the surviving parent (grief counselling, grief therapy, or help with practical matters) may do much to benefit the child. The possibility of providing bereavement counselling directly to the child has also been examined, and voluntary organizations such as 'CRUSE' have recently initiated group discussion sessions for bereaved children. Black and Urbanowicz (1987) initiated a family therapy programme designed to help bereaved children. They arranged for families of children who had lost a parent to receive six home-based therapy sessions, starting two months after the bereavement. The therapists were psychiatric social workers with relevant experience and training in bereavement counselling, and the aims of the intervention were to promote the expression of grief and to improve communication between the surviving members of the family. Compared with controls, the treated group fared slightly better one year after the loss. Overall, a positive outcome was found to be associated with the child having cried and spoken about the dead parent in the month following the loss, and with a favourable recovery by the surviving parent. In the treatment group an improvement in the child's adjustment was found to be associated with increased crying. At a two-year follow-up most of the significant gains associated with treatment had faded somewhat, but treated parents had significantly fewer health problems. The authors concluded that the study demonstrated modest gains as a result of intervention, and that it certainly provided no support for the idea that encouraging children to face their grief might prove harmful. Other interventions with bereaved children make use of play materials to allow children to express their feelings indirectly or symbolically.

Later Effects of Childhood Loss

There has been a good deal of controversy over the question of whether the loss of a parent during childhood is associated with a vulnerability to depression and other difficulties in the adult years. In their study on the social origins of depression, Brown and Harris (1978) found that women who had lost their mother before the age of 11 were more vulnerable to stressful life events in their adult lives and were more likely than other women to experience depression. Although several authors have challenged the evidence from the studies that apparently show such an effect, Brown (1982) has ably defended the proposition, and most recent reviewers agree that there is indeed an association between early death of the mother and depression, alcoholism, and other difficulties during adulthood (Finkelstein, 1988).

THE DEATH OF A CHILD

In the UK about 40 children die every day; in the US the figure is nearer 200. A high proportion of the early deaths in advanced societies now occur as a result of accidents, for these days infectious diseases rarely prove fatal and recent advances in medical techniques have significantly reduced the proportion of children who die from cancer. For those parents who are unfortunate enough to be in the exceptional position of losing a child, however, the emotional consequences are often devastating. Saunders (1979–1980) reported that the death of a child produced more intense grief for the parents than either death of a spouse or an adult's loss of a parent.

Perinatal Death

It appears that grief following a stillbirth or a death in the first few days after birth can be as overwhelming as that caused by the loss of a child with whom the parents have developed a relationship over several years (Kirkley-Best and Kellner, 1982). Parents of the dead baby are often preoccupied with thoughts about the child and frequently exhibit profound grief symptoms. They often express a desire to hold the dead baby, so that they can mourn for a person rather than a 'thing', and they are likely to benefit from giving the baby a name and from attending a simple funeral. Hospital staff are increasingly aware of the importance of such acts and are now less likely than they were formerly to remove the baby and to suggest that the parents try to 'forget' their tragedy, to hold back feelings of grief, and to regard the dead baby as an impersonal object.

Severe psychiatric problems appear to be quite common following the death of a young baby and may persist for a number of years (Tudehope *et al.*, 1986). Mothers usually respond more acutely to the loss and take a longer time to recover from their grief (Benfield, Leib and Vollman, 1978). Better adjustment following perinatal death appears to be associated with emotional support by the partner, relatives and hospital staff, and those who have been given some forewarning that the baby might die are likely to show less intense grief reactions. The speed and quality of recovery do not appear to be associated with the age, religious affiliation or social class of the parents, or with the presence of other children in the family (Murray and Callan, 1988). In a study of parents who had experienced the perinatal death of a baby some two years previously, Murray and Callan (1988) found high levels of depression, compared with a normal sample. Depression was more common in women, in those who expressed dissatisfaction with the support given by hospital staff and other people, and in those who had not had a successful pregnancy since the loss. The factor most closely associated with a low level of depression was satisfaction with the support given by hospital staff at the time of the loss. Positive adjustment was also related to the amount of time the parents spent with the child, and to the time since the loss.

Cot Death

One type of death in infants that has come to prominence in recent years is 'cot death', 'crib death', or 'sudden infant death syndrome' (SIDS). This is the major cause of death between three weeks and one year, and accounts for around 1500 infant deaths each year in the UK (and about 7500 in the US). Cot deaths occur in apparently healthy babies and it is impossible to predict with any degree of accuracy which children will be affected, although it is marginally more common in infants who were born prematurely, who have young mothers, and whose mothers smoke. A change in the pattern of breathing is an important danger signal and parents of high-risk infants (for example, those in families in which there has already been a cot death) may be provided with monitors that sound an alarm if there is some interference with the normal breathing pattern.

Parents who have lost an infant due to SIDS may be helped by counselling, and there are a number of specially important issues that the therapist will need to address (Woodward *et al.*, 1985). The parents need to know that cot death is a recognized medical problem and that they are not to blame for the child's demise. In particular, myths surrounding the condition will need to be dispelled and the parents need to discuss their anxieties about whether any future children will be at special risk (Limerick, 1976). Cot deaths are likely to generate many family tensions, and the counsellor might need to make contact with several members of the extended family to protect the couple from unwarranted suspicions and accusations and to mobilize additional support for the bereaved couple.

Those who have lost a young child as a result of cot death or perinatal death often decide to replace the dead child by having another baby as soon as possible. Bowlby (1981) raises some doubts about the wisdom of this strategy. He suggests that there may be a danger that the parents' preoccupation with the new pregnancy may prevent them from completing their grieving for the child who has died, and that they may see the new baby not as a new individual but as the return of the lost child. This, he suggests, may lead to a disturbed relationship with the new baby, and his advice is that bereaved parents should wait for a year or two before they consider having another child. It is possible, however, that if the parents are alerted to the possible dangers outlined by Bowlby they will be able to avoid such problems, and evidence from studies of stillbirth and neonatal death (Murray and Callan, 1988) suggests that early pregnancy following the loss of a baby is in fact associated with a relatively low incidence of depression.

The Death of an Older Child

When an older child is diagnosed as having a terminal illness the parents often enter into a state of anticipatory mourning. Familiar symptoms of grief begin to be experienced, with the parents suffering shock and feeling numb. Anger is often apparent and there may be disbelief and denial. Furthermore, the habitual struggle between hope and despair may be profoundly taxing, particularly if the parents are 'out of phase' in their alternating optimism and misery. Thus the degree of stress on the parents' relationship is frequently severe (Bowlby, 1981). After the death has occurred many parents experience serious psychosomatic and psychological problems, and the marital relationship may suffer further. Studies of parents who have lost a child through cancer (Kaplan *et al.*, 1973) or accidental drowning (Nixon and Pearn, 1977) reveal a very high level of parental separation and divorce following the child's death.

Many of the factors shown to aid recovery from spousal death and the death of a baby, such as forewarning and social support, have also been shown to aid the recovery of bereaved parents. Thus, when parents lose a child through cancer, those who have experienced anticipatory grief are better prepared for the death and feel less guilt after the child has died (Rando, 1983). Those who have a key supportive relationship that gives them security during the child's illness and the period after death also cope more effectively (Spinetta, Swarner and Sheposh, 1981).

Although little has been written on the effects of childhood death on siblings, the few studies on this subject reveal considerable psychological difficulties for the children who survive. Nixon and Pearn (1977) found that siblings of a dead child frequently exhibited psychosomatic and behavioural problems, and a similar picture emerges from a study of children who had lost a sibling through cancer (Tietz, McSherry, and Britt, 1977). Pettle-Michael and Lansdown (1986) also reported a high incidence of psychological disturbance in a group of siblings of children who had died, and they were also able to show that the degree of post-bereavement distress was considerably less if the sibling had been warned some time in advance that their brother or sister might die.

DEATH BY SUICIDE

When a person loses a family member through suicide they are likely to have special problems in coping with the bereavement (Wallace, 1973). Indeed it has been claimed that the stress following a suicide may be the most intense of any type of bereavement (Stroebe and Stroebe, 1987). It is not difficult to understand why this might be the case. Death by suicide is generally sudden, difficulties in personal relationships between the suicide and family members or friends may have played an important part in triggering the act and, unlike other forms of death among family members, suicide often stigmatizes the survivors. Relatives may have to appear at an inquest and they may have to read newspaper accounts of the tragedy that has hit their family. Thus as well as experiencing an extreme grief reaction that often follows sudden loss, the survivor may be haunted by guilt and shame. Survivors may feel that they 'drove the person to it' and played an active role in causing the death, or they may feel that they ignored signs of torment and 'cries for help' and thus played too passive a role.

There are few general recommendations that can be made regarding counselling help for those bereaved as a result of suicide, for the circumstances of suicide, the motive, and the part played by significant others, are highly variable. In some cases it will be true that the spouse, relative or friend contributed to the intense distress that led the individual to commit suicide. In many instances a friend or relative may be realistic in judging that they did little to protect the person from taking their own life. One of the factors known to be associated with an increased potential for suicide is a deterioration or cessation of communication between the person and other family members.

But it is also true that in many cases surviving relatives or friends assume far too much of the responsibility for a suicide.

Inappropriate guilt thrives in circumstances where the motive for the suicide is ambiguous and, unfortunately, almost all suicides are somewhat ambiguous in this respect. Those who are left behind are frequently bewildered by the action, and in their anxiety to search for an explanation they often take at least some of the burden of guilt upon themselves (Sheskin and Wallace, 1976). In counselling those bereaved through suicide, it is often useful to discuss some of the states of mind that may lead to a person taking their own life. In a number of cases suicide is a failed attempt at 'attempted suicide'. That is, the person meant to make a suicidal gesture and to survive, but things went wrong. Some suicides are 'realistic' in the sense that they follow rational decisions to escape from unbearable pain or embarrassment. Others are symptomatic of a severe psychological breakdown, usually of a depressive nature. In such cases the person may be said to have committed suicide 'while the balance of the mind was disturbed'. In other cases the suicide represents a spiteful act carried out to make someone feel guilty. Shneidman (1973) recognized that those who survive other people's suicides need special help, and he proposed the use of a technique which he labelled 'postvention'. This form of intervention is based on a systems analysis of family and community relationships and focuses on rational discussion rather than on the expression of feelings. The aim of postvention is to reduce the after-effects of suicide by aiding the recovery of surviving family and friends.

REFERENCES

Abramson, L. Y., Seligman, M. E. P. and Teasdale, J. (1978) Learned helplessness in humans: critique and reformulation. *Journal of Abnormal Psychology*, **87**, 32–48.

Bahr, H. M. and Harvey, C. D. (1980) Correlates of morale among the newly widowed. *Journal of Social Psychology*, **110**, 219–233.

Bankoff, E. A. (1983) Social support and adaptation to widowhood. *Journal of Marriage and the Family*, **45**, 827–839.

Benfield, D. G., Leib, S. A. and Vollman, J. H. (1978) Grief response of parents to neonatal death and parent participation in deciding care. *Pediatrics*, **62**, 171–177.

Berardo, F. M. (1970) Survivorship and social isolation: the case of the aged widower. *Family Coordinator*, **19**, 11–25.

Black, D. (1978) The bereaved child. *Journal of Child Psychology and Psychiatry*, **19**, 287–292.

Black, D. and Urbanowicz, M. A. (1987) Family intervention with bereaved children. *Journal of Child Psychology and Psychiatry*, **28**, 467–476.

Bock, E. W. and Webber, I. L. (1972) Suicide among the elderly: isolating widowhood and mitigating alternatives. *Journal of Marriage and the Family*, **34**, 24–31.

Bowlby, J. (1981) *Attachment and Loss, Vol. 3: Loss: Sadness and Depression*. Harmondsworth: Penguin.

Brown, G. W. (1982) Early loss and depression. In: C. M. Parkes and J. Stevenson-Hinde (eds.), *The Place of Attachment in Human Behaviour*. New York: Basic Books.

Brown, G. W. and Harris, T. (1978) *The Social Origins of Depression*. London: Tavistock.

Caplan, M. G. and Douglas, V. I. (1969) Incidence of parental loss in children with depressed mood. *Journal of Child Psychology and Psychiatry*, **10**, 225–244.

Clayton, P. J. (1975) The effect of living alone on bereavement symptoms. *American Journal of Psychiatry*, **132**, 133–137.

Ferraro, K. F. (1985) The effects of widowhood on the health status of older persons. *International Journal of Ageing and Human Development*, **21**, 9–25.

Finkelstein, H. (1988) The long-term effects of early parent death: a review. *Journal of Clinical Psychology*, **44**, 3–9.

Gerber, I., Weiner, A., Battin, D. and Arkin, A. (1975) Brief therapy to the aged bereaved. In: B. Schoenberg and A. Arkin (eds.), *Bereavement: Its Psychological Aspects*. New York: Columbia University Press.

Gleser, G. L., Green, C. L. and Winget, C. (1981) *Prolonged Psychosocial Effects of Disaster: A Study of Buffalo Creek*. New York: Academic Press.

Glick, I., Weiss, R. S. and Parkes, C. M. (1974) *The First Year of Bereavement*. New York: Wiley.

Goldberg, S. B. (1973) Family tasks and reactions in the crisis of death. *Social Casework*, **53**, 398–405.

Gove, W. R. (1972) The relationship between sex roles, marital roles, and mental illness. *Social Forces*, **51**, 34–44.

Kaffman, M. and Elizur, E. (1983) Bereavement responses of kibbutz and non-kibbutz children following death of father. *Journal of Child Psychology and Psychiatry*, **24**, 435–442.

Kaplan, D. M., Smith, A., Grobstein, R. and Fischman, S. E. (1973) Family mediation of stress. *Social Work*, **18**, 60–69.

Kaprio, J. and Koskenvuo, M. (1983) Mortality after bereavement: a prospective study. Unpublished manuscript, Department of Public Health Science, University of Helsinki, Finland.

Kirkley-Best, E. and Kellner, K. R. (1982) The forgotten grief: a review of the psychology of stillbirth. *American Journal of Orthopsychiatry*, **52**, 420–429.

Kosten, T. R., Jacobs, S. C. and Kasl, S. V. (1985) Terminal illness, bereavement and the family. In: D. C. Turk and R. D. Kerns (eds.), *Health, Illness and Families*. New York: Wiley.

Lieberman, S. (1978) Nineteen cases of morbid grief. *British Journal of Psychiatry*, **132**, 159–163.

Limerick, S. (1976) Counselling after a cot death. *Health Visitor*, March 1980, 84–86.

Lindemann, E. (1944) The symptomatology and management of acute grief. *American Journal of Psychiatry*, **101**, 141–148.

Lopata, H. Z. (1973) *Widowhood in an American City*. Morristown, NJ: General Learning Press.

McNeill-Taylor, L. (1983) *Living with Loss: A Book for the Widowed*. Glasgow: Fontana.

Maddison, D. C. and Viola, A. (1968) The health of widows in the year following bereavement. *Journal of Psychosomatic Research*, **12**, 297–306.

Mawson, D., Marks, I. M., Ramm, L. and Stern, L. S. (1981) Guided mourning for morbid grief: a controlled study. *British Journal of Psychiatry*, **138**, 185–193.

Miles, M. S. and Crandall, E. K. (1983) The search for meaning and its potential for affecting growth in bereaved parents. *Health Values: Achieving High Level Wellness*, **7**, 19–23.

Murray, J. and Callan, V. J. (1988) Perinatal death. *British Journal of Medical Psychology*, **61**, 237–244.

National Academy of Sciences, Institutes on Medicine (1984) *Bereavement: Reactions, Consequences and Care*. Washington, DC.

Nixon, J. and Pearn, J. (1977) Emotional sequelae of parents and sibs following the drowning or near-drowning of a child. *Australian and New Zealand Journal of Psychiatry*, **11**, 265–268.

Osterweis, M., Solomon, T. and Green, M. (1984) *Bereavement: Reactions, Consequences, and Care*. Washington DC: National Academy Press.

Parkes, C. M. (1964a) Recent bereavement as a cause of mental illness. *British Journal of Psychiatry*, **110**, 198–204.

Parkes, C. M. (1964b) The effects of bereavement on physical and mental health: a study of the medical records of widows. *British Medical Journal*, **2**, 274–279.

Parkes, C. M. (1972) *Bereavement*. London: Tavistock.

Parkes, C. M. (1980) Bereavement counselling: does it work? *British Medical Journal*, 5 July, pp. 3–6.

Parkes, C. M. (1986) *Bereavement: Studies of Grief in Adult Life*, 2nd end. Harmondsworth: Penguin.

Parkes, C. M. (1987) Research concerning bereavement and grief reactions. In: C. Sutton (ed.), *A Handbook of Research for the Helping Professions*. London: Routledge and Kegan Paul.

Parkes, C. M. and Weiss, R. (1983) *Recovery from Bereavement*. New York: Basic Books.

Parkes, C. M., Benjamin, B. and Fitzgerald, R. G. (1969) Broken heart: a statistical study of increased mortality among widowers. *British Medical Journal*, **1**, 740–743.

Paul, N. L. and Paul, B. B. (1982) Death and changes in sexual behaviour. In: F. Walsh (ed.), *Normal Family Processes*. New York: Guilford Press.

Pennebaker, J. W. and O'Heeron, R. C. (1984) Confiding in others and illness rate among spouses of suicide and accidental death victims. *Journal of Abnormal Psychology*, **93**, 473–476.

Pettle-Michael, S. and Lansdown, R. (1986) Adjustment to death of a sibling. *Archives of Disease in Childhood*, **61**, 278–283.

Ramsay, R. W. (1977) Behavioural approaches to bereavement. *Behaviour Research and Therapy*, **15**, 131–135.

Rando, T. (1983) An investigation of grief and adaptation in parents whose children have died from cancer. *Journal of Pediatric Psychology*, **8**, 3–20.

Raphael, B. (1977) Preventive intervention with the recently bereaved. *Archives of General Psychiatry*, **34**, 1450–1454.

Raphael, B. (1982) The young child and the death of a parent. In: C. M. Parkes and J. Stevenson-Hinde (eds), *The Place of Attachment in Human Behaviour*. London: Tavistock.

Rees, W. and Lutkins, S. (1967) Mortality of bereavement. *British Medical Journal*, 4, 13–16.

Rutter, M. (1966) *Children of Sick Parents*. Oxford: Oxford University Press.

Sanders, C. (1979–1980) A comparison of adult bereavement in the death of a spouse, child and parent. *Omega: Journal of Death and Dying*, 10, 303–322.

Scott, J. P. and Kivett, V. R. (1985) Differences in the morale of older, rural widows and widowers. *International Journal of Ageing and Human Development*, 21, 121–135.

Shepherd, D. M. and Barraclough, B. M. (1976) The aftermath of parental suicide for children. *British Journal of Psychiatry*, 129, 267–276.

Sheskin, A. and Wallace, S. E. (1976) Differing bereavements: suicide, natural and accidental death. *Omega: Journal of Death and Dying*, 7, 229–242.

Shneidman, E. (1973) *Deaths of Man*. New York: Quadrangle.

Spinetta, J. J., Swarner, J. and Sheposh, J. (1981) Effective parental coping following the death of a child from cancer. *Journal of Pediatric Psychology*, 6, 251–263.

Stein, Z. and Susser, M. W. (1979) Widowhood and mental illness. *British Journal of Preventive and Social Medicine*, 23, 106–110.

Stroebe, M. S. and Stroebe, W. (1983) Who suffers more? Sex differences in health risks of the bereaved. *Psychological Bulletin*, 93, 279–301.

Stroebe, M. S. and Stroebe, W. (1985) Social support and the alleviation of loss. In: I. G. Sarason and B. R. Sarason (eds.), *Social Support: Theory, Research and Applications*. Dordrecht: Martinus Nijhoff.

Stroebe, W. and Stroebe, M. S. (1987) *Bereavement and Health: the Psychological and Physical Consequences of Partner Loss*. Cambridge: Cambridge University Press.

Stroebe, W., Stroebe, M. S., Gergen, K. J. and Geergen, M. (1982) The effects of bereavement on mortality: a social psychological analysis. In: J. R. Eiser (ed.), *Social Psychology and Behavioural Medicine*. Chichester: Wiley.

Tietz, W., McSherry, L. and Britt, B. (1977) Family sequelae after a child's death due to cancer. *American Journal of Psychotherapy*, 31, 417–425.

Tudehope, D. I., Iredell, J., Rodgers, D. and Gunn, A. (1986) Neonatal death: grieving families. *Medical Journal of Australia*, 144, 290–292.

Vachon, M., Lyall, W., Rogers, J., Freedman, K. and Freeman, S. J. (1980) A controlled study of self-help intervention for widows. *American Journal of Psychiatry*, 137, 1380–1384.

Van Eerdewegh, M. M., Clayton, P. J. and Van Eerdewegh, P. (1985) The bereaved child: variables influencing early psychopathology. *British Journal of Psychiatry*, 147, 23–29.

Wallace, S. (1973) *After Suicide*. New York: Wiley.

Woodward, S., Pope, A., Robson, W. J. and Hogan, O. (1985) Bereavement counselling after sudden death. *British Medical Journal*, 1, 363–365.

11

Families, Problems, and Communication

COMMUNICATION WITHIN THE FAMILY

Problems often arise or have a more damaging impact because family members fail to communicate well with one another. Within some families, members rarely show their true feelings and there may be little sharing of information, but in other cases particular issues are hidden or denied because it is feared that open discussion would generate destructive conflict. Avoidance of contentious issues is sometimes appropriate, and even 'denial' can be a useful strategy, but the effects of engaging in a dialogue are typically positive. Grievances tend to diminish when they have been aired, and silence allows discrepancies between people's views to widen. Family problems are often solved when each member is able to contribute information and opinion. Open expression of feelings reduces emotional tension and encourages family members to use each other as confidants and 'therapists'. Finally, honest communication promotes healthy relationships and strengthens a family, making it more resilient and more adaptable to change.

'We never seem to talk any more' is a frequent complaint by one married person to their partner, and a marked decline in the intensity, frequency or openness of a couple's communication is indeed a sign that their relationship is in trouble. Close communication is necessary for the maintenance of intimacy, and a deterioration in the quality of exchanges is both a sign of breakdown and a reason why a relationship may degenerate. As things get worse the partners may refrain from any but the most trivial dialogue, or all of their interchanges may become hostile and aggravated. In such circumstances the couple's communication with other people is also likely to be strained, for however antagonistic they are to one another, the partners may conspire to keep their difficulties concealed. Friends and relatives may therefore be surprised and shocked when they eventually learn of the couple's separation.

Couples rarely keep their children well informed about moves towards separation, and although the children are usually aware that there is a crisis in their parents' relationship they are often too fearful or too polite to ask for an explanation. Colluding in an uneasy silence, they frequently remain very confused and distressed. In the absence of sufficient information children tend to construct their own accounts of what may be happening, but these frequently increase their distress and make them feel responsible for the rift between the parents. Misunderstanding and uncertainty may increase the child's susceptibility to psychological and physical symptoms, including withdrawal, irritability, and a variety of psychosomatic complaints.

Even on the matters which most intimately concern them, custody and access by the non-custodial parent, children are frequently not consulted either by their parents or by representatives of the court. A particular preference is often simply assumed, although in many cases the parents' assumptions about the child's wishes are ill-founded. Arrangements made about separation, divorce and custody, and the way in which these are explained, are crucial in determining how children respond to marital breakdown, both immediately and in the longer term. The failure of parent–child communication at this time is therefore especially lamentable. Furthermore, the extent and tone of communication between the parents following the separation and divorce have a significant bearing on whether children develop emotional problems.

Open and honest communication may also cease when a member has a serious illness or is close to death. Some relatives are told by the physician that death is imminent but decide not to tell the patient. Such evasion can have unfortunate consequences and may deny the person the opportunity to enjoy a very special period of closeness with those whom they love. Those who know that they are terminally ill are often relieved to be able to discuss matters openly with their family, and those who reach the state of 'acceptance' are more likely to experience peace at the end of their life. Relatives who manage to confront the issue and to discuss matters openly with the dying person and other members of the family also benefit considerably. 'Denial' may heighten the distress when the patient is dying and impede recovery following bereavement. If the dying person enters a hospice, or a hospital ward that has adopted a hospice philosophy, both patient and family are encouraged and helped to accept that the end is near and to express their feelings plainly. Following a family death, communication between the surviving members may be powerfully restrained. There may be little or no reference to the deceased, and individuals may conceal their feelings of anger, guilt, sadness and anxiety. Such a reaction is again unfortunate because bereaved people who express their feelings tend to recover more quickly, and open communication at this time helps a family to adapt more effectively.

Thus a family's failure to communicate adequately often leads to difficulties or prevents a problem being solved. A breakdown in communication can create serious quandaries for individuals and may weaken the family system. The situations considered here have been examined at length earlier in this volume, but the dangers of communication failure are equally apparent in numerous other areas of family concern. Thus a couple's failure to communicate with one another about their sexual needs, preferences, and distastes is often responsible for sexual difficulties within the relationship, and the promotion of open communication about sexual matters is thus a key feature of almost all sex therapy programmes. The failure of children who have been sexually victimized to disclose the abuse may reflect a general climate of secrecy within the family. Other areas in which communication deficits and the inhibition of emotional expression have been shown to have damaging effects include adoption, stresses generated in the work context, the care of the elderly, drug and alcohol problems, and many aspects of parent–adolescent relationships.

FACILITATING FAMILY COMMUNICATION

Many interventions designed to reduce conflict and to enhance the quality of family life focus on improving communication. Thus many programmes aimed at enhancing marriage emphasize the development of communication skills (Guerney, 1977; Bornstein and Bornstein, 1986; Floyd and Floyd, 1987). Improving the quality of communication within the family system is also a principal goal in many applications of family therapy. Strategic family therapy (Satir, 1967; Watzlawick, Beavin and Jackson, 1967) is sometimes identified as the 'communications approach'. Therapists working within this framework maintain that unclear messages contribute to most forms of family disturbance, and they attempt to disclose important contradictory messages operating within the family system. The 'structural approach' to family therapy focuses on the organization and structure of family interaction and communication. Using this framework, Minuchin (1974) suggested that fear of open conflict often inhibits family communication and thereby contributes to psycho-somatic conditions and other disturbances. Dramatic symptomatic improvements may occur when hidden conflicts are finally aired. The therapist therefore encourages the clear and direct expression of desires, feelings, and opinions, and helps the family to resolve underlying issues of conflict.

When intense hostility prevents certain family members from communicating, another family member, a friend or a professional may act as a 'go-between' or may encourage the antagonists to discuss matters in an atmosphere of moderation and restraint. Divorce conciliation provides an outstanding example of such an intervention. There are substantial advantages in settling matters by negotiation rather than confrontation, and calm bargaining may produce a reasonably equitable solution to contentious issues, thus reducing emotional trauma. Conciliators are trained to guide the couple through contentious issues in such a way that the situation remains relatively calm and the negotiation is likely to end in a mutually acceptable outcome.

When parents find it difficult to tell a child about their marital difficulties and their impending separation, grandparents, family friends, or older siblings may help to report the situation in a sympathetic but realistic way. Children need to be reassured that they are not responsible for the parental strife and that they will continue to be loved and cared for. They should be encouraged to express their feelings and to discuss any doubtful issues. Reconciliation fantasies should be discussed openly, but gently discouraged. A number of intervention programmes have been devised specifically to help children whose parents have recently separated. Younger children often meet together as a group and engage in structured play activities designed to teach them useful coping skills, to increase their understanding of relevant aspects of family relationships, and to encourage their expression of feelings within a safe and supportive context.

COMMUNICATION BY PROFESSIONALS

Families facing difficulties frequently have contact with professionals, including doctors, nurses, social workers, counsellors, psychologists, teachers, the police, and lawyers, and their interactions with these people can have profound effects on how well they cope. Although it is easy to assume that the impact of 'the helping professions' is always favourable, problems are sometimes exacerbated because professionals fail to communicate clearly or fully with family members. Professionals have diverse responsibilities towards families, reflecting their various disciplines and their specialist skills, and while some have the primary function of supporting the family as it attempts to cope with difficulties, others play a more pragmatic role. Their primary task may be to use their medical, legal or educational skills to help an individual, and they may regard the provision of emotional support for the family as a secondary consideration. Nevertheless the communication style of members of any of these professions can have dramatic effects on how the family responds to a challenging situation.

Examples relating to the work of health professionals illustrate many of the relevant points. The fundamental objective of doctors and nurses is to improve the medical condition of their patients, and the more highly skilled they are in the technical aspects of medicine and nursing the better off the patient and the patient's family are likely to be. Proficient diagnosis, surgery and nursing care help the patient and the family to cope because they improve the patient's physical condition, and it is important not to ignore this basic truth when focusing on the psychosocial aspects of family health care. But there is much more to the practice of medicine than identifying conditions and prescribing physical treatments, and health professionals increasingly focus on prevention and on the treatment of 'the whole person' or even 'the whole family'.

Both the style and content of communications by health professionals can have critical effects on family well-being. Members of a medical team can offer the family information, advice, reassurance, sympathy and encouragement. They can provide clients and their families with accurate information about the patient's current state and indicate how things are likely to develop. Information about medical tests and procedures will often reassure family members, who will then be in a better position to support the patient. The strategy whereby health professionals use relatives as intermediaries to inform and reassure the patient is particularly valuable when the patient is a young child.

Medical personnel can also help the family by providing a detailed explanation of the nature of the condition or disorder. In the case of a premature birth, for example, the parents need to understand that their infant is likely to be special and different. Counsellors helping a family in which there has been a cot death need to be fully informed about 'sudden infant death syndrome', and the parents need to be reassured that they are not responsible for the child's death. To take another example, informing the family about the nature of an elderly patient's physical condition, and its psychological consequences, may help the relatives to judge the person's behavioural eccentricities in a more appropriate and more charitable way. Insight into the causes and effects of dementia, for example, will often prompt relatives to revise their judgements about the older person's failings. Thus professionals often play an important educational role. In particular, they are able to disabuse family members of the myths and misunderstandings that frequently cause confusion and engender feelings of guilt, anger or helplessness.

Professionals may also help by referring the family to other sources of information. Many of the topics that concern families are described in useful books and articles that provide facts, explain difficult concepts and give helpful hints. The professional who has a good knowledge of such sources will be able to recommend material appropriate to the family's needs and level of understanding. Similarly, the professional should be fully aware of local community resources. It can be of enormous help to a family caring for an elderly person suffering from dementia, for example, if a social worker or nurse is able to recommend a local dentist, hairdresser or chiropodist who has experience with such clients and is sympathetic and skilled in dealing with them. Informing the parents of a handicapped child about toy libraries and playgroups in the area will often be extremely valuable, offering substantial benefits to the parents as well as helping the handicapped child to develop cognitively, socially and emotionally. Sometimes the most useful contribution a professional can make is to put the family in touch with a local self-help group and to encourage their participation. It needs to be remembered, however, that some families stridently avoid contact with others who share their problem, either because they continue to 'deny' the reality of their predicament, or because they fear that they will become labelled or stigmatized by joining a special group.

Another important task for health professionals is that of providing advice on practical aspects of care. Thus a nurse or social worker may suggest how an elderly person can best be lifted or bathed, or how a child's difficult behaviour might best be managed. Their experience with other families in similar circumstances will allow them to indicate common pitfalls and to suggest how these might be avoided. Thus professionals treating children who are chronically ill will realize that parents often divert their attention away from the child's siblings and that this can cause considerable distress. A sensitive caution about this danger will often be sufficient to prevent the parents from focusing their concern exclusively on the sick child. Families of those who are seriously ill often find it difficult to tell friends and relatives about the patient's condition, and professionals may suggest appropriate ways of doing this.

It is likely that many professionals underestimate the effects they have on families. Ressurance that particular reactions are quite 'normal', for example, may bring intense relief. Even the most casual suggestion by a professional may be taken as a firm directive or as a sign of approval or consent. Thus a comment to the effect that a family should not feel obliged to visit a hospitalized patient every day may be grasped as a welcome 'permission' to visit less frequently. A chance word of appreciation for the patient's forbearance or of praise for the family's resourcefulness can boost the family's morale tremendously. Serious illness in the family often heightens sensitivity to other people's behaviour, and a kindly word, a sympathetic look, or recognition that a doctor or nurse has 'taken time' with them can provide immense encouragement. On the other hand, any apparent lack of interest or abruptness by a professional can generate intense anger or despair. Families expect the professionals who deal with them to be concerned and approachable, and they need to feel that there is someone on whom they can rely in an emergency. The corollary of this is that as a result of the considerable demands that some families make on them, a number of those in the caring professions experience extreme stress and may suffer an emotional collapse (Payne and Firth-Cozens, 1987).

Many professionals are highly skilled communicators, and provide information in a clear, non-evasive and non-patronizing way, but others are less conscientious or less adept at consulting with clients and their families. In a number of the areas reviewed there is evidence that some professionals communicate poorly, maintaining a distant attitude and an unapproachable air. Clients frequently voice dissatisfaction with the way in which information was divulged or hidden from them, and an unsatisfactory interaction can have lasting efects. The way in which the news that their newborn baby is handicapped is given to parents, for example, appears to have an exceptionally powerful effect not only on how they respond immediately but also on how they adjust in the longer term. Many parents complain that doctors and nurses withheld information, or that there was little opportunity for them to ask questions. Those who are immediately told of fears for the child's condition are generally very appreciative of such openness. They value honesty and frankness, and they are especially grateful when professionals remain available for consultation over a longer term.

More physicians now inform patients when they are suffering from a terminal condition, but in many cases it is still left to relatives to decide whether or not they will tell the person that he or she will soon die. Many relatives are grateful that they have been informed, yet feel dissatisfied with the manner in which they were told. In many cases they report that the professional was evasive and distant. Many physicians who confide such news to relatives discourage queries and soon curtail discussion. Family members are often too shocked, embarrassed and inhibited to ask candid questions and are left in a state of anxiety and confusion. Professionals who care for sick children need to be especially skilled in communicating directly to their young patients, and they must also be able to relate well to the parents. Children trust people they judge to be honest and open, and remain fearful and suspicious of those who are unresponsive or difficult to understand. They are more easily able to express their fears and anxieties to those they trust. Parents are better able to tell the child about the illness and to explain various medical procedures if doctors and nurses keep them well informed. Furthermore, if professionals are able to reduce the parents' anxiety, their calm manner is likely to attenuate the child's apprehension and distress.

It is clear that families are often profoundly affected by their direct interaction with professionals, but it is also worth noting that families are sometimes helped by professionals without ever coming into direct contact with them. Thus professionals may work to improve facilities within an area, they can set up groups that will eventually become autonomous, and they can influence the decisions made by politicians and by various agencies, including schools, hospitals, social work departments, and police divisions. Another way in which professionals provide indirect services is by generating, recommending and distributing materials that can form the basis of client 'self-help'. There has been a long tradition of publishing medical manuals and 'practical psychology' guides for family use, but such materials are now attracting more professional attention than ever before. Self-help books continue to appear in vast quantities, and audio- and video-technology is increasingly being exploited. By writing a popular text, producing a tape, or appearing in a radio or television programme a professional can reach vast numbers of people, and the media approach clearly has enormous potential.

Self-help manuals can provide the troubled individual or family with information and practical suggestions relating to their specific problem, or may direct readers through a self-managed course of therapy. Many forms of therapy have been adapted to the self-administered text format, and the use of written materials in this way has become known as 'bibliotherapy'. The effectiveness of such methods is rarely evaluated in any systematic fashion (Turvey, 1985), but it is reasonable to assume that well-presented information and sensible advice produced by experienced professionals may be of substantial benefit to a highly motivated audience. Although most consumers embark on a self-help programme independently, more professionals are now directing selected clients towards appropriate materials.

The quality of the self-help texts and tapes that are currently available is very variable. The following examples illustrate some of the titles and topics within the range. *A Medical Handbook for Senior Citizens and their Families* (Thornton, 1989) deals with both physical and psychological problems of the elderly and includes information on preventive measures, the nature of particular medical investigations, and the value of support systems. Another text, *Coping with Alzheimer's: A Carer's Emotional Survival Guide* (Oliver and Bock, 1987), has a narrower focus and aims to provide help for those who face the long-term task of caring for a demented relative. A number of useful texts have also been written to help the parents of handicapped children to contend with their own difficulties and to help their children develop to their full capacity (e.g. Cunningham and Sloper, 1978; Newson and Hipgrave, 1982).

Several self-help guides are available for couples who wish to reduce the conflict within their relationship (e.g. *The Intimate Enemy*—Bach and Wyden, 1969; *Staying Together*—Beech, 1985), and many books are available to help both adults and children cope with divorce (e.g. *Breaking Even: Divorce, Your Children and You*—Burgoyne, 1984; *Helping Children Cope with Separation and Loss*—Jewett, 1982; *Mum, Will Dad Ever Come Back?*—Hogan, 1980). There is even a book which guides individuals through a behavioural programme to help them fall out of love (Phillips and Judd, 1981). Many books seem to provide comfort, perspective, and advice for those who have recently suffered a family bereavement. A particularly good example is Doug Manning's *Don't Take My Grief Away: What to Do When You Lose a Loved One* (Manning, 1984). And in addition to the many books that provide support for a specific type of problem, a number aim to provide insight and help on a broader range of issues (e.g. *Living with Stress*—Rudinger, 1982; *Families and How to Survive Them*—Skynner and Cleese, 1983).

THE PROFESSIONAL–FAMILY RELATIONSHIP

Some families have positive stereotypes of most of the caring professions whereas others have profoundly negative attitudes. Some families willingly accept professional help with a family problem (some, indeed, become highly dependent) while others assiduously avoid any 'interference from outsiders'. Professionals themselves hold stereotypes of particular kinds of families and may have strong preferences for working with some rather than others. Thus the relationship that develops between a professional and a family reflects stable attitudes and prejudices as well as the particular interactions that transpire. Professionals need to be aware that their contribution will not always be welcome, and that because they often enter into tense and unhappy situations they will sometimes become targets for a family's hostility. Some professionals are called upon to exercise a particular expertise and act primarily as 'technical consultants' to the family, while others act principally as a supporter, advocate or counsellor. There is no single 'ideal model' for the professional–family relationship, but some ways of working together may be more productive and comfortable for the participants than others. In many cases families will prefer to see themselves as 'collaborating with' rather than 'being treated by' the professional.

Thus when a child is receiving medical treatment, or when a child's behaviour gives rise to concern at school, many parents see themselves as collaborating with the doctor, teacher, or psychologist in pursuing the most beneficial course for the child. If family members work with a professional (or a group of professionals) as co-partners, and thus become members of the team, they will be involved in any decision-making process and should have access to any information discovered or generated by professionals. However, when it is considered that there may be a risk of a child being mistreated, parental access to records may be restricted, although many elements of the collaborative approach may still be maintained. Thus professionals may work with the parents to establish an effective and non-abusive way of gaining the child's compliance during disciplinary episodes.

One reason why collaboration is generally preferable to consultation is that it encourages family members to maintain control over their own affairs. It is preferable for such matters as the custody of a child following divorce, housing for an elderly relative, or a woman's accommodation following marital abuse to reflect the clients' wishes rather than the initiative or persuasive powers of professionals. In studies of the outcome of psychotherapy it has been shown that therapists who establish a mutual set of goals with their clients, and forge a 'therapeutic alliance' with them, are far more effective in helping clients than those who simply make assumptions or impose their own treatment goals (Luborsky et al., 1985). A professional who is too directive may inhibit any initiative that a family is developing and thereby induce a 'secondary handicap'. Over-involvement and over-protectiveness are further snares that may hamper the long-term effectiveness of intervention. The most effective contribution is often one which helps the family to help itself. Families benefit most when they are given support and are helped to solve their own problems. The ultimate goal of professional involvement should be to encourage the family's autonomy and self-reliance as far as possible, and to avoid dependence.

Similarly, professionals should avoid relieving family members of responsibilities that they are able to maintain. Thus it is unwise to invite families to relinquish tasks such as looking after the sick, children or the elderly, except when specialist care is essential. Family members may suffer long-term stress and guilt, for example, if they feel that they have too readily surrendered the care of a sick child, an elderly relative, or a dying patient to hospital personnel or the manager of a residential home. Even when a person is being cared for in an intensive care unit, relatives often feel guilty about 'just standing by' while others 'do everything' for the patient. Hospices generally avoid the danger that family members will be made to feel redundant and ineffective by inviting family members to collaborate with staff and to act as part of the team providing care for the dying person.

COMMUNICATION BETWEEN PROFESSIONALS

Many families have contact not just with one professional, or even with several within a single agency, but with a number of professionals from diverse agencies. Thus a family with a chronically sick child might be in touch with social workers, family counsellors, and the child's teachers, in addition to those who are directly concerned with the child's medical treatment. In many cases the most revealing account of the family situation emerges only when all of the available information about the family is consolidated, and the most effective intervention results from professionals acting together as a team. Interdisciplinary cooperation has increased substantially in recent years, and it has become a relatively standard practice in some areas for 'case conferences' to be convened. At their best, such meetings are highly effective in bringing together diverse information and communicating opinions regarding the family's current difficulties. Family members may be present throughout the discussion. Sometimes they function as associates of the professional team, although in other cases the professionals act as an advisory panel of consultants to the family. Alternatively, some or all of the discussion may take place when family members are not present, and some conferences are convened to make recommendations about the family to one or more agencies. Thus some teams do in effect 'pass judgement' on the best course of action for the family as a whole or for a particular member of the family. This circumstance generally arises only when there is a suspicion of violence or some other form of abuse.

Although the integration of professionals' efforts towards helping a particular family usually increases the overall effectiveness of the services offered, the team strategy raises a number of problematic issues. Should all relevant documents be made available to all of the professionals involved with the family, for example, and how should duties and responsibilities be allocated? Newly formed or *ad hoc* teams may encounter organizational problems that impede their successful functioning, but many experienced teams have evolved standard policies and procedures that appear to be highly effective. Professionals who work together are able to share responsibility for joint decisions and can support each other in a number of ways. Helping families to deal with distressing issues is highly demanding and often places formidable emotional pressure on the professional (Payne and Firth-Cozens, 1987). Encouragement and guidance from colleagues have enabled many to survive during times of special stress and the relief derived from membership of a supportive team has enabled many professionals to avoid the syndrome of emotional exhaustion that has come to be labelled 'burnout' (Eisenstat and Felner, 1984).

Even minimal contact between professionals can be very helpful. Thus a telephone conversation between a teacher and a pupil's physician may radically alter the view that each has of the child's response to treatment. Similarly, contact between the police, a social worker, and a Shelter worker may help to ensure the safety of a woman who has been beaten by her husband. There is much to be gained by such collaboration, and any initiative that promotes cooperation may produce substantial benefits for client families. Some community agencies have compiled and distributed an extensive directory of professionals and groups in their district, thus helping to increase awareness of local resources and to facilitate interdisciplinary contact. Opportunities for professionals from different agencies to meet together informally may assist in the development of an interdisciplinary community in which each professional becomes personally known to many others. Efforts to 'network' professionals in this way are likely to reduce any tendency for those within a particular specialty to remain separate, and may therefore bring substantial gains for families who need help from a number of sources.

COMMUNICATION WITH LAY HELPERS

In discussing professionals' communication with troubled families we have drawn principally upon examples from the health field, but many of the points considered have a far wider applicability. Social workers, psychologists, psychotherapists, teachers, lawyers, police, divorce counsellors, the clergy, and many others can have a powerful effect on how well families contend with a distressing event or situation. Many of the issues raised are also relevant to the many lay people who in one way or another become involved with troubled families. Indeed, many of those who experience severe family difficulties have no contact with professionals, but rely on friends to help them, or try to cope alone (Pilisuk and Parks, 1986).

Neighbours, friends, and relatives often act together as an informal support network and offer their assistance when they recognize that a family is in trouble. Major problems often create a good deal of extra work, and if other people help with everyday chores this can lighten the family's burden considerably. Illness, handicap and marital disruption also frequently reduce the family income and may impose additional expense, and relatives sometimes offer financial aid to help the family through an emergency period. Particular friends or relatives may be knowledgeable about resources, or may have useful social contacts from whom they can solicit specialist opinion. And besides the many practical ways in which the support network may mobilize to help a troubled family, other people also give valuable psychological support. Knowing that others are aware of a problem can give substantial comfort, and communication with concerned friends often releases tension. By providing a hopeful analysis of a situation, other people may inspire the family and give it strength. They may also provide a novel perspective on a problem, while reassuring the family that their responses are appropriate and 'normal'.

Many lay people offer their services to others in the community. In many countries telephone 'help-lines' offer advice and friendship to people in need. The Samaritans provide a befriending service for the anxious, depressed, and suicidal, for example, and 'Parents Anonymous' offer support and advice for parents under stress. The volunteers attached to such services are usually carefully selected and receive special training, and there is evidence to show that many voluntary agencies are highly effective in helping clients. In an early programme, Rioch (1967) recruited housewives from parent–teacher associations, women's groups and other such organizations and provided them with a basic training in psychotherapy. The women were selected on the basis of their intelligence, reliability, psychological stability, and their ability to relate to other people. An evaluation study conducted after the training indicated that the women were remarkably competent in their dealings with clients and had developed many useful therapeutic skills.

There are many 'natural therapists' in the community. Even without training or any awareness that they are having a therapeutic impact, such people are highly effective in reducing other people's distress. They are inherently responsive and sympathetic in their interactions and have a intuitive capacity to understand the feelings of others. (It is also worth noting that some people may have quite the opposite effect and tend to exacerbate other people's distress; the psychologist Sidney Jourard once made the colourful distinction between 'natural healers' and 'natural witches'.) Those who work in some occupations, including bartenders, undertakers, taxi drivers, debt collectors and hairdressers, are frequently called upon to play an informal therapeutic role, and this suggests that one way of improving the general availability of psychological help within the community would be to increase the therapeutic expertise of those involved in such work. Following such a rationale, Milne and Mullin (1986) evaluated a training programme designed to increase the listening skills of hairdressers. Not only were the hairdressers' counselling skills enhanced by the programme, but they were also rated as significantly more helpful following training.

FAMILY-TO-FAMILY COMMUNICATION

Different families who share a similar problem or have been through comparable experiences may derive substantial benefits from meeting together. The advantages of such gatherings are increasingly recognized by professionals and by families themselves, and there has been a major growth in such support groups in recent years. They now cover a very wide range of concerns, and it is hardly surprising that there are many self-help groups relating to each of the major areas examined in this book. Thus there are groups for families affected by a wide range of specific illnesses (including leukaemia, cystic fibrosis, diabetes, etc.), and many forms of disability (among these are groups for families with a member who is blind, deaf, cerebrally palsied, mentally handicapped or autistic). Other groups have been developed by those involved in marital and intergenerational conflict, marital violence, and child abuse, and by people whose lives have been profoundly affected by separation, divorce, or bereavement. Many of these groups are affiliated to national and international associations, and the fact that there are now hundreds of specialist associations testifies to the fact that families find their participation in these groups very worthwhile.

There is a wide variation between the groups in terms of their activities, their objectives, and their membership. Some are based in hospitals while others meet in community centres or in a member's home. Some are regarded by the participants principally as friendship networks, some as resource-sharing cooperatives, and others as study groups. While some bring whole families together, others include just one or a few members of several families (for example, 'those caring for a spouse with Alzheimer's disease', 'victims of violence', or 'children of divorce').

One of the most important functions of such groups is the sharing of information. Families can help each other to learn more about the nature of the problems they share, and useful hints or details about local resources can be communicated between families. The groups also provide a valuable opportunity for families to compare notes on their responses to their common problem, and new members often make the comforting discovery that their own reactions and sentiments are very similar to those of others. People may come to identify with particular others and may adopt similar attitudes and coping strategies. Observing that some families have managed to contend successfully with hardship may increase confidence and make the future look more promising. Feedback from group members can also have a useful restraining effect, for the discovery that certain responses are considered 'inappropriate' may lead a family to adopt practices and attitudes that are more generally acceptable. Thus interaction with families in a comparable situation may 'shape' a family's responses in a number of ways.

Being part of a group often promotes a sense of community, and as a group becomes more cohesive participants may come to rely on the group for friendship and support. Families with problems are often isolated, and the availability of a congenial and non-threatening peer-group will often provide a very welcome relief from isolation and furnish a family with a convenient and supportive social network. Wright *et al.* (1987) asked members of a group for those caring for elderly demented relatives to indicate what they felt they had gained from the group. Three major benefits were identified—the knowledge they had gained through discussion, the realization that their situation and their reactions were not unique, and a general sense of 'community' and 'belonging' provided by their membership of the group. The supportive context of group meetings may also encourage individuals to express certain feelings for the first time, although others will remain very reticent about discussing personal and family matters with those they may still regard as 'outsiders'.

Many of the benefits people gain from their participation in self-help groups derive from their attempts to help other members. When people offer personal testimony they construct reflective and integrated accounts of their own experiences. This often involves a valuable process of personal discovery; people learn a great deal about themselves by telling other people about their experiences. Attempting to help others is also rewarding in a number of other ways. It may boost the helper's self-confidence, distract them from their own preoccupations, encourage their compassion, and foster the development of empathy. These effects may help to explain the well-substantiated phenomenon known as 'the helper effect'. The condition of those who have a psychological problem often improves when they attempt to help others with similar problems.

In addition to their educational, supportive and therapeutic functions, self-help groups may also act as 'pressure groups' in calling for improved services and additional resources. Indeed, one of the most important advantages of a group of families coming together may be their greater capacity for requesting and demanding changes in policy of those responsible for providing and allocating resources.

Because self-help groups provide considerable support and are highly effective in helping families to cope they are a very important community asset. They are also highly cost-effective. Programmes aimed at improving the social conditions within a community can therefore achieve a great deal by working with and supporting any existing self-help groups and by encouraging new initiatives. Professionals can extend their services to a large number of families by working with and through self-help groups. They may provide resources and information, act as consultants and facilitators, and may even be able to provide appropriate training to some group members. Such involvement may substantially broaden the delivery of (some) professional services, ensuring that professional help is available to many families who are in immediate need of support. The collaboration between professionals and community groups may also offer valuable opportunities for the implementation of effective prevention strategies.

REFERENCES

Bach, G. and Wyden, P. (1969) *The Intimate Enemy*. London: Souvenir Press.
Beech, H. R. (1985) *Staying Together*. Chichester: Wiley.
Bornstein, P. H. and Bornstein, M. T. (1986) *Marital Therapy: A Behavioral-Communications Approach*. New York: Pergamon Press.
Burgoyne, J. (1984) *Breaking Even: Divorce, Your Children and You*. Harmondsworth: Penguin.
Cunningham, C. and Sloper, P. (1978) *Helping your Handicapped Baby*. London: Souvenir Press.
Eisenstat, R. A. and Felner, R. D. (1984) Towards a differentiated view of burnout: personal and organizational mediators of job satisfaction and stress. *American Journal of Community Psychology*, 12, 411–430.
Floyd, D. S. and Floyd, W. A. (1987) A cognitive–emotional–behavioural enrichment retreat weekend. *Australian Journal of Sex, Marriage and Family*, 8, 184–193.
Guerney, B. G. (1977) *Relationship Enhancement: Skill Training Program for Therapy, Problem-Prevention and Enrichment*. San Francisco, CA: Jossey-Bass.
Hogan, P. (1980) *Mum, Will Dad Ever Come Back?* Oxford: Blackwell.
Jewett, C. (1982) *Helping Children Cope with Separation and Loss*. London: Batsford/BAAF.
Luborsky, L., McLellan, A. T., Woody, G. E., O'Brien, C. P. and Auerbach, A. (1985) Therapist success and its determinants. *Archives of General Psychiatry*, 42, 602–611.
Manning, D. (1984) *Don't Take My Grief Away: What to Do When You Lose a Loved One*. San Francisco, CA: Harper and Row.
Milne, D. L. and Mullin, M. (1987) Is a problem shared a problem shaved? An evaluation of hairdressers and social support. *British Journal of Clinical Psychology*, 26, 69–70.
Minuchin, S. (1974) *Families and Family Therapy*. Cambridge, MA: Harvard University Press.
Newson, E. and Hipgrave, T. (1982) *Getting Through to Your Handicapped Child*. Cambridge: Cambridge University Press.
Oliver, R. and Bock, F. A. (1987) *Coping with Alzheimer's: A Carer's Emotional Survival Guide*. New York: Dodd, Mead and Company.
Payne, R. and Firth-Cozens, J. (1987) *Stress in Health Professionals*. Chichester: Wiley.
Phillips, D. and Judd, R. (1981) *How to Fall Out of Love*. London: Macdonald Futura.
Pilisuk, M. and Parks, S. H. (1986) *The Healing Web: Social Networks and Human Survival*. Hanover, NE: University Press of New England.

Rioch, M. (1967) Pilot projects in training mental health counselors. In: E. L. Cowen, E. A. Gardner and M. Zax (eds.), *Emergent Approaches to Mental Health Problems*. New York: Appleton–Century–Crofts.

Rudinger, E. (ed.) (1982) *Living with Stress*. London: Consumer's Association.

Satir, V. (1967) *Conjoint Family Therapy*. Palo Alto: Science and Behaviour Books.

Skynner, R. and Cleese, J. (1983) *Families and How to Survive Them*. London: Methuen.

Thornton, H. A. (1989) *A Medical Handbook for Senior Citizens and their Families*. Dover: MA: Auburn House.

Turvey, A. (1985) Treatment manuals. In: F. N. Watts (ed.), *New Developments in Clinical Psychology*, Vol. 1. Leicester: British Psychological Society in association with Wiley.

Watzlawick, P., Beavin, J. H. and Jackson, D. D. (1967) *Pragmatics of Human Communication*. New York: W. W. Norton.

Wright, S. D. *et al.* (1987) The assessment of support group experiences by caregivers of dementia patients. *Clinical Gerontologist*, **6**, 35–59.

12

Vulnerability and Resilience

FACTORS THAT HEIGHTEN DISTRESS

As a variety of family problems were examined in earlier chapters, several factors appeared to have a widespread tendency to increase distress. One such factor is 'unforeseen change'. Stressor events that occur without forewarning generally have more harmful effects than similar events which have been expected. Another detrimental factor is 'ambiguity'. Situations that remain unclear are open to subjective interpretation, and people often impose a 'meaning' on an event that heightens the adverse impact, perhaps by generating feelings of guilt or inadequacy. People also underestimate the extent to which their own thoughts and feelings are 'natural' and 'normal' and often feel that their responses to stressful situations are unique, weak, wicked or ridiculous. Social isolation is another key vulnerability factor. Families that live in relative seclusion, detached from neighbours and the community, are more likely to be conflictual and violent, for example, and deal less effectively with the difficulties arising from illness, handicap, marital breakdown, and bereavement.

UNFORESEEN CHANGE

Stressor events that occur suddenly and without forewarning are especially likely to produce serious adverse consequences. In all of the areas reviewed, abrupt and unforeseen changes lead to considerably more distress than those which have been anticipated. Thus chronic illnesses that have a gradual onset generate less acute distress than those which strike suddenly. Serious accidents, strokes and heart attacks often create panic within families and seriously disrupt their normal functioning. On the other hand, although insidious disorders such as Alzheimer's disease and multiple sclerosis ultimately place great strain on the patient and the family, they are less likely to provoke intense dismay and consternation.

Parents who are told immediately after the birth that their baby is handicapped are generally much more distressed than parents who learn of their infant's disability some months later. One reason for the difference is that a later diagnosis will usually have been 'signalled' in advance. Over the course of weeks or months of growing suspicion and concern, and a succession of medical investigations, the parents may gradually adjust their view of the child's condition and prepare themselves for disturbing news. Marital breakdown is another context in which anticipation reduces distress. When a relationship is in serious trouble, both partners are generally fully aware of the fact, and separation usually follows prolonged discord and many threats and warnings. In those rare cases in which a person leaves without any forewarning the immediate effects are often particularly intense, especially if the partner had no idea that the relationship was in jeopardy. Similarly, children who have been 'protected' from learning of their parents' probable separation generally become very distressed when they are suddenly informed that the father (or, less commonly, the mother) has left or is about to leave.

Finally, those who are forewarned that a family member will soon die tend to make a better recovery following bereavement than those who suffer a sudden and unexpected loss. The protective effects of forewarning are often powerful and enduring, and those who lose a family member without warning may remain in a state of confusion and profound distress for a long time ('the syndrome of unanticipated grief'). Forewarning has been shown to have a buffering effect on those who lose their spouse, a child, or a sibling. Bereaved parents who had been given some opportunity to brace themselves for their child's death tend to make a better recovery and feel less guilt, and siblings who were told that their sick brother or sister was suffering from a terminal condition are less distressed after the death, and show fewer psychosomatic and behavioural symptoms, than those who had not been prepared for the loss.

Major unexpected changes are particularly disturbing for a number of reasons. Confidence may be drastically eroded when firm assumptions are suddenly undermined, and life may appear utterly unpredictable and precarious. Plans require drastic revision and new patterns of response are required at a time when normal routines are no longer appropriate. Those who have not had time to brace themselves or to rehearse new strategies may be completely overwhelmed by the sudden upheaval. Because any major change will also affect other family members, each individual suddenly has to contend with a radically different social environment.

A forewarning gives people an opportunity to prepare practically and psychologically for the imminent change, and may provoke anticipatory adjustments in the functioning of the family system. Suppositions are gradually revised, emotional responses rehearsed, and new plans developed. Assumptions about the future may be steadily modified until the person and the system have effectively 'come to terms' with the threatened change. Sometimes the degree of anticipatory coping is so extreme that it actually makes it more difficult for the individual or the family to contend with the immediate situation. Thus adaptation can be premature, as when a person rehearses detailed plans for a life alone before there is any real threat of separation, or when a family engages in 'anticipatory mourning' before the patient's death.

As well as stimulating cognitive changes, a forewarning often leads to the generation of new behavioural strategies, some of which may soften the eventual impact of the change. Thus children who are informed that their parents are about to separate may seek reassurance from the departing parent that they will keep in regular contact. A partner who knows that separation is imminent may take the opportunity to establish why the person is leaving, to extract certain promises, and to discuss practical matters. Furthermore, they may use the occasion to clarify their own position and to regain some control over events. Such actions may pre-empt the extreme frustration and helplessness often experienced when an adverse change occurs suddenly and without warning. Thus adaptive responses made in advance of a challenging event can substantially reduce distress. When family members are aware that a sick member is likely to die, for example, their special efforts to care for the dying person, and the opportunity to show dedication and compassion, are likely to forestall a great deal of distress following bereavement.

Forewarning therefore instigates many adaptive preparatory changes, and professionals and others who are aware of possible developments that might cause distress should therefore give family members every chance to prepare by keeping them fully appraised of the situation. Many circumstances are by their very nature unpredictable, but any temptation to maintain an optimistic silence should be avoided. Naturally, any such disclosure should be made with the utmost sensitivity and without giving rise to unnecessary alarm. Some people find the task of alerting families to potential risks very disagreeable, but they need to be mindful of the possible costs of not providing adequate warning. Thus expectant parents have a right to know that their unborn baby may be handicapped or may die shortly after birth, despite the fact that such information will cause them immediate distress. Those who are forewarned about critical stressor events are forearmed against many of the most harmful effects, and an early, candid and sensitive disclosure is an intervention that can have very powerful preventive effects.

AMBIGUITY

It is often much more difficult to cope with an ambiguous situation than with one that is definite. Not knowing whether a troubled relationship will continue or will soon end, for example, can cause a great deal of ambivalence and distress. A person is often less distraught when an uneasy situation has been clearly resolved, even if the outcome is not the one they would have preferred. Situations that remain indefinite often leave the person confused, emotionally volatile and powerless. And unpredictability is only one type of ambiguity. There are often unanswered questions about the causes of the problem and the extent to which various people (including oneself) might be to blame. It may also be unclear whether a situation is redeemable and how the effects might best be remedied. In the absence of clear information on such matters, individuals and family groups impose their own interpretations, make their own prognoses, and assign blame. The alternatives they consider, however, and the accounts they construct, are often unrealistic and frequently increase rather than reduce their distress.

Subjective Appraisals

People have a fundamental tendency to try to make sense of ambiguous situations and events, and this endeavour (sometimes labelled 'effort after meaning') plays an important part in determining how individuals and families respond to stressful life events. In their struggle to reduce ambiguity people draw upon their general knowledge, myths, and fantasies, as well as on any specific information that may be available. They may search through their past experience for possible clues, and even the most trifling incident may become the raw material for elaborate interpretation. Thus a man who has suddenly been left by his wife may recall tiny incidents from long ago and re-interpret particular comments or behaviours in order to construct an acceptable explanation of why she left.

When a handicapped child is born, the parents and other relatives will search for an explanation of why the child is handicapped, of 'what went wrong', and of 'who is to blame'. If they have little understanding of the real causes of the handicap they are likely to accept any plausible explanation they can discover or invent. An illustration of the consequences of such a process is provided by the results of an early study of mothers of Down's syndrome children (Stott, 1958). When the study was conducted the cause of this condition had not been identified and the hypothesis being investigated was that the handicap might be the result of the mother having experienced 'shock' during pregnancy. When mothers of Down's children and a comparison group of mothers of non-handicapped children were asked to recall any disturbances they had suffered in the months before the child's birth, the mothers of the handicapped recalled significantly more. In the year following the publication of this report, however, it was discovered that Down's syndrome is caused by a chromosomal irregularity. Because the condition is determined at the time of conception it cannot be a consequence of the mother's experience during pregnancy. This immediately raises the question of why, in Stott's study, the mothers of Down's children reported more shocks. It is unlikely that they did actually experience more disturbances than other mothers. A more viable explanation is that, in their search for possible reasons for the child's handicap, these mothers might have spent a considerable amount of time reviewing details of their pregnancy. This would have resulted in a relatively detailed memory of any unfavourable events, thus enabling them to recall more shocks at the time of the interview (Brown, 1974).

Efforts to interpret sensitive situations are subject to a number of recognized biases. Some people, for example, tend to see things in 'black and white' terms, and those who engage in such 'dichotomous thinking' may be particularly erratic in their judgements. When they focus on an unfavourable aspect of a situation they may adopt a totally pessimistic view, while focusing on a single favourable element may lead them to see the whole situation as entirely positive. Another kind of bias stems from over-generalization. A family that has a problem with one neighbour, for example, may develop a widespread mistrust of all of their neighbours. Other types of cognitive distortion involve the misattribution of responsibility, the tendency to focus disproportionately on particular aspects of a situation, and the inclination to decide whether something is real or true on the basis of wishes and feelings rather than facts.

Searching for meaning is a group phenomenon as well as an individual phenomenon. A family faced with a major development may explore a number of possible meanings before arriving at some consensus about the degree of threat, who is responsible, and the probable outcome. As a family engages in the process of 'meaning construction', some of the more idiosyncratic and outlandish interpretations suggested by particular individuals may be discarded in favour of more moderate and rational assessments, but family processes may also introduce new distortions and prejudices. A situation may be judged unrealistically because the family has few facts, or because available information is misunderstood, or because conclusions are based on sentiment rather than sense. Family members often share similar attitudes and perceptions (how families 'construct reality' and form a 'family paradigm' or 'world view' was discussed in Chapter 2). The prevailing consensus about the neighbourhood, social agencies, stressful events, and the strengths and weaknesses of the family group is likely to influence the perception of any new development, and if the family's broad 'world view' is incoherent or unrealistic then interpretations of many novel situations will also be unreasonable.

Most family paradigms include some 'mythical' elements. Myths are sometimes useful, as when they increase family solidarity or help to dispel inertia, but they can be disabling, adding to the family's confusion, delaying precautionary measures, and undermining attempts to deal with existing problems. Thus a 'myth of invulnerability' will encourage the family to believe that nothing terrible will ever happen to them, and a 'rescue myth' will promote the unwarranted assumption that the family will always be saved from serious trouble as a result of some timely intervention by an outside agent.

Self-reproach

Many myths and cognitive distortions serve particular emotional needs. A family may 'require' that a particular explanation be accepted and indulge in various self-deceptive strategies in order to 'substantiate' the preferred account. For example, events are often misinterpreted in such a way that self-esteem is preserved or enhanced. This is an example of a 'self-serving bias', and can result, for example, in families inappropriately assigning blame to other people, rather than to themselves, when things have gone wrong. Some families seem to act together as 'mutual admiration societies', conspiring to exonerate each other, to praise each other and to blame other people for family misfortunes. Their systematic misinterpretations may help them to maintain their self-respect and to sustain family solidarity, but such misunderstandings are likely to reduce their capacity to deal effectively with a difficult situation.

A bias in the opposite direction, i.e. an inclination towards 'self-blame' or 'self-reproach', is also very common. People often feel unduly responsible for problems that occur within their family. Thus parents and siblings frequently experience guilt when a child is ill or handicapped, while sick children themselves may believe that their affliction is a punishment for some transgression. Many children also assume that they are to blame for hostility between their parents, and many imagine that they were in some way responsible for the breakdown of their parents' marriage. Child victims of physical or sexual abuse tend to feel responsible for the assaults made on them, and many believe that they deserved the maltreatment. Adults who have been injured by their partner are no less susceptible to this general tendency for victims to burden themselves with guilt. Many women who are victims of marital violence indulge in self-blame and exonerate and abusive partner. Finally, guilt has long been recognized as a characteristic feature of grief. The 'meaning' of a death is frequently ambiguous and when a loved one dies other family members are frequently left in a state of bewilderment. In the absence of an 'adequate' explanation for the death, survivors often engage in self-blame.

Reducing Ambiguity

Those who are better informed about the real nature of a threat or distressing event have to rely less on subjective judgements and are more likely to develop an appropriate understanding of the situation. Informal discussions with friends and neighbours and meetings of self-help groups can reduce ambiguity and help to provide a realistic perspective. Health professionals have a special role to play in keeping family members abreast of developments and informing them about the causes, nature and consequences of illnesses and treatments. Similarly, by virtue of their training and experience, teachers, lawyers, social workers, psychologists and the clergy (among many others) can help family members to develop a realistic assessment of their difficulties and to avoid misleading assumptions. One of the principal aims of any form of counselling is to enable clients to develop a reasonable view of themselves and their problems. Some approaches place the emphasis on people's ability to develop a realistic perspective spontaneously as they explore their own thoughts and feelings, while others stress the need for the counsellor to be more directive and to instruct and guide the client. Many interventions specifically address the task of ensuring that the family's view of events should be 'rational'. Thus Shneidman (1973) introduced a strategy (labelled 'postvention') for helping survivors of a family suicide to achieve a realistic view of their predicament and their responsibility. Rational-emotive therapy (Ellis, 1962), which is often applied to relationship problems, is based on the fundamental premise that personal and interpersonal distress is largely the result of irrational thinking, and many other forms of therapy focus on changing faulty cognitions, appraisals, or attributions, or on challenging dangerous myths (Beck, 1976; Meichenbaum, 1977; Brewin, 1988).

Several programmes with a powerful didactic component were discussed in earlier chapters. Group meetings arranged for the perpetrators and victims of marital violence, for example, often include detailed tuition regarding the nature of conflict, anger, and aggression. Common myths are exposed, and perpetrators' attempts to discount the seriousness of their abusive actions, as well as victims' tendencies towards self-blame, are explored and challenged. A primary educational component is also found in many of the programmes that have been developed to help children cope with such issues as parental divorce, physical violence at home, or the serious illness of a sibling. Through structured play they are taught about health and relationship matters, and are helped to recognize their own emotional responses.

Many of the misconceptions that increase distress might be avoided if people were generally better informed about family life issues. The fact that there is often little or no discussion of family matters in schools (except in some Scandinavian countries, where relevant courses form part of the core curriculum) is both remarkable and lamentable. Education on matters concerning relationship formation, family interaction, stress management, conflict prevention, and childcare could do much to increase children's understanding and help them to develop a range of practical skills. Opportunities are also missed at later stages. Thus antenatal classes provide a context which has great potential for the coverage of a wide range of family and childcare issues. But although many details of childbirth and the physical care of the infant are usually provided, little attention is generally paid to psychological aspects of the parent–child relationship or to issues concerning the effects of the child on the couple and on other children in the family.

Poor communication endangers marriages and detracts from a family's capacity to adapt to changing circumstances, and one way of encouraging greater openness of communication between intimates would be to provide opportunities for them to discuss family issues with other families, or with a counsellor. In one promising development along these lines, couples about to marry (or cohabit) are invited to meet with a counsellor (often in a group setting) for a number of sessions. Some of these premarital counselling programmes focus on the development of communication, conflict-management, and problem-solving skills, but courses also explore a wide range of family-life issues and are designed to help couples understand common relationship problems. 'Marital-enhancement' programmes are directed at couples with a long-standing partnership who wish to enrich the quality of their relationship and, like premarital counselling programmes, they can be regarded as primary prevention measures. By increasing a couple's knowledge and skills, and improving the overall quality of their relationship, it is likely that fewer difficulties will arise and that they will be better prepared for future challenges.

FEELING UNIQUE

People frequently worry that their reactions to stressful situations are unique, and they are greatly comforted when they discover that many other people react in a similar way. Experienced counsellors are familiar with clients' profound relief on discovering that feelings they supposed to be 'wild', 'pathological', or 'wicked' are regarded by the therapist as 'natural', 'unexceptional' and 'reasonable'. Thus some parents of children who are seriously ill feel so tense during hospital visits that they avoid visiting the child as regularly as they might. These parents may reproach themselves and consider that they are weak, selfish and disloyal to the child. If, however, they learn that many other parents in their position share similar feelings, they are likely to feel more positive about themselves and their relationship with the child. Another example concerns the responses of those with a relatively minor handicap. Such people often have particular difficulties in adjusting to their condition. They are in a 'marginal position' and cannot clearly identify either with the non-handicapped or with those who are profoundly and obviously disabled. When they meet people who suffer from a much more serious handicapping condition, but are well-adjusted, they may regard themselves as feeble and inept. They are likely to be greatly comforted and encouraged when they discover that their feelings are shared by many others with minor handicaps.

People who face many other kinds of difficulty also assume that their responses are peculiar and outlandish when they are in fact rather common. Thus many divorced people are still in love with their ex-spouse, many children still yearn for a family reconciliation years after their parents have divorced, and many non-custodial parents have ambivalent feelings about keeping in touch with their children. Couples with a new baby may feel that they are 'wicked' and 'strange' because they sometimes become very frustrated or angry with their infant. An abused woman may feel that she is quite exceptional in wishing to stay with the man who has severely beaten her. Those who have recently been bereaved may be tortured by the assumption that no-one else has negative thoughts about the person they have lost. In all of these cases, people derive great comfort from being told that they are 'in good company', and that they are neither 'bad' nor 'mad'. Similarly, it is often very reassuring for troubled families to learn that many families experience a breakdown of communication over sensitive issues, often engage in bitter conflict, often find it difficult or impossible to adjust to changing circumstances, and frequently turn to others for help.

ISOLATION

Many problems occur more frequently, or have more deleterious effects, within families that are socially detached. Isolation is associated with family violence, for example, including marital abuse, elder abuse and physical child abuse. Those who are socially integrated and have regular contact with relatives, neighbours, and the local community show better adjustment following separation and divorce, the birth of a handicapped child, the serious illness of a family member, and bereavement.

Many families take pride in their independence and self-sufficiency, but most are willing to confide in others during times of difficulty and are open to offers of help and support. 'Closed families', on the other hand, stridently maintain their separateness even when facing profound difficulties. They conceal their problems from others and may regard even a casual enquiry as highly intrusive. Members of such families may collude together to establish the myth that they can cope with any circumstance and never need help from others. Thus couples who fight bitterly and persistently may keep their difficulties hidden from other people, and parents with a handicapped child may insist on struggling alone, refusing to meet with other families, to use baby-sitters, or to take advantage of any special community resources.

Some families construct a view of reality that includes profoundly negative impressions of neighbours, distant relatives and the community. Evaluating their social context in entirely unfavourable terms they are likely to feel threatened by any potential contact and therefore close ranks and deny access and information to any of those who might be able to help them. Other families live in relative seclusion because they wish to hide some aspect of their family life. Thus some abusive families isolate themselves from relatives and neighbours so that nobody will learn of the violent assaults that happen within the home. In other cases a family is isolated not by choice or design but because there are few opportunities for making social contact. Geographical remoteness, or the absence of any social community within the neighbourhood, may prevent a family from forming or maintaining supportive relationships with others.

A family may consider that there is so much mutual support between members that little would be gained from any involvement in the wider community. People do indeed derive valuable support from intimates, and when members are effective 'therapists' for each other the unit may be emotionally self-sufficient in all but the most challenging circumstances. Yet any family can benefit considerably from integration into the wider community. Friends, neighbours and members of the extended family can be valuable aides when troubles arise, and the fact that other people know of the family's predicament and are prepared to help may be highly comforting to a family that is facing a major upheaval. Families gain confidence through recognizing that they are part of a network of mutual obligation, and they are reassured when they know that reliable sources of additional support are at hand.

The degree of informal support available to families has declined considerably in recent decades. Contact with members of the extended family has become less frequent (largely due to decreases in geographical proximity, a sharp decline in family size, and a weakening of kinship bonds). Geographical mobility, architectural changes, and increased facilities for work and leisure within the home have reduced the scope for individuals and families to meet and form relationships with others in the neighbourhood. There has also been a sharp decline in the strength of 'community feeling', and families now have fewer neighbours or relatives that they feel free to call upon for help. This weakening of community support may have increased the overall stress experienced by families while also decreasing the amount of informal support available to them.

The value of a highly integrated social network is now well recognized, and some agencies have developed programmes aimed at encouraging community renewal. Various 'networking' strategies are used to increase the social integration within particular neighbourhoods. By helping to develop a regular schedule of community meetings, social events and resource exchanges, such programmes aim to bring families together, to reinforce the prevailing social network and to foster a sense of community. It is hoped that by increasing the opportunities for casual contact fewer families will remain isolated, that the quality of life in the community will be enhanced, and that informal support will become more widely available. Although most programmes are based in neighbourhoods (some seeking to promote the development of 'urban villages'), others seek to exploit the potential offered by other social units such as schools, offices, and industrial workplaces. And although some of the more extensive programmes have been generously resourced, many others have capitalized on prevailing structures and have required only a minimal expenditure of resources. Although the benefits of such 'mini-interventions' are often difficult to gauge, it is likely that in many cases they have been very substantial.

RESILIENCE AND ADAPTABILITY

One of the most significant themes to emerge from the reviews presented in earlier chapters is that of individual and family resilience in the face of stressor events, and of the capacity to adapt and recover following a major change. Many studies show that people frequently come to terms with the most difficult situations and the most tragic circumstances. Examples of such resilience are found in all of the areas examined in this book. People often cope remarkably well with chronic illness. Many parents who are profoundly shocked by the birth of a handicapped child soon begin to take a more positive and hopeful view of their circumstances. Victims of family violence sometimes appear to recover psychologically long before their wounds have healed, and they often retain a surprising degree of affection for the person who assaulted them. Some of those who have been separated and divorced report that they experienced relatively little distress when the relationship ended, and most of those who do suffer considerably following marital breakup later recover much of their self-esteem and adjust to their new lifestyle. Many terminally ill patients come to terms with their imminent death and are able to reach the state of 'acceptance', and almost all of those who lose a loved one manage to recover in due course.

Children also show remarkable psychological strength. Many cope bravely with painful illnesses and chronic complaints (Eiser, 1990), while others lead happy and fulfilled lives despite severe disablement. Children also struggle heroically with the disruption provoked by such onerous events as parental divorce, marital abuse, the death of a parent, and the serious illness of a sibling. Child victims of physical abuse often continue to feel affection for the parent who has subjected them to horrific injury, and the assumption that all such victims remain forever traumatized is soundly contradicted by the evidence. Considering the large proportion of children who experience at least one major adverse event or circumstance during childhood, it is very reassuring to discover that psychological trauma, developmental disruption and permanent effects are by no means inevitable.

Of course, many individuals *are* profoundly disturbed when they experience serious upheaval in their lives. Many develop serious physical ailments; suffer a substantial loss of self-confidence; or become chronically anxious, depressed, or angry. The fact that those who are traumatized are more likely to come to the attention of clinicians can mislead professionals into underestimating people's resilience in the face of profound hardship and change. Studies of representative samples of people who experience serious disruption in their lives, however, confirm that many are highly resilient. Such studies have also provided many inspiring accounts of the extent of individuals' and families' endurance and fortitude. It therefore needs to be recognized that for any single class of family problem there will be major differences between families in the degree of adverse reaction, and that not every family will be traumatized. Acknowledging this, however, does not deny or discount the experiences of the many individuals and families who are profoundly disturbed, and such cases obviously deserve the special attention of clinicians and therapists.

Apparent resilience does not mean that the person is untouched by the event, but may indicate that their struggle to cope has been particularly effective. By understanding how some people manage to overcome severe misfortune professionals may be in a better position to help those who are finding it difficult to survive a major setback. Those who maintain their composure and remain in control despite critical adverse changes do so by means of a wide range of practical coping strategies. Some of these are 'problem-focused' and involve behaviours (such as making plans or asking people for advice) that attempt to deal with the problem itself, while others ('emotion-focused' strategies) involve attempts to curb the emotional impact of the problem (Folkman and Lazarus, 1980). Emotion-focused coping includes a variety of perceptual and judgemental strategies (reframing, passive appraisal, etc.) as well as behaviours such as openly expressing one's feelings. Both adults and children use a wide variety of strategies for coping with threat and change, and many of these can be highly effective. Even denial, which is often regarded as a dangerous avoidance tactic, can sometimes have favourable effects.

Resilience and adaptation are evident within family systems as well as within individuals. Some families appear relatively undisturbed by important developmental changes and weather stressor events without becoming unsettled or disorganized. Resilient families are normally adaptable and deploy their considerable resources (including 'family strengths' and 'coping strategies') very effectively. Resilient families are not unaffected by stressor events but are successful in using cognitive, behavioural, interactional and structural strategies to limit the effects of adverse changes. Such strategies attenuate stress rather than totally eliminating negative consequences, and it may take some time for the full measure of their effect to become apparent. Gradual progress towards recovery follows every type of negative family transition, but while it may be tempting to account for this in terms of the maxim 'Time heals', this tends to obscure the fact that recovery results from a number of strategic adaptations and is not simply an automatic or passive process.

When crisis threatens, family systems typically engage in a number of 'damage limitation' manoeuvres. Family members are often especially warm and supportive to one another, conflictual issues may be disregarded, and the family may become more cohesive. Damaged relationships may be urgently repaired, and members who had previously maintained a high degree of individuality may 'join' more closely with the family. Recognition of a common threat encourages people to cooperate with one another, and when family members work together as a team they are more likely to solve the problems that beset them. Frequent expression of support and affection, and acts of selflessness and sacrifice, may increase the degree of emotional bonding between family members, and all of these changes are likely to improve the system's capacity to function coherently and effectively.

Many of the structural adaptations that follow changes in family circumstances can be seen as coping strategies. Thus when a member leaves, or becomes incapacitated through illness or accident, someone usually takes over at least some of the roles that the individual played within the family. As well as changes in role structure, stressor events are likely to instigate adjustments in the boundaries, sub-groupings, and patterns of alliance within the family. The structure and content of communication will also change. While a serious threat may disrupt family interaction, it can also have the opposite effect of enhancing communication between members. An individual who is normally somewhat reticent may suddenly become very forthcoming, and issues that were previously evaded may now be openly addressed. The family may also revise its 'construction of reality' in the light of significant changes, perhaps creating new myths or reviving memories that have suddenly taken on a new relevance.

In its attempts to form a 'convenient' view of its current predicament a family may employ such tactics as drawing favourable comparisons (i.e. things could have been much worse), 'reframing' the event in order to foster a more optimistic view of the likely outcome, and engaging in 'passive appraisal' ('things will sort themselves out'). Some of these strategies avoid confronting the issue directly and realistically, but they may inspire optimism and therefore help to sustain the family. Misperception can also be adaptive, and fantasy may permit the family to preserve a relatively buoyant atmosphere when a more realistic view would result in dejection and inertia. It can be seen that it would be unwise to be too specific in suggesting how families can best cope, for almost any view that a particular family adopts of itself or its problem may prove adaptive. Thus some families reduce stress by casting themselves in the role of 'helpless victim', while others are spurred into effective action by recalling their triumphs over previous adversities.

The evidence affirming that many individuals and families are resilient in the face of dramatic changes suggests that the strategies they use are often appropriate and adaptive. Underestimating the capacity for 'self-protection' and 'self-repair' may lead professionals and lay helpers to pre-empt or to undermine some of the useful devices that clients and families employ. This suggests the danger that some 'therapeutic' interventions may frustrate a family's attempts to deal effectively with a disruptive situation, rather than helping it to recover. Empathic approaches that are congruent with a family's own attempts to cope are less likely to meet with resistance and are more likely to be effective. Indeed, a principle common to many forms of counselling is that the therapist should recognize the existing strengths of individual clients and client families and seek to sustain and reinforce them. Therapies that are 'client-led' have a clear advantage in this respect. Another fundamental tenet is that therapists should avoid clients becoming too dependent upon them, and many counsellors see their primary task as that of helping individuals and families to help themselves, as 'facilitating change' rather than 'directing change'.

Professionals can do much to facilitate resilience. and adaptation. By supplying useful information and identifying useful resources they may substantially attenuate the impact of a stressor. They can reassure families that their coping efforts are sensible and worthwhile, commend their fortitude and determination, and help them to discover new ways of helping themselves. The experienced professional will be aware of the full range of common responses to particular stressors and will rarely assume that the client 'must be' traumatized. Those who recognize the prodigious power of resilience are unlikely to disrupt the subtle processes of survival and self-healing. On the contrary, they will join with their clients in their attempts to normalize any difficult and threatening situation.

REFERENCES

Beck, A. T. (1976) *Cognitive Therapy and the Emotional Disorders*. New York: International Universities Press.

Brewin, C. R. (1988) Attribution therapy. In: F. N. Watts (ed.), *New Developments in Clinical Psychology Vol. 2*. Leicester: British Psychological Society in association with Wiley.

Brown, G. W. (1974) Meaning, measurement and stress of life events. In: B. S. Dohrenwend and B. P. Dohrenwend (eds.), *Stressful Life Events: Their Nature and Effects*. New York: Wiley.

Eiser, C. (1990) Psychological effects of chronic disease. *Journal of Child Psychology and Psychiatry*, **31**, 85–98.

Ellis, A. (1962) *Reason and Emotion in Psychotherapy*. Secaucus, NJ: Citadel Press.

Folkman, S. and Lazarus, R. (1980) An analysis of coping in a middle-aged population. *Journal of Health and Social Behaviour*, **21**, 219–239.

Meichenbaum, D. (1977) *Cognitive-Behaviour Modification: An Integrative Approach*. New York: Plenum.

Shneidman, E. (1973) *Deaths of Man*. New York: Quadrangle.

Stott, D. H. (1958) Some psychosomatic aspects of casualty in reproduction. *Journal of Psychosomatic Medicine*, **3**, 42–55.

Author Index

Subject Index